Further praise for
GOING DOWN JERICHO ROAD

"*Going Down Jericho Road* is a brilliant achievement."

—William S. McFeely, author of *Frederick Douglass*

"Is there a compelling reason for another book on Martin Luther King Jr.? . . . The short answer is yes. . . . In painting the period's landscape through the case of one local struggle that took on international significance, Honey makes a crucial contribution to our understanding of our past—and helps us understand the racial and class landscape of America today."

—Rick Ayers, *San Francisco Chronicle*

"[An] absorbing, definitive history."   —Leonard Gill, *Memphis Flyer*

"Honey's fine book will be the definitive appreciation of the Memphis garbage strike, one of the pivotal human-rights moments in late twentieth-century America. No source seems missing, no pertinent interview untaken, no perspective ignored. *Going Down Jericho Road* is history as it actually was."   —David Levering Lewis, two-time Pulitzer Prize–winning author of *W. E. B. Du Bois*

"A first-rate chronicle. . . . *Going Down Jericho Road* succeeds because Honey tells the story through individuals, putting a human face to the strike, the civil-rights movement and the efforts by Memphis to stop it. . . . Honey's analysis of King's role is sharp and telling. . . . Vivid."

—Charles R. Cross, *Seattle Times*

"Who could imagine there was still so much to excavate and to grasp about Dr. King's last stand? From the poignant glimpses of the lives of Memphis's black sanitation workers, to the back-room maneuvering among leadership allies and rivals, Michael Honey brings it all to life: the last campaign, the last days, the last hours, the final moments. This is a

dramatic and engaging work of history, illuminating an entire era through the glittering examination of the final 'mountaintop' and the crevasse beyond."　　　　　　　　　　　　　　　—Melissa Fay Greene, author of
Praying for Sheetrock and *There Is No Me Without You*

"[*Going Down Jericho Road*] is brilliant in the way it delineates the economic benefits to Southern society of American apartheid. . . . It is also stirring in portraying the strike leaders, ordinary workers who risked everything to establish their basic rights in the face of arrogant and condescending power."　　　　　　　　—Michael Carlson, *The Spectator* (UK)

"*Going Down Jericho Road* is a masterful piece of documentary history. . . . It is also a new look at one man in particular—King, the one-dimensionalized martyr of the civil rights struggle, whom Honey evokes anew through the use of fresh and unfamiliar quotes." —Darryl Lorenzo Wellington, *Dissent*

"*Going Down Jericho Road* provides fresh insight into Martin Luther King's last battle in his struggle against racial injustice. Through the vivid and moving story he tells, Honey takes the reader on a trip back in time. . . . *Going Down Jericho Road* shows how the past is not past, but is intimately linked to the continuing American debate about social justice."
—W. Ralph Eubanks, author of *Ever Is a Long Time*

"Michael Honey knows Memphis—and its labor and civil rights history—from the inside out. . . . A compelling history."
—Bruce Nelson, *Labor History*

"When I put this book down, I could only say, 'Bravo, Michael Honey.' With riveting detail, analytic fluency, and a deep respect for the difficulty of achieving social change, Honey dissects internal leadership struggles, FBI harassment, and King's own, sometimes paralyzing self doubts. I loved, and was inspired by, this deeply human portrait of King."
—Alice Kessler Harris, author of *In Pursuit of Equity*

GOING DOWN
JERICHO
ROAD

GOING DOWN
JERICHO
ROAD

The Memphis Strike,
Martin Luther King's Last Campaign

MICHAEL K. HONEY

W. W. NORTON & COMPANY

NEW YORK • LONDON

For information about permission to reproduce selections from this book, write to
Permissions, W. W. Norton & Company, Inc., 500 Fifth Avenue, New York, NY 10110

Manufacturing by RR Donnelley, Bloomsburg
Book design by Chris Welch
Production manager: Devon Zahn

Library of Congress Cataloging-in-Publication Data

Honey, Michael K.
Going down Jericho Road : the Memphis strike, Martin Luther King's
last campaign / Michael K. Honey. — 1st ed.
p. cm.
Includes bibliographical references and index.
ISBN-13: 978-0-393-04339-6 (hardcover)
ISBN-10: 0-393-04339-8 (hardcover)
1. Sanitation Workers Strike, Memphis, Tenn., 1968. 2. Strikes and lockouts—Sanitation—Tennessee.
3. King, Martin Luther, Jr., 1929–1968. I. Title.
HD5325.S25721968 M465 2007
331.892'81363720976819—dc22

2006032217

ISBN 978-0-393-33053-3 pbk.

W. W. Norton & Company, Inc., 500 Fifth Avenue, New York, N.Y. 10110
www.wwnorton.com

W. W. Norton & Company Ltd., Castle House, 75/76 Wells Street, London W1T 3QT

3 4 5 6 7 8 9 0

Dedicated to T. O. Jones and the Memphis workers and activists
who put King's beliefs into action,
and to my parents, Keith Honey and Elizabeth Miner Honey

You see, the Jericho road is a dangerous road. . . . The question is not: if I stop to help this man in need, what will happen to me? The question is: if I don't stop to help the sanitation workers, what will happen to them?

—*Martin Luther King, Memphis, April 3, 1968*

I choose to identify with the underprivileged. I choose to identify with the poor. I choose to give my life for the hungry. I choose to give my life for those who have been left out of the sunlight of opportunity . . . seeing life as a long and desolate corridor with no exit sign. This is the way I'm going. If it means suffering a little bit, I'm going that way. . . .

If it means dying for them, I'm going that way.

—*Martin Luther King, "The Good Samaritan," Chicago, August 28, 1966*

CONTENTS

II

FIGHTING FOR THE WORKING POOR

III

JERICHO ROAD IS A DANGEROUS ROAD

A PERSONAL PREFACE

FRENCH HISTORIAN MARC BLOCH, AN ANTIFASCIST RESISTER murdered by the Nazis during World War II, wrote that historians adhere to standards of truth, but cannot avoid taking sides. "The solidarity of the ages is so effective that the lines of connection work both ways," between the past and one's present.

I have my own personal solidarity with the history told in this book. As a high school student in Michigan, the heart of organized labor in the 1960s, I supported the rising civil rights movement. As a college student, I witnessed the racial polarization following the bloody Detroit riot in 1967 and worked in the "Vietnam Summer" campaign that Martin Luther King, Jr., helped to initiate. Until the nation stopped spending its fortune on wars abroad, he said, we would never solve the problems of poverty and racism at home. As King encouraged young men to do, I resisted the Vietnam War by filing with my draft board as a conscientious objector to war.

Like many other New Leftists, by 1968 I thought perhaps King was not "radical" enough. Then he began his Poor People's Campaign, a "last ditch" effort to convince the government to shift priorities from military spending to ending poverty. King hoped to build a movement of the poor, beginning in the Mississippi Delta heartland of cotton, segregation, and poverty. He also went to its commercial capital of Memphis, Tennessee, to aid 1,300 black sanitation workers on strike for union rights. When an assassin murdered King there on April 4, 1968, we lost the one person in the Movement (as we called it) who could unite a broad range of Americans in favor of racial and economic justice and peace. Another assassin killed Robert F. Kennedy in June after he won the California Democratic primary as an antiwar candidate pledged to end poverty.

It seemed that the world split apart in 1968. In Prague, Mexico City, Paris, Chicago, Memphis, and many other places, people revolted against the old ways, while government repression intensified. Largely disconnected from unions and the Marxist "Old Left," I followed King's legacy as best I could by joining the Poor People's Campaign march that June in Washington. I worked full-time to end the war in Vietnam and then moved south to work for the Southern Conference Educational Fund in the peace and freedom movement. I sat in a dreadful Kentucky county jail for three weeks for protesting false charges against black activists in Louisville who had been arrested for organizing a community protest of King's assassination.

Then one day in August 1970, Martha Allen and I moved to Memphis as southern civil liberties workers. A dreadful pall still hung over the city in the aftermath of King's death. White police officers had declared war against black youths. State law allowed them to use "all necessary means" to arrest fleeing felons. They killed a black teenager for stealing soft drinks from a truck and shot another in the back when he tried to climb a fence after a petty burglary. In 1971, twenty-three police officers chased down sixteen-year-old Elton Hayes and beat him to death for trying to outrun them in a high-speed car chase—setting off riots in the black community. Police jailed and harassed our friends in the Black Panther Party after they sat in at the Memphis Housing Authority to demand affordable housing for the poor. As economic conditions worsened in the 1970s, workers continued to organize and strike.

One day, responding to an emergency call from the Panthers, I sat on their porch as an American Civil Liberties Union (ACLU) "observer" to discourage white police officers—who were circling the block with their rifles visible and loaded—from initiating a shoot-out. They left. On another day, we followed Reverend Ezekial Bell in an entourage of cars across a bridge over the Mississippi River to help black civil rights activists in the plantation district of Earle, Arkansas. We turned a corner in the cotton fields to see police and other white men brandishing shotguns, leaning against cars and pickup trucks. As we drove into Earle for a rally, they closed the road behind us. We were lucky to be able to leave Earle intact later that day.

One could see the "white backlash" in full swing in 1972, as President Nixon's attorney general, John Mitchell, proclaimed in Little Rock that Republicans would take the country "so far to the right you won't recognize it." In one macabre scene, white Memphians buried a bus in a trench and stomped its roof in to protest two-way busing to integrate the schools. (Black students had previously been bused to avoid integration.) As blacks gained more political power, many whites left the city. White workers at area factories called us Communists for handing out leaflets supporting Democrat George McGovern for president. We organized a rally at Reverend James Lawson's Centenary United Methodist Church to protest false charges against black activist and California professor Angela Davis, a Communist Party member, and we became targets of the local "Red squad." When we made plans on the phone to meet at a factory gate to hand out leaflets, the police were already waiting for us. They tapped our phones and followed us around, as the FBI accumulated a file of 2,400 pages regarding my various Movement activities dating back to my sophomore year in college.

We were part of a small handful of younger activists who joined with the embattled veterans of the Movement. As such, I was fortunate to meet many of the characters in this book. These included the voluble Reverend Ralph Jackson, the inspiring civil rights leader Maxine Smith, the astute attorney Russell Sugarmon, the prophetic Reverend James Lawson, the athletic but gentle Reverend Henry Starks (who called everyone "brother" or "sister"), the acerbic Bill Ross, and the analytical Dan Powell (the latter two, white labor leaders), the feisty community activist Cornelia Crenshaw, the saintly priest Monsignor Joseph Leppert, and the energetic union organizers Leroy and Alzada Clark. These and many others tested in the strike of 1968 organized Memphis for many years after King's death.

We also witnessed devastating poverty in our fast-deteriorating neighborhood in North Memphis. Unions in my home state of Michigan had enhanced the lives of many of my relatives; I asked what had happened to labor in the South? In my organizing, I met some of those in the previous generations who had built southern labor and civil rights movements since the 1930s—people such as Myles Horton, Claude Williams, Anne and Carl Braden, Modjeska Simkins, Fred Shuttlesworth, and Jack O'Dell. But most leftist labor organizers in Memphis had been run out during the anti-Communist purges of the 1950s, and I knew little about what had happened there. I kept asking myself, How did it get to be this way?

My organizing experience sensitized me to a host of issues and people in the South, and it still provides a vantage point for studying history. But after six years in Memphis, I still did not have answers to my questions. So I went off to graduate school at Howard University in Washington, DC, and then to Northern Illinois University outside Chicago, where learned professors introduced me to the study of African American, southern, and labor history. In my research, I learned about the long history of black resistance to racial oppression and found out that labor organizing persisted during eras of slavery and segregation. In *Southern Labor and Black Civil Rights: Organizing Memphis Workers* (1993) and *Black Workers Remember: An Oral History of Segregation, Unionism, and the Freedom Struggle* (1999), I traced the way black and white workers had created a better world. They generously opened their lives to me and helped me to form a bottom-up view of history that I could never have obtained from other sources.

I had arrived in Memphis only two years after King's death, but until I began researching this book, I still only vaguely understood what had happened there during the great upheavals of 1968 and 1969, when the Memphis sanitation strike became a turning point for the Movement comparable to the Montgomery bus boycott of 1955. The Memphis story provides a window through which we can understand the struggles of the 1960s as well as the deep obstacles to King's dream of a united, peaceful, integrated, democratic America. Yet it is a story that has been almost lost to history. Although many people know King died in Memphis, many don't know what he was doing there; they don't know that he died in a struggle for the right of workers to have a union.

Going Down Jericho Road follows King's Poor People's Campaign and the plight of black workers struggling for union rights in the Mississippi Delta region—until their paths crossed in Memphis in 1968. Organizing in Memphis—the Bluff City—proceeded under its own steam and with its own leaders, but eventually the local movement and King's fate became inextricably intertwined. I have traced the history and highlighted the issues that emerged as part of a national debate about the connection between racism and economics. It is a story about King, and it is also a story about the plight of the unemployed and poor people in America who worked "full-time jobs at part-time wages."

In Memphis, King joined forces with black workers, ministers, young people, women, and a broad range of activists who turned the town upside down for sixty-five days in the winter of 1968 under the banner, "I <u>Am</u> A Man." It was the simplest of demands: the right to human dignity, which translated to union power on the job. Union organizer William (Bill) Lucy called this mass community mobilization "the spirit of Memphis." King defined that spirit as one in which the better-off help the poor to change their lives.

King asked people to follow the example of the Good Samaritan, a traveler of a despised race who stopped to help a battered stranger lying by the side of the road between Jerusalem and Jericho, after better-off religious leaders had passed by and done nothing. "Ultimately, you cannot save yourself without saving others. Other-preservation is the first law of life," King said. On April 3, the night before his death, King urged strike supporters in Memphis to follow the Jericho Road as the Good Samaritan had done—by serving the poor despite personal dangers. In his view, serving others was life's highest calling and also of benefit to ourselves, for, "Either we go up together or we go down together."

———

LIKE ALL HISTORIES, this one remains incomplete. I ask the reader's understanding for the book's shortcomings, and I thank all of those who helped me in trying to tell the story (see Acknowledgments). I have incorporated many voices and perspectives, but especially those of people in the Movement. This story is only part of a much longer and continuing odyssey of the world's working poor—taking us not to the reassuring civil rights legislative victories of 1964 and 1965 but to the hard, unresolved issues of racism and poverty that continue to haunt us in the present.

GOING DOWN
JERICHO
ROAD

Introduction

TWO LIVES LOST

Nothing would be more tragic than to stop at this point in Memphis.
We've got to see it through. When we have our march you need to be
there, if it means leaving work, if it means leaving school, be there.
We've got to give ourselves to this struggle until the end.
—*Martin Luther King, Jr., Memphis, April 3, 1968*

L OCATED IN THE HEART OF THE MISSISSIPPI RIVER DELTA, Memphis often drips with humidity so heavy that merely walking outside is the equivalent of taking a shower. When the skies finally burst open, rain falls so hard that people scurry for shelter. On February 1, 1968, Echol Cole, thirty-six, and Robert Walker, thirty, rode out a driving Memphis rainstorm by climbing inside one of the sanitation division's old "wiener barrel" trucks. The walls inside the packer were caked with putre-fying garbage of all sorts—yard waste, dead chickens, moldy food. Any port in a storm, they say.

At the end of a miserable, cold workday, Cole's and Walker's soiled, worn-out clothes smelled of garbage. The city did not provide them with gloves, uniforms, or a place to shower. They did hard, heavy work, lifting garbage tubs and carrying them on their shoulders or heads or pushcarts to dump their contents into outmoded trucks. On this particular day, Cole and Walker rode in a precarious, stinking perch between a hydraulic ram used to mash garbage into a small wad and the wall of the truck's cavernous container. As crew chief Willie Crain drove the loaded garbage packer along Colonial Street to the Shelby Drive dump, he heard the hydraulic ram go into action, perhaps set off by a shovel that had jarred loose and crossed some electrical wires. He pulled the truck over to the curb at 4:20 PM, but the ram already was jamming Cole and Walker back into the compactor.

One of the men lurched forward and nearly escaped, but the ram snagged his raincoat and dragged him back. "He was standing there on the end of the truck, and suddenly it looked like the big thing just swallowed him," said a horrified woman.

T. O. Jones, a union organizer, knew both of the men. He called their deaths "a disgrace and a sin." Two men had already been killed due to a faulty garbage packer that rolled a truck over in 1964. And Jones had already taken a grievance to the commissioner of the Department of Public Works (DPW), asking that this particular truck no longer be used. Instead of junking the old garbage packer, the sanitation division of DPW had tried to extend its life by putting in a second motor to run the compactor after the first one wore out. Workers jump-started it in the morning and let the motor run all day long, pouring in fuel periodically. It was an accident just waiting to happen.

It went without saying that the two dead men were black. Jones was black. Almost everyone working in sanitation was black, except the bosses. Hauling garbage was the kind of work the city assigned to blacks only.

The city provided a voluntary, self-financed life insurance policy covering death benefits up to $2,000, but Walker and Cole could not afford it. Because the city listed them as unclassified, hourly employees (they could be fired on a moment's notice), the state's workmen's compensation didn't cover them. The two men's deaths left their wives and children destitute. A funeral home held the men's bodies until the families found a way to pay for their caskets. The city gave their families one month's salary and $500 for each man, but burial expenses of $900 for each worker used that up.

These avoidable deaths rubbed raw some long-existing frustrations. Workers had sparred with the administration of the Department of Public Works about many issues, including the use of faulty equipment. The city had no facilities for black workers to wash up, to change clothes, or to get out of the rain.

Workers in the streets and gutter crews were also incensed that the new city government had renewed Mayor Henry Loeb's old policies from his days as Public Works commissioner in the 1950s: when it rained hard, the DPW dismissed workers for the day, with only two hours' worth of pay. In a city where sixty inches of rain fell every year, this policy meant many lost days of work that shrank their already-meager wages.

White supervisors, on the other hand, were paid rain or shine. A few whites operated heavy equipment and belonged to a craft union of engineers, but they had little sense of union solidarity with black workers. Blacks did work as drivers, crew chiefs, and foremen in the sanitation division, but whites had all the power and were part of a long tradition of white supremacy that put blacks at the bottom of the city's labor hierarchy.

African Americans constituted nearly 40 percent of a Memphis population of 500,000 in the mid-1960s, and 58 percent of the city's black families lived in poverty—10 percent above the national average and almost four times the rate of poverty among Memphis white families. Many black families shattered under the pressure; the unemployed and people with marginal jobs suffered disproportionately from diabetes, sickle-cell anemia, high blood pressure, and cancer. More than 80 percent of employed black men worked as laborers, while most black women with paid jobs worked in the homes of whites or in the service economy.

These conditions originated in a long history of racism and labor exploitation. Industrial unions had organized some of the manufacturing industries, but most had not reached out to workers in what economists called the secondary labor market. White employers and craft union members alike had barred African Americans' entry into skilled jobs, and the ready prospect of getting fired forced many black workers to take what the white man dished out. Segregation denied them adequate education, training, and promotion ladders to better jobs, and they routinely endured police brutality and unjust incarceration.

Many sanitation workers made so little that they qualified for welfare even after working a forty-hour week. And they couldn't even count on those hours—white supervisors sent them home without pay or fired them on the slightest pretext. Like most whites in Memphis, many of these supervisors were still accustomed to thinking of blacks as their personal servants. They called people like Ed Gillis—seventy-two years old in 1968—"boy."

Gillis belonged to that stream of rural migrants that washed into the city to become the urban working poor. Generations of these black workers built the wealth of the South and the nation but received little in return. By the time Gillis took a job at the Memphis Department of Public Works in 1948, he had already worked half of his life in the cotton-plantation hinterlands at extremely low wages. His father left him at an early age and his mother could not afford him, so white plantation owners had raised him. He worked hard for them, getting no pay and little education, until he finally left. In all his subsequent roles as farmhand, cowboy, railroad construction worker, and sharecropper, he tried not to cross white folks. But he did not grin, shuffle, or take lightly any abuse of his dignity.

By 1968, Gillis had been crushing rock with a hammer and putting down asphalt for the city of Memphis for twenty years. He had not once been late to work, yet his effort and punctuality counted for nothing with his white bosses. In one incident, a white driver who ignored Gillis's admonitions about how much asphalt to dump, and where, poured it in a huge pile that Gillis then had to shovel up. "That stuff was 497 degrees hot in the summertime," he recalled ruefully. The driver got angry when Gillis objected, and Gillis then exploded at the man, telling him, "I'll whip you all over these streets. White people will see me ride you all over town."

Gillis, like black urban factory workers, was skilled at "taking it" from white folks, but he could only stand so much abuse. On February 12, Lincoln's birthday—just over a week after the deaths of Cole and Walker, and a few days after being shortchanged on pay—Gillis and others on the sewer and drainage crew didn't show up for work—nor did workers in the sanitation division.

Nearly 1,300 black men in the Memphis Department of Public Works, giving no notice to anyone, went on strike. Little did they imagine that their decision would challenge generations of white supremacy in Memphis and have staggering consequences for the nation.

I

LABOR AND
CIVIL RIGHTS

■

1

A PLANTATION IN THE CITY

Run tell your mama,
Run tell your papa,
Run tell your grandma too,
I'm goin' up the country,
Goin' where they don't 'low you.
—*Blues song heard on Beale Street in the 1920s*

MEMPHIS STANDS HIGH ON BLUFFS OVERLOOKING THE Mississippi River, part of the transportation network linking cotton and agricultural production in the fertile Mississippi River lowlands and floodplains to national and world markets. With labor stolen from Africa and land stolen from the Chickasaw Indians, slave traders literally sold black people "down the river" for a profit, and entrepreneurs used slavery and then racial segregation to control labor and keep costs low. As black Memphian and scholar C. Eric Lincoln put it in 1968, "Psychologically, Memphis has always been in Mississippi. Its presence in Tennessee is a geographical accident."

As in Mississippi, blacks and whites understood their common history very differently. Near the center of downtown Memphis, in a park named in his honor, stands a corroding, cast-iron statue erected in 1904 "in the honor of the military genius of Lt. General Nathan Bedford Forrest, CSA [Confederate States Army]." It doesn't tell us that Forrest made his fortune selling slaves, that as a Confederate general during the Civil War he presided over the massacre of hundreds of black and white Union soldiers who surrendered at Fort Pillow, Tennessee, or that he organized the Ku Klux Klan to terrorize black voters and their white allies after the war. Generations of whites paid homage to him as a war hero, while blacks remembered him as a mass murderer.

After the war, African Americans who could not get land of their own ended up as sharecroppers or day laborers, or sought to get "upcountry"— out of the plantations and to the city. Emancipation unleashed a flood of former slaves into Memphis, where they competed for jobs with whites. Irish workers at the bottom of the white labor hierarchy, as well as middle-class whites, terrorized these black Delta migrants during an 1866 white race riot in which forty-six blacks and two whites died. But when blacks obtained civil rights and the right to vote during Reconstruction, through amendments to the federal Constitution, even Nathan Forrest had to seek their support to get elected to office. African Americans made up 30 to 40 percent of the city's voters and elected more blacks to the City Council and legislature in the 1870s and 1880s than they ever would again until the 1990s. Blacks and whites in the Republican and Populist Parties throughout the South taxed the wealthy to fund public schools and services until the better-off divided farmer–labor movements with racist "white supremacy" campaigns, lynching, disenfranchisement, and segregation.

In Tennessee, white Democrats passed laws separating "the races," and instead of taxing wealth, they put a tax on the right to vote that accumulated every year it went unpaid—until poorer whites and blacks could not afford to vote. Racial division set back and nearly destroyed efforts to organize southern labor.

In Memphis, a series of yellow-fever epidemics also killed or forced out German and Irish workers, the most pro-union elements of the city's white working class. "Mother" Mary Jones, an Irish woman who lost her family to the plague, might have organized in Memphis but instead left to lead egalitarian crusades for unions and workers' rights across the country. Most blacks stayed and survived, but new generations of Memphians came almost entirely from the Mississippi Delta, the hard core of cotton plantations and white supremacy. By 1900, the city's white business leaders consolidated their control, eliminating blacks and most working-class whites from political power and entrenching segregation and anti-unionism.

African Americans nonetheless continued to fight for equal rights, build churches and businesses, publish newspapers, and demand work and decent pay. Black women played a crucial role. Ida B. Wells was physically thrown off a train for refusing to ride in a blacks-only section, and she published a newspaper exposing how whites used false cries of rape to justify the lynching of black men. She raised a storm of protest when a white mob murdered three black Memphis businessmen in 1892, and angry whites burned down her newspaper offices and forced her into exile. To overcome black resistance, in 1896, the U.S. Supreme Court, in *Plessy v. Ferguson*, allowed states to enforce segregation (also known as Jim Crow), despite the fact that the Fourteenth Amendment to the Constitution grants equal citizenship rights to all.

Legalized segregation set white workers against black workers and kept them both poor. If whites and blacks could not meet, go to school, ride the trains, vote, or use public facilities equally, they could hardly be expected to organize unions together. Jim Crow laws and racial-economic divisions encouraged racism from the bottom up as well as from the top down. Whites of all classes murdered dozens of black sharecroppers and day laborers when they organized a union in Elaine, Arkansas, at the end of World War I, as white racial violence raged across the land. In the Memphis suburbs, on May 22, 1917, the front page of the *Commercial Appeal* announced that whites would lynch Ell Persons, a black youth falsely charged with raping a white girl. Historians described the grisly scene:

Vendors were on hand to sell pop, sandwiches, and chewing gum. Women wore their best clothes to the event. Parents wrote notes to schoolteachers requesting their children be excused to witness the lynching. An estimated five thousand spectators gathered as Persons was tied to a stake in the ground, then drenched with ten gallons of gasoline and burned alive. . . . Later that afternoon Persons's head and one of his feet were thrown from a passing car into the midst of a group of African Americans standing near Beale Avenue. . . .*

*Most people referred to Beale Avenue as Beale Street.

Such nightmarish violence aimed to produce black passivity, but blacks continued to resist Jim Crow. Robert Church, Jr., son of the first black millionaire in the South, who bought up land during the yellow-fever epidemic and later sold it for a fortune, helped organize a branch of the National Association for the Advancement of Colored People (NAACP). It operated as a nearly secret organization and remained pitifully weak until the 1940s, but black business leaders, educators, and clergy continued to push for better schools, black workers still organized, and rural people moving to the city created a unique, expressive urban culture of blues, gospel, and jazz. The black freedom struggle did not die.

THE HIGH POINT OF SEGREGATION came in the first fifty years of the twentieth century, when one man did more than any other to control and stabilize this wild river town. Sanitation worker Ed Gillis recalled E. H. Crump as "the big dog" of Memphis politics, who ruled almost singlehandedly from the 1910s until his death in 1954, shortly before the Supreme Court's *Brown v. Board of Education* overturned the *Plessy* decision. Raised in Mississippi, Crump left in 1894 with twenty-five cents in his pocket. He worked his way into politics and business, and married into wealth in Memphis. With his bulbous nose, a shock of red (later white) hair, his stocky frame pressed into bankers' clothes, a combative personality, and hyperbolic language, Crump almost seemed comical. But there was nothing comical about Crump's virtual one-man dictatorship.

Crump was first elected Memphis mayor in 1908; thereafter, he built his political machine by collecting money from illegal gambling dens, houses of prostitution, and, during Prohibition, from illegal liquor joints. Crump's ward and precinct heelers used these funds to pay for people's poll taxes and for city employees to get people out to vote for his candidates. Under Crump, "The colored people, they voted plenty," recalled Republican black political activist George W. Lee. In fact, he said, "People'd vote four and five times," and they voted just the way Crump wanted them to. Crump modernized city services while entrenching segregation, and his control over the most populated city in Tennessee increasingly gave him power over state and national elections and the Democratic Party.

Generations of whites mythologized Crump as a great leader, but as a labor journalist wrote, under Crump there was "no Bill of Rights in Memphis." Crump put Ku Klux Klan leader Cliff Davis in charge of the police and then made him a congressman for thirteen terms. Only a handful of blacks worked in the police department until the 1960s, mostly on Beale Street, and they could not arrest whites or testify against them in court. On the other hand, white police officers, many of them straight from the plantation districts, functioned like Klansmen in blue uniforms, brutalizing and insulting African Americans and union organizers with support from white judges, FBI officials, and federal attorneys. Robert Church fled the city in 1940 when the Crump machine cracked down on civil rights activity and thugs beat up several independent black ministers with lead pipes. Fear and conformity, pervasive mistrust, and avoidance of independent thought and action had become hallmarks of Memphis life—for whites as well as for blacks. Police "snitches" kept Crump informed of all civil rights and labor activities.

In return for their "cooperation," Crump offered black leaders a greater degree of funding for social services, schools, and public housing (all segregated) than in most southern cities. Like a plantation father figure, Crump claimed to take care of "his" people as if they were children: he rewarded them as long as they obeyed and punished them if they did not. Some called this paternalism; most black folk called it "the plantation mentality."

As he became a millionaire through real estate, banking, insurance, and investments, Crump gained overwhelming white business and middle-class support. He offered tight control over blacks, clean streets, efficient city services, and a mostly nonunion environment. White employers banned blacks from better jobs and relied on them for low-wage labor in domestic employment, woodworking, cotton, laundry, and manufacturing. The Memphis Furniture Company, started by the descendants of slave owners in Mississippi, built a fortune by paying black workers as little as possible, as did the Loeb Laundry Cleaner Company, founded by a Jewish immigrant. Real estate investors, cotton brokers, bankers, railroad and riverboat owners, and local manufacturers all supported Jim Crow and Crump; it was profitable to do so and dangerous not to.

Under this regime, the income of unskilled workers, both white and black, averaged less than half of the average in the rest of the country. Yet most white workers resisted joining unions with blacks, even in industries where they both worked at rock-bottom wages, producing profits for industry but misery for the unskilled. The city's elite of organized white craftsmen, on the other hand, profited from Jim Crow. During slavery, blacks did much of the skilled work in cities such as Memphis, and after Emancipation, white craftsmen organized unions that removed them. This created a scarcity of skilled labor and pushed up wages for a relatively small group of white building tradesmen in the American Federation of Labor (AFL). Blacks held a few jobs in the trowel trades and in laboring jobs, controlled by strictly segregated unions that met in the old slave servants' quarters behind the AFL headquarters on Beale Street. On the railroads, white brotherhoods forced black workers out of the good-paying jobs by killing or brutalizing them; in 1919, 650 white railroad workers from Memphis led a five-day wildcat strike in an attempt to eliminate blacks from the industry. AFL unions routinely excluded blacks from skilled work, even in federally funded construction jobs during the New Deal.

The mix of segregation, low wages, anti-union sentiment, and machine politics in Memphis created a particularly deadly legacy for public employees. Crump turned the city's elite of white AFL craftsmen into allies by allowing city government to set wages at union scale through contracts with the city's builders' association. But the city never formally recognized unions or signed a union contract; when white firefighters, teachers, and police officers tried to organize unions, the city fired and blacklisted them. Crump did not want organized workers exercising any independence or raising the costs of their labor, and opposition to public-employee unionism became a tradition in Memphis. Even President Franklin Roosevelt excluded government workers from the right to organize during the New Deal.

All of this created huge obstacles to black worker organizing, but during the Great Depression, farmers, workers, poor people, and a dispossessed middle class overwhelmingly elected Roosevelt as president in 1932, pressuring him to do something to end poverty and unemployment. In 1935, the federal government enacted the Wagner Labor Relations Act, which established citizenship rights on the job by allowing workers to freely support or reject unions in secret balloting protected by the National Labor Relations Board (NLRB). Southern congressmen prevented the Wagner Act from covering government, agricultural, and domestic workers (in the South, blacks made up the vast majority of the last two groups). The federal government looked the other way as planters crushed the Southern Tenant Farmers Union (STFU), across the river from Memphis, and took no strong actions to stop lynching in the South. The New Deal was hardly paradise for African Americans, who suffered egregious discrimination under its policies.

But hope emerged as a group of unions formed the Congress of Industrial Organizations (CIO) and pledged to organize all workers regardless of race, gender, nationality, or political beliefs. African Americans became the CIO's strongest supporters of interracial organizing, aided by assorted white radicals. Despite all the obstacles, workers in Memphis during the late 1930s and throughout World War II built CIO unions in cotton and food processing, on the waterfronts, in lumberyards, and in factories, but they often paid a terrible price for their activism. Whites beat and nearly killed Thomas Watkins, a black longshoreman who led a strike of black and white Mississippi River workers in 1939, as Crump denounced the CIO as "nigger unionism" and "Communism." Company thugs and white workers fearful of losing their jobs brutally beat white union organizers at the Ford and Firestone factories. Even black workers, fearful their company would close if they unionized, slashed open the stomach of fellow worker Clarence Coe when he tried to organize them. "You had to fight for every inch—nobody gave you anything," he recalled. "We couldn't meet in no single place together. They would kick all our asses," and police "beat the white worse than the black" when they held a CIO meeting on the waterfront. Employers continued to divide workers by race. "You couldn't hardly trust a guy that you couldn't meet with. Twenty years after we had the union, you couldn't trust certain people."

George Holloway, a black worker at Firestone, saw unions as his one hope for a better life. He hated the fact that his grandparents had been slaves, and he hated the segregated schools, theaters, buses, cinemas, restaurants, neighborhoods, and jobs in Memphis. His father, who belonged to A. Philip Randolph's Brotherhood of Sleeping Car Porters, had improved his family's situation through union wages. Holloway followed his father and Randolph, hoping for an alliance between unions and blacks that would enfranchise workers and get rid of Jim Crow. Martin Luther King, Jr., would nurture the same hope.

THE BLACK IMPULSE to resist Jim Crow took many forms. During a seemingly hopeless era of discrimination, black workers created something very special in Memphis. The city's reputation as a wide-open river town with a strong, expressive black culture attracted people from the plantations in a continuing rural-to-urban migration (the "Delta flow," some called it) that channeled people such as Memphis Minnie, Howling Wolf, Muddy Waters, B. B. King, and many more into an area tucked between the ghetto and downtown. As Muddy Waters put it, "Beale Street was the street. Black man's street. . . . So many slick people came from down that way, learnt how to gamble, learnt how to con, how to cheat, from down in that part of the country. And Beale Street was the main line." Here, in the "home of the blues," men and women sang and played guitars, banjos, pianos, and whiskey jugs, and even made a living doing it. Black cultural identity emanated from the churches but also from Beale Street, where sanitation strikers marched repeatedly in 1968.

One of the Beale Street bluesmen was Walter ("Furry") Lewis. His parents separated before he was born—in Greenwood, Mississippi, in 1893—and he ended up at the age of six on Brinkley Avenue in Memphis. Fending for himself, Furry picked up a guitar and made his money singing on street corners; he formed his own band and traveled the South with medicine shows. Lewis survived by his wits, but in 1916 he lost his leg in an accident while trying to hop a freight train. Unable to do heavy labor, he found a job in 1923 with the sanitation division of the Memphis Department of Public Works. Starting at two in the morning, he swept city streets with a broom and hauled garbage with a mule-drawn trailer. He slept in the daytime and at night played in taverns and at private parties, even at the police station. He developed a large repertoire of songs with his clear singing voice and clean, sure, finger-picking style. He picked blues into the night and picked up garbage until dawn.

Lewis recorded classic blues songs in the 1920s, but the blues as a commercial enterprise nearly disappeared after the Depression struck Beale Street. In 1940, Crump shut down its illegal juke joints as a way to clean up his image with white voters, and businesses there took a further downward slide. Furry kept sweeping streets until Sam Charters rediscovered and rere-corded him in 1959, as an icon of the lost days of Beale Street. In the 1960s, white musicians beat a path to Furry's door, seeking the roots of the blues.

Like most bluesmen, Furry rarely sang directly about his trials and tribulations as a worker. He sang about being unjustly accused of crimes, about trying to avoid the death penalty or the penitentiary, about hateful love affairs, about trains and living on the road, about the pleasures of women and wine. When he sang about work, it was about John Henry, who could outwork a machine but died doing it. He believed the best work was no work at all:

> *I left Memphis to spread the news,*
> *Memphis women don't wear no shoes,*
> *Had it written in the back of my shirt,*
> *I'm a natural-born lover, don't have to work.*

Sometime during or after the 1968 strike, Furry retired from sanitation work, but by then the world of black labor had changed immensely. During World War II, Memphis had offered rural blacks something more attractive than the blues: jobs. Suddenly, war industries needed black workers, including black women, and A. Philip Randolph threatened a mass march on Washington in 1941 unless President Roosevelt opened industrial jobs to blacks. Through executive order, the president called for employers to end Jim Crow on the job; then he set up the War Labor Board, which penalized industries for interfering with the right to orga-nize or join a union. Crump met his Waterloo when the federal govern-ment threatened to take away federal contracts if he did not leave the unions alone.

Crump finally let Randolph speak in Memphis in 1944 (he had banned him earlier), by which time many blacks and whites had joined forces in the CIO. The United Rubber Workers (URW) became the CIO's largest union, with 7,000 members during and about 3,000 after the war, about a third of them black. Increasing numbers of white workers realized that unions could not effectively organize factories unless they organized all the workers into one union. From fewer than a thousand members before the war, CIO unions expanded to more than 32,000 members at its end. AFL unions had even more members.

White workers, even in the CIO, continued to resist black equality at every turn, yet the CIO gave black workers a form of leverage they had never had before. The 1940s became the "seedtime" of the civil rights revolution, as the NAACP called for a "double victory" campaign against Hitler fascism abroad and Jim Crow fascism at home. Black leaders such as W. E. B. Du Bois called on CIO unions to democratize American life, and black workers increasingly demanded equal access to jobs, to elected union positions, and to skills and advancement. Union wages spurred bigger donations to churches and civic groups, and Coe, Holloway, and other black CIO members joined civil rights groups, voter registration drives, and black civic clubs to challenge segregation. NAACP membership ballooned in heavily unionized places such as Detroit, and the Memphis NAACP became one of the largest chapters in the South. Black soldiers returning home from the war demanded equal rights, and many of them used the GI Bill and union wages to create a new generation of college-educated youth demanding their due as citizens.

Black women like Irene Branch, a domestic worker who became a Firestone employee, also joined unions during the war as a ticket to a much better life. "Those supervisors would curse you, call you names, do you any kind of way. They'd call you 'nigger' and everything else, and spit on you. Blacks was really treated bad." But union grievance committees changed this. "We didn't see freedom until we got that union in!" Even though many black women lost union jobs after the war, they continued to play increasing roles in service work and public employment, supporting sanitation workers and others who demanded unions. Some 80 percent of black women wage earners worked as domestic workers in Memphis before the war; by 1960, less than half of them did.

Although the CIO unions kept it quiet, Communists also played a crucial role in the upsurge of unions and civil rights demands in the 1940s. Leftist CIO activists led Local 19 of the Food, Tobacco, Agricultural, and Allied Workers' Union of America (FTA), Local 282 of the United Furniture Workers of America (UFWA), and the National Maritime Union (NMU) and provided the key supporters of labor and civil rights organizing. After the war, CIO leftists practiced "social equality" (integration) in their union halls, elected black officers, created active rank-and-file shop-steward councils, socialized over beer and on picket lines, called each other "brother" and "sister" in meetings, and in other ways challenged white supremacy. At Firestone and in most industries, blacks and whites still had separate departments and seniority lines, denying blacks promotion into the better jobs, yet an increasingly active "civil rights unionism" also made headway.

In 1946, the CIO generated great hopes when it announced Operation Dixie—a million-dollar campaign to organize southern workers, support equal rights for blacks, and eliminate reactionary politicians through a voting coalition of black and white working-class voters. This projected voting alliance—coupled with industrial growth, black migration and urbanization, and unionization—threatened to change race relations as the Memphis population swelled from 300,000 to 500,000 between 1930 and 1960 and became nearly 40 percent black. The rise of black-run radio stations WDIA and WLOK, the black-owned newspapers *Memphis World* (begun in the 1930s) and *Tri-State Defender* (begun in 1951), and increasing education and assertiveness among black ministers all ushered in a rising demand for black freedom in the postwar period.

THIS BUDDING REVOLUTION of labor and civil rights was stifled in its infancy, as the nation made a great political U-turn after the war. Lynching of black war veterans, which the young Martin Luther King protested in a letter to the *Atlanta Constitution* in July 1946,* demonstrated that segregationists would strike back hard against black aspirations. At the same time,

---

*Twenty white men shot to death two black couples driving near Monroe, Georgia, apparently because at least one of the black men wore a soldier's uniform.

the U.S. Chamber of Commerce declared that there were "two great menaces to the U.S., Russia abroad and unions at home," and a new breed of Republicans in Congress, such as Richard Nixon, portrayed CIO unions and New Deal Democrats as part of a Communist conspiracy.

Lubricated with money from right-wing oilmen in Texas and supported by segregationists across the South, the rhetoric of anti-Communism throttled social change. One white minister, speaking before the Memphis Lions Club in 1947, said unions had to be stopped to keep Communists from secretly taking over. Southern groups such as "Christian America," the Southern States Industrial Council, and the Christian fundamentalist Harding College in Arkansas, put out blizzards of anti-Communist, anti-union, and anti-integration propaganda on college campuses and military bases. Klansmen, police, and vigilantes arrested, kidnapped, and beat CIO organizers, and many employers routinely fired workers for joining unions.

The climate for unions worsened in 1947 as a more conservative Congress emasculated worker protections under the Wagner Act. The Taft-Hartley Act, section 14(b), allowed states to outlaw the "union shop" that made union membership a condition of employment. It also prohibited secondary boycotts of employer goods, enmeshed organizers in a maze of legal requirements, required union officers to sign an anti-Communist oath or lose the right to participate in NLRB elections, and restricted union political contributions. The Tennessee legislature promptly passed a "right to work" law, allowing workers to gain benefits from a unionized workplace without joining the union or paying dues. "Free riders" made it very difficult for unions to maintain their memberships in an increasingly fearful, anti-union environment.

At the time that Ed Gillis moved to Memphis in 1948, Crump's days as a political boss were numbered, because many unionized workers could now afford to pay their own poll taxes and vote against his candidates. Attorney Lucius Burch, who would serve as attorney for Dr. King in 1968, organized a coalition of blacks, middle-class reformers, and unionized workers that elected Democratic liberal Estes Kefauver (and later Albert Gore, Sr.) to the U.S. Senate. Crump's reactionary candidate failed to decisively carry Shelby County for the first time, a sign that unions had become a major factor in Tennessee politics. But things also took a turn for the worse during the 1948 election. Left-wing unions and many civil rights activists supported the independent Progressive Party presidential candidate, Henry Wallace, formerly the vice president under Roosevelt, who ran the first truly integrated national political campaign in the South and called for an end to nuclear testing and a peaceful détente with the Soviet Union. Nineteen-year-old Martin Luther King and many other blacks hailed Wallace's commitment to integration, as Progressives ran black and white candidates on the same ballot and held integrated rallies. In Memphis, the famous baritone Paul Robeson held a concert for Wallace at Mason Temple, where sanitation strikers would rally twenty years later.

Harry Truman and many anti-Communist liberals disregarded the grassroots character of the Wallace campaign and maligned him as a surrogate for the Communist Party. The CIO did not like Truman but supported him as the lesser evil against Republican Thomas Dewey, and Truman won mainly due to labor support. But after the election, a great "Red scare" swept the nation as Truman and the Democrats led bipartisan repression against the Left at home and national independence movements in the former colonial world. The CIO joined in, purging eleven unions with nearly a million members for having Communists in their leadership. The CIO also cut its financial support to the integrationist Southern Conference Educational Fund (SCEF), and to Highlander Folk School when it refused to ban left-led unions, the strongest supporters of integration. The "Red scare" nearly silenced demands for integration within organized labor in Memphis and the South for the next twenty years.

Attempts to organize southern workers, still the least unionized in the country, fell to pieces, setting precedents that would make organizing black workers extremely difficult during the 1960s. In Memphis, a court injunction forbade workers from picketing and helped the Greyhound Bus Company break a strike in 1946. In 1949, the Memphis Furniture Company fired a black union leader and withdrew union recognition and dues-checkoff rights that workers had won during the war, thus forcing black women—many of them single mothers—to strike. They walked the picket line for months, some of them with burlap bags tied around their feet because they lacked winter shoes. The police escorted strikebreakers into the plant in buses decorated by red, white, and blue banners, and they threatened picketers with long clubs tooled inside the plant by scabs. The segregationist white CIO leader Red Copeland stepped up efforts to purge from the CIO leftists and civil rights advocates, including an important young black leader, UFWA president Rudolph Johnson.

The defeat of unionists at Memphis Furniture set off an employer campaign to decertify other CIO unions. Owners of the American Snuff Company tobacco plant, one of whom later became a prominent John Birch Society activist, provoked a strike of 350 women (most of them white), employed police violence, and replaced union workers with scabs (many of them black), thereby destroying the union. Injunctions against picketing, prohibitions of secondary boycotts (in which nonstriking unions boycott the goods of companies under strike), racial divisions, the use of scabs, and police violence once again became standard ways to break unions in Memphis.

Civil rights advocacy within organized labor soon became practically forbidden in Memphis. U.S. Senator James Eastland, one of the largest plantation owners in Mississippi and a leader of the white supremacist White Citizens' Council, held Memphis hearings in 1951 attacking labor's civil rights supporters. He was particularly angry that black Local 19 members had gone to his state to protest the frame-up of Willie McGee, a black truck driver who had a consensual love affair with a white woman but was nonetheless executed on a rape charge. Leroy Boyd and other protesting Local 19 members were arrested and barely escaped Mississippi alive. Eastland's hearings forced Local 19's white business agent, Ed McCrea—an integrationist and one of the CIO's most able organizers—to leave town. Boyd observed, "If a white person took too much time with a Negro, they'd always call him a nigger lover . . . and also Communists." Eastland again held hearings in Memphis in 1957, attacking, among others, Grace Lorch, a white woman who saved black teenager Elizabeth Eckford from a mob during the school desegregation struggle in Little Rock.

Combined "Red scares" and "Black scares" not only killed union organizing but silenced support for the U.S. Supreme Court's *Brown v. Board of*

Education ruling on May 17, 1954, which overturned segregation as the law of the land. The Communist "conspiracy" remained a staple news item, as did a drumbeat of support for the American military intervention in Korea and elsewhere. As the great reversal of the 1950s shut down public debate, a more bureaucratic, conservative, business style of unionism replaced the thriving CIO labor movement of 1946, and segregation reigned in most southern unions. By the time the mostly segregated AFL unions merged with the mostly biracial CIO unions in 1955–56, organizing had practically stopped—a fact the Memphis *Press-Scimitar* emphasized with a headline in 1955: LABOR? MANAGEMENT? NO ONE COULD TELL THEM APART. AFL and CIO unions in Memphis probably had a respectable 50,000 members among them, but union membership sharply declined as unions ceased to organize the unorganized.

Integrationists tried to use the contradiction between Jim Crow at home and America's espousal of freedom in the world as leverage to make civil rights demands on the federal government, but cold war anti-Communism undermined civil rights as well as unions. The cold war did not create a favorable climate for change; instead, its pressures caused the NAACP increasingly to narrow its framework, away from a broader social and human rights agenda to what people called civil rights. Top NAACP leaders like Thurgood Marshall collaborated with the FBI in rooting out "Reds" from the Movement, just as did the AFL-CIO, thus proving their loyalty to American foreign policy dictates. But purges did not protect the NAACP from the anti-Communist and segregationist backlash.

Memphis NAACP membership had jumped from about 400 in the late 1930s to more than 4,000 in 1947, but by 1949 it dropped to about 1,000 and remained at low ebb for the next ten years. The NAACP nationally and in Memphis ostracized leftists and steered clear of the Willie McGee case, while the Memphis Urban League, ostensibly a supporter of civil rights, cooperated with Eastland to kill Local 19, the most racially progressive CIO union in Memphis. "Memphis is a hard spot," wrote the NAACP branch president in 1954; NAACP regional organizer Ruby Hurley later wrote to her national office: "I could really cry about Memphis." Memphis NAACP President Harold Lockhart in 1955 decried the local NAACP's "pronounced apathy and lethargy," but when he tried to get black teachers to organize youth chapters, the school superintendent put a quick stop to it by accusing the NAACP of being a Communist front. In Mississippi and Alabama, white officials actually declared the NAACP illegal.

THE COLD WAR'S crushing assaults undercut organizing and uncoupled unions from the civil rights struggle. In the South, white supremacy still reigned. Unions failed to reach out to organize the largest group of the unorganized—black workers—and civil rights groups steered clear of union organizing, leaving the black working poor with few champions. The light that CIO unions had once cast upon demands for labor solidarity and workers' rights flickered and faded.

One glimmer of light still shone from Memphis, as blacks and whites from working-class and rural cultures created rock 'n' roll, country, blues, and soul music that helped many American youth break the cultural mold of segregation. Elvis Presley, Johnny Cash, B. B. King, and "a surprising number of the performers recognized immediately anywhere in the world came from Memphis and its environs," wrote historian Pete Daniel.

More importantly, the Red scare could not stop the emerging civil rights revolution, led in part by the young Martin Luther King, Jr.

2

DR. KING, LABOR, AND THE CIVIL RIGHTS MOVEMENT

*The two most dynamic and cohesive liberal forces in the country are
the labor movement and the Negro freedom movement. . . . Together
we can bring about the day when there will be no separate
identification of Negroes and labor. . . . Some will be called
reds and Communists merely because they believe in economic
justice and the brotherhood of man. But we shall overcome.*
—*Martin Luther King, Jr., Fourth Constitutional Convention,
AFL-CIO, December 11, 1961*

IN 1957, *TIME* MAGAZINE PROCLAIMED KING ITS "MAN OF THE
Year." It characterized him as an "expert organizer" but "no radical"—
a Christian civil rights leader, presumed to be quite different from
1940s black socialists with labor politics like Randolph, Du Bois, or Robeson. In reality, King never confined his politics to civil rights. He had clear
links to working-class and poor people through his family, church, and
community, and from an early age he advocated an economic-justice
agenda that went far beyond civil rights. He also developed a labor perspective and connections to unions that influenced his strategy for change.

White journalists may have seen the well-dressed, highly educated, eloquent "Dr. King" as the quintessential middle-class leader, but he came
from a line of people, including slaves, who struggled fiercely against
poverty and Jim Crow. His grandmother took in washing and ironing for
whites but was not afraid to beat up a white man who had assaulted her
son, Martin's father. Martin's grandfather on his maternal side, A. D.
Williams, lost his thumb in a sawmill accident and was no stranger to hard

work. He escaped from plantations and peonage in the countryside by migrating to Atlanta and turning a minuscule congregation of former slaves at Ebenezer Baptist Church into one of the city's largest black churches. Along with Dr. Du Bois, the renowned black scholar at Atlanta University, Williams protested the bloody white race riot of 1906 that killed twenty-six African Americans in Atlanta. He developed the local chapter of the NAACP and led church and civil rights activities there for many years.

"Daddy" King, Martin's father, also escaped lynching terror and low wages by moving to Atlanta from rural Georgia. He married A. D.'s daughter Alberta, and when A. D. died, he boosted a declining membership at Ebenezer and led local NAACP fights for voting rights, desegregation, and increased salaries for black teachers. Preaching a religious Social Gospel aimed at elevating the black urban poor, he took his son Martin—born in the year of the stock market crash of 1929—to see the unemployed people standing in food lines, so that a young man being raised in relative material comfort would understand the privations of the poor.

Martin wrote that he learned at an early age that "the inseparable twin of racial injustice was economic injustice," and that he developed "anticapitalist feelings" as he witnessed dreadful southern poverty and labor exploitation during part-time summer work. He had an optimistic belief in the goodness of human nature and the power of America's democratic ideals, but, like other African Americans, he was constantly tested by the deep-seated racism of most whites. As an undergraduate in sociology at historically black Morehouse College between 1944 and 1947, King studied the systemic links between racism and poverty and how they might be overcome through democratic action. As a master's-degree student at Crozier Theological Seminary outside of Philadelphia, and then as a Ph.D. student at Boston University, King became familiar with Social Gospel indictments of economic inequality and read about Gandhi and his campaigns of nonviolent direct action. He disagreed with Karl Marx's atheism but adopted his biting critique of capitalism as damaging to the poor and workers. King used Hegel's dialectical reasoning to envision a Christian-democratic "third way" between capitalism and Communism, and he adopted an optimistic theology of "personalism," in which a God who valued the sanctity of the individual aided humans who struggled to overcome evil through concerted group action.

King belonged to a generation of highly educated black Christian preachers who came into their own during the labor-based progressivism of the 1930s and 1940s. When he met Coretta Scott in Boston, he found another black Southerner (raised in rural Alabama) who wanted to change the world and who remained a peace advocate all of her life. During the Depression, whites had robbed her father of his earnings and later burned his sawmill to the ground; she did not grow up with a middle-class shield such as the one that had protected Martin. She was a fine soprano, and as a student at Antioch College, she sang in a concert with Robeson, whose singing and acting career was destroyed by the Red scare. She moved on to the New England Conservatory of Music in Boston, where she met and married Martin in 1953. In September 1954, less than four months after the U.S. Supreme Court overturned school segregation, they moved to Montgomery, Alabama.

Their lives changed on December 1, 1955, when Rosa Parks, a seamstress, refused to give up her seat on a bus to a white man and touched off a new kind of mass movement. Parks had recently attended workshops at Highlander Folk School, an interracial meeting ground for CIO unionists in the 1930s and 1940s and for civil rights activists in the 1950s and 1960s. She had long worked as an assistant to E. D. Nixon, past president of the Montgomery NAACP and a leader of the Brotherhood of Sleeping Car Porters, and she also led NAACP youth groups. Her refusal to give up her seat led to her arrest, which set an example that energized black working people—the majority of those who rode the buses. They boycotted them for 381 days, walking or getting rides in car pools to their jobs, using a black bricklayers' union hall as headquarters. Nixon got Parks out of jail, steered King into Movement leadership, and shamed black ministers into taking a forthright public stand against Jim Crow.

King had qualities that allowed him to lead a mass movement that joined working-class people to the middle class through the black church. In a remarkable few moments in his first speech at the first mass meeting of the Montgomery Improvement Association (MIA), King put the struggle against segregation into a moral and world-historical context. "There comes a time when people get tired of being trampled over by the iron feet of oppression," and have to organize, he said. Unions had set the precedent: "When labor all over this nation came to see that it would be trampled over by capitalistic power, it was nothing wrong with labor getting together and organizing and protesting for its rights." King's call for unity in a struggle for "freedom and justice and equality" that he said would reverberate worldwide had a powerful effect in creating the Montgomery movement, which in turn became King's model for a democratic, nonviolent revolution.

Nixon embodied the connection between labor and civil rights, raising hundreds of thousands of dollars as treasurer of the MIA by appealing to union members across the country, and by helping to connect King to Randolph and the world of civil rights unionism and pacifism. Bayard Rustin and Glenn Smiley of the Fellowship of Reconciliation (FOR) came to Montgomery to help King sharpen his understanding of nonviolent direct action, and they convinced him to give up the "arsenal" of guns he had in his home to protect his family. King came to know A. Philip Randolph, Walter Reuther (the social-democratic president of the United Automobile Workers union, the UAW), and leftist Ralph Helstein, president of the United Packinghouse Workers of America (UPWA). The AFL-CIO did nothing to support the Montgomery movement, but these unions with large black memberships donated heavily to the MIA, and in the future King repeatedly would turn for support to them as well as to Local 1199 Hospital Workers and District 65 of the UAW in New York City. Cleveland Robinson, Moe Foner, Carl and Anne Braden of SCEF, Myles Horton of Highlander, and others associated with civil rights–oriented unionism and the labor Left became King's staunch allies.

Racists blew up King's house, the house of E. D. Nixon, and the residences and churches of other activists. Senator Eastland and the White Citizens' Council subjected blacks and their white supporters to economic intimidation and fear, yet the Montgomery movement stayed united and won a Supreme Court ruling against segregation in transportation. King's religious framework, his stunning eloquence, his learning, his ability to place his demands within the framework of the Constitution and the American creed of freedom—all made him a powerful spokesperson, and the mass media gave King phenomenal attention.

In 1957, King and other ministers held a conference on desegregating transportation through boycotts and other protests, producing the Southern Christian Leadership Conference (SCLC), a ministers' group that sought to end Jim Crow and "redeem the soul of America" through nonviolent organizing. Black labor activists such as Russell Lasley of the UPWA, as well as New York City leftists Bayard Rustin, Ella Baker, and Stanley Levison, helped King formulate a platform and tighten his ties to civil rights and labor advocates. King also went to Ghana to celebrate its independence from British colonialism, and he visited India to learn more about nonviolence. Indian Prime Minister Nehru spoke with him about democratic and socialist anticolonial movements in the developing world. King gained an increasingly global perspective and specialized in linking issues. At Highlander Folk School's twenty-fifth anniversary celebration in September 1957, he called for a coalition between organized labor and Negroes to end Jim Crow, adding, "I never intend to adjust myself to the tragic inequalities of an economic system which will take necessities from the masses to give luxuries to the classes."

A month later, he spoke to Helstein's UPWA members in Chicago: "The forces that are anti-Negro are by and large anti-labor, and with the coming together of the powerful influence of labor and all people of good will in the struggle for freedom and human dignity, I can assure you that we have a powerful instrument." King defined integration as "complete political, economic and social equality," and said achieving it required "a whole series of measures which go beyond the specific issue of segregation." This idea of a grand alliance to extend democracy to racial and economic spheres became a fundamental concept for King, as did his strong belief in American democracy—what King called "the right to protest *for* right." Although the media tended to portray him as almost solely a civil rights leader, demanding equal rights within American capitalism, his views went much further than that.

American conservatives and segregationists, on the other hand, increasingly attacked him as a covert Communist. Georgia's Commission on Education sent an undercover agent to take a picture of King sitting next to a reporter for the Communist Party newspaper, the *Daily Worker*, at the Highlander gathering. Right-wing groups turned the photo and headline, "Martin Luther King at Communist Training School," into the most famous billboard of the era. The *Commercial Appeal* ran a picture of the billboard, the John Birch Society sent it out as a postcard, and Billy James Hargis and the Christian Crusade used the allegation against King in its pamphlet titled, *Unmasking Martin Luther King, Jr., The Deceiver.* Bob James, a white Memphis City Council member, recalled that his impression of King as a subversive rabble-rouser first began with this depiction of him as an associate of Communists. Segregationists campaigned for years to close the integrationist Highlander and claimed that King's association with the school proved that he was Communist—and that the school's association with King proved *it* was Communist.

Congressional investigating committees and southern segregationists used the circular reasoning of anti-Communism against King for the rest of his life, imposing guilt by association when he insisted on defending other people's civil liberties. He petitioned to free integrationists Carl Braden and Frank Wilkinson from "Communist" charges made before the House Un-American Activities Committee (HUAC), a congressional committee led by Southerners trying to destroy the integrationist movement. Drawing on HUAC reports, the FBI noted King's efforts to free Junius Scales, the last imprisoned victim of the anti-Communist Smith Act (his conviction was later overturned by the Supreme Court), and Morton Sobel, convicted of conspiracy to commit espionage in the Julius and Ethel Rosenberg case, as well as his support for black Communist Henry Winston, a Smith Act victim who lost his sight while in prison. King was not a Communist by any means, but he did not see them as demons; he was friendly with people such as Benjamin Davis, a black Communist former city councilman from Harlem who was born and raised in Atlanta, and Jack O'Dell, a black former Communist and CIO activist.

King was not the dupe of anyone. Rather, he viewed civil liberties and civil rights as indivisible, and he recognized that denying freedom of speech for leftists inculcated a climate of fear aimed at silencing all movements for change. Along with other leading black intellectuals, such as Morehouse College President Benjamin Mays, King called for the abolition of HUAC, Eastland's antisubversive Senate committee, and other efforts to suppress freedom of speech and thought. Like Mays, he also recognized the failures of capitalism for people of color; encouraged by Coretta, he increasingly opposed America's interventionist militarism abroad. And, like numerous black intellectuals of the CIO era, he continued to appreciate the value of an alliance between the progressive wing of the labor movement and the black community.

King had a broad perspective on issues, but he also recognized that until a people's movement overturned Jim Crow and blacks gained the right to vote, few other meaningful changes could occur. With King's fame as a civil rights leader growing, media accounts often suggested that he alone could almost magically design and lead one victorious movement after another; people besieged him with speaking requests, and he had little time to think or plan an organizing campaign. He developed a reputation as a leader of the masses, but his reputation went far beyond his resources or his experience. The Montgomery movement fell into disarray and division after King moved to Atlanta to become co-pastor of his father's Ebenezer Baptist Church and president of SCLC. King could not export the bus-boycott model to other communities, segregationists stifled grassroots voter-registration drives, and King floundered in his efforts to organize a mass movement. His search for viable tactics and strategies would haunt him for the rest of his life, as he continued to expand his view of the nature of the problems and the possible solutions confronting the freedom movement.

KING FIRST WENT to Memphis on July 31, 1959, to speak at a massive freedom rally at Charles H. Mason Temple, owned by the Church of God in Christ, a rapidly growing Pentecostal denomination. King's demand— "Give us the ballot and we will change the South," made at a rally of some 27,000 people in the nation's capital in 1957—had especially resonated in Memphis, where more blacks already had the vote than in any other southern town and a voter-registration movement was going strong.

The *Brown* decision, Crump's death in 1954, the Montgomery move-

ment, and the murder of young Emmett Till in Mississippi had all galvanized a younger generation of black freedom fighters in Memphis. Black
postal employee O. Z. Evers sued to end bus segregation even before the
Montgomery bus boycott began. Clarence Coe and other black unionists
at Firestone—represented by a labor attorney named Anthony Sabella,
who later represented black workers in the 1968 sanitation strike—
collected money to sue both their employer and their union for discrimination, using *Brown* as a legal precedent. After the Tennessee legislature
repealed the poll tax in 1951, African Americans had also formed dozens
of civic clubs to register black voters, whose numbers increased from 7,000
in 1951 to 39,000 in 1954.

Black unionists and civil rights supporters campaigned against police
brutality and segregation and vowed to elect blacks to office, as they had in
the late nineteenth century. Black minister Roy Love ran for the school
board in 1954 and received 20,000 black votes, and attorneys Russell Sugarmon and A. W. Willis, Alma Morris, and others created the Shelby
County Democratic Club to unify black voting clubs. (Black activists in
Nashville took similar action.) After white officials disqualified Evers, Sugarmon ran for city commissioner and led an effort to elect a Volunteer
Ticket to unify black voters. Three of the five candidates were ministers, a
sign of growing activism among the black clergy. Birmingham's Reverend
Fred Shuttlesworth, Little Rock's Daisy Bates, gospel singer Mahalia Jackson, and SCLC's Reverend Ralph David Abernathy all came to Memphis to
support the campaign.

When King appeared on July 31 to support Sugarmon's effort, more
than 5,000 black people "rocked Mason Temple," according to the *Tri-State
Defender*, a black weekly, and they displayed the fervent spirit that became
characteristic of the city's mass meetings. Sugarmon said King's speaking
style electrified his audience. "He was tremendously eloquent. . . . I never
heard anybody who could give voice to the emotions and aspirations like
he could in the idiom of the Negro church." King used a pattern of making
a statement of fact and then saying, "We just want to be free." He got about
three of these statements out before the audience spoke back in a kind of
call-and-response. "Every time he got to the refrain, five thousand people

would join in. It was fantastic. You could feel the feedback . . . the rapport between him and everybody in that room." Sugarmon added: "I'll never forget that because you could feel the assemblage acquire a personality of its own. It was like a brain relating to the limbs."

Like King, Sugarmon was born in 1929 and led an educated group of middle-class militants driving the civil rights movement forward in the late 1950s. Sugarmon remembered his first racial incident as a child, when police arrested him and slapped him around for riding a new bicycle, claiming blacks never had new bikes so he must have stolen it. "From that point on, a uniform was an enemy and I wanted to do something about it." He recalled that Crump's political machine had posted police officers out-side the drugstore of his father's friend, black pharmacist J. B. Martin, for expressing political independence, thus driving away his customers and putting him out of business. Sugarmon left Memphis to go first to Rutgers University and then to Harvard Law School, determined to return and change his hometown.

King told black Memphians he was "delighted beyond power of words to see such magnificent unity," and added that he "had never seen such enthusiasm at a meeting of Negroes." He suggested that something never seen in the Movement before would happen in this city on the river. Other speakers denounced blacks in schools, government, and anywhere else who maintained their allegiance to the old Crump establishment and said any black voting for Henry Loeb (at this point running for mayor) would be considered a "Tom" for the white man. A black reporter wrote, "The rally turned out to be a funeral for local Uncle Toms."

But at-large districts and runoff elections made it impossible to elect black candidates unless a significant number of whites voted for them. Most blacks thought the best they could do was to collaborate with racially moderate whites, so they had voted overwhelmingly to elect a business-man named Edmund Orgill as mayor in 1955. But in return, Orgill endorsed not a single black candidate, failed to support integration, and then withdrew after the 1959 primary for health reasons. Blacks expected support from organized labor for their candidates in the August 20 pri-mary, but the AFL-CIO didn't support Sugarmon, nor did they support black attorney and minister Benjamin Hooks in his quest for a judgeship. In a move they would long regret, the AFL-CIO also supported Loeb in his race for mayor. Unionized whites and blacks together had previously elected Orgill, considered a racial moderate, but the Negro–labor voting alliance had come unglued.

In the 1959 primary, two-thirds of black registrants voted, and 90 percent of them voted for African American candidates; many followed Sugarmon's "single shot" strategy of voting for only one candidate out of a field of many in order to bring a black candidate to the top when whites split their votes among competing white candidates. But almost no whites would vote for blacks, and whites even changed the rules so that all school board candidates had to run at large, making it impossible for a black to win. Blacks had built a strong voters' movement, but "We won everything but the election," complained Sugarmon.

Meanwhile, the segregationist movement advanced. Loeb, the outgoing Public Works commissioner, said, "A lot of good white men" might suffer if Sugarmon got elected as a commissioner of Public Works, and he called for a "white unity" ticket. In a stormy, closed-door meeting, Loeb forced various whites to withdraw from that race to avoid splitting the white vote. Bill Ferris, who became the sole white candidate running against Sugarmon, won. The two white-owned commercial newspapers campaigned against all of the black candidates, and although blacks made up nearly 40 percent of the electorate, none were elected to office. Loeb won the mayor's race with overwhelming white support, destroying Orgill's previous strategy of appealing to both working-class whites and blacks.

Southern whites had begun their historic desertion of the Democratic Party as a way to resist black civil rights. In the 1960 presidential election, the majority of Memphis whites for the first time voted for a Republican, Richard Nixon, while Memphis blacks voted two-to-one for John Kennedy, after he helped get King released after he was imprisoned in Georgia for his civil rights activities. "Though the white man is divided on many issues which affect our local scene, he is together on one issue—the Negro," said black political activist (and Republican) George W. Lee, co-chair of the Volunteer Ticket Committee.

HENRY LOEB WAS a personable man and a natural politician. Born in 1920 to descendants of Yiddish-speaking Jews who left Germany and moved to Memphis in the 1860s, the six-foot, five-inch Loeb received an Ivy League education at Phillips Academy prep school in Massachusetts and then at Brown University in Rhode Island. The business-oriented Civitan Club gave Loeb its Outstanding Citizen Award and praised him for his sincerity and his "daily living" that "evidenced a faith in God." Loeb and John F. Kennedy had been friends, and both served on P.T. (patrol) boats during World War II. Loeb's presumed military heroism gave him enormous appeal among white male war veterans. In 1951, Loeb married Mary Gregg, the 1950 queen of the Memphis Cotton Carnival, an annual event that romanticized the bygone days of slavery and the Confederacy in an era when whites still celebrated the birthday of Nathan Bedford Forrest. Newspapers began touting Loeb as a possible unifying white politician and successor to E. H. Crump.

The gregarious Loeb was "the politicking-ist son-of-a-gun that ever came down the pike," according to an associate, Frank Miles. He first gained attention by raising money as chairman of the American Legion's Red Cross fund, shaking hands with people in elevators and hallways. Post Number One was one of the American Legion's largest in the country, with 7,000 members, most connected to the Millington Naval Air Station outside Memphis. Devoting itself to "God and country," law and order, and "100 percent Americanism," Legion Post Number One provided a base for many aspiring white politicians. Although supported unofficially by Crump, Loeb said, "Nobody owns a piece of me." He called for an end to one-man control of the post, a secret ballot, and a "two-party system." He won the commander race in 1952 and made the American Legion his political base.

This segregated organization differentiated itself from the White Citizens' Council by making Communism, not integration, its sole target. Loeb led "Americanism months" and public rallies against Communism and charged the Veterans' Administration with "pushing socialistic aims" for insisting that its hospitals alone should care for veterans. Loeb emphasized a tight fiscal policy, saying, "The American Legion should realize that the cold war with the Communists is an economic war, and every time we spend money needlessly we lose a battle in that war." He doubled the membership of the post, and his glad-handed approach to politics endeared him to many white middle-class and business leaders, as did his fiscal conservatism and appeals to patriotism.

Loeb first ran for the City Commission in 1955, and many blacks voted for him for suggesting that, as a Jew, he would be sympathetic to their plight. Each of the four elected commissioners ran a department of government more or less independently and had as much power as the mayor. Running the Public Works Department, handling drainage and sewage, repairing city vehicles, and doing road construction and repair and park improvements seemed the least desirable commission spot, but Loeb took it on with great zeal. He changed the name of the garbage department to the sanitation division and set out to run it as if he were running the city itself, holding open-office hours on Thursday afternoons. He made a reputation for penny-pinching, absolute honesty, and attention to the last detail of every transaction. Focus on the letter of the law became his trademark. He said city employees should not be forced to be ward workers for those in power—as they had been during the Crump regime—and he pledged to a black Boy Scout unit that he would improve public streets and gutters and trash collection for blacks as well as whites.

Loeb built up a following far superior to that of other white politicians by aggressively resurfacing streets, fixing potholes, improving curbs and gutters, draining ditches, clearing weeds and snakes from drainage pipes, undertaking huge trash collections, and beautifying the increasingly affluent white communities in Mid-Town and East Memphis. Loeb advertised his work to the white community by employing two full-time secretaries and dictating up to a hundred letters a day. The city engineer called him "Hurricane Henry" for his prodigious work routine.

However, black workers actually did the heavy lifting at all ends of the Public Works Department, and Loeb financed his expansion of services by increasing "efficiencies" that came at their expense. He hired black men with arrest records who were unlikely to organize, held down wages, and bought the cheapest trucks and equipment, which quickly grew obsolete. One of these obsolete trucks led to the deaths of Echol Cole and Robert Walker in 1968. Worker morale declined and grievances accumulated throughout his tenure as commissioner of Public Works (1956 to 1960).

Loeb played softball with his employees and tried to establish the image of a friendly boss, but his relationship with blacks remained strictly that of an employer. He closely followed the business teachings of his father and his grandfather, who made the family fortune in the notoriously low-wage laundry business, where black women did the great bulk of miserable, hot, steamy work at poverty-level wages. Becoming the head of Loeb's Laundry Cleaner Company in 1946, he had successfully resisted efforts by black workers to organize unions, tightly monitored his workforce, and kept his company's wages low in an industry that remained a bastion for highly exploited and cheap black labor. When a white resident reported that black workers were selling scrap metal, rags, and bottles they picked up, Loeb charged them with infringing on the city's "right of contract" and punished them with an extra hour of work every day without pay.

Loeb put the letter of the law above the basic human needs of his workers, who desperately needed raises. When Loeb went to speak to the men about donating from their meager wages to Shelby United Neighbors, a charity to which most government workers donated, they rather meekly asked him for improvements in their working conditions. He abruptly changed the subject and left. Loeb did make some improvements in worker conditions, putting canvas tops on open-bed trucks and improvising a pension system, but his reforms often came with a catch. He provided paid vacations for workers for the first time in 1956, for instance, but he made them work unpaid overtime to cover the benefit. His penny-pinching ways embodied the Calvinist tradition, according to his boyhood friend Ned Cook: "His household budget is always balanced. Everything is in order. Everything is in place."

Loeb's friends said that he knew few if any African Americans on more than a superficial level. Arkansas Governor Orval Faubus made his political career by exploiting the Little Rock school-integration crisis in 1957, and, like Faubus and many other politicians of the era, Loeb increasingly espoused segregationist views in order to unify his base. He bluntly stated, "I am opposed to integration," but he also said, "I believe in treating negroes [sic] fair," which meant "separate but equal facilities and fair economic treatment." But when Loeb ran for mayor in 1959, he vowed, "I would fight any integration court order all the way. I am not for anarchy."

Black residents' hopes that Loeb, as a Jew, would be an ally proved to be a great delusion. As the White Citizens' Councils increasingly enforced white conformity, Memphis Jews remained largely silent. Southern Jews made up less than one percent of the South's population, and many of them had fully assimilated into white supremacist culture. Few of them, especially businesspeople, would jeopardize their positions by speaking out for black rights. Loeb increasingly established himself as a dedicated, straight-talking segregationist who would do more to unite white voters against racial liberalization than any other politician after Crump.

Among whites, Loeb gained a reputation as hard-working, fiscally smart, and a dedicated and fair public servant; among blacks, he became a clear enemy. He shifted Memphis politics away from former Mayor Orgill's formula of appealing to both working-class whites and black voters, in favor of appealing to white prejudices and ignoring blacks. In 1959, he supported Andrew Taylor, an overt segregationist running for governor, as part of the evolving "massive resistance" of white politicians to school integration. Saying he was not prejudiced, Loeb urged blacks to throw in their lot with white southern conservatives. But he also urged them to reject white Northerners posing as friends—as they supposedly did during Reconstruction, when black allies from the North "placed the Negro in places of political responsibility for which he was not prepared." Insultingly, Loeb admonished them for "always asking and never giving," and he urged them to reject the "shade tree" philosophy of the welfare state.

Whites elected Loeb as mayor in 1959 with the largest number of votes in the city's history, and white voters sustained his mayoral career for the next sixteen years. Loeb converted to his wife's Episcopalian religion in 1963, removing the sense that he was Jewish at all. Among blacks, Loeb's popularity evaporated: he received 12 percent of their votes in 1956 but only 2 percent in 1959. Maxine Smith of the NAACP bitterly mocked Loeb's early election appeals that Negroes and Jews should "stick together." Instead of following that road, "somewhere along the way he thought it would be more expedient politically to become a segregationist. He's just like all other politicians. . . . They do what's politically expedient at the time."

LOEB'S ELECTION as mayor occurred at a time when African Americans felt under siege. Racists had killed Florida NAACP leader Harry T. Moore and his wife Henrietta with a bomb on Christmas Eve, 1951, for registering voters; they continued regularly to blow up black churches and homes in Mississippi and "Bombingham," and they demolished a public school in Clinton, Tennessee, to stop desegregation in 1957. In Memphis, police brutality remained the most oppressive form of white terror. A casual perusal of the *Tri-State Defender* on any given week at the turn of the decade documented shocking and random police brutality against blacks. When the newspaper's black editor went to the police station in West Memphis, Arkansas, across the river, to bail out an employee involved in a minor traffic accident, a white police sergeant jumped over the counter and struck him repeatedly for questioning something the sergeant said.

Cases of police brutality before the NAACP included an instance in which white police beat up a young black man for having convulsions and another in which they attacked and arrested two teenagers merely for being at home and answering their door (officers apparently didn't like their attitude). Police routinely used a long strap and clubs to beat up arrested blacks en route to the police station. Officers attacked U.S. Army veteran Everett Johnson at the door to his church after he urged a black woman being manhandled by them on the street not to resist arrest. The police called him a "nigger" and beat him so badly he went to John Gaston Hospital on a stretcher. They arrested him for disorderly conduct, resisting arrest, disturbing the peace, and interfering with police—typical charges used to cover up police brutality.

Attorney Sugarmon, Firestone worker Matthew Davis, and many other black civic leaders used neighborhood and voting clubs to protest police violence, yet most whites seemed unaware of it. The editors of the two major newspapers, both members of the Memphis Committee on Community

Relations (MCCR), kept stories of police brutality and black protest out of the white press, and few whites read the black press. One black man put it simply: There was "no justice for Negroes" in Memphis, and there also was no common understanding of the problem between whites and blacks.

In the workplace, blacks suffered in their own portion of hell. When Clarence Coe, playing the "Jackie Robinson role," broke into a previously "whites only" machine job at Firestone, white workers nearly killed him in two separate incidents. When George Holloway at International Harvester also broke into a "whites only" job, someone sabotaged his punch press. "I was the committeeman for the man in the department who tried to kill me," said Holloway. "That's how relations were with whites at the time." Holloway represented hundreds of whites as a union shop leader, yet some of them still called him "nigger." The White Citizens' Council took control of the union hall and resegregated it, forcing the national UAW to take over the local. White vigilantes broke out the windows of Holloway's home; Coe said, "Here in Memphis, this was the worst place on earth," and he kept a gun in every room of his house for self-defense. Most industrial unions failed to live up to nondiscrimination clauses in their constitutions and contracts, and NAACP labor secretary Herbert Hill proved it, publishing several devastating reports on pervasive union discrimination that were widely publicized in the black press. Even industrial unions like the UAW preached equality but practiced white supremacy: blacks composed only 1.5 percent of its skilled members nationally in 1963.

Fortunately, in Memphis a distinctive cadre of activists emerged from the black middle class to organize a new civil rights movement. Said union organizer Alzada Clark, "We didn't have CORE or SNCC or anything else, because we had sophisticated leadership with college degrees in Memphis. You had to have degrees to have any power here. . . . This made Memphis different than some cities." These middle-class, educated activists were "prudent realists," in the words of one historian, filing suits rather than organizing demonstrations. In some ways, though, they were very much in the King mold.

In a region marked by poor education, the NAACP's college-educated cadre included former Army officer and accountant Jesse Turner, president of the black-owned Tri-State Bank; lawyer Russell Sugarmon and his educator wife, Miriam (Laurie) Sugarmon; attorneys Benjamin Hooks, A. W. Willis, and James Estes, among others. With an expanding black population to support them, they increasingly challenged segregation at every level and, by the early 1960s, created one of the most active NAACP chapters in the Deep South. They campaigned to desegregate all public facilities, including the city's zoo, parks, playgrounds, and public libraries; petitioned the school board to end segregation; and pressed hard to elect and appoint African American leaders in the public schools.

When Maxine Smith teamed up with NAACP President Turner, they became driving forces to make the Memphis NAACP a fighting organization. Maxine—as African Americans affectionately called her—had a deep reservoir of anger. She remembered as a child trying to visit her sick father, a postal worker, at the local veterans' hospital. "I want to see Mister Joseph Watkins," she asked. The clerk told her, "We don't refer to niggers as 'Mister' around white folks." She was only nine when her father died; her mother worked as a secretary at the Baptist church, which provided a rock of support in her youth.

She met King when he was a student at Morehouse and she was a student at Spelman, and she remembered him as quiet, unassuming, and younger than most of his peers because he had skipped grades and gotten into college early (so had she). She later went to Middlebury College in Vermont because the University of Tennessee would not admit blacks into graduate school. There she found good white friends and obtained a master's degree in French. She taught for two years at colleges in Texas, where she married Vasco Smith, a black Memphian in the Air Force. They spent two years living at various air bases before returning to Memphis, where he became a dentist. Maxine Smith joined Laurie Sugarmon, a Phi Beta Kappa from Wellesley College who also had a master's degree in French from Middlebury, in applying to Memphis State University graduate school. It claimed they were "not qualified" to enter a state college. The two women sued, defeating segregation at MSU in 1959. Sugarmon went on to earn a Ph.D. from Johns Hopkins University and to become MSU's first black faculty member.

Smith and Sugarmon belonged to a group of black women at the center of black community and work life in the Mississippi Delta who drew on the fighting tradition of antilynching crusader Ida B. Wells. Ida Leachman, a distant relative named after her, migrated to Memphis from Mississippi, along with thousands of other black women whose discontent helped to fuel the city's labor and civil rights movements. Leroy and Alzada Clark organized many of them in low-wage furniture-related shops in the 1960s, and black women of all classes kept movements alive in factories, churches, and neighborhoods. Alma Morris and other women organized clubs to get out the vote and later became involved in the 1968 Memphis strike.

Maxine Smith and a number of other women and men ultimately built the membership of the NAACP in Memphis into the largest in the South, while Jesse Turner initiated court suits challenging segregated facilities and obstacles to voter registration. They briefly ran a boycott against the Memphis *Commercial Appeal* for refusing to use honorific titles for African Americans. (Editor Frank Ahlgren said the paper used "Mr." and "Mrs." and other titles only for "people of substance," without regard to race, but apparently very few blacks qualified for this status in the minds of white editors.) The power of the black vote forced the ruling elite to make concessions to the black community, and the white power structure refocused on dividing blacks, as Crump had done.

It angered Smith that the strategy worked. "There are folks that can be bought that can be bought; folks who bask under the smile on the part of the white man. . . . The white man has very effectively slanted us politically." Mayor Orgill's supposed moderation in the 1950s had done little for blacks, who became used to the idea of progress through biracial accommodations. Having an open enemy as mayor could be a kind of advantage, for Memphis clearly needed more than an election. It needed a movement, and Smith thought Loeb might stimulate one.

"SOMETHING IS GOING to take place that never took place before" in Memphis, King had said in his 1959 Mason Temple speech. And then, in March 1960, it happened: a direct-action campaign started by black students willing to go to jail for freedom. Black youth had been waiting impatiently for something like the Montgomery movement to come along, but not much had happened. On February 1, the first lunch-counter "sit-ins" began in Greensboro, North Carolina; weeks later, in Memphis, a handful of black students followed their example, sitting in and getting arrested for breaking the segregation laws at the city's segregated public libraries. Industrial union member George Isabell's daughter was among the first to go to jail.

Black high school and college students rallied at the city's historically black LeMoyne College and Owen Junior College (later combined as LeMoyne–Owen College) and fanned out from there to "integrate" downtown stores. Student sit-ins occurred at department stores, lunch counters, restaurants, and the zoo and touched off daily mass meetings in black churches, picketing, and lawsuits by the NAACP. Black Memphians displayed what Sugarmon called a remarkable "religious fervor" in mass meetings, and at least 300 black students were arrested in the next several months. They even "sat in" at several white churches on a Sunday and at a citywide religious gathering in Overton Park. The city arrested them, claiming the United States would become a "godless" Iron Curtain country if whites lost their right to worship as they chose (without blacks). Black attorney Benjamin Hooks tried to persuade the court to be lenient by using the story of the Good Samaritan helping the less fortunate and citing the admonition, "Love thy neighbor as thyself." An all-white, all-male jury returned felony convictions.

When school let out and students went to work, the desegregation movement began to lose its steam, so adults began picketing the downtown stores; the direct-action movement among adults and students lasted a year and a half and perhaps produced more sit-ins than in any other southern city. Maxine Smith estimated that there were more than a thousand arrests over eighteen months, and, as membership secretary of the NAACP, she recruited 2,000 members in two years. The NAACP picketed segregated downtown stores and filed suits to desegregate public eateries, libraries, and stores. The direct-action movement transformed the consciousness of many black Memphians, undercutting old patterns of accommodation and "taking it."

A new sense of citizenship and of urgency emerged as the result of direct action—in much the way that King had said it would. By this time, he had moved from Montgomery to Atlanta, and he played no direct role in instigating the sit-ins in Memphis or anywhere else. SCLC's Ella Baker encouraged the youth to create their own organization—one less compromised by cautious adults—and they followed her advice by founding the Student Nonviolent Coordinating Committee (SNCC) in Raleigh, North Carolina, where King spoke. The sit-ins and President John Kennedy's 1960 election gave many African American youth a new sense of optimism. Then, in May 1961, a new phase of struggle began, as young people led "freedom rides" to desegregate interstate transportation, suffering murderous beatings and frightening imprisonments.

King supported but did not participate in the freedom rides, yet his preaching for equal rights and freedom nonetheless had a tremendous effect, as African Americans and whites absorbed what he had to say via newspaper, radio, and television. The two weekly black newspapers (the *Memphis World* and the *Tri-State Defender*), the two black-run radio stations (WDIA and WLOK), and black ministers broadcasting on several smaller radio frequencies kept African Americans in Memphis abreast of the desegregation of Ole Miss in 1962; the Birmingham desegregation struggle and the March on Washington for Jobs and Freedom in 1963; and the Selma-to-Montgomery march for black voting rights in 1965. Black Memphians participated in all these struggles, which produced defining legislative victories in the federal Civil Rights Act of 1964 and the Voting Rights Act of 1965.

As the Movement overturned segregation laws, demands for desegregation of American economic structures came increasingly to the forefront in Memphis and everywhere else. When SCLC held a two-day board meeting in the Bluff City in 1963, it sought to build a broader base among black ministers to address a range of ills plaguing blacks. On April 30, King addressed 700 people at Metropolitan Baptist Church about the mass movement that he was currently leading in Birmingham to desegregate accommodations and employment in downtown stores. He said some 2,000 protesters had gone to jail, and masses of students left their schools to challenge Police Chief Bull Connor's fire hoses, snarling police dogs, and armed police. They were following a strategy of "jail, no bail," and filling up the jails—making it difficult for the white power structure to suppress the Movement, which he (correctly) predicted would spread rapidly across the South. The Memphis *Press-Scimitar*, which had not yet gotten around to capitalizing the word *Negro*, quoted King: "This is a quest for equal opportunity. We will promote selective buying where negroes will trade only with those who agree to employ negroes."

In many of its details, Birmingham previewed the Memphis movement of 1968, which would also combine street demonstrations and mass protest meetings with an economic boycott to force business and city government to support justice for black workers. The Birmingham movement aimed at both desegregation of downtown stores and decent jobs in those stores for blacks, and it used an economic boycott during the Easter shopping season to pressure businesses and a newly formed city government uncertain of its powers. Bayard Rustin later wrote that Birmingham introduced the "package deal," which required an array of measures for economic and social advancements, not just civil rights measures, and highlighted "the concept of collective struggle over individual achievement as the road to Negro freedom."

In Memphis, economic issues could not be ignored, for black family income averaged one-third of the white average, while housing, education, and health issues cried out for solutions. Concurrent with the Birmingham campaign, the Memphis NAACP in the spring of 1963 focused on jobs, pressuring 100 retail firms to change their hiring policies and to desegregate at the same time; then it moved on to make similar demands of hospitals, restaurants, and hotels. Reverend James Lawson, an instigator of the sit-in movement in Nashville and a consultant to King and SCLC in Birmingham, had moved to Memphis the previous year. He and Jesse Turner led some 600 Memphis protesters, including high school students, in demanding black employment gains, desegregation, and an end to total white control over the school board based on an unfair, at-large election system. Lawson and black lawyers from Memphis aided the West Tennessee voting rights struggles as well, barely escaping Somerville, Tennessee, with bullets whizzing overhead, in July 1963.

Although not highlighted by the mass media, economic demands always remained a critical part of the civil rights movement. The NAACP in Memphis held workshops on Title VII of the 1964 Civil Rights Act, prohibiting employment discrimination, and the organization lodged many protests against both businesses and white unions for employment discrimination. Following the Selma-to-Montgomery march for black voting rights in March 1965, Memphis ministers and activists led a "mammoth" Good Friday march demanding black employment in downtown banks. This and other marches began at the African Methodist Episcopal (AME) Church's Clayborn Temple and went through downtown to put pressure on both businesses and the city government.

One by one, the barriers to more-or-less-equal public accommodations fell. By 1964, some 250 blacks attended Memphis State University (today known as the University of Memphis), and the city had desegregated 131 parks, under court order, and 100 restaurants. The local NAACP chapter regularly received awards from the national organization for its activism and membership gains. Memphis became known primarily as "an NAACP town," one in which the movement relied heavily on court suits and electoral politics. Some people now praised what they called the "politics of moderation" in Memphis, as the business-oriented Memphis Committee on Community Relations and the two major newspapers called for modest compliance with the Supreme Court's *Brown* decision. The city did not experience the violent upheavals that marked the freedom movement in Birmingham, and blacks in Memphis already had the voting rights that black people in Selma and Mississippi would die to achieve. A certain self-congratulatory complacence set in among the city's ruling circles, as the Southern Regional Council, a supporter of integration, reported in 1964 that Memphis "has begun to shine as a beacon of reason and decency in the Deep South."

But the job problem had not been solved, and white thinking remained mired in the past. Out of 1,200 police officers, only forty-two were black. Like black workers in other jobs, they were concentrated at the bottom of the department's hierarchy and worked in a dual, segregated justice system, with no opportunity for advancement. Blacks in both city and private employment could not find decent jobs, and the black working class remained stuck at the bottom of the economic order. Hence, many potential youth activists like Marion Barry (later the mayor of the nation's capital) left and never returned. C. Eric Lincoln, who became a noted black journalist and scholar, said, "The police in Memphis represented to most black people the possibility, even the probability, of an incident which could lead to sudden death. . . . I left because, among other reasons, I felt that I could never live in Memphis and attain my manhood."

HENRY LOEB RESIGNED as mayor at the end of 1963, in order to take over his father's business after he died, and the *Tri-State Defender* hoped it would be the end of his political career.* This "young, handsome man with a backward look who afforded himself the folly of dreaming of turning the clock back to Ante Bellum days" had disillusioned blacks by taking "every opportunity to declare loudly and long in a coarse manner that he is a 'segregationist.' " The newspaper blamed Loeb and other segregationist politicians for stirring up a violent political climate that led to President Kennedy's assassination in November 1963.

For a moment after Kennedy's death, things seemed to move in a promising direction. During the 1964 elections, voters overwhelmingly elected Lyndon Johnson as president and Democrats in Memphis replaced Crump's Congressman Clifford Davis with George Grider, a supporter of unions, black voting rights, and Johnson's War on Poverty. Blacks elected attorney A. W. Willis as the first black representative to the legislature since Reconstruction and joined with whites to elect William Ingram as mayor. Blacks thought that Ingram, a white judge who had served as a buffer between black defendants and the police, would be the truly moderate leader that they had hoped Edmund Orgill would be in 1955.

But the 1964 election proved to be another electoral mirage. Grider became a congressman only because nearly all blacks voted for him. A majority of the whites voted for Bob James, a favorite of the American Legion who

---

*He ultimately divested himself from the Loeb dry-cleaning and coin-operated laundries, some of them attached to Loeb's Bar-B-Qs in black neighborhoods. His brother William took control of most of the family business.

had received a medal from Federal Bureau of Investigation (FBI) Director J. Edgar Hoover for his efforts to "fight Communism." White voters overwhelmingly supported Republican presidential candidate Barry Goldwater, who solicited the segregationist vote by supporting "states' rights," a code word for defending segregation. Alabama Governor George Wallace ran for president in the primaries, fomenting a rabidly anti-Communist and pro-segregationist following. The John Birch Society (formed in 1959 by Robert Welch, who spoke in Memphis in 1961 and denounced Freedom Riders as Communists) opened a Memphis bookstore in 1965. It called for a return to the unfettered capitalism of the late nineteenth century, when neither workers nor African Americans had rights under the law and claimed that Supreme Court Chief Justice Earl Warren and perhaps even former President Dwight Eisenhower were secret Communists.

In a polarizing political atmosphere, a majority of working-class as well as middle-class white voters—except for many members of organized labor—switched from the Democratic to the Republican Party, which in Tennessee jettisoned any pretense of support for civil rights. In 1966, Memphis white voters dumped Congressman Grider and replaced him with a militaristic, anti–civil rights, free-market Republican named Dan Kuykendall. According to the Memphis *Union News*, business groups led by the anti-union National Association of Manufacturers heavily bankrolled political action committees that put many such conservatives in power.

One consolation for blacks and unions seemed to be the election of William Ingram as mayor. But, even more than Orgill, he turned out to be a huge disappointment. He "completely captivated the black community in Memphis without doing anything for us," Maxine Smith summarized. She thought Ingram was "the most dangerous thing that ever happened to the black community," because he could control its vote while giving nothing back. Sugarmon, elected to the state legislature in 1966, and his Shelby County Democratic Club felt the same way. In 1968, they organized blacks to vote for black mayoral candidate A. W. Willis. Still supporting Ingram were O. Z. Evers and his allies in the Unity League, in alliance with T. O. Jones and others trying to organize the sanitation workers. Blacks split their votes.

Black political leaders, each on their own turf, were not united, and electoral politics alone could not alleviate the crushing burdens of poverty. The civil rights movement had made advances in Memphis through court suits, sit-ins, boycotts, picketing, and voting, but, said Smith, "The gains we thought were considerable have been only token gains." By 1968, she thought white leaders of the city government had become even more racist, and the economic problems of blacks had scarcely been addressed. Young black males especially grew frustrated and angry that civil rights gains failed to alleviate their poverty and unemployment.

AS THE FREEDOM movement progressed, Martin Luther King increasingly stressed that voting and civil rights were not enough to emancipate African Americans from the effects of slavery and segregation. Following the lead of Rustin and Randolph, he turned repeatedly to what commentators often called the "Negro–labor coalition" as the core of a broad movement for change. In a 1961 speech at the National AFL-CIO Convention titled, "If the Negro Wins, Labor Wins," King said that blacks and labor remained historically tied in a common destiny, that the civil rights movement in the 1960s had picked up the spirit and many of the methods of nonviolent direct action and protest methods from the union movements in the 1930s. "Negroes are almost entirely a working people," he pointed out. "Our needs are identical with labor's needs, decent wages, fair working conditions, livable housing, old age security, health and welfare measures, conditions in which families can grow, have education for their children and respect in the community." He optimistically projected a coalition in which registered blacks and organized labor would vote together to improve the conditions of all Americans.

Yet King did not shirk from condemning union racism, nor did Randolph and the NAACP, leading to open conflict with AFL-CIO President George Meany. The AFL-CIO could expel unions that organized blacks because their leaders were thought to be Communists, yet it refused to expel unions that openly banned blacks from membership. King warned that white racism could stop unions and civil rights from moving forward together. He also warned of "the ultra-right wing," an alliance between "big military and big industry," and "southern dixiecrats and northern reactionaries." King said, "These menaces now threaten everything decent and fair in American life. Their target is labor liberals, and the Negro people, not scattered reds. . . . This period is made to order for those who would seek to drive labor into impotency."

King continued to urge unions to fully include blacks and other minorities and to build an alliance that could take political power and turn back the American Right. He told the United Electrical Workers in 1962 that freedom for blacks "is a key to unlocking the social and political machinery" for white workers as well, and he later suggested to Walter Reuther that it might be a good idea for the UAW to train the SCLC staff, so that "we will find the civil rights movement really engaged in the organization of both the workers and the unemployed." Yet few unions moved in that direction—in a place like Memphis, the AFL-CIO barely mentioned the term *civil rights*—and King increasingly worried that the failure of a black–labor coalition would leave black workers and the poor in the lurch.

In his "I Have a Dream" speech at the March on Washington for Jobs and Freedom on August 28, 1963 (which he first delivered in June before union and civil rights supporters at a huge UAW-backed march in Detroit), King said the "promissory note" from the nation's founders for full freedom and equality had "come back marked 'insufficient funds.' " As a result, "The Negro lives on a lonely island of poverty in the midst of a vast ocean of material abundance . . . an exile in his own land." In a speech usually noted for its optimism, King issued a dire warning that without rectifying the disastrous economic effects of slavery and segregation, civil rights would not bring true freedom. The UAW, Hospital Workers Union Local 1199, the Brotherhood of Sleeping Car Porters, and Distributive Workers District 65 endorsed the March on Washington, but the AFL-CIO did not, and most unions still failed to organize the South or to overcome racism in their own ranks. As King called for an economic bill of rights and a multibillion-dollar "Marshall Plan" to rebuild the cities, he could not rely on the American labor movement to support such demands.

TWO NIGHTS BEFORE Christmas in 1964, King stood on picket duty at midnight with black women strikers at the Scripto pen and pencil factory in his Atlanta neighborhood, known as Sweet Auburn. The workers made $400 a year less than the minimal poverty level—for full time, nonunion work—and had little chance to succeed in their struggle for union rights and wages without the help of the civil rights movement. C. T. Vivian, King's director of SCLC affiliates, had always been a strong union supporter, and electrified a mass meeting of the workers, declaring, "The mainstream of America's life is labor. Labor's demands are our demands." SCLC helped the workers to unionize and win their strike, and King concluded, "The time has come for the civil rights movement to become more involved with organized labor."

Vivian said the victory at Scripto demonstrated that the civil rights movement by 1964 "had the ability to move the nation in another way that labor seemingly had lost the ability to do." But neither civil and voting rights movements nor the unions could change the country by themselves. Even as blacks knocked down barriers to public accommodations and voting rights, the Movement had not yet made serious inroads on the problem of black poverty. The need for unions and the civil rights movement to jointly redress black economic grievances would be nowhere more obvious than in Memphis.

3

STRUGGLES OF THE
WORKING POOR

They would give us handouts. We had gotten tired of those handouts.
You could tell a worker when you saw him in the streets because his
hat was too big, his coat was too long, his shoes were too big . . .
from handouts. We worked every day, and let us have the
money and pick [clothing] as other people do.
—*Sanitation worker Clinton Burrows*

"I WAS JUST SOME SORT OF SLAVE," MRS. JAMES T. WALKER, president of the African-American Bluff City Education Association, told the U.S. Civil Rights Commission. Its 1962 hearings in Memphis clearly documented vast employment discrimination against African Americans. Mrs. Walker said conditions for public school teachers weren't much better than when she began teaching at age fifteen, thirty-four years earlier. White supervisors and principals were disrespectful of black teachers, who worked at low wages, with no union rights. She said the teacher was "the mother, the nurse, the teacher, the doctor, and everything else" for black students, who often couldn't learn because they were too hungry. They were bused to distant schools, often passing white schools closer by. Although more blacks than whites went to the lower grades, twice as many whites went to the upper grades, because so many blacks had to drop out of school to work. Overall, blacks made up 45 percent of the public school students, but no blacks served on the school board. And, despite woeful funding of black teachers and black schools, Superintendent of Schools E. C. Stimbert testified, "there is no barrier placed in the path of any pupil."

The hearings documented how pervasive racial discrimination in education and employment kept black workers at the bottom of the labor force. The U.S. Army's Memphis General Depot employed 1,718 people, including many black workers, but only four of them worked in nonlaboring jobs—as clerk typists and stock control clerks. Southern Bell Telephone and Telegraph claimed it could not hire blacks in high-end jobs because of "compatibility problems, customer resentment." International Harvester claimed it trained employees "without regard to race, creed, color or national origin," yet of 2,025 workers (547 of them black), there were no black supervisors and no blacks among the 617 salaried white-collar employees. "Whites only" and "colored" signs still demarcated toilets, locker rooms, and drinking fountains. Very few blacks held even semiskilled jobs in Memphis factories in the early 1960s.

White government, business, and union officials all participated in Jim Crow, but few admitted it. Prentis Lewis, president of the Memphis AFL-CIO Labor Council, when asked whether building-trades unions discriminated, said, "I wish I could answer, but I just don't know." Yet everyone knew that building-trades unions had been freezing blacks out of craft occupations for years. The AFL-CIO's United Brotherhood of Carpenters local had less than one percent black membership and only one black in an apprenticeship. Twenty years earlier, 250 to 300 blacks had been bricklayers and carpenters; now there were only forty or fifty, about one percent of the workforce in a town almost 40 percent black. Since the *Brown* decision, said Joseph Cowan, a black business agent of a black carpenters' local, "We have not had a single Negro carpenter on a single school job." Though Memphis was having "one of the biggest building booms in its history," funded in part by state and federal governments, blacks got none of the skilled jobs—not even, incredibly, for building the Crump Memorial Hospital for Negroes. "The old pattern of employment (the Negro is the last to be hired and the first to be fired) is deeply rooted and used by nearly every contractor in the city of Memphis," said Cowan. Eighteen craft unions had almost no blacks, and not a single African American had an electrician's license in Memphis because whites would not train them.

Local, state, and federal agencies responsible for overseeing government spending and contracts all participated in freezing blacks out of skilled jobs. The Federal Housing Authority funded segregated housing construction, black builders could not get FHA-insured mortgages, and federal agencies employed scarcely any blacks. Whites sued to stop the construction of housing for blacks in the suburbs, while local governments used zoning ordinances to keep them out. The Civil Rights Commission hearings only skimmed the surface. Increasing mechanization of farming and factory jobs sent black unemployment and poverty rates soaring, while new jobs in white-collar, nonunion, suburban employment went to whites only. When a Tennessee advisory committee to the commission held another hearing in 1964, it found that only 2.2 percent of black workers held white-collar jobs, compared with 41.5 percent of white workers.

More and more jobless young black men joined the military and went off to be killed or maimed in Vietnam, conscripted by an all-white draft board. Black women showed up as factory workers, but only at the lowest wages and in the worst jobs; or they worked in the homes of whites for $3 to $5 a day. Black women cleaned the schools for 58 cents an hour and worked full-time in the city hospital for as little as $80 a month. Except for the small black middle class, poverty pervaded the Memphis black community. New interstate highways allowed whites to speed away from the city to sprawling suburbs, where they did not see the poor, yet they remained readily visible in the city. Black female domestic workers stood waiting for buses to go into and out of white neighborhoods; unemployed black men who did casual labor (when they could find it) stood idly on street corners; open drainage ditches, crumbling streets, and dilapidated houses abandoned by previous white immigrants marked black neighborhoods.

Most whites chose not to see the black working poor, but these workers nonetheless provided the glue that held Memphis together. Black women cooked, cleaned, emptied bedpans, took care of children, and relieved whites of household labor; black women and men did hot, heavy, dirty work on the streets and in restaurants, hotels, hospitals, wharves, homes, fields, and factories. They filled factory, sawmill, cotton-warehouse, and other laboring jobs, but increasing numbers of them, under the pressure of mechanization, had no jobs at all. Those who could find nothing else hauled garbage.

SANITATION WORKERS EXISTED in a netherworld between the plantation and the modern urban economy. Their desperate plight exemplified the larger crisis of the black working class. Said Maxine Smith, "Whenever you have a bloc of black people doing one kind of job, you know there are racial overtones—well, not overtones—it's just a racial problem." Even though the NAACP complained about their conditions, "We just aren't heard. We have been down for the same number of years hollering about police brutality. Nobody listens. Nobody listened to us and the garbage men through the years. For some reason, our city government demands a crisis. . . . They seem not to hear black people. . . . We're invisible."

The invisible sanitation worker was just as important as the doctor in preventing disease, Martin Luther King sometimes said. Indeed, for lack of a good sanitation system, yellow-fever epidemics had devastated Memphis twice in the nineteenth century. Since then, the city had made "sanitary services" one of its "most important municipal functions." The Department of Public Works did a "giant housekeeping job," as a city report described it in 1955, with its work encompassing sanitation, maintenance, sewers and drains, engineering, plumbing, and traffic engineering. Black workers in blue-collar jobs did most of its heavy labor, which included "collection and disposal of garbage, cleaning streets and alleys, keeping the drainage system free of rubbish, cutting weeds on vacant lots, and a host of other services." Workers also kept the city's motor vehicles cleaned, tuned, and running, and paved the streets. Assisted by interconnected open ditches that carried away storm water, these workers provided the first line of defense against the rats and diseases that accompanied garbage.

In the early twentieth century, blacks did this work with mules and open carts, later moving to enclosed steel-body trucks and electrical compactors. They still picked up dirty, rotting waste by hand; cut down and hauled prickly shrubs and trees; and removed monster weeds. The fertile Mississippi Delta climate produced several crop rotations per year, so collecting trash meant not just picking up garbage but also serving as an all-purpose yard-waste collection service. Clean city streets and parks had been the pride of Memphis since the Crump days. By 1955, the DPW accounted for more than a third of the city's budget. But most of its sanitation workers lived a bare notch above the level of domestic workers; some 40 percent of their families lived below the poverty level, and many of them qualified for welfare despite working full-time jobs.

Those living in the white suburbs and attending the white schools of East Memphis scarcely noticed the city's glaring disparities. "East Memphis was like another country," said Reverend J. L. Netters. "They knew nothing about the sanitation workers," even though they came into their yards weekly to pick up refuse. Even the black middle class of preachers, teachers, businesspeople, and professionals often did not "see" the poor, said Reverend Samuel ("Billy") Kyles. Just as white people took maids for granted, "We took the garbage workers for granted . . . like they are invisible." They suffered in ways that people who wore white or clerical collars could scarcely imagine.

Reverend Henry Starks, however, did notice their plight. One man in his congregation had continual health problems. Doctors operated on him twice, but his employer would not give him enough time to recover before sending him back to work. Starks said that in the city's view, "a man had to get sick and well almost in a few days," with "no kind of fringe benefits to sustain him." This man "was at the mercy of the people who were his superiors. There were no safeguards. [If] they didn't like his attitude, and they didn't like the way he worked, and they didn't like the way he moved about, then they could transfer him [or] just put him out on the street. Now, who would like to go down to the mayor's office on a grievance and complain every time something went wrong out there?" The man died a premature death.

Another sanitation worker in Reverend Stark's congregation had nine children:

He was on the streets when I saw him, receiving checks from the government, and working: picking cotton, hauling cotton, chopping cotton, doing what he possibly could to make a living. Now he had worked for a number of years with the city, but when his back was wrenched, they found out that they could not use him, even though they did have jobs where men did not have to carry a tub.... And this was sickening. And he tried and tried to remain. But because he couldn't carry a tub, that fellow—I preached his funeral. He was only forty some odd years when he passed. Hypertension and other things just carried him away....

Reverend Starks felt such conditions did incalculable damage to human personality. Black men had to beg for what should have been theirs to begin with—a decent job at decent wages. This situation forced many workers to adopt what Starks called "slave mannerisms": "The slave out on the field, he had no recourse to justice except if he went to the master and the master could give it to him if he wanted to at his own dictates, his whims. Well, no man wants to stand that way any longer, and then be denied, because that is exactly what happens." Black labor exploitation, in his view, inherently involved civil and human rights abuses.

A steady stream of migrants fed this labor exploitation. In the eastern Arkansas, northern Mississippi, and West Tennessee cotton country, plantation owners replaced black laborers with mechanical cotton pickers and pesticides; the percentage of cotton harvested by machines went from 5 percent in 1950 to 50 percent by 1960 and 95 percent by 1970. In Fayette County, Tennessee, black unemployment reached nearly 70 percent, and 80 percent of blacks lacked plumbing in their homes. The Memphis sanitation division drew heavily on this poor county for workers who they thought would put in long, hard hours without protest. Leroy Bonner left this rural area in his twenties and bounced from one low-wage job to another until, at age forty-eight, he migrated into sanitation work. Another sanitation worker from Fayette County expressed his plight simply: "There is no worst job. I would take anything."

Such men found sanitation jobs in Memphis through friends or family, just as Ed Gillis had. Many of them hoped to use Memphis merely as a stepping-stone to better jobs in Chicago or elsewhere in the North, but economic contraction in the late 1950s, and mechanization of urban factory jobs, forced most migrants who came to Memphis to remain, locked in dead-end jobs and working ten-to-twelve-hour days at less than minimum wages. James Robinson exemplified the familiar pattern of displaced workers from the rural areas:

> I was born in Earle, Arkansas, June 27, 1937. We lived out in the country. When my father was a sharecropper, the five of us boys together, we could pick a bale of cotton a day. Five boys, five bales a week, thirty or forty bales of cotton. But always come out in the hole. Didn't make enough to get nothin'. I went to 10th grade, it was somethin' like a one-room school house, forty, fifty students, one teacher.

Robinson went to school only five months a year (instead of the seven months for most white students), as employers called on him to plant, weed, and harvest cotton.

Brutal struggles over labor rights had gone on in this plantation district for many years. Whites had responded to black worker organizing with the Elaine Race Riot in 1919 and repression against the sharecropper movement during the 1930s. Similarly, in Fayette County, landlords in 1959 evicted black people en masse from their rented farm homes for trying to register to vote. They survived by living in tents, and a brutal struggle over equal rights in Fayette and Haywood Counties continued for years.

Rural laborers left such environs as quickly as they could. Robinson got out of the cotton fields as a teenager by taking a laboring job with the Army Corps of Engineers, working on river dikes. He then moved north to Michigan and worked in a unionized Ford plant for ten years, but he couldn't stand the cold in the North. When his father became ill, Robinson returned to take care of him. He ended up taking odd jobs in Memphis until an uncle who worked at the sanitation division got him a steady job. Robinson started a family and survived by working on a garbage truck.

Unlike classified city employees, unclassified day laborers could be fired on a moment's notice, with none of the civil service protections extended to those considered full-time workers. This nonclassified system also reinforced arbitrary white power on the job. White supervisors, in classified occupations, operated heavy equipment and ran various divisions of the Public Works Department. Not many white men wanted to work as foremen or drivers in garbage collection, but they bossed street repair crews, ran the bus barns, did the hiring, made the job assignments, and largely followed their own rules.

"Before the union, it was whatever they decided they wanted to pay you. If they wanted to pay you they did, if they didn't want to they wouldn't," said Robinson. "I wasn't makin' a damn thing. You can't pay the light bill on no 96 cents an hour." His wages did go up slightly in the 1960s, but not enough to keep up with inflation. "I'd been there fifteen years and I made $1.65 an hour" in 1968, five cents above the federal minimum wage. "We were workin' every day then for welfare wages," said Robinson.

Ed Gillis, who had taken up residence in Memphis in 1948, made a mere $7.80 a day after twenty years of employment in the DPW. Such workers could not keep up with the rising cost of living, and they gathered junk and discount coupons from garbage piles to supplement their incomes. Supervisors always found various ways to squeeze more work out of their employees without increasing their pay. Bosses assigned workers to cover a certain district within a week, regardless of rain, snow, or sleet. Said Robinson, "You had to stay out there as long as it would take you. You'd work ten, twelve hours a day. But you didn't get paid but for eight. You stayed out there until you'd get through. We were out there sometimes till dark. You'd start at seven o'clock in the morning, no extra for overtime."

Workers tried to curry favor with white supervisors by giving them bribes of whiskey or money. The city's outmoded labor relations truly resembled those of a plantation more than of a modern metropolis. Sanitation worker Clinton Burrows said, "It was the same thing that you would put on farmhands. That means get up as early as you can and leave when they tell you . . . sunup to sundown." The disrespect of supervisors galled the workers, who thought they had left this plantation mentality behind in the cotton fields. Robinson said, "Sanitation was the worst job I ever had. The job wasn't really as bad as the folks you were workin' for."

Since many white bosses came from the plantations themselves, they treated black workers much like landlords in the Mississippi Delta treated their sharecroppers and tenants—or like bosses treated convicts on penal farms. Some bosses even carried sidearms. Robinson remembered whites sending blacks home from work if they came in a minute late, or firing them for "talking back": "You work two weeks, and payday your money ain't right. You go in there and tell the man, 'Look, I worked eighty hours this payday, how come I ain't got but sixty?' [He'd say] 'Get out of here, you don't know what you're talkin' about.'" Under such conditions, Ed Gillis said, he couldn't "feel like a man," and he had trouble facing his family on the rainy days when he was sent home without pay.

Workers had no regular breaks, no place to go to the bathroom to wash up or relieve themselves, and, in the blazing heat of the Mississippi Delta, nowhere to eat their lunch, for which they were allowed no more than fifteen minutes. Robinson recalled one instance in which a supervisor made him and his crew get out from under a shade tree and eat their lunch under the truck because a white woman complained about their lounging near her property. Heat and humidity in the Mississippi Delta often shot the thermometer up to a hundred degrees; finding shade was a necessity. But sitting under the truck might have been worse than sitting in the sun. "Truck had maggots and things all fallin' out of it. [But] he [the boss] said, 'You gotta get out from under the shade tree and sit under the truck to get some shade.'"

Not only white supervisors, but also white citizens, had disdainful attitudes toward black sanitation workers. The city did not require residents to pack their garbage in bags or take it to the curb. Workers had to clean up everything in their area of work—which could include cutting and hauling downed trees out of someone's private property. Sanitation men walked through people's yards, picked up discarded boxes and wastepaper, grabbed tree limbs by the armloads, carried buckets of grass clippings, wrestled with the refuse of thorn bushes, picked up dead animals on the road. Garbage lay in cans without any covering, rotting in the Memphis heat. S. T. Thomas, who left sharecropping in Arkansas to come to Memphis, said white homeowners could be particularly insensitive:

> We were the pickers, with our hands. A lotta people used barrels, but most of them used those 50-gallon drums. They would set it right

under the edge of their house or the garage to where the water run off the house right down in the cans. They didn't want you to pour that water out in the yard, off of the garbage . . . you had to carry it out. And they didn't want you to roll the barrels out—"You don't roll that barrel across my yard and cut up my yard!" Extremely heavy. So we'd team up on it and tote the barrel out . . . . it's gonna be stinkin' and have flies and things. That's what we had to do. So, it was pretty bad.

The next problem was "gettin' it off the cart and up in the truck." Men strained themselves all the time, getting hernias and bad backs. Said Robinson, "We had to pick up trash out of the backyard. You had to tote it on your head in a tub. The tub's full of water, rain, garbage, maggots, everything else running out." And the city did little to make the work any easier: "Back then you had to supply your own clothes, own gloves, they didn't give you anything but the tubs. If you'd get a hole in it the water'd run all out the tub down on ya." The indolence of the white bosses made this work all the more galling: "Boss would sit around drinkin' coffee, come around once or twice a day to check on the truck."

After passage of the 1964 Civil Rights Act, which forbade racial and gender discrimination on the job, unionized blacks in Memphis increasingly fought for equal access to better jobs, but it was nearly impossible to fight for such rights where unions did not exist. For the lack of a strong union, black sanitation workers suffered backbreaking work that only earned them low wages, few benefits, and no job security. In 1960, the city had paid them anywhere from 94 cents to $1.14 an hour. By 1968, this went up to 5 cents more than the minimum wage of $1.60 an hour for laborers and $1.90 an hour for those who drove trucks. The city claimed that the average wage was around $1.80, more than many other city laborers received. But these were still poverty wages.

White arrogance and racism further reduced the real value of the men's work. If someone became sick or was injured on the job, most white supervisors did not afford them such elemental human decencies as a ride to the doctor or home. Gillis said white drivers sometimes dropped off their black road crews and made them find their own transportation home, instead of taking them back to the city yard. Many black sanitation workers could not afford cars, and often a bus stop might be miles away; when they got there, they might have to wait an hour for a bus.

Poor wages and long hours of work had a shattering effect on home life. As Clinton Burrows put it, "We were victims of the system." Men had little time for leisure and little energy to give to their families—sometimes working two or three jobs to make ends meet, as well as working unpaid overtime in sanitation. Low wages forced them to draw housing subsidies, food stamps, or other sorts of federal and state welfare payments that subsidized the city government for the rotten wages it paid to the working poor. In 1968, James Robinson and his wife and three children lived in LeMoyne Gardens, one of the largest housing projects for the black poor. "At that time I didn't pay but thirty dollars a month, that's includin' the light bill," he recalled. "Quite a few were livin' there. We couldn't live nowhere else, we weren't makin' enough money to live nowhere else." Sanitation worker Robert Beasley likewise lived in a housing project designed for unemployed people on welfare.

A COHORT OF sanitation workers joined together in the early 1960s, determined to break arbitrary, personalized, racist oppression on the job. James Robinson knew from his factory job in Michigan that it was not unreasonable to set limits on working hours or to allow workers some say over their conditions of employment. He recalled, "The job I [had been] working on up north was a union job. After thirty days they gave you a paper and said, 'Sign this.' You'd sign it and give it back to them and you belonged to the union. You didn't sign, you didn't work. That was the United Auto Workers. You didn't have to worry about the boss, he wasn't gonna mess with you or you'd put the union on him. He's messin' with somebody and they blow the whistle. Everybody stopped workin'. You didn't take no stuff from the boss." The contrast to nonunion work in the South could not have been more obvious, and a number of sanitation workers had experienced both situations.

A number of sanitation workers had also been in the military, in either World War II or the Korean War. Veterans had enthusiastically taken up organizing during the CIO's Operation Dixie, and Robert Beasley, Taylor Rogers, Clinton Burrows, Joe Warren, T. O. Jones, and others had also worn the uniform of the United States. They formed a core of organizers for a union.

Beasley went into the U.S. Army in 1943, knocked around in various jobs, and then went to work for the Memphis sanitation division in February 1957. Ten years later, he became one of the activists leading the union. Like Robinson, Beasley recalled how utterly degraded he felt by his work conditions. In winter's cold rain or summer's boiling temperatures, "whether it was zero or one hundred [degrees], you just keep going." Employers sometimes loaded workers on the backs of trucks that hauled dead animals off the road. He experienced numerous dog attacks in people's yards, and when he hit an attacking dog to fend him off, a white homeowner screamed at him for doing so. The men got no respect. "We were called garbage men, walking buzzards," he said.

Burrows, after serving in the U.S. Navy, worked for the Southern Pacific Railroad and Republic Steel in Chicago, and then in a foundry; he, too, had experienced the benefits of union organization. But with the post–Korean War recession, he couldn't find a good job and went to work in Memphis for the sanitation division, also becoming part of the core of veterans who began to organize. "I thought changes was going to be made, and I came home and there weren't any changes that I could see." He felt like a farmhand, or like a prisoner:

> It was worser than being in the penal institution. They didn't want you to enter the office to get a drink of water. If you did, you had to take your hat off, wipe your feet off. . . . Eating without washing your hands, working in the snow without [a] fire. These are inhumane treatment. People in the penal farms were being treated better. We had traveled the world, we knew people were living better than this.

Burrows saw unionization first of all as a way to change the workers' psychology of subservience, a step toward self-respect. Many workers "acted like they were working on a plantation, doing what the master said. And the master was Henry Loeb." He wanted to change that.

Not all the sanitation workers came from rural backgrounds. Born in Memphis, Taylor Rogers attended Manassas High School through the tenth grade, went into the Navy during World War II, worked in the Army's Memphis General Depot, did custodial work, and then worked for Coca-Cola Bottling Company. In the late-1950s recession, nothing lasted. "There wasn't too much opportunity for a black man at that time. Really wasn't no other jobs hardly to be found. I was at a point I had to take what I could get." Rogers joined a sanitation crew, and one rainy day, while trying to take one of the tubs from a coworker's head to throw it onto the truck, his fingers slipped and the tub fell back on the man's head. He nearly broke the man's neck.

By 1968, Rogers had eight children to feed, and he hated his work conditions. "You got home you had to take your clothes off at the door 'cause you didn't want to bring all that filth in the house. We didn't have no decent place to eat your lunch. You didn't have no place to use the restroom. Conditions was just terrible." Without a union, "We didn't have no say about nothing. Whatever they said, that's what you had to do: right, wrong, indifferent. Anything that you did that the supervisor didn't like, he'd fire you, whatever. You didn't have no recourse, no way of gettin' back at him. We just got tired of all that."

Something had to change. Sanitation workers who went on strike in 1968 would say, as Rosa Parks and Dr. King had said during the Montgomery bus boycott, that they "just got tired."

But who would lead the organizing? Beasley recalled, "Anything could scare a sanitation worker at that time," because the job market offered them nothing else if they got fired for union activity. Thomas Oliver Jones, who worked with Beasley on a truck, seemed unafraid. Jones had little education, few options, and a family to feed, but he became obsessed with getting workers to see that they had rights and should use them, and he possessed a dogged belief in the ability of workers to change things. Gillis, Beasley, and other workers saw Jones as someone who cared enough to take on the risk of organizing. Gradually the men gained confidence in Jones and in themselves.

Born in Memphis on September 24, 1924, Jones grew up the hard way, like most black men, doing what he could to survive. Short and stocky even as a young man, he went to Douglass High School on the city's north side but joined the Navy before he graduated. After the service, he moved to California and worked in the Oakland shipyards, where he, too, learned of union wages and work conditions. He returned to Memphis in 1958 after the recession in West Coast naval shipyards eliminated his job. On December 12, 1959, he took a job with the Memphis Public Works Department. He got married, had kids, and went into chronic debt. When he risked what little he had by insisting on organizing a union, his family life became difficult. He could not pay his bills, yet he insisted on spending his extra time organizing rather than making money.

After he returned to the South, Jones looked around him and noticed the "world changed" since he had left: black people everywhere were fighting for their rights and demands for unionization were sweeping through the ranks of public employees. The world had changed, but "some people involved in the world weren't aware of it. . . . That's the same instance with these men. They didn't realize that they could do this [organize], you know." Jones went for advice to black unionists struggling in other industries, like George Holloway at International Harvester and Matthew Davis at Firestone, and white unionists also tutored Jones and other sanitation workers in unionism.

Jones drew on his own reservoir of ambition, pluck, and anger, and his determination probably made the difference between failure and success. If there had been no T. O. Jones, there might never have been a sanitation union in Memphis. Reverend Ezekial Bell, who became one of the union's strongest supporters, said, "If there were any heroes in the strike situation, it was T. O. Jones. Not the preachers who came to the front and made the orations, and raised the money, and so rallied the community. I think it was T. O. Jones. He is a man who certainly deserves everything that can be said kindly about Memphis." Bill Ross, executive director of the Memphis AFL-CIO Labor Council, said Jones's dedication and humility won over other sanitation workers. They believed in him "because he understood their problems. He had a certain amount of charisma with them. He talked their language. He was just another tub toter." He thought Jones "was a highly motivated, honest person when it comes to his relationship with his fellow man."

Jones had little organizing and no negotiating experience, knew little about the finances and organizational structures of unions, and often had difficulty making his ideas understood. This would cause untold problems with his international union and lead to his downfall after 1968. But as an organizer, he played the most essential role of all: Jones helped his fellow workers to realize that they had rights. Because he was one of them, he could do what no one else could: agitate and organize them into a conscious force for change. His only power was his faith that they could change their lives and his refusal to back up or quit.

Jones saw the old world of white paternalism and subservient labor relations falling, but it took time for poor people to grasp the power that they potentially held in their own hands. For about nine years, Jones experienced pain and desperation as he sought, often in vain, to convince his fellow workers that they had the right to a contract, to a grievance procedure, and to collect the dues needed to keep a union functioning. Most of the city's white business and civic leaders regarded these simple precepts of unionism as foreign concepts. In the early 1960s, Jones seemed to be a man lost in the wilderness.

Although he had no training, Jones understood the first principle of union organizing: that the workers themselves had to take action. He talked to them constantly about their need for a union and their own ability to do something about it. He told his son Jesse, "these people don't realize that they don't have to live like this. They don't realize that if they come together, that they can overcome these things, you know, although they don't think they can win, but they can."

Jones scraped together whatever money he could find to help people with their personal needs and create a union treasury of sorts. Joe Warren, an Army veteran who had worked for nine years at the Firestone Tire factory, became his assistant. Warren had a fighting attitude. He only took the Firestone job to pay off a loan on his new red Cadillac, a luxury blacks were not supposed to have—which is exactly why he bought it. Once laid off at Firestone, he worked in the sanitation division for the rest of his life.

J. L. McClain, Haley Williams, Beasley, Burrows, and a few others worked with Jones as a cadre of activists.

It took years for that circle of organizers to prepare a base for unionism among rank-and-file workers, and Jones meanwhile lived with a great deal of doubt and uncertainty. Jesse Jones followed his father's work, characterizing him as the Good Samaritan: "The Bible says, 'No greater love hath a man than this: that he would lay down his life for his friends.' And that's what my father did." He did not seek wealth or fame—"He just seen himself as a person that was doing something that needed to be done." He also agonized, however. Jesse said his father's lack of education caused him "to feel, you know, like he was inferior." White supervisors labeled him a "troublemaker," and most workers remained highly skeptical of his union campaign. Jesse said his father prayed a lot, looking for strength to continue. "Before the strike, it was like he was just a gust of wind, you know, just blowing."

JONES SOUGHT ALLIES in the black middle class of civil rights activists, politicians, businesspeople, educators, professionals, the clergy, and union members. He turned first to one of the city's most active black politicians, Binghampton neighborhood's Unity League President O. Z. Evers. He had fought police brutality in his neighborhood, successfully sued to end segregation in the zoo, and sued the city bus system, but a judge ludicrously ruled that he had no standing as a plaintiff because he owned a car and therefore presumably didn't ride the buses. Inspired by King's 1959 speech urging blacks to use the ballot to change the South, Evers ran to become the city's first black commissioner since Reconstruction, but the city's election commission used a technicality to disqualify him.

Evers never seemed to give up. Some suspected that he intended to create a personal power base in order to strike backroom deals with white politicians—a standard practice for black leaders in Memphis. But Evers also knew what it meant to belong to a union. After living in Chicago and California, he had become a U.S. postal worker in Memphis. Black postal workers held desirable jobs: they did not work in the grease and grime of a factory or the sweltering heat of a cotton compress, and they were the first to organize when President Kennedy allowed federal government workers the right to join unions in 1962. Evers saw unionization as a way out of poverty.

In February 1960, Evers started signing up sanitation workers into Local 984 of the International Brotherhood of Teamsters, Chauffeurs, Warehousemen and Helpers of America. The Teamsters already represented sanitation workers in Nashville, Knoxville, and Chattanooga, and they had a local base among truck drivers at several Memphis companies. Teamster business agents James Brannon (white) and Samuel Baptist (black), and secretary-treasurer Paul Kuhns (white), held a press conference with Evers to announce an organizing drive. Fearing they would be fired, not a single sanitation worker sat at the table with them.

Evers said some sanitation workers at that time made as little as 94 cents an hour but should be making at least $1.65 to rise above abject poverty. He urged that their wages be raised to $1.90 but said they would accept less if Public Works Commissioner William Farris would guarantee them a full day's wage regardless of weather conditions. Evers attacked the exclusion of blacks from top supervisory positions and their lack of rights on the job. He complained that the men had to carry leaky tubs and were victimized by arbitrary layoffs by racist foremen. Commissioner Farris, part of a semiliberal group of Democrats endorsed by the AFL-CIO, would not negotiate with Evers or any other "outsiders," saying, "There will be no union." He also threatened to eliminate the sanitation division and replace it with private contractors if workers organized.

More than 200 sanitation workers responded with a rally at Rock of Ages Church in the second week of March to demand union rights, with Evers and local union leaders sitting right up front. In early April, they held another mass rally, this time including "over 70 workers' wives stomping and cheering wildly at the promises of the union officials," according to the *Tri-State Defender*. Evers said 700 (he later said 900) of the division's 1,400 workers had signed union cards. Farris countered that many other workers had signed a petition saying they did not want a union. Evers said of Farris: "He's lining men up at all the stations with these petitions and trying to force the men to sign. Sign up or be fired is what he's telling them."

In the first week of May, Evers organized another mass meeting at

Mason Temple to inform the community about the plight of the sanitation workers. They demanded a raise to a base pay of $1.90 an hour, locker-room facilities, uniforms and boots, guarantees of full-time work even during bad weather, and recognition of their union. Farris responded that if sanitation workers struck, "I have 1,500 men waiting for their jobs." Suddenly, Teamsters leaders put off a strike and abruptly cut off all communication with Evers. Henry Loeb had apparently met with and intimidated the Teamsters, who withdrew from the campaign. "I think the Union has sold the men down the river," a disappointed Evers told the black press. Lacking a union to work with, Evers dropped his organizing activities.

At this point, sanitation worker organizing easily could have died, but Jones kept looking for outside support and telling workers that the union *is* the workers. Former Firestone worker Joe Warren knew George ("Rip") Clark, the president of the United Rubber Workers union, who connected Warren and Jones to two white men named Leon and James Shepard, of the Retail Clerks Union of Memphis, Local 1529. Leon, the Union's secretary-treasurer (and its business agent), gave Jones a key to the union's office and let him use its phones in a flat above Robilio's Restaurant, thus providing a rent-free base of operations and a crucial opening to other white-led unions.

Jones and his colleagues began calling their organization the Independent Workers Association (IWA). As poor workers with marginal union or legal support had done in the past, they took it upon themselves to create their own structures. These self-activated efforts came to fruition on June 16, 1963, when a hundred Public Works employees turned out for a meeting in the Retail Clerks' hall. They complained of leaky tubs, lack of raingear, trucks with bad brakes and faulty equipment, and other health and safety problems. What they most wanted were uniforms in which to work and showers made available after work.

Mayor Loeb and the city commissioners reacted to this protest by discussing a law to ban all city employee unions, and rumors circulated that the city would fire anyone who joined the union. Loeb said the city would never formally recognize any union, even though city departments since Crump's days had been making informal agreements with unions to set wages and hired many white building-trades workers through their unions. Sanitation employees probably would have been satisfied to exercise the informal prerogatives that white craft unionists already had, but Loeb thought allowing them such prerogatives would set off demands among the many other black city employees making poverty-level wages.

White elites, according to the NAACP's Jesse Turner, believed in the "domino theory," thinking, "If we give in to these folks, what's going to happen to all the other Negroes who are working here?" Blacks in hospitals, parks, and other city jobs needed to organize, and so did white firemen working seventy-two-hour weeks, white police officers who had miserable pay and work conditions, white and black teachers, and other underpaid civil servants. The lowly black sanitation workers had stepped out in the front line of the struggle for the rights of all Memphis public employees, many of them white.

True to Memphis traditions, the city squelched this initiative by sending informers into the Independent Workers Association's first big organizing meeting. Based on names forwarded by these "snitches," the Public Works Department drew up a list that included T. O. Jones and thirty-two other men. Ten days later, on June 27, Farris fired them all. He told the press the firings had nothing to do with the union; rather, he charged those fired with "inefficiency." These longtime city employees, most of them middle-aged or older, must have been inefficient a very long time, wrote the *Tri-State Defender*.

Warren, Jones, and other workers picketed Farris's office, but they had no union international to back them up. Jones turned to attorneys Sugarmon and Willis, UAW leader Holloway, and the black Ministerial Alliance, cultivating support from Henry Starks, Samuel Kyles, James Lawson, and other ministers. Black civic leaders pleaded with Farris to give the men their jobs back, and ultimately he did, but he accepted none of their union demands.

Faced with the opportunity to go back to his job under what he considered humiliating conditions, T. O. Jones made the fateful decision not to return and to keep organizing. He continued holding secret meetings and talking to individuals one-on-one, trying constantly to get them to pay union dues. He also talked with white union leaders. In effect, he appointed himself a volunteer organizer. "He started from scratch and from what the Lord was giving him and the people around him," said his son. The Shepard brothers kept Jones and his family from starving by creating a part-time job for him as a janitor at the Retail Clerks' hall. Working sporadically for wages, Jones dodged creditors at home and borrowed money from one person after another. Politicians offered Jones payoffs to stop his organizing, said Bill Ross, but he refused. Meanwhile, his inability to make a decent income widened a split between Jones and his wife. His dedication to unionism, his son Jesse said, shattered his family life.

JONES SAW THIS as the time to organize, and he seized it. The political climate, he reasoned, had everything to do with success or failure. The high tide of struggle had just crested in Birmingham, and throughout the South, thousands of black students, workers, and church members took to the streets in civil rights protests during 1963. Public employees had also grown restless. U.S. population and economic growth caused the number of government employees to leap from 5.5 million in 1946 to 11.6 million in 1967 (state and local governments employed 9.5 million of these). Teachers, nurses, police, highway workers, street cleaners, garbage collectors, office and hospital workers, researchers, and others still suffered from low wages and few rights on the job. In 1962, President Kennedy changed this with Executive Order 10988, making it legal for federal workers to join a union (though they had no right to strike). Federal postal workers led the way, and then in 1966, the U.S. Department of Labor signed an exclusive union contract with its employees.

Yet state and local governments acted as if public employee unionizing was a crime. In the Memphis sanitation division, white supervisors singled out men who attended union meetings, sent them home early, and docked their pay. After concluding that he needed outside support, Jones asked Memphis Labor Council Director Bill Ross if he could find an international union to support the local. Ross went to Washington to see Jerry Wurf, the new president of the rapidly expanding American Federation of State, County, and Municipal Employees (AFSCME). Unlike the Retail

Clerks union, AFSCME had a strong vested interest in organizing sanitation workers and was already doing it in a number of cities. And at its head was one of the most dynamic leaders of the labor movement.

Idealistic and pragmatic at the same time, the irascible Wurf had grown up in the tough Depression era on the Lower East Side of New York City, in a Jewish household that encouraged sharp wits and tongues and bred a militant belief in social justice. As a child, he suffered long bouts of illness with polio; as an adult, he remained in great pain much of the time due to a deformed foot and a lame leg. His physical weakness made him angry, inclined him to fight for the underdog, and forced him to use his wits and his intellect rather than muscle. He became a dedicated, militant socialist in the anti–Communist Party Left.

Wurf played political hardball, developing his cutting wit and explosive speaking style in street-corner and union political battles. He began in the 1930s as a member of the Young People's Socialist League, part of the Socialist Party under its leader Norman Thomas. He had a quick temper and made fast, hard judgments about people, and he wandered through the 1940s as a marginal labor activist. Wurf recalled, "I used to make these speeches and denounce public officials with such fervor and such a lack of facts." An acerbic, profane, and extremely critical and self-critical man, Wurf became increasingly experienced in collective bargaining; over time, his dedication to workers won him a place in New York City's labor movement. And Wurf immediately supported Martin Luther King during the Montgomery bus boycott and subsequent civil rights protests.

Wurf took over the presidency of AFSCME in 1964 as part of a movement opposed to the old business unionism of Arnold Zander, whom Wurf first served and then replaced. Before 1964, AFSCME looked like a lot of other AFL-CIO unions: bureaucratic, government-dependent, led by professionals and lawyers. Business unionism, for many workers, functioned like a guaranteed slot machine—you put your money in and money came flowing out. Personalities struggled for power, but issues relevant to the rank-and-file worker fell by the wayside. Wurf took over as part of a movement of younger people trying to change the union's culture, and that included overthrowing Jim Crow. Like most such unions,

AFSCME had long practiced racial discrimination. In Atlanta and other places, the union had separate black and white locals, and "It really didn't do a goddamn thing about the basic problems of race and indecency," said Wurf. The union had no women and only one African American on its executive board. Even though blacks and women were surging into government work, the membership remained about 70 percent white before Wurf took over.

After Wurf's election as president in 1964, an insurgent group—which included Catholics, Jews, Puerto Ricans, and African Americans—took over. AFSCME integrated its staff, no longer organized white and black workers separately, and began to build a solid core of organizers. Black AFSCME activists included James Farmer and others who initiated freedom rides and other civil rights protests. Based on this history, said Wurf, "in many respects this union was uniquely prepared to deal with the very difficult problems that existed in Memphis" around the issue of race.

When Bill Ross met Wurf, it must have been a study in contrasts. Ross was a southern, white, working-class, cold war liberal. As a printer, he had tried to organize various newspapers where he worked, and each time employers squelched him. Finally, he said sarcastically, "I was asked to leave the state." He became director of the Memphis AFL-CIO, where he had to please labor conservatives, racists, and business unionists, even as he served a membership in Memphis industrial unions that was at least one-third black. Wurf could not quite comprehend the complex blend of conservatism and liberalism that Ross carried within him, and he was never even sure whether Ross was an enemy or a friend. Nonetheless, Ross interested Wurf in supporting the Memphis sanitation workers.

AFSCME prepared a charter for Local 1733—a number chosen by the workers to recognize the thirty-three men who had been fired in 1963—and the workers held a charter dedication ceremony on November 13, 1964, at the historic W. C. Handy ("Father of the Blues") Theater. Memphis Labor Council President Tommy Powell presented the charter to T. O. Jones, and Father James Murray stressed, "Catholic moral theologians are practically unanimous in holding that it is morally wrong for civic or other authorities to refuse recognition to freely chosen unions of public servants." Leon and James Shepard, civil rights activists Maxine Smith, Russell Sugarmon, and A. W. Willis all appeared. The meeting embodied the kind of community support for public-employee organizing that Jones had sought since 1959. When the workers chose their first slate of officers, they elected him as president. Frank Parker and Holston Cooperwood served as first and second vice presidents, Robert Beasley as recording secretary—all three had been fired—and Marvin Costner served as secretary-treasurer. Freddie Lee Walker, Boston Brooks, and Otis Caldwell were elected as trustees and James Moss as the chaplain.

With an AFSCME charter (effective in January), the workers became increasingly assertive. Race relations based on subservience crumbled as the civil rights movement convinced many blacks of the effectiveness of taking group action. And now that Jones had significant union backing, his son Jesse said, "People are beginning to really listen to him and to see that his point of view is real."

IN JANUARY 1965, William Ingram became the mayor of Memphis and Pete Sisson became Public Works commissioner. It seemed an auspicious moment for the union. Jones supported their election campaigns, during which both men said they would support unionization of Public Works. The union's charter took effect on Martin Luther King's thirty-fifth birthday. Within fourteen days of taking office, however, Sisson fired five of the union's newly elected officers. The power structure in Memphis had let him know that recognizing a public-employee union was out of the question. Jones and Ross and the AFL-CIO pressured Sisson to return these men to their jobs. Three of the five got their jobs back, but it was another three years before the other two were reinstated.

Meanwhile, according to the Memphis AFL-CIO's *Union News*, an "overwhelming majority"—perhaps 80 percent—of sanitation workers had signed union authorization cards, although very few paid dues. That month, the AFSCME national field director, Tom Morgan, put Jones on the union's payroll as an international representative. A group of workers picketed Sisson, but he said that the city charter forbade formal recognition of a union and that he would fire anyone agitating on the job.

Mayor Ingram did nothing for the men. City commissioners held hearings in which AFL-CIO representatives—including white officials from the post office—explained how grievance procedures and seniority clauses meshed with the needs of government. Black ministers Henry Starks, Samuel Kyles, and James Lawson all testified to the needs of the workers. But commissioners voted four-to-one against recognizing the union, saying that if they gave it to the sanitation workers, they would have to grant recognition to other unions, which they did not want to do.

Sisson responded to the union campaign with numerous informal agreements—reducing the weight of the containers the workers had to carry, standardizing pay scales, putting heaters on some trucks, and bringing the workers into the modern world by making them eligible for Social Security. He gave them the option of dropping their additional city-run insurance fund (set up by Loeb in the 1950s)—and those who did deeply regretted it when they got older and had big medical bills to pay. White supervisors still fired workers at whim and blacks had almost no access to promotion. The basic conditions of worker indignity and employer abuse remained.

Jones still had no legal standing to obligate Sisson to do anything. In a city where it typically rained sixty inches per year, often in torrential downpours, the men wanted adequate raingear, and they wanted the city to repair the faulty brakes and dangerous packing mechanisms on some trucks. Without recognition of the union, such minimal demands received little attention.

The workers began to talk about taking direct action—a strike. Informants within their ranks, however, passed the word to Sisson, who sent out 700 letters to former city employees, offering them jobs if a strike began. On August 18, 1966, Jones met with AFSCME's international organizer Pete Brown; 500 workers met that weekend and voted to strike the city on Monday. In contrast to the February 1968 strike, they chose a good time to do it. Garbage left unattended in August stank to high heaven. Workers prepared picket signs and planned to march on city hall on Monday. But the city was a step ahead of them.

Mayor Ingram met with city commissioners to plot a strategy. Before the men could hit the picket lines, a Memphis chancery court issued an injunction that threatened Jones and union organizer Pete Brown with jail if the workers struck, or even if they picketed work sites. City Attorney Sam Weintraub personally read Brown the injunction, which he said was based on two Tennessee Supreme Court rulings declaring strikes against the public illegal. Some workers began picketing at midnight Sunday, but T. O. Jones appeared in the morning and told them the city had as many as 350 men at city hall ready to take their jobs. Brown and Jones abandoned the strike and AFSCME did not even appeal the court injunction, leaving it in effect indefinitely.

Scabs and a court injunction—methods to crush union activity used in Memphis since at least the 1930s—defeated Local 1733's strike before it even began. Fear of informants and firings now haunted the workers, and union dues dried up even further. Ingram said the city could never give any written agreement to a union. Wurf was angry that a strike had been threatened without adequate preparation, and that Jones and Brown had been so quickly intimidated by the injunction. Never strike in anger or frustration; only strike if you know you can win. And if you can win, ignore the injunction and go to jail if necessary, Wurf said. He fired Pete Brown and developed a profound lack of confidence in Jones.

Wurf believed that after this aborted strike, Jones reverted to the kind of backroom deal-making with white politicians that had characterized Memphis race relations since the Crump era. He questioned his skill and his veracity. ("T. O. Jones, who the hell knows what he says, because he's almost a pathological liar," he later told interviewers.) AFSCME's director of field operations, Peter (P. J.) Ciampa, later characterized Jones as "a cheap little hustler" who conducted union affairs by trying to make deals with Ingram and his cronies. But Jones had the workers' loyalty, and he remained the president of Local 1733 and an AFSCME staff member.

THE STRIKE FAILED not just due to inexperience or a lack of nerve by organizers. Black ministers, the NAACP, and political clubs felt that Mayor Ingram, whom they had strongly supported, would continue to open the doors to integration. The black middle class did not want to upset Ingram and would not get strongly behind a strike at this time.

The threat of a strike at least produced more improvements. Sisson purchased three-wheeled pushcarts to replace the open tubs men had been carrying on their heads; he replaced open-bed trucks with mechanical packers; he gave out raingear and a 10-cent-per-hour raise. And he ultimately returned all the fired workers to their jobs. But none of this established union rights.

Ross and the Memphis Labor Council supported Jones but did almost nothing to prepare the groundwork for the battle to come. Barely a word about the civil rights movement appeared in the Memphis *Union News*, even after the passage of the Voting Rights Act in 1965. The AFL-CIO in Memphis did not help white workers to see civil rights as part of the advance of labor, and vice versa. The "Negro–labor coalition" that Martin Luther King sought remained on extremely weak grounds in the Bluff City.

4

STANDING AT THE
CROSSROADS

*Something is wrong with capitalism as it now stands in the United
States. We are not interested in being integrated into* this *value
structure.... [A] radical redistribution of power must take place.*
—*Martin Luther King, to a ministerial advisory committee
in New York, November 24, 1967*

JAMES LAWSON FIRST LEARNED ABOUT MARTIN LUTHER KING,
Jr., by reading a newspaper account of the Montgomery bus boycott
while he was a Methodist missionary in India. Lawson leaped out of
his chair, clapped his hands, and shouted for joy. This was the movement he had been waiting for. He had lived in the land of Gandhi since
1953, absorbing anticolonialism and nonviolence as part of his being. He
was eager to build a movement to overturn what he called the interlocking
"cruelty systems" of colonialism, racism, and war, using a revolutionary
philosophy called nonviolence.

Before going to India, Lawson spent part of a year in federal prison for
resisting the draft. He could have accepted a student or ministerial defer-
ment, or filed for conscientious objector status; instead, he returned his
draft classification card to Selective Service. Said Lawson, "I sensed that
racial injustice and the whole motif of military conscription were akin to
each other in their basic denial of what I understood to be the purpose of
life." In an April 1951 trial, during the Korean War, a judge sentenced him

to three years of a five-year possible sentence for refusing to cooperate with the draft. Observing the humanity of even those called "criminals" while he was in prison, Lawson became "very persuaded of the inability of a person to say that a man is bad." After that, he refused to count anyone out of the human family.

Lawson's belief in nonviolence as a spiritual way of life grew out of his family's struggle against racism. Born in Uniontown, Pennsylvania, in 1929, he grew up in the steel town of Massillon, Ohio, one of the places organized by the CIO. His father had been a Methodist preacher in Alabama, where he carried a pistol to protect himself from white racists, but then he moved his family to Ohio for their safety. He organized NAACP chapters as he traveled the Methodist circuit and taught his five girls and four boys to resist racism. Young James struck a white classmate who called him a nigger, but when he told his mother about it, she said, "And what good did that do, Jimmy?" She taught her children to use their minds instead of their fists, and all four brothers became conscientious objectors to war. James began a "personal experiment with love . . . a resolve deep inside me that I would never hit out at people when I got angry, that I would find other ways to challenge them."

Through no choice of his own, racism became a life-defining issue. Lawson grew up with whites in a school and neighborhood where blacks were a small minority. An eighth-grade teacher inspired him, and he excelled in school, but the principal tried to steer him away from college as being unsuitable for an African American. As he moved about in Berea, Oberlin, and Cleveland after high school, Lawson experienced numerous racial conflicts with whites, but he never went along with racial conventions and sat in "whites only" areas whenever he encountered them. He decided, "I'm not going to be disciplined, or contorted into some form that I'm not."

In his freshman year (1947) at Baldwin Wallace College, a Methodist school, he decided he would study to be a minister and serve in the South. The overwhelmingly white student body elected him as class president. Lawson read the works of Gandhi, Sartre, Muste, Niebuhr, and Tolstoy and thought deeply about the problem of nuclear proliferation. He joined the

Fellowship of Reconciliation (FOR), a group dedicated to ending racism and war. He met pacifist A. J. Muste, a former labor organizer and America's foremost proponent of revolutionary nonviolence, who connected him to Bayard Rustin, James Farmer, and Glenn Smiley—some of the same people who also influenced King.

Reading widely about world affairs and nonviolence, Lawson became "committed to change, revolution, getting rid of the monkeys on the backs of myself, people, Negroes, poor people." Lawson defined revolution as a "radical overturning of the systems that oppress and hurt and cripple people," and he found his alternative to these systems in the "life and ministry of Jesus or the Prophetic Tradition." He defined nonviolence as an "aggressive engagement in seeking to apply a style of life tempered in love."

After college and prison, Lawson met socialists and nationalists in India and toured Africa. Observing a parallel freedom struggle building among colored peoples of the world, he vowed to become a part of it. Like King, he did not feel conflicted about who he was; he felt proud of the history of struggling for freedom in his own family. One of his ancestors had escaped slavery through the Underground Railroad, and another had become an influential free black and abolitionist in Philadelphia. Lawson believed it was time for a new form of abolitionism.

Lawson and King finally met at Oberlin College, where Lawson studied for a theology degree, in the winter of 1957. Still in their twenties, both men instantly recognized their common perspectives and goals. They knew many of the same ministers, read many of the same texts, and were both fully committed to overturning segregation. Both had excelled in their studies and received widespread support among white students and professors. Lawson had already been to prison and to India; King had already led a mass movement, and he would later go to India and Ghana to learn about the anticolonial struggle. At Oberlin, King gave an exciting series of talks. Lawson said, "I told him I wanted to work in the South and that I was waiting for the right time. He said: 'This is the right time. Come now. We don't have a person with your experience in nonviolence.'" Lawson called Muste, who called Smiley; they appointed him as southern field secretary of the FOR, and in 1958 he moved to Nashville to become only the second African American admitted to Vanderbilt Divinity School.

Lawson decided, "Montgomery was not an accident; you can repeat it, from the bottom up," and that's what he intended to do. In Nashville, he met Dorothy Wood, who worked in the office of Will Campbell, a field representative of the National Council of Churches; in 1959, Lawson and Wood married. She was as committed to bringing about change as Lawson was, even as they quickly started a family. Lawson began teaching nonviolence to groups of people on behalf of FOR and then SCLC. Like King, he spoke of "soul force," or *satyagraha*, as the crucial ingredient needed to keep the world from committing the suicide of nuclear war and to defeat racism. For him, pacifism meant: "We will make the choice according to the methods that we use, not according to the ends that we seek." He knew of the deep origins of nonviolent direct action in the United States—from the antislavery and women's movements to the labor movement and struggles for religious liberties. Historians taught American history in terms of conquest, but Lawson studied it to find out how ordinary citizens had effected change through nonviolent movements from below.

Like King, Lawson rejected Communism, but also anti-Communism. Lawson said that 90 percent of anti-Communism "is really another form of racism . . . because it projects all of our nation's problems . . . upon the outsider," instead of on their systemic roots in the American experience.

King asked Lawson to chair SCLC's direct-action committee and he accepted. Together the two conducted nonviolence training in Jackson, Mississippi. In Nashville in the fall of 1959, Lawson held nonviolence workshops aimed at developing a cadre to eliminate the "colored" and "whites only" signs in bus stations, airports, department stores, banks, and everywhere else. Participants in these discussions did not define their movement as a civil rights struggle but rather as a campaign to transform human relations, to create what people came to call "the beloved community." When the student sit-ins began, the Nashville movement proved itself one of the most successful at getting a city to desegregate public accommodations.

In the midst of the sit-in movement across the South, King invited Lawson to become director of nonviolent education for SCLC. Both spoke about the power of nonviolence at the Student Nonviolent Coordinating Committee (SNCC) founding convention in April 1960, and Lawson's call for young people to take events into their own hands especially roused the students. He shared their impatience with old forms of organizing and its compromises, saying, "This Movement is not only against segregation. It's against Uncle Tom Negroes, against the NAACP's over-reliance on the courts, and against the futile middle-class technique of sending letters to the centers of power." These sharp comments caused NAACP President Roy Wilkins to tell King he would get no further support from the NAACP if he appointed Lawson to the paid staff. King didn't, but Lawson continued, unpaid, as SCLC's director of nonviolent education and as a board member. Later, in the midst of organizational turmoil within SCLC in 1966, King asked Lawson to take a paid staff-director position, but he declined. By this time, he had his own congregation to tend to, and he thought trying to discipline SCLC staff members might be impossible.

Lawson remained one of the most morally committed and uncompromising forces in the nonviolence movement. He went on the freedom rides protesting interstate bus segregation, which landed him in prison in Mississippi in 1960. He spoke to the SCLC national convention in Nashville in August 1961 and called for the development of a "nonviolent army." Drawing on the Book of Jeremiah in the Bible, he defined the freedom movement as a "spiritual, moral, social, cultural revolution" that aimed "to overturn all of the systems of slavery and racism across the board." Lawson's teachings pushed the Movement in profoundly militant directions as he taught nonviolence to Movement activists in Nashville (1959–60), Albany (1962), Birmingham (1963), and Chicago (1966). He developed the tactical position of "jail, no bail" and authored ten rules of engagement for the Birmingham movement. He considered confrontational methods part of his ministry.

Another aspect of Lawson's politics was his focus on economic justice. Research by the Nashville protesters showed that blacks constituted 33 percent of the downtown shoppers: "We ought to have therefore a decided and visible percentage of the clerks, the tellers, the secretaries, the receptionists, the supervisors, the managers across the board." Being able to eat at a lunch counter was not enough. "Jobs, economic opportunity, access, the breaking down of the bad pay, the breaking down of a workplace climate that was insulting and demeaning of black people was from the very beginning a concern without reservation. . . . Black people being the last hired and the first fired was always on the front burners in all of the meetings and workshops, and in all of our negotiations."

In March 1960, Vanderbilt University expelled Lawson for his role in the sit-ins. In an unprecedented act of solidarity, the dean of the Divinity School and twenty-five white faculty members threatened to resign in protest, and two of them did. The school reinstated Lawson, but he felt truly hurt by its action and transferred to Boston University, King's alma mater, where he received his master's degree in theology in August 1960. Lawson then took a brief pastorship in Shelbyville, Tennessee; in June 1962, he moved to Memphis to become the minister at Centenary United Methodist Church.

Centenary Church, located on Mississippi Boulevard, had started in 1866, the year of a horrific Memphis race riot. It had sponsored literacy classes and served as a bastion of hope for freed slaves. By the time Lawson got there, however, it had become "in-grown and comfortable," in his words. With 800 to 1,100 members, it was the largest black Methodist church in the Mid-South. Civil rights lawyer A. W. Willis belonged, but few of its other members were activists. Lawson ran the church in true nonviolent style—giving low-key, quiet sermons, not calling for people to be saved or even to join the church. He took no collection; people dropped money in a platter as they left, if they were so inclined.

The sit-ins had dwindled, and Memphis now lacked a dramatic movement that could change what Lawson called its "smothering" racial climate. He noted that many of the same people led both the NAACP and the Shelby County Democratic Club, and he thought the civil rights movement had become a bit insular and parochial. Establishment whites used the interracial Memphis Committee on Community Relations (MCCR) mainly for dampening the fires of revolt. Schools were poor and still segregated, masses weren't involved in the Movement, and no other movement organization challenged the NAACP. White business elites turned to

A. Maceo Walker (of Universal Life Insurance Company), Dr. Hollis Price (president of LeMoyne College), and a few other black business and educational leaders, who "tended to be very conservative, and they were very suspicious of newcomers, black newcomers like myself, and were very suspicious of union activity." The NAACP had to be "dragged along" into direct action and building a solid base in the community, and Lawson thought Memphis remained "very much a plantation city."

In December 1963, Lawson joined NAACP picketing to get the twenty largest Memphis restaurants to desegregate. He became the chair of the NAACP's education committee in 1965, and he also chaired the War on Poverty agency called Memphis Area Project South (MAP South). He ran for the school board and led picket lines against the escalating Vietnam War in 1967. His concern with economic justice issues heightened as inner-city rebellions broke out in 1964 and 1965; in the summer of 1966, he joined with King to help build the Chicago freedom movement for equal access to jobs, housing, and education. As economic issues came sharply into focus, the civil rights movement took a sharp turn in the direction of Black Power.

AT LEAST TWENTY-SIX black and white civil rights workers had been murdered since 1960. All-white juries continued to acquit their murderers even as King and Lyndon Johnson shook hands on August 7, 1965, after the president signed into law the Voting Rights Act. Four days later, brutality by members of a nearly all-white police force in a nearly all-black ghetto, combined with rampant unemployment and miserable slum conditions, set off the massive Watts riot in Los Angeles, which left thirty-four dead and a thousand injured, as fires burned for four days. King arrived to calm the situation, but many black youths jeered him as too "middle class" and out of touch with the ghetto. Most whites, on the other hand, blamed black inferiority, Communists, or King's civil disobedience campaigns for the riots. Only a few whites besides the region's United Auto Workers union leader stood clearly with King in decrying the socioeconomic conditions that gave birth to the upheaval.

King told the UAW's District 65 in New York in September that the explosion in Watts required "a shift in the focus of struggle [that] is going to create tensions in the north which will not abate until the root causes are treated." He defined these causes from a labor perspective, emphasizing that a "destructive hurricane" of automation was "sweeping away jobs and work standards" and leaving many young blacks unemployed. Mechanization of unskilled jobs would not only destabilize black communities but also undermine unions, for "where there are millions of poor, organized labor cannot really be secure."

As riots exploded and industrial jobs and unions declined, King watched the Movement fragment. Many New Leftists cast aside coalition-building and said King was not radical enough. Malcolm X, Robert Williams, and others had condemned King's nonviolence as unmanly and ineffective. Responding to the crisis in the inner cities and to his critics on the left, King increasingly called for fundamental restructuring of the American system. In 1966, Coretta, Martin, and their children moved to the ghettos of Chicago in hopes of building a northern-based freedom movement. Chicago impressed upon King the depths of the economic and social problems blacks faced in America, but his campaign for black freedom in the North put him into conflict with some of his supposed liberal allies in the Democratic Party.

In the midst of the Chicago freedom movement, James Meredith, who in 1962 had "integrated" the University of Mississippi, decided on his own to hold a "march against fear" from Memphis to Jackson, Mississippi. In 1963, whites had murdered William Moore, a white integrationist postal employee from Baltimore, when he tried to walk across the Deep South in an appeal for brotherhood. When Meredith tried to do the same in 1966, a white World War II veteran with a Purple Heart, a Memphian named Aubrey James Norvell, appeared from behind a bush and blasted him with a shotgun on June 6. King and other national civil rights leaders immediately converged at Meredith's bedside at St. Joseph Hospital in Memphis; the next day, a number of them took up Meredith's march where he had left off. King provided the driving force in insisting that white violence against blacks could not be allowed to go unchallenged.

That night, June 7, some 600 people rallied at Lawson's church. The

NAACP's Roy Wilkins said, "Just a few miles south of here there is another country. We are going to show the people of Mississippi that they are part of the 50 states." King said, "There is nothing more powerful to dramatize an injustice than the tramp, tramp of marching feet," adding that the Memphis-to-Jackson march, beginning at Lawson's church, would be "the biggest, most momentous march" in Movement history.

Later that night at the Lorraine Motel in Memphis, Wilkins and the national NAACP and Whitney Young of the Urban League met with King, Floyd McKissick of the Congress of Racial Equality (CORE), and SNCC's Stokely Carmichael. Wilkins and Young sharply objected to the participation of the Deacons for Defense, a Louisiana group composed mostly of working-class military veterans. The Memphis police had stopped a carload of Deacons who pulled into town with M-1 rifles and bandoliers of bullets to support Meredith. Carmichael—the charismatic SNCC leader and fiery speaker born in Trinidad and raised in New York City—argued that local people in Mississippi should control the march rather than national leaders. King agreed that the Deacons could participate as long as they did not carry guns and adhered to nonviolence, but Wilkins and Young objected to the militancy of both the Deacons and Carmichael. They left, but King remained to push on.

In days to come, the mass media focused on debates over whether the Movement should support "Black Power" or integration, self-defense or nonviolence—exaggerating and simplifying differences that existed within the Movement. Together, King and Carmichael in Mississippi led some of the most dangerous, frightening, and provocative marching and rallies of the era, as police viciously attacked demonstrators and blacks fought back. The Deacons, without weapons, did provide some protection, and the March Against Fear, with almost no federal protection, lasted for nearly three weeks. Black Mississippians often were armed and most were not ideologically committed to nonviolence. King did not argue against people protecting their homes and families, but he continued to speak for nonviolence and integration. Carmichael said, "Integration is irrelevant," and Meredith, recovered from his wounds, said he had been foolish to march without a gun.

King broke away to hold his own witness in Philadelphia, Mississippi, where he was confronted by police officers who had helped to murder three civil rights workers during Freedom Summer in 1964. A mob of whites attacked the marchers, with King among them. That night in Indianola, King condemned the use of violence by anyone, whether they were in the Movement or attacking it. The next day, blacks exchanged gunfire with several carloads of marauding whites that had fired into the Mississippi Freedom Democratic Party headquarters.

Lawson, Reverend Ralph Jackson, the white minister Malcolm Blackburn, and a number of other Memphians participated in the marches. The March Against Fear became a turning point for twenty-year-old Coby Smith, who went to Mississippi with his father, a UAW union steward at the Memphis International Harvester factory and a friend of black UAW leader George Holloway. Smith had been student-body president at all-black Manassas High School and then one of the first two black students at the private, liberal arts–based Southwestern College. He recalled, "I was going to be somebody, man, I was trying to make some money. I was going to be rich. We thought that all we had to do was desegregate America, be the best we could be, the smartest, the brightest." In high school, Smith received an American Legion award that could have led him into becoming a career officer in the military, and a photo showed him proudly, earnestly dressed in uniform. But his life turned in another direction because of the Movement.

In his view, supposed conflicts over self-defense or pacifism, Black Power or integration, in large measure came down to differences in emphasis between younger and older people in the Movement. Russell Sugarmon, A. W. Willis, and especially James Lawson, had influenced Smith. "I, like everybody else, admired and loved the man. He's tremendous and we all wanted to model our lives after what he had been able to accomplish." Yet when Smith tried to work as a student leader with the adult leaders of the NAACP, he thought they made too many decisions for the students, and he did not like the way Lawson himself had to "fight for credibility" with more mainstream civil rights leaders. Younger people could come up with more effective strategies for social change, he thought.

He began to feel the famous "generation gap" of the 1960s between himself and older leaders over questions of integration and nonviolence.

Smith ran errands for both Carmichael and King and sometimes went with others to prepare communities for the arrival of the marchers. In Canton, he witnessed what looked like an army of muscular white football players from Ole Miss (who were actually law enforcement officers) wading into crowds of black people and beating and teargasing them until blood and tears rolled down their faces. Officers shot Carmichael in the chest with a tear-gas canister, while King calmly urged people not to panic as they choked on gas and suffered police blows. Smith noticed that King continued to work with Carmichael, no matter how incendiary his rhetoric, and that Carmichael and other SNCC people had a strong appreciation for King's courage and his militancy. Carmichael said of King in Mississippi that it was "as if he were out of a straitjacket. We sensed that this was the aspect of the Movement that he liked best, where he was most free to be himself," among his own people, even while "every racist with a rifle, shotgun, or stick of dynamite" threatened to kill him. Klansmen in Natchez murdered sixty-seven-year-old Ben Chester White, a plantation worker unconnected to the Movement, in hopes of luring King to the area so they could kill him, too.

Getting his Movement education during the Mississippi march, Smith concluded that the supposed divisions between "violent" and "nonviolent" black leaders were mostly media exaggerations, and that King and Carmichael each had their own kind of militancy and integrity. Smith considered himself a student of King, saying that his language "was like poetry." But he asked why whites condemned blacks for taking up guns in self-defense yet never objected to blacks using them against other people of color in Vietnam. Violence remained as American as cherry pie, as H. Rap Brown said, and Smith thought the main question for African Americans was how to react to it. It seemed to him that whites largely ignored King's nonviolent demands except when they feared a credible threat of counterviolence by blacks. Meredith himself said he would shoot back at white vigilantes in the future. Smith, too, saw nonviolence as a tactic only, and he noticed that King, despite his nonviolence, never backed down from a fight. Smith went back to Memphis with the idea that blacks of all persuasions and classes needed to create a "black united front" to pose a credible threat of violence that would force whites to negotiate.

Black Power—in Malcolm X's terms, black economic, political, and cultural control over black communities—swept into the forefront of Movement politics. The idea had deep historical roots in black movements for autonomy and justice, and many blacks in Mississippi and elsewhere considered "integration" irrelevant compared with the need for economic and political power. The mass media made a great to-do over the shift in rhetoric and emphasis during the Meredith march, where "Move On Over or We'll Move Over You" and "We Shall Overrun" competed with "We Shall Overcome." In the aftermath of the march, Carmichael wrote in the *New York Times* that whites in the Movement corresponded in many ways to white civil servants who worked in and controlled colonized countries. "Whites can only subvert our true search and struggle for self-determination, self-identification, and liberation in this country. . . . If we are to proceed toward true liberation, we must cut ourselves off from white people." He condemned the NAACP as "reactionary . . . one of the main roadblocks to black freedom," and said interracial organizations made too many compromises.

This new emphasis largely rejected the strategy of Randolph, Rustin, King, and others who believed they could change the country by combining labor and civil rights struggles and broad constituencies to create a "coalition of conscience" that could be a majority political force. As the foremost advocate of interracial mass coalitions, King necessarily bore much of the criticism from Black Power advocates. SCLC could hardly be indicted as a puppet for white interests, since African Americans led and staffed it, yet it clearly represented southern preachers with an older, religion-based vision, one that many New Leftists considered less revolutionary than their own. Some saw nonviolence as an outmoded concept left over from a time "when it was considered a noble deed, man, to lay down in the street and let some cat beat you up," as black Memphian Calvin Taylor put it.

King never argued that everyone had to be a pacifist, and he conceded the right of individual self-defense, but he argued that a mass movement could not afford the luxury of publicly taking up weapons or speaking in the language of violence. If violence occurred, media coverage would obscure who started it, and the Movement would lose both its moral standing and its appeal to public opinion and government leaders. King soberly refuted the idea that urban guerrilla war or violent revolution could prevail against the foremost military machine in the world, or that third-world revolutionaries like Mao Tse-tung would aid the Black Revolution in America. He saw riots not as acts of revolution but as desperate and fruitless cries of despair from powerless people that would only lead to more repression. Lawson felt the same way, and actually calculated just how many guns it would take for guerrilla warriors to outflank the police or the U.S. Army. He said it could not be done.

The issue was not just violence versus nonviolence, but also the role that self-defense should play in the Movement, and whether its goals mainly concerned integrating into the existing system or radically changing it. The divide in the Movement was not as wide as the mass media suggested, for most organizers agreed on the need to attack institutional racism, not just segregation, and to support black solidarity. In Chicago, King attacked institutional racism and convinced some street-gang members and younger activists that nonviolent direct action could be militant, disruptive, challenging, and effective. Even so, a major riot broke out in Chicago in July, which King and his organizers struggled to control. Yet false dichotomies between Black Power and nonviolence led many to think that King had fallen behind the times; people constantly challenged him to explain why integration and nonviolence remained relevant in the era of Vietnam and Watts.

KING RETURNED TO Memphis on September 9, 1966, fresh from a frightening open-housing march in the Chicago suburbs in which he was hit in the head with a rock as some 5,000 working-class and middle-class white homeowners screamed for his blood. Whites in Chicago reacted violently to his calls for integration, as if he wanted to tear their world apart. In Memphis, he opened the Progressive National Baptist Convention, representing some 400 churches, as his Chicago campaign to attack urban poverty and discrimination wound down to an inconclusive finish. Before some 3,000 black Memphians, King spoke for seventy-five minutes at the Metropolitan Baptist Church of Reverend Ben Hooks.

"We must persist in the struggle against injustice, but we must use the proper methods in doing it," he said. America had placed blacks behind "a huge, tragic, invisible wall." King demanded to know, "Who perpetuates the wall?" The Ku Klux Klan, the John Birch Society, white "moderates" who urged caution, and a government "more interested in winning the war in Vietnam than in winning the war right here"—they all perpetuated the wall, as did "some Negro preachers more interested in being Uncle Tom than in being just." King said that even the Black Power slogan could be a form of acceptance of segregation. "We must never adjust to being behind the wall."

King took a positive position on the goals of Black Power, mixed with caution about its methods. If Black Power meant "amassing political and economic power to achieve our goals . . . a belief in ourselves and our heritage," then King favored it. But if it meant riots, which were happening that very week in his hometown of Atlanta, "I want the record to show I'm against it. Our power does not lie in Molotov cocktails and rocks and bottles. It lies in unity and the willingness to suffer for righteousness." Nor did power lie in all-black movements. "I'm not going to believe, no matter who says it, that the Negro can make it by himself. We are one-tenth of the nation's population, and we can't move without some good will from the other nine-tenths."

Yet King did not blame the Black Power movement for riots, as many whites did; he blamed riots on the wall of white indifference and "winters of delay" by the government in the War on Poverty. Lawson and King both rejected the idea that a much-publicized "white backlash" would subside if the Movement only slowed its pace; they felt the backlash merely expressed a long-standing white opposition to black equality. Society needed to bring its prejudices to the surface in order to resolve them.

The *Tri-State Defender*'s Nat D. Williams praised King for "pulling the blankets back and showing what's happening under the cover" to African

Americans. But the *Commercial Appeal* did not praise him or regard him as a better alternative to Carmichael. Instead, it criticized him for taking up the March Against Fear, which it deemed provocative and riotous, and said King's prophecies of potential trouble ahead belied "his professed devotion to a course of nonviolence." Letters to the editor denounced King more sharply. A White Citizens' Council activist called King and the march "a Communist plot to take over the South" and a new form of "Black Supremacy." King came under attack from those who called themselves moderates, from his presumed allies on the left, from the right, and most of all from powerful forces in the federal government.

FBI Director J. Edgar Hoover had been in power in Washington longer than most congressmen had been alive, starting with his role in the Red scare against unions, raids against immigrants, and the harassment and deportation of Marcus Garvey that followed World War I. Raised in a segregated city, the nation's capital, Hoover had always viewed the rise of Martin Luther King with alarm. He knew King had defended the civil liberties of Communists and supposed Communists and had received support from leftists, and that socialist and class politics had increasingly seeped into his speeches. King's sought-after strategic alliance of workers, the peace movement, and the black freedom struggle mirrored a similar "center-left" strategy of the Communist Party.

But mostly Hoover saw King as a racial threat. To his aides, Hoover called King a "burr head." He detested his fame, which only grew when King brought hundreds of thousands to the nation's capital in 1963. His assistant, William Sullivan, had drawn Hoover's ire when he said King was *not* a subversive threat, so to curry favor with Hoover, Sullivan ripped King's performance at the Lincoln Memorial as a "powerful demagogic speech" that proved King was now "the most dangerous Negro of the future in this Nation from the standpoint of communism, the Negro and national security." Hoover pinned his accusation that King was a closet Communist to his relationship with a white New York City businessman named Stanley Levison, who wrote much of King's 1961 speech to the AFL-CIO and, as a close adviser, steered King toward coalitions with unions and middle-class and religious allies. When he was grilled at a Senate Internal Security Subcommittee (SISS) hearing on subversion in 1962, Levison told Senator Eastland that he had never been a Communist Party member; he probably had been, and clearly had raised funds for it and other leftist groups. Based on Levison's advisory relationship with King, Hoover applied for and received permission from Attorney General Robert Kennedy to secretly wiretap King and his associates.

Hoover also complained of King's relationship to Jack O'Dell, a former labor organizer and Communist Party (CP) member who had been expelled from the National Maritime Union as part of the purge of the CIO's Left, and who helped King organize and raise funds. Hoover knew that both Levison and O'Dell had cut their previous ties to the CP, but he did not tell that to either President Kennedy or President Johnson. King believed that people had a right to their own opinions, and he said anyone could work on his staff as long as they were no longer CP members. Personal pressure from President Kennedy forced King to disassociate himself from both men, but he did so only temporarily and not completely.

The FBI had an ongoing "counterintelligence" program called COINTELPRO, which had been used to decimate the CP by planting informers and provocateurs within it. COINTELPRO also targeted King to prove his Communist connections. In March 1962, FBI agents secretly broke into Levison's offices to plant bugs and phone wiretaps; in November 1963, they used break-ins again to install wiretaps in King's offices and on his home phone. Hoover developed a round-the-clock surveillance campaign aimed at destroying King. FBI agents bugged his hotel rooms and sent an anonymous, threatening letter and tape to his home, urging King to commit suicide or be exposed as sexually promiscuous. Hoover continually poisoned the president and other top government officials with memos on King's supposed Communist sympathies and his sex life. Angered by the 1963 March on Washington, Hoover publicly called King "the most notorious liar in America," and privately ordered FBI agents not to warn King when they learned of plots against his life (as they had done previously). After King won the Nobel Peace Prize in 1964, and especially after he spoke out strongly against the Vietnam War in 1967, Hoover grew even more determined to destroy King.

King did not expect to be a target of repression by the federal government, which had been something of an ally, especially under President Johnson. King did fit the profile of a revolutionary, but not the kind Hoover and the paranoid Right imagined. King's radicalism stemmed from his understanding of Christianity as a moral belief system that called upon people to apply uncompromisingly the egalitarian teachings of Jesus to the world around them. King outlined this view at the European Baptist Assembly in Amsterdam in August 1964, saying the times required revolutionary Christians "willing to bear the burden of the cross" to end poverty and bring about lasting peace in the world. "It was Christian preaching that first spread the idea of the Brotherhood of all mankind throughout the world," and that gave hope to the slaves of early America and now to the semi-slaves of the colonized world. "Feeding the hungry and clothing the naked . . . must be done, and God has called us as his children to see to it that it is done."

King's demanding, even harsh, agenda called upon dedicated people to suffer whatever it took to bring about social change, and his commitments always went far beyond civil rights. Lawson said, "A nonviolent person has made a major decision and a major analysis about violence" that is all-encompassing. It included a commitment to end not only the violence of racism but also the violence of poverty and of war. But the mass media in the United States largely portrayed King as a civil rights or a black leader without understanding his deeper reasoning and his calling as a Christian minister. One of the great problems with understanding King, said Lawson, "is our typing him as a civil rights leader. We do not type him as a pastor, prophet, theologian, scholar, preacher . . . and that allows conventional minds across the country to thereby stereotype him and eliminate him from an overall analysis of our society." Perhaps this also blinded Black Power advocates and New Leftists to the full scope of King's radicalism.

On August 25, 1967, J. Edgar Hoover issued a new COINTELPRO memo to all FBI offices titled, "COUNTERINTELLIGENCE PROGRAM, BLACK NATIONALIST—HATE GROUPS, INTERNAL SECURITY" (caps in original), defining the FBI's purpose as not just surveillance but attack:

The purpose of this new counterintelligence endeavor is to expose, disrupt, misdirect, discredit, or otherwise neutralize the activities of black nationalist, hate-type organizations and groupings, their leadership, spokesmen, membership, and supporters, and to counter their propensity for violence and civil disorder. . . . No opportunity should be missed to exploit through counterintelligence techniques the organizational and personal conflicts of the leaderships of the groups . . . to insure the targeted group is disrupted, ridiculed, or discredited.

Hoover emphasized the power of the mass media to perform this function if properly led by the FBI's information.

The FBI had no legal authority to attack individuals and groups exercising their free-speech rights under the First Amendment of the Constitution, but that did not matter to Hoover, who placed SCLC on his list of hate groups and King on his short list of people to be discredited. Memphis was one of the key cities that received his August 25 memo.

BY 1967, THE Movement had reached a turning point. Too many crises erupted at the same time, so that whenever King tried to address one set of circumstances, another set would quickly arise. The Meredith march diverted him from his Chicago campaign, and to counter the Movement's fragmentation, he increasingly tried to find a unifying theme and strategy in a "second phase" that would lead to the realization of economic and social justice as well as civil rights. Without a second phase, he told Teamsters shop stewards and organizers in New York on May 2, the gains of equal legal rights and voting rights won in the first phase would be severely compromised. He titled his speech "Civil Rights at the Crossroads." King still pushed for the coalition between labor and civil rights that had triumphed in passing the Civil Rights Act of 1964 and the Voting Rights Act of 1965, but King's second phase required a more radical demand: to resolve centuries of intertwined racial and economic injustice by overhauling American capitalism.

As if that were not enough, King felt compelled to open yet another front of conflict. In a stunning speech at Riverside Church in New York on April 4

—one year to the day before his death—King offered the most severe moral indictment of imperialism of his generation. He boldly condemned America's Vietnam War as an unjustified, cynical, and hopeless slaughter of poor people of color. He critiqued the origins and effects of the war, in which a million Vietnamese had already died, but he went further, saying, "The war in Vietnam is but a symptom of a far deeper malady within the American spirit." He spoke of corporate investments abroad and American support for military dictatorships, and of greed. "We must rapidly begin the shift from a 'thing-oriented' society to a 'person-oriented' society. When machines and computers, profit motives and property rights are considered more important than people, the giant triplets of racism, materialism, and militarism are incapable of being conquered."

King attacked the war as damaging to the Vietnamese but also to Americans, and particularly to African Americans. The nation's conduct abroad taught people at home to accept violence while it consumed society's resources like a "demonic suction tube." President Johnson's War on Poverty, he said, had been "shot down on the battlefields of Vietnam," while the "flame throwers in Vietnam fan the flames in our cities." King did not just say the war was wrong; he indicted the system that brought it about. He called for "a true revolution of values," a reordering of priorities to "develop an overriding loyalty to mankind as a whole," to join the world revolution on behalf of the poor, the colonized, and the oppressed. Everyone must protest the war, he said, for "silence is betrayal." He feared "there is such a thing as being too late. . . . [I]f we do not act we shall surely be dragged down the long, dark, and shameful corridors of time reserved for those who possess power without compassion, might without morality, and strength without sight."

In delivering this sharp critique, King sacrificed his ties to the American political establishment and to the most powerful leader in American government. Two weeks after his Riverside Church speech, he told the press: "We seek to defeat Lyndon Johnson and his war." Johnson, for his part, raged at King, and Hoover told him that King had a "propaganda line" similar to the Communist Party. When King spoke at a mass antiwar rally on April 15 in New York, Hoover stepped up his efforts to connect

King to "Communist Influence in Racial Matters," with total support from the president.

While King's moral and political agenda kept expanding, that of the NAACP remained within the narrower framework of cold war civil rights. King's moral indictment of America's course in Vietnam caused the NAACP board of directors to condemn him unanimously, and other black leaders criticized him as well. The *New York Times* said, "King has diminished his usefulness to his cause, to his country, and to his people." The *Washington Post* and other media attacked him as either naïve or too radical. Carl Rowan, a black journalist who also worked to support American foreign policy as part of the United States Information Agency (USIA), wrote in *Reader's Digest*, a conservative magazine with millions of readers, that King had "an exaggerated appraisal" of himself and was influenced by Communists. An adviser told President Johnson that King had "thrown in with the commies."

Lawson recalled taking a long walk with King in which he expressed great pain over the attacks made against him, especially by blacks, because of his antiwar stand. Yet Lawson and King remained in complete agreement that the nonviolent movement had no choice but to reject violence and blind anti-Communism as tools of American foreign and domestic policy. Socialism had moral appeal to masses in Africa, Asia, and Latin America not because people there were duped, Lawson said, but because it had "put a bottom on life, below which no one is falling." Both he and King said that if the United States wanted to compete with the socialist world, it had to offer a moral alternative. War was not the answer.

Lawson and King had worked in tandem against the war since 1965, when Lawson flew to Vietnam on King's behalf for a three-week peace-seeking mission. Stopping the war, said Lawson, was always a part of their economic and moral justice agenda, and was especially important for black soldiers, who were victims of an "economic draft" that made the military attractive as a source of employment. As more and more blacks came home maimed or dead from Vietnam, and more Vietnamese civilians died, SCLC organizer James Bevel urged King to make opposition to the war the top priority of SCLC.

King's antiwar position opened a huge gap between him and the AFL-CIO, its member unions, and its president, George Meany, who strongly supported the war. When fifty dissident unions and some 500 unionists gathered at the University of Chicago on November 11, 1967, to disagree with Meany and form the Labor Leadership Assembly for Peace, they chose King as keynote speaker. Amid a rising antiwar chorus of intellectuals, students, businessmen, and politicians, King said, "One voice was missing—the loud, clear voice of labor." The war "has given the extreme right, the anti-labor, anti-Negro and anti-humanistic forces a weapon of spurious patriotism" and "smothered and nearly extinguished the beginnings of progress toward racial justice." He called on unions to disassociate themselves from U.S. war policy, but most of them continued to support it.

The more King spoke about the war, the more he began to lose his traction as a "civil rights leader." Rather than making the war his top priority, as James Bevel urged, he thought the Movement should merge its issues—linking racism, poverty, and war as parts of an oppressive system that needed to be changed. At a staff retreat in Frogmore, South Carolina, in November 1967, King argued that ghetto rebellions demonstrated that the Movement had hardly touched the problem of pervasive poverty. He called on SCLC to move from an "inadequate protest phase to a stage of massive, active, nonviolent resistance to the evils of the modern system." Rather than seeking to integrate into existing values, he said, blacks had to change those values and the system that produced them. To do it, King said, required "a method that will disrupt our cities if necessary, [to] create the crisis that will force the nation to look at the situation, dramatize it, and yet at the same time not destroy life or property." He wanted to dramatize the plight of the poor, even if it required "nation-wide, city-paralyzing demonstrations."

King had shifted from civil rights to a human rights agenda, said Lawson, based on the trajectory of social movements, which "don't spring up fully developed" but rather evolve organically, based on experience. "Our initial concerns were concerns for the spiritual, psychological wounds caused by the indignities that segregation heaped upon black people," but as some barriers to freedom fell, other obstacles appeared and had to be

challenged. King responded to that challenge, calling not for an armed revolution but for a revolution in values. The black freedom movement, he
said, "is forcing America to face all its interrelated flaws of racism, poverty,
militarism and materialism. It is exposing evils that are deeply rooted in
the whole structure of our society." Life itself, not theory, had revealed
"that radical reconstruction of society itself is the real issue to be faced."

KING HAD PONDERED these issues during the SCLC convention in
Atlanta in August 1967, wrestling with how to create a strategic response to
the crisis of the black poor, the working poor, and American society more
generally. In a "somewhat subdued, resigned manner," he spoke with a
reporter outside the convention hall, telling him that the United States had
reached a crossroads, with many people feeling tremendous bitterness at
the shallow gains of the black freedom movement and the ongoing crisis
afflicting the black urban poor. He said he planned to create a nonviolent
campaign to attack the problems of war, poverty, and racial oppression all
together, and he projected sit-ins and camp-outs in the nation's capital,
combined with massive economic boycotts and calculated disruption to
demand that the nation reorder its priorities.

"This is something like a last plea to the nation to respond to nonviolence." If the strategy failed, King said, all he could do would be to "say to the
nation, 'I've done my best.'" He would call it the Poor People's Campaign.

5

ON STRIKE FOR RESPECT

*We just got together, and we decided to stand up and
be men, and that's what we did.*
—*Taylor Rogers, sanitation striker*

*We were so proud of the fact that the sanitation folk had stood as
men ... and they showed a kind of togetherness that maybe
some of us had never shown. ... When you are very
poor and you don't have very much to lose anyway,
just maybe you can get together a little better.*
—*Cornelia Crenshaw, strike supporter*

IN THE FALL OF 1967, HENRY LOEB ONCE AGAIN RAN FOR MAYOR of Memphis. His "Law and Order" and "Be Proud Again" rhetoric appealed to those who feared high taxes and integration and wanted clean streets and efficient city services at low cost. As a fiscal conservative, he pledged to eliminate the Memphis city government's operating deficit of $65,000 (and an expected fiscal-year–end deficit of $2.2 million) by cutting jobs and expenses. Russell Sugarmon and other civil rights activists (including Charles Cabbage and Coby Smith) tried to elect attorney A. W. Willis as the first black mayor, but in the primary blacks voted overwhelmingly for incumbent mayor William Ingram, a supposed racial moderate who had done little for blacks. In the November runoff between Loeb and Ingram, Loeb won, despite fierce black opposition, by receiving more than 90 percent of the white vote.

Loeb came into office in January 1968 "over the determined opposition of practically the entire black community," said Reverend Benjamin Hooks. "And so you had the Negro community at a very critical point. Possibly in the hearts of the black community there was a feeling that the political process is a fraud. That we did what we were told to do if we wanted to have freedom, we registered, and we voted, we voted overwhelmingly for our choice . . . and he was defeated . . . by a segregationist . . . an uncompromising, unyielding segregationist." Maxine Smith, equally disgusted at the failure of electoral politics to bring change, voted for Loeb in the November election because she thought he would stir the black community into opposition, whereas Ingram would continue to put it to sleep.

During this period, Local 1733 of AFSCME struggled just to stay alive. T. O. Jones had only about forty dues-payers, out of nearly 1,300 sanitation workers in the Public Works Department. Getting a dollar a week in union dues from poor people making nonunion wages proved nearly impossible. As Jones approached workers outside the gates of the Public Works Department for the quick and furtive donations out of a worker's closed hand over the fence (he called them "fist collections"), supervisors took note of who responded. Said Jones, "The men knew how the city felt about the union," and they feared they would be fired. Yet going to their homes individually for the dues took too much time for too little money.

Desperate to cut a deal, T. O. Jones and Joe Warren had gone to Loeb on July 4 and pledged to support his election bid if he would promise to recognize and bargain with their union. "He told us there would be no union," remembered Warren. "You can have it, but you can never get no dues checkoff or recognition by the city. He wouldn't take no money either, he said that would be wrong. 'I want all of you all to go fishing on election day, I'm gonna win anyway.'" When Warren threatened that the union would strike, Loeb responded, "You'll be the first one fired."

WHEN LOEB TOOK office in January 1968, he immediately tightened the city's labor policies. Public Works employees sometimes had to work late into the night to clear the roads, and Loeb insisted that they start another workday the next morning, with no overtime pay. Loeb wouldn't spend money on new equipment, and if a vehicle broke down, workers had to stay with it until it could be removed from the street, again without overtime pay. As workers retired, died, or were injured, he did not fill their positions, forcing those who remained to do more work without more pay. Cutting costs by doing more with fewer workers created mounting hours of unpaid labor, and workers considered it outrageous for the city to balance its budget this way.

Loeb disrupted the informal bargaining relationship Jones had developed under previous Public Works Commissioners William Farris and Pete Sisson. The new mayor–council form of government that took effect in January required the mayor to appoint the formerly elected directors of the Public Works, Police, Fire, and other departments. Loeb named his political crony Charles Blackburn—an insurance man and linen-supply company manager with no previous government or negotiating experience—to run Public Works. P. J. Ciampa, AFSCME's director of field operations, said Blackburn "was a guy who didn't know a sanitation truck from a wheelbarrow." The mayor told Jones to deal directly with Blackburn, but when he tried to do so, Blackburn told Jones that Loeb made all the important decisions. The union's previous arrangements meant nothing, and Jones had nowhere to turn to resolve worker grievances.

Under the new administration, those grievances piled up quickly, and workers started talking about a strike. Commissioner Sisson had previously allowed the sewer and drainage men to work in the rain or to wait until the rain cleared up, with no loss of wages. Loeb reinstated his Public Works policy of the 1950s—paying only two hours' wages and sending workers home on a rainy day. "That's when we commenced starving," said Ed Gillis. He made only $7.80 a day, even when it didn't rain. With so little to show for his work, "Lot of times I just got ashamed to come home."

Around 7 AM on Tuesday, January 30, Gillis's coworker L. C. Reed arrived at the sewer and drainage division on High Street. A city employee for fourteen years, Reed had formerly been a sharecropper in Mississippi. His wife worked in a beauty salon, and they had three children and a home to pay for. He and a group of twenty-one other blacks prepared to do their usual things: lay pipes and sidewalks, haul broken-up rocks to create concrete walls and drainage areas to prevent erosion, dig sewers, and the like. Before they could start work, recalled Reed, "There come a shower of rain and it rained about half an hour after we checked in and they told us to wait a while and then they come out and . . . the superintendent sent us home. And after they sent us leaving, the sun come out. There wasn't anything new. They cut the crew and 'fore the crew leaves the barn the sun would be shining pretty, but still us go home. White men worked shine, rain, sleet, or snow."

They reported the incident to a steward for the union, who reported it to Jones. The next morning, Jones stopped the sewer and drainage men at one of the city's five truck depots (formerly mule barns) from going to work. Blackburn came down to the depot to find him sitting on a table surrounded by black men. Jones demanded full pay for the previous day before the men would go to work. Blackburn predictably refused, but he agreed that the rainy-day policy should be studied and perhaps changed. Jones got the impression that Blackburn would also get the men more than two hours of show-up pay for their lost day of work. Several days later, Blackburn posted a bulletin saying superintendents would now try to make sure everyone worked a full week, even during bad weather.

The next day, February 1, AFSCME field director Ciampa flew into Memphis from Washington, DC, hoping to establish good relations with the new Public Works director. He and Jones met with Blackburn and emphasized the need for a written grievance procedure; Blackburn said that existing informal procedures were better. They called for union dues checkoff; Blackburn said that doing this would exceed his authority. Jones tried to impress upon Blackburn that he already had an informal grievance procedure, established under Sisson; Blackburn said he had no power to act on grievances without Loeb's approval.

That afternoon, during a driving, cold rain, Jones dropped Ciampa off at the Memphis airport. As he drove back into town, a Public Works supervisor's car raced by, going in the opposite direction to the Democrat Road barn for sanitation trucks. Jones turned his car around and followed the car, then quickly learned that the Public Works Department's disdain for safety had produced lethal consequences: Echol Cole and Robert Walker were dead, chewed up like refuse in the back of a garbage compactor. Workers held Loeb directly responsible for their deaths because of his unwillingness, going back to the 1950s, to invest in new equipment. Two other men had died in a truck accident in 1964, but Loeb continued to prioritize saving money for the city over saving workers' lives.

During the week following the deaths of Cole and Walker, workers grew more and more angry at the paltry benefits the city offered to the dead men's families; and sewer and drainage workers opened their pay envelopes to find only two hours' wages for their day of missed work. Now, according to Ciampa, "The thing just got away from" Jones, who "had to run to stay out front" of a spontaneous strike movement.

On Sunday afternoon, February 11, Loeb convened his "kitchen cabinet"—including city attorneys James Manire and Myron Halle—at his house, along with Blackburn, who told them about the situation in sanitation. Manire thought older men with families to feed were unlikely to strike; the other city officials thought "the fear was still there, that these men wouldn't stand up for their own self, you know," said Jones. They were wrong.

On Sunday night, between 700 and 900 black men packed into the Memphis Labor Temple at 126 1/2 South Second Street for an outpouring of grievances. Many of them had never attended a union meeting, but a spirit of collective anger had taken hold. "Jackleg" preachers in the workers' ranks started the meeting: Reverend Turner and Reverend Sammy Bumpers prayed, and the men preached and sang. Reverend Theodore Hibbler asked the men whether they could really stay out if they went on strike, and one man's comment summarized their feelings: "We don't have anything no how, and there ain't no need in our standing around 'cause we ain't got anything under the situation we have."

Jones laid out the basic issues: pay of less than $70 a week, no guarantees of acceptable wages on rainy days, old equipment and inadequate safety provisions, fear of being fired for belonging to the union, and no prospects for any improvements. A few men wanted to vote immediately to strike, but the failed strike of 1966 still hung heavily over their deliberations. The majority wanted Jones to meet again with Blackburn to discuss a list of specific proposals to improve safety, grievance procedures, wages, and the like.

In fact, Jones had already made an appointment with Blackburn and also had already told Joe Warren that if 500 or more men showed up at the union meeting, they might proceed with a strike. The men waited at the union hall while a group of some fourteen union stewards, including Haley Williams and J. L. McClain, met at 8 PM with Blackburn and two superintendents, Charles Woodward and Maynard Stiles. Jones listed the workers' demands and suggested possible solutions. Blackburn suggested they go see Loeb, but, Blackburn recalled, "They didn't want to see any mayor in any plush office. They wanted an answer right then and there." Blackburn then offered to take their demands to Loeb, but told them he couldn't support all of their demands. One union steward summed it up: "You ain't gonna do anything for us. It's the same old runaround." When Blackburn pleaded that the city budget was out of balance, a man responded that the workers had it much worse: "*We* are in the red. We ain't got no money, ain't seein' no raise in sight."

Jones recalled, "I knew it was out to go back to the men and say, 'We didn't get anywhere but give me till tomorrow.' I knew that was out." Jones asked Blackburn to go to the hall and speak to the men himself, and steward Nelson Jones (no relation to T. O.) added, "We got to tell the men something when we get back down there because the men got their minds made up and they want an answer." Only at this point did Blackburn realize that a large group of workers were waiting on his decision. Ciampa had sent him a letter outlining union demands, but Blackburn apparently had not taken it very seriously, and Jones had not made the strike threat entirely clear, Blackburn said later. For whatever reason, he passed up his one chance to stop the strike.

Jones later said Blackburn might have mollified the workers if he had talked to them directly and offered them minor concessions. For about $44, he calculated, Blackburn could have paid for the lost hours of the twenty-one workers sent home on the rainy day, but instead, he had "nothing to offer us." Labor attorney Anthony Sabella commented that former Commissioner Sisson "once had authority to follow his conscience in such matters, but Blackburn didn't. . . . He couldn't even extend the common courtesy of going to the meeting T. O. Jones asked him to attend, because he knew Loeb would not allow him to make such decisions."

Jones walked out of the room and returned in gray khaki pants and a jacket—jail clothes—and told Blackburn: "Call the chancellor. I'm ready to go to jail." Blackburn asked quizzically, "Why are you going to jail?" Jones told him he was about to violate the 1966 injunction against any action that might lead to a strike. Blackburn, in his naïveté, told him, "No one is going to be arrested." He did not think a strike would occur, for he could not see a burning, central grievance. Perhaps a more skilled unionist might have better impressed the moment's significance upon him, or perhaps a negotiator more experienced than Blackburn might have been more perceptive. But it really didn't matter: Henry Loeb never would have made significant concessions anyway.

When Jones and his union stewards returned to the waiting men at the Memphis Labor Temple, it was after 11 PM. Many workers had gone home, but the sentiments of those who remained crystallized instantly. "He gives us nothing, we'll give them nothing," shouted one man, and others took up the call for a strike. The men did not vote; they simply shouted out approval and filed out of the building. According to Gillis, who participated in the meeting, "It wasn't T. O. Jones. It was all us labor got together and we was going to quit work till we got a raise and got a better percentage, see, and could get justice on the job from the way they's treating us."

The workers set out with no organization or plans; they just went home. Some began to call their friends, urging them not to go to work. Jones spent the night waiting to see what would happen next. He "didn't set no type on no strike or nothing. We did that ourselves, the labor," said Gillis. Using one of King's stock phrases, Taylor Rogers summarized: "You keep your back bent over, somebody's gonna ride it." These men had decided to stand up to the City of Memphis.

L. C. REED took the bus to work on Monday, February 12. He had not attended the Sunday evening meeting. It was freezing cold, a mere twenty-two degrees. "The union stewards met me at the gate and said, 'Don't work.' I asked one of them what it was all about and he tried to tell me. I don't think he knowed exactly, but he knowed to tell us not to go to work. And I told him, 'Well, it suit me because they didn't pay me for that rainy day when they should have.' I took heel and turned around."

As he drove up to the Scott Street station, Blackburn realized that no one had come to work. By the city's count, 930 of 1,100 sanitation workers and 214 of 230 sewer and drainage workers did not show up. Loeb and Blackburn spent all morning trying to replace them. They finally got thirty-eight trucks out the door, leaving 150 behind, but many of those who went to work quickly returned, saying strikers had harassed them on the streets. The city normally handled 2,500 tons of garbage every day, but on this day they handled less than a tenth of that. Angry strikers told men going to work to quit. "I didn't know nothing about no strike," said Jesse Ryan, until workers confronted him and called him a scab. They knew where he lived, only a few blocks away, and Ryan decided to find another job for the strike's duration. He was glad he did: someone later shot into the home of another worker, and the man's wife left him for continuing to work during the strike.

Bill Ross meanwhile went to the AFL-CIO labor hall with no idea that a strike was underway. Hundreds of sanitation workers greeted him, and T. O. said, "I've got a strike on my hands." Said Ross, "It looks like it." He gave an impromptu speech to the men, feeling more than a little incredulous at what they had done. "With no assurance whatsoever" that they could get union financial support or feed their families, these men had simply refused to work. "Telling me that you could get that many people out is unbelievable. . . . I mean, they were determined. I have never seen a group more determined."

Jones had told no one in labor circles about the Sunday night meeting and had stayed awake all night, wondering who would go to work in the morning. Jones didn't even call this a "strike," because that implied the normal procedure of canvassing people, taking a vote, and preparing. None of that had happened. "The public works employees did not strike; they withheld their services," Jones said. He called it a "work stoppage." The workers said they had actually quit their jobs. The 1966 injunction had outlawed strikes, but it did not prevent them from quitting. Union lawyers would later use this same rhetoric as a device to avoid citations of union leaders for contempt of court.

The anger and determination of the workers instantly became a palpable force. "I've never worked in a group of men that was as eager to get something for themselves as these men were," Jones recalled. After their previous failures, the workers had been wary of the union. But now, "You know, it had come to the point where they followed and they'd begun to trust someone, and that someone was me." It was not his strike, it was theirs, and he decided to do everything in his power to support them.

Sometimes no one really knows what will happen until masses of people make their move. In Montgomery, Martin Luther King and others had waited breathlessly one Monday morning to see if blacks would boycott the buses, and they were elated to see the buses empty. Similarly in Memphis, the workers themselves didn't know how many would boycott work until it actually happened. By the union's count, all but seventy-five workers on the first day and all but thirty on the second day of the strike quit work. They neither put up a picket line nor handed out leaflets; they simply refused to go to work, and they began to harass those who didn't.

How this could happen remained a mystery to many whites. Television reporter Don Stevens told viewers that night that a man named T. O. Jones "seems to be the leader" of the group. He also reported that the strikers seemed willing to do whatever their spokesman said to do. No closeup camera interviews with various workers telling their conditions, no names matched with faces, no background on the 1966 walkout or any of the issues involved appeared on the news. Superficial media coverage made it easy for the average white Memphian to believe that outsiders interested only in collecting union dues had led a group of gullible workers to strike against their own interests.

To the contrary, AFSCME organizer Bill Lucy noted, "Supposedly an organizer, a staff guy, can sell ice cubes to Eskimos, but that's not true. You cannot convince a guy against his will that a course of action is the best one to take." AFSCME's professional organizers in fact feared the decision of the workers would be a disaster. February was the month when agricultural work dropped off in the surrounding area, and unemployed workers could flood Public Works looking for jobs—as they had during the threatened 1966 walkout. Scab workers had defeated black women at Memphis Furniture Company in 1949 and white women at American Snuff Company in 1950; to stop scabs, white construction workers on strike in the early 1950s resorted to beatings and brandishing shotguns. "I would have bet anybody that they could have hired at least 500 or 600" strikebreakers quickly to break the 1968 strike, Ross said.

AFSCME leaders in Washington, fully aware of the prevalence of strike-breaking in the South, had the same fears and felt more outraged than excited by the walkout. No one had consulted them or asked them to pre-pare for a strike. Jones did not call the international, he said, because it "wasn't going to do but one thing," and that was to order him to "tell those people to stay on their jobs." Jones believed that national staff would "get their heads together against these men down here" and make agreements with city leaders that did not meet the men's demands. AFSCME leaders did object to a strike in the dead of winter and to the fact that no prepara-tions had been made. This strike broke all the rules that AFSCME Presi-dent Jerry Wurf followed: not to strike in anger, to strike only if you knew you could win, to be mindful of timing, to get financial backing, and to be well prepared to support unemployed workers. Local 1733 had done none of these things. But Jones said, "The men weren't thinking of strategy; they were thinking of justice and injustice."

Lucy, the union's associate director for legislation and community affairs, recalled, "We heard about the strike quite by accident. A newspaper reporter called headquarters and wanted to know what our strategy would be. We didn't have the foggiest idea what he was talking about." At the time, "in the public sector, things were going wild," said Lucy, with strikes and organizing escalating: "When we looked at Memphis, the city was cer-tainly not on our agenda." Lucy thought it was "one of the great ironies of all times" that this unplanned and unwanted strike would become a turn-ing point for the whole international union.

Very shortly after receiving a phone call from the Memphis *Commercial Appeal*, P. J. Ciampa had Jones on the phone at the AFL-CIO hall. Said Ross, "Ciampa was an explosive kind of a fellow, and I could just hear him bouncing up and down" as Jones spoke with him. The first words out of his mouth were, "Good God Almighty, I need a strike in Memphis like I need another hole in the head!" Ross understood Ciampa's reaction but reflected, "Hell, T. O. nor anybody else couldn't have stopped those people from coming out. Hell, if you would have gone back there Monday morning and told those people to go back to work, they'd have killed you." He recalled his own phone conversation with Ciampa:

> So he says Bill, you go out there and tell those people to go back to work and I'll come down there and see what I can do. I said buddy, I'm the only one white man in this building with 1,300 black souls out there. I'm not about to go out there and tell those people to go back to work. Now if you want to tell them to go back to work, you come down here and you do it yourself. He says okay, I'll be down there. And he caught the plane and was down there that afternoon.

Ciampa's anger had to do with fear as much as frustration at the way Jones had handled the situation. Later, he recalled, "My God, what in the hell am I going to do with a strike in the South? I'd heard so many horror stories about them." He knew CIO efforts had been crushed during Operation Dixie after the war and that the South remained full of violently anti-union groups. He confessed, "I had a feeling of impending doom before I even started." After Ciampa arrived in Memphis, however, his feelings about the strike began to change. On Tuesday, February 13, when he met with the workers, their determination, anger, and resolve impressed him. He recalled looking out at his audience, "looking at 1,200 eyes. Six hundred men staring, you know, and in dead silence while you're trying to transmit to them: 'I am here. I am for real. I want to believe and bleed and do what I have to do with you.' . . . As I was talking to them they looked at me with such intentness. . . . 'Who is he? Where are you from? What does he represent?' . . . I was very uneasy all that night."

Panfilo Julius Ciampa, a second-generation Italian American, understood their suspicion and instinctively identified with them. His father, who had fought for the rights of some of the most oppressed workers in the United States as a member of the United Mine Workers, had had an eye gouged out by Pinkerton thugs during one of the most intense labor-management mine wars of the 1930s in Pennsylvania. At age six, Ciampa watched union members carry his father home after this terrible beating, and the Depression later forced him out of college and into the Pittsburgh steel mills. He became a voluntary organizer in the tumultuous CIO struggle to organize the United Steelworkers' Union and then worked in aircraft construction. Eventually, Walter Reuther appointed him as a regional director for the United Automobile Workers, one of the largest unions in the United States. Although he later served as one of the pallbearers at the UAW president's funeral, Ciampa had fallen out of favor with Reuther and ended up working for AFSCME as Jerry Wurf's leading field organizer. Ciampa, an angry man who understood all too well how the news media could turn the general population against a union, would testily counter every media insinuation that the union, not the men, had called the Memphis strike.

Although not welcoming the strike, the AFSCME national office took it very seriously. By Monday night, it had an interracial team in Memphis, consisting of two whites (Ciampa and Joe Paisley from Nashville) and two African Americans (Jesse Epps and Bill Lucy from the national office). Lucy probably understood the situation best. Born in Memphis in 1933, he had moved to California in 1941, but only after imbibing the feelings, sounds, and tastes of the Bluff City during the depths of the Depression. He went to college to study engineering in California, took a government job, and joined AFSCME. In 1966, he became its associate director for legislation and community affairs and an all-around organizer. AFSCME's 400,000 members in 1968 made it the fastest-growing body in the AFL-CIO, and the kind of "powerful vehicle" that King said unions could be. Lucy saw it as part of the Negro-labor alliance King sought.

Lucy had been directing an AFSCME district council in receivership in Detroit, but he dropped everything to go to Memphis. He left his car at the Detroit airport, thinking he was going "to settle what appeared to be a minor problem" and would be gone only a few days. He knew city governments in Nashville and Knoxville had allowed public-employee unions, and the Tennessee state government had recognized unions as bargaining agents, so he thought Memphis would do the same. But Lucy didn't return to Detroit for his car until nine weeks later—when he had a huge parking bill to pay.

When Lucy reached Memphis on Monday night, he began to have a strange feeling: it seemed like not much had changed since he had left

Memphis as a young boy. Trade unionism was not popular in the South, and many blacks, especially in the middle class and the religious community, were anti-union. Many unions had a long history of racism, and blacks knew it. And Mayor Loeb was completely unwilling to bend. But one thing had changed: the sanitation workers. Their determination seemed quite remarkable to Lucy. During the early 1960s civil rights movement, younger black people with few family obligations had been sparkplugs for direct action, but here Lucy saw many older men who "had lots of time with the city and these are the last ones who want to become involved with the union. The last. Because they've got the least to gain and the most to lose." The working poor with families and bills to pay could not afford to lose even a day's work, but they "simply put life and limb on the line."

Since previous strike attempts had resulted in firings and injunctions, most people, especially Mayor Loeb, thought the men would go back to work after they blew off steam. In one of the first television news broadcasts, a reporter guessed that the strikers might last two or three days. Instead, Lucy said, it became "a thing where they had just committed themselves to a fight, and there wasn't anything that was going to change their minds or turn them around." They "felt that as long as they stood together that everything in the end was going to come out right regardless of what they had to go through in the meantime." Their steadfastness lent a special character to the strike.

Ed Gillis had avoided fights with whites most of his life, but once a fight commenced, he refused to back down. According to Taylor Rogers, the situation "just got to the point that we had to do something. You didn't have no benefits. You didn't have no say-so about what you did or how you did it. You did it like they said to do it. That's why we wanted a union, we wanted somebody to represent us, so that we could have some say about our hours and working conditions."

BILL LUCY SOON realized there would be no quick compromise. Mayor Loeb was no Bull Connor, who had galvanized the civil rights movement by using fire hoses and dogs against black children. Loeb was often polite and sometimes even gracious to blacks. But he was a polarizing figure nonetheless. Without Loeb, said Jesse Epps, "We never would have been able to be successful in our efforts here." The former Mayor Ingram "had enough political ingenuity to have either influenced, bought, or hook or crook divided the Negro leadership," and if he had been reelected, "we would not have gotten the united Negro front that we got in Memphis." Epps said Ingram would have further divided blacks but Loeb united them.

Lucy and Wurf both said that mayors antagonistic to unions often proved to be AFSCME's best organizers, and Loeb proved their point. He had been in office a mere forty-three days when the strike began, and Taylor Blair, a business agent for a white craft union (International Brotherhood of Electrical Workers) and an acquaintance of Loeb's, immediately went to him to encourage an early settlement. But Loeb "said that his daddy would turn over in his grave if he knew that he had ever recognized a damned union. . . . I knew there wasn't much point in arguing with a fellow like that because he was trying to uphold what his daddy had said." As a former employer in the low-wage laundry industry, it revolted Loeb to think of the city recognizing and enabling a union to function. White attorney Lucius Burch explained, "When you say 'recognize' to a businessman that means 'to recognize-as-the-exclusive-bargaining-agent.' These words run together. Now every businessman that you run into, the last thing he wants is an exclusive bargaining agent agreement." Loeb and the business class saw this as a violation of their property and contract rights.

Tied to this view was Loeb's racial outlook. He saw black workers as subordinates; as a former laundry executive and commissioner of Public Works, he expected them to come to him, hat in hand, to resolve their problems. On February 11, he told the news media, "I represent these men, and have been available, and will be available, to discuss their problems." Loeb waited at his office all day, but none of the striking workers appeared. That night on the evening news, he said the problem was a "lack of communication." But he also announced, "This new administration is not going to be pushed around right off the bat in office. If it does, it's in for a mighty tough four years." Loeb thought AFSCME had picked out Memphis as a target for unionization following the just-ended, successful New York City garbage strike (though that strike was conducted by Teamsters, not AFSCME). He declared the Memphis strike illegal and said the union was taking advantage of the new form of city government merely to line its pockets.

Already, Loeb had called the Commercial Appeal editors to make these same points in hopes of influencing their coverage, and he had asked the Police Department's Intelligence Bureau to begin surveillance of Local 1733 and its supporters. "Much planning and study had been given to the means of controlling possible disorders," wrote the bureau's Lt. Ely Arkin, a dark-haired man with a heavy mustache and piercing eyes who looked like a private eye out of a crime novel. He concluded that Memphis "had been picked out as a Target City" for black revolution. It was only one of many erroneous conclusions drawn by the Intelligence Bureau—one of many "Red squads" in cities across the country that existed to maintain files and information on labor, civil rights, antiwar, and presumed radical organizations and individuals. If the problem was "lack of communication," as Mayor Loeb said, it wasn't for lack of intrusive government surveillance. Arkin's "Red squad" shared its information with the FBI, and surveillance by both organizations escalated as soon as the strike began.

AFSCME staff members Ciampa, Lucy, Paisley, Jones, and AFSCME's national communications director, John Blair, immediately tried to increase communications with the city on Tuesday, February 13, when they held their first meeting with Loeb, City Attorney Frank Gianotti, and his assistant Myron Halle. They met at the mayor's office, where vivid red carpets covered the floor and dark wood panels lined the walls. Loeb sat behind a desk that had been jacked up to accommodate his height, while visitors sat in low couches and chairs and had to look up at him. Ciampa remembered, "He looked like he was about fifteen feet tall and he said in that southern accent, 'Mister Chiampy, I heard a lot about ya. Glad to see ya. Welcome to Memphis.'" As the square-jawed mayor jocularly greeted the union's emissaries, Lucy thought, "He sort of struck me as you know, a wild-west type," a kind of John Wayne in the city.

Loeb made references to having been a PT boat commander (a lieutenant) and being a "rugged individualist" and exuded southern charm, but it didn't work on the wary union veteran Ciampa. He quickly said the men would return to work and all issues could then be worked out—but only if Loeb first recognized AFSCME as their bargaining agent. Loeb shot back that the only way he would talk to the men (not necessarily the union) was if they went back to work first: "The mayor can't be in the position of bargaining with anyone who is breaking the law." Ciampa asked, "What crime have they committed, Mr. Mayor? They are saying they don't want to pick up stinking garbage for starvation wages. Is that a crime?" Their discussion quickly grew heated. After the meeting, the mayor told the press that he would not bargain with people breaking the law, thus cutting off his options for compromise by publicly making the strike an issue of legality and morality.

While Loeb debated with union representatives, some 1,300 sanitation workers held their first official strike meeting at noon. Bill Ross did not have enough space at the AFL-CIO labor hall, so he sent strikers to the much larger hall of Local 186 of the United Rubber Workers (URW), in the heart of industrial-union power. The union hall fronted on a busy thoroughfare in North Memphis, home to a great portion of the city's black industrial working class. Behind it, in former cotton fields, sat the Firestone Tire factory, belching smoke and a distinct smell of rubber. Thousands of young black students went to nearby Douglass and Northside High Schools, and many of them were just waiting to work at Firestone. Taylor Rogers and many other strikers lived in the area. With the largest black union membership in Memphis, Local 186 provided a physical home for strikers. Clarence Coe, Matthew Davis, and many other blacks had fought for equal job and union rights for two decades in the city's premier industrial union. No workers had a stronger organization, better wages, or more willingness to strike; some joked that Firestone workers had "strikitis."

At the epicenter of industrial-union organizing since the 1930s, Local 186 had 2,700 members, one-third of them black and some of them women. Its white president, George ("Rip") Clark, had advised Joe Warren and T. O. Jones and now he openly supported their strike. Although some of his white members vigorously objected, the hall quickly became the scene of daily mass meetings at noon, followed by afternoon marches and evening mass meetings at various black churches. Nearly every week during the strike, Warren and others would go to the Firestone and International Harvester factory gates to get hundreds of dollars in donations from unionized workers.

At this first meeting in the Local 186 hall, convened by Jones, black community activists immediately made their presence felt. Cornelia Crenshaw spoke first. An energetic, well-dressed, imposing black woman, she regularly challenged all conventions regarding black people and women. Crenshaw had worked as a manager at the Memphis Housing Authority (MHA) for more than twenty-seven years—one of the few black women in city employment (outside of the schools) with a white-collar job. When the MHA fired her, she filed suit against them for discrimination in 1965 under Title VII of the U.S. Civil Rights Act. She got nowhere, but maintenance workers in the housing projects came to her for help when they tried to unionize. She took their case to Pete Brown of AFSCME and to the NAACP. Neither group proved ready or able to take on the powerful MHA director.

After her experience at the MHA, Crenshaw recalled, "I can understand them coming to a breaking point just the same as I did." She hailed the strikers for their courage, told them that their struggle represented the hopes and aspirations of the whole black community, and admonished them to stay united. That afternoon, she began recruiting women as typists, telephone callers, picketers, and fund-raisers. For the next two months, she worked until late into the night making sure the workers' families—some of whom had as many as eighteen children—received food and financial support. The women proved to be "as strong as the men" in supporting the strike, Bill Lucy said, and Crenshaw was an example of that. She had participated in the black community's political factionalism, working with T. O. Jones and O. W. Pickett in support of Ingram; yet she also hoped the unity of the strikers and their families could galvanize and unify the black community to overcome political schisms and turf warfare.

A youthful Ezekial Bell, the city's only black Presbyterian minister, followed Crenshaw to the podium. Bell said that because they had tried to strike once before, with no results, many people would assume they would fail, but he urged them to stay out at all cost. The first minister T. O. Jones had called on for strike support, Bell became one of the workers' strongest and most militant advocates. Born in Clarksdale, Mississippi, in 1935, he moved to Memphis in 1943 and had known Jones since they both went to Douglass High School. Bell was first academically in his class, president of the student council and his senior class, and later won scholarships to Harvard and Tennessee State (choosing to attend the latter). He did a graduate fellowship at the University of Chicago's theological seminary, finishing there in 1956. He ministered to churches in Knoxville, Tennessee, and Huntsville, Alabama, where Martin Luther King and Ralph Abernathy once stayed at his house. Bell, like other well-educated members of the NAACP in Memphis, burned with anger at the city's racial backwardness. Rhetorically, he would raise support for the workers' demands to incendiary levels.

Bell and Crenshaw took a crucial first step toward creating a bridge between unions and the black community. Like many African American ministers, Bell had rarely spoken in a union hall, and it gave him mixed feelings. At the NAACP office, he had read many complaints of discrimination against the Memphis craft unions. Everyone knew white workers used these unions as job trusts, giving apprenticeship training and jobs to their sons and relatives while denying access to blacks. But Bell's father had been a Mississippi sharecropper and then a sanitation worker, so Bell knew the pain these men suffered. Bell said he felt it wasn't his place to tell them to join or not to join the union; he would support their struggle for economic justice however they defined it.

Jones and Lucy both urged Bell to focus on the union and downplay race so that they could get the support of white unionists in the city. He ignored them, calling the strike primarily a racial issue. The city government, the union, and the newspapers at first tried to define the strike as a labor issue only, but civil rights leaders never agreed. Bell, Vasco Smith, and Jesse Turner of the NAACP all spoke to the men at the union hall during the first week of the strike. Turner said the union asked them not to identify the strike with the NAACP or racial issues, but, "I let them know in no uncertain terms that the NAACP was behind them, that this was a racial matter and we're going to tackle it as such."

P. J. Ciampa, fresh from that morning's discouraging meeting with

Mayor Loeb, told workers that their own solidarity remained the key to everything. "We've got to stay together in the union to win the victory. Strength in numbers. We must stay together for however long is necessary— a day, a week, a month." Workers roared their approval. They were angry, disgusted, fired up. Ciampa saw these men as "indestructible"—not militant, exactly, but very determined. Lucy, in his calm manner, emphasized the need for the men now to convince their relatives and their neighbors not to steal their jobs and to stand strong behind them. Defeating strikebreakers would be the key to victory. He said the strikers themselves must be an active force and make alliances with people in churches and the community if they wanted to win. Hopes for solid support from organized labor soared when Memphis Labor Council President Tommy Powell presented a check for several hundred dollars to Ciampa and said the unions would aid the strike "both morally and financially in any way they see we can be of assistance."

WORKERS BECAME RESTLESS. Accustomed to hard physical work, they could not be contained in a union hall, so Jones and Lucy led the boisterous mass of workers into the street. Walking four or five abreast in the winter sun, they quickly found motorcycle police riding beside them. Joe Warren drove his red Cadillac out front, as if leading a parade. More than 800 striking workers marched five miles from the belching smokestacks of the Firestone factory in industrial North Memphis to the clean streets and new city hall on downtown's Main Street, so prized by business elites and "good government" progressives.

Clapping, shouting, singing, "We shall not, we shall not be moved," the workers exuded a spirit that neither the civil rights nor the labor movement had seen in some time, and the sheer size of this group eclipsed many movements of the past. When workers went into the street or held a rally, their numbers gave people a sense of power and scared the powers that be. Very shortly, this mass of rowdy workers crammed into a City Council chamber designed to hold only 400 people. The council was in session, and forty to fifty police appeared in the aisles to control the workers. Black council member J. O. Patterson objected: "I can't see anything that necessitates this many police officers. I don't think there is going to be any violence. I certainly would like them [the police] removed from the council chambers." He deadpanned, "I wonder just who is protecting the city." Massing large numbers of police had long been a tactic to intimidate protesters in Memphis, and he knew it.

Lucy, meanwhile, went straight to the mayor's office. "The men are here. You said, 'Any men you want to bring down to talk to me, I'll talk to them.' Here they are." Unruffled, Loeb directed the crowd to the city's old auditorium, South Hall, one of the places the civil rights movement had desegregated. The assembly quickly turned into a fruitless mismeeting of minds. Engulfed by boisterous workers, Loeb tried to command them back to work: "City employees can't strike against their employer. This you can't do!" He appealed to them to safeguard the health of the city and told them flatly, "You are in effect breaking the law." To his surprise and consternation, they erupted in laughter and heckling. When he mentioned Charles Blackburn, boos erupted. "He's a straight shooter," cried Loeb. "Yeah, but he shoots the wrong way," a man yelled.

To the mayor's surprise, many of the older men proved unruly, angry, and not at all ready to go back to work. He asked them to come to him about their grievances, "just as you used to ask me," and appealed to their memory of him as their employer in the 1950s as Public Works commissioner. The men remembered, all right. As Loeb spoke, Jones propped his feet on a chair, cocked his head sideways with a somewhat incredulous look on his face, and chuckled in amusement. Others guffawed without restraint. "He even said that he would give the shirt off his back" for the men, Lucy recalled. "Someone from the audience said, 'Just give me a decent salary and I'll buy my own.'" Men from the plantation districts didn't seem as humble as most whites assumed they were.

The mayor felt terribly affronted by the men's derisive reactions, which confounded his sense of propriety in employer-employee as well as racial relations. This first meeting angered him and hardened his position. He told the men flat out, "This is not New York. Nobody can break the law. You are putting my back up against the wall, and I am not going to budge."

But Loeb's response also angered the men. Taylor Rogers recalled why people could not restrain themselves: "The thing he was saying is what he would do for us. But he did nothing. His open door policy was a joke. There is no way a worker could get close to his office. Everything he said was a joke—that is why the people would laugh. We knew if they had tried, they would have gotten thrown out. You couldn't even talk to your station manager or supervisor if he was white. If you couldn't talk to them, how was you going to talk to Loeb?" Rogers believed what many other black folks believed: "Loeb was a racist. He cared nothing about black folks." They could not take seriously his pleas for man-to-man discussions.

During this meeting, Ciampa and Lucy also took the microphone. "After you've worked for the city for ten or fifteen years . . . what do you get?" Lucy asked. "A brand new garbage tub," one man jested, while others muttered, "Nothing," or cursed under their breaths, as disgust and anger rippled through the crowd. Ciampa voiced the thought on the minds of many: "They are going to have to come up with some bread and some decency or this city is going to smell awhile." Ciampa asked the men to affirm to the mayor, "This was your decision, right?" and they shouted out affirmations. He called out a list of demands based on ones the local had discussed on February 11. Wage demands had been scaled back slightly, and their original demand of a full day's pay for the twenty-one workers sent home because of inclement weather had now been subsumed under a larger set of issues: a written contract, dues checkoff, a formal grievance procedure with binding arbitration, wage increases, fair promotion, pension and fringe benefits. The workers paid close attention to each detail, and they shouted their approval.

Every short quip from union leaders roused tremendous enthusiasm from the workers, while they treated Loeb's entreaties as absurdities. They really let loose when Ciampa enunciated the main issue as one of freedom. "As a free American citizen," he said, "I am going to express myself and you are going to express yourself by not working for those stinking wages and conditions!" As he reached the end of his sentence, Ciampa's speech accelerated and he nearly shouted out his conclusion. The men burst out in applause and shouts, destroying the decorum hoped for by the mayor. By confronting Loeb, Ciampa won the trust of the workers. The more the mayor and the city's middle class hated Ciampa, the more black workers liked him. "The amazing thing is, you know, their suspicions at first, and [then] their absolute, total, complete loyalty," he said. Workers began to feel that Ciampa truly represented them. He later told the television media, "The men are making the decisions, not I." The solidarity of the men moved him. Their determination and moral strength, he said, "is something I haven't seen since strikes when I was a kid" during the CIO's great organizing drives.

Lucy next took the microphone from Ciampa, but an agitated Loeb seized it from Lucy. "I suggested to these men today," he said, pointing at their representatives, "that you go back to work." Then he shouted, "Go back to work!" Some men laughed and others shouted, "No! No!" Neither Loeb's paternalism nor his stern warnings worked. When he became more assertive, Jones recalled, "The people just booed him right down." Loeb's veins bulged out from his neck as he made his last statement: "I have sat here and taken quite a bit of abuse and I don't appreciate it, and I have not given any abuse back. Your jobs are important. I promise you the garbage is going to be picked up. Bet on it!" Loeb strode out of the meeting.

AFSCME organizer Jesse Epps recalled, "That was the first time in the history of Loeb's life that he was no longer the master. There was an insurrection among the slaves." Having been elected on a "racist ticket," Epps said, "he couldn't have predominantly black men telling him what to do. And he just drew the line."

For the rest of the strike, Loeb became two people. To the white community, he seemed stern but reasonable, while to the black community he seemed totally out of touch with reality. To Bill Lucy, Loeb demonstrated "just a complete detachment from the issues." Many whites saw him quite differently. *Commercial Appeal* reporter Joe Sweat, an admirer who followed Loeb around every day, emphasized the mayor's personal virtues. "I never, ever heard Loeb treat a black person with anything but respect. I never heard him make a derogatory statement about Negroes in general. But he couldn't say 'Negro' correctly, poor bastard, he just couldn't say it." It always came out "nigra." The problem was not Loeb's etiquette, Sweat explained. "He was very bound up in helping individuals with their personal problems," and made special efforts to accommodate handicapped employees, "but he was just not progressive."

————————

LOEB AND THE unionists went back to his office and talked late into the night, clearly at cross purposes. Loeb thought the union had come to Memphis hoping to ride the momentum of the favorable settlement won by sanitation workers in New York City, which received daily treatment in the Memphis newspapers. "I don't care what [Governor Nelson] Rockefeller did. I don't care what [Mayor John] Lindsay did. You're talking to a country boy. This is not New York. This is Memphis. I live here and my kids live here and I am not going to play around with the health of this city." Ciampa shot back, "You try to put yourself in a sanctimonious little cubicle. You can't solve problems like that."

They could find no common ground. Loeb immediately gained a public-relations advantage by insisting on media presence, which unionists said created a "fishbowl atmosphere" during talks. Predictably, the media picked up only select tidbits of the conversation and replayed them to the public as representative of the whole discussion. Loeb and Ciampa had one particularly sharp exchange in which Ciampa told Loeb, "You have not behaved like a public servant, but like a public dictator through the whole damn thing, and that's tragic." Loeb retorted, 'I'm sorry you feel that way," and proceeded to repeat that the union was breaking the law. Ciampa had seen "the law" crush workers and their unions and found Loeb's constant references to its sanctity infuriating. Shaking his finger at the mayor, he raised his voice to say, "You're a liar when you say that. If I'm breaking the law, then take me into court. If I'm not breaking the law, then shut your big fat mouth."

Media treatments depicted Ciampa as a vulgar outsider attacking the integrity of the mayor. Loeb referred to his insistence that the media be present at all negotiations as "open government"; Lucy considered it a setup, making it impossible for give-and-take to occur, and encouraging Loeb to make every statement for public consumption. "We'd be sitting there just talking and all of a sudden the TV lights would go on and the mayor would leap up and say something real militant and then the lights would go off. And he'd sit back down." Said Lucy, "We were somewhat amazed. It was the first time, I think, that we'd ever come up against this type of individual."

Over and over, television news replayed images of Ciampa in the mayor's office shaking his finger in Loeb's face. The *Commercial Appeal* wrote that the mayor and his aides had "suffered uncalled-for insults from union manipulators." Wrote strike historian Joan Beifuss, "Looking back, few people remembered the early issues of the strike, but everyone could recall that moment on TV when Ciampa, roaring with Italian gusto, poked his finger under the Mayor's nose. . . . Loeb began to emerge as a combination Sunday School teacher and Western sheriff while Ciampa began to look like a Mafia hood sent into town to make off with the gold. . . ."

During the parts of negotiations seen by the public in newsreels and in the newspapers, Loeb kept his famous temper in check; he seemed open, calm, and controlled. By contrast, "Ciampa blustered, shouted, waved his arms and tossed his head like any one of the dozens of tough guy scenes you've seen on the screen," wrote political reporter William Street. Lucy said the discussions were not that heated, and by all accounts Loeb in private was a profane man, not averse to calling a friend "son of a bitch." Cursing came naturally to the former PT boat commander, yet in public he presented himself as a paragon of virtue and civility.

Loeb was simply playing the same shrewd political game that had gotten him elected repeatedly by white landslides. Wrote Beifuss:

> He knew that his support was centered in those classes of the city who innately distrusted unionism, in the older folks caught on fixed income in the mildly inflationary cycle of 1968, and in that cross section of the white community which longed for frugality in government, absolutist morality in leadership, and a surcease of the confusion caused by groups trying to redefine their status in the old structures of society. When he spoke, he spoke for them, and they heard him loud and clear.

Loeb confidently played to a strain in the American electorate that produced Richard Nixon's "Southern Strategy" to further the conservative agenda of the rising Republican Party. Playing to the TV camera, Loeb's law-and-order rhetoric helped to ignite white backlash against the strike.

He thought (wrongly) that no other mayor in the South had recognized a public-employee union, and he refused to be the first to do so.

DURING HIS FIRST administration, Loeb had attacked the media for not giving him favorable coverage, and the *Commercial Appeal* had not endorsed him for mayor in 1967. Now the newspaper backed him up. "As to the legal situation, it is crystal clear," the paper confidently editorialized. A 1957 Tennessee Supreme Court decision concerning the giant Alcoa Aluminum factory in East Tennessee had enjoined the International Brotherhood of Teamsters "from striking or picketing to compel a municipality to bargain collectively." That ruling, combined with the Memphis chancery court injunction against the abortive garbage strike in 1966, meant that "Mayor Loeb could be accused of ignoring legalities if he bargained with union leaders who actually have no legal standing as representatives of the garbage crews."

The Tennessee Supreme Court did draw a line in the sand against public-employee strikes, but not public-employee unions. Buried in a news story on February 16, 1968, AFSCME representative Joe Paisley pointed out that Nashville, Chattanooga, Clarksville, and Elizabethton all allowed city workers to have union dues taken out of their paychecks (dues checkoff), and Tennessee allowed state highway workers to belong to a union. "When the governor of the state allows something, it seems little less than bullheaded for the mayor to claim it's so wrong," said Paisley. President Kennedy's 1962 executive order had already legalized the right of federal government workers to have unions, though not to strike, and twenty states allowed limited union rights for their employees. "There is nothing in the law that says a city can't sign a contract or a memorandum of understanding with a union! There is nothing," said Memphis labor lawyer Anthony Sabella. "The one case that they relied upon merely states that you can't strike for that purpose! . . . [It] doesn't make it illegal for the city to sign such an agreement."

True, unionized teachers in Florida went to jail for striking during the same month that the sanitation strike began, and public workers often faced arrest for striking. But such strikes often succeeded in getting governments to bargain and to recognize union rights. Reverend Hooks compared the Memphis situation to Michigan auto workers taking over General Motors factories with sit-down strikes in 1936. They obviously did not have the right to take over private property, yet state government refused to use troops to storm the factories. This finally forced GM to recognize the union, and workers went on to sit in and sit down everywhere to realize the federal Wagner Act's guarantee of the right to organize. The civil rights movement had also broken laws repeatedly, until Congress and the courts declared segregation statutes void. One can say something is illegal, said Hooks, but in the end, "You had to deal with it anyway." Put another way, Ciampa said that nothing in the law "says a man has to work in indentured servitude."

Unionists and city leaders were in fundamental conflict over both language and the practical issue of union maintenance. The union said that for talks to proceed, Loeb needed first to "recognize" it. Loeb said he did recognize the existence of unions, but the law prevented him from bargaining with strikers. In any case, he insisted that he would never sign a contract with one or allow the city to take union dues out of workers' paychecks. Union representatives countered that nothing in the law prevented him from doing these things and that recognition implied accepting conditions that allowed a union's continued existence. That included a contract and allowing dues to be automatically deducted from the paychecks of union members and deposited in the union's account.

Loeb said a good union should go directly to every worker for dues, and that worker should be able to say yes or no to it. The reality, however, was that workers would agree to deductions before they were paid, but few of them would relinquish money from their meager salaries once they got it. Memphis United Furniture Workers President Leroy Clark struck employers in the furniture industry repeatedly to get automatic dues checkoff; without it, he could not afford to organize the unorganized or to service unionized workers. As union attorney Sabella put it, "The employers know that money is the source of strength as far as a union is concerned, and if they can cut off that income, they are just out of business!" As a former employer in the laundry business, and as former commissioner of Public Works, Loeb knew this too.

Another, more elemental issue troubled the mayor and other white employers. Black worker organizing threatened the subordinate and low-wage relationship of blacks to whites, exploded the myth of black passivity, and implied that poor black men indeed had rights other people had to respect. Labor-management specialist Frank Miles recalled that in the past, many employers had refused to deal with CIO unions simply because they had blacks on their bargaining committees, which put white employers in a "catastrophic" face-to-face bargaining relationship with African Americans. "You had a two-fold resentment there" against blacks and unions, and employers "just resented the fact that these people now were going to be coming in their offices and sitting down and telling them what they were going to have to do." They considered this "a complete reversal of the way of life for all these years."

In the context of the 1960s, many whites saw the battle against black union organizing as a way to resist the civil rights revolution. Jesse Epps said that the mayor and many whites who supported him simply wanted to "hold onto yesterday" in race relations. For African Americans, on the other hand, the word *recognition* had important connotations of citizenship rights; for black workers, it meant a union, a written contract, and hope for fair treatment and respect on the job.

At loggerheads over language and conflicting worldviews, the talks between unionists and Loeb proved frustrating and fruitless. Ciampa rhetorically asked reporters after the first morning of talks, "Loeb will talk, but will he say something?" Exasperated, Ciampa said, "I pushed, prodded," but he could get no concession that would allow him to ask the men to go back to work. Loeb was quite willing to talk but not to bargain, and he talked merely to wear down his opponents to accept his terms.

However, late in the evening on February 13, a breakthrough occurred when Lucy, Paisley, City Attorney Gianotti, and assistant attorney Myron Halle met without Loeb or Ciampa. "In this sub-committee room we had boiled everything down . . . and had actually reached almost a tentative agreement on the question of the deduction of union dues," said Lucy. But at one or two in the morning, the mayor came in and blasted his subordinates for even considering such an agreement. Wearily, the AFSCME negotiators agreed to let the mayor make a statement to the media the next morning, saying simply that nothing had been gained.

Instead of following this cooperative strategy, the next morning Loeb told reporters at a press conference that Ciampa had taken him aside during the first night of negotiations to say that all he cared about was union dues. Loeb later gave this version of Ciampa's comments: "Look, Mayor, all we're interested in is a dues checkoff. The dough, give me the dough and you can write the rest of the ticket yourself. . . . Everything else you can have the say on, but we're gonna get that money. That's what we came for." Labor attorney Sabella said that even the brash Ciampa would never put union demands in such crass terms, nor would it suit the union's interests to do so. Recognition and bargaining rights were far more important than dues. But this is what Loeb believed.

"He didn't mention the other items that had been resolved," said Lucy. "That was when he made this the central issue involved in the strike. And what, you know, dawned on us then was that we were not dealing with a person of good faith. Because we had made no public statement whatsoever" about union dues. Ciampa was furious—both because of Loeb's misrepresentation of his comments and because he told reporters about comments supposedly made in confidence: "It was the cheapest, lowest trick that a man could play, because if you go off the record you're off the record." Next, Loeb stunned the unionists by announcing that he was breaking off negotiations. Ciampa, wrote reporter Joe Sweat, "broke into angry profanity at the mayor," and AFSCME leaders "stormed out of the mayor's office as talks broke off in a hostile atmosphere."

According to Lucy, something quite premeditated had happened. At the news conference, Loeb was in his shirtsleeves in an office packed with people. But that night, Lucy watched the news incredulously: it showed a dignified, solitary mayor, reading his statement. He was "fully dressed, black suit, black trousers"—clothes Lucy remembered him wearing in the afternoon of the previous day, before the late-night breakthrough by negotiators had occurred. Loeb had prerecorded for the evening news his statement opposing a settlement, and he wasn't about to change his position.

In this announcement, Loeb took a dispute that began with workers demanding rainy-day wages and turned it into a war to keep their jobs. "If work is not resumed by 7 AM Thursday, February 15, 1968, we will immediately begin replacing those people who have chosen to abandon their jobs and their rights," Loeb announced. Frank Holloman, Loeb's new fire and police director, canceled days off and vacations for police officers and put them on twelve-hour shifts, seven days a week, and he ordered police to escort all garbage trucks. He put police guards with Loeb around the clock.

On the evening of February 14, after talks between Loeb and AFSCME collapsed, Ciampa addressed the Memphis Labor Council. Its executive board, chaired by H. B. Griffin of the United Rubber Workers, endorsed the strike and a boycott of the newspapers and downtown businesses. The council represented 50,000 AFL-CIO members in Memphis, 60 to 70 percent of them white, supported by the Tennessee AFL-CIO Labor Council, with 100,000 affiliated members, an even larger majority of whom were white. The AFL-CIO became the most significant interracial group supporting the strikers.

The next morning, February 15, AFSCME convened a mass meeting at the union hall of the United Rubber Workers Local 186. AFSCME negotiators told sanitation strikers that they had gotten nowhere with the mayor and that Loeb would begin replacing them that day if they did not go back to work. By no means sold on the wisdom of this strike, Lucy gave them the option of backing down: "We told them there are no hard feelings if they go back to work, but when we gave them a choice, not one guy left." AFSCME's Joe Paisley told a reporter, "They stood in unison—1,000 plus, they're not going back." Impressed by their resolve and happy that the Memphis Labor Council had also resolved to back them up, Tommy Powell told the strikers, "You have pulled the labor people in Memphis closer together in the last few days than they have been in years."

On February 12, perhaps 300 workers had considered themselves members of AFSCME, and far fewer had paid dues, but by now some 700 of them had officially joined. It could not be claimed that they jumped on a union bandwagon in order to get strike benefits, for even at the international level, AFSCME did not have a strike fund. Yet fewer than a hundred sanitation men remained at work. Loeb might have offered minor concessions that would have resolved their strike, but his hard-line stance had instead angered the strikers and strengthened their solidarity.

AFTER THE NEGOTIATIONS failed, Tommy Powell called Loeb and arranged to meet him at his home. H. B. Griffin, president of the United Rubber Workers and vice president of the Memphis Labor Council; a union man named Gabe Talarico (later a state legislator); and International Brotherhood of Electrical Workers (IBEW) representative Taylor Blair went with him to convince the mayor to compromise. According to Powell, it was a strange evening:

> We didn't get but two blocks from the house when we see policemen who spot us as labor leaders and ask us what we were doing there. Now damn it, we had been invited to come! So we walk in the man's house and he's got a shotgun, a bat, and a big dog. I begin to think, "now what am I doing here? What does this man think is going to happen?" So I say, "What's going on Henry?" And Loeb says, "Look, H. B, I've been knowin' you and Tommy Powell always was crazy, but you got some sense, now you tell those niggers to get back to work!" Well, we talked until two o'clock a.m. or something and finally his wife comes in and says, "Henry, they're makin' a lot of sense to me. Why don't you listen?" He said, "Oh, shut up, Mary." She whopped him upside the head, WHAP! and slammed the door! He said, "See what you made my wife do?" And I said, "Man, I didn't make your wife do nothing. She saw what was right."

Loeb kept calling the strike illegal and Powell kept urging Loeb to rethink the consequences of his hard line: "I gave him a scenario of what was going to happen if he didn't stop this. I said, 'It's gonna snowball. If we can't win it we're gonna get the civil rights people here. We don't intend to lose this, our prestige is on the line.'" But Henry Loeb wouldn't budge.

6

HAMBONE'S MEDITATIONS:
THE FAILURE OF COMMUNITY

We who engage in nonviolent direct action are not the
creators of tension. We merely bring to the surface
the hidden tension that is already alive. . . .
—*Martin Luther King, Jr., "Letter from Birmingham Jail," 1963*

STRIKES, LIKE OTHER FORMS OF NONVIOLENT DIRECT ACTION, provide one means for bringing issues into the open so they can be resolved. But what most white Memphians read, saw on television, or heard on the radio did not help them to see or understand issues related to unions or the black revolution of the 1960s. For example: The *Commercial Appeal's* cartoon, *Hambone's Meditations*, printed since the 1910s, appeared six days a week, usually on the second page, reproducing degrading caricatures of blacks and silly homilies associated with the bygone days of minstrel shows. The grinning simpleton Hambone, through his exaggerated lips, spoke in dialect, saying such things as, "Ef tomorrow evuh *do* come, I reck'n Ole Tom gwine be de busies' man in de *whole worl*'!!!" Judge Benjamin Hooks* related this image to "total and colossal indifference to Negroes and their achievements. We are relegated to an Amos and Andy

---

*Attorney Hooks, also an ordained Baptist minister, was appointed the city's first black judge in 1965.

Darktown Strutters' Ball type of thing. We are ludicrous or ridiculous or comical." Instead of the mass media focusing on black comedy or black crime, he asked, "Why can't there be something about what Negroes are doing, not as Negroes but as citizens of this city?"

Despite many black protests about it, the *Commercial Appeal* published *Hambone's Meditations* throughout the rising tide of civil rights and Black Power movements. Mass-media racism symbolized, Hooks said, that most whites were either blind or hostile to the plight of blacks and that a failure of communication and community existed in Memphis. Yet white editors thought they were at the forefront of change. Of the city's two daily newspapers, the *Commercial Appeal* had the largest circulation, with nearly 220,000 readers, nearly half of them in the Mississippi Delta outside of Memphis. It had once been a defender of the Confederacy, but in the 1920s the paper had won a Pulitzer Prize for exposing the depredations of the Ku Klux Klan. The competing *Press-Scimitar*'s semi-liberal Unitarian former editor, Edwin Meeman, had campaigned against Mayor Crump's dictatorship for years, but the conservative, anti-union Scripps-Howard national chain of media outlets owned both newspapers. Three television stations and a score of radio stations in Memphis had a wide listening market, but after Crump's death, the print media filled a power vacuum. Many considered *Commercial Appeal* editor Frank Ahlgren the most powerful man in Memphis. Those politicians the newspaper endorsed for public office usually won.

Editors at both papers denounced violence during white rioting against James Meredith's attempt to integrate Ole Miss in 1962, and they urged compliance with Supreme Court desegregation rulings. They considered themselves racial moderates but followed "the principle of quietness in trying to promote racial harmony," according to a former reporter, by suppressing news of the civil rights movement and generally ignoring black life. In 1968, the *Commercial Appeal* employed five blacks, none of them as reporters. It employed one black student intern, Calvin Taylor. Black and female faces simply did not appear with notepads or microphones in hand in Memphis, except at the black-run *Tri-State Defender* and WLOK and WDIA radio stations. These outlets provided crucial communications for black Memphis, but few whites read or listened to them.

"In reading white papers Black people have already adjusted to the misdirection of the news—and the non-reporting of the news, or the untrue reporting of the news," black activist Charles Cabbage observed. "They kind of siphon out the truth," knowing that the media "cannot go against the power structure. It's a part of that. We all know that." The newspapers identified criminal suspects by race only when they were black; published segregated job ads; failed to expose the dire conditions facing blacks or to give favorable attention to black leaders like King; and often distorted events and ignored key issues. Both commercial newspapers refused in most cases to carry courtesy titles for blacks as they did for whites; the NAACP had boycotted them briefly in the 1950s for that reason.

Reverend Ralph Jackson said that getting African Americans to stop reading the white commercial press provided a crucial step toward consolidating black solidarity behind the strike. Cabbage thought this was a mistake, cutting off blacks from knowledge of what the whites were thinking. Blacks of course had their own sources of information—not only black-run media but also black churches, unions, and social organizations. Many African Americans knew brothers, husbands, fathers, other relatives, neighbors, or church members involved in the sanitation strike, and they heard firsthand appeals in their churches. But most whites gleaned what little they knew of the sanitation workers through a commercial mass media that largely blocked interracial communication. And this was not simply a Memphis or a southern phenomenon.

In February 1968, President Johnson's National Advisory Commission on Civil Disorders, chaired by Illinois Governor Otto Kerner, began to release its report on inner-city riots and their causes (the report appeared as a paperback on March 1). The Commission's Report concluded that the country was "moving toward two societies, one black, one white—separate and unequal." King's testimony to the Kerner Commission (as it became known) had emphasized the worsening economic conditions of black youth, and the report documented massive structural unemployment for huge numbers of young black men, inadequate housing and recreation facilities, deteriorating schools, poor-to-nonexistent health care, low wages, ineffective antipoverty programs, endemic police brutality, and widespread racism and discrimination. It warned of the failure of community between the races, writing that segregation and poverty had created a destructive environment for most blacks. And yet, these conditions remained "totally unknown to most white Americans." Why?

Among other reasons, the report pinpointed media racism, finding that African Americans constituted less than 5 percent of newswriters and less than 1 percent of editors (most of these worked for black-owned news organizations), and that the mass media failed to let African Americans speak for themselves. Biased white media coverage actually misinformed the reading public and obscured issues of police violence, high black unemployment, and the plight of the black working poor. As a result, the report quoted a black man saying, "The average black person couldn't give less of a damn about what the media say. The intelligent black person is resentful at what he considers to be a totally false portrayal of what goes on in the ghetto. Most black people see the newspapers as the mouthpieces of the 'power structure.'"

THIS FAILURE TO communicate, in Memphis as elsewhere, helped to produce a failure of community. Unions and civil rights organizations had always complained that the "news" shut them out. When the *Press-Scimitar* on February 14 wrote that Loeb spoke "for all of us," for example, it ignored the fact that African Americans constituted nearly 40 percent of the city's population. The way the newspapers covered the strike hardened the opposition to the workers and the union. On February 13, even before Loeb and the workers had met, the *Commercial Appeal* called the strike "a shallow attempt at blackmail" by outsiders trying to capitalize on the successful sanitation strike in New York City. AFSCME wanted to "find out how easily the new city government will give in to such assaults," and to open a wedge to unionize the city's 20,000 public employees and service workers in the private sector. AFSCME of course did want to organize, but media accounts did not explain why the workers themselves might also want to do so.

Character assassination began the same day. The *Commercial Appeal* wrote that the "heavy set" T. O. Jones, at forty-three years of age, had been repeatedly discharged for work absences and had no stable address. It dredged up a story that creditors had filed bad-check charges against him (the charges had been dropped) and characterized him as a "roly poly" character who fell asleep in the mayor's office during negotiations. Jones felt that disparaging media treatment set him up for harassment by the police. He took to living away from his home and a small group of young black men often accompanied him as bodyguards.

On February 15, the newspaper began an editorial barrage against AFSCME, saying its main objective was to get the city "to act as collector of dues," and that the city's mayor had "suffered uncalled-for insults from union manipulators." In an editorial on February 16, "Loeb Takes Right Course," it wrote: "The bluster, swagger and insolence of the men purporting to represent the city garbage workers cannot be construed as 'bargaining.' They 'negotiate' with Mayor Henry Loeb and the City of Memphis somewhat like the Viet Cong and Hanoi do with South Vietnam and the United States." Loeb, on the other hand, showed "proper firmness, and yet has listened to the most brazen and abusive language from union leaders," whose "ultimate aim, supported from the top level of the union, is to collect dues from workers." Its editors advised citizens to take care of their garbage themselves and to support "their" mayor, since "reason has not worked in dealing with this wildcat strike. Strong measures have had to be taken," such as firing strikers and replacing them. Accompanying the editorials, cartoonist Cal Alley (a younger but no less inflammatory cartoonist than his father, J. P. Alley) depicted a fat white man in a rumpled suit standing atop a stinking pile of garbage and holding a sign, "The Right to Strike Is Above Public Health."

The *Commercial Appeal* continued with a barrage of visceral, old-fashioned anti-unionism. "Make no mistake about it. Memphis was a carefully selected target for the garbage strike," according to a February 18 editorial titled, "Memphis Is Being Used." Bias extended into news accounts, one of which told of the "union command post" set up by the "fast-talking" and "profane" P. J. Ciampa at the Peabody Hotel. "Soon after the garbage workers strike began Monday, out-of-state labor leaders arrived to take charge. It became increasingly apparent that Memphis had been designated a target for the hard focus of big-time union power." Newspaper headlines indelibly cast Loeb as an uncompromising leader on behalf of the public. Although reporters and white-collar workers at the newspaper had been among the first to form a CIO union in Memphis in the 1930s, they had also led the Red scare and the expulsion of civil rights unionists from the CIO. The all-white American Newspaper Guild chapter ultimately endorsed the strike, and some reporters, such as Richard Lentz, had considerable sympathy for the strikers. But these reporters could not moderate the anti-union bias of editors at both the *Commercial Appeal* and the *Press-Scimitar*.

The call to defend the city from strikers brought forth vigorous volunteerism from whites, and television coverage showed whites applauding white Boy Scouts as they loaded garbage onto city trucks or picked up their own garbage and hauled it in station wagons to an emergency dump site (which consisted of little more than an open field with paper and garbage strewn everywhere). Television news also showed white and black strikebreakers working together and portrayed whites taking garbage out to the curbs as acts of citizenship. But when television cameras recorded Reverend Bell and a group of workers protesting as garbage trucks left a city depot, viewers probably wondered why these boisterous people would sit down in the middle of a wet and oily street with picket signs. Few reporters engaged strikers or their supporters with in-depth questions— or, if they did, their stories did not get past their editors. Through the media lens, workers and their supporters largely remained caricatures— picketing, chanting, making noisy speeches and demands, but rarely engaging in thoughtful discussion.

By contrast, televised sequences showed Mayor Loeb (albeit with body-guards) speaking cordially to black and white picketers or saying he was "protecting the men" from a union that "would like for us to reach in the men's pockets" by giving the union a dues checkoff. Most whites lacked other sources of information and accepted what they read in the newspapers, heard on the radio, and saw on television. "I don't believe he can be bought, intimidated, or manhandled by any forces working against him," Louise Carley wrote of Loeb in a letter to the *Commercial Appeal*. "His whole bearing, when confronted by a union leader in such an insulting, vulgar way, was one we should all applaud."

Strike supporters complained constantly about biased media coverage—expressed through omission as well as inflammatory images. James Lawson had long wondered, Did editors purposely decide to offend black readers, or were they just blind to their own racism? He felt that media racism created a daily schism between the white and black communities. Media portrayals of King exemplified their bias: "You would not see a single photograph of Martin King that had him deliberative or calm. Almost every photo in those years was a photo with his mouth wide open at some point of speaking somewhere, so making him look as though he was a rabble rouser." Not surprisingly, many whites saw King as an associate of Communists and a lawbreaker, and they ignored his role as a responsible minister and public leader. Lawson thought this treatment of King revealed the Memphis media's attitude toward blacks as a whole: "Never did you see any kind of a story that put us in the context of being a human being like any other human being." While Lawson tried to build a "beloved community" beyond race, he felt the media reinforced the barriers of racism.

The commercial news media continually played upon such "outsider" stereotypes instead of closely examining the issues related to the strike. Early on, AFSCME officials pointed out that workers had contracts in Nashville and Chattanooga; that the law did not forbid government from recognizing or bargaining with a union; that even the 1966 injunction against the union in Memphis did not prevent the city from negotiating with the union if it wished. But the newspapers did not explain these facts to the public. The *Commercial Appeal* focused instead on union "illegality" and wrote, "It's the Mayor's Job," and only he could settle the strike, when in fact the City Council had policymaking powers and could create a resolution to the strike if it chose to do so.

HENRY LOEB BEGAN recruiting strikebreakers on Thursday, February 15. His father taught him that if you have a strike on your hands, introduce workers to take the place of strikers, gradually increase their numbers, and outlast the strike. He counted on white supervisors, on white college students looking for extra money, on Boy Scouts and other volunteers to get garbage out to the curbs or pickup sites. Black workers, however, would need to be the critical component of any movement to replace the strikers, for most whites would not take "black" jobs. Starting with only twenty new men, thirty supervisors, and forty nonstriking workers, the city began its campaign to pick up the garbage, but these nonstrikers still picked up less than one-tenth of the normal amount. Striking workers gathered at various work sites and barns, heckling scabs and demanding that they go home.

Undercover black police detectives who attended the union rally on February 14 alleged that Local 1733 activist Peter Parker told strikers to "beat the living hell" out of undercover police, and that Ciampa said, "If a man seeks your job, then he is a thief and has stolen it. I want you to treat him as a thief and do a good job." Police spies consistently exaggerated or twisted the comments made at mass meetings, but strikers no doubt did try to frighten scabs away from work. According to the police, strikers attacked one of them and tore his clothing. In another incident, seven or eight strikers chased scab workers away from garbage pickup, one of the strikers allegedly jumping up on a truck's running board and waving a .38-caliber pistol. A young white Youth Corps fellow named Jimmy Crunk grabbed his .22-caliber rifle and pointed it at the pistol-packing striker and threatened to blow his brains out. The man jumped off the truck and fled. Crunk worked in the city's Youth Corps, paid by federal funds as part of the War on Poverty, which claimed it had not authorized anyone to be a strikebreaker. Fire and Police Director Frank Holloman said the city had authorized no workers to carry weapons on the job.

The next day, newspapers pictured Crunk grim-faced and determined, with his rifle raised and standing next to the seal of the city at the side of the garbage truck, and they showed other white scabs carrying rifles. Frank Miles, personnel director for the E. L. Bruce lumber company, immediately called the *Press-Scimitar's* editor Null Adams and warned him that such provocative images could turn a strike into a racial conflagration. Adams agreed and ordered that no more such pictures be printed.

To solve the problem of accumulating garbage, the mayor asked people to take garbage out of their yards, where sanitation men had always gone to get it, and carry it to the curbs themselves. This cut labor costs and the time required to pick up garbage, and the mayor liked it so much that the sanitation division never returned to yard service. The city further economized by reducing pickups from twice to once a week, another practice the city adopted on a long-term basis.

The newspapers notified people where and when garbage would be picked up, and most whites in suburban East Memphis dutifully carried their garbage to the curbs, while most blacks let their garbage pile up. It was their act—though not a pleasant one—of labor solidarity. A strike support leaflet urged, "Leave your garbage where it is. Let it pile up. Let the wind blow it where it will. Let there be no full garbage cans on the front porch where you live. When the police escorted garbage trucks roll through your neighborhood let them go back empty!" The African American community soon became a huge garbage dump, while white neighborhoods remained more or less immaculate. Memphis thus supplemented the Kerner Commission's characterization of America as "two societies, one black, one white—separate and unequal" with an image of two communities—one mostly clean and the other piled high with refuse.

"Ciampa Go Home" bumper stickers mysteriously appeared all over white Memphis a day or two after the strike began; the Memphis Labor Council's Bill Ross thought they emanated from the John Birch Society's bookstore. Ciampa received hundreds of threatening letters at the Peabody Hotel. Real estate broker Charles Owen wrote to Ciampa that he had united white Memphis with his "uncouth, detestable, objectionable, rude" behavior, and that "hundreds of professional men" of all sorts—from doctors and small business owners to plumbers—welcomed the opportunity to face down his union's "punks, hoods, and nuts." Owen enclosed the photo of Ciampa pointing his finger at Loeb that had received so much play in the press. "Go back to New York, or wherever in the *hell* you came from. . . . Go home, Yankee," he wrote, demanding, "You hoodlums" should "get the hell out of Memphis."

"The resentment of the so-called outsider" had been a weapon against civil rights and unions in the South since Reconstruction, according to Frank Miles. "When the CIO came into the picture, and they were real socialists, real radicals; they were communists in the eyes of a lot of people in those days. They were being sent in by these big international unions to tell 'us' how to run 'our' business." Many white Memphians reacted in just this way to Ciampa, and also to King, whom they saw as the ultimate outsider, even though he was a Southerner. Racism exacerbated anti-union attitudes. When a boycott of downtown stores began to emerge as part of the strike support strategy, Jack Boker, a member of the International Brotherhood of Electrical Workers, a white craft union, wrote to Ciampa, "It will be a great day when nice people can go into our best stores and not be insulted and brushed against by those smelly, arrogant, rough, shop lifting BURR HEADS." Boker once had lived in Detroit, where "lousy negroes [sic] do actually push you or your children off the sidewalks." He preferred the South, where strikes were settled "with NO negroes [sic] to contend with." He denounced Ciampa for his "YANKEE interference."

Ciampa did receive some white support: Memphian J. S. Clark wrote, "Written contracts and due[s] check offs are legal and customary in America" and should be accepted as part of American freedom. Across the country, rank-and-file unionists, delegates to union conventions, presidents of major unions such as Walter Reuther of the UAW, and national AFL-CIO President George Meany all offered strike support in the next month and a half. Even Loeb received some letters opposed to his handling of the strike, but most of them came from outside Memphis and impressed him not in the least. Instead, he constantly referred to "bushel baskets" of letters and petitions supporting his stand, and he kept piles of them close to his desk to prove that Memphians stood behind him. Loeb spent enormous amounts of time and energy responding personally in writing or by phone as he cultivated his network of business and college friends, fraternity brothers, and American Legion members.

What Loeb never admitted was that public opinion was completely split along racial lines. The great majority of blacks supported the strikers, but as Loeb added replacement workers, increasing numbers of whites rallied to his side, often brandishing cold war metaphors. "Nothing can be gained by appeasement," wrote Katherine Treanor, who urged Loeb to "stop the issue of food stamps" so that taxpayers, "against whom the strike is directed," did not foot the bill for the sanitation workers' time off. Gene Lowery also objected to strikers' getting food stamps: "Mr. Mayor, I believe you know as well as I know that if these strikers were making twice the money they make now, they would still find a way to get the government to supply them with food stamps and they would spend their money on 'rot gut' liquor, women and dog racing." Blacks did not vote for Loeb anyway, he wrote, "so why should you give an inch?" James Hendrick, a doctor at the University of Tennessee Medical School, called union activists "the Communist Labor Crew" and urged Loeb to "pick up their leaders on vagrancy and put them on the chain gang." In Crump's days, that might have happened, but Loeb merely offered his polite thanks for the doctor's support.

ONE POTENTIAL BRIDGE existed between Memphis's white and black communities. On Friday, February 16, AFL-CIO and AFSCME union leaders went to a City Council hearing to plead with them to intervene. Tommy Powell, president of the Memphis Labor Council, became the first white Memphian to speak forthrightly to the city government on AFSCME's behalf. His appearance inaugurated a reign of recriminations and threats against him from whites.

A tall, muscular man with blond hair and a crew cut, Powell hardly looked the part of a labor agitator. Born in 1928, he grew up on a cotton farm near a little town called Possum Hollow, ten miles from Jackson, Tennessee. His family hired Johnny Cash and Carl Perkins—later famous as country singers—as day laborers. His mother told him "not to fool around with them trashy boys," but Powell sympathized with them, since they were "poor guitar pickers, and we were poor cotton pickers." He believed in doing unto others as he wished them to do unto him. His father died young and Tommy went into the military. In the 1950s, Powell and other poor whites in the countryside grew desperate for jobs. He escaped the cotton fields through an athletic scholarship to Tennessee State University, but when he took his fellow football players out on strike to protest their mistreatment by the coach, TSU took away his scholarship and he landed back on the streets.

Hungry and with no apparent future, Powell migrated to Memphis and got a job at Armour Packing Company. A fledgling union made him an officer because "I had been to college and they said they wanted somebody who could read and write." A frenetic, five-pack-a-day cigarette smoker, Powell became an equally frenetic advocate for workers. His international union, the Amalgamated Meat Cutters and Butcher Workmen of North America, was an older AFL craft union that rivaled the United Packing-house Workers of America, one of the CIO's most racially progressive and leftist unions. Because of his union's significant black membership, Powell could not stand aloof from civil rights issues, especially as he engaged in tough battles to organize black and white workers in Mississippi. Black packinghouse workers had generated a powerful civil rights movement within organized labor and increasingly used the 1964 Civil Rights Act's Title VII prohibition against employer or union discrimination to fight for better jobs. Powell became increasingly aware of the importance of civil rights, and even more so when the Amalgamated and Packinghouse unions merged in 1968.

Powell catapulted to the presidency of the Memphis Labor Council, its youngest leader ever. White workers tended to trust him because of his "good old boy" rural ways, while blacks could see what a journalist called an "angry energy" on behalf of the working poor. Powell received his salary from his international, not the Labor Council, and he did not have to compromise with conservative white unionists as much as a paid AFL-CIO functionary like Bill Ross did. Powell also served three terms during the 1960s and early 1970s in the Tennessee House of Representatives. With one foot in the working class and the other in the legislature, he also knew that public workers provided the only potential new base for the AFL-CIO expansion as industrial-union membership declined.

In supporting the sanitation workers, he was not out of step with the other leaders of the Memphis AFL-CIO. The Memphis *Union News* called for white unionists to support the sanitation workers' rights to collective bargaining and deduction of union dues, as well as to choose their own leaders and to strike. "These are all trade union principles that men and women have fought and died for down through the years and are still prepared to fight and die for," said its front-page editorial in early February. It condemned Loeb's "anti-labor views and his utter disregard for the rights of the employees and his callousness toward the dignity of the individual." AFL-CIO support for the strike gave Powell and other white unionists a way to bridge the gap between the white and black working class. Although the craft and building-trades unions had long kept blacks out, and some white unionists supported Loeb on racial grounds, many of these white trade unionists turned against Loeb when he began to hire strikebreakers.

When Powell spoke before the City Council, however, he ran into a stone wall of opposition. Councilman Thomas Todd, from the white working-class district of Frayser, utterly opposed public-employee unions and served as one of Loeb's most dogged defenders. Todd owned plantation lands in Mississippi and had fought off several union drives among black workers at his Chisca Plaza Hotel in Memphis. He had called AFSCME unionists "creatures" and "gangsters" interested only in exploiting the workers, and he now asked Powell, "Why have you in the labor movement been keeping the Negroes out of your unions if you are so concerned about these poor, underpaid workers?" Councilman Bob James answered Todd's question: "Because he knows that this one is all-Negro and he won't have to worry about taking them in."

James was no critic of racism, but rather an angry transplanted Northerner and owner of a cleaning company that employed blacks. He started life as a moderate on racial issues but turned to the right after being deeply influenced by the film *Communism on the Map*. Supported by the American Legion, he showed it at least 300 times. He changed from Democrat to Republican and ran for Congress in support of Barry Goldwater's 1964 bid for president. James lost, but he was elected to the City Council in 1967. He considered strikes and social movements part of a Communist conspiracy to manipulate blacks and the poor.

Tommy Powell objected to James's characterization of unions, and Bill Lucy also responded by saying, "I'm sorry the council has seen fit to inject the race issue." Todd, James, and other hostile, pipe-smoking, white male council members continued to act as if they and the mayor were on the side of the workers protecting them from the unions. James said the union was bad for the workers because better pay would force the city to mecha-nize away their jobs. "That's fine," black council member Fred Davis coun-tered sarcastically, "but who's going to pay the welfare?" Councilman Billy Hyman said, "We are concerned" because many sanitation workers might lose their jobs and "are not qualified to do anything else." James asked Ciampa to preserve "the basic dignity of the city" by sending the men back to work and negotiating after that. Ciampa retorted, "The basic dignity of the city has never gotten them anything in the past, why should it now?"

This first attempt to persuade white council members to bypass the mayor fell completely flat. Council members had been in office for just six weeks, and most of them had campaigned for a new mayoral form of gov-ernment that supposedly offered the advantage of creating a strong execu-tive authority to run the city. For sixty years, Memphians had elected a mayor more or less equal in authority to city commissioners, each of whom ran a part of the city. In 1966, voters approved a referendum creat-ing a new system with a strong mayor and thirteen City Council mem-bers—six elected at-large and seven elected by districts, without party identification. In the old mayor–commissioner system, Henry Loeb had been a major irritation to blacks as mayor from 1960 to 1963, but then he had limited powers. Now, as a powerful mayor, he became a greater threat. But the new government structure, implemented in 1968, also introduced an element of confusion. If unionization was a policy decision, council members might enact a law to allow it, but others considered contracts the province of the mayor. Strike supporters didn't know for sure where to put pressure.

Many hoped that a more democratic system had been created that could favor the workers. Elections based on districts had made it possible to elect blacks for the first time since Reconstruction. Elected from a majority-black district, Reverend J. L. Netters supported the sanitation workers throughout the early 1960s and wanted to speak out boldly on their behalf, but he felt constrained by the huge white majority on the City Council. Reverend J. O. Patterson, also from a majority-black district, was the son of J. O. Patterson, Sr., bishop of the Church of God in Christ (COGIC), a Pentecostal denomination that was the fastest-growing church in the city. The younger Patterson, also elected to the state legislature, supported the workers but felt the political constraints of working with whites. Fred Davis, a black insurance-company owner elected from a barely majority white district, had a much more tenuous political base that caused him constantly to seek compromise.

The ten white council members, elected from districts with few blacks, had little sympathy for the strikers and were glad to let the mayor handle it. W. T. McAdams was a white fiscal conservative whose district included many black industrial workers in North Memphis; Billy Hyman, a white Mississippian who ran a lumber company in black South Memphis; Philip Perel, a jeweler active in the Retail Merchants Association, which was concerned about stopping any threats to boycott downtown stores. Wyeth Chandler was a lawyer and Democrat-turning-Republican whose father had been mayor during Crump's era, and he would become Loeb's successor as mayor in 1972. He said flatly that Loeb should handle the strike and the council should stay out of it. Yale-educated businessmen and attorneys Jerred Blanchard and Lewis Donelson, and car dealer Downing Pryor, were conservative Republicans. It appears that every male member of the council had served in World War II or the Korean War, and had been thoroughly indoctrinated by the Red scare and American patriotism. All the whites were strongly anti-union.

Gwen Awsumb, the one woman on the City Council, was a civic-minded Republican from an upper-middle-class East Memphis family who some hoped would be a compromiser, but she believed the "ultimate destruction of the country could come through the municipal unions." Privately, she said, "It was time somebody dug their heels in [against unions] and said, 'This has gone far enough.'" Only the three black council members, all Democrats, had clear interests in intervening in the strike, but they had no allies among the whites, most of them Republicans.

Loeb insisted that anything to do with contracts was an executive question, and he alone had the decision-making power; he successfully imposed this view on the City Council. In fact, he had met with council members earlier on February 16, practically commanding them to stay out of the strike. Hence, as police began ordering extra quantities of mace and disabling gas and prepared to go on long shifts, the city government offered little hope for positive government intervention in the strike. The Wagner Act and the National Labor Relations Board had not covered federal-government employees, and President Kennedy's 1962 executive order allowing unionization only covered federal, not local, workers. Thus, the sanitation workers faced a determined mayor, and had few allies on the city council who could moderate or buffer his power.

BETWEEN 900 AND 1,000 workers met at the United Rubber Workers union hall at noon on Friday, February 16, the same day as the City Council hearing. Epps, Ciampa, Jones, Powell, Lucy, and Crenshaw denounced Loeb's strikebreaking, and the NAACP's Reverend Samuel Kyles called for people to lie down in front of garbage trucks to stop scabs. Kyles, chair of the NAACP's labor and industries committee, and Maxine Smith, NAACP director, held a press conference that morning in which they charged the city "with racial discrimination in the treatment of the sanitation workers." Composed, determined, and articulate, both leaders represented the NAACP board that had voted its support for the strike on Thursday night. But why call a struggle over union rights an issue of discrimination, a reporter asked. "It is only Negroes who are relegated to this type of position," Smith replied. "We can't afford to wait—there is very high feeling about this in the Negro community." Kyles added, "The purpose of the NAACP is to attempt to improve the economic conditions of Negro citizens," and it had complained to the city about the plight of the sanitation workers for many years. In an earlier report, the NAACP had thoroughly assessed the "poor, depressing and disturbing plight of Negro employment," finding that not a single African American led one of the city's thirty-four departments, and that city jobs remained coded "white" or "black."

White police and public officials expressed alarm at NAACP support for the strike and thought the civil rights and labor movements had teamed up, but it was not so. Kyles would not have cared if the strikers pressed their case without the union; in his press statement, he never mentioned the word *union*. He had a gut-level distrust of white unionists, and several years later he commented in the press that a Jew (Jerry Wurf) should not have so much control over black men (AFSCME members). Kyles said, "My interest was in the men, not the union, and that was my attitude straight through. . . . I mean I don't have any faith in the union." Kyles came from a better-educated segment of black Memphis that also had no faith in Ciampa. "One thing that did disturb me was that Ciampa was too crude," he later said. Far from being involved in a conspiracy, the NAACP entered the fray without any approval from AFSCME. "We didn't ask them. We said whether you want our help or not, you got it," said Kyles.

Kyles's distrust of AFSCME's white leaders reflected the failure of most white-dominated unions to act on civil rights issues. Kyles and Smith had processed many worker complaints of racism in unions, and they frequently saw unions as obstacles to black advancement. Lawson, who knew the terrain of movements for social change as well as anyone, said industrial unions had made many workers into "middle-class people," but most of them had "failed then to include the poor workers of the country, and particularly to include the black workers . . . [and] in many instances . . . sought to exclude them."

Despite such reservations about unions, the NAACP proved itself a significant ally to the workers. Many NAACP branches were reluctant to use direct-action tactics, such as sit-ins and picketing, but the Memphis NAACP had been built on them during the student movement in the early 1960s. At the February 16 press conference, Kyles immediately urged strike supporters to pull out all the stops to pressure the government, including tying up police and city-government phone lines with calls, and picketing and boycotting downtown merchants. He urged people to join the NAACP for an all-night protest vigil at city hall on Monday, February 19.

The NAACP projected a civil rights–style pressure campaign to support the workers, even while Kyles knew the union did "not [want] to make it a racial thing if you're going to get local union support." The union's first flyers, for example, called the strike an issue of justice rather than a question of race. Bill Lucy told Kyles that no NAACP statement could be read to a mass meeting of the workers without first taking it before the union executive board. Kyles refused to do this and was irked that the NAACP's Friday statement—though broadcast on television and printed in the newspapers—was not read to the strikers. Nonetheless, as soon as unionists and civil rights advocates began to converge, alarm bells went off in white Memphis.

The *Press-Scimitar*, in an editorial titled, "This Illegal Strike," condemned the NAACP. "It is regrettable that anyone should attempt to make a racial issue out of the garbage strike, when the real issue is the fact that it is illegal in Tennessee for any public employee to strike against the public." FBI agents began conducting surveillance of the strike only two days after it began, with "Red squad" and FBI agents soliciting information on the strike from at least five individuals involved in the civil rights community. The FBI's special agent in charge, Robert G. Jensen, said the NAACP had "injected itself into the strike" and thereby gave it "racial overtones." He wrote to J. Edgar Hoover in Washington that the Memphis FBI would follow the strike closely "through racial sources." The Memphis Police Department, including its black undercover agents, closely coordinated surveillance with the FBI, which then distributed reports to U.S. Army Intelligence, the U.S. attorney general, the Secret Service, and other government and police agencies.

The state legislature in Nashville also became involved. As soon as Tennessee Senator Joe Pipkin heard of the NAACP's role, he and Senator Hugh Stanton introduced draconian bills to make it a felony punishable with one to five years in prison "to encourage, advise, abet or otherwise seek to bring about any stoppage or impairment of police and fire protection, garbage removal, or other governmental functions necessary to the health, welfare and protection of the people." A second bill prohibited payroll deductions for union dues. A third bill allowed for a prison sentence of up to five years for anyone convicted of disrupting communication with fire and police departments; it passed in the State Senate, 21 to 0. Lawmakers across the South were introducing bills in reaction to public-worker organizing and strikes, such as that of 40,000 to 50,000 of Florida's 60,000 teachers, who "resigned" in February to protest inadequate salaries and school funding. "Whatever you do," don't let sanitation workers get a checkoff system for collection of union dues, a New Orleans official told the *Commercial Appeal*.

Conservative Victor Riesel, whose syndicated national column Red-baiting unions and leftists had been carried by the *Commercial Appeal* for years, warned, "Just look at a profile of the New York garbage strike and you have the profile of thousands to come."* "Big unions," political power plays, and major disruption of a city's life would be the price of public-employee unionism, he wrote.

Fortunately for AFSCME, despite the state's right-to-work law, unions already represented about 20 percent of Tennessee workers and had more influence there than perhaps in any other southern state. The Tennessee Labor Council donated funds to the strike, opened their meetings to AFSCME speakers, and issued statements of support. Labor Council Director Matt Lynch and other unionists swarmed over the legislature on February 26, opposing the proposed anti-union laws. Senator Pipkin continued to hold his proposals over the heads of strikers and community supporters, but because of AFL-CIO opposition, he could not get them out of committee.

Nonetheless, white union leaders in Memphis feared the racial repercussions of the sanitation strike. Taylor Blair of the International Brotherhood of Electrical Workers told the mayor that Memphis "had been sitting on a powder keg since August 1967," when a race riot nearly occurred. Born and raised in Tennessee, Blair had worked in northern cities, considered southern segregation wrong, and became involved in the city's War on Poverty and race-relations work through his church. His wife worked for the Retail Clerks Union, which had provided the first support for T. O. Jones and Local 1733.

Because of the racial conflicts simmering in Memphis, Blair warned Loeb, "This thing ought to be stopped as quick as possible." Yet Loeb appeared unconcerned and "insisted that there was no racial problem in Memphis." It shocked Blair that the mayor could be so oblivious to the danger that "this town could start burning," and he went to Frank Miles, who knew Loeb quite well, to suggest, "Henry is getting some real bad advice . . . maybe he'll listen to you."

---

*Sanitation workers in New York struck on February 2 and won a favorable settlement on February 11.

Miles, who had been president of the Memphis Labor Council when Loeb took his first steps toward public office in the 1950s, had been a bus driver during a 1946 bus strike, when a bullet intended for a scab hit a passenger in the back. He dreaded a prolonged and bitter strike, fearing that strikers might resort to firearms, beatings, and sabotage and that police might use tear gas, clubs, and guns. Miles spoke with AFSCME leaders Ciampa and Jones, who assured him that wages were not the main issue and that room to bargain existed. So he decided to try to mediate with Loeb.

On Friday, Blair and Miles went together to Loeb's office, and Miles warned that hiring permanent replacement workers could drag the strike on indefinitely, like the St. Petersburg teachers' strike. Loeb told him the city had already hired eighty-five people, further alarming Miles, who thought, "It looked like he was going to replace everybody within a matter of two weeks," creating more worker grievances. Loeb said he would not hire any more replacements if the union would let the city assemble garbage trucks in the shopping centers and have people take their garbage there, but when Miles took that proposal to AFSCME leaders that night, they turned it down flat, because it would have looked as if they approved of the city's hiring scabs. Ciampa rejoined, "You take the scabs off the streets and we'll collect the garbage at hospitals and schools, and we'll do it free." But Loeb said no.

In this standoff, Miles feared for his company, E. L. Bruce. "Here we are sitting out here with a large stockpile of hardwood lumber in a predominantly Negro neighborhood," where someone could easily throw a Molotov cocktail across the fence and burn the lumber to cinders. He also feared that Bruce's black workers also might go on strike. The sanitation strike unsettled black workers in a number of Memphis factories, including a new RCA Television plant, and Blair also noticed with some alarm that black ministers had begun to support the strike "without any whites involved in it at all." He thought it "spelled racial trouble any way you looked at it, when there was an all-black movement."

Miles became frustrated that Loeb could not be more flexible, saying, "The mayor seemed to have a record running in his brain that kept coming out the same way." On Saturday, February 17, Miles and Blair again talked to Loeb—for nearly eight hours. Again they accomplished nothing. Loeb offered only one ray of hope, saying no workers on strike would lose their jobs after the strike ended, and the men's insurance accounts would remain paid up—a sign that he did not plan to dispense with them. The city indeed continued to pay premiums for workers who made medical claims to Blue Cross, which cost the city nearly $23,000 during the course of the strike. County agencies—to which the city contributed—paid more than $7,000 for food stamps for strikers. These seemingly humanitarian gestures toward the families of workers kept ministers and the labor community hoping that Loeb's intentions were honorable.

But others didn't buy it. The newspapers earlier in the week quoted Reverend Bell as saying that if Loeb "wants to play rough, we know how to play rough too," and at the Saturday-noon union meeting, he denounced strikebreakers as "rats." Bishop J. O. Patterson, as well as O. W. Pickett and the leader of the local Teamsters union, also spoke, and strikers voted overwhelmingly to reject the mayor's telegrammed request that they go back to work. Black teenagers that morning had harassed strikebreakers and police dispersed them without violence or arrests, but they claimed that someone that day had fired on a sanitation truck.

That Saturday afternoon, just as Blair and Miles left their discouraging talks with Loeb, a group of black and white ministers went in to see him, including Loeb's longtime friend Reverend Frank McRae. Loeb told them that as long as talks were not defined as "mediation" (and therefore binding on the city), and as long as all discussion could be channeled through the ministers, he would resume talks with AFSCME. But he also said he would not compromise.

Miles thought that too many people had now become involved. Bargaining should consist of careful and private discussions between principals to the dispute. Instead, everyone in the city seemed to be giving Loeb advice, while he constantly gauged his political support and media coverage. This was not good bargaining. Under these conditions, Miles thought, the strike showed every sign of escalating from being a labor dispute into a much wider social conflict.

———

THE FIRST TRULY mass meeting of community members and strikers occurred on Saturday night, February 17, as some 2,000 people listened to speeches by black ministers and white and black labor leaders at Bishop Charles Mason Temple, the home base for the rapidly growing Pentecostal Church of God in Christ. The current bishop, J. O. Patterson, told them, "What's mine is yours if you need it." His congregation donated food and money, and people in the audience helped to bag food and give it out to strikers. Black strike supporters, already frustrated by biased media coverage, excluded *Commercial Appeal* reporter Charles Thornton. He waited outside and described a diverse group going in and out of the meeting, including members of the NAACP and black political clubs, and "a woman dressed in the white, flowing robes of the Black Muslim organization." He also noted a few whites. The newspaper published the names and even the addresses of several white Memphis State University students who attended, potentially inviting retaliation against them.

Typical of the white media's approach to the civil rights struggle, Thornton suggested that some black leaders wanted to use the strike "as a convenient vehicle to help whip up support for the militant black power philosophy." He began probing for weaknesses and divisions and asked Ciampa "if he intends to use race as a weapon in the strike." Ciampa refused to take the bait, simply saying he could not turn down any community support. However, Thornton wrote, AFSCME officials feared that any suggestion of racial turmoil would be a quick way to lose that support among unionized whites.

The unity of the sanitation workers and the actions of both the NAACP and the AFL-CIO established a sense of momentum on behalf of Local 1733 in the first week of the strike. On Sunday, workers fanned out to speak to every church congregation with which they had any connection, personalizing the issues by attacking Loeb's unbending attitude and asking for support. Most African Americans were poor and could readily identify with their plight, and they gave it.

———

ON SUNDAY AFTERNOON, something surprising happened. Out of the media's sight, Memphis City Council members held a secret meeting at the home of Fred Davis—undoubtedly the first time that most white City Council members had ever been to a meeting in a private home in the black community. They decided to ask the mayor to offer the workers a 10-cent-per-hour increase in wages, followed by another 5-cent increase in July. City Council President Lewis Donelson believed a raise would send the men back to work and thereby avoid the strike's main demands of formal recognition and a union shop. The workers had always been pragmatic, open to any sign of accommodation by the city.

The next morning, Donelson told Loeb of the proposal, and the mayor hit the roof. He said the council had overstepped its authority and had no business getting involved in the dispute. Had the proposal been implemented, it probably would have ended the strike. But Loeb told Donelson, "The city is going to beat this thing." He wanted to win, not to settle the dispute.

7

TESTING THE SOCIAL GOSPEL

*I felt that white ministers, priests and rabbis of the South would
be among our strongest allies. Instead . . . some have been outright
opponents . . . all too many others have been more cautious
than courageous and have remained silent behind the
anesthetizing security of stained-glass windows. . . .*
—*Martin Luther King, Jr., "Letter from Birmingham Jail," 1963*

K ING WROTE HIS "LETTER FROM BIRMINGHAM JAIL" IN MAY
1963 as an appeal to white "moderates" to take sides in the civil
rights revolution, disputing a newspaper ad by eight white ministers who called the Movement's protests and marches "unwise and
untimely." King rejected their implication that piecemeal improvements
and time itself would change society for the better. "We will have to repent
in this generation not merely for the hateful words and actions of the bad
people, but for the appalling silence of the good people."

In the first days of the sanitation strike, Reverend Henry Starks, a minister
of the African Methodist Episcopal (AME) church in Memphis, similarly
noted an "appalling silence" among white religious leaders. "The individual
or local congregation really found itself paralyzed" by the politics of race, he
said. Reverend Frank McRae, a white "moderate" and Methodist district
superintendent, born in Memphis and raised across the street from Henry
Loeb, said this paralysis came from pervasive racism. "The [white] church
was asleep" in "a sleepy southern town run by a plantation mentality." While

many "blacks knew the white community 'cause they worked in their homes and cut their grass," most whites suffered from complacency, ignorance, and fear when it came to blacks. "I believe the most devastating fear I have ever known is the southern white man's fear of the black man. Why does the southern white man fear the black man? Because he knows he has kept his foot on the neck of the black man all these generations." He said whites feared blacks "would become a majority and rise up and take over."

Of necessity, Memphians saw race relations in a religious context. It was said that Memphis had more churches (some 600 of them) than gas stations. Less than 10 percent of those attending religious services were Catholics, about 2 percent were Jews, and nearly 90 percent were Protestants. Of the latter, perhaps 100,000 whites and a similar number of blacks were Baptists. They preached from the same Bible and praised the same God, but they differed dramatically on what the stories in the Bible meant. Religion might have bridged the gaps between whites and blacks over the strike, but it mostly exacerbated them.

King offered an alternative to southern religious conservatism, preaching the Social Gospel of labor and social reform movements that had emerged with industrialization and urbanization. King demanded a righteous religion that resisted racial and economic oppression, and his version of the Social Gospel struck a rich chord among African Americans, who had used Christianity as a means to resist exploitation going back to slavery. But such talk had been largely rooted out of the southern white church. McRae said that most whites thought religion should be a salve to individuals locked in poverty but not a basis for social action to end that poverty. Fundamentalists believed in a literal interpretation of the Bible that could be read to include justifications for slavery, racism, and the idea that workers should be meek servants. White ministers were "fine to give invocations at football games and annual meetings," said McRae, but their congregations and superiors commanded them "to leave social issues alone."

White churches helped to run the abolitionists out of the South before the Civil War, as well as radical white preachers who sought to organize the "brotherhood of man" in the CIO in the 1930s and 1940s. By contrast, black churches and ministers had often (not always) welcomed CIO and civil rights organizers. Black communities, and Memphis in particular, had also been divided by a multitude of sects and institutions within churches, organized around strong leaders concerned about controlling their own turf. But in response to the sanitation strike, black ministers began to come together. Many of them had had some taste of black proletarian life. Reverend Roy Love of Mt. Nebo Baptist Church, previously a laborer in a hardwood flooring factory, in 1943 joined forces with the minister of the historic Beale Street Baptist Church, Reverend George Long, to bring black labor leader A. Philip Randolph to speak in Memphis. Long famously declared, "Christ, not Crump, is my Boss," before the Crump machine ran him out of town. Love stayed, ran for the school board in 1954, and became president of the black Baptist Pastors Alliance. He had long supported sanitation workers' efforts to organize.

On the second day of the strike, Love called a meeting of black Baptist ministers and appointed Reverend James Jordan, of Beale Street Baptist Church, to head a committee of seven black ministers to intervene in the strike. Jordan felt white ministers could settle this strike, and so he contacted white Baptists, Methodists, Catholics, Presbyterians, and Jews to try to interest them in a meeting. He felt the basis existed for a strategic biracial alliance. Reverend Starks, Jordan, and perhaps fifteen other African Americans had previously "integrated" the Memphis Ministers Association, a group of more than a hundred white ministers, after the association mistakenly invited a black minister, thought to be white, to join. Starks not only belonged to the Memphis Ministers Association but he now presided over the Interdenominational Ministerial Alliance, which included nearly a hundred black ministers.

The nominally interracial Ministers Association had begun study groups on racial and economic problems after the near-riots in the summer of 1967. In May 1967, the ministers had elected Rabbi James Wax, the only Jewish member of the Memphis Ministers Association, as its president. Reverend Jordan and Father Nicholas Vieron of the Annunciation Greek Orthodox Church also cochaired a race relations committee, and the association had even designated February 11—the very day that the sanitation workers met to call their strike—as Race Relations Sunday. The Ministers

Association had previously issued a statement condemning racial prejudice as immoral. Apparently the white churches were not quite asleep.

Out of this mix, Jordan brought together a selected group of blacks and whites in a meeting held at Lane Avenue Baptist Church, chaired by Presbyterian Ray Dobbins of the Ministers Association social action committee. One white minister said the ministers should not get involved, and at this point Reverend McRae agreed with him. But the majority formed a small interracial committee to work on the issue. Reverend Starks followed this up by asking Rabbi Wax to initiate some action. Wax and his white colleagues had a "relationship with the power structure [that] is different from mine," said Starks, and could "save the city a lot of anguish" by talking directly with Mayor Loeb. Black ministers decided to stay in the background.

Wax seemed like a good choice to take the lead. His broad concern for social justice set him apart from the more individualistic worldview of personal salvation held by most Protestant ministers. He saw how the ancient Hebrews' struggle against slavery applied to African Americans, believed in the Social Gospel, and had an abiding admiration for Dr. King. Judaism, Wax said, dictated a "reverence for life," which "means to be concerned with the conditions under which people live." For twenty-two years he had been the rabbi of Reform Judaism's Temple Israel in downtown Memphis. He had also become a pillar of the city's respectable religious community. He had long worked with middle-class civic, religious, and business leaders to quietly improve government and race relations through the Memphis Committee on Community Relations (MCCR). This group included "moderate" blacks such as LeMoyne College President Hollis Price and Universal Life Insurance President Maceo Walker, as well as influential whites such as *Commercial Appeal* editor Frank Ahlgren and attorney Lucius Burch. Wax grew accustomed to "reasoning" behind closed doors. "That's how we worked in this city for a long time," he recalled.

Assimilation had long been a survival strategy of the southern Jewish community, which well remembered Leo Frank, a Jew in Atlanta falsely charged with rape and murder and then lynched by a mob. Memphis Jews maintained their own religious institutions but did not challenge the "whiteness" of the dominant population. Wax said, "Almost all native-

born Southerners whose families lived in the South for two or more generations have segregationist attitudes," and Jews were no different. He
belonged to a Jewish community with an insular, middle-class quality and
little familiarity with the black community. Jews owned Lowenstein's and
Goldsmith's downtown department stores, which blacks had picketed in
the early 1960s, demanding an end to segregation. Jewish business leaders,
like others, had acceded to this demand but otherwise had provided little
help to the civil rights movement in Memphis.

Although it had required picket lines and sit-ins to do it, Wax felt proud
that Memphis had quietly taken Jim Crow signs out of the downtown stores
and opened its parks, the zoo, libraries, and other public places to blacks.
He believed in the city's reputation for moderation. Tennessee's Catholic
Bishop Joseph Durick recalled that when he had lived in Birmingham in
1963, "All I would hear would be the great progress and strides that Memphis and Atlanta are making, that the businessmen and the city fathers have
gotten together and they are not going to let racial difficulties get in their
way of moving forward. And that was the story that we were getting."

Unfortunately, this story was a delusion of moderate whites, particularly
when it came to the churches. The Ministers Association mainly represented
upwardly mobile congregations, and Wax's was one of them, but almost no
Baptist and fundamentalist sects—rooted as they were in the "vast lower
middle class" of insecure, rural-oriented Protestants—belonged. Reverend
Lawson and many other blacks scorned the MCCR for using studies and discussions as substitutes for action. Lawson presented the MCCR with a Freedom Manifesto in 1967, calling on it to act more boldly and to talk less, but
Rabbi Wax, at that time the MCCR's secretary, opposed it, and the NAACP's
Vasco Smith walked out of the organization, complaining that the MCCR
wanted to put fires out, while he wanted to start them. Wax found it difficult
to fully understand the black community's anger; he believed talking with
influential whites was more effective than picket lines. Like Isaiah in the Old
Testament, Wax urged people to "come and let us reason together," but Lawson thought "reasoning" in the Jim Crow South occurred best under the
pressure of black community mobilization.

When such mobilization occurred, most white religious leaders typically responded with alarm, and so it was during the sanitation strike. After the collapse of talks between Loeb and AFSCME, Wax led a committee to see Ciampa at 10 PM on Friday night, February 16. Wax told Ciampa, "We have had in this city good race relations," that "we have worked long and hard at it," and that he didn't want to see racial progress destroyed by the strike. He said he did not officially represent the Ministers Association, but he personally urged the union to end the strike for three weeks as a "cooling-off period." In return, he offered to convene talks with the mayor.

Not quite the madman characterized in the media, Ciampa voiced his own fears of a racial disturbance, saying, "It is not gonna be too many days until the lid blows off . . . some hothead, and away we go." But Ciampa knew the city would never negotiate if the strike ended, and said he did not have the power to end it even if he wanted to. Under AFSCME's rules, only local union members could make that decision, and they weren't about to end the strike. Ciampa did agree to hold more talks if the mayor would, and on Saturday, February 17, a group of white ministers, including Loeb's friend Reverend McRae, went to the mayor. Loeb agreed to talk further with AFSCME as long as the ministers mediated.

ON SUNDAY, FEBRUARY 18, at 7 PM, nearly two dozen men met in the midst of the city's urban poverty, in the basement of St. Mary's Episcopal Cathedral. Loeb had stipulated that the news media must be present, and reporters and TV cameramen sat around the room. In the middle sat a U-shaped table, with Memphis City Attorney Frank Gianotti, his assistant Myron Halle, and Loeb on the left and an interracial group of union representatives (Ciampa, Lucy, Joe Paisley, Jones, and five strikers) on the right. In the middle sat Rabbi Wax, William Dimmick, dean of St. Mary's, and Reverends McRae and Frank Tudor Jones, as well as Father Nicholas Vieron and one black minister, Reverend James Jordan. Wax presided and began by reading through the nine demands raised by the union, including recognition and a written contract, dues checkoff, a formal grievance procedure, pay raises, and various benefits.

City leaders began by saying they could not talk to people breaking the law and would not participate in talks unless the union representatives

agreed immediately to end the strike—something only the full membership of Local 1733 had the power to do. This refusal to talk to strikers or
their representatives nearly aborted the meeting, until Vieron suggested
that Wax ask all the questions and that all answers be directed back to him.
Ciampa objected, "Father, please! This is an exercise in futility. . . . We're
adults here. We're struggling with serious problems. Are we going to play it
like children?" Speaking directly to Loeb, Ciampa asked, three times, as if
speaking to a deaf person, "Mayor Loeb, will you discuss the matter of
recognition with me?" Loeb looked away from Ciampa as he responded: "I
feel strongly about obeying the law. . . . There's very strong inherent respect
for the law in Memphis. I've gone about as far as I can go until we get to
the point where the law is being obeyed. . . . My position with the union is
well known. Mr. Chiampy understands this."

Long before this meeting, "Chiampy" and Loeb had lost patience with
each other. Ciampa asked in exasperation, "How can men talk when they're
not here on an equal basis? If we can't agree to sit down and recognize the
existence of one another?" Loeb said he would only talk to the ministers.
Ciampa then asked Rabbi Wax to please ask the mayor, "What law would
Mayor Loeb be violating if he discussed the problem at hand with the representatives of the people involved?" City Attorney Gianotti suddenly turned to
Ciampa and blurted out, "Tell those men in no uncertain terms—not the way
they've been telling them—that these men are violating the law!" Looking
directly at the five workers in the room, with cameras rolling, he pounded his
fist on the table and shouted, "Go back to work—immediately! I mean now!"
Ciampa shouted back sarcastically, "Thank you for talking to our men!"

Rabbi Wax got the meeting back on track only by asserting the legitimacy of the absurd device of the two sides speaking not directly to each
other but to him. As they did so, the mayor played primarily to the television cameras. "The right of these men to come in and see me will never be
terminated," he said, and the city wanted to "have the same happy relationship" with the sanitation workers' union that already existed with other
unions. "What *is* that relationship?" an exasperated Bill Lucy asked. For
nearly five more hours, almost pointlessly, the parties talked around each
other through the ministers.

Around midnight, AFSCME International President Jerry Wurf sham-
bled in, with "rumpled gray hair, horn-rimmed glasses, one leg dragging
slightly in a polio limp, gesticulating hands, the sharp clipped accent of
New York," strike historian Joan Beifuss wrote. Wurf did not look like a
firebrand; indeed, he was exhausted. He had come directly from a full-bore
organizing drive of public employees in Pennsylvania, a state with a
collective-bargaining law and 100,000 public workers ready to join
AFSCME, and he had profound misgivings about diverting his attention
to Memphis. Privately, he had said, "You are stupid if you have a garbage
strike in January or February . . . [and] you don't go after a politician the
minute he gets into office. You haven't had time to get people mad at him.
. . . [Y]ou are a fool to do it and I'm not a fool. I didn't call the strike, and I
would have advised anybody against it; but now they're out, it's got to be."

Wurf did not welcome strikes, particularly not in the South, for they
always spawned mistakes and confusion and exacerbated human weaknesses.
The unplanned character of the Memphis strike made it "one of these situations where strategy was made by events instead of events resulting from
strategy," and he feared it could lead to a major defeat that would undermine
AFSCME's momentum nationally and undercut any hopes of ever organizing the South. AFSCME's national communications director, John Blair, had
been in town for a week and had already briefed him, in Wurf's words, about
"these ridiculous negotiating sessions in front of television cameras."

Wurf also feared that his best organizer had blundered. A strike in the
South "calls for diplomacy, sensitivity," Wurf said later, but Ciampa had
"played right into Loeb's hands." Ciampa's blunt statements might work in
Baltimore and Michigan, where "the first thing you do is call your boss
four-letter words cause you're rallying your workers," but not in Memphis.
"Maybe we will eventually have to holler and scream, but that should be
last, not first. . . . The mere sound of his [Ciampa's] name sends tremors,
not only through the white community, but even through responsible elements in the black community." Already, Wurf felt concerned about the
appalling hate mail Ciampa was receiving at the Peabody Hotel.

Sensing disaster in the making, Wurf hoped to succeed where Ciampa
had failed—by appealing to the "middle of the spectrum" in Memphis. To

do this, he had to alter the "fishbowl" situation that made frank discussion impossible. "I sensed that Loeb was horsing around for the cameras, you know, this nonsense. You know it's not possible to negotiate with television cameras and public officials. . . . There has to be confidential exchange, give and take, and men are not willing to show that they give and take. The role of the public official is that he has to take a position and never yield an inch because it's essentially a moral position—however phony that stance is." Wurf had to get the negotiations out of their confrontational, public mode.

Participants at the church took a midnight break as AFSCME staffers briefed Wurf, who concluded that Loeb had "missed the signal" from the union that it was "available for some wheeling and dealing" and did not want to sustain a strike under such unfavorable circumstances. Loeb had never engaged in full-blown labor negotiations, but surely he knew that a national labor leader would usually put his institution's preservation above the interests of local workers. Indeed, with Wurf in the room, and after reporters went home, Loeb began speaking directly to him instead of to the ministers. He never spoke again to Ciampa, who now went silent during negotiations.

However, Wurf and Loeb made little progress. According to Dean Dimmick, the meeting went back and forth over the nine points in dispute "about 900 times," and it all seemed childish to him. Loeb called for a cooling-off period during which the strike would end and he would stop hiring replacement workers—but this would have killed the union just as the failed strike of 1966 had done. After much talking, however, it appeared that solutions to some issues might be at hand. Dimmick thought the whole conflict could have been settled that very night. By four in the morning, disagreements had boiled down to only two points: formal recognition of the union and a means for checkoff of union dues.

Rabbi Wax now made an impassioned plea for compromise. As Wurf recalled his words, he said, in effect, "The red necks were coming across the bridge and the town would burn. . . . He really carried on, both in terms of the possibility of violence and . . . about the division that would take place between the races." During a period of urban riots and Black Power, Wax's argument really worried Wurf, who made what he called a "cold decision . . . to get down to the nitty-gritty and give our ultimate position" in order to end the strike quickly. Wurf proposed a memo of agreement rather than a contract, to get around Loeb's opposition to full union recognition. And then he decided to "show our aces, give the Mayor his way out," by dropping the demand for direct and mandatory deduction of union dues from the men's paychecks. He proposed that dues could be deducted or not, voluntarily for each worker, through the credit union, which presumably operated independently of both the city and the union. For the first two years, AFSCME headquarters would turn over its share of the dues collected to local charities.

Wurf thought he had just proposed a face-saving compromise for Loeb: It would not be a union shop, in which workers had to belong to the union; the city did not have to participate in institutionalizing the union through dues deductions; it did not have to sign a contract, only agree to let the union function at the workplace.

Loeb said (erroneously) that the credit union had no standing separate from the city, and then he rejected the rest of the offer out of hand. Wurf thought that Loeb at least would leave the possibility of dues payment through the credit union as a later bargaining point, even if he wasn't yet prepared to accept these proposals. Instead, Loeb rejected all of it; he "threw it away and then it was gone." Wurf suddenly realized that Loeb "was not the least bit ready to deal . . . out of intransigence, stupidity, [or] lack of experience." He felt foolish for having presented, so early in negotiations, an option that would normally be his last proposal for compromise, and he was angry at Loeb for his unwillingness to bargain. Exhausted, everyone went home as the dawn began to break.

AT NOON ON Monday, February 19, Wurf met nearly 1,300 strikers at the United Rubber Workers union hall. He presented Jones with a $5,000 check and said AFSCME would do everything necessary to sustain the strike. Reverends Jordan, Bell, and others made statements assuring the strikers that the community was behind them and they were on the side of right. That afternoon, Wurf and AFSCME representatives returned to more fruitless discussions with the mayor and his men. The Memphis Citizens Association, connected to the White Citizens' Council's crusade to preserve segregation, issued a statement of support for Loeb.

That night, AFSCME and the NAACP began a tactical alliance; Wurf and his organizers attended an all-night vigil, sponsored by the NAACP, starting at 6:30 PM with eighty people at city hall. The NAACP was already calling for an escalating stream of vigils and protests and an economic boycott of downtown businesses. A few black college students appeared and picketers sang, "We Shall Overcome," and carried signs reading, "Watts also waited too late," and "Jobs, Jobs, Jobs." At 3 AM, three black men were still picketing, finally quitting at 6 AM. On Tuesday, February 20, when workers held another noontime rally at the Local 186 union hall, Jesse Epps announced AFSCME support for a boycott of white businesses. These included Loeb's Bar-B-Q, a chain of fast-food restaurants located in black communities, many of them attached to coin-operated laundries, and owned by the mayor's brother William. (The two men were at odds, and Henry had divested his holdings in the company.) The boycott also included the Oldsmobile car dealership owned by City Council Chairman Downing Pryor. "Keep your money in your pockets and let the garbage stay in the streets and alleys until justice is done," Epps declared.

The raft of speakers at the union rally that day included Taylor Blair, Paisley, Ciampa, Jones, Starks, Crenshaw, Bell, and City Council member J. O. Patterson, Jr. The former black Republican political leader George W. Lee said, "There will be no peace until the Iron Curtain is removed from Russia, the Bamboo Curtain from China, and Jim Crowism from the United States." Reverend Baxton Bryant, director of the Tennessee Council on Human Relations, also had entered the fray. Son of an Arkansas tenant farmer, a war veteran, a southern Methodist, and a populist Democrat who began preaching at age sixteen, Bryant spoke at this and subsequent union meetings and talked to everyone in city government who would listen, in his attempts to resolve the strike.

Wurf held more discussions with the city that afternoon, but he became just as frustrated as Ciampa, Lucy, and other AFSCME representatives. He also grew disillusioned with Rabbi Wax. Wurf said that Loeb "knew what I didn't know . . . that Wax wouldn't or couldn't stand up" to him. Wax left for a previously planned trip to Florida and turned over discussions to Dean Dimmick, who seemed even less able to influence Loeb. Wurf also grew frustrated by the media. "The thing that I found hard to believe was . . . the absolutely, totally irresponsible attitude of the press. . . . I have never encountered what we encountered in Memphis. . . . They knew that the strike had come from the inside, that the outsiders had nothing to do with it. They knew the workers had legitimate grievances. . . . They knew what the real issues were and were unwilling to print it."

That night, four young whites and seven young blacks, men and women, picketed Loeb's home, sponsored by the NAACP.

Wurf gratefully accepted NAACP support, which had the potential of turning this into a community-based movement, but differences clearly existed. Kyles, Turner, and Maxine Smith felt this was a black issue, and they intended to mobilize the black community independent of union control. Even more than AFSCME, the NAACP had a clear fight with Loeb and held no illusions that he would make any compromises without intense black community pressure. T. O. Jones already felt some anger at black ministers and civil rights advocates for their emphasis on race, at a time when the union still hoped to resolve the strike as a strictly labor issue. Kyles said Jones had pressure on him "from the local union people," but Jones clearly did not want black ministers and NAACP middle-class leaders to take away control of the strike from him and his members.

Yet the NAACP's confrontational stance made increasing sense to Wurf. He had talked to Loeb for three days in various downtown Memphis churches, with no resolution in sight. Wurf wanted to leave town, but he found himself stuck in a tactical bind. Because black workers appreciated Ciampa's obvious devotion to their cause, Wurf said, "I could not get Ciampa out of town then without doing serious injury to our stance or even our credibility with our rank and file membership." He therefore could not replace Ciampa, but he also didn't want him (or T. O. Jones) to run the Memphis negotiations. Wurf had no choice but to provide much of AFSCME's leadership for the rest of the strike. And he, too, increasingly viewed this as a civil rights issue as well as a labor issue.

By Wednesday, February 21, a regular routine had been established: a union meeting of nearly a thousand strikers at noon, addressed by community supporters; a march to the downtown from Clayborn Temple; and mass meetings in various black churches. At the Local 186 meeting, Epps again echoed the NAACP's original demand for a boycott of downtown businesses, saying, "We must stick together and God will help us win."

ECONOMIC PRESSURES ON workers increased after they received their last paychecks on February 20, and so did temptations to go back to work. Costs to keep the workers going amounted to $15,000 a week—a heavy burden for an international union with no strike fund. O. W. Pickett led relief efforts and talked to the mayor's assistant, who assured him that food stamps would continue for strikers. By the end of the first week of the strike, Loeb had hired approximately 150 scabs, increasing the strikers' fear of permanent replacement.

That is why Reverend Bell kept emphasizing at the Local 186 meetings the possible misfortune that could befall people who took other people's jobs. The tension between strikers and scabs became very evident to S. T. Thomas. He and a group of twenty-five to thirty strikers went in the mornings to the bus barns to see who was striking and who was working. One morning, with the police looking on, a nonstriker pulled out a .22-caliber rifle and pointed it at Thomas, who said, "What's wrong with you, man?" The strikebreaker cursed Thomas viciously and threatened to kill him. Thomas responded, "You better be glad I ain't got mine this morning. I'll blow your goddamn brains out!" The police took the side of the nonstriker and began using racial epithets against Thomas. He barely avoided a beating. Police arrested him and charged him with "night riding" and "intimidating people."

A judge convicted Thomas and told him he was going to send him to the Shelby County Penal Farm for eleven months and twenty-nine days, but the judge died before Thomas's sentencing date came up, and a second judge gave him two years of probation instead. This and other confrontations suggested to Local 1733 members that they should avoid openly confronting strikebreakers at the gates of the sanitation depots. "The ones that the city was hiring at the time, we didn't bother with them too much. Everywhere they'd go they had to have a police squad car escorting them," said Taylor Rogers. Incidents of intimidation against strikebreakers occurred throughout the strike, but striking sanitation workers mostly used moral pressure. Said Rogers, "Some of the men was goin' back in and we'd have a prayer meetin' with them, and they didn't go back no more. We'd talk to them and tell them, 'It's our job y'all are trying to take out there.' We'd talk to them wherever we'd meet them. Right on the spot we'd tell them so, trying to tell them not to go back. . . . Some of them wouldn't go back the next day. Some of them wouldn't go. We never resorted to violence, to do anything to nobody."

S. T. Thomas resented the scabs intensely, but he later absolved them for working during the strike. In his view, they had simply put their fears for their families' immediate welfare ahead of their long-term advancement.

AFSCME staff members made a policy decision to avoid open conflicts with scabs in order not to give the police an excuse to attack strikers. Bell and many other community supporters, including students, yelled at strikebreakers and sometimes sat down in the street, but threats of full-blown civil disobedience in front of the truck barns failed to materialize. Social pressure from ministers, neighbors, and the larger black community remained the chosen method to prevent other black workers from breaking the strike. And labor–community solidarity began to take hold quickly.

Police surveillance intensified just as quickly. On February 20, Bill Lucy protested, "Twelve or 14 police intelligence men have been tape recording all union meetings with bugs and reporting everything directly to the mayor." Black plainclothes police officer E. D. Redditt had attended the very first meeting held by the strikers at the Local 186 hall, and he continued to keep track of strike activities from his vantage point as a well-known "police–community relations" officer, and so did black officers Willie B. Richmond, Louis McKay, and Jerry Williams. Some of these men had more respect in the community than others, but anytime African Americans saw black police working undercover, they tended to associate them with the tradition of "snitches" employed by the Crump machine, whose reports had so often led to repression by those in power.

Yet these officers had their own labor grievances, for the Memphis Police Department (MPD) kept blacks in the same lowly, underpaid positions as black workers in general. Redditt sympathized with the sanitation workers and knew civil-rights and black youth activists on a first-name basis. Raised on Beale Street, and an all-city track star, he got a community college degree in health and education but had to join the military when he could not get a teaching job. He went to Korea and then came home to work for the MPD for lack of better opportunities, and opened its first community-relations center. He wanted to work with young people, but the MPD shifted him into plainclothes work, thereby putting him in an uncomfortable position in the black community. Everyone knew him, so he was not "undercover," and yet he was assumed to be a "snitch."

The use of plainclothes officers resulted from an escalation of "intelligence" activities in Memphis. The FBI had always worked closely with the MPD, but even more so after Frank Holloman became fire and police director in January 1968. Holloman had worked directly under J. Edgar Hoover in the FBI's national office for twenty-five years before coming to Memphis, and he had also been in charge of the Memphis FBI for a short period. He made increasing police intelligence one of his top priorities. Police officers received training in crowd and riot control from the local FBI, and the MPD in turn provided undercover police to attend strike and community meetings.

Given the "antisubversion" orientation of top officials, FBI and police "counterintelligence" agents in Memphis could not accept the sanitation strike at face value—as a protest against racism and a demand for just compensation and treatment. Rather, they explained this struggle to Hoover and Holloman as something created by outsiders or conspirators to serve more devious purposes. The FBI took the names and addresses of white college students who attended the Saturday night rally and searched its bureaus around the country. The agency connected two students to the W. E. B. Du Bois Clubs on the West Coast—presumably confirming the theory, enunciated by the *Commercial Appeal* as well as the FBI, that workers were "being used" by outsiders. FBI agents sometimes ignored the names of blacks listed in news stories, as if only white participation proved that radicals were involved. Such reports of course justified expanded surveillance.

But FBI agents also followed the strike through "racial sources," some of whom saw the strike as a "power struggle" in which black leaders tried "to out-do the other in an effort to become the ultimate spokesman for the blue collar and heretofore unorganized Negro factions in the city of Memphis." FBI agents pinpointed every sign of disunity. According to one FBI memo, "Negro leaders feel that the Union is not sincerely concerned about the welfare of the average Negro worker, feeling that the Union is more interested in getting Union dues and getting a power base established in the city of Memphis whereby it can later organize the City Hospital workers and other low-paid City employees." Some in the NAACP, like the mayor and the City Council, felt uncomfortable that AFSCME or other unions might organize the South's largest medical center for blacks at John Gaston Hospital, headed by a black man, Odell Horton.

FBI and police agents cultivated black ministers and NAACP board members, and a number of them regularly provided insights on the strike. Civil rights activists spoke to federal law enforcement officials in hopes that they would be more neutral than the Memphis Police Department. Some ministers also felt it was their duty to maintain dialogue with the police in hopes of minimizing violence, according to Lawson. While some NAACP members tried to open communications with the police and the FBI, AFSCME labor veterans thought they had too much: they had few illusions about intelligence agents, who apparently had already bugged their hotel rooms and tapped their phones. During labor and civil rights struggles in the past, white FBI agents had done very little to protect people's rights to speak and organize, and Martin Luther King's first altercation with Hoover occurred when King publicly pointed out how FBI agents often worked hand in glove with southern segregationists. FBI and police agents viewed civil-rights, Black Power, and union activists as subversive of the established order, and were not about to help out anyone in the Movement.

WURF VERGED ON walking out of the talks with the mayor by the end of the day on Wednesday, February 21. He had one hope left—that he might get through to the personable Loeb in a "man to man" dialogue. Unlike most politicians who said one thing in public and something else behind closed doors, Loeb remained consistent in his views—to a fault. Wurf thought Loeb was "wallowing in the confrontation" and had "allowed the bitterness of the quarrel, the outsider issue, the black issue, and so on, [to] obscure the very fundamental problems that were involved here." Perhaps he could get the mayor to see that the welfare of the city and the workers required a compromise. Perhaps their shared Jewish heritage could break down personal barriers.

As the clergy-organized talks stalled out, Wurf said he took Loeb aside for a frank conversation: "I says to him, 'Look, you silly son of a bitch, I'm not getting out of town; I'm going to fight you and you've won a few battles, but you know, in the long run you can't win. And in the long run you've got to live with us. . . . I've mobilized the total union. If we spend money on nothing else—I'm bringing in anything that I have.' And this was true and I said, 'You've got to understand that we cannot walk away from these men. We just can't.'" Loeb "began to give me this bull about if I was a Memphian, if I understood, and I told him that was a lot of shit. And he went on—but he was not in anger—and he said, 'Son of a bitch, you're getting to me. Look, why don't we go to this banquet tonight . . . perhaps we can get talking to each other.'"

Thus it came about that the two men went to the Brotherhood Award banquet that night, put on by a local chapter of the National Conference of Christians and Jews and attended by prominent business and political leaders. This event confirmed Wurf's deep suspicions about the Memphis Jewish community. "'Let's take a Jew to lunch this week' or something, you know, never impressed me as a substantial effort to save the world," said Wurf. "By this time I was beginning to learn something about Memphis, that it always had a sort of redneck Jewish community, and incidentally a Jewish community that is totally alien to me." Loeb was a Jew born to aristocratic privilege in the Deep South, and Wurf was a Jew born to polio and poverty in New York City. They saw the world from opposite ends of the social spectrum.

At this dinner, *Commercial Appeal* editor Frank Ahlgren received the Brotherhood Award for his supposed politics of moderation during the desegregation of the downtown in the early 1960s.

Most of the African Americans in the room were waiting on tables, but Eddie Jenkins, a Memphis State University student and a member of the black ROTC glee club, sang for the mayor and the other dignitaries. He felt like "a darkie on the plantation. There was a bunch of us token niggers

down there—all of us clapping and saying 'yeah! yeah!' " as Loeb acknowledged not just one, but two standing ovations, followed by muted applause
for Wurf when Loeb introduced him to the audience. Loeb, said Wurf,
"was showing me that although in some ways he was *geshmadt*,* that he
had busted loose from the Jewish community in his own way [and that
they] approved of what he was doing." Said Jenkins, "I noticed Jerry Wurf
didn't stand up. He didn't clap a lick."

After singing, Jenkins sat next to Wurf and Loeb, whose glad-handed
sincerity nearly floored him. As Loeb shook hands enthusiastically with
Jenkins, however, the student asked him, "Why are you holding out on the
strikers?" Loeb said he could not hear because of the din, but Wurf interjected, "You heard him. He asked you why you're holding out on the strikers." Loeb surprised Jenkins by taking down his phone number, calling
him that very night, and then writing him a personal letter. Jenkins
thought, "Gee whiz, maybe the guy ain't so bad after all. . . . Maybe he is
trying to be relatively fair. Maybe we got him all wrong." He changed his
mind after attending Loeb's weekly open house at city hall, after which
Jenkins realized Loeb was merely exercising a politician's charm and wasn't
about to budge on the strike.

"Loeb . . . at that banquet was showing me he had the community on his
part," said Wurf. "And I, of course, told him at the banquet when he drove
me home that, 'So what?' This had nothing to do with it. I was not running
for mayor. I didn't care if I had community approval and I didn't care if I
had establishment approval. But I pointed out to him . . . that these people
would grow to hate him. Because the price he had to pay to win would hit
these people where they lived."

On Thursday morning, rather than returning to negotiations, Wurf and
his men went down to city hall to talk to the City Council. He sent word
that he hoped the mayor, too, would attend the council meeting. Loeb took
offense and said that AFSCME had walked out of negotiations. He
declared the talks over. Rabbi Wax's "let's reason together" strategy had
failed. Loeb and Wurf would not talk face-to-face for the next six weeks.

*A Yiddish word for a Jew who converted to Christianity.

Reverend Starks and the other black ministers had hoped white ministers would exert real pressure on Loeb, but Starks concluded that white ministers were "paralyzed" by the norms of white society. Men like Wax got their understanding largely "through secondary sources such as newspapers, and were swayed by what they read. They did not readily identify this as a struggle for justice which required their participation." And they did nothing further to force Loeb to bend.

For his part, the more Wurf understood Memphis, the less he liked it. "It was clear that white workers would not have been treated this way," and that Loeb "thought that these goddamned people were inferior; he understood that portion of his constituency that one would refer to as the cracker constituency, the redneck constituency, and pandered to them and at the expense of these men."

In weeks to come, black ministers, the NAACP, and AFSCME would all be blamed for injecting the race issue into the strike. Said Wurf, "I didn't make it a racial issue nor did Loeb make it a racial issue. . . . It was. It was the desire for a man to have access to a job that had been denied him . . . all of this spoke of one thing: that blacks were not worthy of social or economic concern by the establishment."

THE FAILED NEGOTIATIONS with the mayor only made black minister James Jordan more angry about the plight of the sanitation workers. After the first all-night meeting at St. Mary's Cathedral, he took home a worker who had not spoken up in the meeting. Jordan observed that, for "people of limited education . . . it's pretty hard to try to express yourself in front of so much royalty, especially when you don't have the words at your fingertip."

In the car, however, the worker unburdened his feelings. He reminded Jordan of recent newspaper stories about the horrors of convict labor at Tucker and Cummings prison farms in Arkansas, and then told him, "That condition exists here in Memphis. We work under conditions worse than that."

What Loeb did not understand, and what remained at the crux of the conflict, said Jordan, is that these men went on strike because "they worked as slaves before. Now they have a union."

II

FIGHTING FOR THE
WORKING POOR

∎

8

MINISTER TO THE VALLEY: THE POOR PEOPLE'S CAMPAIGN

I wish today, that Christians would stop talking so much about religion, and start doing something about it, and we would have a better
world. But the problem is that the church has sanctioned every evil in
the world. Whether it's racism, or whether it's the evils of monopoly-
capitalism, or whether it's the evils of militarism. And this is
why these things continue to exist in the world today.
—*Martin Luther King, Jr., Ebenezer Baptist Church, Atlanta, January 7, 1968*

D URING JANUARY AND FEBRUARY OF 1968, KING FOLLOWED a
parallel path to that of workers and their allies in Memphis. As
they challenged the old racial order in Memphis, he challenged
the larger system of poverty, racism, and war. As they fought for a living
wage, King struggled to get his Poor People's Campaign off the ground.
Nearly half a million U.S. troops in Vietnam were besieged in the deadly
battle of Khe Sanh and in the Tet Offensive in January. More than 500 GIs
died in one week in February. A disproportionate number of young black
men—who could not get decent education or jobs—came home every
week in body bags to Memphis and other cities. Across the country, repression escalated against Black Power, civil rights, antiwar, and student
activists. In Orangeburg, South Carolina, on February 7 and 8, state troopers gunned down some fifty unarmed black students from two all-black
colleges who had protested segregation at a local bowling alley. Three
teenagers died, all of them shot in the back.

King tried to make up for what his movement lacked in organization and resources by maintaining a stupefying whirlwind of speaking and organizing activity—what Andrew Young called King's "war on sleep." King's life had become, according to his wife, Coretta Scott King, "like a political campaign three hundred and sixty-five days of the year, but you never take a break, it never ends." Under tremendous stress, King spoke more eloquently and prophetically than ever, shifting his emphasis from desegregation and voting rights to the war and the plight of the working class, to changing the country's priorities and even its social and economic structure. He still insisted on "integration," which he defined as a society in which everyone would share equally the nation's power and wealth. But was anyone listening?

"Two-thirds of the peoples of the world go to bed hungry at night. These are the least of God's children," he told his congregation at Ebenezer Baptist Church in Atlanta. In India, Nigeria, and the Mississippi Delta, "I have met people by the hundred who have never had any money in their hands in their lives," he said, yet "in God's economy, the man who lives in the slum, and in the alley, is as significant as Henry Ford, or John Rockefeller." Perhaps better than anyone else, King understood the need for a broad multiracial alliance that included the middle class as well as students, workers, religious, unemployed, and angry young people. "I can never be as I ought to be unless you can be what you ought to be," he repeated. "Injustice anywhere is a threat to justice everywhere."

KING'S FOCUS ON middle-class obligations to the poor provided a guiding theme as he kicked off the Poor People's Campaign during a three-day staff retreat and a press conference in Atlanta on January 15–17. Black professionals and the middle class had improved their lot through the civil rights movement, he told his staff, but "the plight of the Negro poor, the masses of Negroes, has worsened over the last few years." He said "an underclass" separate from the working class, including "thousands of Negroes working on full time jobs, with part time income," lived in conditions that would be described as a depression if they existed in the white community. To forestall more inner-city riots, he called on the Movement to "take this rage, that's all around us now, and transmute it into a powerful force for social transformation."

King wanted to match civil rights and voting rights laws with laws creating jobs or income. These were not new demands. Rustin, Randolph, the NAACP, the Urban League, and economists for several years had been discussing a "Freedom Budget," a "Bill of Rights for the Disadvantaged," and a "Marshall Plan for the cities" to wipe out the poverty that plagued thirty-five million Americans. The Kerner Commission's report would also call for jobs, housing, and economic development programs, and media outlets such as *Newsweek*, nonprofit organizations such as the Ford Foundation, and even conservative economist Milton Friedman proposed some form of negative income tax to create a guaranteed annual income. The 1966 SCLC convention had supported these measures and a renewed labor–civil rights alliance. It had also called for repeal of the Taft-Hartley Act's section 14(b). "We must guard against being fooled by false slogans, such as 'right to work,'" King said. "It provides no 'rights' and no 'work.'"

Now, King proposed to abolish poverty directly through government redistribution that allowed poor people enough money to pay for their own housing, education, and other necessities. Shoring up their incomes while training displaced black workers would keep the economy growing while reducing the crime, drugs, and prison terms that accompanied poverty. Self-sufficient citizens could then work their way out of poverty. If the government applied the equivalent of the tax dollars paid into the federal budget by African Americans toward job creation and housing subsidies, in ten years it might wipe out poverty. King was not a dreamer, for many academics and policymakers were considering such proposals. Although some polls showed a lack of concern about poverty, one Harris poll showed majority support for ending it through government programs. With all of its billions of dollars of wealth and its great technology, King said, America had the resources to end poverty at home and in the world—if only it could exercise the will to do it. King drew upon mainstream economists but he also differed from them by linking economic revitalization to demilitarization. The money spent on the Vietnam War, he said, could wipe out poverty in America; structural economic reform could not happen without ending the twin bloodbaths in Vietnam and the nation's cities.

King also proposed to attract youth to his campaign and away from riots by using something "as attention getting and dramatic as a riot, without destroying life or property in the process"—a "dislocative" thrust of civil disobedience aimed at federal power in Washington, DC. King envisioned SCLC recruiting and training some 3,000 demonstrators from fifteen impoverished major cities and rural areas, who would go to the nation's capital and camp out in a tent city—joined by thousands more in mass rallies—until Congress and the president either created jobs or a livable income for the poor. Andrew Young recalled, "We were prepared to stay in Washington on this campaign as long as we needed to," and to risk terms of up to a year in prison for civil disobedience. King and Young suggested that the peace and human rights movements might coalesce to use sit-ins and protests to shut down the Pentagon, block roads, and keep the government from functioning normally—civil disobedience on a higher level than ever seen before.

"Distributive justice" would be much harder to win than desegregation and voting rights, King told his staff at their January retreat. Earlier civil rights and voting rights demands "clearly [were] mirrored in the Constitution" and "didn't cost the nation one penny," but "there's nothing in the Constitution that says a man should have an adequate income." Hence, the Movement had to appeal to God-given rights inferred from the demands for "life, liberty and the pursuit of happiness" in the Declaration of Independence.

Privately, King said American capitalism had failed African Americans and that the mixed socialist and capitalist social democracies of Northern and Western Europe worked better. "Something is wrong with capitalism as it now stands in the United States," he had told a gathering of ministers in December. "We are not interested in being integrated into *this* value structure. Power must be relocated, a radical redistribution of power must take place." Publicly, he asked people to recognize that slavery and segregation had created a cycle of black poverty that only special programs could end. "In this instance, we will be confronting the very government, and the very federal machinery that has often come in as our aide. In a sense we're going for broke," he told reporters in Atlanta on January 16, in order to "lift the hopes, and thereby diminish the tensions in our communities." He said that, given the possibility of new urban riots, the greatest danger was doing nothing.

Within the SCLC staff, King's proposals set off heated discussions. In announcing the campaign, King said SCLC had 270 affiliates and sixty staff members in thirty cities and would train an additional cadre of black ministers. It sounded good, but King's staff actually was spread very thinly and was ill-prepared for such a campaign. Staff members complained that they did not know where to find the people for this march or how to get them excited about the campaign. King argued that anyone could understand a simple demand for jobs or income, and that a more complex program would only confuse people. Yet many staff members felt at a loss to explain how they could win such broad demands from a recalcitrant Congress that refused even to pass a rat-control measure in early 1968. What back-up plan would they have to claim at least a tactical victory if the campaign failed to win its larger demands?

King argued that "a radical reordering of our nation's priorities" through the Poor People's Campaign could potentially unify the Movement, but SCLC staff members felt as if they were adrift at sea. They had spent their lives in the civil rights movement and the black church. Now King called on them to organize a new multiracial constituency around class issues among Mexican Americans, Indians, and poor whites as well as African Americans. SCLC did not have the resources and organizing structure to make it happen. Almost alone, King had to convince not only the civil rights community and a broader public, but also his own reluctant staff members, that they could organize the poor. King in 1967 had argued that the Vietnam War was the biggest obstacle to improving conditions in America, but he now argued that fighting poverty and the war together could unite the broadest segment of the population. Yet the movements of the 1960s encompassed many diverse groups, many of them middle-class–oriented and with little focus on class issues.

If King lacked the means to launch the Poor People's Campaign, as a spiritual leader he had an almost mystical belief in the ability of people to overcome seemingly impossible odds through struggle. Speaking to fifty or

sixty staff members, he explained the Poor People's Campaign in such eloquent spiritual and psychological terms, that the greatest skeptic would
have had difficulty opposing the idea. Movements keep hope alive and
renew the individual's sense of "dignity and destiny," King said, pointing to
one of his staff members who had left a life tainted by crime to become "a
man, and a person committed to moral purposes" through nonviolent
direct action. Since the Montgomery bus boycott, King had said that the
first step toward liberation for black people was to "desegregate their
minds," to change their spirit and mentality, and he still emphasized that
mass action remained the way to do it, and to banish the disunity in the
Movement. He asked his staff to go on faith. If people had taken this long to
think through the Montgomery bus boycott, they never would have done it,
he said. Disunity in the Movement reflected "derivative confusions" due to
the Vietnam War and the violent state of race relations, and only a unifying
goal and mass action could overcome it. King seemed to suggest that even if
the Movement failed to achieve its immediate goals, the more important
thing was to bring people together to take a course of moral action.

Veterans of the black freedom struggle had good cause to question
King's perspective. His plan seemed to stress mobilization rather than true
grassroots organizing, and it relied heavily on the ability of ministers and
organizers. In the past, King had specialized in flying into crisis situations,
drawing on the momentum of a local movement, publicizing it, and
inspiring great crowds. But Ella Baker, a community organizer in Harlem,
an NAACP southern regional organizer, and SCLC's first staff member,
had long criticized such an approach to movement-building, as well as
King's leadership-centered organization based on preachers. At the founding of the Student Nonviolent Coordinating Committee (SNCC) in 1960,
she had told students: "It is important to keep the Movement democratic
and to avoid struggles for personal leadership," and she continually advocated "group-centered leadership, rather than a leader-centered group pattern of organization." Baker parted company with King and became a
trusted adviser to SNCC, seeking a movement that did not wait on anyone
else and one that involved women, poor people, and youth in creating
their own movements from below.

King saw the Poor People's Campaign as a way to go beyond past limitations and to create a new, interracial, class-based movement among the poor, but it could still be criticized as another example of mobilizing people rather than organizing a grassroots movement, and it required a hard sell to get other Movement strategists on board.

Bayard Rustin, King's longtime ally, in a January 29 meeting of King's advisers in New York, argued that a poor people's disruption of the nation's capital would only exacerbate white backlash and thereby facilitate a victory for the right wing in the 1968 elections. In early March, Marion Logan, a respected member of the SCLC board, circulated a memo to the rest of the board, opposing the campaign for the same reason. King spent countless hours trying unsuccessfully to get her to retract it. SCLC's most charismatic organizer, James Bevel, still argued that SCLC should put all of its energies into ending the war in Vietnam, which had sidetracked all domestic legislation, while Jesse Jackson wanted to put SCLC energies into Operation Breadbasket, which used locally based economic boycotts to force industries to hire blacks and improve economic conditions in the ghetto.

Clearly, King's campaign to attack poverty at a national level would be difficult to pull off. His agenda put the Movement on a dangerous collision course with the national power structure, but King did it deliberately. He told an audience at Jesse Jackson's church in Chicago in early February, "We've got to find something that avoids riots on the one hand, but also timid supplication for justice on the other. We must face the fact that pressure-less persuasion does not move the power structure of our nation. I'm sorry it's that way. Privileged groups seldom, if ever, give up their privileges voluntarily and they never do it without resistance. . . . Freedom is never voluntarily given by the oppressor."

IT WAS A dangerous time for prophecy, and the news media quickly interpreted King's projected campaign as a "capital siege," casting doubt on whether such a movement—even though King called it "a search for an alternative to the riots"—could really be nonviolent. King repeatedly said SCLC had worked successfully with street gangs and black nationalists in Chicago and elsewhere, but in fact the main precedent was the 1932 encampment of World War I veterans—the Bonus Marchers—who came to the nation's capital to beseech Congress for early payment of their pensions to offset the Depression. The government responded by beating, routing, and even killing them. Only Randolph's threatened all-black mass march for jobs on the eve of America's entry into World War II provided a hopeful model: President Roosevelt responded with an executive order barring employment discrimination in defense industries, and Randolph canceled his march. King may have been using Randolph's strategy of brinkmanship, hoping for concessions that would allow him to call off his proposed confrontation.

Alternatively, the powers that be might ignore his demands and use occupation of the capital as an excuse to unleash widespread repression; King could be setting a trap for himself. He betrayed his own inner worries by telling reporters in Atlanta on January 16, "I hope we don't come to the point where we have a kind of fascist development in our country that will destroy every value that we hold dear." As he traveled the country speaking against the Vietnam War and in support of the Poor People's Campaign, bomb and assassination threats delayed his flights and heckling held up some of his speaking engagements. Politicians Ronald Reagan, Richard Nixon, George Wallace, Georgia Governor Lester Maddox (who had threatened to beat with an ax handle anyone who protested segregation at his store), Mayor Loeb, and others used the rhetoric of backlash against civil rights, the peace movement, feminism, and the New Left to win white working-class and middle-class votes. Congress blocked rent supplements and other measures to help the inner cities yet spent billions to build missiles and develop other military programs, while state and federal governments threatened to use "anti-riot" conspiracy laws to silence "agitators" like King.

As King publicized his Poor People's Campaign, the clamor against him reached a new high. When he seconded the Kerner Commission's warning that inner-city riots would escalate unless the government addressed intertwined problems of poverty and racism, white conservatives attacked both King and the commission for fomenting rebellion. When King continued to demand a political settlement of the war in the wake of the stunning Tet

Offensive by Vietnamese insurgents, President Johnson sent in more troops and targeted King as a traitor. As King's links to the federal government disintegrated, right-wing extremists increasingly focused their frustrations and their wrath on him.

One irate patriot wrote FBI Director J. Edgar Hoover on February 12, the day the sanitation strike began: "This power hungry, evil black devil, posing in a dirty black cloth of Christianity is a bigot, rabble rouser, Communist bedfellow, and an anti-American screwball." He added that King's proposal for "guaranteed wages for Negroes is sickening," a plot financed by Russia and China. Congress should stop King by passing a law prohibiting the advocacy of civil disobedience, another man wrote. Right-wingers also claimed King had purchased 12,000 Remington automatic rifles to use in ghetto uprisings, and the FBI, incredibly, sent agents to the Remington Company to investigate the charge. On February 16, a man who was upset about Communist allegations against King wrote to Hoover, "If I am mistaken about this, please correct me." Hoover did nothing to correct him; he merely reiterated his past warnings of subversion within the black freedom movement.

Such fantastic charges against King had long been circulated by the FBI through the House Un-American Activities Committee and antisubversion committees headed by segregationist Senators James Eastland of Mississippi and John McClellan of Arkansas. McClellan, whose committee suggested the existence of sinister subversive plots behind race riots, asked the FBI in January for information on King's plans for the Poor People's Campaign. The FBI supplied derogatory information not only to him but also to Speaker of the House John McCormack, Senate Majority Leader Mike Mansfield, all of the military and intelligence agencies, President Johnson, and his cabinet members. Ohio Representative John Ashbrook of HUAC insisted that riots had always been part of King's master plan, while Senator Frank Lausche of Ohio passed on to Hoover letters from his constituents complaining about King's "extensive Communist background."

Immune from libel laws, segregationist politicians made outrageous charges against King in the Congressional Record, with no fear of correction or sanction. Although Attorney General Ramsey Clark in January denied the FBI the right to extend its longstanding wiretapping of King, FBI agents kept track of his conversations by tapping the phones of his advisers. Hoover intensified his efforts in March, assembling a major program within the FBI to undermine and discredit King and the Poor People's Campaign.

FBI surveillance and shock attacks from the Right were to be expected, but dissension among his own followers unnerved King. Movement unity had vanished. Few blacks had ever supported nonviolence in principle or as a way of life in the first place, and some in the Black Power movement now said that guerrilla war, modeled on race riots in American cities, provided a more likely means of overthrowing old structures of power. King and integration were obsolete, many said, and even the black press gave him diminishing coverage. A considerable segment of blacks in the middle class worried that King's challenge to take up the struggles of the poor might hinder their own progress, and they looked askance at the impoverished and unlettered masses of migrants streaming from the countryside into the cities. Many blacks rejected King's antiwar stance as unpatriotic, reflecting a long tradition of black participation in war to "prove one's manhood" and gain equal citizenship rights. Others feared that the Poor People's Campaign might set off another round of urban riots within the most heavily armed power in the world.

King persisted in delivering his message, as he traveled during January and February through the District of Columbia, New York City, Alabama, his home state of Georgia, Kansas, Los Angeles, Mexico, and even England. Despite the controversies swirling around him, Coretta said, King was still much like "the President of the Negroes"—in demand and still loved by many. King spoke not as a political candidate, however, but as a prophet in "the heart-changing business," as he put it, whose job was to overcome fear and instill hope as part of a larger liberation movement. In his last book, *Where Do We Go from Here: Chaos or Community?* (published in 1967), King called on black people to form their own enterprises, to engage in protests and boycotts, to fight for jobs through movements such as Jesse Jackson's Operation Breadbasket in Chicago, to organize unions and voter-registration drives, and to become sophisticated, "intensive" activists and educators in order to create "a conscious, alert and informed people."

But actually building grassroots coalitions and persuading the poor to take up his plan for a movement proved extremely difficult. Some 10,000 welfare mothers already belonged to the National Welfare Rights Organization (NWRO), and King's workers began turning to them as organizers in a number of communities. On February 3, King and his lieutenants (Ralph Abernathy, Andrew Young, Bernard LaFayette, and Al Sampson) met with NWRO chairperson Johnnie Tillmon, founder George Wiley, and a total of thirty NWRO leaders at a YMCA in downtown Chicago. The women sharply questioned him about his lack of support for Senator Robert Kennedy's efforts to defeat Republican and Southern Democratic legislation to freeze welfare funds and force recipients to work at below minimum wages. How could King possibly claim to speak for the poor when he did not even know about the various provisions concerning welfare mothers?

In fact, King had previously criticized these measures and had visited Chicago earlier to expose the miserable conditions of welfare recipients to the media. But King and his all-male entourage came from a patriarchal upbringing in which women stayed home with the children while men spoke from the pulpit or led movements for social change, and it may have rankled Mrs. Tillmon. She remarked, "You know, Dr. King, if you don't know about these questions, you should say you don't know, and then we could go on with the meeting." To his credit, King replied, "You're right, Mrs. Tillmon. We don't know anything about welfare. We are here to learn." Young thought King had never been criticized so sharply as in this meeting with the NWRO, but they nonetheless agreed on "basic principles such as jobs, income, justice and democracy and will work closer together," an informant told the FBI. King began to more clearly incorporate welfare issues into his talks.

Women of color made up the great bulk of the working and unemployed poor, but, except for Dorothy Cotton, they had no prominent role in the top leadership of King's campaign. Only a few women—notably, Ella Baker, Septima Clark, and Cotton—had ever played major organizing roles in SCLC, and their marginalization reflected its male and middle-class dominance. Andrew Young freely admitted, "In SCLC we were working with college students, with independent business people. The civil rights movement, up until 1968 anyway, was really a middle-class movement. . . . Cesar Chavez and George Wiley had poor people's movements." Yet, as it turned out, women actually became the backbone of much of the organizing for the Poor People's Campaign at the local level. Geraldine Smith of the NWRO organized for King across Mississippi, while Carol Williams of the Southern Consumer Cooperative set up much of his tour in Alabama, and women made up a great number of those who registered to go to Washington.

On another front, King tried to overcome the split within the black freedom movement between nonviolence and Black Power advocates—highlighted during Meredith's March Against Fear in 1966. On February 7, King went to the District of Columbia to meet with Stokely Carmichael, who had left SNCC to set up a cross-class, militant alliance he called the Black United Front, and Chairman H. Rap Brown and others from SNCC.

Brown and other Black Power advocates showed what they could do in Washington by taking over a church where King and SCLC board members met, displaying walkie-talkies and bodyguards, forcing out the press, and blocking others from coming in. In another meeting, one young black woman angered King by lecturing him for having "sold out" by turning marchers back at the Edmund Pettus Bridge in Selma. King's attempts to make alliances with militant young blacks remained immensely problematic. According to the FBI, former businessman William Rutherford, SCLC's new executive director, later privately condemned Carmichael and his friends as "black fascists." Yet King thought they were essential for gaining support of disaffected young African Americans in the inner cities.

According to wiretaps by U.S. Army Intelligence of a conversation between King, Carmichael, and H. Rap Brown at the Pitts Motor Hotel in Washington on February 7, King tried to convince Black Power advocates to adhere to nonviolence in the coming campaign. "Is killing and burning . . . in your own people's streets your answer?" he asked. Carmichael answered, "It's time. We can't wait anymore, and the people . . . are tired of waiting." King rejoined, "Nobody is as tired as me." Carmichael said, "We got guns. Marching for peace—shit, you seen it. What's it got us?" King secured a pledge that they would not interfere with the campaign when it came to town, although they did not say they would support it, either. According to the *Chicago Defender*, in an article titled, "King, Stokely Join in Capital Camp-In," the "worry here is that the militants may seize the King campaign and take over." Some 7,000 troops were already receiving riot-control training at nearby military bases. Meanwhile, according to FBI wiretaps, King and his advisers worried there could be a "double cross" from Stokely.

Only an hour after meeting with Carmichael, King spoke to a predominantly white and middle-class peace conference of some 400, organized by Clergy and Laity Concerned about Vietnam. King proposed a Selma-style interracial alliance, something Black Power advocates completely opposed. King adviser Stanley Levison also worried that New Left and peace groups made problematic allies; when King had spoken at the National Conference for New Politics in Chicago the previous fall, Black Power advocates nearly hooted him off the stage for adhering to nonviolence and integration.

Everywhere King turned, he met controversy and attack as well as adulation. Speaking to a mass meeting in a black church in Washington, he ruminated on the "dark days" of the present. He asked people to look on black poor people and young people not as criminals or deviants but as "the ones who've been overlooked, and who've been left on the outskirts of hope" but who could be part of a progressive movement. King also saw the times moving in a more repressive direction. He warned a Washington gathering of black businesspeople about "the Wallaces and the Birchers" and his fears that "the sick people and the fascists will be strengthened."

As King tried to mobilize African Americans, one of the questions on the mind of Bayard Rustin remained unanswered: Where are the unions? Most of them wanted little to do with either the Black Power or the peace movement with which King wanted to create alliances. Walter Reuther, King's best-funded union benefactor, had not come out against the war and even had opposed black caucuses—which he saw as divisive—within his own union. Most AFL-CIO unions had opted out of poor people's politics, and King did not articulate a clear role for them in a movement on behalf of the unemployed and underemployed "underclass." The nature of the Negro–labor alliance had become exceedingly murky.

Another contradiction concerned how or whether SCLC could create strong coalitions among poor whites, African Americans, Native Americans, and Mexican Americans. Each of these groups had its own constituencies and issues, as did welfare recipients and women. SCLC had agreed to support a demonstration for welfare women's rights in May, but otherwise King had few answers to these organizing problems. Ella Baker's longstanding criticism—that King and SCLC relied too much on charismatic leaders rather than the rank and file—hit home. King's organizers usually came in to develop local movements already underway, but now they had to create a grassroots movement from scratch. No one knew how to organize the truly desperate poor, who, as King said, struggled merely to exist, and SCLC had only a vague notion of how to create a truly multiracial movement. Lack of unity between racial and ethnic minorities would become evident when the encampment in Washington finally did begin.

KING TRIED DESPERATELY to get the Poor People's Campaign off the ground by making a mid-February speaking tour in the South aimed at recruiting ministers and others willing to lead the campaign on a local level. On February 15, the day that Loeb broke off talks with the workers in Memphis, King met with 600 members of the Alabama Christian Movement for Human Rights at St. Thomas AME Church in Birmingham. He gave a speech that encapsulated many of his arguments for distributive justice and emphasized the limits of the civil rights revolution: It had not eliminated racism, nor had it penetrated "the lower depths of Negro deprivation" across the country.

"Now we are dealing with issues that cannot be solved without the nation spending billions of dollars, and undergoing a radical redistribution of economic power," King said. To understand the depths of the problem, he added, "I only ask people to read history." Slavery and segregation denied blacks a significant land base, while federal and state subsidies shored up businesses and white farmers. "So often in America, we have socialism for the rich, and rugged, free enterprise capitalism for the poor. . . . Nobody has lifted himself by their own bootstraps." Farm and factory mechanization had eliminated low-wage jobs, while laws, taxes, and government policies had mainly benefitted the wealthy and reinforced economic inequalities. The more apt metaphor for blacks was not that of the bootstrap but rather that of a man kept in prison for many years and then released. "And then you just go up to him and say, 'Now you are free.' And don't give him any bus fare to go to town. Don't give him any money to get some clothes to put on his back. Don't give him any money to get on his feet in life again. Every code of jurisprudence would rise up against this. And yet, this is exactly what America did to the black man."

King called on the black middle class to break with their own illusions that because they had succeeded, everyone else could too. "I'm trying to get it over to the Negro 'partial-haves' to join hands with the Negro 'have-nots,'" he said in Birmingham. "You know, we have too many Negroes who have somehow, through some education and a degree of economic security floated or . . . swam out of the back waters" of poverty, but now they had "forgotten the stench of the back waters." Like Dives in the Bible, they "forgot about the poor." Dives did not go to hell because of his wealth; "Dives went to hell because he passed Lazarus every day but he never really saw him." King used the example of Dives as often as the parable of the Good Samaritan to get middle-class people to empathize with the poor. "Every Negro in this country," he said, should take up the cause of the poor:

> We need this Movement. Not only for black people. . . . [W]hen you
> stand in action, and you begin to move together, you don't go arguing
> over whether white people should be in the Movement. That argu-
> ment never should have come up anyway. We don't enlist races in the
> Movement, we enlist consciences. And anybody who wants to be free,
> and make somebody else free, that's what we want. I'm not only con-
> cerned about the black poor. I'm concerned about the white poor. I'm
> concerned about the Puerto Rican poor, the Indian poor. I'm con-

cerned about the Mexican-American poor. We are going to grapple
with the problem of poor people. And we're going to do it in spite of
the philosophical debate, black and white together.

Stopping at Baptist churches in Montgomery and Selma on February
16, King said the freedom movement in these places had infused "a new
sense of dignity and a new sense of destiny," but a new challenge now confronted it. "We have been robbed economically. . . . We need bread to eat,
we need clothes to wear, we need shelter. And that is what our Poor People's Campaign in Washington is all about." But even though hundreds
came out to hear King wherever he went, the lack of a visible organized
base of poor people became increasingly obvious during his tour, as did
King's fatigue and depression. Speaking to his own congregation in Atlanta
on February 18, King reflected the intense pressures upon him, saying that,
like the Good Samaritan, he had to push on despite the fear of death. "You
know the Jericho Road is a dangerous road."

Under immense pressure to create a meaningful movement, King
hoped black preachers could be the spark plugs for a new struggle to end
poverty. Backed by a Ford Foundation grant of $230,000 for ministerial
training, SCLC gathered about 150 ministers from fifteen cities at its Ministers Leadership Training Program in Miami. Its purpose was "to create a
common force of grass roots people to affect [sic] positive change in the
ghetto." A SCLC document circulated at the conference said that "the Black
Preacher and the Black church" had "the greatest potential power" to
rebuild black communities, and warned, "America is at a crossroads of history" and must "choose a new path" or face "chaos, hatred and violence." A
"nation gorged on money" needed to rededicate itself to education, health
care, housing, jobs, and respect for the poor.

Exhausted and ill, King remained secluded throughout the Miami conference. For two nights, police would not let King or the delegates go out of
the hotel because they were so concerned about threats against King's life.
King had stressed his vocal cords so heavily in his touring that he could
hardly speak, but on February 23 he addressed the ministers in a talk
titled, "To Minister to the Valley," telling them that they, rather than he,

would make the choices that could change the nation. He urged ministers to return from the "mountaintop," after five days of inspiring speeches, to the "valleys filled with men and women who know the ache and anguish of poverty." He called on them to follow the example of Jesus, "the greatest revolutionary that history has ever known," a far more potent leader for the poor than Karl Marx. Ministers had the power "to completely change the course of the United States of America"; by mobilizing the poor they could force the nation to pay its "promissory note" of economic justice as well as civil and political freedoms.

King asked the ministers to practice "dangerous altruism" in solidarity with the poor. "The nation needs this," he said. "Christianity is not a euphoria or unalloyed comfort and untroubled ease. What is it? It means taking up the cross. Taking it with all of its tension-packed agony and bearing that cross until it leaves the very marks of Jesus Christ on your body, and on your soul." King demanded community work and political commitment, not just alms or religious salve for the souls of the poor. But FBI reports said most black ministers in Miami remained noncommittal about the Poor People's Campaign.

At a time when the campaign should have been a month away from going to Washington, King said in private, "Our staff has not gotten to the people we are talking about . . . the hard-core poor people." King complained to his staff: "There's no masses in this mass movement." Roger Wilkins, after talking to King during the Miami conference, said that King had "a profoundly weary and wounded spirit," and that "a profound sadness" had come over him. "He was just a different person. He was sad and depressed."

MOBILIZING THE PEOPLE King called "the underclass" in near-starving conditions in the valleys of the Mississippi Delta and the city slums seemed a nearly impossible task. King faced a contradiction of means and ends, trying to build a poor people's movement with essentially middle-class ministers. His doubts grew exponentially. Was the nation listening? Would the black middle class ally with the poor? Would unions help? How could he find people to make his dream of a mass movement for economic justice and peace a reality? He did not know.

In his address to the Miami ministers, he acknowledged, "The bitterness is often greater toward that person who built up the hope, which could say, 'I have a dream,' but couldn't produce the dream because of the failure and the sickness of the nation to respond to the dream." He felt the pressure of that reality every day.

Not incidentally, one of SCLC's target cities for action was Memphis. And, moments after King's speech in Miami, Memphis ministers attending the meeting, Reverend Samuel Kyles and Reverend Benjamin Hooks, talked to friends back home, who told them the Memphis police had just attacked sanitation workers and ministers with mace and billy clubs.

9

BAPTISM BY FIRE

I was reared in Birmingham, Alabama. All of my ministry and work
has been in the South. So I have 30 years of discipline . . . that comes
to a black that has been born in the South and who has made any
type of attainment in the South . . . and I have said all of this
discipline of 30 years was lost in that moment. . . .
—*Reverend Ralph Jackson*

MEMPHIS CITY COUNCIL MEMBER FRED DAVIS ENTERED
into politics from the all-black enclave of Orange Mound,
where he built an insurance company and then created
precinct clubs from groups of policyholders. Growing up, he had picked
cotton in Mississippi and waited tables at the Peabody Hotel, had served
in the Air Force, and later picketed the Memphis fairgrounds and even
had been arrested in order to end segregation in public accommodations.
With thick black-rimmed glasses, a short haircut, and quiet mannerisms,
he did not appear to be a fighter for black rights. In fact, he was not.
Reflecting a district that was 52 percent white (Orange Mound was only
one part of it), Davis entered the City Council in January 1968 as a con-
ciliator. To that end, as chair of the city's Housing, Building, and Public
Works Committee, he scheduled a hearing on Thursday, February 22, at
the newly built, lushly carpeted council chambers, hoping to find a way to
a strike settlement via the council.

The hearing began calmly. Councilman Lewis Donelson allowed that the council did have the authority to pass an ordinance in response to worker grievances. He and the other committee members, Davis and black councilman James Netters, prepared to take questions from union leaders, ministers, and a few strikers. Council members Pryor, Blanchard, James, Chandler, and Awsumb came in and out of the meeting. Among the ministers was King's close ally, James Lawson. Cornelia Crenshaw, who had been distributing food to the strikers, upset the council's decorum by asserting that the city had denied the strikers decent treatment because they were black, as a white council member grumbled, "What has she got to do with it?" Union leaders got up next and spoke to the economic issues.

After listening impatiently, Davis finally said, "Now we would really like to hear from the men themselves. Do any of you want to speak?" Five sanitation workers sat in the audience, and several raised their hands. Jesse Epps did not know the men, and he feared they could have been planted to say that the men wanted to go back to work. T. O. Jones led them out of the room for a conference, and when they returned, Davis once again tried to get them to speak, but now they would not. Epps responded that the men "don't feel comfortable in such plush surroundings," and "they are not equipped to come in here and speak. That's why they want to have some representatives to speak for them and that's the union." Jones later insisted that neither he nor the rank and file had prepared for this encounter with city officials, and he was afraid the workers might confuse the issues or be drawn into making statements they would later regret.

Davis was not satisfied. "We insist on hearing from the men themselves," he interjected. Like many in the black middle class (including some NAACP leaders), he seemed to accept Mayor Loeb's belief that the union simply was using these men to get their dues. Jerry Wurf thought Davis was using a despicable ploy to split the workers from their leaders, and he rebutted his question by saying, "There has been an attempt here today to distinguish between the union and the men. . . . [Y]ou've got to understand that the men are the union and the union is the men."

The union made a tactical mistake by not bringing rank-and-file members and preparing them to speak, but Memphis Labor Council President Tommy Powell, sensing an opportunity, stood up and said, "Okay, if you want the men, we'll get them here for you. They're at the union meeting right now. Give me a few minutes." While Epps and others monopolized the microphone for nearly an hour, striking workers left their daily meeting at the United Rubber Workers union hall and marched downtown. When they filed into the City Council chambers, a mass of boisterous union partisans confronted Davis and his committee. City Council members "thought they had been tricked," said Epps. "They had not been tricked. They had tricked themselves."

As some 700 men and women packed chambers designed to hold 407, the atmosphere in the room changed completely. Davis tried to keep order, repeating, "I will preside," but he could not quiet the crowd. Someone shouted, "You didn't trust us. Here are the men!" Ministers got up so workers could sit down. Reverend Zeke Bell moved to the back but shouted as he went, "You're not going to put us back in the balcony. We're out of the balcony. You've had us there for three hundred years and we're not going back." The sergeant-at-arms asked Davis to clear the aisles to meet fire codes, but the crowd ignored Davis's entreaties to do so. Epps yelled to the men, "Do you want a union?" They shouted back, "Yes!" in unison. "I am up here" to keep order, Davis exclaimed, pounding his gavel. Reverend Lawson interrupted to shout, "You're up there because we put you up there," while someone else yelled, "And we're going to get you down."

For black City Council members, who had been in office only a little more than a month, the scene in the City Council chambers seemed like a nightmare. Suddenly, Netters felt, "I'm on the other side. It was the most weird feeling. I felt sick inside." Davis tried again to appeal to blacks in the crowd by saying, "I have to walk both sides of the street" (representing the city and the black community). Lawson told him, "You can't do it. You're with us or not." And the workers yelled, "You're not with us!" A line had been drawn between black moderates and militants. "A whole part of what the black revolution and confrontation movement represents is that the old form of politics must go," Lawson later recalled. "A black politician must be identified with the people."

Seeing trouble ahead, Councilman Chandler arranged to move the meeting to the city's much-larger Ellis Auditorium, but as workers got up to leave, someone shouted, "We ain't going nowhere. We're staying right here." O. Z. Evers urged people to "stay until Council recognizes the union and recognizes they can overrule the Mayor. If they want to take someone to jail, they can take all of us." Davis sternly intoned, "I do not recognize Mr. Evers," but, one by one, Evers, Jones, Bell, Wurf, and others took the microphone to insist that they would not leave until they got justice. Workers began to sing, "We Shall Not Be Moved." In the newly carpeted City Council chambers, wrote Joan Beifuss, "A combination union meeting, religious revival, picnic and sit-in began"—one that would affront the sense of propriety and ownership over city government by many of the city's whites.

Hemmed in for years by paternalism, passivity, and the city's feigned "good race relations," workers and their supporters threw aside conventions, and a festival of resistance ensued. AFSCME organizer Joe Paisley led workers in singing, "We're waiting for the council, we shall not be moved," and "We're waiting for the mayor, we shall not be moved," as well as hymns and "God Bless America." As 142 police officers and thirty or more squad cars surrounded city hall, Tennessee Council on Human Relations Director Baxton Bryant (from Nashville) suggested lunch, and Reverend Bell called his church to ask them to bring supplies. Wives of strikers cleared the table where the city's lawyers normally sat, as union supporters brought in "a hundred loaves of bread, twenty or thirty pounds of bologna, fifteen pounds of cheese, ham, mustard, and mayonnaise," according to Beifuss. While sanitation workers' wives made sandwiches, ministers preached, and workers sang and shouted out their support for the union. City hall no longer belonged to the rich and white; the rancorous and unorganized voices of workers and their supporters took center stage.

White labor leaders Powell and Wurf met in a side room with several council members, trying to convince them to settle the strike right then and there. Councilman Donelson, conservative but also pragmatic, went upstairs to the mayor's office and told Loeb that Wurf was losing the strike and probably would settle for a small wage increase and a limited form of union recognition. Why not give it to him? If the city did nothing, he warned, racial conflict would intensify. Loeb waved in Donelson's face what he said were 500 letters supporting his stand against settling the strike, and he said his duty was to enforce the law. "Henry, I don't think you were elected to count letters. . . . I do know how the white people feel. But you're Mayor of the other 40 percent too," Donelson responded. Loeb ignored this entreaty. Said Donelson, "After that he didn't consult me very much."

Meanwhile, police proved unwilling to try to dislodge 700 people from the City Council chambers. Their inability to control this demonstration rankled them and fueled plans for revenge. Council members Davis, Netters, and Donelson went back to face the crowd, but they still could not bring it under control. It was like "spontaneous combustion," said Netters. Black ministers gave unscripted speeches connecting union issues to the historic struggle against black oppression, and no one could turn off the oratory. E. H. Arkin, the agent for the Memphis Police Department's Intelligence Bureau, wrote: "The situation became rather tense because of some of the inflammatory speeches being made by Negro leaders" trying to one-up each other with militant rhetoric.

Sharp statements and disorder outraged white council members, as NAACP President Jesse Turner called on people to bring buckets of garbage to the City Council chambers, and others threatened dire consequences if the council did not act. But Reverend Bell won honors for the most "inflammatory" statement, pointing to the city's insignia of Old South steamboats, industry, and cotton balls and its slogan, "City of Good Abode," engraved above the City Council podium. Bell contrasted these idealized images to the city's history of slavery and exploitation, of black women who "nursed white babies for hundreds of years," of slaves sold on a downtown auction block, of black men fighting in Vietnam but denied their rights as citizens at home. He warned that toilets in the City Council chambers could not accommodate the overflowing crowd, and, pointing to the insignia, said, "I'm not going to get up there and tear it down . . . but I wouldn't care if someone else tore it down."

Accounts of his remarks in the next day's papers enraged many whites who thought Bell had threatened to desecrate the new City Council chambers, as if blacks would urinate in the aisles. Councilman Tom Todd said,

"Those people had been talking that 'We're going to burn the city down, tear the council chambers apart, and if you don't give us what we want we're just going to make this place a shambles.'" Bell corrected such reports, but he offered no reassurances: "I said that I would probably burn it down myself if I thought it were worth it, but I don't think it's worth it." Bell played the role of "rhetorical conjurer of dark doom and destruction upon the collective head of white Memphis," according to strike historian Beifuss. He was motivated not by radicalism but by anger at his father's painful experiences with sharecropping and sanitation work, and at the obstacles that racism continued to put in the path of both middle-class and working-class blacks.

Few whites could understand the rhetorical fireworks of Bell and others who later made even stronger statements. Councilman James complained that protesters were rude and always making demands instead of requests: "The worst thing that happened was when the Council decided to hear some of the grievances." Most whites were not open to hearing impassioned statements by blacks, and they fundamentally rejected the idea that injustices in the past placed obligations on them in the present. In this and subsequent protests, the apparent blindness of most whites to black reality pushed Bell and others to become more and more militant in their statements.

Davis recognized that he and his committee had to do something. Behind closed doors, Davis and Netters voted for, and Donelson against, a resolution to recognize the union and give it checkoff rights. At 4:15 PM, they told the assemblage that they would call a special meeting of the full City Council for the next day and bring before it this resolution to "recognize the union as the collective bargaining agent and that there be some form of dues check-off." It took them an hour to convince Jones and others to accept this delay, but at 5:30 PM, Davis promised to forward the resolution to the City Council, and he adjourned the meeting. The audience stood and cheered.

It looked like a great victory. The people's elected representatives would go around Loeb, and government would finally do right by the sanitation workers who had struggled for so many years. The "inflammatory" Reverend Bell stood up and said he was willing to put his faith in the word of "brother Davis," but he also warned the strikers: "When you go home, don't sleep too soundly. We may be calling for you again. I am coming up here tomorrow and I'm bringing my garbage because if the decision is not right, by jingo, I'm not going home."

"COMMITTEE GIVES IN to Sit-in of Strikers, but Loeb Holds Firm," read the *Commercial Appeal* headline on page one. Jerry Fanion, the white Shelby County human relations director, had witnessed the "picnic-in" and worried through the night. Sleepless, he picked up a copy of the *Commercial Appeal* before dawn: "It's the Mayor's Job," read the lead editorial, to fulfill his duties as the city's executive. "He is faced with an illegal strike, is representing the public, and through him the public is being pushed by scarcely veiled threats of 'trouble' for Memphis. Mr. Loeb's stand is that we will maintain law and order and proceed through this situation in a lawful manner, and that is what this community wants." Wednesday's "belligerent show of force" should not "intimidate" or "stampede" the City Council into "imprudent decisions." In effect, the news article and the editorial made the City Council look like weaklings and called on the mayor not to compromise.

Below the editorial, another one decried "Viet Cong Resistance" to the United States in Vietnam; to the right of it, an article headlined, "Vietnam Reds 'Go For Broke' in Test of LBJ," highlighting the need for the country to stand tall against Communist aggression. The juxtaposition illustrated what Jesse Turner said: Whites fought sanitation-worker demands because they feared, much like American policymakers in Vietnam, a "domino" effect of increasing victories for insurgents. The accompanying cartoon by Cal Alley, titled "Beyond the Bounds of Tolerance," suggested that, as in the case of Communist aggression, Americans should resist both unionists and blacks as threats to existing society. Alley depicted a thuggish character astride a garbage can labeled "City Hall Sit-In," amid tipped-over cans and trash strewn about and the reeking odor of garbage. In contrast to the docile simpleton Hambone, Alley sketched a dark, animalistic figure wearing a long coat and slouched hat—part mobster and part bum—that looked much like the racist portrayals of supposedly corrupt black politicians during Reconstruction. In wavy letters over this sinister figure atop the garbage can hung the words "Threat of Anarchy." This inflammatory drawing reverted to a racist image of black men as dangerous, almost bestial, and strike supporters would repeatedly hold up this cartoon as an example of media contempt for the workers, their union, and the black community.

That morning, police reported bomb threats to Loeb's home and office and rumors that black student and military veteran John Burl Smith would lead disturbances at Owen Junior College. The City Council members held a closed session for four hours and rejected the resolution by Davis and his subcommittee that could have resolved the strike. They adopted instead a substitute that reiterated what the mayor had already agreed to: the right to join and be represented by a union, a better promotion procedure, continued hospital and insurance and pension coverage, and wage increases at some unspecified future date. But they rejected a dues checkoff through the credit union and left out any mention of a written contract. The mayor had come into their meeting several times, telling them that council action was not needed because this was an executive matter. To assuage his feelings, the council added a last sentence to its resolution, saying it "recognizes that the mayor has the sole authority to act in behalf of the city as its spokesman."

Meanwhile, some 600 workers met at the Local 186 hall. Wurf waved the morning newspaper with its ugly cartoon and shouted, "The papers are still against us." Jones urged people to march to city hall, but in a peaceful manner. "We don't want to give the police no excuse to arrest us. So if you have been drinking, please don't come down." Powell, too, criticized the newspaper, and reiterated, "We are not coming down there for violence. We are coming in a peaceful manner, but determined." Cornelia Crenshaw said she had received word from Councilman Patterson that the City Council had altered the settlement proposed the day before—a fact that Bill Ross confirmed. He added, "It's about time for this city to realize that we are tired of being kicked around like dogs." Reverend Bell said he had his sleeping bag and would not leave the City Council chambers until their demands were met.

That afternoon, about a thousand people—many of whom had not been at the City Council hearing the previous day—showed up at Ellis Auditorium, as did hundreds of police. Lawson and others who had not been to the noon union meeting had no idea that the proposed resolution to the strike had been altered. He said, "We thought the City Council was going to approve its sub-committee's recommendation that the union be recognized and the dues check-off be given. In other words, we thought we had won," bypassing Loeb to make an agreement with the council.

Strike supporters sat in stunned silence as council members quickly approved a resolution that ignored the strike's major demands and endorsed Loeb as the sole decision-maker in the strike. The three black council members voted no, as did white conservative Tom Todd—but only because he thought the resolution did not give full enough support to the mayor. As workers rose to their feet, shouting in anger, police quickly switched off all microphones and began to escort the council members out. These actions, according to the FBI, "tended to antagonize the audience," and "several inflammatory speeches were made."

While police escorted the council members, Lawson called out, "Get us some mikes! Will you please listen to us? Will you please let us speak to you? Let us talk to our people! Please get us some microphones!" There were no microphones, and the only light in the room came from outside the building. Lawson jumped onto the dais and, in his loudest street voice, urged people to calm down and sit down. "Let's look at it for a few minutes and see what we're going to do next."

Sitting nearly in the dark, Vasco Smith held up the morning paper: "This is what they think of you. You are living in a racist town. They don't give a damn about you!" Everyone booed. He told them, "You'll get only what you're strong enough to take." Lawson, too, criticized the Alley cartoon and the distorted media coverage, as did Wurf. Jones shouted out, "You see what promises are? They have lied to us again. . . . You can see the Councilmen are with the mayor . . . we are ready to go to their damn jail!"

A. W. Willis, Reverend Ralph Jackson, and other respected middle-class leaders of the NAACP were there. Turner again threatened to dump garbage at city hall, and Evers threatened to call in Black Power militants

Stokely Carmichael and H. Rap Brown. "If they want trouble, we will give them trouble!" A Memphis police informant told the FBI that something at that moment crystallized in the psychology of the Movement: "Heretofore, there had been very little racial hatred injected in speeches to strikers, but that in his considered opinion the statements enumerated above tended to incite the workers and have tended to turn the strike into a racial situation." The informant said Jones got up and shouted, "We're going to march in the street this time. We tried to keep this a union issue, but it's now a racial issue. I'm not responsible for what you do."

Led by Jones, the crowd now poured from the auditorium onto the steps of city hall, prepared to march to Clayborn Temple, but police blocked the streets. Everyone milled around in front of city hall. A crew of policemen locked arms and told the crowd it lacked a permit to march. At another intersection, police "walked across the street to the curb and blocked us," striker Ed Gillis recalled. "They said we was pushing. We wasn't pushing. We was just standing there . . . and we was singing . . . wouldn't nobody fight." He found himself at the front of the group, singing, "We Shall Not Be Moved."

Wurf watched with apprehension. Most of the crowd consisted of strikers—"tired, beaten men, making a struggle that before they died they would stand up and be men. They were not bomb throwers." But, "scratching and clawing and humbling themselves" to make a living, they were "tired" of miserable conditions and disrespect. "They were really worked up. And when that kind of guy gets worked up, he's [really] worked up. And I was scared." He decided they should march not to Clayborn Temple but to Mason Temple—a much longer walk, of about three miles, which he hoped would burn off some of their anger.

WURF PLEADED WITH Assistant Police Chief U. T. Bartholomew, who said he had no authority to let them go. U.S. Civil Rights Commission staff member Bobby Doctor ran to tell Jacques Wilmore, the director of the commission's southern field office, located in Memphis, "You'd better come down. I think the police are going to kill a lot of black people." James Lawson reached Frank Holloman by phone and told him that to maintain a disciplined, nonviolent movement, the workers had to vent their anger and frustration in action. David Caywood, the white president of the West Tennessee American Civil Liberties Union, and Jerry Fanion both rushed to the office of Mayor Loeb, who broke the impasse with a call to Holloman, ordering the police to let the people march. Inspector Sam Evans and Assistant Police Chief Bartholomew agreed they could march four abreast on the west side of Main Street so as not to interfere with traffic.

Fifteen minutes before 4 PM, the march began. But "the march could scarcely have been called an orderly march," the police reported. Indeed, few people even knew about the order to march four abreast, and fewer still understood its purpose. Whoever heard of a protest march with more than 600 people marching four abreast? A. W. Willis had told people in the auditorium that the civil rights movement in Nashville had been trying to stop the police from forcing marchers to stay three abreast in the streets, which infringed on the right to protest. In this case, if marchers stayed four abreast, the sheer mass of the crowd would force many to walk on the sidewalk and run into shoppers; if they walked only in half of the street, they could hardly avoid crossing the center line. And to vent the anger of the workers, it made more sense to take over the streets. Jones refused to cooperate and told Inspector Evans that the men would march eight abreast.

Once the march got underway, however, an almost festive mood ensued. Bill Ross picked the polio-challenged Wurf out of the march and drove him to Mason Temple. Civil Rights Commissioner Wilmore sighed with relief and headed back to his office. Lawson tried to create rapport with an officer, telling him that he too should join a union to improve his terrible wages and work conditions. Memphis State University's white Presbyterian chaplain, Dick Moon, and Reverend Bell had an amiable conversation with another officer. "He was a friendly looking fellow," Bell recalled.

Then, about halfway back from the front of the march, police cars suddenly appeared, each packed with five officers openly displaying rifles and billy clubs. They drove their cars into a closed formation, bumper to bumper, and began pushing up against Gillis and other marchers to force them toward the sidewalk and into one lane of the street. Police later complained that the marchers "harassed and cursed" them, had their arms locked, and would not budge. Reverend Lawson turned, stopped, and told the police, "Get that car back and away from us." A veteran of violent police attacks on protesters in Birmingham, Lawson saw where this was going. He told the workers, "Let's keep marching. They're trying to provoke us. Keep going." At that point, the police began what Lawson thought was a deliberate effort "to teach us a lesson."

Gillis said police used their vehicles as weapons, one car in particular. The police "done run that car right up against me twice!" and "his front fender there was just rubbing my side. . . . I didn't say nothing. And finally he rammed up and bumped against me and I still didn't say nothing. And he looked around at me and rolled his eyes. I still didn't say nothing. I just backed up some, away from the car." Then, the vehicle ran over the foot of Gladys Carpenter, a veteran of the 1965 Selma-to-Montgomery march and the 1966 March Against Fear, and a worker for Councilman J. O. Patterson, Jr. She exclaimed, "Oh! He runned over my foot!"

Police claimed that a striker in a green sweater (later identified as John Kearney) led "approximately fifteen unidentified male Negroes" toward the police car, filled with six officers, and that Jones stood in front of the car to stop it and then yelled, "Yeah, tip it over." Wilmore, a sober and veteran observer of marches, saw workers rocking the vehicle but not trying to tip it over. They were trying, he thought, to get the car off Ms. Carpenter's foot and to stop it from pushing against the crowd. This occurred at 3:56 PM, according to the police. At 3:57, a police radio ordered the officers to put on their gas masks, and Bartholomew ordered them to disperse the crowd.

"I was behind her," Gillis said, and the next thing he knew, "The police was out there macing all of us." In a manic fashion, police officers came charging out of cars yelling, "Mace, mace," and holding up little squirt bottles full of what Police Chief J. C. MacDonald called "a new debilitating type chemical aimed to render defenseless those upon whom it is used." It consisted of tear gas mixed with a chemical that broke down protective skin oils, causing skin to peel, damaging nerve endings, and causing excruciating pain. He observed that it "worked most satisfactorily" on this "recalcitrant and obstructive crowd which refused to move." Police shot this burning, blinding, numbing, disorienting, and gooey gel directly into the eyes and noses of their victims, who typically fell to the ground, lost their vision and sense of direction, had difficulty breathing, and began crying copious tears. The military had developed mace for use in war, but police departments now stockpiled it to use against urban rioters. Lawson believed this was the first major use of the new chemical on a civilian population.

As the police charged, the elderly Gillis recoiled in shock: "There was about 15 or 20 police with that mace just gassing us, pushing us over to the wall . . . and there was nobody cussing, nobody fighting. Just walking down the street." As "that gas was flying everywhere . . . I pulled my cap off and tried to keep it out of my eyes—put it over my eyes—and they come around and shoot it up in my nose . . . them polices [was] shooting that mace all in our eyes and faces." Mace burned like fire, and it left skin red, disfigured, and peeling. "It like to put my eyes out," he said; it left "a scab all the way around my head here, all through my hair."

Gillis and others could not run away because the police "had kept us right up against the wall and just started shooting that mace on us." One black officer pulled out a pump shotgun and elevated it so that it could be seen easily, as the police pushed the crowd south toward Beale Street. "They done us awful bad. And then they jabbed me three times in the side with a nightstick. . . . One old man there, 62 years old, they busted his head. . . . I didn't see that, but . . . I seen his head the next day where they busted all his skin off."

The police marked their targets well. Jones said he was near the front of the line of marchers and nowhere near the car-rocking incident, but police quickly located and maced him. The next thing he knew, a police officer had his gun pointed right at him. But this was not his day to die, said Gillis, because workers "snatched T. O. Jones out of the way." According to the FBI, "T. O. Jones escaped."

P. J. Ciampa was not as lucky. He had been marching only a vehicle away from Ms. Carpenter, and he made a perfect target. Ciampa had a bad knee and could not move quickly. He was talking to some of the marchers when three officers said, "That's him." Ciampa recalled, "I looked up at him, and said, 'Just a minute, mister,'" but the officer responded, "Yeah, we'll take care of you." Ciampa described what happened next:

The mace hits me in the face, and I start heading for the curb and I stumble, and grovel, and then I feel awful. I feel this stuff all over me. You can't breathe, you can't see, you know. . . . I was completely disoriented. . . . I was just groveling for something to hold onto. And the earth was the best thing I could find. And some hands started grabbing me, and I thought, "My God! They're going to—this is it! This must be the cops!" . . . I was totally helpless. I thought, "I've had it," you know. . . . I thought they were going to tear me apart.

Black photographer Whittier Sengstacke, Jr., said Ciampa was "just in miserable shape. He was crying, he couldn't walk." Ciampa must have had flashbacks to the way thugs had so brutally beaten his father in the 1930s. But to Ciampa's relief, the hands that grabbed him were not those of the police but rather of sanitation workers, "a few courageous souls that just moved in amongst the mace and everything else, and drug me out of there." The men carried him away, got him to a restroom in a bank, and began washing out his eyes with water. Police had sprayed him repeatedly, he had bruises and abrasions, and the skin began to peel off under his left eye.

From Lawson's perspective at the front of the march, "We are now in the retail business section and the office building section of Main Street when, suddenly, out of these side streets comes squad car after squad car." Four or five officers poured out of each one. "They do not just emerge out of one street . . . it was a maneuver, not accidental." When Lawson turned to a group of police officers and asked them to stop, an officer ran right up to him and sprayed the chemical in his face—not once but twice. His eyes partly protected by glasses, Lawson tried to recover his balance. In true nonviolent style, he turned to face the police a third time. They hit him full force with mace again, so that he could not function at all. Around him, all semblance of order collapsed as police attacked men in dungarees and clerical collars, women, and anyone else in their path. People ran in all directions, screaming and cursing and crying out. Even shoppers coming out of department stores got maced.

Presbyterian chaplain Dick Moon and Zeke Bell had been having what they thought was a friendly conversation with an officer when "he just wheeled and started putting mace all over me," said Bell. The police pushed Moon up against a department-store window along with a crowd of many others, and he feared they would all crash through the plate glass. "There was an old man next to me and I saw a club come right down on him and it broke the skin and blood spurted every which way. . . . An old Negro woman was down on her knees," trapped by the police and the crowds.

Civil Rights Commissioner Wilmore noticed several black officers in the police contingent; one sprayed mace aimlessly and with a look of shame on his face. Wilmore had not yet made it back to his office, and the march had not turned out to be as tranquil as he had expected. In front of Goldsmith's Department Store, he saw police spraying their mace everywhere and watched as officers grabbed a thirty-eight-year-old sanitation striker named John Kearney by his green sweater. The man did not resist:

> And at that point I pulled out my identification badge and I said, "Okay, now you got him in custody, you got him, you don't need to hit him." And at that point they cracked down on his head with a terrible crack. And at that moment I became aware of a policeman coming from the other angle out of the corner of my eye with a mace can. And I turned around towards him and I just did like this in his face [showed his badge] and he just reached . . . around my badge and gave me about two or three squirts squarely in the face. . . . The police officer just saw the color of my skin . . . he just operated automatically, that at that moment the enemy was anybody with a black face.

Black photographers Sengstacke and Edward Harris took photos for the *Tri-State Defender* as the police pushed people from the streets to the sidewalk and methodically maced official observers such as Baxton Bryant and Wilmore. Many officers took off their badges as they attacked and became especially incensed at the black reporters. "Don't take a picture, give me that camera," an officer commanded, as Harris snapped a photo of him with his nightstick raised to strike someone. Credentials "didn't mean anything to policemen," said Harris. "We were the only

Negro newsmen on the scene and we were the only ones that I observed that were sprayed with mace." Up until this point, the *Tri-State Defender* had given the sanitation workers very little coverage, but now Sengstacke and Harris took up a crusade to expose their plight and the police brutality against the black community.

It seemed inexplicable to Lawson that, after having averted a potential riot at city hall, the police would now move on the crowd in such a vicious manner. No doubt, some police had been dying to get at the marchers, and the car-rocking incident simply provided the excuse to do so. He recalled one officer who "in his facial expressions demonstrated just pathological hatred the entire distance" of the march. But Lawson concluded that the police attack was planned, not a spontaneous act—although he thought the decision to attack was made by the officers in the field rather than by Frank Holloman or the mayor. Police records reflected that the orders came from Bartholomew and MacDonald, on the street, when marchers would not stay four abreast.

The "police assault," as Lawson called it, would profoundly influence the course of the strike. "A number of the police officers were very angry, and they took it out on the community wherever they could" from then on, said Lawson. "Police brutality increased in that period. I mean, here we are marching every day and walking every day and resisting every day, and they could not publicly put us in our place as they were used to doing in the police force in Memphis, Tennessee." The police "were so hostile to us, they saw us as the enemy and not violence as the enemy. They could have easily kept public order if they wanted to," as Police Commissioner Claude Armour had done during the early 1960s sit-in movement, said Lawson. "But the reality is that they didn't want to." This attack was only the first act of police retaliation against the Memphis movement.

"I BELIEVE IN dramatizing evil," said Reverend Henry Starks. He had participated in marches as symbolic demonstrations in the past, and he had not been fearful going into the streets on this day, because he believed the older men in the union "don't care for violence at all." The city's young Black Power supporters could cause trouble, but "most of them don't march." Starks walked right behind Ciampa, and he was horrified when the police dragged him away and turned their mace on him.

The events of that day gave him great emotional pain. Having grown up in segregated Memphis, he had experienced all of its humiliations. Police violence had always been pervasive, but the city had avoided the violent civil rights confrontations that had rocked Birmingham, St. Augustine, and Baton Rouge. He hoped for reconciliation between white and black, but now he felt sickened to see the angry expressions and violent actions of the police. He experienced the macing as a form of humiliation, and it frightened and immensely saddened him. He did not want to continue the march, but he put personal feelings of hurt and outrage aside and helped to reorganize the marchers. Said Starks:

> The continuance was born of sheer desperation. . . . You couldn't let the march fail for the symbolism involved. See, you *had* to continue . . . because otherwise it would have been disastrous to the cause. . . . I didn't want to go myself but I had to do it. . . . I was really sick in a way. I was disgusted and broken. Here I had on my clergy garb, too, and here I was hurting on the inside because of what I had seen them do to a lot of my people. And, of course, it was a painful ordeal for me all the way, but we had to do it.

Starks also recognized that repression spawned resistance, galvanizing both the black clergy and the black community as a whole: "I mean this was the cause of the unity that swelled up in the Negro community almost over night . . . when we had our night rally, we could hardly hold the people." The organization of the black ministers "was born, see, born by this episode, this experience."

One of the biggest mistakes the police made that day was to attack the Reverend Ralph Jackson. He came from an old school of southern preachers who had survived the Jim Crow South by working the system of paternalism and creating a niche for himself in the black church. He had participated in the Meredith March Against Fear, but he had largely stayed out of the way of confrontations with whites. Smoking nice cigars, wearing three-piece suits and silk ties, driving a Cadillac, with diamond rings and gold stickpins in his ties and slicked-back hair, Jackson hardly looked like an advocate for sanitation workers. Now he was mad as hell.

First of all, he was infuriated that "you had a bunch of councilmen who acted like cowards and children" and did not listen to the opinions of people like him on that fateful day. Then, he had been "laughing and talking more or less in a picnic fashion" with other marchers, and even exchanging pleasantries with the police, when, to his shock, "I was gassed and maced and that's when I got mad." He recalled:

> I have always prided myself, coming from Birmingham, living in the midst of racism and all, the only encounter I have ever had with a policeman was a ticket . . . all of it lost, because I saw this for what it was. This was done to me for one reason and that's because I was black, no other reason.

By their actions, police baptized him into the world of the working poor and told him just where he stood, in their eyes: at the bottom. Thus began a new relationship among black ministers, workers, and union organizers. With tears streaming from his eyes, as soon as Jackson could see, he left the march and got into his limousine. He found Ciampa stumbling down the street and picked him up. Ciampa recalled that Jackson "was almost speechless. He was so furious he could hardly talk. And I was so kind of whipped that I didn't feel like talking. And I got into his car, and it's spacious. . . . I looked at his spats. What kind of a . . . I begin thinking, 'What is this preacher?'" When they came across the march's stragglers, Ciampa got out of the car and joined them, while Jackson drove on.

Ciampa joined Gillis and others who went on foot down Main Street to Beale Street and east toward Mason Temple. The police attack had scattered the march, and, amid rumors of window breaking and looting, stores closed and shoppers fled. Only about seventy of the thousand or so who began the march remained together. When the bedraggled marchers finally reached Mason Temple, *Tri-State Defender* reporter Harris said, the police had also arrived, now holding four-foot-long billy clubs. They appeared ready to inflict even more mayhem. But instead of fear, their presence elicited outrage.

When Ciampa and others entered Mason Temple, Reverend Jackson was up at the podium, on fire with emotion that no one could ever put out. The FBI speculated that various leaders (all of them men) were now attempting to outdo each other with inflammatory rhetoric. T. O. Jones, almost apoplectic with anger, sputtered, "I feel like we have been assaulted by the police department." O. Z. Evers shouted, "I've been pleading for the last ten days to keep this movement in labor [and] you see what we got. I've been pleading with the hot heads in this town to be cool, you see what we got. If this is what Memphis wants," the Movement should bring in Black Power advocates Stokely Carmichael and H. Rap Brown to "kick 'em in the teeth."

Newsreel footage showed Wurf's mostly deliberate, sober-speaking style giving way to a barely suppressed rage. He pointed out, "Yesterday, this group was behaved, it was peaceful, it sought nothing but the right to speak up, without a sign or semblance of violence." But the City Council members "lied to me and they lied to you. I regret that I believed them." He again referred to the "filthy, rotten" cartoon in the *Commercial Appeal*, accusing the newspaper of setting them up for this attack by its distorted reporting and inflammatory editorials. Tommy Powell was just as angry. After leaving the city hall confrontation, he told a reporter, "I don't know what it's gonna take.... The union has tried to keep it strictly a union matter, but no longer it's a union matter, no longer." The responsibility for whatever violence might ensue now rested on the city and the mayor, he said. FBI reports made it appear that he made this statement at Mason Temple as if to incite a riot.

Jones later summarized the altered situation: "A union has always tried to keep an issue as a union issue ... but where there are as many blacks involved as was there ... it finally becomes a racial issue, let's face it. ... For some reason the civil rights group is going to get in there. And you cannot tell them no. Especially when you're reaching out for support." Events propelled him toward a much more militant stance than he had wanted to take. He had defined the strike primarily as a labor issue, but now his rhetoric sharpened in mass meetings and he began to define it as a civil rights issue, too.

Wurf also concluded that the strike had now taken on added meaning. He had built AFSCME in the 1960s partly on energy created by the civil rights movement. James Farmer, who became the leader of the Congress of Racial Equality (CORE), began as an organizer in Wurf's union, as did others involved in the Freedom Rides into the segregated South. Wurf and his AFSCME colleagues had picketed employers in New York and elsewhere for discrimination. "So with that kind of a background, it wasn't hard for me to sense that I was in the middle of a race conflict and a rights conflict, perhaps that was at least as important as the union conflict."

AT MASON TEMPLE, strikers and their supporters vented intense anger at the police and the white establishment. Many times in the days ahead, protesters would repeat the threat made at this meeting to bring in the ironically misnamed "Black Power boys." When people felt angry, they talked about bringing in Stokely Carmichael or H. Rap Brown, not the pacifist Martin Luther King, Jr.

Gillis said it was fortunate that at this moment black ministers began to play a determining role in the strike. "If the ministers hadn't gotten into it, there would have been a lot of bloodshed. . . . They was just like Martin King. They didn't want no violence."

When Reverend Starks told the last holdouts from the march to go home and resist the temptation to retaliate with violence, they did as he said. The power of hundreds of workers picketing, marching, and meeting provided a discipline and momentum to the Movement that undercut calls for retaliatory violence.

Following their baptism by fire, sanitation workers hardened their decision to stop "taking it"—accepting demeaning treatment and overwork from the white man—and they encapsulated their determination in a slogan that would echo through the history of black labor and freedom struggles. After the macing, four simple words appeared everywhere on their placards: "I Am A Man."

10

MINISTERS AND MANHOOD

"I <u>Am</u> A Man" meant freedom. All we wanted was some
decent working conditions, and a decent salary.
And be treated like men, not like boys.
—*Sanitation worker Taylor Rogers*

I and others had become unaware of conditions in trying to make
it under the system. We had really gotten away from the things that
go on and the conditions under which people live and work, the
types of wages and salaries they received, the types of homes
they live in. All of these things were unfolded to us.
—*Reverend Ralph Jackson*

O N SATURDAY AFTERNOON, FEBRUARY 24, JAMES LAWSON
introduced a crucial defining idea to the larger public. Loeb
"treats the workers as though they are not men, that's a racist
point of view," he told reporters at an afternoon press conference. "For at
the heart of racism is the idea that a man is not a man, that a person is not
a person." As a minister, he defined the key idea of the strike in King's per-
sonalist terms. Lawson told workers: "You are human beings. You are
men. You deserve dignity." The idea, he later explained, "is rooted in the
Negro spirituals. It's rooted in the early slave preachers who told people,
'You're not a slave, you're a man. You're not birthed for slavery. You were
birthed for liberty and truth.' . . . This is classic black reaction to oppression. It's quite historic."

Workers knew exactly what he meant. Since slavery, whites had asserted
control over black lives. In the case of Ed Gillis, white bosses had even
interfered with his mother's ability to raise her own children. Clarence Coe
at the Firestone factory still felt outraged when white men half his age

called him "boy." Black newspaper columnist Nat D. Williams wrote, "From earliest childhood the average Negro has been drilled in the habit of being a Negro. That means subservience, obsequiousness, adjustment to little or nothing, swallowing of insults and mistreatment, low paying jobs . . . a list almost limitless." Reverend Starks said black workers had to adopt "slave mannerisms" merely to get by with white folk. "I <u>Am</u> A Man" rejected all that.

Bill Lucy told workers on February 13, after their first and only meeting with Loeb: "He's treating you like children, and this day is over because you are men and must stand together as men and demand what you want." "I <u>Am</u> A Man" meant self-determination, freedom to choose, the right to organize. Lucy first used the phrase in a strategy session, Epps spoke of it, and strikers took it over wholesale. James Robinson first heard the phrase from a striker, preacher, and singer named Theodore Hibbler. Robert Beasley said workers finally "got the fear out of them in some kind of way," and the slogan helped them to do that.

Strikers decided to use the phrase on the picket line, and Reverend Malcolm Blackburn, the white minister of Clayborn Temple, printed it up on hundreds of placards. Carl Montgomery carried the "I <u>Am</u> A Man" placard every day. "That is the only sign he would wear," said Beasley. "I guess in his mind he was, and [that's how] he wanted to be treated. . . . I guess it did mean something, didn't it? When you are grown you are supposed to be a man."

The phrase had roots on Beale Street, too. Sanitation worker Furry Lewis heard Muddy Waters sing about manhood in his 1955 hit single, "Mannish Boy." Declaring, "I'm a MAN, spelled M-A-N," Waters, himself a refugee from Mississippi plantations, tied manhood to sexual prowess and personal independence. Blueswomen did, too, singing, "I'm a WOMAN, W-O-M-A-N."

Throughout most of American history, and especially for workers and the racially oppressed, exercising one's "manhood" meant standing up for one's rights to freedom and full citizenship. By using the first-person pronoun "I," the sanitation workers constructed themselves as the authors of their own liberation. But this wasn't just about workers in the sanitation division or only about black men, for the strike quickly set off a contagion of insubordination. Hazel McGhee, a laundry worker who was tired of her bosses talking to workers "like you was their child," went on strike around the same time as her sanitation-worker husband did. She cheered him on, saying, "Stand up and be man. If you can be a man, I can be a woman. If you can be strong, I can be strong." Erverlena Yarbrough later used the slogan to encourage men at her factory to "stand up" by organizing a union. A number of black women strike supporters later joined the National Welfare Rights Organization, carrying the idea into the ranks of the unemployed poor.

The slogan resonated beyond the working class and across black Memphis—among the middle class, men and women, young and old. Practically every male spokesman for the black freedom struggle, and many women, had equated "manhood" with standing up for your rights, come what may, either through self-defense or nonviolent methods. For emphasis, workers underscored the verb: "I _Am_ A Man." Everyone got the message. Put in more prosaic terms by striker Robinson, "I _Am_ A Man" simply meant, "We ain't gonna take that shit no more."

Black ministers in particular recognized the significance of this new strike slogan. Jesse Epps recounted, "They said to themselves and to their congregations, 'This is no longer 1,300 men fighting, but it's this whole Negro community fighting. And if we lose we're all lost.' " Police and mace turned a strike into a community movement. "The lord moves in mysterious ways," Epps cracked dryly.

The idea of fighting for manhood rights for black workers and the poor especially seized Reverend Ralph Jackson. He solidly inhabited the black middle class, and white city leaders had praised his efforts at supporting urban development. His wife, Hattie Jackson, was the first black principal of a predominantly white school in Memphis. His African Methodist Episcopal Church (AME) was the first black Christian denomination in America, and it had long provided education and social-uplift programs. Jackson directed its minimum salary program to ensure decent pay for traveling AME preachers.

After police assaulted him, however, Jackson concluded that the black middle class had been living a lie, ignoring the poor and deluded into thinking the white power structure truly accepted them. He quickly turned his outrage into energy and used his preacher's fire to indict the white power structure. He used his knowledge of church organization and administration to raise and account for funds, his mimeograph machine to produce memos, and his church offices as a nerve center for the sanitation strike. Jackson's AME Minimum Salary Building sat on the outskirts of a decaying downtown district that included Beale Street bars, pawnshops, houses of ill repute, the NAACP office, black-owned businesses such as Universal Life Insurance Company and Tri-State Bank, as well as Foote Homes and other housing projects for the poor.

Next door stood the weather-beaten, soot-blackened Clayborn Temple of the AME Church, first built in 1891 as a white Presbyterian church. With its busted-out neon sign on a metal pole, the forlorn-looking yet magnificent temple had a small black congregation and a white minister named Reverend Malcolm Blackburn, a Canadian who had met Jackson through the National Council of Churches. Jackson brought him to Memphis, where he became a journeyman printer as well as a preacher, and the most consistent white supporter of the strike. Blackburn, who lived alone in a black neighborhood, knew few Memphis whites. He picketed and marched, suffered numerous arrests, and printed most of the leaflets. Day after day, people gathered at Blackburn's Clayborn Temple to march fourteen blocks, 1.3 miles, to protest at city hall. Behind Clayborn Temple sat St. Patrick's Church, once a refuge for the Irish but now an outpost for a few black and white social-justice clerics ministering to black Catholics. About fifty black churches radiated out from this core area. They became the organizing center for the Movement.

In Miami, Martin Luther King had called on black preachers "to minister to the valley," and black ministers in this escalating labor dispute did just that. "If there's any man who can speak and who can denounce the power structure, it's the black clergy," said Reverend Starks, "for the simple reason that he doesn't make his living off the power structure. . . . He's lived, in and around the edge of poverty all his days and he knows what an awful thing poverty is when it comes to defacing personality, and distorting human personality. Whenever possible, he gives himself to the eradication of such evils." Said Reverend Blackburn, "It was so obvious why the ministers were involved; because these were our people."

Out of this nexus between workers and ministers emerged "the spirit of Memphis," as Bill Lucy called it. Black ministers knew the importance of winning the strike. Said Wurf, "If these black workers with the power of the black community could win this beef, then the black community had achieved a measure of freedom that did not exist before. That is not merely symbolic!"

AFTER THEIR BAPTISM by fire on Friday, February 23, Jackson, Lawson, Baxton Bryant, Jesse Turner, and others met with Fire and Police Director Frank Holloman. Jackson demanded disciplinary action against the officer who gave the order to unleash mace and those who carried it out. Holloman had been in office only since January, and he relied heavily on his subordinates to make decisions. Lawson gave him the benefit of the doubt, asking Holloman whether or not he knew of his department's long history of brutality and its poor relationship with blacks. Holloman merely responded that mace was better than bullets, and he did nothing to discipline any of the officers. When Claude Armour was police and fire commissioner, he had avoided violent incidents during the civil rights protests in the early 1960s, but Lawson saw little evidence of that restraint now. It appeared that police officers within the ranks had declared open season on black men, and Holloman would do little to stop them. Police repression in the ghettos of Watts, Newark, and Detroit, and in the Chicano barrios in East Los Angeles, had set off riots and heightened racial and ethnic solidarity. Memphis appeared to be going in that direction.

On Saturday, February 24, police placed the blame on marchers for the violence at city hall on Friday. They arrested seven marchers, including a seventy-eight-year-old man, charging them with assault and battery, disorderly conduct, and "night riding"—a charge aimed at Ku Klux Klan vigilantes who rode on horseback to terrorize black communities during the Reconstruction era. Those arrested included Eugene Brown, who had approached a police officer to complain that other officers had hit him on the head and gassed him without cause. Only on his way to jail did police take him to the hospital to have his wounds treated. The police additionally charged John Kearney—whom they had beaten badly during the march—with intent to commit murder, claiming he had drawn a knife.

"Justice" in Memphis was still colored white. Assistant Police Chief U. T. Bartholomew now claimed that T. O. Jones (described by the newspapers once again as the "heavy set Negro") had incited workers to rock the police car. Although Jones had been clearly visible as a speaker at Clayborn Temple after the macing incident, the police claimed they could not find him and that he had "escaped." Ed Redditt had tipped him off that the police were looking for him, and Jones went across the bridge to Arkansas. He did not turn himself in to the police until Saturday morning, when he became the eighth marcher arrested. Police charged him with assault to commit murder, "night riding," and disorderly conduct.

The *Commercial Appeal* that morning blamed Friday's violence on "the incitement" of "an organized group which does not want to talk out problems, but wants to create problems." This nameless group had tried "to turn a labor issue into a racial issue, which this is not," the paper said, and the police should be praised for their "extreme restraint" and "self-control" in "protecting" downtown businesses. "Memphis can take deep pride in the prompt and efficient way its law enforcement officers handled the volatile situation. . . . They had guns, but they didn't shoot." The mayor also praised the police and pledged that he would preserve "law and order." A police internal report later concluded that the police had been "attacked by a large and unruly crowd," that officers had "re-acted cooly [sic] and efficiently, [and] prevented a serious tragedy from occurring."

The city government on Saturday morning did what the newspapers urged, petitioning the chancery court to stop AFSCME leaders from carrying out their duties. City attorneys alleged that union leaders had violated the August 20, 1966, injunction against the union. Chancellor Robert Hoffman, who had made that ruling, now declared, "No principle of law is more firmly established than the principle that public employees do not have the right to strike . . . it is illegal for any person to authorize, induce or engage in a strike against the city of Memphis." As he had in 1966, Hoffman put his injunction in place even before setting a date for a hearing. He named AFSCME national staff—Wurf, Ciampa, Lucy, Epps, and Paisley—as defendants. He also named workers and union officers who had been cited in the 1966 injunction: T. O. Jones, Nelson Jones, J. L. McClain, Joe Warren, Booker T. Bonds, Oscar Middleton, Lent Willis, Alvin Turner, James Jordan, Lee Washington, and Peter Parker. If any of these people should march, picket, or make public speeches, they would be arrested.

This draconian injunction went beyond the question of whether a public-employee strike was legal. The injunction practically voided First Amendment rights to freedom of speech and association. The city's personnel director promptly sent a letter to all sanitation workers saying the injunction applied directly to them as part of the union's "officers, agents and members." City attorneys thought the threat of jail would scare people back to work, as it had in 1966.

The city had now ended negotiations with the union, criminalized the strike, and extended twelve-hour, seven-day-a-week shifts for police, with no days off. It also expanded "internal security" spying operations. All of this created a huge strain on the department's 850 officers, who had to police a city of more than 400,000. Crime rates had increased by 18 percent between 1966 and 1967, but under Loeb's fiscal stringency, patrolmen had fewer resources to fight crime. They earned between $500 and $900 a month—less than many unionized factory workers. To the extent that officers received any training at all in human relations, much of it consisted of conservative ideological indoctrination at the local FBI Academy. Lawson told police they, too, needed a union, and it was true.

The increasing strain on the overwhelmingly white police force, in a city with 200,000 black people, guaranteed escalating racial conflict. State law authorized police to use "all necessary means to effect the arrest" of fleeing or resisting suspects, encouraging officers to rely on pistols and nightsticks rather than quick footwork or less lethal methods.

The degree to which police violence had enflamed black sensibilities became evident as workers gathered at the Local 186 union hall at noon on Saturday. The city had already sent black police officers into union meetings disguised as sanitation workers, infuriating many blacks who remembered how Crump used "snitches" to divide their past movements from within. Taylor Blair of the city's AFL-CIO was at the podium, speaking to 500 angry strikers, when he suddenly heard shouts and cursing from the back of the room as workers discovered Memphis Police Department agent Louis McKay. They took away his gun and his mace and threatened to beat him to a pulp. Gladys Carpenter—the woman who said the police had run over her foot the day before—and Cornelia Crenshaw intervened. The press quoted Crenshaw as saying, "The ladies at the meeting put our bodies between him and the crowd," but she later said the press misquoted her. "I did not shield him, and I felt that he was worse than dirt to come out there."

Blair strode to the back of the room, where workers handed him the man's mace and his gun, which Blair quickly unloaded and stuck in his belt. He dragged the man to the podium, making a great show of force to mollify the angry crowd. "I asked him if he wanted to tell the people what he was there for, and so he mumbled something into the microphone about he was there on instructions." That sounded to the workers like McKay was an agent of Henry Loeb, and people went wild. "I thought . . . we were gonna lose control of the crowd," Blair said, so he grabbed the man "by the back of the belt like they normally handle prisoners" and pulled his arm up behind his back. Blair, Gladys Carpenter, and a black minister hustled the hapless informant out of the building and handed him over to white police officers, saying they had made a citizens' arrest. Black plainclothesman Ed Redditt stood by, partly amused at the police department's bungling. They took McKay away but never prosecuted him for anything.

THE CITY'S WHITE leaders proved themselves too clever by half. Instead of frightening people away, they had galvanized a broader movement in support of the strikers. The black community, Reverend Jackson said, would not be trampled by "some slap happy policeman." The city's severe injunction also opened a leadership vacuum that forced black ministers to take a more active role. If AFSCME leaders went along with the injunction and ceased being leaders, or if they violated it and went to jail, the strike's organization could collapse. But though the injunction could stop union-ists, it did not apply to ministers, who remained free to instigate secondary boycotts, give speeches, and organize picket lines.

Dan Powell, the AFL-CIO's white southern political director, said the injunction created the one situation that could defeat the city: It took the strike out of the realm of collective bargaining and placed it in the context of a communitywide freedom struggle led by black ministers. Mayor Loeb thereby ushered in one of the last unified mass movements of the civil rights era.

The ministers responded almost instantaneously. Only hours after the macing, Cornelia Crenshaw and community activist Alma Morris came up with a list of all the black ministers in town and gave it to AFSCME orga-nizer Epps. He sent out 200 to 300 telegrams calling them to a citywide meeting. On Saturday, February 24, in an unprecedented show of unity, at least half of the city's black ministers—some 150 of them—convened at Mason Temple. In the basement of the church, black ministers of all denominations put aside their usual turf and ego wars to form a support group they called Community on the Move for Equality (COME). They took their name from Lawson's favorite biblical injunction (also Rabbi Wax's): "Come, let us reason together."

The meeting included both longtime civil rights advocates like Rev-erend Roy Love and relative newcomers like Bell and Lawson. Ministers from huge churches, like Bishop J. O. Patterson, Sr., of the Church of God in Christ, as well as ones from many small storefront churches, showed up. This gathering pulled together what King said in Miami was the most powerful potential organizing force available to black America. Picking up on the NAACP's proposal at the start of the strike, they called for an eco-nomic boycott of downtown merchants. They urged ministers to speak about the strike in their pulpits and take up goodwill offerings to support it. They called on ministers to open their churches for mass meetings and to encourage all church members to join marches to the downtown, to walk picket lines, and to turn out for mass meetings.

That afternoon, Lawson, Starks, Bishop Patterson, and Bishop B. Julian Smith held a press conference announcing that 100 ministers had formed the new organization. The ministers both broadened the strike's agenda and sharpened its tactics. They demanded not only justice for the sanitation workers but also more jobs for blacks in government and the private sector, including white-collar and professional jobs long denied to blacks. COME later defined this as pursuit of "racial balance in all kinds of jobs, public and private." To highlight their economic boycott, the ministers projected a slogan, "No new clothes for Easter." Bishop Patterson respectfully requested the press to notice that the organization of black ministers proved that outsiders were not running the show. He said they would adhere strictly to nonviolent methods.

At 6 PM, some 600 people assembled upstairs at Mason Temple, sounding themes that would echo throughout the next weeks: "Buy no new clothes for Easter," "Keep your money in your pocket," "Boycott!" Speakers focused on the humiliation of the macing, the plight of the workers, the importance of united action. People donated food for the strikers, signed up to join picket lines, and pledged to leave their garbage in the streets. Tarlese Matthews led people who joined hands and rocked back and forth, singing, "We Shall Overcome," "Leaning on the Everlasting Arm," "Ain't Gonna Let Nobody Turn Me Around," and other church-based anthems and civil rights songs. Matthews came up to officers Willie Richmond and Ed Redditt, attending the meeting in plain clothes, and warned them that Stokely Carmichael was on the way, while Lawson called from the podium to expel members of the two commercial newspapers and any police informers. Richmond and Redditt left of their own accord.

With little instruction or supervision, people passed around fifty-gallon garbage cans to take up donations, and no one worried about someone stealing the proceeds. They passed the pail many times in the weeks to come. "The people did it themselves, you know. It was just really a beautiful expression of common purpose and unity," said Lawson. This and other mass meetings evoked the power of community unity that fired up countless civil rights struggles.

Lawson left to attend to several hospitalized members of his church, and the mass meeting went on into the night. In his absence, a self-selected core of strike supporters discussed leadership issues. NAACP President

Jesse Turner might have been a logical choice to the lead the Community on the Move for Equality (COME), although that would have made the new organization almost a creature of the NAACP. Turner declined nomination because, as a tax accountant in the middle of tax season, he was too busy. Lawson had more experience with the nuts and bolts of building a mass protest movement than anyone in Memphis, and COME was primarily a ministers' organization, so he was the logical choice. Later that night, Harold Middlebrook reached him at home and told him the new organization wanted Lawson to chair the group. Lawson agreed, with the proviso that it include SNCC activist Charles Cabbage.

On Sunday, February 25, nearly every African American congregation in the city had something to say, sing, or shout about the strike. AFSCME workers went into churches and spoke or asked their ministers to speak about the strike. Sanitation worker Nelson Jones had told Bishop Patterson about the strike before it even happened, and Patterson and other ministers broadcast live on WDIA, WLOK, and a small religious station, KWAM. Black ministers spread the word far and wide over the airwaves. A whirlwind of preaching and teaching rolled through black churches, and people were urged to come to Monday events.

Sunday's church meetings were very practical. Ministers urged their congregations to support the "blueprint for action" adopted the previous day: to form action and telephone committees; to promote a boycott of the two mass-circulation commercial newspapers as well as Loeb's Laundry and Bar-B-Q and Pryor Oldsmobile; to picket and boycott downtown stores; to march; and to attend mass meetings. The blueprint also charged black ministers with talking to white ministers to "set them straight," and to preach "soul force" to whites.

Churches took up offerings for the strikers. In weeks to come, evening mass meetings rotated among various denominations and neighborhoods. Mass meetings gave the movement its own means of communication—keeping people informed about what to do next, the status of negotiations with the city, where to go and when to meet. They provided a forum for discussing a strategy for action, for connecting generations, for spiritual awakenings. "We wanted people to hold together," said Lawson. Preachers "tried to give the movement a rationale and make it a personal commitment" for each person. They also connected "Christian theology and biblical theology and biblical stories to the struggle, so that people have something to work on intellectually and spiritually themselves."

Mass meetings included inspiring music and prayers; most important, both unionists and ministers called upon individuals "to consecrate themselves to it, to be committed to it, and committed to the struggle," in Lawson's words. This was "the psychological arena for people, because we don't deny death or deny pain, we don't deny the struggle [in] the world in which we live, we . . . help provide folk with ways of understanding it and then dealing with it . . . in a constructive fashion." The black church provided "a way of therapy, an analysis of thought" that could keep mass movements energized and strong.

Black ministers, almost all of them men, often operated in a hierarchical and sometimes selfish manner, but at their best they voiced a people's aspirations. King excelled at this, and mass meetings in the black church during the King era often transformed the individual's sense of self and the group's sense of power. The black church was the Movement's secret weapon: whites could not fully control what went on there, in a space where black people could join a mass movement, overcome internalized oppression, and liberate themselves from deference, self-deception, and self-denial.

Memphis in many ways replicated the church-based freedom movement seen in Montgomery and elsewhere, but with an added element: the zone of freedom went beyond the church to the union hall. Black workers had their own "jackleg" preachers in the ranks, as well as ministers who came to their noon union-hall meetings, which took on the air of a revival. Catholic priest William Greenspun observed,

> Firestone hall should have been on film. You'll not see it anywhere else in the world. It was . . . worth coming to Memphis for. Here were a thousand workers and a minister who'd stand up and begin a liturgy in which the secular and existential were so united with Scripture and hymns you felt you were on a mountainside listening to Moses or with the Israelites marching around Jericho's walls waiting

for them to crumble. . . . there is this reawakening sense of personhood. The most phenomenal movement in the world is the passion
for personhood. You find it in the church, in teenagers, in Negroes, in
the poor, worldwide.

Ministers, congregants, union leaders and workers began to build a
movement aligning the poor and the middle class very much in the way
that King had in mind for the Poor People's Campaign. The *Tri-State
Defender* noted the new convergence in its headline: "Negro Community,
Labor, Ministers Back Sanitation Workers." A few weeks later, the *Commercial Appeal* recognized what had happened with a headline, "Negro Pastors
Take Reins as Garbage Strike Leaders in Switch to Racial Pitch."

On Sunday, when the NAACP board met, ministers asked the organization to escalate strike support. Board members unanimously voted to do
so. Vasco Smith, president of the Shelby County Democratic Club, also
spoke to his members that day, urging them to show city officials that "for
one time we're going to stick together—and in the end we're going to get
just what we want."

THE DOMINANT WHITE opinion backed the mayor and the police. One
letter to the editor on Sunday morning claimed, "Lawbreakers are being
led by professional union organizers, a dangerous combination that
deserves no sympathy." Another blamed "outsiders sent in here to stir up
trouble in order to enlarge their union kingdom and enrich their pocket-
books," derided Ciampa for his "bullying and profanity," and praised the
mayor for standing up to him and union "goons."

One group of white businessmen, however, met late into the night on
Sunday with four members of the City Council and with U.S. Civil Rights
Commission staff members to find a way for the mayor to "save face" and
end the strike. They got nowhere. On Monday, February 26, the president
of the Memphis Chamber of Commerce, Thomas Faires, and the Memphis
chapter of the National Alliance of Businessmen held a press conference
urging employers to hire more African Americans, but they pleaded that it
was up to the U.S. government, not business, to lower the massive unem-

ployment that plagued black Memphis. This ineffectual appeal did nothing to resolve the strike.

At 11 AM on Monday, Lawson, Jackson, and Baxton Bryant led about 130 sanitation workers and their supporters from Clayborn Temple at 280 South Hernando. They went west on Beale to Main Street and then north to city hall at Main and Adams. Police officers—tense and primed for another confrontation—lined the march, while police helicopters droned ominously overhead. Lawson had advised the police of all of the group's plans, and marchers accepted severe police limits that forced them to walk on the sidewalk in single file, each marcher separated from the next by two car lengths. They went downtown without incident and then retraced their route back to the temple.

This adherence to strict police rules convinced Frank Holloman to pull some of the uniformed police back into less-visible positions in order to avoid provocations. No one seemed to want a repeat of the previous week's confrontation. Another 122 people marched again that afternoon, carrying signs that read, "Stay Away, No Shopping Today," "Keep Your Money in Your Pockets," "Jim Crow Must Go," "Decency and Dignity for Sanitation Workers," "King Henry, We Will Not Turn Back." Young black women chanted, danced, and sang freedom songs, while picketers handed out flyers asking shoppers to boycott downtown stores. The police left the exuberant protesters alone and only arrested an older white man from River Rouge, Michigan—possibly a member of the United Auto Workers' militant Local 600. Police accused him of using profanity as he jeered the Loeb administration.

The movement under Lawson's leadership thus began a strenuous regime that continued for the rest of the strike: two marches a day—the first following a morning mobilization at Clayborn Temple and the second following an afternoon mass meeting of union members at the Firestone union hall, with a mass meeting held at a different church each night.

On this first day of downtown picketing, the *Commercial Appeal* ran its only major story that let sanitation workers speak for themselves. Willy White, age forty-four, told a reporter he was determined to win union dues checkoff and bargaining rights despite the temporary hardships. Out of work and out of money, he and his family were staying with his sister. "It's crowded all right, with my wife and 11 kids and me," but "union dues have to come out because, man, you got to pay for somebody to protect you and represent you." Charles Justice, fifty-nine, said, "I've been with the city 14 years and this is the first time we really stood up for what we wanted." Oliver Jones (not T. O.), forty-one, said, "I want a written contract between the union and the city," adding that Loeb's proposed 8-cent-an-hour wage increase was unfair. James Randall declared, "I'm going to stick with it 'til the end. We need this union. . . . You think it's cold today, hell it don't bother none of us. We work in any weather." Said Leon Hill, thirty-seven, "I got a wife and four kids and you know what I've been making . . . $1.65 an hour. How you gonna live with a wife and four kids on that."

Interviewed workers gave the lie to their image as docile men being led by outsiders. Unbelievably, a layout artist juxtaposed this article featuring worker voices with a *Hambone's Meditations* cartoon. It depicted an Uncle Tom sort of character in an apron with a feather duster in his hand, mouthing a simpleton's platitudes. Blacks indignantly viewed this image of emasculation as reason enough to boycott the newspaper. As Reverend Jackson said at a mass meeting, "Anybody who buys an insult to himself is a fool. Let it be known that we are not fools! Maybe they don't know it, but all the Hambones are dead." And yet, under the title "A Negro's Reaction," an unnamed black letter writer said he had lost confidence in his minister and the NAACP, adding: "The strikers are, as is often the case with people with limited educational backgrounds, incapable of thinking for themselves and therefore are easily persuaded by glib persons like Lawson." He blamed blacks for not wanting to work or get an education.

Commercial Appeal political editor William Street undercut reader sympathy for the strike by explaining that black leaders supported it merely to jockey for power—a theme constantly exaggerated by the media and the FBI. It seemed the strike was never about the issues black workers said it was. "When does a labor problem become the politics of race?" Street answered, "When there is money to be raised and power to be gained by expanding a local labor situation into a civil rights demonstration." He never explained what "power" came out of the self-sacrifice such a movement required.

Only one outraged voice of white strike support made it into the *Commercial Appeal*. Reverend C. O. Basinger, a minister from suburban East Memphis, blasted the newspaper:

> The one thing your scabbing, strike-breaking prone newspaper has never come to grips with is the fact that union leaders were called in after local members of the union, unrecognized by the city, walked off the job. Your newspaper should be sued by the union for suggesting that Memphis was a planned target city for this knockout blow by the union. . . . You have repeatedly attempted to induce public opinion through the falsification of facts, through slanting, by innuendo, and every other technique. May the Scripps-Howard reap in the whirlwind by having the Justice Department break up your lousy syndicate controlling public opinion in Memphis. . . . Start looking at the garbage worker as a human for a change.

The Memphis Police Department immediately put Basinger's letter and his name into their files for investigation. They were alarmed by a report in which the FBI reviewed Lawson's leading role in 1960 in helping to found SNCC, which it called a dangerous revolutionary organization; his participation in a peace mission to Hanoi on behalf of Dr. King in 1965; and his Memphis picket lines opposing the Vietnam War. The FBI's "Source one" advised that Lawson had plans to go to Czechoslovakia, "a Communist country," to attend a Christian peace conference; other informants said Lawson was trying to bring the dreaded Stokely Carmichael to Memphis. The FBI also cited an informant's version of an interview Lawson gave to reporter Clark Porteous on WHBQ-TV in May 1967, in which he supposedly said, "The Communist program had many good points and much to offer the United States." The FBI did not bother to get a transcript of the program. It simply repeated this unverified information whenever Lawson's name came up, and it continued to do so in subsequent reports, as if Lawson supported Communism.

FBI agents routinely accepted such falsifications, which came routinely from the notoriously inaccurate House Un-American Activities Committee (HUAC), and then repeated them as if they were known facts. Lawson made a point not to associate with known Communists, but intelligence officials seemed to have no more comprehension of Lawson's politics than they did of King's. They never discussed the men's Christian framework or their rejection of violence and simply regarded as a threat anyone who organized for change. They did not appreciate that Lawson, as an experienced nonviolent strategist and leader, might provide a stabilizing force in the Memphis movement.

POLICE AND FBI agents became even more alarmed about Lawson when he asked Charles Cabbage in a phone call on Sunday to join the strategy committee for the Community on the Move for Equality. Cabbage had responded to Lawson's request with a lengthy analysis, saying that black people in Memphis had been waiting much too long for a bottom-up movement to fight poverty, and that the strike raised larger issues about "the generally archaic, outmoded conditions of living that black people are forced to live under." He and Lawson did not disagree on any of this, so Cabbage agreed to serve on the committee.

The strategy committee membership kept changing, but it initially consisted largely of ministers and people from their mid-twenties and up, including Reverends P. L. Rowe, Starks, Bell, Jackson, Turner, and Middlebrook, and community spark plugs Cornelia Crenshaw and Tarlese Matthews. Lawson felt fortunate to be able to involve someone who could draw black youth into the Memphis movement. "Cab," as his friend Calvin Taylor said, lived "down in the hole," among the urban poor in the South Memphis slums. Lawson and the ministers probably agreed with Cabbage's goals, as he explained them: "We want what people generally refer to as Black Power, or just black liberation for black people. Black people need to control . . . the economics, the politics, the social life as well as the cultural life of their community." But how to get Black Power was another matter. Cab conceded that nonviolence could organize mass movements but felt that white elites only responded to it when they feared worse alternatives—namely, organized counterviolence from the black community.

When the strategy committee met on Monday morning, Cabbage began his ambiguous and contentious relationship with the ministers of COME by arriving at the meeting more than an hour late.

"I WAS CLASS CLOWN" at Carver High School, Cab recalled. Such reputation as he had as a teenager he created on the basketball court. As a high school student, he was not involved in the civil rights movement, and he had no interest in education or religious studies. In his view, schools had failure built into them, operating like "meat markets"—or perhaps packing houses—trying to put through many children as quickly as possible while cramming a little knowledge into their heads.

Cabbage came from that part of the population that King called "the working poor." His father, Irvin, shuffled from one job to the next for miserable wages, too preoccupied with survival to communicate much with his family, while his mother, Jessie, struggled to keep eight children alive. Later, during the sanitation strike, Cab didn't need to boycott the downtown stores—he and his family had never had enough money to shop there. Born in 1945, Charles spent much of his young life with his grandparents, who had built a well-crafted home in an area called Arcadia Hills in South Memphis. This was his one secure place in the world.

One of his black high school teachers got Cabbage interested in going to Owen Junior College, a tiny, underfunded black school run by Baptists. There he met other black teachers who interested him in ideas and in going to Morehouse College, part of Atlanta University and considered a Mecca for black men in higher education. Certainly it was a big step up from Memphis's historically black LeMoyne College, Cab's other alternative. Founded by the American Missionary Association after the Civil War, LeMoyne had a conservative leadership and less intellectual vitality than Morehouse. In the 1950s, the white chairman of LeMoyne's board of regents had been an open segregationist. Its black president in the 1960s, Dr. Hollis Price, tried to maintain a quiet atmosphere among students even as he tried carefully to improve the racial atmosphere in Memphis.

Morehouse and Atlanta University gave Cabbage a different perspective. Here, too, trustees beholden to white benefactors tried to keep students quiet. But at Spelman, the university's flagship women's college, where Maxine Smith had gone, and at Morehouse, the men's college, students imbibed black politics and history and dreamed big dreams. Morehouse President Benjamin Mays cultivated young black leaders like Martin Luther King, and many of the college's students plunged into activism. Cabbage studied history, sociology, and political science, and in Atlanta he met white activists from the American Friends Service Committee (AFSC) and black activists from SNCC—all united by their common opposition to the Vietnam War. SNCC said the war revealed all the iniquities facing Black America's young men: poverty and unemployment mixed with death and destruction. SNCC's Julian Bond, also a "Morehouse man," was elected to the Georgia legislature, but whites denied him a seat because of his opposition to the draft and the war.

Cabbage found his calling in draft resistance. He would later be indicted for refusing induction. His opposition to the war and what he termed American imperialism came out of his own class roots. Speaking of President Lyndon Johnson, he said, "If he wants to win it, let him go on ahead and fight it. He can keep on sending his son-in-laws over there . . . but don't send me, don't send me 'cause I ain't even got no job, Jack. So I really ain't got no stake." Cabbage also became engrossed in reading revolutionary texts, some of them Marxist, some of them Leninist, and others based on the experiences of colonized people. He took special interest in Frantz Fanon's *The Wretched of the Earth*, which argued that colonized people had to "experience themselves as men" and liberate themselves from dependency by turning violence against their oppressors.

In Atlanta, Cabbage met Cleveland Sellers, Stokely Carmichael, Willie Ricks, Ralph Featherstone, and young black women in SNCC whose boldness charmed and excited him. That included Edwina Harrell, the daughter of a Memphis Firestone worker. "My political process accelerated," he said. Cabbage also felt strengthened by radical white students in Madison, Wisconsin, where he went to speak against the war. In April 1967, he also attended a huge antiwar rally, predominantly white, with King as the main speaker, in New York City. There was talk of SCLC or SNCC sending him to Baltimore as an organizer. But Cabbage disagreed with the idea of organizing mainly among students, since they were but a small and unrepresentative portion of the black community; he thought it would be stupid to go to another community where he did not know the people. He wanted to go back to Memphis.

Around this time, he met Coby Smith, who had arrived in Atlanta from Memphis looking for SNCC activists. Cab posed questions to him. Where would the new American revolutionaries come from? The black middle class? The black working class, like Smith's or Cabbage's fathers? No, people in these social classes were tied down, controlled by the system. Revolution comes from the dispossessed. Like "the wretched of the earth" in Algeria, the unemployed and marginalized of the ghettos could rise up from below, shaking all the structures of power in America, even the imperialist war machine. Marginalized people had already done it in Watts, and conscripts from the ghetto were even rebelling in Vietnam. Angry and dispossessed black people—young men especially—only needed guidance from a well-informed revolutionary leadership.

Such a movement could not pledge itself to nonviolence. Black poor people regularly fought each other and the police, and they suffered daily from the violence of poverty and unemployment. Fanon said you could turn the internalized violence of the oppressed against the system. Malcolm X urged building a new base of power; Fidel Castro, Mao Tse-tung, and Ho Chi Minh had successfully organized oppressed peasants, intellectuals, workers, and the dispossessed. Why couldn't black revolutionaries do the same? Coalition-building with integrated organizations such as unions had little appeal. Poor people needed to build confidence by creating their own organizations.

Cabbage and Smith drew up the outlines for an umbrella organization for young black militants they called the Black Organizing Project (BOP). Its agenda did not include organizing the working class per se. BOP wanted to do "grassroots organizing" among young black men living in housing projects and slums, playing in pool halls and hanging out on street corners, students in college and high school, inmates in jails and prisons. "This was our approach to the black united front," said Smith. "We wanted to organize blacks everywhere we were. We knew the places we were most predominant were in churches and the jails." Vietnam War veterans could provide the most volatile recruits.

The two young men returned to Memphis in the summer of 1967 and started BOP. Without membership cards or lists that might reveal identities, their work was highly local in its orientation and amorphous in terms of its goals. Cab believed in a tightly organized vanguard of leaders to set forth tactics and strategy, but black youth in Memphis had little experience with full-blown rebellion, and they lacked the dense urban culture of places such as Oakland, California, where the Black Panther Party for Self Defense began. They had plenty of anger, however. Mired in the crisis of the black working class, society offered them no training and little future beyond low-wage jobs and living in slums. Young black people questioned the value of civil rights achievements in a city where race relations remained in a kind of time warp and so many blacks remained trapped at the bottom.

They could not have gotten started, however, without James Lawson. Professor Vincent Harding, one of King's associates at SCLC in Atlanta, put Cabbage in touch with Lawson; he and his neighbor A. W. Willis, met with Cabbage at Lawson's house. According to Lawson, the young SNCC activist told the two Movement veterans that he did not believe in nonviolence and would "steal, cheat and lie" if necessary to bring about change; it was apparently his version of "by any means necessary." Lawson viewed such talk as a kind of "nihilistic romanticism" but thought he would grow out of it. As chairman of the War on Poverty program's Memphis Area Project South (MAP South), Lawson hired Cabbage (age twenty-three) and Coby Smith (age twenty-one) and paid each $20 a week to reach out to disenfranchised young people in what MAP South called the Neighborhood Organizing Project.

The government had charged antipoverty agencies with creating maximum feasible participation of the poor, and the young organizers intended to fulfill this mandate. But as soon as they did, white political and business leaders—who wanted antipoverty programs to co-opt, not accelerate, movements for change—attacked the program. To complicate matters, racial conflicts broke out in a number of cities, and on the hot weekend of

June 23, Memphis Police Commissioner Claude Armour declared a five-day alert. Police tactical units kept the city under surveillance as whites and blacks armed themselves for trouble. Several incidents in which white police beat and shot black youth in Memphis put black community relations with the police on a hair trigger. Then massive urban rebellions broke out in July in Newark and Detroit. In one incident that easily could have led to a shoot-out, five carloads of white officers surrounded John Burl Smith—a twenty-four-year-old black military veteran, part-time college student, and Army Depot worker—after he had a verbal dispute with a white gas-station attendant. They also arrested his passenger, Charles Cabbage. The young men's crime, in Lawson's words, was that they "talked straight" to police rather than cowering in fear.

Congressman Dan Kuykendall demanded that Cabbage and Coby Smith be rooted out of the antipoverty program after rumors associated them with SNCC, which various agencies of the U.S. government listed as a "subversive" organization. Mississippi Senator James Eastland followed up with an investigation into the antipoverty program in Memphis, and he attacked one in Mississippi as well. Lawson defended the young organizers, saying the FBI had checked and they had no subversive associations. MAP South held a public hearing in Lawson's church, and white attorney Lucius Burch did a brilliant job of defending their right to organize. Cabbage spoke eloquently of the dire conditions of the black poor. He told a reporter, "Just look at these people, the shacks they have to live in . . . the bitter, angry young men. Sure they're angry. They can't find jobs. They can't earn a decent living. Riots? Riots are started by just this sort of mess. These people feel that their backs are up to the wall. What does it mean when his back is up to a wall? He fights back." But in his testimony, Cabbage frankly said he had been organizing poor people for rent strikes, something MAP South Director Washington Butler could not justify. He fired both Cabbage and Coby Smith.

Cabbage's eloquence drew more attention. The police began "still watches" against him and his associates, parking their cars outside their homes and using binoculars and wiretapping to track their activities. "If you said 'Black Power,' you were an immediate threat. And we were saying it," said Smith. In response to summer riots, President Johnson also expanded domestic spying—not only by the FBI but also by the U.S. Army's Military Intelligence Division (MID)—to alert the White House to possible civil disturbances. The Memphis FBI had used surveillance on labor radicals and black activists since at least the 1930s. When former FBI official Frank Holloman took over the Memphis Police Department in 1968, he immediately set up a stronger domestic intelligence unit, using some of the MPD's approximately 100 black officers as plainclothesmen to target black youth. Police officers also obtained student records from Memphis State University administrators and private bank and phone records of Movement leaders such as Lawson. The FBI nationally had also escalated its COINTELPRO surveillance operation against so-called Black Nationalist hate groups, including SCLC and its pacifist leader, Martin Luther King, Jr. The military, the police, and the FBI targeted anyone speaking strongly for black rights or against the war.

Coby Smith and Cabbage, both unemployed, cast about for a new direction to build Black Power. They found it in the fall mayoral bid of black candidate A. W. Willis, who hired them as campaign workers but then publicly rejected the Black Power slogan. Incumbent Mayor William Ingram put out a rumor that Willis had been paid off by Henry Loeb to divide black voters, most of whom voted for Ingram. White voters unified behind Loeb, and Lawson, running for the school board, was the only black candidate to receive a significant number of white votes. Cabbage and Smith, discouraged by the lack of black unity, turned back to the Black Organizing Project, aided by black MSU student Calvin Taylor.

Cabbage stopped giving interviews to the media, and he tried to carry on his work below the radar screen of the authorities, with no money or credible employment. He worked with Black Power activists at MSU and LeMoyne College, and activists cemented their bonds with a specialized, interlocking handshake. Not many people could cross the line from higher education into the ranks of the lumpen proletariat, but Cabbage had the charisma of the street, an engaging manner, and an athletic bearing—and he could talk for hours. Cut loose from a job, with no funds, and isolated from mainstream black politics, Cab smoked marijuana, took hallucinogens, and identified with the black youth subculture to the point that he nearly disappeared into South Memphis. Listening to music by Richie Havens and Jimi Hendrix and "rapping" at all hours in juke joints or people's homes, he created a mostly male youth cadre, teaching them revolutionary politics in the language of the ghetto. He moved about and stayed in different houses, calling people from phone booths to avoid police wiretaps.

Despite their revolutionary image, according to Coby Smith, "Most of us were very religious young people, as most of the people in the Movement were. Even on Beale Street. We'd go to places and we could always relate to people based on some central ideas that were pragmatic truths. They understood. They wanted to protect their families and themselves. It was so easy to organize. All we had to do was talk to somebody." Cabbage in South Memphis and Smith in North Memphis organized small groups under names such as the Memphis Mobilizers. Cabbage recruited Lance Watson (know as Sweet Willie Wine)—a "natural leader," in Cabbage's words—who came straight out of prison into street organizing. (Wine and Cab had been friends as adolescents.) Cabbage thought that perhaps as many as 2,000 black youth had some connection to his network by the spring of 1968. No one could know if this was true or a gross exaggeration: Calvin Taylor estimated that Cab had about fifty people in his South Memphis network, but Coby Smith had only about five people on whom he could rely in North Memphis. It didn't much matter. An FBI informant said Cabbage thought a moment of crisis would come when people would turn to him as the person who could "keep the lid on" by controlling militants in the street. In return, he hoped to leverage funding to support projects among ghetto youth.

Although James Lawson had defended Cabbage and Smith, their firing by MAP South, chaired by Lawson, exacerbated a personal rift between them. Lawson was set in his nonviolent beliefs and did not hesitate to express his opinions—and his opinion was that their strategy did not make much sense. Calvin Taylor said Lawson did not appreciate that "we were representing the threats that Lawson and them would need in order to sort of make the white man afraid." That did not mean to burn down your own neighborhood, said Taylor, but to keep "people hopping . . . keep them afraid" by using "the threat element" of some "fire power." This required developing an armed wing of the movement—"phase two" of the Black Organizing Project.

Very few people had ever heard of BOP, but during the sanitation strike, many people began to hear of a youth group called "The Invaders." Said Coby Smith, "The name Invaders comes from the fact that the kids were watching TV and they saw some alien space movie and they said, 'That's just like us; they [whites] treat us just like we're from outer space.' " The Invaders idea drew on science fiction, in which alien beings moved in on earth people, who could not distinguish them from normal people. Anti-Communist films in the 1950s had used the same motif: Communists looked like regular people, but they had a plan to take over the world. Black people could not so easily efface their identities, but who would know if a smiling black man was really a revolutionary?

The threat of black revolutionaries gave the Invaders their reputation and appeal among black youth, who desperately needed to get to know each other and to unite. "When I grew up you couldn't go into another neighborhood," said Smith. Cabbage, too, had been threatened or beaten up by other black youth when he tried to cross over into their neighbor-hoods. Smith said they wanted to tear down these territorial, turf-driven, and violent divisions among black youth. "Wasn't no big deal. Just a simple thing. Every day we would come and we would talk with young people, folks that other leaders did not want to talk to. And we would say, 'Look, you don't have to fight each other, you don't have to gang bang anymore.' " They weren't nonviolent, Smith said; they were "antiviolent"—that is, they opposed violence, but they would fight if attacked.

Cabbage's South Memphis network could move quickly to express alienation and outrage, without the resources of an office, a phone, or membership lists. U.S. Civil Rights Commission investigator Bobby Doctor appreciated these "young, aggressive-minded black people in the city." They helped blacks to develop "a new self-image, an image of strength, dignity, pride." Nobody else worked with unemployed young men hanging out at pool halls, as well as pimps, drunks, prostitutes, and others who had completely fallen out of the economy. The Invaders name was "catchy," said Taylor. "People who weren't even members of the Invaders would put on a jacket and put 'Invaders' on it because it made them somebody big, somebody important. This is what the talk of the town was. The Black Power people are here to lead us."

But organizing casual contacts into a coherent force proved impossible. Cabbage called himself the executive secretary of BOP and projected a chain of command that could take action quickly and protect people from the police. In reality, his group's subunits operated autonomously, beyond the reach of any command-style leaders. Cabbage's group of street leaders could not agree with each other and lacked the ability to carry out disciplined, coordinated mass action. "There was no control," Cabbage admitted.

Cab's sixteen-year-old brother, Richard, helped to start the Invaders. Like many teenagers, he did not know how to "digest what was going on." Trying to function as a revolutionary at age sixteen undermined normal life for Richard, and he never recovered from it. The Invaders did not want to attend meetings to hear slightly older people talk and orient them. They even resented the better-educated Coby Smith and Cabbage, and angry words were exchanged during the very first meeting of the group. According to Taylor, some people were angry at Coby for talking too much, and they even considered "wasting" him.

Teenagers had no patience with older leaders, but they didn't always understand each other, either. They wanted action, not talk, and began to follow John Burl Smith, who became the best-known leader of the Invaders after he came out in public with the name "Invaders" stenciled on the back of his jacket. He had been in the military, had the dress and bearing of a military leader, and represented veterans, who went from being teenagers to carrying rifles in the blink of an eye, as the Vietnam War began to influence the politics of the Movement at home.

Once the Invaders image became public, it seemed that every young high school student wanted a jacket with that name on it. Style and image appealed to high-schoolers. Afro hair, sunglasses, army fatigues, sandals, and amulets differentiated younger "militants" from older civil rights leaders and ministers in more middle-class apparel. Cabbage's close-cropped

hair and conventional dress in the summer of 1967 soon turned in that
direction, too, but John Burl Smith immediately took the militant image
and ran with it. An although he started out with little theoretical knowledge, he accelerated toward the idea of total revolution faster than anyone
else. He believed armed struggle was around the corner, and he would not
back down from any conflict. He took seriously Black Panther Party
founder Huey P. Newton's principle of "revolutionary suicide," taking confrontations with authorities up to and beyond the limits of survival. Soon
he tried to wrest leadership from Cabbage.

Great confusion existed about where youth organizers and Black Power
advocates might be going. The sanitation strike presented them with a
prime opportunity to define themselves and claim a public constituency.
"In 1968, when the sanitation workers strike started, this was for us the ful-
fillment of our concept of the Black United Front," said Coby Smith. "Hey,
we got 'em now. Tell all the bourgeoisie, white people, that . . . we'll go over
here and work with the sanitation workers, with people in prison, with
youngsters on college campuses, with all kinds of disaffected and ignored
forces in our population." The strike solidarity movement came into being
entirely without them, but young militants now saw it as a way to take the
struggle for freedom to a higher level than it had ever before reached.

"It was now or never, really, you know," said Taylor. "Do or die. And I
think that this was the most beautiful time that I have ever seen black people really united. God almighty, man, black people all over the city . . .
wasn't nothing going on but the sanitation strike. They didn't care if you
were a Black Power militant, if you were an Uncle Tom, but if you were
behind the sanitation strike you were a brother. Come on into the house. It
was really a beautiful thing."

AS THE STRIKE-support movement drew in increasing numbers of
younger people, they added a harsher rhetoric and a major difference in
tactics that would be debated behind closed doors in the strategy committee of COME and elsewhere for weeks to come. Cabbage said the ministers
were not taking militant enough action to defeat the city's strikebreaking,
so their strategy of nonviolence inherited from the civil rights movement

was "doomed to fail." They "introduce the possibility of hope but they can't take the struggle any further when it is necessary," because when they excluded the threat of violence, they excluded the very thing that could wring concessions from the power structure.

Lawson, for his part, did not see anything "radical" about calls for armed resistance. He said blacks who used violence "are essentially well-conditioned Americans" who merely confirmed the dominant pattern:

> I have an utter disdain for people running around talking about you're a militant revolutionary because you think that you can get something to happen at the end of the barrel of a gun, when what you get to happen there is death and injury, mayhem. You don't get justice there, and you don't get people's power for change there. . . . Whether you're violent or nonviolent, you'd better have a philosophy of suffering. You'd better be willing to take some pain and injury and hurt. No soldier picks up a gun going to a battlefield pretending I'm not gonna get killed. He'd better face the reality of his own death. Well, you do the same in nonviolence.

Lawson's definition of manhood ran counter to that of many young people who considered themselves revolutionaries. He regarded the revolutionary talk of the Invaders as nothing but "rhetorical radicalism." In strategy committee meetings, ministers complained that the Invaders made inflammatory speeches about "picking up the gun" and "revolution" but actually did little to advance concretely the cause of the strikers. They came into meetings with "ideological, rhetorical displays," said Lawson, but they never put forward a plan of attack and rarely even participated in picketing or joined in other actions to support the strike. Reverend Starks called them "sideliners in the Movement." He and other ministers came to feel that the Invaders also had hidden agendas—the main one being a quest for money to support their own organization.

But Cabbage criticized the Movement and the ministers for failing even in nonviolent terms, for not putting people's bodies on the line to stop the garbage trucks and the scabs from going out. Taylor said, "The feeling among us was that the strike had gone on for so long that it was now time for them to cease this business about picketing" and stop the strikebreakers; Lawson, he said, was brilliant as a nonviolent theorist but weak on tactics and implementation. Cabbage and others felt that made it all the more important to hold out the threat of violence to get the city to settle the strike.

PRIOR TO 1968, few people would have thought anyone more radical or militant than James Lawson. But none of his credentials from earlier years necessarily impressed people coming of age in the late 1960s. What the Invaders saw in Lawson was a somewhat older minister with conventional clothing, very clear diction, precise ideas of how a movement should be organized, and a belief in nonviolence as almost a litmus test for activism. They didn't see him or his group bringing the system to a halt. They viewed Martin Luther King, Jr., in the same way. Having put his body on the line many times, however, Lawson resented people who put "King and others of us" in the category of "maybe counter-revolutionaries, reactionaries."

Clearly, it was time to fight, but with what weapons? This would be a preeminent issue in the weeks to come.

11

CONVERGENCE

> Sometimes I felt like we was going back to work shortly and then
> after a couple of weeks rolled around, sometimes I didn't feel like
> we was going back to work at all. But we all started participating
> in the meetings and that gave me a little more courage then.
> I knowed if we would stick together we would win.
>
> —*Striker L. C. Reed*

As the strike's third week began, the city was operating thirty-eight garbage trucks manned by 225 strikebreakers. Loeb and the newspapers used calls for law and order to strengthen the unity of the white community, insisting that outsiders from AFSCME had instigated the strike to take advantage of black racial grievances. The city had every reason to think it would win: macing, permanent replacement of strikers, and court injunctions could squash the workers' movement even more effectively than the firings of workers who had threatened to strike in 1966.

The very health of the city was at stake, according to columnist Stanley Levey, in a *Press-Scimitar* article titled, "Behind Strike of Memphis Garbagemen." He described the Memphis strike as part of a national pestilence of irresponsible unionism that had to be fought:

> Public employees by the hundreds or thousands have been signing
> union cards, striking and picketing—activities not long ago consid-

ered illegal, unethical or unprofessional. . . . Firemen have abandoned fire trucks. Hospital workers have left their patients. Transit workers have left subways and buses. Policemen have reported "sick." All or most have won higher pay and better working conditions, generally without punishment.

The "aggressive and articulate" Wurf had turned AFSCME into the country's fastest-growing AFL-CIO union by taking advantage of rapid job growth in education, health care, and government and a "fever of union militancy" among public employees.* Levey thought taxpayers would end up paying dearly for this militancy unless the city of Memphis stopped it.

Racial polarization also could hardly be denied, but it was unclear whether it would aid the strike or kill it. In the black community, garbage piled up, and black ministers, students, and civil rights activists were infuriated by the police attack on Friday. In the white community, garbage collection went easily and most people united behind Loeb and defended police action as maintenance of law and order. Lawson and other black leaders first of all tried to build black unity, but they also sought white allies who could pressure the city government into a settlement.

Union members provided one possible bridge over the city's racial and class divides. Prior to the strike, Dan Powell, the southeast regional representative of the AFL-CIO's Committee on Political Education (COPE), at a conference of unionists from six southern states held in Memphis on February 7, had brought into the open the idea of combining labor and civil rights agendas. Based in Memphis, Powell had joined the CIO when the American Newspaper Guild organized the city's two newspapers in the 1930s. He and his union participated in purging the Left from the CIO, but Powell regretted the resultant loss of civil rights supporters from the southern labor movement. Hoping to reconnect labor and civil rights causes, Powell on February 7 brought in Bayard Rustin to give a keynote

---

*Public employment had increased by 60 percent over ten years, and AFSCME's membership in 1967 had jumped to 375,000 from 250,000 eighteen months earlier. Public workers held 142 strikes in 1966, and teacher strikes delayed school openings in twenty cities.

speech to the labor delegates. Rustin directed the AFL-CIO's A. Philip Randolph Institute, which focused on addressing civil rights issues within organized labor. Rustin strongly advocated coalition politics.

Not "love or affection" but mutual interests dictated an alliance between blacks and the labor movement, Rustin told delegates. Reiterating themes raised in King's 1961 AFL-CIO speech, he told them, "You can't win without us [blacks], and we can't get a damn thing without you." Rustin promoted moving "from protest to politics," based on an expanded black franchise in the wake of the Voting Rights Act, and he listed reforms that would benefit both blacks and labor, including a "freedom budget" funding full employment, improved education and wages, and other antipoverty measures. Rustin, like King, wanted to shift the freedom movement from "phase one" to "phase two."

The problem—as black Memphians knew all too well—was that so many white working-class voters had already shifted their own allegiances to racist white politicians like Loeb and Wallace and to Republicans like Goldwater or Nixon, all of whom supported business over worker interests. Rustin and Alexander Barken, the white director of COPE for the AFL-CIO, both warned against right-wing extremists as well as Black Power "demagogues." Neither Rustin nor Barken, however, offered an antidote to building trade unions that excluded blacks, to industrial unions and employers that kept them locked in the worst jobs, or to backlash by working-class white voters.

And few white workers in Memphis had ever heard much about the Negro-labor alliance from their own AFL-CIO leaders. Whether unionized white workers would fully support the strike remained a crucial unresolved issue. Bill Lucy said he received a lot of encouragement from white unionists at the start of the strike, but with a caveat: "We had people telling us that 'I'll help you all I can, but if the NAACP becomes involved, you can forget about me.'"

WHO WOULD BE willing to come to the immediate aid of the strikers? Who would be willing to confront the police? Who would be willing to go to jail? And who would maintain nonviolence and who would not? These questions preoccupied James Lawson and other strike supporters. If one wanted troops willing to go to jail, previous experiences pointed not to white unionists but to black youth, whose boisterous picketing had practically shut down businesses in Nashville and Memphis in 1960 and in Birmingham in 1963. Black youth, however, demanded disruptive, exciting action, and few of them believed in nonviolence as a principle.

When COME held its first strategy committee meeting on Monday morning, February 26, Lawson, Jackson, and other black ministers knew what needed to be done almost without discussing it. First on their agenda was to involve more black teenagers in the movement, and they selected twenty-six-year-old black postal clerk Harold Middlebrook to take charge of doing it. He had studied at Morehouse College, gone to jail with King to protest segregation at Rich's Department Store in Atlanta, and helped to organize the Selma and Meredith marches. He wanted to do in Memphis what SCLC had done in Birmingham: fill the jails. FBI agents and the police pegged Middlebrook as a "protégé" of Lawson and claimed that both of them incited racial hatred. An informant warned the FBI of their efforts to organize black youth, who "can be emotionally stimulated to commit acts or utter statements which could create chaos in the community." Nearly 5,000 black schoolteachers would receive their paychecks on Thursday, and COME needed to activate black youth to convince the teachers to keep their money in their pockets rather than to shop downtown.

Workers held their noontime rally on Monday at the Local 186 union hall, and two separate groups marched downtown—one group leaving from Clayborn Temple around 11 AM and another in the afternoon.

Monday night, a defiant, charged-up crowd of more than a thousand people filled Clayborn Temple. Jerry Wurf defied the court injunction with a vigorous speech proclaiming, "With the solidarity of the men and the solidarity of the black community, we've got to win." Reverend Jackson roared his support for the strike—waving his hands, pounding his fists, and sweating profusely as he excoriated the Loeb regime. He exhorted the crowd not to rest until "justice and jobs" prevailed for all African Americans. A genius at raising the emotional temperature of a mass meeting, Jackson also raised nearly $1,600 from those in attendance. Jackson also widened the movement's agenda, saying that after the workers won their demands, the movement would campaign to end police brutality and improve housing, jobs, wages, and education across the city.

The movement might have faltered after the repression on Friday, but strike supporters considered Monday a great success. People had marched and picketed downtown without any violence, and there was much celebrating of the fact that the Memphis movement seemed to be on track despite—or perhaps because of—the police attack. But not everyone agreed with marching under strict police controls, as they had done that day. During the evening mass meeting, John Burl Smith indicated he wanted to speak, and Clayborn's white pastor, Malcolm Blackburn, turned the podium over to him. Smith looked the part of a returning Vietnam War veteran. The FBI reported, as if it were ominous, that Smith "had two or three individuals with him who were obvious Black Power advocates" with "natural Afro hair-dos, dark glasses, and some wear amulets around their necks." He also had the name "Invaders" emblazoned on the back of his jacket.

Smith made a fiery speech that poked fun at ministers like Starks and Jackson, saying, "All of their praying would not solve the strike or not get justice for the Negro." He urged people to dump their garbage on the streets and challenged the ministers: "We've got to do some fighting. We must fight the power structure whether it is Henry Loeb or Richard Nixon. . . . You'd better get some guns. . . . You're going to need them before this is over. You can't pray your way out." An FBI informant also quoted him as saying, "You preachers do the praying and we'll do the other work." Reverend Starks immediately told the audience that Smith's ideas were not those of the strategy committee, but Reverend Blackburn countered that the feelings of young people needed to be heard if the movement wanted their support.

How to involve the Invaders, who did not adhere to nonviolence, without tainting the movement now became a problem for the ministers. Lawson and other ministers did not believe that "rhetorical radicalism" by black youth necessarily produced violence, but FBI agents and police took their words literally. The FBI reported to J. Edgar Hoover and a variety of police and military leaders unverified rumors of "two bearded, natural hair-do male Negroes" in town to meet with T. O. Jones in order "to assassinate Mayor Henry Loeb," and of "various black powerites and participants in riots in other cities . . . coming to Memphis to exploit the strike." Police also reported rumors that Loeb's home and Lowenstein's and Goldsmith's Department Stores would be burned, that "the incipient SNCC-oriented Black Power movement" might burn the homes of scabs and take over the strike. Each alarmist report lengthened the list of potential conspirators and heightened police and FBI fears.

The open rift aired at the Monday-night mass meeting suggested not a Black Power conspiracy, however, but a generational and ideological divide. Lawson and the ministers, as well as AFSCME, continued to project mass marches and peaceful confrontations with city authorities as the only way to win. On Tuesday, February 27, some 300 people gathered at Clayborn Temple. Given that police had attacked them a mere four days earlier, they felt tense, but they mobilized their forces and marched to city hall. Others came by their own routes and overfilled the City Council chambers once again. The council attended to all sorts of mundane business, recalled Reverend Dick Moon, while protesters "waited and waited" for their issues to be addressed. Council Chairman Donelson proposed an affirmative-action program to open upper-level city jobs to blacks, but everyone already knew that the mayor was opposed to it, and the council did not adopt it.

The council put Wurf on its agenda to testify, but before he could do it, he received a summons from Chancellor Robert Hoffman, ordering Wurf and twenty-two others to chancery court for a hearing on charges that they had violated his antistrike injunction. The council told Wurf it would wait for his return, and meanwhile gave strike supporters thirty minutes to testify. Civil rights leaders, including Maxine Smith and Jesse Turner, many ministers, and James Shepard and a few other white unionists, all joined in. Reverend Kyles protested that police had lined up their vehicles outside and seemed prepared to gas them again. "Whose City Hall is this? We are being treated like criminals. They won't even let us use the rest rooms." Lawson protested the "two sticks" of brutality used against blacks—one wielded by government and the other by the police. He said, "It appears that we are surrounded by the Gestapo." About fifty white businessmen watched, and Emmette Baker, president of the Memphis White Citizens' Council, passed out flyers urging segregationists to defeat the strike.

Finally, Wurf returned from chancery court, hoping to persuade council members that they could end the strike painlessly: the mayor did not even have to sign a contract but could simply write a letter. The city did not have to deduct union dues from worker paychecks directly, only allow the supposedly independent credit union to do so. AFSCME would accept phased-in 5- and 10-cent raises, written assurances of future union representation and grievance procedures, and continuance of existing fringe benefits—conditions the mayor's attorneys had already accepted. Wurf told the council that AFSCME would sign a no-strike clause as part of a new bargaining relationship. He said the mayor had adopted a no-compromise posture that had become more important to him than the substance of the issues, which Wurf said could be resolved easily.

Wurf thought his moderate proposals would produce a settlement. On Sunday night, Wurf and Lawson had met behind the scenes with Ned Cook—a close friend of the mayor's and an international broker of millions of dollars in cotton, land, grain, and lumber—to compose various drafts of a compromise letter for Wurf and Loeb to sign. He thought this indication of business concern would sway the City Council. But when Wurf finished his testimony, the council ended its meeting without taking any action, leaving protesters sitting in the council chambers having achieved nothing. Fire and Police Director Frank Holloman ordered police not to arrest them or even to remove them if they held a sit-in. He did not want another dramatic confrontation, and with none at hand, the protesters left.

Council members met again later in a secret session, but they failed to come up with a consensus on any action. No one in the white power structure wanted to set the precedent of accepting AFSCME into bargaining. On that same day, the federally funded Memphis Housing Authority denied AFSCME's request to represent 113 of their maintenance workers, even though President Kennedy's Executive Order 10988 in 1962 clearly allowed federally funded agencies to recognize public-employee unions. The temper of the whites on the council was hostile to AFSCME. "All of us had a built-in resentment to labor unions," said council member Bob James, who particularly resented Lawson's educated demeanor and moral stance, which did not rectify the "original sin"—an illegal strike. African Americans, James said, didn't know how to "sell their ideas" and simply tried to browbeat the council into submission.

Meanwhile, when Wurf returned again to chancery court, Judge Hoffman said that he and twenty-two others had violated his 1966 injunction by speaking at mass meetings and other activities, and he bound them over for a trial. Attorney Anthony Sabella, pleading, "These men are not criminals," won release on their own recognizance instead of the $500 bond requested by the city. He then began a fruitless series of appeals to overturn the injunction as a violation of constitutional rights to free speech. City leaders clearly planned to wear down the union through court actions.

That night, a relatively small crowd of 300 rallied at St. Paul Baptist Church. Black undercover patrolman Willie Richmond reported that Reverend Kyles said, "This was a labor issue in the beginning, but it is a race issue now, and we are at war." Kyles pledged that if the courts put the AFSCME leaders in jail, preachers would take over leadership of the strike and go to jail too. Reverend Blackburn stressed, "We are not violent. We come in peace. We want justice." He told the audience, "I know you are proud that you are black. I am proud that I am white. Everyone should be proud of what they are."

The next day, Wednesday, February 28, about a hundred "primarily middle-aged and elderly Negro women," according to the FBI, led the picketing of the downtown, joined by some 300 strikers. It was one of many instances in which black women played a leading role in strike support, raising money, walking picket lines, leading the singing in church and community meetings, taking over much of the work in the AFSCME office. The actions of black women were critical to the strike, but they did not get much press coverage. Black women seemed almost invisible in the media and the historical record.

That morning, the *Commercial Appeal* revealed that secret negotiations among Lawson, AFSCME, and business and civic leaders, had reached an agreement. A front-page headline, "Loeb May Offer Compromise Plan to

Collect Dues," destroyed it. The mayor immediately held a press conference to say that the "news of a compromise is news to me," and that he would never accept a dues checkoff or sign a union contract. Councilwoman Awsumb observed, "We could have ended it that day if they had not used that word 'compromise' because this is a word that to our Mayor is as bad as 'nigger' to the Negro. It is like waving a red flag. And he backed off . . . and you could never get him back to that middle ground again."

The mayor sent a letter to sanitation workers on Thursday, February 29, calling public-employee strikes illegal in this "nation governed by laws" and saying, "The strike must end," before any agreements could be considered. He reiterated his previous offers of small wage increases and a continuance of vacations, insurance, and other benefit policies already in place. Workers had the right to belong to a union and to pay dues, but they had to do it without the city's help. He assured them of "fair, dignified treatment," that he was "sincerely interested in your welfare," and that "you know that I keep my word." There would be no reprisals, the mayor said, but he also warned: "I should remind you that some of the regular jobs have been filled and others are being filled daily." The police reported that 317 workers now manned sanitation trucks, including sixty-two men who had first gone on strike but then had returned to work.

Also on Thursday, Harold Middlebrook's efforts to mobilize youth started to pay off. Lawson met with thirty high school and college students at his church to plan mass picketing on Saturday in order to shame teachers and others away from downtown stores. Twenty-seven black and two white teenagers marched from Clayborn Temple in miserable, rainy weather to picket Goldsmith's and Lowenstein's Department Stores, singing, "Don't buy from that store no more." A mass meeting that night at Mt. Pisgah CME Church warmed up attendees with speeches, songs, and chants, while outside, officers ticketed dozens of cars and recorded license-plate numbers. When Jerry Fanion, community relations director for Shelby County, questioned the police about this, they promptly arrested him. Ed Harris, a young *Tri-State Defender* employee, took their picture, and they arrested him too, charging both of them with "jaywalking." The arrests caused pandemonium inside the church, and even Fire and Police

Director Holloman recognized this as a foolish provocation. He took the unusual step of going to court to get the charges dropped the next morning, Friday, March 1. But federal judge Robert McRae also denied jurisdiction to AFSCME's appeal for free-speech rights and sent it back to Hoffman's chancery court.

The most crucial event that morning, however, occurred not in the courts but at the noontime meeting at the United Rubber Workers union hall, where the strikers stood up in unison and thundered their rejection of Loeb's letter demanding that they go back to work. They could potentially make a few modest gains and keep their jobs by going back to work, but they were willing to lose their jobs, if necessary, to get a union. "The basic issue is not pay, but recognition of the union," explained Jesse Epps. "There has never been the unity in the Negro community of Memphis that there is now, and the reason is that recognition of the union involves recognition of the workers as *men*. The mayor wants to say, 'Go on back to work and then we'll do right about your complaints' . . . Just as if Memphis were a Delta plantation."

Marches continued that day into downtown, and, for the first time, at Memphis State University, thirty-three black students and eleven white students marched together in support of the strike. Councilman Jerred Blanchard tried to get the City Council to initiate a pay raise and to negotiate a settlement behind the scenes, but both of his efforts failed. (Later Blanchard joined with conservative Councilman Tom Todd to propose a strike moratorium and a citywide referendum to be held in August to decide whether or not workers should have a dues checkoff, a proposal that would have killed the strike. Ciampa rejected it.)

Hopes for a compromise with the mayor among middle-class people still died hard. About seventy-five black ministers met with him at the AME Minimum Salary Building that afternoon, and he then invited a smaller group to his office; they met from 7 to 10 that night. Having been briefed by the police about the threats of armed force heard in Monday night's mass meeting, Loeb thanked the ministers for "helping contain extremist elements within the Negro community." He then talked about the city's tight budget and inability to pay higher wages. Both of these comments made Reverend Jackson even angrier than he already had been. He did not want to contain militancy, and, "It was not the mayor's prerogative to decide what the men wanted. . . . Listening to him made us realize that there was no position that we could take that would be compatible with his thinking." Loeb reemphasized that fact by telling a reporter, "There is no change in my position. Be sure you put that in the story."

Interdenominational Ministerial Alliance President Henry Starks concluded, "There was only one thing that the mayor wanted to do—continue to talk. . . . [W]e were as far apart at this particular meeting as we'd ever been." Starks thought one good thing had happened: Black ministers lost their illusions about Loeb, and they concluded that the movement would have to escalate its pressure on city hall.

Yet for most white ministers, *moderation* remained the watchword. That Friday night, the AFL-CIO's Bill Ross pleaded with the Catholic Human Relations Council to support the strike, but Monsignor Joseph Leppert, a white Mississippian with progressive views on race, objected that strike supporters at city hall on Tuesday had stirred up racial hatred and had even made obscene comments. Alberta Turner, wife of NAACP President Jesse Turner, couldn't believe her ears. "Obscenities! I'll tell you what obscenity is. It's answering the phone at 2 o'clock in the morning and hearing someone say, 'Your husband will be dead by tomorrow night.' It's having people write letters saying, 'Get out of town, you goddamn niggers.' It's watching your children go off to school and not knowing if they'll come home again because they've been threatened too. That's obscenity!"

Later that night, someone smashed several of the windows at Loeb's home.

THE POLICE CALLED Lawson and Middlebrook "incipient interlopers," and their informants said they might wrest control from "middle of the road Negroes . . . extremely stable, cautious and law-abiding ministers," such as Bishop Patterson and his son J. O., Jr. They put Reverend Jackson in this category, and they did not seem to understand that politics in the black community had shifted because of the police actions. Intelligence agents, however, held Lawson and others stirring up black youth as responsible for an apparent escalation of vandalism and youth actions over the weekend of March 2 and 3.

The FBI and the police intensified surveillance of the Invaders as well. They identified the leaders at this point as Charles Cabbage, John Burl Smith, Charles Ballard, Charles Harrison, Donney Delaney, Verdell Brooks, and Clinton Roy Jameson. Agents considered it ominous that Cabbage had talked with Lawson outside Tuesday's City Council meeting. They said Cabbage and Coby Smith had gone to Atlanta to discuss strategy with other SNCC members, and they noted that John Burl Smith had once attended a New York meeting of the Socialist Workers Party, a group on the U.S. Attorney General's list of "subversive" organizations. They were shocked that the black Ministerial Alliance had given John Smith $75 to pay his rent, and an FBI source quoted Coby Smith as saying that Memphis needed a "good race riot" to shake it up. Police reported trash fires and vandalism and said someone had found a cache of dynamite near one of the sanitation barns.

Youth involvement did accelerate over the weekend. On Saturday morning, some 175 people picketed downtown and handed out leaflets, led by Reverend Starks, and police identified 75 percent of them as being of high school or college age. Surprisingly, about 25 percent of them were white students from Southwestern College and Memphis State. In the afternoon, an even larger group of about 900—half of them women and youth, and including 300 sanitation workers—marched through downtown. This day was a powerful testament to increasing community and youth involvement in disciplined action, but many others chose spontaneous action. That night, someone tossed bricks through the windows of a Loeb's Bar-B-Q and a Molotov cocktail through the window of a scabbing sanitation worker, and anonymous assailants physically attacked two scabs. Others dumped garbage in the street and set fires throughout South Memphis, Cabbage's turf, forcing the fire department to make fifty-two emergency runs to put them out. Police attributed these actions to black youth stirred up by black clergy in COME.

Black ministers continued to preach and practice nonviolent discipline through mass meetings and marches, however. On Sunday afternoon, twenty-one different groups of religious singers, consisting mostly of black youth, held an eight-hour gospel-music sing-in at Mason Temple. O. W. Pickett and his Concerned Citizens Committee for Sanitation Workers and Family announced that $50,000 to $60,000 had been raised over the first three weeks of the strike to pay for food, clothing, and rent for strikers. People held smaller meetings at a church on the fringes of Shelby County and at Reverend Bell's church, where black police plainclothesman Ed Redditt tried to explain their being there as part of an effort to improve "police–community relations." Blacks told Redditt and his colleague, Willie Richmond, that they did not appreciate their presence. Rosetta Miller supposedly later told Richmond he would end up in the hospital if he didn't stay away from movement activities.

Sunday morning's *Commercial Appeal*, in a story titled "Marchers Draw Little Attention on Main Street," downplayed the effects of the downtown economic boycott. "Shoppers either ignored the marchers or stopped to read the signs they carried," the article read, and a salesman even reported that "three men who had picketed his store in the morning, came back after the march and bought shoes they had seen in the window." The newspaper seemed to suggest the futility of sedate tactics such as picketing, thus strengthening the argument within the movement for more disruptive tactics. Reverend William Fields told the mass meeting Sunday afternoon that if "any of you are arrested the movement will get you out of jail," and the Interdenominational Ministerial Alliance met to discuss physically blocking garbage trucks. WHBQ-TV reporters asked Lawson on an afternoon news show if he would bring in what they called "the Black Power boys," and Lawson said yes, he would bring in Stokely Carmichael or anyone else who could strengthen the city's united front.

The movement had settled into a pattern of picketing, meetings, and mass demonstrations, but it proved impossible to form a coherent organization. Lawson ran daily COME strategy committee meetings at the AME Minimum Salary Building based on consensus, and meetings often took the form of a free-for-all. One participant exclaimed, only half in jest, "Who's running this thing?" Reverend Starks called the movement a work in progress that was "open on both ends"—one could come into the movement or leave just as quickly. Starks tried to run his church, take care of his parishioners, give his sermons, and march in the street every day. By early March, he was physically spent and becoming ill. People felt exhilarated and then exhausted by the intensity of movement activities.

MAINTAINING UNITY REMAINED especially hard in Memphis, where a triangulated civil rights leadership consisted of the NAACP and the Shelby County Democratic Club on one hand, the Interdenominational Ministerial Alliance on the other, and the Unity League (headed by O. Z. Evers) as a distant third force. Beyond that lay the amorphous organization of the Invaders and an incipient Black Power movement among youth, as well as the possibility of a fledgling SCLC. In the swirling day-to-day events of the strike, leadership carried with it heavy sacrifices, personal losses, and danger, and Reverend Jackson complained that few black business or professional people or teachers took on these burdens. Jesse Epps noted that many black ministers only became involved later, when Martin Luther King came to town, in order to get up on the podium and be seen with him. The black middle class did not provide reliable supporters.

As a result, Lawson and the COME strategy committee suffered little restraining interference from more conservative black leaders. A few people taking on huge burdens made the difference between success and failure, and most people preferred to relinquish day-to-day leadership to Lawson. Yet some people resented Lawson for filling a key leadership role, and a degree of competition for leadership always existed. Lawson led in part by example and in part by default: he could survive on amazingly little sleep, getting up at six and going to bed at two or three in the morning. Despite all his activities, he and his wife, Dorothy, and their three sons met for dinner almost every night. Few others could keep up his pace. And no one else had his long experience in and theoretical knowledge of nonviolent direct action.

Strong union and worker action provided the glue that kept the movement solid. By contrast to the fluctuating ministerial and community support group, AFSCME had full-time national and regional leaders staffing the strike, including Bill Lucy, P. J. Ciampa, Jesse Epps, Joe Paisley, and

President Jerry Wurf, plus T. O. Jones and rank-and-file activists Joe War-ren, Robert Beasley, S. T. Thomas, J. L. McClain, Taylor Rogers, James Robinson, and Haley Williams. These men and others kept the rallies, picket lines, and marches going every day. The threat of fines and jail time for violating the court injunction put them all under tremendous pressure, as did police recording devices in hotel rooms and constant surveillance.

Given the failure of the 1966 strike, Wurf considered it a cardinal rule to largely ignore the injunction still in effect in Memphis. Without flaunting their activities, AFSCME leaders continued to speak at the Firestone hall, in churches, and before community and union gatherings, and to mobilize picket lines and marches. But they avoided arrests and confrontations with scabs. Wurf said, "This was not an ordinary strike. It was not handled in an ordinary way." Jimmy Crunk, the scab worker who pulled a rifle on strikers during the first week of the strike, demonstrated the possibility that some-one could get killed. Rabbi Wax had warned Wurf that armed racists might come into Memphis from the surrounding areas. If the union physically confronted scabs, Wurf feared, "All we would do is give the police excuses to break heads and throw teargas at us." Instead, AFSCME leaders relied heavily on civil rights–style mass meetings, picket lines, and the economic boycott.

Their one concession to the injunction was that they ceded much of the strike's public leadership to the black ministers. Wurf, Epps, and others attended strategy committee meetings, but AFSCME staff had their hands full primarily with keeping the workers unified and active and in provid-ing for their families. AFSCME worked with Evers, Pickett, Crenshaw, and others in the community to direct food and funds to more than a thou-sand families, itself a huge logistical undertaking. All funds raised went through the ministers' organization, COME, and how it got spent became a big issue later. Tri-State Bank (and NAACP) President Jesse Turner saved many a family from eviction by letting COME and the union write checks to them, even when it wasn't clear whether there was enough money in the account to cover them. Strikers didn't have much, but they feared losing what little they did have. Lucy remembered a man who owed more to a loan company on his 1953 Buick than the car had originally cost: "These companies had lent the people more than they could ever afford to pay back at phenomenal interest rates."

Without a great deal of discussion taking place, the ministers and the AFSCME leadership neatly divided their responsibilities to create a labor–civil rights alignment unparalleled in southern movement history.

BUT MOST OF the "good people" in white Memphis still remained silent. The predominantly white Memphis Ministers Association had done nothing since the failure of negotiations in the strike's second week. On Monday, March 4, the group finally resolved to set up a meeting of black and white religious leaders, but Rabbi Wax hesitated and the proposed meeting stalled. Timidity and compromise killed numerous white initiatives to do something to resolve the strike.

A handful of whites played a more forthright role. Father William Greenspun at St. Patrick's Church attended strike-support meetings and gave more than $1,000 of diocesan funds to provide food and aid to families of the strikers. AFL-CIO leader Dan Powell raised several hundred dollars from a goodwill offering at the Unitarian Church. A number of clerics without congregations, such as MSU campus chaplain Dick Moon, sided with the strike, but none of them could leverage enough white community pressure to offset the mayor's claim to speak for white Memphis.

When whites supported the strike, FBI agents became obsessed with discrediting them. FBI informants viewed Reverend Blackburn, the most consistent white strike supporter, as an "enigma." They could not peg him as a leftist, but they claimed he had a violent temper and undefined subversive politics. The FBI also closely tracked white students who worked with Lawson against the war or who supported the strike. While searching for subversives among white youths and liberals, however, police agents ignored the strike's most important group of potential white allies: unionized workers.

On Monday, March 4, some 300 sanitation workers marched from Clayborn Temple to city hall at 3:45, led by ministers Starks, Jackson, and Blackburn. The FBI estimated that at least 150 white union members joined them; people in the movement said 500. They carried placards that read, "Memphis AFL-CIO Labor Council Supports Sanitation Dept. Employees." Memphis Labor Council President Tommy Powell, Vice President H. B. Griffin of the United Rubber Workers (URW), and COPE regional director Dan Powell led them in picketing downtown stores. George Clark, white president of United Rubber Workers Local 186, whose union hall AFSCME workers used every day, brought the largest contingent to the demonstration.

The Memphis *Union News*, edited by Bill Ross, defined the strike as a classic labor battle representing "the same type of revolt we had in the early period of the building trades, railroads, coal mines." It ran a front-page editorial that denounced "ultra-conservative community leaders [and] the labor-hating press" that had been "spewing forth their biased and prejudiced views." It accused the mayor of using tax money to pay for the police to bring in scabs from outlying counties and asked why the city allowed schoolteachers and bus drivers to deduct union dues from their paychecks but would not let sanitation workers do the same. "Organized labor in Memphis is growing weary of the shabby treatment that it is receiving and has received in the past from the ultra-conservative community leaders," Ross wrote.

By placing the strike in a labor context and ignoring racial issues, Ross appealed successfully to a number of white union members. According to Beifuss, "During the first month of the strike, locals of textile workers; electrical, radio and machine workers; hotel and restaurant workers; typographers; maintenance of way workers; butchers; steelworkers; oil, chemical and atomic workers" all contributed money to the strike. The URW made the largest union donation to the strike when AFSCME workers collected $835 from rubber workers at the gate of the Firestone factory. Unionist Taylor Blair and former labor representative Frank Miles continued to mediate, as they had been doing from the beginning of the strike. Also on March 4, State Senator Frank White, an ally of organized labor, introduced a bill to create a mediation board that could force Mayor Loeb to accept binding arbitration by a third party. The Tennessee AFL-CIO kept pressuring legislators, successfully, to keep in committee anti-union bills spawned by the strike. "Even rural lawmakers aren't anxious to have organized labor down on them" in an election year, wrote the *Commercial Appeal* on March 16.

Donations to the strike from national unions would accelerate throughout March, especially after King voiced his support for the strike. The Seafarers International Union presented AFSCME with $5,000 and pledged an additional $1,000 a week. The International Longshoremen's and Warehousemen's Union (ILWU), one of the few CIO unions to survive the CIO purge of Left-led unions, also gave financial and moral support. When fifty union officials from ten southern states met in Memphis for an AFL-CIO Social Security conference on March 15–16, they passed a resolution backing the strike and criticized the conduct of the city government as "a throw-back to the dark ages."

At the local level, however, much division remained among white trade unionists. Taylor Blair had taken Wurf to the Memphis Building and Construction Trades Council meeting during the second week of the strike. Normally, local unionists would honor the visiting head of a national labor union, but the building tradesmen shunned him. Dependent on city government for construction jobs, in segregated unions, they barely acknowledged Wurf. Lucy said, "We got absolutely nothing from them, not even the time of day." The American Newspaper Guild executive committee, including editors and reporters, did endorse the strike, but its predominantly clerical and advertising membership virtually censured the committee's action.

Wurf said unions, like other American institutions, reflected the "good, bad, indifferent" character of human beings, and even if white union support for AFSCME was not unanimous, he considered it significant—especially when compared with the overwhelming hostility from most quarters of the white community. Most white AFL-CIO unionists recognized that if the Loeb administration destroyed Local 1733, it would destroy Memphis public-employee organizing and set back the labor movement for a long time to come.

Memphis represented the "convergence" of labor and civil rights that King sought, but it also represented the racism of the era. Epps and Lawson both observed that when white unionists rallied on March 4, they took a different route to the downtown, and most of them stayed to themselves when everyone gathered at their common destination. This could be explained by the fact that the Memphis Labor Council explicitly sought to highlight white support for the strike. Yet "convergence" undeniably remained stuck in a racial minefield. Dan Powell said that the strike had to be treated predominantly as a civil rights issue to attract black support, but AFSCME would lose the support of many white unionists as a result. School desegregation and racism, fear of increased taxes to pay for increased wages to sanitation workers, and political allegiances to Loeb all undercut white labor support for the strike.

George Clark and the URW's Local 186 at Firestone Tire and Rubber Company came under sustained attack from some of its white members for supporting AFSCME—so much so that Clark issued a leaflet to his local, denouncing Loeb as well as some of his own white union members. "The right-wing people in our plant, that are supposed to be union members, will not prevent this union from supporting this, or any other group of workers, in their efforts to have a union." Someone later bombed the concession stand outside the union hall in anger at AFSCME's continual use of the Local 186 hall.

Many whites at the International Harvester plant's UAW Local 988, the largest union local in Memphis next to Local 186, also resisted supporting the strike. Some of them had fought the desegregation policies of UAW President Walter Reuther, and black UAW leader George Holloway had battled for years with White Citizens' Council and John Birch Society secessionists at his local. UAW regional representative Carl Moore prompted Local 988 to give a check for $600 to the strikers, but few of the UAW's white rank-and-file members came out publicly to support the strike.

Despite these contradictions, AFSCME's Epps saw the Memphis movement as a first step to revitalizing the southern labor movement. As he put it, "Either Memphis was the dam or it was the gate. And to lose it was not losing it for State-County but losing it for the whole AFL-CIO in the South." But Lucy observed that many white unionists supported the strike as an economic issue only; as soon as it became a racial struggle, most of them jumped ship. After March 4, racial issues came increasingly to the forefront, and there would be no other major AFL-CIO demonstrations.

This white-worker ambivalence made Memphis AFL-CIO President Tommy Powell's unrelenting support for the strike all the more remarkable. He demonstrated, picketed, spoke at mass meetings, played a key role in negotiations, and served as an unpaid adjunct to the whole AFSCME effort. T. O. Jones appreciated the role of Powell, Ross, the Shepards, and other whites who had helped him start Local 1733. After the macing incident on February 23, a number of black activists at Clayborn Temple had urged that Stokely Carmichael and H. Rap Brown come to Memphis. With Wurf and Powell standing next to him, however, Jones emphasized that the movement did have white allies. "I want to criticize some folks for some of the things they have had to say up here. All white folks are not low down. No, sir, all white folks are not low down."

THE "SPIRIT OF MEMPHIS," as Lucy called it, encompassed a revitalized community mobilization on behalf of both labor and civil rights, even though it was filled with contradictions. Many white workers looked askance at the strike, but a greater number of indigenous southern whites involved themselves in the Memphis movement than in any previous southern civil rights or black labor struggle.

Privately, Jones wondered where many of the more conservative black leaders and even some civil rights activists had been for all those years prior to this strike, when the Memphis Labor Council and a few white union leaders had kept his local alive. He did not want labor issues to be overtaken by the politics of race, but events swiftly moved in that direction.

12

ESCALATION:
THE YOUTH MOVEMENT

> Our Henry, who art in City Hall,
> Hard-headed be thy name.
> Thy kingdom C.O.M.E.
> *Our* will be done,
> In Memphis, as it is in heaven.
> Give us this day our Dues Checkoff,
> And forgive us our boycott,
> As we forgive those who spray MACE against us.
> And lead us not into shame,
> But deliver us from LOEB!
> For OURS is justice, jobs, and dignity,
> Forever and ever. Amen. FREEDOM!
> —*"Sanitation Workers' Prayer,"*
> *recited by Reverend Malcolm Blackburn*

FOLLOWING THE TRADE-UNION DEMONSTRATIONS ON MARCH 4, some 300 souls met that night at Eastern Star Baptist Church, and Reverend Ralph Jackson denounced white ministers who would not join demonstrations as "unfit for the honor of minister." Lawson called on this small audience to widen the Memphis battle over union rights into a struggle for human rights and to escalate it by courting mass arrests in the streets. When Reverend Bell said, "Memphis is going to be a better city to live in, or there won't be no Memphis at all," a youth shouted out, "We will burn it!" Reverend Henry Starks announced they would march at 1:30 the next day to the meeting of the City Council, which had "lied to us the same as the Mayor did. . . . They are not going to fool us out of there anymore. We are going to stay until they do something about our sanitation problem." The consensus was that victory required escalation, not moderation.

The next afternoon, March 5, Bell and Moon led workers and sympathizers from Clayborn Temple to the City Council chambers, where they once again filled all 407 seats. Another seventy-five protesters, who could not get in, stood outside. Two hundred police also filled the room, and a hundred sheriff's deputies surrounded the building. Police officers cautioned council members not to move through the crowd if they did not want to be caught in the middle of a mass arrest. Gwen Awsumb walked into city hall to find "the whole basement . . . teeming with police. I've never seen so many police in my life."

Speakers addressed the council in tones of outrage. Lawson said the city could have already raised wages substantially with the money it had spent on extra police protection for scab workers, and he reminded the council that sanitation workers had been fighting for six years for union rights. Their pay had hardly moved up a notch during that time—in a job that had never paid enough to live on. He turned toward the audience and declared, "We will sit in this Council room until you get a settlement or until they put us out." Reverend Moon read from the Book of Jeremiah about leaders who would not listen to the people, and Awsumb quietly gasped in dismay when he ended with a passage that read, "We will burn this city down," clapped his Bible shut, and walked away from the microphone. A white man, his name lost to history, rose to beg the council to settle the strike, warning that his white neighbors were arming themselves to fight blacks.

Councilman Patterson hoped to pass his ordinance authorizing union dues checkoff, but he lacked the unanimous agreement needed even to put it on the agenda. When white council members refused to debate the substantive issues in the strike, saying that only the mayor could settle the strike, Reverend Bell rose to indict them for their seeming indifference. Later, he said the media quoted him out of context; that context was the pent-up frustration many African Americans felt not only about Memphis but the country as a whole:

We're not going to leave this building until we get what we came for. We will be gassed or killed. We are going to stay until Shiloh comes. We didn't come down here to reason with you gentlemen. If you were reasonable, it would have already been settled. The white preachers are too damn scared to tell you what you need to hear. I don't like black rats or white rats, or rats. There are rats on the Council. . . . All these men are asking for is dignity and respect. You talk about whether it's the Mayor's or the Council's responsibility. If these men were white, you would have already done something.

Bell purposely overstepped the bounds of racial etiquette and widened his attack to include national issues: "This is a racist town, this is a racist country. You call our sons off to be killed to protect your way of life. They come back here and don't have a place to live. It takes about $350,000 to kill a Vietnam soldier. We ask for the right to have a dues checkoff and you say we have no right. The kind of garbage in the newspapers is not worth reading." Bell shook his finger at council members: "I say you men don't have any backbone and you are all going to hell."

With a flushed face, Councilman Donelson jumped to his feet, "shaking with rage," according to a reporter. "Mr. Bell, we have listened to you patiently. Either you speak to us in respect or I will move for adjournment." Reverend Bell would not back down: "My mother didn't raise any half-witted children. If I insult you by telling the truth, I'm going to keep on telling it." Councilmen Donelson and James fought over the privilege of moving for adjournment, and only Patterson and Netters voted against it. White council members abruptly left, turning off the public-address system.

The City Council's three black members—and, surprisingly, the conservative Republican Jerred Blanchard—stayed behind. Elected to the council as an at-large member, Blanchard believed he should represent the nearly 40 percent of the city's population that was black as well as the 60 percent that was white. He felt disturbed by the massing of police and also thought the public-address system should have remained on, so that citizens could address their government. "I wanted to find out how the police handled them and how they [strike supporters] handled themselves," he said. Blanchard had already begun to sense tragedy in the making.

The audience ignored police orders to move and began singing freedom songs, cheering, and yelling. Benjamin Hooks later said their zeal may have seemed disproportionate to the circumstances, but it came from the macing incident and the expectation that the police would assault them once again. Someone offered up a prayer "before they gas us down," and Cornelia Crenshaw shouted out that she was "prepared to die." She later recalled, "I meant that very strongly that day. I was so angry until I just [stood] there and with the force of my own voice without a microphone it could be heard all over the city council." She felt fearful of the police but angry at council members who "would just sit there and insult your intelligence, as a person, just make a toy with you, you know, and make a fool of you."

Lawson organized people for a mass arrest as they chanted, "We want jail, we want jail!" The powerfully built, tall assistant police chief, Henry Lux, locked the doors to the City Council chambers as police closed ranks. At the same time, American Civil Liberties Union (ACLU) President David Caywood, an attorney, rushed to the mayor's office to plead with him to prevent another police attack. At 5:30 PM, Lux ambled to the front of the room, shaking hands with people he knew and joking with them. Lux surveyed some 400 people holding a sit-in and tried to break the tension by joking that he hoped they would not make him carry them out—"You don't want me to have a hernia." For the next forty-five minutes, he negotiated with Lawson about whether protesters would walk out or be carried out.

Outside, a group of marchers, comprised mostly of black students newly-arrived from Clayborn Temple, linked arms, and wouldn't let anyone in or out. Malcolm Blackburn went outside and convinced them to let the police through, while inside Lawson told the crowd no one would be blamed if they didn't want to be arrested, but also reminded them: "It is not dishonorable to go to jail for the right reason." At 6:15, arrests began. Rather than going limp, protesters lined up two by two and walked under their own power to the city jail, escorted by police. Young people in the street formed a cordon around them, singing and chanting, "Down with Lux, down with Lux." Some of them, said Moon, "were cheering and crying at the same time"—thrilled that adults had stood up to the white power structure. Those arrested marched as if through a battle line, singing:

> *Leaning, leaning, leaning on the everlasting arm,*
> *Leaning, leaning, leaning on the everlasting arm.*

Lux enforced restraint upon his angry white officers, some of whom could barely control themselves, but Moon said one officer kept commanding Reverend Starks, " 'Get along, boy. Go on, boy. Move it, boy.' And I remember Rev. Starks saying, 'I'm not a boy. I am the Rev. Mr. Henry Starks and if you call me 'boy' just one more time you are going to arrest me for assault.' " NAACP Director Maxine Smith had not planned to get arrested, but she joined hands with Bell as they sang their way to jail. She had never been arrested and was embarrassed about it. "I wanted my debut to be memorable," she said, and would have preferred being dragged to jail, because "I wanted to be a little troublesome to the police department."

Instead, a black officer arrested her in a gentlemanly fashion. At the jail, however, white officers she did not know kept referring to her as "Maxine" and refused to address her husband, Dr. Vasco Smith, by his title, even though they addressed white ministers Moon and Blackburn by their titles. As police photographed, fingerprinted, and booked her and other protesters, she said they treated them "like common criminals," taking their wallets and rings and going through their pockets. Her organization had long chronicled the degradation African Americans felt at the hands of the police, and she now experienced it herself.

At one point an officer—probably unintentionally—shoved her into a room with a man using a urinal. She protested and was removed quickly, but she felt claustrophobic when police put her in a small cell. She waited five hours to be bailed out. At least five black women protesters were placed on the women's floor of the jail, where one officer told her the police would never use titles of respect for black women. Smith later protested to Fire and Police Director Holloman about the generally "degrading, insulting, and humiliating" treatment, and she demanded he fire disrespectful police officers. Holloman said his policy was not to use titles for anyone, regardless of their social status, and he took no disciplinary action against the police. Much worse things happened as standard practice in Memphis jails.

Police had arrested 121 people at city hall, including one Firestone worker, eight ministers, and thirty-nine sanitation workers, charging them with disorderly conduct. Police also arrested two members of the Invaders, Charles Ballard and John Burl Smith, who had been downtown to support that day's rally, and charged them with reckless driving. Reverend Blackburn listened in his jail cell as Smith argued with one of the ministers that getting arrested in a protest was a waste of time and would not do any good.

That night, "militant young Negroes," according to the *Commercial Appeal,* held a boisterous rally at Clayborn Temple, where Reverend Ralph Jackson roused them with his fiery preaching and Lawson came fresh from jail to urge them to march on police headquarters the next day and get arrested. People passed around words to a new parody on "The Lord's Prayer," titled, "Henry, We're Going to Tear Your Kingdom Down."

Charles Cabbage and forty of his followers passed out a mimeographed, five-page manifesto titled, "Afro-American Brotherhood Speaks: Black Thesis, Black Power." It demonstrated the gap between young black revolutionaries and black ministers. With the image of a raised black fist on the front page, the thesis attacked "Uncle Tom" black leaders who "skin and grin" for the white man, and it called Memphis a "massive plantation." It attacked the military draft and "a war we have no stake in," and defended imprisoned SNCC leader H. Rap Brown as a martyr. It called inner-city rebellions "the initial phase of a black revolution" and urged black students at Carver and Douglass High Schools to reject their black principals as surrogates for whites. It called on them also to reject white liberals, "who not only know very little about the need and wants of Black youth, but have no real genuine concern." The thesis attacked black unity around the strike as a false unity—one that had put misleaders in charge. It condemned preachers "who inevitably *quite [sic] the struggle too soon*" (emphasis in the original), and indicted AFSCME for failing to physically stop strikebreakers. Cabbage and other Invaders, when they went to COME strategy com-

mittee meetings, criticized preachers who would not use "any means necessary" to stop scab workers. It concluded: "There must be some real fighting. We all know the preachers can't fight or won't fight."

The "Black Thesis" included a letter from H. Rap Brown, written in New
Orleans Parish Prison, that countered King's classical defense of nonviolence in his 1963 "Letter From Birmingham Jail." It began, "Manhood is
the continuing battle of one's life and one loses a bit of manhood with
every stale compromise to the authority of any power in which one does
not believe. No slave should die a natural death. There is a point where
caution ends and cowardice begins." Brown urged people to move from
"revolt to revolution," to realize that for every freedom fighter murdered
by the police, "there must be 10 dead racist cops. And for every Black
Death there must be a Dien Bien Phu," referring to the bloody battle in
which Vietnamese armed forces defeated the French military. The thesis
finished with a drawing showing exactly how to make a Molotov cocktail.

At the end of Tuesday night's meeting, the FBI noted, young people
chanted, "Black Power, Black Power." The Memphis police and the FBI predicted violence would result as more and more young people got involved
in the movement. But not all black youth ideologically opposed nonviolence or the ministers' approach to the Memphis conflict. The *Commercial
Appeal* quoted Central High School student Pat Mayweather, a young
woman deemed "Chairman of the Negro Youth Movement," saying, "We
are not militant. We are not for Black Power. We just want equality. You
might say we don't know what we are doing here, but we know this is a
cause and that it involves black people and we are black and we believe logically that we are involved." Edward Carter, Jr., the only white youth in the
group, urged more whites to support the strike. These March 5 actions, as
intended, increased the sense of a movement in the process of escalation;
Lawson further emphasized this by announcing that he had invited Martin
Luther King, Jr., to come to Memphis.

The escalation in Memphis reverberated out into the surrounding Mississippi Delta. On the same day, Memphis police received a telegram from
nearby Brownsville—a hotbed of racism where a lynching had occurred
after World War II—signed by V. Doyle Ellington, grand dragon of the

Tennessee branch of the United Klans of America. The group's national leader, Robert Shelton, was complicit in the Klan bombing of Birmingham's Sixteenth Street Baptist Church, which killed four young girls and wounded twenty-two in 1963. Angry about the suspension of the three Memphis police officers who had arrested movement supporters for "jaywalking" the week before, Ellington's telegram read:

> MEMPHIS IS ON THE VERGE OF AN ALL OUT RACIAL WAR. . . . WE ARE SWORN CITIZENS OF THE STATE OF TENNESSEE TO UPHOLD LAW AND ORDER AND I HEREBY COMMIT THIS OFFICE TO THIS DUTY. WE FURTHER COMMIT THAT WE WILL NOT STAND BY AND SEE ANY DULY AUTHORIZED OFFICER BE CUT DOWN WHILE ENFORCING THE LAW. WHATEVER IT TAKES TO STOP THIS WE STAND READY. YOURS FOR GOD AND COUNTRY.

The *Commercial Appeal* also published a letter that day from Mississippian Robert Patterson, secretary of the White Citizens' Councils, who disputed the Kerner Commission and identified civil rights activism, not racism, as the root of the nation's racial problems. Incited by King, he wrote, "The Negro has been told that he has the right to disobey laws that do not suit him and even has the right to riot." A solution to the race problem would only come "when our nation's press finally decides to tell the American public the truth, that the races are different."

Bill Ross of the Memphis Labor Council had long kept track of white supremacists and right-wing hate groups, and he feared the strike would bring out violent people with guns, such as the white Memphian who shot down James Meredith in 1966. Epps, Lawson, other activists, and even white City Council members constantly received threatening hate calls and letters. The FBI tracked Lawson's outgoing long-distance phone calls, but it ignored the many hate calls he received and provided neither Lawson nor anyone else in the movement with one iota of security.

ON WEDNESDAY, MARCH 6, students began to play a significant role in escalating the Memphis movement. At Memphis State, a campus of 15,000 students, black and white youths were strangers to each other, but on this day, an interracial group of 150 students marched and held a sit-in and speak-out at the student-center patio. Other students incredulously "peeped from classroom windows" as a self-assured, neatly dressed black student named Eddie Jenkins stood on a table to address his classmates, and began to discuss not only the plight of the sanitation workers but also their own powerless condition. "Black and white students have established a common ground on which we may attack, not meet and merely discuss, but solve the problems or ameliorate the situations that threaten the common good of us all, black and white," Jenkins told a student reporter.

White student Laura Ingram commented: "I could not believe that this was Memphis State. I was so encouraged by it. . . . I think the entire demonstration was a success in communication between black and white students." Black and white students discussed the Black Power slogan without sharp disagreements, and both the campus newspaper and the assistant dean praised the event. In the days that followed, up to 300 black students began to congregate in the student center to discuss the strike and related racial issues. The alarmed head of campus security called this "veiled black militancy." In 1968, as student movements swept campuses across the country, Memphis police and FBI agents suspected a radical conspiracy to overturn campus peace. They continued, however, to focus not on black students, the obvious leaders, but on white students who they thought had "the reputation of being agitators," and had led the demonstration, "along with a large number of unknown Negro students." The FBI now had George Leon, Susan MacDonald, Sidney Chilton III, and Laura Ingram under national surveillance because of their presumed ties to the Southern Student Organizing Committee (SSOC), the W. E. B. Du Bois clubs, and Students for a Democratic Society (SDS).

Police soon did focus on a few black students, particularly Edwina Harrell, whom they linked to Black Power advocates off campus. One informant said she had a "fine reputation" and had worked in a local law office, but "she is now wearing a natural Afro hairdo" and had been "indoctrinated" when she was a student at Spelman College by Cabbage, who was now priming her for "militant and if necessary violent action." A leaflet

Harrell wrote and distributed at the March 6 event suggested otherwise. It recounted the history of strikes in the United States and warned that when management failed to make concessions, "It is an historically proven fact that violence follows." The flyer did not call for violence; rather, it called on students to take sanitation-worker grievances to all-white East Memphis by picketing shopping centers and to challenge the university's hierarchical conservatism. "Now is the time to change Memphis and Memphis State University!! Now!" The FBI apparently could not distinguish analysis and demands for democratization from calls for revolution.

Downtown, 117 people (charges had been dropped against four others) came before Memphis Judge Ray Churchill for the city hall sit-in on March 5. He adopted a surprisingly conciliatory tone: Protesters did not have to put up bond and charges would be dropped against all of them if they did not get arrested again in the next sixty days. "I think perhaps it was bad judgment going there and saying you would not leave," Churchill said, and the city had "come a long way in the last two weeks," moving from the violent clashes on February 23 to these more civil arrests in March.

Judge Hoffman in chancery court proved far less conciliatory, convicting seven leaders of AFSCME for contempt of his court order prohibiting strike activities and sentencing them each to ten days in jail and a $50 fine. He set bail at $1,000 each for Wurf and Ciampa; $500 each for international organizers Lucy, Epps, and Paisley; and $250 for T. O. Jones and Nelson Jones, a union steward. Hoffman cited Wurf's talk to the City Council as well as testimony from police agents and *Press-Scimitar* reporter Clark Porteous that Wurf was indeed leading the strike. Lyle Caldwell, who had first gone on strike but then returned to work, testified that T. O. Jones had threatened him on the phone shortly before someone threw a brick through the window of his home with a note tied around it, saying he should quit scabbing. Hoffman said AFSCME leaders could purge themselves of contempt at any time simply by calling off the strike.

Union leaders claimed they were "helpless" to stop the strike, had not encouraged it or even known about it, and merely had come to Memphis to settle it. Hoffman tried to get Wurf and Loeb (who came to press the city's case) to settle the strike in his court—to no avail. Hoffman then dismissed charges against fifteen local union stewards after attorney Anthony Sabella said the men had simply quit work and technically speaking were not on strike. Hoffman told these local men they would not suffer penalties if they would just go back to work, but international union staff members who persisted in strike support would go to jail—an apparent ploy to divide the rank and file from staff members. Sabella appealed the judge's ruling.

Out in the streets, Harold Middlebrook had succeeded in firing up high school student protests of these proceedings. He had set up youth action committees in a number of black schools that had called upon students to skip school to protest the arrests. A number of them did, rallying that morning at Clayborn Temple and marching that afternoon to city hall. Moon and Starks later led one group of marchers to the sixth floor of police headquarters and right into Judge Churchill's court. Another "unruly" group of black and white youth, according to police, marched two abreast to the courthouse carrying placards reading, "Justice Is Dead in Memphis" and "Your Kingdom May Burn Down, King Henry." Red squad leader Lieutenant Ely Arkin wrote: "As they progressed, the marchers became louder and more boisterous, shouting, yelling, and singing." Six young black men carried a coffin to symbolize the burying of freedom, and, surrounded by 200 singing students (one of them white), placed it on top of the city hall stairs. Middlebrook read from the Bible and Blackburn conducted a mock burial of justice, saying, "In this casket is justice. In this casket is the freedom of not just the black people, but of all the people of Memphis."

Marchers encircled city hall and sang, "We Shall Overcome," ending with shouts of "Freedom!" Marchers hoped to produce a cascading series of arrests, but the police did nothing, only leaving Reverend Malcolm Blackburn to say that they would march again and again until justice was done. They marched back through the downtown, accompanied by sixty police officers, and when students turned off Main Street and onto Beale, several of them kicked overflowing garbage cans into the street. Still, police officers did nothing, knowing from past experience that arresting students would only produce sympathy in the black community and expand the movement.

Lawson and Middlebrook had seen the powerful effects of the black high school student movement that had saved the Birmingham movement from failure in 1963, and they knew that black youth required confrontation to get fired up. Quiet, disciplined marches were a little too predictable to energize youth shock troops, and organizers welcomed their creative actions. Sure enough, police began to have great difficulty in controlling hit-and-run actions by small groups in the streets. On the night of March 6, after the students "buried freedom," seventeen young people picketed Loeb's Laundry at Parkway and Lauderdale; later, someone broke one of its windows. Roving picketers moved on to the Harlem House restaurant and then Loeb's Bar-B-Q at McLemore and Mississippi, joined by Reverend Blackburn. In the early morning hours of March 7, youths broke out windows of Loeb's at Fourth and Vance and at grocery and department stores elsewhere and pulled false fire alarms throughout black Memphis. Someone threw a rock through the window of a Red Ball Freight Company truck, sending its black driver—who had nothing to do with the strike—to the John Gaston Hospital to have glass fragments removed from his head and face.

Most of these incidents, Lieutenant Arkin believed, stemmed from "vandalistic youths" not connected to the strike, but Police and Fire Director Holloman nonetheless publicly blamed their actions on the ministers. The newspapers quoted him the next day as saying, "They [the young people] go to meetings, are inflamed by fiery speeches, then disperse in small groups and are able to create havoc. How their [the ministers'] consciences can condone it is far beyond me." Northside High School's black principal immediately suspended two students for handing out Black Power flyers, and Juvenile Court Judge Kenneth Turner warned adults not to encourage youths to become truant from school on pain of fines and jail terms for parents. Black youth kept authorities unsettled and guessing about their next moves.

On Thursday, March 7, as the City Council finally considered Patterson's dues-checkoff proposal and voted it down, Pat Mayweather and another group of nearly 100 black students met at the Minimum Salary Building to make placards. They marched through downtown, led by Harold Middlebrook, in what Arkin described as "a loud, boisterous and disorderly march," shouting "Down with Loeb" and "Down with the mace-spraying cops." Lawson led a second, more quiet and orderly, march—

quite in contrast to that led by Middlebrook. Another group of twelve—mostly adults—also picketed and sat down in front of the entrance to the Democrat Road sanitation facility that morning, but no one was arrested.

Escalation was the order of the day. That night at St. John's Baptist Church, Reverend Bell told some 200 people: "Memphis is sitting on a powder keg, and the only thing holding it together is the ministers." Trash fires continued throughout South Memphis. Encouraged by Mayor Loeb, 3,000 members of the Tennessee Army National Guard began massive riot-control exercises in Memphis, as well as in other Tennessee cities. A U.S. judge refused to halt the exercises, despite a complaint filed by 500 African Americans in Nashville.

An FBI "Racial Matters" memo on Friday, March 8, warned (capitalized in original):

BITTER HATRED ON PART OF NEGRO LEADERS AND NEGRO YOUTH IS RAPIDLY DEVELOPING. THIS OVERALL HATRED AND CONTEMPT FOR AUTHORITY, COUPLED WITH YOUTHFUL EXUBERANCE, SOURCE FEELS, MAY TRIGGER A RASH OF PERIPATETIC AND SPORADIC UNOR-GANIZED INCIDENTS OF VANDALISM, BURNINGS, AND HIT AND RUN ASSAULTS ON POLICE OFFICERS.

That night, trash fires abounded throughout heavily black South Memphis, where Cabbage had his strongest base. A number of adults warned Lawson and other ministers that bringing militant black youths into strike support risked chaos, while various community sources told the FBI that Black Organizing Project leaders sought to provoke open warfare with the police.

But black youth more often than not took action on their own. On Saturday, March 9, about fifty black male teenagers, hanging out at a restaurant in South Memphis, threw rocks and bottles at both a squad car and then the wrecking truck that came to get it. More police vehicles arrived, and the incident almost turned into a brawl. The police feared such events could escalate until "some uniformed patrolman will catch some youth in the act and the youth will run, ignoring the officer's order to halt and will be shot," triggering an all-out riot. At the Democrat Road sanitation facility, black youths joined a crowd of fifty strike supporters who heckled scabs, while another group of seventy-five youngsters (including five whites) ignored heavy rains to march downtown chanting, "Freedom now." Strikers also marched that afternoon, and that night Lawson and AFSCME leaders at Olivet Baptist Church outlined a schedule of continual marches, picket lines, and rallies.

A few of the city's more privileged white college students began to get involved, including Bill Casey and the editors of the student newspaper at the private Southwestern College (originally a segregated Presbyterian school). Prompted in part by Coby Smith, one of the first black students to attend Southwestern, sixteen white students went to white churches in East Memphis on Sunday, handing out a flyer that said the strike was "no longer a simple labor dispute but a fervent protest against the outdated racial attitudes of this City that has united the entire Negro community." According to Casey, "A few of the kids looked like beatniks and people were shocked and scared. . . . I had several sheets wadded up and thrown at me." Otherwise, their actions elicited little response, while the FBI took special note of "ill groomed" white students supporting the strike.

On Monday, March 11, the Northside High School student-body president, Murray Austin Ervin, and another student named Alex Johnson passed out flyers at school, calling for a walkout. Despite a driving rainstorm, ninety-one students left the school at 12:30 and marched three wet miles to Clayborn Temple, upending garbage cans in what they called "turn over day." After rallying, thirty of them linked arms six abreast and danced their way through the downtown shopping area, chanting, "Black Power" and "Down with Loeb." They thoroughly "harassed the police," according to a reporter.

Many people considered Northside the finest predominantly-black school in the city, with 1,100 students, 77 percent of them African Americans, nestled in a neighborhood close to the Firestone factory, where the parents of many of these students had repeatedly gone on strike. Northside's principal called on students "to use common sense," warning them of truancy charges and suspensions. But increasing numbers of them joined downtown marches and picket lines. They set off a chain reaction. At Humes Junior High, a smaller number walked out; at Carver High School in southwest Memphis, John Henry Ferguson, a twenty-year-old school dropout, and Willie Jenkins, who had been suspended from school in January, brazenly went through the cafeteria, calling on students to leave. They lay down on the floor when school officials brought in the police, who arrested them.

A number of black informants told the FBI they condemned the COME strategy of "injecting more youth," whom they called excitable and "impulsive by nature." By contrast, Reverends Bell and Jackson congratulated the Northside students for their actions. That afternoon, Reverend Jackson led another 175 marchers in an orderly procession from Clayborn Temple to the downtown. Twenty-five feet behind them, another, more rowdy group of 125 to 150 black youth shouted, "Down with Loeb" and "We hate hunkies" (white racists). The police tried to get them to march single file, but they marched four abreast, and the police could not get them to remain orderly. Disruption of the downtown, said Reverend Bell, "is going to continue. We're not going to tell the police what we're going to do because the police are cooperating with the mayor."

Middlebrook enthused: "We had the kids totally involved." Police became "very much uptight about the youth marches," said Lawson. Middlebrook recalled a white woman who walked out of a department store; confronted by black youth dancing and singing, "Before I'll be a slave I'll be buried in my grave," she fainted. Such incidents increasingly drove white shoppers away from the downtown.

GOING INTO ITS fifth week, the movement remained strong, but doubts existed about whether strikers and their supporters could hang on long enough to reach a victory. Testimony in Judge Hoffman's court revealed that only thirty workers had paid dues to the union before the strike, raising questions about how well organized AFSCME really was. The city on March 8 put sixty-five of its 180 garbage trucks onto the street and, the next day, increased that to seventy-five. Public Works Director Charles Blackburn said 90 percent of the people could now get their garbage picked up at the curb. Black community informants told the FBI that some NAACP leaders and ministers "are hopeful that the strike will soon end." Tennessee Governor Buford Ellington sent his black administrative assistant, Hosea Lockard, to urge both black leaders and Mayor Loeb to make a compromise. Loeb said no; he had nothing but disdain for the Democratic governor.

Lieutenant Arkin felt confident that strikers would have to return to work out of economic necessity (although an FBI report indicated "no end in sight"). The city increased pressure on the workers after the *Commercial Appeal* published articles headlined, "County Taxpayers to Pay Half of Food Stamp Tab" and "Strikers Find Haven in Food Stamps," causing scores of conservative whites to write to Loeb that he should cut off food stamps and life insurance for workers. Loeb kept the latter, but on March 29, he canceled the city's contributions to the Shelby County Welfare Commission for food stamps for strikers, toward which the city and county paid a total of $15,000, in two increments. Workers paid 50 cents for $12 in food coupons, and more than 750 of them had signed up—at a total cost of some $300 to $400 a day.

It was unclear whether or not the mayor had the authority to cut off these funds, but the city's share of food-stamp money stopped. Striker Matt Randle said food stamps made the difference between food and no food for one's family. "We lived on food stamps." After the food stamp cut-off, Cornelia Crenshaw broke down in tears at a workshop of the Council of Jewish Women, telling them that strikers' families did not have enough to eat. "I told them at that time that I knew nothing about Castro, I had no communist's learning . . . but I swore that I was going to write to Castro and ask him for some money to feed these men. I think we became so possessed with this thing until we would go to almost any end." Crenshaw, O. W. Pickett, and AFSCME redoubled efforts to raise funds and food for the strikers.

Loeb had even less authority to stop the credit union from serving as a vehicle for union dues, since it was an independent agency with its own board, but, said Councilman Patterson, "That was one of the greatest ways to kill off a union, is to make sure that the union can't get its dues." Loeb had put workers—many of them losing cars, homes, and appliances—in a squeeze. "When you don't have income, you get discouraged," recalled striker Clinton Burrows. "Children would be crying at home, the next day they would talk about it" at the union meeting. Strikers "were getting weaker and weaker," and by mid-March, he thought about half of them wanted to go back to work. Fortunately, some of the children marched with their fathers, and most of the wives stayed solidly behind the strike.

With movement escalation, racial polarization over the strike only intensified. A barrage of letters in the newspapers pressed for more draconian actions by the city. One claimed, "No business can be efficiently operated with union labor in this country"; another called garbage collection itself "a socialistic venture" and warned that American freedoms "may soon be gobbled up by a godless, atheistic, materialistic socialism." Clearly, black ministers now played the key role in keeping strike support alive. On Tuesday, March 12, the *Commercial Appeal* published an article headlined, "Negro Pastors Take Reins As Garbage Strike Leaders in Switch to Racial Pitch." Writer Joe Sweat quoted Reverend Jackson as saying, "I have become a union leader." But he and other ministers, Reverend Blackburn said, walked "on a tightrope," trying to help a "pretty mild mannered group assert their right and on the other hand we are trying to hold down the young militants who want to tear the place up."

Some eighteen demonstrators on that Tuesday morning, led by Reverend Starks, protested scabs entering at the Democrat Road sanitation facility. Harold Middlebrook led more than 200 black students to the weekly City Council meeting, pleading for action. Two of them were arrested in the city hall auditorium, lending a new air of intensity to the proceedings. Councilman Patterson put forward his resolution supporting payroll deductions through the credit union, and once again the council rejected his measure. For the first time, however, a white council member, Jerred Blanchard, voted with Patterson, Davis, and Netters. To many of the city's whites, said Blanchard, "I became the fourth 'nigger' on the Council. That was the night the phone started ringing." Now he, too, was barraged with anonymous death threats and derogatory comments.

Lawson bluntly told the City Council: "All right, if you want to leave it to Uncle Bubber [indicating Mayor Henry Loeb] and say that you don't have any responsibility in this thing, go ahead. Then the black ministers will just go fishing and let what happens in this town happen." But Lawson was not about to go fishing and let so-called Black Power militants take over. He and other ministers increasingly framed the strike as part of a larger struggle for black access to good jobs, better housing and schools, city leadership positions, and an end to police brutality—"only part of a broad spectrum of grievances in the Negro community," according to reporter Joe Sweat. T. O. Jones privately chafed at this politicization, but there was nothing he could do about it.

After the council vote against dues checkoff, Patterson tried to propose another resolution, but the council did not let him bring it to a vote. Reverend Bell wanted to provoke another mass arrest, but instead Reverends Lawson and Kyles and Maxine Smith led a walkout of some 300 people from the meeting into a press conference. Kyles said, "There is no justice for blacks at City Hall," while Lawson pledged to "escalate our fight" and have "a whole series of people coming in here from all over the Country to help you march and lead you on to victory." Lawson wanted to raise the level of publicity and action in days to come, but Bell wanted to raise the level of disruption immediately. That night, at a rally at Lawson's church, Bell said that if Memphis did not become a "city for all the people, there would be no city at all." He urged students to skip school and picket Loeb's planned speech at Central High School the next morning. Reverend Jackson also raised the level of his rhetoric, warning "police snitches" that he would not stop people from beating them up, and Dr. Vasco Smith and others urged people to unite and not be intimidated by police.

At one mass meeting, Reverend Jackson pulled a gold-plated lighter out of his pocket and said conditions now called for fire, not water. But militant rhetoric aside, black ministers feared the consequences if Loeb or the City Council did not make concessions soon. At various times, Martin Luther King, Jr., had pleaded with whites in power that "I need some victories" to keep the black masses from turning to violence, and Memphis's black ministers felt the same way. The level of threats against scab workers, firebombings, and acts of vandalism escalated throughout the week, and Charles Cabbage spoke openly of armed self-defense should police or white vigilantes attack. Police claimed that T. O. Jones reportedly said he had seventy-five volunteers willing to burn the community—if that is what it took to bring about a settlement. Jones probably did not mean this literally, an FBI agent conceded, but such talk exemplified the frustration felt by many African Americans.

Combined actions by workers and students provided the key to keeping alive a direct-action movement in the streets. On Wednesday, March 13, late in the morning, 150 to 170 people, many of them teenagers, marched downtown and held a prayer- and songfest in front of city hall. A smaller group split off on the way back to Clayborn Temple and threatened shoppers and police, and another 125 to 200 adults marched later in the day. The movement's hectic schedule now included up to three marches downtown, a union meeting at midday, and a mass meeting at night, as well as picket lines and boycott actions at sanitation depots and various stores. Workers could carry some of this burden, but student reinforcements had become crucial to the effort.

Authorities did what they could to discourage them. Police arrested nine black youths, ages eighteen to twenty-three, including nineteen-year-old Willie Henry, and charged them with disorderly conduct and "night riding." In the words of the police, their crime was "shouting, acting boisterous and threatening people," while refusing to march single file on downtown sidewalks. One seventy-year-old white man claimed that two marchers struck him and broke his false teeth, but he could not identify them. That night, at a mass meeting at St. Paul Baptist Church, ministers again appealed to the youths for their support. Elsewhere, at Cypress Junior High School, after a talent show attended by a thousand people, a group of youths went on a rampage and smashed rocks and bottles against police cars. Fifteen carloads of police at the scene dispersed them, with no arrests. Someone broke out another window at a Loeb's Bar-B-Q, and seventy-five black students stayed away from Northside High School the next day. School boycotts and student marches had become a regular feature of the strike.

The confrontation in Memphis had reached an explosive stage, in part because the city proved increasingly successful in replacing strikers with scab workers. Reportedly, 120 strikers had now joined thirty-five other workers who had refused to strike in the first place—along with 156 other new recruits—so that more than 300 workers manned eighty trucks. At the cost of between $4,000 and $5,000 a day, all 800 Memphis Police Department officers worked seven days a week. The strike itself offset this huge financial drain by reducing the number of paid workers and garbage pick-ups. Bolstered by police escorts, increasing numbers of scabs went to work, despite heckling by strike supporters. Loeb's strategy of gradually intro-ducing strikebreakers seemed to be working.

Hence, a number of activists cried out for a more militant response to stop the strikebreaking. Reverend Malcolm Blackburn felt that the picket-ing and marches had become too predictable. The movement had failed to stop scabs, yet every time the topic of civil disobedience came up, the sub-ject was dropped. On Thursday morning, March 14, he decided to block the sanitation trucks at the Democrat Road depot with his body. When he picked up Willie James Kemp and two others at his church, Kemp told him, "Well, we're not gonna let you go to jail by yourself." On the picket line, Blackburn refused to move out of the way of the trucks; next thing he knew, a phalanx of police threatened to beat up the picketers. Blackburn and Kemp were arrested, each of them for the second time, and so were four other strikers. Down at the police station, Blackburn recalled with amuse-ment that a white officer called him "boy," making him an honorary Negro, and charged the six of them with conspiracy to endanger public health and to obstruct trade and commerce.

Later that day, Reverend Middlebrook teamed up with Reverend Roo-sevelt Joyner, John Burl Smith, and Charles Ballard to lead a total of thirty people, including ten teenage girls, to sit down in the street at Third and Pontotoc in black Memphis; they were all arrested for blocking neighbor-hood garbage pickups. Several girls complained that police maced them; seventeen of those arrested were under eighteen years old.

Juvenile Court Judge Kenneth Turner struck back, directing police to arrest any school-age children under the age of sixteen they found on the street during school hours—"no matter what they're doing." Police promptly arrested a thirteen-year-old and a fourteen-year-old trying to make their way downtown to join demonstrations. Turner said he would charge such youths with truancy, and five truancies could result in expulsion from school. When hauled into court, a number of black students flaunted their disdain for the judicial system. As City Judge Bernie Weinman heard disorderly conduct charges against thirteen young adults (under sixteen) and seventeen youths (under eighteen), they laughed derisively and talked over the proceedings, until Weinman burst out, "This is no game—no picnic," rebuking them as a classroom teacher might.

It seemed that repression only accelerated protest among black youths, and even some white ones. At Memphis State University that Thursday, whites in Students for a Democratic Society (SDS) and blacks in the Black Student Association (BSA) enlisted the student Liberal Club in picketing Mayor Loeb. MSU had called off morning classes so that all students could hear him, and Loeb spoke without incident, but as he began to drive off, about 150 students confronted him with a picket line on the sidewalk. True to form, Loeb popped out of his car and promptly began trying to convince them of his views and inviting them to his open house at city hall. The head of campus security had a fit: the television cameras recorded it all—which, police complained, only "built up the egos" of the demonstrators.

Authorities feared that the Invaders would get a foothold among rebellious youth—a fear that Cabbage cultivated. He told an informant that he purposely stayed in the background, but that the Black Power movement might challenge Lawson. John Burl Smith remarked that he would soon bring Stokely Carmichael to town, and that Carmichael had gone to Cuba to get weapons. Such comments were part of BOP's calculated strategy of raising white fears of black rebellion in order to get more bargaining leverage. The FBI and the Memphis Police Department had them under constant and suffocating surveillance, following them day and night. When Cabbage complained of this to the FBI, an agent told him the police had the perfect right to follow them. Obviously, they weren't about to stop.

IF INCREASING ARRESTS provided one form of escalation, increasing national publicity provided another. Up to this point, said Jerry Wurf, the Associated Press correspondent in Memphis had deliberately suppressed news of the strike, which had barely been covered by national media. Desperate to break the news blackout, movement supporters had threatened for weeks to bring in "Black Power boys," such as Stokely Carmichael. But Lawson, Epps, and others who knew Martin Luther King sought to remedy the lack of media exposure by trying to pry him away from his impossible schedule ("King Implored by Ministers to Come Here," read a page-one story in the *Commercial Appeal* on March 14). However, in a town dominated by the NAACP without a functioning SCLC chapter, bringing in King first could set off organizational rivalries and offend national NAACP leaders.

Jesse Turner, president of the Memphis NAACP and a member of the organization's national executive board, believed the strike was faltering, so he called NAACP President Roy Wilkins. The national NAACP had already sent $1,000 to support the strike, but Wilkins had just finished serving as one of the Kerner commissioners and said he was too exhausted to come. Undeterred, Turner went to New York City on Sunday, March 10, for an NAACP executive board meeting, and he pleaded for three days that "this was a fight we could not [afford to] lose." At the same time, unionists contacted Bayard Rustin of the A. Philip Randolph Institute. Coincidentally, Turner brought Wilkins back with him, and Rustin flew in separately on Thursday, March 14; both men ended up speaking at Mason Temple that night. Both represented the more conservative end of civil rights leadership at this point—Wilkins typically favoring court challenges over demonstrations and Rustin calling for moderation and electoral alliances within the Democratic Party.

Turner believed that Wilkins could bring out the mass of Memphis NAACP members, and he was right: nearly 9,000 people showed up at Mason Temple, creating the largest event of the strike to this point. Middle-aged and older black women and men appeared in their Sunday clothes, as did many sanitation workers. The mass meeting demonstrated why the Memphis NAACP had earned top honors within the national organization for five of the previous six years, boasting the largest membership of any local branch in the South.

T. O. Jones helped to lead the meeting, and Jesse Epps told the crowd,

"There will be little talk from this union from this day forward, for we are preparing for action." Reverend Ralph Jackson, with his hair slicked back and wearing a shiny suit, pumped up the crowd's emotions with raucous tones of outrage. People circulated huge garbage cans, labeled, "Dump Loeb Not Garbage," and filled them with cash donations. Lawson called on people to stand in unity, saying, "There is no freedom without dignity," and "no dignity without justice and manhood and power." When Rustin took the stage, most young people knew about him only what they saw: a middle-aged black man in an unpretentious suit and tie, with large glasses and graying hair that seemed to stand straight up on his head. His conventional dress accentuated an earnest style of delivery. He looked and spoke like someone who had been struggling hard for most of his life, the veteran of an earlier generation of nonviolent radicals now at odds with the New Left and Black Nationalism.

Rustin's position in the Movement at this point abounded with ironies. He had been among the first outsiders to help King in Montgomery create a thoroughly nonviolent movement and connect to labor and civil rights supporters across the country. He continued to advise King from the shadows, fearful that his homosexuality and past ties to the Young Communist League of the 1930s would be used to destroy King. Regarded by many as an organizing genius, Rustin had played a key role in the 1963 March on Washington for Jobs and Freedom, but lately he had urged the Movement to steer away from confrontations such as the Poor People's Campaign. Instead, the nonviolent Rustin wanted to build electoral coalitions with AFL-CIO unions, most of which fully supported the U.S. war in Vietnam.

Lawson had a long relationship with Rustin, however, and was not disappointed by his performance in Memphis. Pointing his finger for emphasis, Rustin laid out the simple proposition that black people could not get justice in the larger sense if black workers did not win this fight. "How can you get rid of poverty if working men don't get decent wages? If you can't get a decent salary for men who are working, in the name of God, how the hell are you gonna get rid of poverty?" Until the federal government recognized the plight of poor people who worked in the inner cities, it never would end poverty, and justice for black workers would never happen in Memphis unless trade unions and black people "stand together, man to man."

Rustin disparaged what he considered Black Power's cultural distractions. In New York City, he said, "Nothing's happening" because African Americans kept struggling over hairstyles or whether to use the name "Negro," "Black," or "colored"—or debating what is or is not soul food. By contrast, "In Memphis there is a real fight going on. Here people have a fight on your hands and don't have time for this foolishness." He drew his heaviest applause when he likened the Memphis fight to the Montgomery movement and called the Memphis strike "one of the great struggles for the emancipation of the black man today." "This becomes the symbol of the movement to get rid of poverty . . . [and] this fight is going to be won because the black people in this community and the trade unions stand together."

Rustin told his audience that the power to bring change was in their own hands, supported by the national Movement. "I am sure your papers do not report and debate the truth of what's happening here," but "people who believe in justice and democracy are behind you and have not forgotten the struggle that is going on here nor its profound importance." Rustin's audience followed his every move and applauded his articulate and frank statements. As sweat streamed from his face, Rustin then led the crowd—including well-dressed elderly women, students in cardigan sweaters, and church elders in suits and ties—in singing. He was a grand singer, one of those in the Movement who had helped to transform spirituals into labor and civil rights anthems:

> Ain't gonna let nobody turn me round, turn me round, turn me round,
> Ain't gonna let nobody turn me round, gonna keep on a-walkin',
> Keep on a-talkin', marchin' to the Freedom Land.

Rustin was not a well-known figure, but he provided a good warm-up for Wilkins, who was, and an aroused audience gave a long, loud, standing ovation when Wilkins stepped to the podium. He, too, had chided Black Power advocates, and he had also criticized King for opposing the Vietnam War. Like Rustin, he wore a conventional suit and tie, not a dashiki or army jacket, yet people knew that Wilkins had devoted himself for decades to the NAACP, to which many in the room belonged. They expected Wilkins to take a middle path in his discourse, and that is just what he did—yet he also delivered his message with acute rhetoric and strong feeling.

He expressed shock that men could work forty hours a week and still qualify for welfare and food stamps. "When you have a situation like that you ought to stay here and fight until hell freezes over. . . . I say the city of Memphis, Tennessee, ought to be ashamed of itself. If I were the mayor, I would be ashamed. I wouldn't want these men to not be able to feed their families on the lousy pittance they are paid." Wilkins criticized police brutality, saying, "Mace is to curb a riot, people running wild. Mace is not made to be used on orderly people marching down the street in orderly fashion." To rising applause, he told the crowd, "You have given enough in forbearance" and should fight hard for change. "I don't mean go out and tear up the town. This is your town just like it's a lot of other people's town and you've got to live in it. Don't foul your nest but don't give an inch. . . . I didn't come here to make threats, but anyone who picks on peaceful people is building for trouble. . . . I don't mean riots," he said, but Memphis "has got to make a clean break with the past."

Wilkins spoke sympathetically of the difficulty of changing an entire culture built on segregation, saying, "It's hard for old Negroes to change their minds . . . and you know it's hard for whites to change their minds, even the good ones." To laughter and applause, he added, "And the bad ones just get worse."

Wilkins knew Memphis. He had first come through town in 1929 with Walter White and George Schuyler to investigate secretly the conditions of black levee workers in Mississippi, who then made a mere 10 cents an hour. He later told interviewers that "Negro peasants," as he called them, had escaped from Mississippi to Memphis "with a plantation economy in their bones." Unionization gave them their only means to move from a dismal past to a better life, but to do it they had to fight bias against unions as well as the old plantation mentality. The struggle in Memphis thus represented "the overflowing of the final developments of the black worker in the South."

Wilkins had seen this transition in his own lifetime, and, true to his own

optimistic brand of politics, he offered a vision of incremental but significant change: "There must be new pay scales, new security, new life for the
people—a new deal all the way around." A change in the status of black
workers, along with the black vote, could transform the city, he said,
adding, "Look at the unity that has been forged here. The Negro population is like a unit on this. It can be done, with that kind of unity." He urged
his audience "to get people who are blocking the way *out* of the way," and
concluded, "Pray God that you may spread it [the Movement] to the rest of
Memphis."

AFTER THURSDAY NIGHT'S mass meeting, a more widespread sense of
unity gripped the black community, along with the demand for action that
gripped many black youth. Friday, March 15, marked five consecutive days
of youth marches, and police arrested five black males (ages thirteen to fifteen) from Humes Junior High School for carrying placards and blocking
traffic at Hernando and Union. None of their parents even knew they had
skipped school. On the same day, a Shelby County grand jury indicted
eight strike supporters arrested on February 23—including seventy-two-
year-old O. B. Hicks. For supposedly rocking a police car, the grand jury
charged them on two counts: for "prowling" and "traveling for the purpose
of intimidating citizens." Judge Weinman's court held in abeyance the
cases of the thirty people arrested for blocking trucks the previous day, and
Judge Churchill released Charles Ballard and John Burl Smith on probation. Fire and Police Director Frank Holloman complained that the courts
were being too lenient.

The police reported increasing verbal threats aimed at sanitation workers, Molotov cocktails used to start garbage fires, some seventy false fire
alarms, and an attack of beer bottles against police cars by some fifty
youths on Danny Thomas Boulevard. Authorities confiscated weapons at
Porter Junior High and Booker T. Washington High School. Police said a
hundred teenagers marched up and down Main Street, some of them
shouting, "Burn, Memphis, Burn," on their way back to Clayborn Temple.

Holloman said, "I deplore the use of our youths in such a manner," and
he advised parents that "it would be wise to know where their children are

at all times." On Saturday, March 16, black youths picketed downtown and Eastgate, Southgate, and Poplar Plaza Shopping Centers in white Memphis, led by Reverend Middlebrook. That night, police arrested four youths between fifteen and seventeen years of age for throwing a Molotov cocktail against a grocery-store wall. City Councilman Netters warned, "Black Power people in Chicago are thinking about coming down here." Holloman warned that teenagers found downtown during school hours "will be arrested no matter what they are doing and charged with truancy."

THE COMMERCIAL APPEAL condemned youthful demonstrators and the adults who supported them, but also admitted to a "stalemate." In a Saturday editorial, "Time for Council to Move," the editors suggested the mayor's hard line had opened a racial chasm, and now called on the City Council to intervene in order to resolve the strike.

On Sunday, March 17, oratory supporting the strike rang out in black churches, and the movement used the churches as a mass outlet for its own four-page newspaper which mocked the despised *Commercial Appeal* with its own title, the *COME Appeal*. Police intelligence agents reported pickets in front of the public library, verbal threats, and vandalism around the city. With alarm, they also noted another sign of Movement escalation: an article in the Sunday *Commercial Appeal* titled, "King to Lend Vocal Support at Rally." Lawson's ally would arrive in Memphis the next day.

13

"ALL LABOR HAS DIGNITY"

All labor has dignity.... You are reminding, not only Memphis,
but you are reminding the nation that it is a crime for people
to live in this rich nation and receive starvation wages.
—*Martin Luther King, Memphis, March 18, 1968*

A S THE CONFRONTATION IN MEMPHIS ESCALATED, MARTIN
Luther King, Jr., promoted the Poor People's Campaign. Much
like the strikers, he confronted a stone wall of opposition from
the American power structure. Trapped in an escalating whirlwind of controversy over his outspoken condemnations of poverty, racism, and war, he
clearly had stepped beyond the reigning consensus in the Democratic Party,
the mass media, and even among many middle-class blacks. King had called
into question "fundamental patterns of American life," said Andrew Young,
and, as a result, "We had become the enemy" to the country's establishment.
FBI Director J. Edgar Hoover, in particular, plotted King's ruin.

The FBI paid close attention to his every move. On February 23, the day
that police had first attacked marchers in Memphis, King had left SCLC's
conference of ministers in Miami to join hundreds of others in New York
City honoring W. E. B. Du Bois at a Carnegie Hall event sponsored by *Freedomways* magazine. The Kennedy administration had forced King to fire
its managing editor, Jack O'Dell, from the SCLC staff in 1963, for O'Dell's

ties to the labor Left, yet King had continued to work with him. King and others acknowledged Du Bois as one of the great scholars and civil rights advocates of the twentieth century, but the U.S. government had taken away his passport for advocating peace with the Soviet Union and an end to U.S. nuclear testing and had indicted him for his peace activities. Partly as an act of defiance, Du Bois publicly joined the Communist Party in 1961, declaring, "Capitalism cannot reform itself" and "No universal self-ishness can bring social good to all." He died in exile in Ghana on the eve of King's famous speech at the 1963 March on Washington for Jobs and Freedom.

King appreciated this spirit of resistance and kept in his files a copy of Du Bois's defiant statement made when he applied for admission to the Communist Party. At the *Freedomways* banquet, King blasted "our irra-tional obsessive anti-Communism" and praised Du Bois as "a model of militant manhood and integrity." The FBI thought King's statements proved he was a Communist sympathizer, and it peddled this view in memos to the mass media, which proved especially responsive in the South. The *Hattiesburg American* in Mississippi seized on King's Du Bois tribute, writing, "People become so deluded with the causes behind which King operates that they refuse to see his radical left tendencies and connec-tions." The *Birmingham News* ran a front-page story on King's association with O'Dell, headlined, "King, Red Ex-aide Team Up Again," and another titled, "King Shows Kindly Disposition toward Reds." The Jackson, Missis-sippi, *Clarion-Ledger* claimed, "Secret FBI records definitely tie Martin Luther King with Communism."

On March 4, big-city mayors endorsed the Kerner Commission's dire warnings about the urban racial crisis and King announced that poor peo-ple would march toward the nation's capital on April 22—using the Kerner Commission's recommendations as demands. On the same day, Hoover ordered FBI field offices to "prevent the rise of a black messiah" and create a new "racial intelligence" section that would, among other things, "publi-cize King as a traitor to his country and race." The FBI created a compre-hensive list of informants to counter the Poor People's Campaign and "serve again to remind top-level officials in Government of the wholly disreputable character of King." The FBI also held a "racial conference" to plan ways to sabotage the Poor People's Campaign, dubbing its operation "POCAM." Agents spread rumors in Birmingham's black community that welfare recipients who joined the campaign would have their benefits cut off, and they promoted stories in the media that King was only using the campaign to manipulate the poor and boost his own ego. The president, his cabinet officers, the attorney general, various arms of the military, the Pentagon, the Secret Service, and members of the media continued to receive various FBI memos with the title, "Martin Luther King, Jr.—Security Matter—Communist."

The FBI and the media campaign reinvigorated a far-right attack against King. The John Birch Society put African American Julia Brown on tour to speak in advance of King in cities he planned to visit (her salary paid by the FBI) and publicized Brown as a former FBI secret agent within the civil rights movement who claimed Communists had taken control of the Movement. (When Brown had visited Memphis in February 1966, the whole John Birch Society in Memphis had turned out.) The FBI campaign circulated claims by Representative Albert Herlong of Florida in the February *Congressional Record* that would be used against King in Memphis and elsewhere: "As is usually the case whenever one of these so-called nonviolent demonstrations is organized it will result in violence. When this happens, King will sanctimoniously retreat to his ivory tower, after having ignited the fires that cause violence, and say he could not help it, it got out of hand."

In the latter part of February and throughout March, scare stories appeared in the mass media that King's campaign would "lay siege" to the U.S. capital. Even sympathetic columnist Mary McGrory wrote that King was "playing a last, desperate card" and "fighting desperately to regain sovereignty over his people. The Spring Campaign represents his last stand." The rightist *National Review* accused King of "making a bold play for leadership [out] of this year's insurrectionary development" that would turn "a haphazard series of events into a coordinated rebellion . . . [that] can only end in bloody race war." *Reader's Digest* editorialized that King's campaign would create "a Washington paralyzed" and "that Communism's worldwide propaganda apparatus is set for a field day." It quoted Roy Wilkins accusing King of "bowing" to "ultra-militants" whose goal is "not freedom of speech but Mafia-like dictatorship."

King complained to newsman Daniel Schorr that the mass media ignored him if he did not make statements as militant as those by Stokely Carmichael but then pilloried him if he did. He continued to lose allies in the New Left who derided coalition politics. His long-time ally Bayard Rustin warned that King would do better to drop the Poor People's Campaign and try to elect Democrats in the fall. And, according to SCLC Executive Director William Rutherford, "Almost no one on the staff thought that the next priority, the next major movement, should be focused on poor people or the question of poverty in America."

The state of the American labor movement also remained a vexing problem, causing King to vent his frustrations in a speech before the Hospital Workers Union Local 1199 in New York City on March 10. "I'm often disenchanted with some segments of the power structure of the labor movement," he said, because most unions failed to take up the burden of organizing the poor and challenging racism inside or outside of the unions. The AFL-CIO strongly supported the Vietnam War, and complacency and apathy reigned in some of the most successful unions. By contrast, he said, Local 1199 provided financial support to the Movement and helped to create the Labor Leadership Assembly for Peace. "If all of labor would emulate what you have been doing over the years, our nation would be closer to victory in the fight to eliminate poverty and injustice," King told his cheering audience of largely female, black, and Puerto Rican workers. The purges of CIO leftists had decimated social movement unionism, but Local 1199 still maintained "the radiant and vibrant idealism that brought the labor movement into being." The United Farm Workers, headed by Cesar Chavez, whom King had met only briefly, came the closest to reviving the old CIO spirit of grassroots organizing, but most unions did not see themselves as part of a poor people's movement, and King had no clear strategy to get them involved.

On March 14 and 15, a promising gathering of Chicanos, Native Americans, and poor whites met with African Americans in Atlanta to discuss uniting behind the Poor People's Campaign. But King was elsewhere. On

March 14 in Grosse Pointe, an all-white and wealthy suburb of Detroit, a city wracked by racial polarization following the massive riots of 1967, King told 3,000 listeners, "The most critical problem in the other [black] America is the economic problem." White flight from the cities and the explosion of suburbs were producing two Americas divided by "a kind of socialism for the rich and rugged, hard, individualistic capitalism for the poor." A white Navy veteran shouted out, "I didn't fight for communism [and] traitors, and I didn't fight to be sold down the drain." As he tried to continue, white hecklers repeatedly interrupted King. "I think it would be rather absurd for me to work for integrated schools and not be concerned about the survival of the world in which to integrate," King protested. He appealed for unity, saying, "The destinies of white and black America are tied together," and we have to "live together as brothers or we're all going to perish together as fools." But members of Donald Lobsinger's anti-Communist group, called Breakthrough, famous for picketing and physically attacking antiwar protesters, continued to shout that King was a "traitor" because of his opposition to the war.

A discouraged King left for Los Angeles. A few days later, the news media revealed that American soldiers had murdered more than 300 unarmed Vietnamese civilians in the village of My Lai; along with the Tet Offensive and the bloody battle of Khe Sanh, it illustrated the worsening situation in Vietnam and the racism gripping America. The disturbing pressures of 1968 led to a visible change in King's demeanor. Exhausted, depressed, guilt-ridden, angry, ill with sore throats and low-grade fevers caused by his lack of sleep and rest, King worried out loud about the possibility of a kind of racial fascism in America. He remained acutely aware of Harris polls showing that most Americans, including most African Americans, disagreed with his antiwar stand. Constant criticism and controversy had a tremendously corrosive impact on him, according to King biographer David Garrow.

King's dream for a fair and equal America—so clearly enunciated at the March on Washington in 1963—had been brutally pounded by riots, white backlash, and war. Yet, without hope, one dies, he had told his staff at the beginning of the Poor People's Campaign. Hence, in the midst of his seemingly hopeless campaign against poverty, war, and racism, and despite the odds against him, King told Lawson he would come to Memphis. It was thirty-four days into the strike.

JAMES LAWSON HAD been keeping King up to date by phone, and the two men understood implicitly that Memphis strikers personified the plight of the black working poor and unemployed all over America. But King's staff practically begged him not to go to Memphis. "We had charted out fifteen cities that we were going to try to organize," said Andrew Young. "We were trying to organize poor whites, Hispanics, southern blacks, northern blacks—I mean, there was just a tremendous organizing job and I didn't know how you could take on anything else." King decided, however, to go to Memphis. To do it, he had to fly from a speaking engagement in Los Angeles to New Orleans, then to Jackson, Mississippi, and then on to Memphis. He moved SCLC's planning conference on the Poor People's Campaign from Jackson to Memphis and said he would begin his planned speaking tour through the Mississippi Delta from there. Memphis would be just a one-day diversion. Young complained, "We had been through this too many times to think Martin could just go to Memphis, make a speech, and leave." King's deep and problematic involvement in Albany, Georgia, in the Meredith march, and other major campaigns had begun similarly— with one little speech.

As King flew to Memphis on Monday, March 18, a crowd of between 9,000 (a police estimate) and 15,000 (a Movement estimate) had already filled Mason Temple by 7 PM. Many more crowded into the doorways and aisles—and they would stand there for the next four hours. Some wore suits and ties, brightly colored church clothes, while others wore work clothing, as the working poor and the middle class mixed together. It began much as any church meeting would. Many ministers who had not been involved in the strike came out to see and be seen with King. Reverend L. R. Donson of Belmont Baptist Church presided, Reverend Charles Thomas read scripture, Reverend W. L. Varnado offered a prayer, and Myrtis Ewell sang, "God Bless America."

The mass meeting had heavy religious overtones, but it also extolled the gospel of labor rights and the black freedom struggle. Memphis Labor Council President Tommy Powell excoriated Mayor Loeb, and the crowd cheered enthusiastically as he passed around a petition and called for 100,000 signatures to remove Loeb from office. Jerry Wurf, with his gray hair and dark glasses, might have been mistaken for a rabbi—until he opened his mouth. Soberly, deliberately, he recounted the origin of the strike among the sanitation men, whose hours of work had been shortchanged one too many times. He told of the deaths of two workers ground up in a garbage packer on February 1. His talk sped up and his volume rose as he described inhumane conditions of work, his finger poking at the air. He hoped that in the future, striking workers could not only sing, "God Bless America" (as they did that night), "but that America would also give some of them its blessings." Outrage flooding into his voice, Wurf said the city took money out of workers' paychecks for debt collectors, so why couldn't they do it to support their right to have a union?

As his anger rose, so did shouts of "Tell it," "Yes," and "Right on!" "These men tell us that all their lives they've been wanting to be men. As men, they've been struggling to be dignified. And they tell us that this may be their only chance. And they're not giving up!" On this night, as on many others, Wurf recalled, "I had the extraordinary experience of standing and pounding a New Testament" in a Christian church. The workers did not mind either his Jewishness or his New York accent. Wurf felt secure and welcomed before black audiences in Memphis, repeatedly describing the labor struggle as part of the struggle of African Americans for dignity and a better life, and fusing his message with that of the workers.

Church was a good place to do it, and Ralph Jackson had become extraordinarily good at it. Reverend Jackson bellowed, "Loeb said we could pile up garbage as high as the roof tops. Let's help him pile it up!" Jackson challenged black doctors, barbershop and beauty-shop owners, teachers, and insurance executives (who had resisted a strike among their own workers several years earlier) to give financial support now. "The preachers have been carrying this thing on their backs for two weeks now. It's about time for us to hear from some of the professional people who make their money offa black folk!" Jackson seemed to form his mouth into a trumpet shape—shouting, waving both arms for dramatic effect. His voice grew harsh and raucous as he shouted his conclusion: "We will not stop until every black man gets a chance to lift himself up! We are on the march, and we will stay there, nothing can stop us!!"

By now, black youths were standing up, rocking back and forth in unison, singing:

> *We shall not, we shall not be moved,*
> *We shall not, we shall not be moved,*
> *Just like a tree, standing by the water,*
> *We shall not be moved.*

This church hymn, transformed into a labor-movement anthem by the Southern Tenant Farmers Union in the 1930s, had returned to the freedom struggle in the 1960s and now was part of both movements through the sanitation strike. Black youths also sang another old church song, transformed by the freedom movement:

> *I woke up this morning with my mind stayed on freedom,*
> *You know I woke up this morning with my mind, stayed on freedom,*
> *I woke up this morning with my mind stayed on freedom,*
> *Hallelu, hallelu, hallelujah!*

The mass of people joined in on yet another hymn-turned-labor-turned-civil-rights anthem, sung first in black churches, then by black women on strike in Charleston, South Carolina, in 1946—members of the Food, Tobacco, Agricultural, and Allied Workers (FTA), one of the CIO's civil rights unions expelled during the cold war purges. That song was finally imported into the civil rights movement via Highlander Folk School, and people in Mason Temple now swayed back and forth, arm in arm, singing as people had done in mass meetings throughout the 1960s,

We shall overcome, we shall overcome,
Oh, deep in my heart, I do believe,
We shall overcome, some day. *

The unity created by their common musical expression took practical forms. While people sang, they donated canned food and clothing, and church leaders passed garbage cans and buckets through the audience for donations to the strike. O. W. Pickett, AFSCME staff, and COME—which that night announced its donation of $10,000 to the strikers—all raised money and channeled it through COME. Ministers and youth passed out the *COME Appeal* newspaper, educating people about the demands of the workers, the status of public-employee organizing throughout the United States, and the support of white union members for the strike. It pointed out: "The Negro minister has taken an irrevocable stand on the side of the sanitation workers in their strike and has issued a ringing challenge to the antagonistic and personality degrading white power structure in the City of Memphis." It listed "ten things you can do" to support the strike and called on all of the educated and professional classes to join in the fight.

Henry Loeb still hoped to split apart black organizations and factions over money, organizational turf, and tactics, but this mass meeting made that appear far less likely. Crammed into a church auditorium, this cross-class alliance of African Americans—as well as a few white union, church, and academic activists—by their presence and spirit brought back memories of the unity and uproarious street demonstrations of Birmingham, Selma, and Montgomery. This meeting proved that the strike was not about to fail.

LAWSON TOLD KING on Sunday night that on Monday, March 18, he would probably be speaking before the largest indoor mass meeting ever seen in the civil rights movement. No other black facility in the South held as many people as Mason Temple. But when he and Jesse Epps met King at

---

*Charleston striker Lucille Simons adapted this song to the picket line and Zilphia Horton, Pete Seeger, Guy Carawan, and others passed it on. When King first heard it sung at Highlander he remarked on what a powerful Movement song it had become.

the airport, Lawson said, "Martin, I'm sorry. I said you would probably speak to 10,000 people tonight. . . . I'm sorry. I don't know what happened, but it doesn't look like you're going to speak to 10,000 people." King's face fell. Epps chimed in, "Yeah, it looks, doctor, . . . as though you might speak to 25,000 people." Lawson laughed, "He just lit up like a lantern."

At 9:07, an hour and a half into this mass meeting, King made his way through a side door at Mason Temple, escorted arm in arm by S. T. Thomas and other sanitation workers. Lieutenant Jerry Williams and a handful of black detectives waited in the wings, welcomed at this point by Lawson as a security detail for King. King and his entourage of James Bevel, Andrew Young, Ralph Abernathy, and local supporters, "had to squeeze our way through standing-room-only aisles with people all over the parking lots," Lawson recalled. "And it was clear that Martin was their man. That obviously was the case, which I had been telling him all along, you see. That he represented the aspirations and the struggle of our people." King's spirits soared as the huge crowd greeted him with a long, loud, standing ovation. With fists raised, thumbs upturned, fingers pointed in a victory signal, black Memphians greeted him as a brother. In this "sardine atmosphere," as Reverend Lawson called it, no shouts of "Black Power" or cries of "sellout" assailed him. The "spirit of Memphis"—unity, determination, and mass participation—reinvoked the power of the early 1960s black freedom struggle.

"Martin was visibly shaken by all this," said Lawson, "for this kind of support was unprecedented in the Movement. No one had ever been able to get these numbers out before." This meeting brought together the labor struggle, civil rights, and the black religious tradition of prophetic oratory in a marvelous new convergence. Ella Baker famously said that King didn't make the Movement, the Movement made King, but he now demonstrated why the Movement also needed him. King reached beyond his anxiety and depression back to his strengths. Speaking for more than an hour, using almost no notes, King helped people to see the strike as something much larger than a local issue and to gain spiritual strength for the fight ahead. The Memphis crowd shouted out support and punctuated his statements with shouts of "That's right," "Yeah," "Tell it, doctor," and they interrupted his speech dozens of times with strong, swelling applause.

He began quietly, speaking almost in a monotone:

> I need not pause to say how very delighted I am to be in Memphis
> tonight, and to see you here in such large and enthusiastic numbers.
> As I came in tonight, I turned around and said to Ralph Abernathy,
> "They really have a great movement here in Memphis." [applause] You
> are demonstrating something here that needs to be demonstrated all
> over the country. *("That's right.")* You are demonstrating that we can
> stick together [applause] and you are demonstrating that we are all
> tied in a single garment of destiny, and that if one black person suffers,
> if one black person is down, we are all down. [applause]

Memphis showed the ability to "unite beyond the religious line," King
said—something he had been preaching and teaching about for years. "We
have Baptists, Methodists, Presbyterians, Episcopalians, members of the
Church of God in Christ, and members of the Church of Christ in God, we
are all together. [applause] And all of the other denominations and religious bodies that I have not mentioned." He could barely get a sentence or
two out of his mouth before people broke into cheers and celebration.

King warmed up to his subject and spoke with increasing emphasis and
rising tones of excitement. The other great need, King said, "is to unite
beyond class lines. The Negro 'haves' must join hands with the Negro
'have-nots.' [applause] And armed with the compassionate traveler's
check, they must journey into that other country of their brother's denial
and hurt and exploitation. [applause] And this is what you have done.
You've revealed here that you recognize . . . that the no D is as significant as
the PhD, and the man who has been to no-house is as significant as the
man who has been to Morehouse. [applause]"

King spoke as both a religious moralist and a political analyst, and with
increasing satisfaction, for the members of his audience appreciated his
every nuance. They were also very fired up. "It's been a long time since I've
been in a situation like this and this lets me know that we are ready for
action," he said, pledging SCLC's financial and moral support. "You are
doing many things here in this struggle," but particularly, "you are demand-

ing that this city will respect the dignity of labor." He reminded his audience that the person who picks up garbage was as essential to the health of society as the physician, and he made a ringing declaration: "All labor [*Ralph Jackson reiterated*, "all *labor*"] has dignity." Yet the nation had devalued the labor of the working poor and of African Americans:

> You are reminding, not only Memphis, but you are reminding the nation that it is a crime for people to live in this rich nation and receive starvation wages. [applause] And I need not remind you that this is our plight as a people all over America. The vast majority of Negroes in our country are still perishing on a lonely island of poverty in the midst of a vast ocean of material prosperity. [applause] My friends, we are living as a people in a literal depression. . . . Now the problem is not only unemployment. Do you know that most of the poor people in our country are working every day? [applause] And they are making wages so low that they cannot begin to function in the mainstream of the economic life of our nation. ["*That's right*."] These are facts which must be seen, and it is criminal to have people working on a full-time basis and a full-time job getting part-time income. [applause]

The sanitation strike raised not just local issues about one benighted administration but a national problem of the unemployed and working poor across America; a victory in Memphis would be a victory for the nation. "You are here tonight to demand that Memphis will do something about the conditions that our brothers face as they work day in and day out for the well-being of the total community." The poor had become invisible to most Americans, but, "You are here to demand that Memphis will *see* the poor."

People who had marched, stood on picket lines, been maced, beaten, and suffered privations for more than a month knew his next point very well, as King buttressed his speech with the biblical story of Dives, the rich man denied entrance to heaven. King left room for the better-off to identify with this parable, saying Dives went to hell not because he was rich but because he passed by Lazarus every day and refused to see him and recognize his plight. "Jesus never made a universal indictment against all wealth"— rather, his target was self-centered greed and lack of concern for others. As he did throughout his Poor People's Campaign tour, King used this story to encourage the black middle class to see and stand with the poor. But he also used it to connect the racism blacks experienced at the local level to the insensitivity of the country as a whole: "If America does not use her vast resources of wealth to end poverty and make it possible for all of God's children to have the basic necessities of life, *she too is going to hell* [applause]."

It was this sort of anger and audaciousness that made people feel they had a power behind them greater than armies. To cheers and cries of "Go ahead" and "Talk to us," King said that God would some day indict the nation's leaders, telling them that despite the nation's technology, spaceships, highways, and massive wealth, they had ignored God's commandments to feed the hungry and clothe the naked. "This may well be the indictment on America. And that same voice says in Memphis to the mayor [*crowd says*, "*Yeah*"], to the power structure, 'If you do it unto the least of these, of my children, you do it unto me' [loud applause]."

In his inimitable way, King combined scriptural teachings and the black Social Gospel with a direct political attack on the American power structure. He politicized issues of wealth and poverty that ministers usually left at the level of generalities. People in the crowd understood the difference. He reminded the leaders of America that God's voice would render a judgment that it could never enter the kingdom of greatness by ignoring the poor. By speaking of God's coming "indictment on America," King brought a larger power to bear.

King did not leave social change to God, however, for he believed people themselves had to change their history and define their own needs. "You are highlighting the economic issue. You are going beyond purely civil rights to questions of human rights. That is a distinction." The Memphis movement would prove once again that organized people could triumph over forces of oppression. History had already proved it. Twelve years earlier, for 381 days, "Fifty thousand strong, we substituted tired feet for tired souls," drawing upon the "best in the American dream" to force a recalcitrant white ruling class to yield in Montgomery, in a movement that carried "the whole nation back to those great wells of democracy"—the Constitution and the Declaration of Independence. In Birmingham, too, black people defeated Bull Connor's dogs and fire hoses with "a fire that no water could put out" and "literally subpoenaed the conscience of a large segment of the nation" to help win the 1964 Civil Rights Act, followed by the great march from Selma to Montgomery that helped to win the 1965 Voting Rights Act. Movement history provided King's best argument that organized people could win their just demands.

According to King, the struggle for black equality had logically brought the Movement to Memphis and to a new direction: "With Selma and the voting rights bill one era of our struggle came to a close and a new era came into being. Now our struggle is for genuine equality, which means economic equality. For we know that it isn't enough to integrate lunch counters. What does it profit a man to be able to eat at an integrated lunch counter if he doesn't earn enough money to buy a hamburger and a cup of coffee? [applause]"

Through a series of questions, King brought into focus how poverty prevented people from exercising God-given, inalienable rights, and then he poured forth a litany of complaints that he had heard on the lips and seen on the faces of poor people in Watts, in Chicago, in Mississippi, in Alabama—all over the United States and in other parts of the world. He spoke in terms used regularly by sanitation workers, Rosa Parks, and King himself in his very first civil rights speech, in Montgomery. There comes a time, he said again in Memphis, when people get tired:

We are tired of being at the bottom [*crowd replies, "Yes"*]. We are tired of being trampled over by the iron feet of oppression. We are tired of our children having to attend overcrowded, inferior, quality-less schools. [applause] We are tired of having to live in dilapidated, substandard housing conditions [applause] where we don't have wall-to-wall carpets but so often we end up with wall-to-wall rats and roaches. [applause and cheers] We are tired of smothering in an airtight cage of poverty in the midst of an affluent society. We are tired of walking the streets in search for jobs that do not exist. We are tired of working our hands off and laboring every day and not even making a wage adequate to get the basic necessities of life. [applause]

King also pointed out how poverty corroded black family life, saying, "We are tired of our men being emasculated so that our wives and our daughters have to go out and work in the white lady's kitchen [applause], leaving us unable to be with our children and give them the time and attention that they need. We are tired." King spoke to black women and men alike about the psychic pain they endured due to racism and poverty, but he added the master touch based on his own experiences that not many others could command—the certainty that there could be a better world, optimism mixed with outrage at oppression.

"And so in Memphis we have begun, and we are saying, 'Now is the time' . . . to make real the promises of democracy," to make an adequate income a part of American citizenship, to make city hall "take a position for that which is just and honest. Now is the time [applause] for justice to roll down like water and righteousness like a mighty stream. Now is the time."

Shouts and clapping, laughter and cries of recognition nearly drowned him out, as King evoked a kind of jubilation in his listeners. Why? People like James Lawson and Andrew Young, who had heard King so many times, instantly recognized King's stock phrases and rhetorical flourishes, yet they marveled at their effectiveness when he brought them into a struggle like the one in Memphis. With one foot planted on the Bible and the other on the Constitution, King had long ago perfected a powerful oratory that matched the timing and the rhythm and the feelings and the needs of the southern black working class. His rhetoric helped poor people get beyond feelings of despair, helplessness, and unworthiness encouraged by lifetimes of poverty and racism. King confirmed that black poverty resulted not from people's lack of initiative or hard work, but rather from powerlessness inflicted by unjust structures of power. He convincingly argued, using history as his guide, that they could change all that.

Instead of closing his speech as he often did with grand generalities, glorious phrases out of the Bible, or the words of a hymn ("His truth is marching on"), he spoke directly to the issue at hand:

> Now let me say a word to those of you who are on strike. You have been out now for a number of days, but don't despair. [*Voices say*, "*Oh no.*"] Nothing worthwhile is gained without sacrifice. [applause] The thing for you to do is stay together, and say to everybody in this community that you are going to stick it out to the end until every demand is met, and that you are gonna say, "We ain't gonna let nobody turn us around." [cheers, loud applause]

After many years of preaching before unions, King spoke to workers as a labor leader as well as a Christian moral leader: "Let it be known everywhere that along with wages and all of the other securities that you are struggling for, you are also struggling for the right to organize and be recognized [applause]." Instead of Black Power, he spoke to them about union power. And what is power? He explained:

> We can all get more together than we can apart; we can get more organized together than we can apart. And this is the way we gain power. Power is the ability to achieve purpose, power is the ability to effect change [applause]. And we need power. What is power? Walter Reuther said once that 'Power is the ability of a labor union like UAW to make the most powerful corporation in the world, General Motors, say 'Yes,' when it wants to say, 'No.' " That's power. And I want you to stick it out so that you will be able to make Mayor Loeb and others say, "Yes," even when they want to say, "No." [applause, cheers]

King urged workers not to accept any paternalistic reassurances to "my men" from the mayor that he would solve their problems:

> Don't go back on the job until the demands are met. [cheers] Never forget that freedom is not something that is voluntarily given by the

oppressor. It is something that must be demanded by the oppressed. Freedom is not some lavish dish that the power structure and the white forces in policy-making positions will voluntarily hand out on a silver platter while the Negro merely furnishes the appetite. [applause] If we are going to get equality, if we are going to get adequate wages, we are going to have to struggle for it.

In this almost unscripted speech, King forged an interaction with his audience that drove his narrative toward action. King knew that his role in a situation like this was not just to inspire but also to direct people toward specific ways to organize, mobilize, create a spirit of resistance, and produce results. After this high-powered, emotional speech, the issue came down to, What should we do next? Amid cheering and applause, a new level of energy had been created—so much so that King could not end simply with rhetoric. He needed to take the Movement to a higher level. He paused for a moment and seemed to be thinking out loud. "You know what?" he asked the crowd. "You may have to escalate the struggle a bit." Then he dropped a bombshell: "I tell you what you ought to do, and you are together here enough to do it: in a few days you ought to get together and just have a general work stoppage in the city of Memphis!" One man rose from the audience, rhythmically shouting, "Yes! Yes! Yes!"

Pandemonium broke loose. King had invoked a latent power that black workers in the Deep South possessed because they did so much of the hard work, and they recognized it when they heard it. Now King helped them to envision what it might be like to use this power: "And you let that day come, and not a Negro in this city will go to any job downtown. When no Negro in domestic service will go to anybody's house or anybody's kitchen. When black students will not go to anybody's school and black teachers. . . ." His voice got lost amid another thunderous ovation from the crowd. People stood, cheering and yelling, clapping, dancing, singing, celebrating the very audacity of his idea: black people could shut down Memphis! Merely by withholding their labor, in good, nonviolent fashion.

Jerry Wurf sat close to King and watched in wonderment as all this unfolded. King's "eyes lit up," said Wurf, as he recognized the charged situation in Memphis and what it could portend for the Movement as a whole: "He had not seen this kind of a response to a situation for some time," Wurf noted. "If you'll recall Dr. King, starting in Chicago, had a series of discouraging experiences. And here was a very encouraging experience. And in a strange way he gave life to the strike and the strike gave him warmth and excitement and involvement—the two came together in a very beautiful way. Spontaneously he stood there and he looked about him. He had no intention of coming in to lead a march, but I was sitting next to him and talked about it and he just felt he couldn't let this thing go."

As King turned to confer with colleagues on the podium, a new set of considerations must have run through his mind. During the civil rights movement, no one had ever proposed a general strike of the whole black population, and general strikes had occurred in American labor history only during periods of very sharp confrontation and turmoil. In Seattle in 1919, San Francisco and Minneapolis in 1934, Oakland in 1946, workers had stopped entire cities from functioning. The general strike of slaves during the Civil War had led to a revolution that overturned an outmoded and unjust labor system, Du Bois had written, while general strikes of railroad and factory workers in the late nineteenth century had led to mass repression. These experiences suggested the almost revolutionary character of King's proposal. Black workers in alliance with the community could shut down all of Memphis.

His rather stunning proposal placed King in his usual dilemma: now that he had envisioned such a path-breaking historical movement, people would of course want him to come back to lead it. And apparently he could not resist. When King sat down, Lawson recalled that he said, "I ought to come back and lead a march." Andrew Young may have been cringing inside, but he instantaneously came to the same conclusion. Hastily, AFSCME and ministerial leaders conferred with King and his aides. King returned to the microphone to announce that he had agreed to return to lead such a protest on March 22. King pledged, "We will not go to schools, places of work or deal with merchants downtown," and after the rally he made a statement to the press appealing to whites, saying, "I wish all my white brothers and sisters would aid us in our hour of need."

IN JUST THIS way, King had found himself in so many jails. His life was not his own because he went where the people asked him to go, striker Taylor Rogers later said. In some cases—now in Memphis as in Montgomery—the struggle matched the vigor and purity of the moral vision he articulated. In a dialectical process, the Movement provided the context, the power, and the hope, and King articulated the vision. At that moment, King came to see the Memphis struggle as a "significant watershed for where the Movement had to go," Lawson said. King had told him even before the mass meeting, "Jim, you all are doing in Memphis what I hope to do with the Poor People's Campaign." And whereas he lacked the troops for that campaign, in this campaign some 15,000 to 19,000 people stood before him ready to fight for the rights of the poor.

Bill Lucy viewed King's response to the situation in Memphis as the work of a genius, based on "the incredible ability that King had to understand and interpret the issues and what was taking place." With only "the most minimal of briefings," he said, King had quickly understood that Memphis represented a shift from civil rights to economic justice for the working poor. It "was really about a new kind of people, people who worked forty hours a week and still lived in poverty, and he was able to arrange his presentation to demonstrate to the crowd that he understood this, and to give them a sense that their struggle was a legitimate struggle, that they had every right to carry on."

As thousands of jubilant strikers and their supporters left Mason Temple after four hours of singing, speeches, and prophecy, something new had been born. Lucy's "spirit of Memphis" became a tangible fact, a feeling that ran through thousands of people and could not now be easily quenched. Perhaps the movement emerging in Memphis, Lucy thought, could break the resistance of southern employers and politicians to unionization of the black working poor. Perhaps this moment could alter the distribution of wealth and power in the South as much as the civil rights struggle had begun to alter its political and social customs.

On March 19, the powers that be in Memphis tried to put the genie back in the bottle. The *Commercial Appeal* editorialized that King had once again cynically used a local movement for his own ends, as he "saw how many Negroes were aroused and quickly decided to attach himself to the local issue." His pledge to return to Memphis, the paper announced, was aimed merely to create a march that would get him "a spot on the evening television broadcasts" and build him up as a preeminent national leader. King's discovery of "ready made followers" led him to pronounce Memphis as the first real step of the Poor People's Campaign out of egotistical opportunism. Councilman Bob James denounced King's proposal for a general strike as "vicious and senseless" and "demagogic," while FBI agents sent out memos calling his speech "a series of demagogic appeals to the baser emotions of the predominantly Negro audience."

In an editorial two days later entitled, "King's Eye on Washington," the *Commercial Appeal* again accused King of simply using other people for his own gain and ominously warned him to remember that federal troops had shot and beaten unemployed Bonus Marchers in the nation's capital during the Great Depression. The editorial also said that King's Memphis campaign gave him publicity but would do nothing for the workers. Everyone seemed to agree, wrote Lieutenant Arkin of the MPD's Red squad: King was simply using Memphis as "a handy starting point to make his pitch for bigger things." King the manipulator—not the King who energized people and raised their vision of themselves and their country—that's the one many white people in Memphis believed to be the real King. They did not see how King's vision of a better world might encompass their interests as well as those of poor and working-class African Americans.

Others saw things differently. When he innovated and moved with the spirit of the times, that was King at his best, wrote journalist David Halberstam. This seemed to be another one of those moments. His speech had raised his own spirits and suddenly changed the trajectory of the Poor People's Campaign. It had focused almost exclusively on the country's poorest ghetto and rural residents, people with no jobs. Now King found himself highlighting the plight of the working poor, placing his campaign into the context of a classic labor struggle combined with a movement for black unity.

On a practical level, King's speech awoke the national media to the importance of the strike. As Lawson put it, King was like "a megaphone for the movement": where he went, the news media often followed. He was one of the few people who could bring national attention to local struggles just by giving a speech. Some in SNCC and other civil rights groups had long resented King for this, yet they also knew that the struggle for social change often hinged on media coverage. More than a month into the strike, "Nobody knew it except us and the city of Memphis," Lucy recalled, but now the media began to give it attention, and many union and civil rights supporters across the country took note.

After March 18, AFL-CIO member unions sent increasing financial support, which totaled more than $100,000 by the strike's conclusion, and they began to see that future union organizing in the South hung on the outcome of the Memphis strike. National media coverage also prompted some downtown businesspeople to wonder whether Loeb's hard-line stance really served their interests. The civil rights movements in Montgomery, Nashville, and Birmingham—and now Memphis—had demonstrated the power of economic boycotts, and King's entrance caused some whites to fear that negative publicity might hurt the city's image of racial moderation and discourage northern investments. Support for Loeb's unwavering position began to waver. Very few whites wanted to see Memphis at the center of a national campaign against poverty and for labor rights.

Yet many continued to hope that they might still find some blacks willing to jettison support for the strike—and indeed, not everyone in the black middle class supported King's labor politics. *Tri-State Defender* columnist Nat D. Williams celebrated poor black strikers and better-off black preachers fighting for a new dispensation from white Memphis leaders, but he also noted "an undertone of criticism in some circles of Negroes" that wondered whether outside leaders such as Wilkins, Rustin, and King "actually did any good other than to focus an unfavorable national spotlight on Memphis."

AFTER THE MARCH 18 mass meeting, King planned strategy late into the night at the Lorraine Motel with Abernathy, Young, Bernard LaFayette,

Bevel, James Harrison, William Rutherford, Dorothy Cotton, and Reverend T. Y. Rogers from Atlanta. As if to top off his energizing evening, a traveling gospel choir of black teenagers who were staying at the hotel serenaded King and his colleagues. The next day, King left Memphis to begin a Poor People's Campaign organizing trip into Mississippi and Alabama. Abernathy and Bevel stayed behind, as the FBI put it, to "confer with Negro ministers masterminding strike support activity."

Memphis gave King hope, but his tour into Mississippi during the next few days would demonstrate depressingly just how dreadful conditions had become for rural blacks driven from their jobs in the cotton economy by mechanization, and how difficult it would be to rouse a movement to go to Washington. King looked forward to returning to Memphis on Friday, March 22, with every reason to believe he would help launch one of the most spectacular days of nonviolent protest in the history of the southern freedom movement.

14

"SOMETHING DREADFUL"

It had never snowed that late in March. Never. And some of us
felt that just really something was just in the air and that it
was going to be something dreadful going to happen.
—*Lanetha Jewel Branch, teacher and strike supporter*

MOVEMENT CRITICS OF KING OFTEN CLAIMED THAT HIS sudden appearances in support of local movements diverted attention from organizing, did little to advance the struggle, and merely inflated his ego. King's strength, said Bayard Rustin, was not in organizing a campaign from the bottom up but rather in mobilizing people to support one already in motion. At this, King was superb. His March 18 speech mobilized black Memphis more than anything that had yet happened. Strikers felt King's words gave deeper spiritual and political meaning to their struggle, and he strengthened their belief in ultimate victory, while others who had stayed on the sidelines began to recognize that the outcome of this struggle might determine the fate of Memphians for generations.

Loeb thought that the power to determine events remained in his hands. As the strike continued into its fifth week, it had failed to truly inconvenience the city's white citizens. Even with its reduced workforce, the sanitation division managed to dispose of most of the white community's trash, and cold winter weather kept garbage from rotting very quickly during a reduced pickup schedule. The day before King's speech, eighty-four of the city's 180 trucks picked up garbage—ninety-two went out the day after, an indication that more blacks were doing scab labor.

Many young people, unionists, and ministers, however, believed they had reached a new and more powerful stage of struggle. The COME Appeal asserted, "Never before in the history of Memphis has the Negro community been more united." Strike supporters widely distributed a leaflet titled, "Dr. Martin Luther King, Jr., and the Community on the Move for Equality Invite You to March for Justice and Jobs." They urged ministers to turn out their congregations for "a momentous event for Memphis and this country," and told public-school teachers: "His march will be the most important event in this country since August 28, 1963, in Washington." In another leaflet, COME linked labor and civil rights explicitly and urged people to "March for Justice and Jobs" in order to make Memphis "a city for all people. A man is a man. God requires that a man be treated like a man." It urged participants to "walk gently" in "a march of dignity. The only force we will use is soul-force which is peaceful, loving, courageous, yet militant."

In another widely circulated leaflet, black ministers urged whites to "be united in harmony and cooperation, not separated by hate and discord," to see the strike in the broad context of brotherhood that King had always emphasized. "To the white people of this community, we say: Let the settlement of this sanitation men's strike constitute a new beginning for Memphis—a drive for jobs, housing and education for blacks and whites alike. Let us strive for equality and friendship. Let us build a better city on a foundation of mutual respect and progress towards the American ideal of liberty and justice for all."

Lawson and his colleagues in the clergy aimed to create a nonviolent coalition that the civil rights movement had never seen before—bringing together unions with civil rights groups, black workers with black preachers, alienated students and young black men disconnected from work with the black middle class, and black and white religious followers of the Social Gospel with each other. In the aftermath of King's visit, however, Memphis was anything but peaceful.

———

KING'S CALL FOR a boycott of work and school and a mass march had set the movement abuzz, yet some felt mass marches were outmoded, and they criticized Lawson for not being militant enough in his tactics. But what did "militant" mean? "Whites interpreted militant as meaning force and violence; blacks interpreted it as meaning unrelenting direct nonviolent action," according to one study. Lawson and the ministers clearly adhered to the latter meaning, but others in the Movement believed in using the rhetoric of armed self-defense to put pressure on the white establishment. Reverend Bell and others kept raising the specter of bringing in Stokely Carmichael as one way of exerting that pressure. Lawson too said he would invite Carmichael if it would unify the black community, yet his presence seemed more likely to splinter than unify the emerging Memphis coalition. Bell ultimately dropped his proposal, but rumors of Carmichael's imminent arrival persisted.

On a more substantive level, black youth increasingly criticized Lawson and other ministers for not stopping the garbage trucks through civil disobedience, nonviolent or otherwise. Lawson did not shy away from civil disobedience—in fact, he had been urging it—and at the March 18 mass meeting, Ralph Abernathy also urged people to place their bodies in front of garbage trucks. But, except for the March 5 mass arrest and the more recent arrest of thirty picketers for blocking garbage trucks in the street, it hadn't happened. In truth, most ministers preferred marches, speeches, and mass meetings. Bell, Lawson, Middlebrook, and other COME strategists hoped to remedy this by recruiting hundreds to get arrested on Friday morning before King's projected mass march. The plan also included a mass boycott of schools. "We are expecting to have 10,000 in the march—school children included. We'll fight the truancy verdict in the courts if need be," Lawson told the media.

COME's youth group fanned out all over town on Tuesday night, spreading leaflets urging blacks to march on Friday, while COME sent a letter from twenty-two ministers and other identifiable black leaders to black teachers and businesspeople. Calling the Memphis movement the most significant since Montgomery, they urged people to put aside their fears. Internal-security police reported that "Black Power Advocates" used more coercive tactics to get people to the march: people calling themselves "Invaders" supposedly had told teachers leaving King's speech that they would burn their cars if they opposed the Friday school walkout. Police reported threats to burn down two white schools and said the Invaders were agitating at schools in South Memphis for classes to be canceled. John Burl Smith went directly to the principal of Douglass High School, demanding to address the students, but he was told to leave, and he did. Police also reported threats to strip cars and damage buildings at four other schools if teachers and principals did not support the walkouts.

Police agents were alarmed to learn that King had left behind James Bevel, perhaps his most incendiary SCLC organizer. With a receding hair-line, a full beard, manic energy, and a prophetic, egalitarian vision of social change, Bevel had saved the movement in Birmingham from failure by unleashing the "children's crusade," in which thousands of students walked out of school, faced Bull Connor's dogs and fire hoses, and packed the jails when the adult movement was flagging. In Memphis, he planned to con-centrate on gaining more black youth support, which had clearly become crucial to the future of the Memphis strike.

Bevel began holding meetings and, true to his ultra-egalitarian Chris-tianity, did not stick to one issue. He said blacks had to overcome a great range of ills engendered by racism, including the war and capitalism itself. Bevel spoke at Warren Temple and Lane Avenue Baptist Church, saying that if the city didn't settle the strike by Friday, schoolchildren should boy-cott classes for the entire following week. He gathered students at LeMoyne College on March 20 to give what one FBI agent called "a viru-lent black power talk" and an MPD agent called "an incendiary anti-war speech." He urged students to read Frantz Fanon's *Wretched of the Earth* and the Nation of Islam's *Muhammad Speaks* newspaper, saying they should accept support from white liberals and clergy but not trust them. He also said he planned to form a new Black Power organization linking black nationalists across the country. Intelligence agents saw Bevel as a kind of ideological wild man—visionary, spontaneous, rhetorically unpre-dictable, and focused on the idea that black people themselves had to run their own communities and stop relying on others. "Bevel is organizing for the future," said a black community informant. Bevel asked students to prepare themselves to lead revolutionary change, but he apparently said little or nothing about the Poor People's Campaign or the strike.

As with King, Bevel's specialty was not methodical organizing but powerful rhetoric that aroused people to action. A number of black activists in Memphis likewise tried to effect change simply by escalating their rhetoric. Reverend Bell made a comment—seemingly designed to provoke the authorities—that he had resumed smoking just so he'd have an excuse to carry matches around the city in case he needed to burn it down. Cornelia Crenshaw supposedly threatened the Memphis Housing Authority with destruction if it did not close down during King's proposed march. Reports circulated that black workers at Baptist Hospital would walk out, and an active rumor mill in black Memphis kept the police off guard and apprehensive about what would happen next.

But AFSCME staff members, as well as James Lawson, questioned whether such agitation really produced constructive action. Jerry Wurf said that a lot of what passed for "militancy" in Memphis consisted of loose talk and bravado, especially among young people. Willie Jenkins, John Henry Ferguson, and a group of about twelve unemployed "young militants" hung out at the AFSCME headquarters, sporadically following the leadership of COME's Reverend Middlebrook, but AFSCME gave neither this group nor the Invaders any formal support because Wurf said they could not be controlled. Even as young blacks complained that the ministers had failed to stop strikebreakers and trucks from leaving the city garbage depots, Wurf said AFSCME had already decided, "We couldn't win the strike on the picket line. . . . We in effect let the city hire scabs." Wurf avoided such confrontations in part because he worried at the phenomenal number of guns floating around Memphis in the hands of both whites and blacks—including "these goddamn crazy kids with their five dollar pistols coming into the situation, invited by T. O. Jones," who used some of them as bodyguards and let them hang out in the AFSCME office. Ciampa called them Jones's "palace guard."

Wurf, like Lawson, shunned rhetorical radicalism but thought it infected King's staff. He described Bevel, Hosea Williams, and other SCLC staff members who came to Memphis as "a nice bunch of people but . . . arrogant beyond belief." He said, "King was a reasonable man to deal with. The staff . . . was totally impossible. He seemed to assemble every egocentric character in America." Wurf tried to warn them about Memphis—that "they were not in control, that the people weren't prepared"—but they ignored him. Wurf said, "I spent half my time to keep that city from burning down while the goddamned mayor was pouring gasoline on the situation and I ran around pulling matches out of people's hands." King's visit had the ironic effect of bringing new recruits to Cabbage's young group— including James Elmore Phillips, Clinton Roy Jameson, Charles Harrington, Charles Ballard, Hurley Gibson, and Don Neely—and a Memphis movement insider told the FBI that Wurf was "doing his best to talk the younger element of the Negroes in Memphis out of committing violence and burning."

Sanitation workers, by contrast, could be relied upon to adhere to non-violent discipline. They attended mass meetings in churches and at the United Rubber Workers union hall, marched in a line under the control of AFSCME marshals, and led picket lines and other forms of protest. But workers sometimes decided to take stronger measures, and police reported increasing incidents of vandalism and threats directed at strikebreakers and white businesses after King's visit. Historically, strikers have often used sabotage when overt picket-line confrontation proved too dangerous; Lawson knew this, and he thought the city's intransigence might justify putting sugar in the gas tanks of sanitation trucks. He distinguished sabotage against property from violence against people—a distinction that white "law and order" advocates did not make. And in truth, distinctions between violence directed at persons and destruction of property were easily blurred. The day after King's visit, according to police, fifty-eight-year-old John Hart, a sanitation worker who refused to strike, had a brick thrown through his car window; another barely missed the window of his house and hit his roof. Bricks also shattered three windows at the home of strikebreaker Richard Givens, who fired his shotgun out of the window in response. Someone threw a kerosene-laden beer bottle with an ignited rag against the home of sanitation supervisor Leonard Ward, but it failed to ignite. Someone even fired a shot through the glass of a scab's front door. Such anonymous attacks made it increasingly risky to scab.

Sporadic property destruction against white businesses also escalated. Someone shot a hole in the window of a Loeb's Laundry, and someone else broke a window at a Loeb's Bar-B-Q; people frequently pulled fire alarms in the middle of the night or started trash fires. In one bizarre incident, a striker named Leslie Robinson, forty-one, kicked a woman's garbage cans into the street, spilling their contents, because she would not stop putting them on the curb for pickup. Robinson cursed her and threatened to burn down her house, until she pulled out a pistol and fired it twice into the air. He left. It appears that she and he were both African American; police later arrested Robinson for assault and her for firing a gun inside city limits.

Actions by young people increasingly unsettled the schools. The city courts indicted two young African Americans who had disrupted Carver High School, Willie Jenkins and John Henry Ferguson, under an 1858 law charging them with "unlawfully disturbing and disquieting a school assemblage." Police singled out Ferguson for arrest numerous times and in one incident stomped on his sandal-clad feet, temporarily crippling him, on President's Island, where police had threatened to kill black labor organizer Thomas Watkins in the 1930s. They told Ferguson that the next time they arrested him, he might end up in the Mississippi River, along with "that nigger-lovin' preacher," Malcolm Blackburn. The police also charged twenty-two-year-old sanitation worker Willie Kemp, another of their favorite targets, with assault and battery on a police officer, in retaliation for roughing up black police plainclothesman Ed Redditt outside the Firestone hall several weeks earlier.

Loeb still insisted that racial violence could never happen in Memphis, but FBI agents and the police warned that events were moving fast in that direction. "Loeb is deeply hated by many of the Negroes," said an informant. "People will be swayed by Black Power groups, mainly composed of young Negroes of Memphis who will not sit still for the same treatment that 'old time' Negroes in Memphis have gone along with." Something much more dangerous was also going on as well: WHBQ-TV reporter Don

Stevens reported to the police on March 21 that someone had called the station to say King would be shot if he returned to Memphis. (Police traced the call to a telephone booth.) King's talk on March 18 hardened the attitudes of some whites, and the buildup toward the March 22 mass demonstration increased racial tensions.

Right-wing activists put flyers and newsletters targeting King, Lawson, Bayard Rustin, and others as secret Communists on car windshields and in homeowners' doors. One flyer, "The 'Real' Martin Luther King, Jr.," put out by a Memphis group calling itself "Enlightened People on Communism," repeated Hoover's allegation that King was "the most notorious liar in the country" and quoted testimony before the House Un-American Activities Committee (HUAC), linking King to supposed subversives Anne and Carl Braden, Bayard Rustin, Jack O'Dell, Fred Shuttlesworth, and Stokely Carmichael—and linking all of them to a Communist conspiracy to "create a Soviet America." Small cells of white hate groups—some of them based in the John Birch Society, the KKK, and the White Citizens' Council —bombarded people connected to the strike with frightening phone calls and letters. "Rev. Dick Moon's wife Glenda got phone calls describing in vivid terms her intercourse with black men and the parts of her anatomy that must be black," wrote strike historian Joan Beifuss. In an era before personal answering machines, Maxine Smith recalled, if you did not pick up the phone, it rang all night long. But if you picked it up, the caller might say, as one did to T. O. Jones, "You black son of a bitch, we're gonna get you." Wrote Beifuss: "It was as if a whole host of people with twisted minds were thrown to the surface by the tension boiling in the city."

But violent views did not come just from the margins of society. Congressman Dan Kuykendall, speaking to students at Southwestern College on March 22, described demonstrators as people who would "pillage, burn, loot and destroy." He attacked flag burning as treason, social programs as the work of the Democratic "pick pocket party," and dissent as "subversion and infiltration." He said the internal revolt of citizens in the United States, like that of the Vietnamese, represented the spreading effects of "communism everywhere." Kuykendall's cold war view of the world as polarized into good and evil suffused the news media and much of the culture in white Memphis, leaving little room for critical assessment of social problems or their origins.

With no framework for analysis upon which whites and blacks could agree, anger and resentment spread in every direction. Someone dumped garbage on the lawn of white Councilman Downing Pryor for merely considering compromise; black children teased the children of black Councilman James Netters for not marching on behalf of strikers; when black youths picketed white Councilman Billy Hyman's lumber store, someone shouted out, "Kill whitey." Loeb received anonymous death threats and traveled with personal guards, and he kept a shotgun readily available under his desk.

Police agents themselves held a paranoid view of the strike—even more so after King entered the picture. The Memphis FBI dredged up an old and uncorroborated memo that "a Communist Party functionary described Martin Luther King, Jr., as a confirmed Marxist in February 1962," while police agents profiled Lawson, too, as a Communist-oriented subversive. The FBI and local police said black ministers and unionists had purposely allowed black radicals to get out of hand and to unleash violent elements among black youth. The police constantly cited what they considered aggressive behavior by black youths—from harmless acts like singing, shouting, and dancing in the streets to taunting and making obscene gestures at people shopping downtown. White agents saw the strike itself as an affront to supposed racial peace, as did whites generally. One letter to the editor alleged that black downtown boycotters harassed a white woman and engaged in "shouting and gesturing obscenities" at another white shopper. In a previous era, the mere allegation of such acts could have led to lynching.

ALL OF THIS should have alerted the city's white leaders to an escalating situation and the need to dampen the crisis with a few swift decisions, but this they would not do. Lawson said a "moral blindness" existed in leading circles in Memphis, and the *Commercial Appeal* demonstrated it in a blunt front-page editorial: "To Dr. King and His Marchers." Placing the blame on King and the Movement for the city's tensions, it read, "If you don't watch out, Dr. King, you, and some of your fellow ministers here in Memphis just might undo what has already been accomplished" in improving race relations.

A handful of whites had begun to struggle to get through to Mayor Loeb the importance of settling the strike, but it was rough going. Dick and Glenda Moon and others started a group called "Save Our City." The group began sending out mailings the first week of March and put an ad in the paper urging people to get involved in settling the strike. A number of middle-class white and black churchwomen and civic activists had been holding interracial social meetings, and they began workshops on racial issues just before King's visit. Joan Beifuss, Carol Lynn Yellin, Glenda Moon, and several others from this group met with Loeb on March 14, telling him they were more interested in obtaining racial peace than saving the city's budget. Loeb stopped them, pointing his finger at women who did not have southern accents and asking them, one by one, "Where were you born, honey?" He told a woman with a master's degree from Oxford University in England, "Well, you're sweet and you're a pretty little thing, but you just don't know what you're talking about." He told them, "I wouldn't do a single thing differently." Groups of white middle-class women who came in to support Loeb got a much warmer reception.

After their disconcerting encounter with Loeb, Mary Doughty and some of her friends who wanted a strike settlement went to a meeting of Local 1733. "Upon entering the Union Hall we were given a standing ovation by the approximately 700 men present," who praised them for meeting with the mayor on their behalf. In the white community, however, such women were called Communists and worse. Trying to get the mayor or the white community to change was difficult indeed.

The City Council still provided the one hope for a pragmatic response before the mass march scheduled for March 22. On Tuesday, March 19, the day after King's speech, some 200 strike supporters attended the council meeting, again supporting Councilman Patterson's resolution that had been tabled on March 12—to let the credit union take money directly out of worker paychecks and deposit dues in the union's account, something already allowed to charitable organizations. Council members discussed

Patterson's proposal until 8 PM, holding two recesses behind closed doors, as strikers and their supporters sang hymns in the City Council chambers. Seemingly on the verge once again of settling the strike, the council took no action. Chairman Pryor recessed the council until 4:30 on Thursday, March 21, the evening before King's return. The *Press-Scimitar* called it a "Hurry Up Try for Ending Strike" and said the council was considering three different ordinances.

A potentially encouraging sign occurred on the night after Tuesday's council meeting, when AFSCME at last found a white audience willing to consider its case. The Tennessee Council on Human Relations sponsored a meeting at St. Louis Catholic Church in a well-to-do white East Memphis suburban area, where Bill Lucy "deftly fielded questions about the strike and received applause several times although the audience apparently was predominantly opposed to the union's position," according to the *Commercial Appeal*. Whites apparently preferred a well-spoken African American to the more blustery P. J. Ciampa, and a white constituent named Louise McComb wrote to Councilman Donelson that they gave Lucy "a standing round of applause at the conclusion of the two and a half hour meeting which included many questions asked and fully answered." As a surprised Lucy later said, "I think people found out that the union fellows didn't carry machine guns . . . and that there were legitimate problems that had to be solved."

Mayor Loeb spoke at the church the next night, and McComb wrote that he "was definitely on the defensive," subjected to sharp questioning, and "often his answers were not to the point." Loeb said union officials could be present and collect union dues from individuals when workers got their checks, but he would not allow the credit union to deduct dues automatically. Why? Because unions were not always "in the best interests of all the residents of the city." Loeb still substituted his own judgment for that of the workers. Only if the voters themselves, in a citywide referendum, approved a dues checkoff would he go along with it.

Labor negotiator Frank Miles belonged to St. Louis Church and attended this meeting. Afterward he approached the mayor with one of Loeb's close friends, who said, "Frank and I were just saying how absolutely silly this whole darn thing is and how dangerous it is." In Loeb's expression, Miles said he thought he saw that the mayor had finally glimpsed dangers ahead: there had been a long period of failed negotiations, "and now here comes Dr. King." Loeb invited the men to his house for a sandwich and then agreed to resume nonbinding discussions between the city and the union. He accepted Miles's conditions for doing so: The city would raise no legal questions (despite the injunction) over the union's right to negotiate; meetings would be held without the media and the parties would make no statements to the press; the City Council, not the mayor, would invite Miles to mediate, so that he did not appear to be Loeb's pawn. Any form of mediation could buy time until things cooled down and eventually produced some form of recognition, Miles thought.

Meanwhile, the movement tried to place maximum pressure on the city. An insider predicted to the police that 10,000 to 20,000 marchers would turn out on Friday, and he reported that mass leafleting was going on among black high school and junior high students, as well as university and college students. At least a thousand black workers—including members of the United Rubber Workers, the Teamsters, and a few members of the UAW local at International Harvester—planned to participate. The UAW's Fair Practice Council that week warned the mayor that he should not use penal-farm workers to pick up garbage, as rumors had suggested he would. Black businesses such as Union Protective Life, North Carolina Mutual, and Atlanta Life Insurance, and even Universal Life, which had broken a strike by its own employees a few years earlier, gave their workers the day off to support King's march.

The MPD's Lieutenant Ely Arkin said pressures had built up to the point that the city had no alternative but to allow King's mass march, which could dwarf anything that had ever happened in Memphis. Even the mass media took notice: WMC-TV news director Norm Brewer on the preceding Friday night had editorialized for resumption of talks. The *Press-Scimitar* ran a letter from Memphis State academics David and Carol Lynn Yellin, calling for mediation leading to a settlement, along with a story and editorial in a similar vein. For the first time, the newspaper explained that the city already bargained with hundreds of craft-union members, that the Memphis Transit Authority allowed bus drivers to have dues checkoff and binding arbitration, and that the Memphis Board of Education did the same with teachers who belonged to the Memphis Education Association. The city already guaranteed a variety of relationships with union members through contracts and would not fall apart if black workers also got a union contract. Unionists had known these facts for years, but most Memphians had not. "The printing of that information and the shift in editorial emphasis presaged a change in the handling of strike news by the two daily papers," wrote Beifuss. But Reverend Benjamin Hooks said the shift in media coverage came too late: the pendulum of opinion had swung so far against the strike in most of the white community that it became "almost impossible to change it."

On Thursday, March 21, at 6:30 PM—the last possible moment before King's march—the City Council passed Chairman Pryor's resolution asking Frank Miles to mediate the strike. They knew Loeb had already agreed to do it, and since mediation was not binding, he could easily reject its results. Patterson, saying this was toothless, cast the only dissenting vote. Had the council instead passed his alternative proposal, allowing dues checkoff, it might have settled the strike right then and there. But Loeb privately had already convinced a majority of council members to support a proposal forbidding dues checkoff. The council would not take a forthright stand against him.

A white woman named Carroll Richards that week wrote a letter to the *Commercial Appeal*, urging Loeb to rethink his position: "If one is to gamble so much, namely the city of Memphis, on principles, his principles should be worth it." She asked Loeb to reconsider the possible disastrous consequences of his uncompromising position. "It is in your power to mold Memphis into a genuine city, or to reduce it to a pile of stinking rubble. May history praise you as a man of wisdom—not condemn you as a fool."

WHILE THE MEMPHIS movement prepared for King's return, he traveled the Deep South to drum up support for the Poor People's Campaign. On March 19, he had left Memphis to speak in small towns across the Delta, including Batesville, Marks, Clarksdale, Greenwood, Grenada, Laurel, and

Hattiesburg, Mississippi. In each place, hundreds of people came out to hear him. He drove to the state capital of Jackson, arriving at 4 AM, after a twenty-one-hour day, and for the next several days he continued on through the Black Belt of Alabama and Georgia. In one week's time—from Los Angeles to Memphis to Mississippi and Alabama—he delivered thirty-five speeches.

Mississippi had always put a special chill in his heart. In Philadelphia, Mississippi, in 1966, he had been directly confronted by one of the sheriffs who murdered civil rights workers there during the 1964 Freedom Summer. Now, speaking in the Delta, the bitterness that African Americans felt about the lack of progress welled up in King, too. In Grenada, where whites had responded brutally to SCLC's voting rights and school desegregation efforts, King attacked racism as stridently as any black nationalist. "We are tired of our men not being able to be men, because they can't find work," he said. "Negroes are poor in Mississippi for one basic reason, and that is that white people have exploited us, they have trampled over us with their iron feet of oppression, and they have denied us opportunity." He told a rally in Laurel, "The thing wrong with America is white racism. White folks are not right. . . . It's time for America to have an intensified study of what's wrong with white folk. Anybody that will go around bombing houses and churches, there's something wrong with him."

As he attacked racism, King also offered a class analysis: black exploitation went back to the taproot of slavery and segregation, he said in Clarksdale, and he called for compensation for this history: "We want some land," the proverbial "forty acres and a mule." Widespread white poverty should demonstrate to Mississippi whites that "you can't keep me down unless you stay down yourself. Now, by trying to keep black people down, white folk have kept themselves down. So they're poverty stricken too. They are half educated too." One white man in Mississippi, acting nervous and conflicted, gave King a hundred-dollar bill to support his campaign, but otherwise he met hardly any whites. King still preached hope, saying, "When you can finally convert a white southerner, you have one of the most genuine, committed human beings that you'll ever find."

King despaired at Mississippi's poverty, but also at his own failure to raise funds and volunteers there for the Poor People's Campaign. He met hundreds of people, but few joined up. When he asked who from Clarksdale could go to Washington, only two people raised their hands. King and his entourage, although hopping across the region by prop plane part of the time, fell behind schedule, and the energy imparted to him by the Memphis movement began to dissipate. On March 21, he canceled his last speeches in southern Alabama due to bad weather, leaving hundreds waiting for him. Hard pressed, he still hoped to reach Memphis for the next day's march and then leave to campaign in Georgia later on the same day.

Instead, at midnight King found himself stranded at the Birmingham airport, impossibly waiting to get to Atlanta for a SCLC strategy meeting on his way to Memphis. Foul weather shut down most flights in the Mid-South. He spent much of the night just getting from Birmingham to the Atlanta airport, and there he stood at 8:15 the next morning, after another night destroyed in what Andrew Young called King's "war on sleep." He waited, but no flights took off for Memphis.

In a bizarre twist, in the middle of what had seemed like an early and warm spring, more than sixteen inches of snow fell on Memphis, the second-largest snowstorm in its history. From the Gulf Coast to the Great Lakes, temperatures dropped more than fifty degrees in less than twenty-four hours. Snow clogged the already-budding magnolia trees and azaleas, and at least nine people died in Tennessee and Kentucky. "Snow Blanket Bundles Dixie," proclaimed a news headline. No one went to work, and no one went to school. The Memphis Public Works Department sent out three trucks, but they all became stuck in the snow. Trees and power lines came down, cars and buses couldn't move, telephones went out. Nature had gone on strike.

James Lawson awoke very early that morning, anticipating the largest mass march since Selma, but then he had to postpone it. Talking by phone to King, he jested, "We've got a perfect work stoppage, though!" Twenty hardy souls showed up at Clayborn Temple to march, including striker L. C. Reed and his son, who came to Memphis for the march on his way from negotiating a pro football contract with the Minnesota Vikings. Ministers told them all to go home. Only Thomas Moore, a white worker from a UAW local in Detroit, marched through the snow that day, holding a handmade picket sign reading, "Do Right Mr.? Mayor." Loeb, who showed up for work at city hall despite the snow, asked him in for a cup of coffee.

Lawson that day spoke to a hardy band of teachers at Mt. Olive CME Church, and nearly a hundred strike supporters turned out for a strategy session at Clayborn Temple. Someone shot into a strikebreaker's home that night, and several acts of vandalism occurred, but not much else happened. Samuel Kyles joked that an act of God had closed down the entire city—the perfect general strike.

After the snow melted, King continued to Waycross, Albany, Macon, and Augusta, Georgia, on Saturday, with his children Marty and Dexter in tow. For once, he was able to campaign with his children, but it was not a happy time. The seemingly solid unity of Memphis had lifted his spirits, but his own tensions and fears had only multiplied since he left the city. Typical of the discouraging news he received from his field organizers, SCLC's representative reported that not one of 120 invited black ministers had come to an organizational meeting for the Poor People's Campaign in Virginia. The campaign was in deep trouble, and so was King. When a reporter in Albany asked him why he did not have any bodyguards, a discouraged King told him, "There's no way in the world you can keep somebody from killing you if they really want to kill you." It was much on his mind.

On Sunday, after less than twelve hours at home in Atlanta, King flew out again to New York. That night, in a Harlem church, King's nerves seemed to reach a breaking point, as he invoked God's promise made to him during his time of terror in Montgomery in 1956, "never to leave me, never to leave me alone, no, never alone, no, never alone." King had used this same refrain at Ebenezer Baptist Church on March 3 when he spoke of the "unfulfilled dreams" of people who tried to change history. "It gets very discouraging sometimes. Some of us are trying to build a temple of peace. We speak out against war, we protest, but it seems that your head is going against a concrete wall. It seems to mean nothing." In the shelter of the black Baptist church, King revealed the huge strain he felt. He told his congregation, "Life is a continual story of shattered dreams. . . . So often as you set out to build the temple of peace you are left lonesome; you are left discouraged; you are left bewildered."

THE SNOWSTORM SEEMED providential in some ways, but in truth it provided a huge setback to the Memphis movement. The community had mobilized and reached a moment of maximum unity, but now it would take at least another week before King could return, and efforts to prepare the groundwork for King's general strike began to lag in the meantime. In industry as well as household and service employment, few black workers could afford to lose their jobs, and now they had extra time to think about what would happen if they boycotted work for a day. Nervous whites half expected it to happen, but neither the civil rights movement nor the unions were prepared for it, and few white unionists would have supported it. The movement carried on as usual, Taylor Rogers recalled, but "we never did follow up on the work stoppage. Not too much was done about it."

In truth, the movement in Memphis, like the Poor People's Campaign, was not as well organized as many people believed, said Maxine Smith. The sheer numbers of the sanitation workers always made the movement appear to have more widespread support than it actually had. She thought that workers made up at least 100 out of the 121 arrested on March 5, for example, while only eight out of some 500 ministers in town submitted to arrest. Demonstrations downtown typically included 300 to 500 people, but again, most of them were workers. Out of a black population of 200,000 African Americans, how many were ready to sacrifice for the strike? Longstanding black disunity around political and organizational turf remained a fact of life.

Loeb knew all this, and when union representatives renewed talks with the mayor's men over the weekend, they quickly sensed that these negotiations were a public relations gimmick to make Loeb appear reasonable. Miles convened the first nonbinding mediation session on Sunday afternoon, March 24, with Jones, Ciampa, and Lucy representing the union and H. Ralph Jackson representing COME, while attorneys Myron Halle and Tom Prewitt, Director of Finance Harry Woodbury, and Tom Todd of the City Council represented the city. But Halle dropped a bombshell, saying he did not think the city could meet legally with people who had been convicted of violating the court injunction—namely, Jones, Lucy,

Wurf, Ciampa, and other AFSCME leaders. "We were amazed and surprised at the city's position," said Lucy, and Miles, too, was flabbergasted as the meeting suddenly dissolved. The next day, the city's representatives went before Chancellor Robert Hoffman, who told them they certainly could meet with union representatives.

On Monday afternoon, March 25, city and union representatives again met behind closed doors for more than four hours, but the mayor would not participate because the media were banned. AFSCME thought he had agreed not to make public statements during negotiations, but on Tuesday, he announced that strikers would no longer receive food stamps; on Wednesday, he told the Lions Club that he would never sign a union contract or allow dues checkoff. He reiterated, "The strike is illegal—and you can't deal with illegality." Loeb had already violated all the rules Miles had established for resumed negotiations, and his men undermined the talks further, saying they were not official representatives of the city, had come only to talk, and that only the mayor, who would not attend, could make binding decisions.

On Wednesday, Reverend Jackson burst in on the COME strategy committee meeting to inform them that the talks with the city had once again turned into a farce. The union could not even get city representatives to use the word *recognition*. Some AFSCME negotiators seemed willing to dispense with that word, but Reverend Jackson insisted that no agreement could be made without it: " 'Recognition' meant the rights of black men to be treated as people with rights, able to speak for themselves. And the City has the obligation to recognize that they have this right. . . . This is what these men were saying, 'I _Am_ A Man, we don't need any Great White Father. I _Am_ A Man, this is what I've decided I want for my family, and as a man I have the right to make that decision,' " said Jackson. This was nonnegotiable, and he made sure that union negotiators understood that, too. From now on, they insisted that the word *recognize* or *recognition* had to be in any agreement to settle the strike.

At the end of the day, Jackson and the AFSCME negotiators all walked out, telling the press, "After three days of meetings the city's representatives have failed to observe and acknowledge the union as a designated representative of the workers."

As mediation once again collapsed, COME announced that King would lead a mass march and one-day work stoppage and school boycott on Thursday, March 28. On Friday night, Reverend C. L. Franklin, formerly of Memphis and now of Detroit, would lead a rally at Mason Temple with his famous daughter, Aretha Franklin—a phenomenon then blasting the American airwaves with her powerful, church-based rhythm and blues. Another giant march with King, the Franklins, and others would then take place on Saturday. The AFL-CIO Labor Council ran full-page ads supporting the march in both newspapers, and handbills appeared everywhere, including among black workers at the Methodist Hospital. Universal Life and Union Protective Life Insurance Company black executives once again pledged to close their doors, as did the black managers of the Harlem House chain of restaurants. Two daily marches into the downtown had already resumed, after the break caused by the Friday snowstorm.

Police expressed increasing concern, particularly because strike supporters had begun to communicate with each other through walkie-talkies and to use citizens band radios to monitor the radios used by police mobile units. The Invaders also allegedly began telling picketers to put down their signs and burn the stores. Black detective Willie Richmond reported, "They were shouting as they walked the streets, 'To Hell with all this picketing and prayer. We are not getting nowhere with all that kind of stuff. Let's fight.'" The climate became so tense that presidential candidate George Wallace indefinitely canceled his plan to speak in Memphis on Wednesday, March 27.

At the same time, a police informant said, nerves were frayed and a great deal of anguish was expressed at COME strategy committee meetings. At one of them, "Those present agreed that the strike cannot last much longer, with Epps stating that the union had already spent over $15,000 and the union has to do something, that it just cannot go on day by day marching downtown." Everyone was exhausted. Reverend Starks may have broken his health, and many others could not attend to their ministerial duties. Fear constrained many blacks—especially black teachers, who could be easily fired by the city. Lanetha Jewel Branch, who had taught in black schools for years, tried to collect a dollar a head to support the strikers; out of forty teachers at her school, only seven would donate. Speaking of King, she later said, "You have to recognize that during that time there were many African Americans who did not participate, and did not believe in what he was doing. Because some African Americans also thought that he was a trouble maker."

Knowing these constraints, COME decided to limit mass meetings to three times a week, instead of holding them every night, and to rely on "big name" speakers such as King and the two Franklins, who could ramp up mass meetings through infusions of soul power. At the other end of the spectrum, Cabbage argued forcefully with the strategy committee that not enough had been done to stop the sanitation trucks from going out or to bring the city to a halt. He felt that tactics should include not only blocking garbage trucks but also various types of sabotage and intimidation against strikebreakers.

Cabbage also opposed bringing in King—first from a turf-conscious viewpoint and then for tactical and political reasons. "We had worked organizing people for two and a half years, while the ministers had done nothing," in his view. The Invaders had in a few cases taken over the pulpits of churches to speak about the strike, and they felt growing support among young blacks. But once King came back, Cabbage thought the movement would adhere more tightly than ever to ineffective picketing and marches. Cabbage felt that people at some point had to be prepared for armed struggle, but the ministers refused even to hold it out as a threat to the city's white leaders—who in the end responded only to pressure and fear. Ministers couldn't be faulted for following their ideology of nonviolence, said Cabbage, for they were sincerely exercising their Christian beliefs, yet he thought this was a losing strategy.

Cabbage and his group believed that young black people were riled up and already had the power to disrupt the city—if only the movement cared to use it. The movement did not need King to use this power. Harold Middlebrook, from a nonviolent perspective, agreed that nonviolent direct action had not been fully tried at the local level: "Dr. King never really needed to come to Memphis. Because we had not done what we could have done."

Yet most of the ministers in COME were not impressed with Cabbage's argument. They didn't see many troops behind him, and it was largely ministers and students, not members of the Invaders, who had brought young people into the streets. Reverend Starks called the Invaders "sideliners in the movement" who talked militancy but actually did little in terms of leafleting, marching, organizing, or any of the other things that built a movement. He thought the Invaders posed no real alternative to bringing in King, in terms of mobilizing a mass movement that could force the city to deal with the strike.

Growing personal strains also separated Cabbage and his group from the ministers. Individual Invaders, often motivated by a desire for personal gain, sometimes took actions that discredited the group. One Invader pilfered the checkbooks for COME and put them into the trunk of Cabbage's car; when police stopped Cabbage on the street, they found the checks and an illegal concealed weapon, which they happily displayed to the media after arresting him. Another Invader in the downtown group named Roy Turks denounced Reverend Jackson in a meeting, calling him an obstacle to the movement. He later mailed or took the minister a bullet, with a note saying that this bullet had his name on it if he did not start going along with the Invaders. Such intemperate attacks, reminiscent of street gangs, divided Cabbage and his group from the mainstream Memphis movement. In his Leninist view of organizing, Cabbage had planned to "direct traffic" behind the scenes, but instead he was exposed by the actions of others as personally untrustworthy and politically unreliable.

Cabbage felt some of this resulted from the work of police agents who had infiltrated his group, yet he did not know who they were, and he had no way to expose them. Nor did he have a way to impose discipline among his members. As the day of King's march approached, tensions skyrocketed between the police and people identified as "black militants." Police detectives felt threatened. Redditt reported that reputed Black Nationalist karate experts and sharpshooters wearing what appeared to be hats identifying themselves as Muslims had arrived from the Watts area of Los Angeles. His partner, Richmond, claimed that John Henry Ferguson and several other Invaders had surrounded him and Redditt at a mass meeting as T. O. Jones declared, "If you are a policeman, I am not going to be responsible for what my boys do to you."

Among Cabbage's group, antagonism toward police agents grew stronger, as police continued to keep Black Power leaders (as well as AFSCME staff) under intensive surveillance, illegally searching hotel rooms, bugging phones, and following people everywhere. Cabbage complained to the FBI about police behavior, in hopes that federal agents might intervene, but the FBI merely said that the police "have a right to surveil anyone on the streets of Memphis." To his chagrin, because he had approached the FBI, some people labeled Cabbage himself as an FBI informant. Anyone who protested anything seemed to end up immediately in an FBI or police file, and it was absurd, Cabbage decided, to think that the FBI would protect the rights of anyone in the movement. And equally absurd to say, as the FBI did, that surveillance had no intimidating effect.

One place FBI surveillance could have a very chilling effect was among students at Memphis State, where some were considering whether to make a major plunge into the strike but also were concerned about jeopardizing their possible careers after graduation, or even their ability to stay in school if cooperative university officials went after them due to FBI inquiries. Ron Ivy, a charismatic student who had experienced the February 23 macing, so distrusted the police that he carried a .22-caliber pistol. He and others in the emerging Black Student Association (BSA) continued to hold forums on black identity, to define what they called black "strength in union." An FBI informant said that at one meeting, "All present agreed that the NAACP was outmoded; that it was too legalistic, too mild, too respectable; and that a militant aggressive black movement was needed," but he also commented that "the group lacks unity and strength."

The BSA discussed the role of black athletes in the upcoming Olympic Games, celebrated the theme, "Black is beautiful," pledged to better the condition of blacks at MSU, and welcomed white participation. The FBI surveillance revealed that black students chafed at the way racism intruded into their lives, but what most of them wanted was democracy and economic advancement, not armed revolution. BSA members produced a document that said black students should help to raise the "bottom class" that "exists in the misery and pessimism of our city," including the sanitation workers, rather than merely try to advance themselves into the black middle class.

CHARLES CABBAGE FELT pained by the contradictions of Memphis. He admired King's personal courage and dedication and did not want to confront him over tactics and strategy, as Carmichael had done in Mississippi in 1966. But if King insisted on coming back, Cabbage felt, history had put the Invaders in a position from which they could not shy away. "By being at the right place and the right time you can bring about big changes," he believed. It was time to end the reign of preachers who still clung to moderation and refused to go all the way toward revolution. A rebuke to King's nonviolent philosophy on the streets of Memphis would have the same kind of effect that Carmichael's cry of "Black Power" did in Meredith's March Against Fear: it would hit front pages all across the country. Black Power revolutionaries in Memphis could demonstrate that King's nonviolent methods and ideology no longer worked. "In our meetings, we had decided that nonviolence had to be challenged, and we decided to disrupt the march. I saw it as an opportunity to stop King," if it became necessary.

He hoped, however, that King would not come back to Memphis, for he did not relish any confrontation with him. He thought that, even in King's terms, the mass march was unwise: people were angry and stirred up, but not well organized, and few of them accepted the nonviolent discipline needed to make a mass march successful. Cabbage considered his alternatives. One would be to circulate through his network and put out the word to stay away from the march. That's what he told some people to do, and he decided to do that himself. Alternatively, he could actively urge his people to disrupt King's march. He concluded that he did not actually have to do that. In fact, he did not have to take any action to challenge King. For neither he nor anyone else one could really control the decentralized movement of young people—most of them unemployed, bored, annoyed, angry, looking for something, anything that might change their conditions.

All Charles Cabbage had to do was sit back and wait.

Martin Luther King spoke repeatedly before unions and called for a labor–civil rights alliance. His support for striking workers at the Scripto factory in Atlanta helped them to win their strike in 1964. *(Reuther Archives)*

By 1966, T. O. Jones (second from left) had organized Memphis AFSCME Local 1733, and workers threatened to strike. *(Reuther Archives)*

On February 1, 1968, two workers died because of outmoded equipment on a truck much like this one. *(Mississippi Valley Collection)*

Sanitation workers struck on February 12, and marched to City Hall the next day. *(Barney Sellers, Mississippi Valley Collection)*

Police officers guarded sanitation workers who stayed on the job during the strike. *(James R. Reid, Mississippi Valley Collection)*

Mayor Henry Loeb, a former laundry owner and public works commissioner, ordered them back to work. *(Barney Sellers, Commercial Appeal)*

T. O. Jones (foreground) and other AFSCME staff, including William Lucy (the third man behind Jones facing the camera), negotiated fruitlessly with Loeb. *(Tom Barber, Mississippi Valley Collection)*

On February 22, protestors took over City Council chambers; Tarlese Matthews and Rev. P. L. Rowe led the singing. *(Robert Williams,* Commercial Appeal*)*

AFSCME's international president, Jerry Wurf, organized a march after the city council abruptly shut protestors out of city hall. *(Vernon Matthews,* Commercial Appeal*)*

Police attacked with mace, a chemical designed for use in war, outraging civil rights and labor supporters. (Commercial Appeal)

Reverend James Lawson (holding sign), shown here with young people and white AFSCME organizer Peter J. Ciampa, led the strike strategy committee. (*William Leaptrott, Mississippi Valley Collection*)

Black women played a crucial role in mass meetings and picketing to enforce a boycott of downtown shopping. *(Mississippi Valley Collection)*

On March 5, 150 to 500 AFL-CIO members rallied and picketed, providing crucial interracial support. *(Mississippi Valley Collection)*

That day, police arrested 117 protestors, who walked to jail surrounded by singing and chanting black students. *(James R. Reid, Mississippi Valley Collection)*

Youthful community organizers Charles Cabbage (speaking) and Coby Smith (right), shown here when fired from the anti-poverty program in 1967, criticized the Movement as not being militant enough. *(Mississippi Valley Collection)*

Anger grew against strikebreakers, as picketers tried to shame them not to work on March 8. *(Tom Barber, Mississippi Valley Collection)*

Reverend Zeke Bell (center, sitting) is shown here speaking to Reverend James Starks (standing). Picketers blocked garbage trucks until forced to move. *(Mississippi Valley Collection)*

On March 14, Memphis State University students supporting the strikers confronted Mayor Loeb. *(Fred Payne, Mississippi Valley Collection)*

Rev. S. B. "Billy" Kyles took donations in a garbage can at Mason Temple on March 14, when Bayard Rustin and Roy Wilkins spoke. *(Jack E. Cantrell, Mississippi Valley Collection)*

A Training School For Communists

Rightists and segregationists regularly depicted King as a Communist supporter. *(John Birch Society Postcard, in author's possession)*

POST CARD

PLACE
STAMP
HERE

1. Martin Luther King, Jr. The association indicated here is not unusual for Dr. King, who belongs to several important Communist front organizations, and who regularly employs or affiliates with known Communists.

2. Abner W. Berry, of the Central Committee of the Communist Party.

3. Aubrey Williams, President of the Communist front, the Southern Conference Education Fund.

4. Myles Horton, Director of the Highlander Folk School (for Communist Training), Monteagle, Tennessee. This school was later abolished by an act of the Legislature of the State of Tennessee.

These postcards (No. CR2) are available at any American Opinion Library, at 20 cards for $1.00; or directly by mail, postage paid, from

AMERICAN OPINION
Belmont, Massachusetts   02178

King is shown here meditating before a March 17 speech near Detroit, where "Breakthrough" members denounced him as a traitor for opposing the Vietnam War. *(Tony Spina, Reuther Archives)*

King is shown here on March 18, conferring with Jerry Wurf at a packed rally at Mason Temple. Behind them are AFSCME's P. J. Ciampa and strike supporter Cornelia Crenshaw. *(Copyright © Richard L. Copley, Reuther Archives)*

King's call for a general strike of black workers and students set off pandemonium at Mason Temple. *(Ken Ross, Mississippi Valley Collection)*

On March 28, community supporters nearly crushed King, Ralph Abernathy, and Henry Starks (both to King's left), as Bernard Lee tried to clear a path to march. *(Sam Mellhorn, Mississippi Valley Collection)*

Police blocked the way, as riots broke out behind King and James Lawson removed him from the march. *(Mississippi Valley Collection)*

Martial law descended upon Memphis, yet workers continued their protest under National Guard occupation. *(Reuther Archives)*

Police attacked looters and marchers indiscriminately. Police killed Larry Payne (standing, right) that afternoon. *(Jack Thornell, Associated Press Wide World Photos)*

The wounded huddled at Clayborn Temple or streamed into John Gaston Hospital. *(Barney Sellers, Commercial Appeal)*

On April 3, a marshal served King and his staff (left to right, Ralph Abernathy, Andrew Young, James Orange, and Bernard Lee) a federal injunction banning them from leading a national march in Memphis. *(Barney Sellers,* Commercial Appeal*)*

Jesse Jackson spoke to King before his April 3 "Mountaintop" speech, in which King urged people to follow the example of the Good Samaritan on the Jericho Road. *(Reuther Archives)*

Mayor Loeb, a shotgun under his desk, is shown here on April 5, greeting clergy who demanded a strike settlement. *(Robert Williams,* Commercial Appeal*)*

On April 8, Coretta Scott King, with her children Dexter, Martin III, and Yolanda, led marchers through the streets of Memphis. *(Sam Mellhorn,* Commercial Appeal*)*

Thousands honored King and what he stood for, and in succeeding years workers continued to march in Memphis on April 4. *(Mississippi Valley Collection)*

III

JERICHO ROAD
IS A DANGEROUS ROAD

CHAOS IN THE BLUFF CITY

Be cool, fool,
Thursday's march is King's thing
If your school is tops, pops, prove it.
Be in the know,
Get on the go,
Thursday at 10.
See you then.
Together we stick,
Divided we are stuck, Baby.
C.O.M.E.

—*Flyer distributed in Memphis schools and*
housing projects, March 27, 1968

MARCHERS BEGAN TO ASSEMBLE OUTSIDE CLAYBORN
Temple as early as 8 AM on Thursday, March 28, buoyed by a
massive leafleting and word-of-mouth campaign. The temperature was sixty-one degrees and climbing, a clear day, the sun beating
down. The heat reflected from pavement and sidewalks; downtown would
soon be stifling. Yet, as strikers and their families and supporters gathered,
expecting King at 10 AM, their mood was festive. This was the big day. Ten
to twenty thousand marchers would show Mayor Loeb the power of a
united black community allied with unions, students, and people of goodwill, white and black. Hundreds of workers carried placards reading, "I <u>Am</u>
A Man." No one expected trouble. Eleven incidents of vandalism had
occurred during the night, but this had become normal.

The police made no move to restrict the march—the streets downtown
belonged to the people. At Lester, Northside, Douglass, South Side, and
Booker T. Washington High Schools, youthful strike supporters began

confronting students and teachers, urging them to march. James Lawson had already stopped by Washington, encouraging students to leave school.

At Hamilton High School, on the south side, students milled around in front of the school, and at about 8:30, a small group heaved bricks at passing vehicles with white drivers. Shortly, a garbage truck accompanied by a police car drove right by them, and more bricks, rocks, and bottles began to fly. Police cars came zooming in from everywhere. Officers sealed off the area, got out of their cars, put on helmets, pulled out their nightsticks, and began walking ominously toward the students.

Two to three hundred students, "in a rather boisterous manner," according to the police, began trying to march toward the downtown. Teenage girls flounced in their skirts and boys did quick dance steps and joked around; other students ducked into alleys and behind buildings, picking up stones, bricks, and bottles. Police ran at them to force them back to their campus, while students dodged this way and that, some of them throwing things. Police began to swing clubs and fists, sometimes knocking students in the head, sometimes tripping and falling over themselves. Black teachers who had been observing moved back into the school building out of the police line of attack, but the students would not retreat. At some point, someone locked the doors against the police, and now students could not get back inside even if they wanted to.

At 9:14, police headquarters sent a message by radio to use tear gas, and officers put on their gas masks. As a surveillance helicopter went into the air, Police Chief MacDonald sent word to march headquarters at Clayborn Temple that they needed an adult to intercede. Jesse Turner of the NAACP came over, as did Harold Middlebrook, and a number of mothers—at least one of whom had a gun—also turned up to defend their children. Police claimed they had used no gas, but the FBI reported they had. A number of students were hurt; fourteen-year-old Jo Ann Talbert was hit in the head by either a police club or a projectile. An ambulance came and medics carried her away on a stretcher. It took twenty-three stitches to close her bloody head wound, and a rumor spread that police had killed her.

By 9:30, a torrent of human beings had amassed at Clayborn Temple, including ministers in their frocks; strikers dressed in work clothes or Sunday jackets; well-dressed professionals; mothers holding the hands of their children or pushing them in strollers. Increasing numbers of high school students (a few wearing jackets that read "Invaders") arrived, and cheers went up as a group of teachers wrote, "Memphis City School Teachers" with lipstick on the back of a placard. Probably ten white priests and fifteen to twenty nuns attended (with the blessings of Bishop Durick), along with a few white college students and professors. Tommy Powell, Bill Ross, Dan Powell, and a few other white labor leaders stood at the front of the gathering crowd, waiting to be led off by King and the ministers, followed by sanitation workers and protesters. It would be a grand march.

Few people expected any violence, especially since Dr. King would lead the march. Joyce Palmer, a young white mother of three, came on her own, knowing no one. At first she saw no whites at all, and then she finally fell in with a good-spirited group of white and black women. Before she knew it, someone had stolen her billfold from her purse, with money, credit cards, and a driver's license. She began to bawl, shocked by this tawdry act on such a grand occasion.

The celebratory atmosphere changed as word spread through the crowd that cops had killed a young girl at Hamilton High; one rumor said she had been stomped to death. Rumors also passed through the crowd that King would be killed that day, that Stokely Carmichael was in town and militants would start trouble. Such rumors flew all the time through the black community; in Watts, Detroit, and Newark, among other places, rumors had led to full-scale riots.

Jo Ann Talbert was not dead, and organizers tried to dispel rumors that she was. But the mood turned increasingly tense as teenagers from Hamilton and elsewhere recounted their conflicts with police. "Some of those children from Hamilton were so mad they never got in the march with us. They were ready to fight anybody at that time," Reverend Jackson recalled.

The growing influx of black high school students hugely affected the day's events. Authorities estimated that 22,000 students had left or never showed up at Memphis schools; more than half of Booker T. Washington's 2,200 students skipped class; some 200 students marched from LeMoyne College. When a contingent of Lester High School students joined via a side street after the march had begun, a cheer went up. The presence of students energized the event, but also brought an element of unpredictability. The police could hardly keep track of all the separate incidents occurring at black schools, where numerous conflicts would erupt with officers throughout the day. White schools remained perfectly normal.

As black students appeared, their youthful energy and impatience suffused the gathering. Older people carried placards authorized by the COME strategy committee, reading, "JUSTICE AND EQUALITY FOR ALL MEN," and "UNIONIZATION FOR THE SANITATION WORKERS," and "I AM A MAN." Many youngsters created their own signs, such as "JOBS, JOBS, JOBS," and "LOEB EAT SHIT," and "FUCK YOU MAYOR LOEB." Many students were in a carnival mood, but others were vulgar and angry. Reporter Kay Pittman Black recalled one teenager who walked through the crowd saying, "We're going to get some white folks today."

At this point, police estimated that only 3,000 to 6,000 people had gathered, but half of them were teenagers and their numbers were swelling. Police also identified a number of people recently released from penal institutions. Their informants also spotted John Burl Smith and John Henry Ferguson, supposedly making fun of marchers for being too timid, handing out picket sticks, and saying, Don't be afraid to use them. James Elmore Phillips and Samuel Carter, the latter known to the FBI as a Black Organizing Project member at LeMoyne, made sarcastic comments about students who were "too chicken" to leave school and suggested that it was time to take strong action. Along with another LeMoyne College student, Clinton Roy Jameson, and someone named Sam, they went into the alley with fifteen to twenty youths to gather sticks and bricks. Cabbage appeared, and an agent claimed he urged a marcher to "tear up" the city.

Police agents wanted something to pin on the Invaders, but they had only bravado and a few inflammatory remarks to record. When the march finally moved forward, BOP organizers stayed behind. Although some black youth came to the march with "Invaders" or "Black Power" stenciled on their jackets and shirts, an FBI agent reported, "Many high school age students have done this for effect and are not necessarily affiliated with the BOP movement."

BY 10 AM, many people had been standing around for two hours; the sun just got hotter and the air more stifling. High spirits and enthusiasm gave way to frustration and anxiety as police helicopters buzzed annoyingly overhead; one student from LeMoyne said, "It seemed as though we were in a cage with guardsmen flying over us to keep watch." On the outskirts of the gathering, disheveled men, young and old, trickled in from Beale Street and a surrounding area lined with pawnshops, bars, and liquor stores. The boycott of downtown businesses had hurt *their* business: when people didn't shop, the work of petty hustlers and thieves slowed down. "You deprived us of our work," one man resentfully told Reverend Lawson. Some of these men began their drinking early, thinking about the opportunity that lay before them.

The swelling crowd vastly outnumbered Lawson's marshals. In Nashville, Andrew Young recalled, Lawson had led "a textbook example of how to organize for social change." In any march, Young observed, "The participants *must* have some prior knowledge of what kind of behavior is expected of them," and "give up the freedom to react in the way they might normally" to provocations and discomfort. This is the discipline people expected of a march organized by Lawson, but he did not have enough marshals to handle such a large crowd; some people never even saw them. And only some of those gathering that morning had adopted nonviolent discipline. A LeMoyne College student spoke to a group of men sipping wine and beer and talking about how much money they could make by looting pawnshops and liquor stores. They had their eyes on the famous Lansky's clothing store, where Elvis Presley bought some of his duds. Street people and some students were "drinking anything they could get their hands on" behind Clayborn Temple and the Minimum Salary Building. According to the LeMoyne student, some of them "had been led to believe that this could be the day, man, that we could really tear this city up . . . or getting this whitey, you know."

A gulf had emerged between the careful planning of the adult leaders and organizers and the youth and street people—just the problem Cabbage had predicted. Thus far, black workers had been the core of most marches, and their nonviolent discipline remained rock solid. Not so with many of the new participants in the movement. Reverend Jackson told a man who had been haranguing the crowd that this was a nonviolent march, and if he could not accept its discipline, he should leave. Jackson, Starks, Lawson, and others asked such people to leave, but they just disappeared into the immense crowd. "There was an element in the crowd that we couldn't get rid of at that time. Nobody could do anything with them," said Fred Davis. City Council members James Netters and Jerred Blanchard were also there, feeling increasingly uneasy. The "white presence wasn't exactly overwhelming" in the ranks of the marchers, said one participant, making the crowd especially vulnerable to police attack.

One question now formed in many minds: "Where *are* the police?" Except for the helicopters and a small group at the front led by Assistant Police Chief Henry Lux, they showed little visible presence. In reality, police had circled the area and nearly all officers had been mobilized, including some 300 Memphis police and fifty Shelby County sheriff's deputies. Most of these people had been working long hours, seven days a week, since the strike began. Their tempers were short. Sitting in cars or standing in the boiling sun, sweat rolled off of them and soaked their clothing. They carried .38-caliber pistols and shotguns and billy clubs, and were quite ready to use them.

Because almost all officers were on duty, they did not have enough city-owned shotguns or portable radios or riot helmets, so some carried their own private weapons. The helmets they did have lacked plastic shields to protect their faces from flying objects, so they, too, felt vulnerable. In fact, 350 law-enforcement officers could hardly control what looked to some like 6,000, to others like 15,000 to 20,000 people in the street. To supplement their power, the police had an emergency squad, called the TAC Unit, which consisted of three cars, each of which held four men. A commanding officer could order a unit to a location, where officers would quickly form a flying wedge and charge down the street. But whether such tactics would calm disorder or merely spread it was an open question.

Harsh force always remains an option when a small group of police deals with a large crowd. The police department had purchased a number of new items since the strike began: eight cases of 12-gauge rifle shells, 100 Remington 12-gauge shotguns with twenty-inch riot barrels, 100 gas masks and 100 extra gas canisters, 1,500 mace aerosol cans and holsters, 50 handheld radios, and other items. The police had already spent more than $150,000 on new equipment and overtime hours from February 12 up to March 4.

They kept this repressive power out of the sight of the massed marchers and street people, on the theory that organized force would be less provocative if kept hidden. But the police might have done better to be more obvious about their presence. At 10:03, about twenty-five men raided a liquor store on Vance Avenue; at 10:15, some young people tried to break into a liquor store around the corner from the Clayborn Temple. With no police in sight, ACLU attorney David Caywood took it on himself to break it up. A few minutes later, he looked aghast to see someone holding a branch with a sign that read, "LOEB'S HANGING TREE." The tenor of the crowd was changing, and no one had counted on King being so late. Samuel Kyles urged Lawson to go ahead without him, but Lawson insisted on waiting.

Where was King? His overcommitted schedule, which always held up his appearances, had created a tactical nightmare. In the midst of overwhelming obligations, King had engaged in countless hours of dialogue with vastly diverse audiences in New York, trying to get their support for the Poor People's Campaign. On Sunday, he had spoken to black Baptists in Harlem. On Monday, he spoke to the sixty-eighth annual convention of the American Rabbinical Assembly in the Catskill Mountains of upstate New York, invited by his ally Rabbi Abraham Heschel, asking them to join a "coalition of conscience" that could "get something moving again in America." Tuesday and Wednesday, he spoke to poor people, students, politicians, and community leaders throughout the New York area. Seeking a rapprochement with advocates of Black Power, he called the slogan a "psychological call to manhood," a demand to pool black political and economic resources. "Let's get the power," King said, "but somehow we managed to get just the slogan."

King continued to insist that a real program for change, as opposed to a slogan, had to include "a sharing of power" in which blacks had equality and whites took responsibility for racism and its effects. He believed "militant nonviolence," something "as attention getting as a riot," but without violence, remained the only viable tactic for a mass movement.

King had stayed at the home of SCLC board member Marion Logan and her husband, Arthur, in New York City. They argued late into the night over her insistence that the Poor People's Campaign would not work. King defended it ever more combatively, drinking and smoking and increasingly agitated. She feared that he was "losing hold" over his faculties and his emotions, and they finally left the discussion unresolved in the early hours of the morning. King was exhausted. He had originally been scheduled to be in Memphis to speak at a rally on Wednesday night, but he stayed in New York and had Ralph Abernathy take his place. He worried so much that he would miss his flight to Memphis that he had another sleepless night.

On Thursday morning, he boarded a plane for the Bluff City, barely functional and with a bit of desperation etched across his features. Immediately after the Memphis march, he planned to leave for Washington, DC, to plan logistics for the Poor People's Campaign. "Martin must have been so fatigued he was almost in a daze," Andrew Young recalled. King's plane was late, and he feared his absence would jeopardize the march's success. Frustrated and agitated, King finally arrived at the Memphis airport at 10:30 AM.

At the march, COME handed out hundreds of thin, four-foot-long pine sticks attached to placards, to make sure signs could be hoisted in the air. The movement had never used sticks in previous marches, only placards—and it never would again. Many youths ominously tore the signs off the sticks and waved them in the air. Marshals took some of them away, but many other youths faded into the crowd with the sticks.

AFSCME organizer Jesse Epps finally made a grand entrance with King, bringing him in like a head of state in a white Lincoln Continental on loan from the R. S. Lewis Funeral Home. But when the car arrived at Linden and Hernando, said Lawson, "Pandemonium broke out." Everyone wanted to see King up close, and so many young people swarmed around that Epps could not maneuver the car and King and his aides could not get out. Ralph Abernathy thought it took him and King an hour to get out, but they couldn't have taken more than ten minutes; being surrounded by a crush of agitated young people made these very long minutes. Ministers locked their arms and cleared a space so King could get out, but he did not like the feel of the crowd. "The people were trampling over my feet . . . crowding around me. The atmosphere was just wrong."

Surrounded by an unruly sea of young people pressing in on him, King had an apprehensive look on his face. He talked with Lawson and initially agreed to wait to take leadership of the march until Lawson could get it better organized. But SCLC staff said King had been in such chaotic situations before, and they urged Lawson just to start the march and it would probably straighten out. Lawson cleared people out of the way with great difficulty, but he got the crowd moving. Within a block, King took the lead, linked arm in arm with CME Bishop Julian Smith, Abernathy, Bernard Lee, and Lawson. It was 11:05. King's admirers continued to charge up from the back and push ministers out of the way, and reporter Kay Pittman Black heard King exclaim that someone should "make the crowds stop pushing. We're going to be trampled."

March organizers had strategically placed L. C. Reed and other sanitation workers right behind King. The workers had gone from Clayborn Temple to city hall and back many times, and they could lend a great deal of discipline to this march. But as the workers passed W. C. Handy Park, said Reed, "Well, we got mixed up some kind of way. And they had a lot of youngsters in there, and they were running up through the crowd hollering, 'Let me get by. I want to get to the front.'" Youngsters moved ahead of the workers and cut them off from the march's leadership, and then, "They really got unruly."

The NAACP's Jesse Turner and the top-ranking police officer at the scene, Henry Lux, independently considered the possibility of aborting the march, but both concluded that stopping it at this point might precipitate the very thing they were worried about: a riot. As the crowd moved down Hernando to Beale, marchers grew more confident and strode down the street singing, "We Shall Overcome" and chanting, "Down with Loeb." A mass work stoppage had not occurred that morning, but they estimated that 10,000 to 15,000 people marched. As film footage shows, however,

King was in distress. Pressed upon by the crowd, his eyes glazed, his head falling to the side, he looked as if he was asleep on his feet or might pass out at any moment. King's colleagues practically carried him along.

As they crossed Second Street and moved toward Mulberry and Main, LeMoyne student Ronald Hooks noticed that "people were trying to walk much too fast for a crowd of that size. Dr. King was being pushed and people were walking on each other's heels." The small police escort at the front of the march could not maintain control, and King was still "engulfed in young people," said Bill Ross.

Kay Pittman Black remained behind, standing on a flatbed truck with Shelby County Community Relations Director Jerry Fanion, watching people pass by, waving and smiling in a happy parade. She also watched as a group of about thirty teenagers with "Black Power" insignias on their shirts tore apart an abandoned iron bedstead and walked off with the iron pipes in their hands. A police helicopter observed that a band of youths who had torn off their signs were now moving with sticks down Beale to Main Street. Bystanders moved too quickly along the sidewalks, out of the control of marshals in the street. Almost no communication existed between marshals at the front and the rear of the march. The title of Kay Pittman Black's newspaper story seemed to sum up what happened next: "It Began Like a Carnival—And Then It Ended Like a Horror Show."

The march had progressed from Clayborn Temple toward the downtown on Hernando Street, turned left on Beale, and then turned right going north up Main Street. It had taken twenty-five minutes to cover a mere seven blocks. Before they got to Main, Lawson, King, and others at the front of the march heard the resounding crack of storefront windows behind them on Beale Street. Lawson sent marshals back to see what was going on, but the frightening sound of shattering glass continued. They couldn't see it, but a riot had begun behind them. Ed Gillis spotted a violin in the street "all tore up" at Second and Beale. "We hear glass flying, bricks throwing and so everybody kind of stirred up, you know," L. C. Reed recalled. Attorney Walter Bailey saw a group of young men attacking a pawnshop window with their sticks. He had his wife and children in tow, and he thought to himself, "Good heavens! What the hell are they trying to do to us? Get us all shot?" Others in the march exclaimed, "Windows! They're breaking windows!" Someone shouted, "Damn it! They're ruining the march!"

Tri-State Defender writer and photographer Whittier Sengstacke, Jr., said the police did nothing to stop the window breaking. When the march began, he saw black youths waving two-by-two picket sticks, with heavy objects bulging from their pockets, while "hardened men in their twenties and their thirties" spread out on the sidewalks. Walking alongside Henry Lux, Sengstacke had asked why no officers were in evidence, and Lux said they didn't expect any trouble and wanted "to interfere with the march as little as possible." But the police had left those operating outside the discipline of the march a free hand. Maxine Smith, at the front with King, thought the continuing lack of police presence was "uncanny," under the circumstances. Now, as Lawson, King, and a phalanx of marchers turned right onto Main Street from Beale, kids ran up from behind, smashing windows. People began to yell, "Burn it down, baby!"

Ralph Jackson had wondered why he hadn't seen more police, but where he did see them, "They weren't looking at us very kindly at all." Up ahead on Main Street, at Gayoso, a large number of them formed a line to block the marchers from continuing toward city hall. With windows breaking behind, ahead, and all around, King found himself leading a group of seemingly riotous marchers into a potentially deadly confrontation with the police. In Chicago and elsewhere, King had been the victim of mob attacks, but never had he seemed to be *leading* a mob. The thought that King might be killed crossed the minds of a number of people.

Lawson noticed several people breaking windows near police officers who made no move to stop them. It looked like a setup. He sent runners back to the main body of the march to stop it. Lux gave Lawson a bullhorn, and he used it to get the front line of marchers to stop. Neither the marshals nor the marchers in the back knew what was going on up front, as the march came to a confused, abrupt halt. Lawson's second concern was to remove King. "Take Dr. King down McCall and out of the way," he told King's aides. King hesitated to leave the march, saying, "Jim, they'll say I ran away." Lawson recalled: "Martin balked, so I said directly to Ralph Abernathy something about 'I understand Martin not wanting to, but I

think he should go on.' And Henry Starks backed me up immediately."
Abernathy said King also concluded, "I've got to get out of here." Reverend
Starks and several others surrounded King, putting their arms through his
to lead him down McCall, a side street.

King's lieutenant Bernard Lee flagged down two black women in a
white Pontiac, and the driver let Lee take the wheel while King, Abernathy,
and two other unidentified black men got in the back. At McCall and
Front Street, about fifty people who had broken away from the march surrounded the car, and they could go no further. Lee asked motorcycle cop
Lieutenant Nichols to get them to the Peabody Hotel, where AFSCME had
a suite of rooms, but Nichols said the rioting made it impossible. "Just get
us away from trouble," Lee said. Joined by three motorcycle cops sent by
Police Chief MacDonald, Nichols escorted King to the Holiday Inn Rivermont. Nichols himself checked King, Abernathy, Lee, and the two others
into Room 801, a suite at the hotel, and then remained in the lobby after
they went to their rooms. Lieutenant Nichols had no desire to make a
martyr of King, but that didn't mean he respected him. Nichols disparag-
ingly told the MPD's Arkin that King's "only concern was to run and to
protect himself."

After King left the march, Lawson used his bullhorn, saying, "This is
Reverend Lawson speaking. I want everyone who's in the march, in the
Movement, to turn around and go back to the church." His marshals began
moving the crowd back, shouting, "Turn around! Go back! Go back to the
church!" As they tried to get marchers to retreat, the police kept moving in
on them. At 11:18, Police Chief MacDonald used a bullhorn to order the
march to disperse, while his officers put on gas masks and began moving
south from their blockade across Main Street. At 11:22, Fire and Police
Director Frank Holloman called the chief of the Tennessee Highway
Patrol, and a helicopter crew used its radio to order motorcycle cops to
clear people out. "The police somewhere got their word to get tough, and
believe me they did," said Reverend Jackson. Patrolmen and motorcycle
police waded into the crowd, using clubs and mace, shooting tear gas or
rolling tear-gas grenades on the ground. This was, as the police report later
put it, their effort to "restore order."

Chaos descended on the marchers. Besides the police, two groups of rioters were in motion—young kids breaking windows as an act of defiance against the power structure, and looters who simply wanted to steal. Lawson tried to move the kids out of the situation. "You don't have to show your manhood this way," he told them through his bullhorn. "If you want to show your manhood, come on out on the football field with me some afternoon." But it was too late. Looting and police attacks escalated. Police actions, far from stopping violence, spread it. A flying wedge of policemen came through the area, and the young people started throwing rocks and bottles at them. Black youth would not suffer blows passively. Their resistance infuriated the police, their faces red from exertion behind plastic windows of green tear-gas masks and some of them bloodied by flying objects.

SOME MARCHERS WALKED away quickly, some held their ground, and some ran. AFL-CIO President Tommy Powell had been a football player in college, and he could outrun the police anytime he chose to, so that's what he did. Dan Powell and Bill Lucy pushed up against a building to avoid the moving bodies, and then they went forward to investigate. T. O. Jones ran for cover, knowing he would be a special target. "It was every man for himself," he recalled. His two sons became separated from their father, and Jesse reported that an officer drew his gun and fired a shot at his younger brother. Terrified, they ran until their father found them. Jesse recalled that when he embraced them, they all cried.

Some sanitation workers were picked off. John Kearney ran, but the same officer who had beaten him savagely on February 23 called out to him, "Hey, nigger, stop!" The officer attacked him once again, but this time Kearney did not submit—he came up swinging, and a number of other officers knocked him senseless. They took him to the hospital, and their testimony later sent him to prison. Robert Beasley knew he would be a target for officers: "I was in the middle of the line. They recognized who I was and they got right in my face." The mace burned him badly and still affected his vision years later. He would get another dose of it later that day at Clayborn Temple. P. J. Ciampa, with his bum knee, could not run, and strikers hoisted him into the cab of a sound truck to get him out of the way of the police. An officer spotted him and smashed the glass to get at him but never could hit Ciampa.

Most of the sanitation workers managed to stay in a group and turned back toward the church under their own discipline. They had their own marshals and mostly avoided police assaults. "We didn't have trouble with the tub toters," one of the police remarked. Other experienced people also managed to avoid police attacks. Leroy Boyd, a member of the old CIO Local 19, said, "I didn't run and none of the police never did attack me. I held my ground. I just continued on. I didn't stop." When one of the less-experienced marchers pulled on Maxine Smith's coat, pleading, "Let's go, let's go!" Smith said, "I will die before I run because as long as I live I'm never running from a policeman." She had seen too many people killed by the police for the crime of running. But her son Smitty was with the children of the Sugarmons, and she temporarily lost him in the swirling crowd.

Many people did not have the practiced solidarity of the strikers and the civil rights leaders. When police started swinging clubs and spraying mace, people scattered in every direction, as police seemed to make no distinctions between marchers and looters. Black police detective Ed Redditt, wearing army fatigues, had blended into the march all too effectively: white officers threatened him, and he barely escaped. A Southwestern student said, "It looked like just a big steamroller of people," running or walking as fast as they could to get away from the police. In the pandemonium, children lost their parents, older people who could not run became trapped, people ducked into doorways or into people's homes for refuge. Fear surged through the crowd. Police kept coming, shooting tear gas, swinging clubs, cracking heads, and, in Smith's words, "using vile language," calling people "niggers," "bitches," and "motherfuckers."

Farther back in the march, demonstrators did not know what was happening and could easily imagine the worst. Frankie Rogers, a sophomore at LeMoyne College, along with her sister, who was trying to organize an AFSCME chapter at John Gaston Hospital, had been marching along peacefully. "That was an exciting time in 1968 with the Vietnam protests, campus unrest all over the country, and the Civil Rights Movement not only in Memphis, but all over the South. I wanted to be a part of the changes that were taking place," she recalled. Suddenly, "All hell broke loose ahead of us. My sister and I heard noises and screams, and we saw people running back toward us yelling, 'A riot just broke out! Run!' My sister and I turned around and ran with the rest of the crowd back toward Clayborn Temple as we could smell the Mace that was being fired by the police."

At the rear of the march, reporter Kay Pittman Black had started to leave, thinking the march had been a success. Suddenly, marchers "came roaring back down the street. We kept asking, 'What happened?' Then we saw bloody heads." A fleeing minister urged Jerry Fanion, "Get this woman reporter out of here," but Black and Fanion found their way blocked by groups of teenagers running toward them and away from the gas.

Only James Lawson with a bullhorn and a number of marshals averted complete panic. Lawson remembered vividly how Reverend J. W. Williams, a tall and distinguished man, stood amid the rushing police and, "calmly, but with great dignity," directed marchers to go back to Clayborn Temple. Larry Seward drove a pickup truck around the area of Beale and Hernando, speaking in a booming voice, "All marchers, young and old, go to the temple. You have hurt the cause. We don't want violence." Jesse Turner and others in suit coats or minister's collars calmly motioned people ahead, while outside the temple, Joe Crittendon—"one of the good strong men in the community," according to Lawson—stood on top of a truck telling them to go inside.

Elsewhere, Reverend Starks had been getting people to move back, when policemen charged into them. Reporters taking pictures especially enraged the police. Whittier Sengstacke, who had been maced on February 23, witnessed police opening up with tear-gas shells and running at the crowd of marchers, swinging their clubs wildly. When Sengstacke identified himself as a reporter, one officer squirted mace into his eyes and another attempted a smashing blow to the back of his head but missed. A white TV cameraman who had filmed a sheriff beating a black man was backhanded with a police club so hard that it sent him through a broken window. Stumbling around Beale Street through a fog of mace, Sengstacke said, "I saw women, young children and citizens of all age groups fleeing in terror in front of the officers."

Harold Middlebrook and other marshals kept control over the core of disciplined marchers, but they couldn't control the others. Ron Ivy said it looked like the police chased everyone "except the people that had looted," who grabbed what they wanted and left; and Sengstacke, too, thought most of the looters had gotten away. "The police seemed slightly reluctant about apprehending the group that was doing the damage and dashed head-long into the peaceful marchers." In his view, Movement participants saved the day. "The marchers conducted themselves very well, being caught in the cross-fire of police gas, guns and the looters' rocks and bot- tles," he wrote, in an article headlined, "Cops Wage War on Black Commu- nity." Lawson concluded afterward that Holloman, Lux, and MacDonald had no control over their officers. The black-run radio station WLOK later concluded that marchers and police shared the blame for the chaos.

A *PRESS-SCIMITAR* reporter, Barnes Carr, documented the kind of police brutality that infuriated the marchers. He witnessed two police officers chasing a man down and continuing to beat him even after he was sub- dued; he saw two officers beat another man on the ground in the same fashion. Police ran into bars and other establishments, swinging batons and throwing people bodily out of the premises. They pushed bystanders, including women and the elderly, into the street, and one officer turned and hit a passing young boy with his club, although the youth had done or said nothing. When the same officer saw a man walk by with a bloodied face, for good measure he smashed him in the back of the head with his club. When one outraged black man tried to wrestle a rifle out of the hands of a patrolman, four police jumped on him and beat him into unconsciousness, and intervention by other officers probably stopped them from killing him. When an officer spotted a group of male and female employees standing inside an establishment making comments, he tore open the door and swung his club at anyone he could reach until they retreated farther into the building. At another establishment, an officer ordered a man to get inside, but the door was locked, and the officer beat him while he screamed for someone to open up.

Reporter Clark Porteous had covered Ole Miss in 1962, where white rioters had killed two people in their efforts to stop James Meredith from registering for classes. Porteous began the day watching thousands peacefully carrying "I Am A Man" placards and chanting, "Loeb must go, Loeb must go," but soon Beale Street looked "like a battlefield." New suits and fixtures in front of Paul's Tailoring, dummies from Lansky's, and goods from Schwab's Sundries and Harris Department Store all lay scattered on Beale, and at Willie's Drive-In on Linden, a looter handed out liquor. Police tear-gas bombs caused a woman to collapse, and the fumes forced the police to turn back until they could get more gas masks. Incredibly, Porteous wrote, "I didn't see any police brutality. Many of the officers were taking a lot, and doing it bravely."

Police did get victimized. One officer, surrounded by a crowd, escaped injury only because two black women drove up in a Cadillac and took him out of the area. Numerous officers were hurt by broken and flying glass or injured while fighting with people in the crowd. One gruesome news photo showed an officer with blood streaming from a wound to his head, and another pictured an officer being chased by a mob after he tried to break up their looting. One officer standing with a walkie-talkie was pushed through a storefront window.

Looting spread like wildfire from the downtown to nearby business and residential districts, especially to the south. In a scene all too familiar in many American cities, people reached into shattered windows and pulled out liquor, clothing, and dry goods. Looters tried to steal guns from York Arms, a sporting-goods store, but the management wisely had put locks on the guns before the march began, and no one could loosen them; by the end of the day, police had arrested ten men with pistols, but few had obtained weapons by looting. Police in helicopters, however, reported that up and down Beale and adjacent streets, an urban carnival had erupted in which opportunistic young men, some students, and even children (many of those arrested were between the ages of eight and twelve) ran off with televisions, alcohol, musical instruments, and anything else they could get their hands on at pawnshops, clothing outlets, and liquor stores. In an area of concentrated poverty, the angry unemployed, drunks, drug addicts, the disabled, and other members of the huge "underclass" of black Memphians had fully seized the time—looting, drinking, cursing, and fighting the police.

Street rage was aimed at symbolic targets as well as expressed randomly. One youth, stomping on a twisted white mannequin pulled out of a store window, declared, "I wish this was a real live one, that's just what I wish." Some threw bricks and bottles with great abandon, and one man hurled an empty whiskey bottle into the crowd, where it smashed into and cut the head of an older black woman marcher. In one incident, fifteen to twenty people battered and torched a car on Front Street. One black man began wildly swinging a stick, crying, "You white folks get on out of here. We're gonna burn down this mother-fuckin' city!" Personal security was gone. Instead of King's nonviolent "dress rehearsal" for the Poor People's Campaign march on Washington planned for April 22, the Memphis march left behind a wasteland, with "Main Street and historic Beale Street littered with bricks, blood and broken glass," according to a newspaper account.

By comparison with the deadly rage that took scores of lives in Watts, Newark, and Detroit, this was still a minor affair, but local police did not have the manpower or gear to handle it. Private ambulances refused to go into the area, and all city buses stopped running after rumors began that a bus driver had been stabbed. By 11:32 AM, Fire and Police Director Holloman asked Mayor Loeb to call Governor Buford Ellington to declare a state of emergency; that evening, tanks and trucks rolled in from National Guard units. Meanwhile, the main threat to peace seemed to be roaming police tactical units that continued attacking anyone who could not get out of their way. Black attorney Walter Bailey said, "I was terribly frightened because I lost track of my wife and little boy. I didn't want them to get trampled in the process of people panicking." Clayborn Temple provided the only hope for salvaging the march and finding families.

AT THE REAR of the march, Kay Pittman Black had made her way to Clayborn Temple and Ralph Jackson's adjoining AME Minimum Salary Building. "Inside the A.M.E. building was a horror show," she wrote. "I saw a man with a mangled bloody arm. People's eyes were streaming and red from the effects of Mace. I saw an 8- or 9-year-old child with a bloody head and a woman on the floor moaning and crying. The skin across her forehead looked like bloody pulp." Upstairs, NAACP President Jesse Turner exclaimed, "I was trying to help police get things orderly. Someone shot me with Mace. Lord, what a mess." A shortwave radio reported that many injured people remained hidden in private homes, where they had gone to get away from the police. One woman shouted, "Those damn kids. Between the kids and the cops the whole town's going to blow up."

The interior of Clayborn Temple looked like the aftermath of a war. The church held 1,500 people, who filled every seat and space in the aisles, as ministers read the names of lost children and instructed people on how to get treated for tear gas. A little boy took tissues to people, and a Southwestern College student took a bucket of water around to bathe people's faces. Reverend Blackburn, Clayborn Temple's pastor, found a man in the chapel beaten into a semiconscious state, a girl with asthma suffering terribly from tear gas, and, on the trunk of a car in the alley, a man that he feared had a broken back. People sick from gas or wounded by broken glass lay everywhere. Reverend Starks pleaded, "All of you that are on our side, we are asking you to go home. Tonight we are asking you to go home and prepare for this weekend." But until things calmed down outside, they couldn't leave.

James Lawson had managed to shepherd many marchers back to the temple. During his ordeal walking through the streets with a bullhorn—tear gas and violence all around him—Lawson worried about what had happened to his wife and son, but his singleminded purpose was to move marchers back to Clayborn Temple, where they could get medical aid and sanctuary from the police. When Kay Black saw him at the Minimum Salary Building, however, he "looked ashen. His hands were shaking. He was on the phone to Police Director Frank Holloman. 'We've got to have some police here. We've got women and children in the temple. We've got to get them out and home. The Black Power boys are in there haranguing and we can't get them out.'"

While the wounded tried to regroup and Lawson talked to police headquarters, Cabbage and other BOP members had reappeared to formulate a strategy of resistance to the police. And even though police commanders told Lawson on the phone they would do everything to help, their officers in the streets had determined to take revenge. When people tried to leave Clayborn Temple, police attacked them with mace and clubs. As Kay Black fled the scene, she reported, "Behind me I could see bottles beginning to fly as the police moved down the street toward Clayborn Temple to disperse the crowd inside the Temple." She concluded, "The battle of Clayborn Temple had started."

Outside, police moved down Hernando in a wedge formation, while young men in front of the church and on nearby roofs hurled at them anything they could get their hands on. The police cleared the street, but the men regrouped. Various police cars arrived, disgorging men with shotguns and riot sticks. But the TAC Unit could not muster overwhelming force, because police constantly had to interrupt their duty at Clayborn to leave for various other crisis points. One group of youngsters decided to march back to Beale Street, and the police formed a line and rebuffed them. A young man suddenly appeared with a rifle, and the police jumped on him and beat him with their nightsticks. He was lucky they didn't shoot him.

At 11:43, police again ordered protesters in front of the temple to clear out. When rocks and bottles flew their way, higher-ups gave permission to use tear gas, which police shot onto the steps of the building. Ed Gillis was inside, wondering what to do. "We knowed they was all out there cause folks done come in with their eyes and heads full of gas," and the residue affected everyone inside. "It was burning me awful bad—my eyes." L. C. Reed was also there, his eyes already burned during the march. As he sat daubing his eyes, police entered the temple, clubbing people and shooting tear-gas canisters onto the floors and against the walls, leaving stains that remained many months later. People ran from the canisters, but as the gas spread through the sanctuary, they were forced to the floor to get air—eyes watering, gasping for breath. Robert Beasley, who had been maced earlier in the morning as well as on February 23, was maced again: "I don't know what sparked it off, but I got caught in the middle of it." As gas filled the room, some people panicked and jumped out of the windows. The *Tri-State Defender* published a photo of at least thirteen officers with gas masks, helmets, clubs, and pump tear-gas guns walking out afterward.

AFSCME's Bill Lucy stood speechless in amazement. Like Lawson, he thought that Holloman, Lux, and MacDonald had completely lost control over their men. "They were doing things that were just unbelievable," he said. Baxton Bryant thought the police handled themselves with some restraint under a direct command, "but once the command was given and they moved out on their own, they were a totally different breed." Councilman Netters came into the temple, recognizing constituents who had been beaten. He asked a group of young people threatening to burn buildings to leave. "Everyone was either hurt or mad or scared, emotional in every way," he said. "I had reached a point of numbness."

Outside, for an hour and a half, police and black youth continued a running cat-and-mouse game. At 12:13, some 250 people took a stand in front of the temple and would not let the police near it. Inside, ministers frantically called police headquarters, asking for help in getting hurt people and suffering families out. The police momentarily backed off, only to use gas once again when people threw things at them. Next door, at the Minimum Salary Building, in a series of phone calls, Reverend Jackson and Frank Holloman tried to resolve the crisis. Jackson first asked for the police to help people leave, but he soon realized that the people feared they would be attacked and would leave only if the police went away. Police Chief MacDonald ordered officers not to use tear gas, but within ten minutes, the officers were using it again. Jackson finally asked Holloman to come to the temple personally to assume control over his officers, but Holloman said that riots all over town prevented him from leaving his command post.

Ministers Darrell Doughty, Dick Moon, Zeke Bell, and National Council of Churches observer Sam Allen huddled in the Minimum Security Building, conferring about the situation. Suddenly, people desperately trying to escape from the temple broke through the door and gas poured in, forcing those already inside to the floor, tears pouring from their eyes. At 1:20 PM, Holloman called back, asking the ministers to stop kids from getting bricks from behind the buildings and throwing them at police, insisting his officers had not used gas in the church. The room was so filled with it that Doughty could not even continue the conversation, and the church leaders crawled out through the window.

By 2 PM, police lifted the state of siege at Clayborn Temple. Taylor

Rogers had been inside with his family, but then, "We left to get to my car and we got maced." As people left the building, Charles Cabbage stood on the steps and coolly commented that they should not run, and that they shouldn't start something they didn't plan to finish.

AS VIOLENCE CONTINUED downtown, the question of who was responsible for it was already on people's minds. *Commercial Appeal* reporter Thomas Bevier saw a patrolman running down the street, tears streaming down his face from the effects of tear gas, clutching a sawed-off shotgun. The cop shouted, "We're trying our damnedest. Write that down. We're trying our damnedest. The police didn't start this. Write that down. Treat us fair." The police said they were creating order out of disorder, but most blacks felt outrage at their methods and blamed Loeb. One man shouted out to Bevier, "That man, that Loeb, better sign the paper or this town is going to tumble down." An hour later, a few blocks away, someone threw a firebomb into a Loeb's Laundry.

By 12:30, police had cleared the downtown sidewalks but continued to spread terror as they fanned out into restaurants, pool halls, and bars. One of the more egregious examples of wanton police violence occurred at the Big M restaurant at Danny Thomas and Linden, a popular dining place for black business and professional people. Out in the parking lot, about thirty helmeted police attacked young men coming out of the restaurant, knocking them down and beating them on the pavement and breaking out their car windows and windshields. Victims included the cousin of a black politician and a visiting staff member of the Kentucky Human Relations Council.

The police then entered the Big M and demanded that the diners leave. Owner Melvin Bond asked the police to let them finish their meals, and someone else asked them to show their badges. Instead, "They began beating and dragging people out," said soldier Kenneth Cox in an affidavit. He and a local Firestone worker and another friend tried to leave, but police trapped them in the parking lot inside his car, with vehicles parked in front of and behind him. The police smashed in his windows, beat the people inside, then pulled him out and maced him. They clubbed him on the head and he ran, not realizing until someone pointed it out that blood was flowing down his face from a gaping wound that took eight stitches to close.

Union Protective Life Insurance President Harold Whalum, dressed in a suit and tie, was helping older women into the NAACP's glass-fronted lobby at nearby 280 Hernando when several police officers burst in, cursing them as "black bitches." Whalum responded quietly. "I told them that there were women present who should be respected and one shouted, 'Shut up, you black ——— and knocked me down with his club. While I was down on the floor, one sprayed me with Mace, called me the same filthy name again, [and said,] 'If we could, we would kill all of you black bastards.'" Maxine Smith, standing next to Whalum when this happened, said the police called all of them "sons of bitches" and "MFs."

Her office was well away from the riot area, and she couldn't understand what the police were doing there. "Any riotous condition that was created on Hernando . . . I think I can truthfully say was created by the police officers." She was horrified to watch six or more officers beat a young woman and a young man in a parking lot across the street—part of a family that included kids, parents, and grandparents trying to get to their car in order to leave the area. The young man "must have gotten more of the blows because he was leaning over her [his sister] to try to pick her up. She had been knocked down when all of them just started beating." By the time they got done, "He was obviously unconscious. A squad car came up the street and he was dragged and just thrown in the squad car . . . but he looked limp."

Chaos surrounding the downtown began to reverberate far out into the city's black neighborhoods, causing panic and consternation among parents worried about the fate of their children. People had seen a young girl lying on the sidewalk downtown, and a rumor spread that a police officer had shot her. One woman far outside the riot zone went door-to-door, telling her neighbors, "Get your children from school. Get them quick before they are killed. The white folks is murdering them in their classes." Such rumors did not seem unbelievable, given the racial history of Memphis and its environs. Many people knew of the bloody riot of 1866, in which scores of blacks had died. "Honey, anything you can name, the white folks is evil enough to do it," one old woman remarked.

Although whites weren't murdering black students in their classes, black parents had plenty of reason to be concerned. At Booker T. Washington High, where 75 percent of students lived in surrounding housing projects for the poor, seven or eight carloads of police arrived after someone pulled the fire alarm. Students and teachers stood outside the school, because the bell had been ringing and they had been waiting for the police for more than an hour and a half. When the police finally arrived, they tore off their badges, rushed from their cars, and attacked. Assistant Principal Mose Walker said they "began swinging at people's legs and just knocking them out from under them on the street." He told his teachers to stay on the school grounds as observers, but the police "shot a gas grenade right in the middle of this group of teachers, almost hitting one 70-year-old man who's retiring." When other teachers went to their aid, the officers threatened them and forced them back into the school building—where they could not so easily witness events—and continued swinging clubs and grabbing people.

"Why—why would they shoot tear gas?" Walker asked incredulously. "There's not a child, not a running person, not an obvious looter . . . not one officer had on a name plate, a badge. Not one." The police hauled twenty to thirty students and adults off to jail.

At John Gaston Hospital, the city's segregated public hospital for the poor, victims of mayhem in the streets began pouring into the emergency room. Doctors treated many people attacked by the police, including a seventy-five-year-old man who had been beaten, an eleven-year-old with a deep cut from a nightstick, and a fourteen-year-old who had been knocked down in the street. People suffered from lacerations to heads and shoulders, broken bones and teeth, skull concussions, buckshot wounds, facial injuries, body bruises, and tear-gas and mace irritations of their lungs and faces. Police or the relatives of victims brought in young black males primarily, and a few policemen also arrived with cuts or bruises.

Most victims came into the hospital in a flood on early Friday afternoon, but another flood came in that night. Doctors treated bruises and sewed up skulls in a rush and sent people on their way. Hospital records noted a number of people shot in the back by police during the following week, but the strike's first fatality occurred during the riots of March 28.

Sixteen-year-old Larry Payne lived most of the time with his father, Mason Payne, just outside the city. On the morning of March 28, he left Mitchell Road School to go to the march downtown, where a UPI photographer pictured him standing next to a looted window, watching as police beat a black teenager. Payne escaped from police and left the downtown around noon; he went to the apartment of his mother, Lizzie, in Fowler Homes, a low-income project ten blocks south of Beale. Apparently he was carrying some stolen cloth. Another boy told Larry of someone he knew in the projects who could sew that cloth into pants, and Larry went out to find him while his mother watched the soap opera *As the World Turns* on television. Larry ran into another group of young men who were debating whether they wanted to go to the Sears store two blocks away. Not everyone did, and it is not clear if Larry went with them or not.

Early that morning, a white woman had called the police to pass on what her maid had told her—that some youngsters from Mitchell Road School, just outside the city limits, were planning to rob a Sears, Roebuck store at 903 South Third. Sure enough, at 12:45, police got a call about youths looting Sears. Two white police officers, Leslie Dean Jones and Charles F. Williams, drove to Sears and found a broken storefront window. Then they cruised until they spotted young men carrying TVs and stereos. According to their account, they followed them to Fowler Homes, where officer Jones chased a youth carrying a television—until he ducked into a basement door. Jones banged on the door and he wouldn't come out, but after more pounding Larry Payne eventually emerged. When the officer told him to put up both hands, Payne pulled out "the biggest knife I ever saw," according to Jones.

Jones pressed the barrel of his single-shot 12-gauge shotgun into Payne's stomach and pulled the trigger. Payne flew backward into a wall and then slid to the ground. The *Tri-State Defender* later published a picture of Payne lying against the basement stairwell, his eyes and mouth wide open, both hands above his head. After he was pronounced dead at John Gaston Hospital, police produced a rusty butcher knife that they said belonged to Payne, yet they were unable to lift any fingerprints from it.

After the incident, a reporter did a more extended investigation. Nearly a dozen eyewitnesses claimed that Payne did not have a knife and was pleading for his life. "He had his hands up. I saw the white palms," said one witness. Another said the shot made "a muffled sound, like busting a sack. The gun was touching his stomach." According to this newspaper account, Payne's mother had heard the shot and ran out from her apartment, pleading with the police to let her reach her son's body, screaming, "You killed my son! You killed my son!" The officers pushed her back and cursed her, and one of them waved a gun in her face, yelling, "If you don't get back, nigger, I'll kill you." She fainted, and friends dragged her into her apartment. More police arrived, and more tenants, and beatings ensued. The *Defender* ran a photo of Leona Jackson, a grandmother, with bandages on her arm and stitches on her head after the encounter. More witnesses came forward to say the police officer coldly and deliberately murdered Larry Payne.

The Memphis Police Department exonerated Jones; he was not even suspended during the investigation, nor did a grand jury ever indict him. No one in the black community believed that anyone faced with a shotgun would try to pull a knife on a police officer, and they knew of other instances when police had planted weapons on people they killed. In 1971, Payne's parents unsuccessfully sued the police for civil damages. In the court proceedings, Henry Lux, at that point the chief of police, admitted that none of Payne's fingerprints were found on the knife. He also said that police had thrown the knife, shotgun pellets, and Payne's clothing into the Mississippi River five months after the incident, so no evidence remained for investigation of the case. The police produced no reason for why they had destroyed evidence or why they would throw evidence into the Mississippi. African Americans saw Payne's death as a simple act of vengeance—an execution committed by one more violent white police officer and covered up by his superiors.

Meeting in emergency session with the City Council on Thursday afternoon, Fire and Police Director Holloman claimed that black people in Memphis had taken up "general guerilla warfare." When reporters questioned his inflammatory language, he told them, "Yes, we have a war in the city of Memphis," and ominously suggested that much more violent action could have been taken. "I think you should realize what the police department did. They used restraint." The next day he reiterated, "We were in a civil war yesterday."

By contrast, most black Memphians felt they had just witnessed a war on themselves and their community. Black real estate broker Harold C. Moore said, "Police charged into the crowd, clubbing and gassing everyone in sight." Jesse Turner, whom police had attacked despite his suit and tie, had watched police beat a twenty-year-old man senseless: "It was one of the most brutal attacks I've ever seen." He characterized police actions as "brutal and inhuman treatment" of people trying to exercise their constitutional rights. He added that not all police officers should be judged by the acts of some—just as not all blacks should be judged by the acts of a few looters. James Lawson concluded that, as on February 23, rank-and-file police had declared open season on black people.

BLACK MEMPHIANS HAD seen it all before—in so many cases documented in the black press and by the NAACP. They suspected that, just as before, the white media would cover up or rationalize the police violence, and that the marchers, Dr. King, and the black community would get all the blame. The *Tri-State Defender* edition titled, "Cops Wage War on Black Community," carried a photo of a once energetic, precocious Larry Payne in a white shirt. Next to it was a "Poem on Memphis Racism," a few lines of which summed up the day.

The looters got away very early in the game.
Have you ever seen a thief linger around to be contained?
They claimed our Negro leaders could not control the crowd.
Unfounded lies and accusations, they denounce our leaders loud. . . .
They lay everything on Black Power, but them boys are college bred.
And are too smart to rob a pawnshop, while the coppers beat their heads. . . .
Will they lump us all together forever and a day?
Or will . . . a new awakening, humane and fairness, be their way . . . ?

16

"THE MOVEMENT LIVES OR DIES IN MEMPHIS"

We are now saying to the city, will you please listen?
Will you please recognize that in the heart of our city
there is massive cruelty and poverty and indignity,
and that only if you remove it can we have order.
—*James Lawson*

A T THE HOLIDAY INN RIVERMONT, KING HUDDLED UNDER HIS bedcovers. In the middle of a sunny day, Memphis seemed to him as black as night. He had told everyone for the last two months that nonviolence remained the only effective weapon of struggle. He had assured the media and elected officials of his ability, even in a time of riots, to lead a nonviolent march through the streets of the nation's overwhelmingly black and poor capital. He thought Memphis would be the beginning of the Poor People's Campaign, but instead, on the morning of March 28, a trap door opened and King and his movement seemed to be in free-fall.

Secluded in his room, away from reporters' questions, wondering what to do next, King felt deeply hurt and betrayed by what had happened. He listened to and watched news reports, despairing to learn that the police had killed sixteen-year-old Larry Payne, others had been shot, hundreds had been arrested, and scores had been taken to hospitals. The height of the police violence had passed by about 2 PM, but the south and central portions of black Memphis remained a battle zone, and more people

poured into the hospital again that night as the police enforced a city curfew by beating people's heads.

From King's room, Abernathy and Lee called back to Hosea Williams at
SCLC headquarters in Atlanta, as SCLC's bookkeeper and controller, James
Harrison, who was secretly on the FBI payroll, listened in. Atlanta FBI
agents, informed by Harrison, described King as "extremely dejected," and
possibly giving in to fears for his personal safety. Agents wrote to J. Edgar
Hoover that Williams, Abernathy, and Lee "strongly feel some elements
which caused disturbance in Memphis . . . may cause personal harm to
King," and King also believed "the violence was caused by a Negro group
who dislike him." Black Power advocates had verbally thrashed King more
than once, but he had never feared them. Now he didn't know what to think.

Very shortly, Samuel (better known as Billy) Kyles came in and sat at the
foot of King's bed. He said King "really didn't have any idea of what had
happened," and he "was very disturbed." Lawson soon arrived, and he and
Kyles both said that the Invaders had instigated the riot. King had numerous times faced young people who wanted to fight the police; he immediately said that the Memphis movement would have to make some
accommodation with them. Lawson vowed to hold a nonviolent march the
following day to prove it could still be done, but Abernathy and Lee said
they would not participate in another march until they were sure there was
better planning. Their confidence in Lawson and the Memphis movement
had been badly shaken.

King felt mounting anxiety about what the day's events meant. He knew
the FBI followed his every step and tapped his advisors' phones, and that
Hoover wanted nothing more than to destroy him and his movement.
James Orange and a number of King's aides, as well as Bill Lucy, believed
police agents initiated the riot to destroy King's leadership—and a congressional investigating committee later concluded that it might have been
true. While King and his aides worried, Memphis FBI agents reported to
Hoover in Washington every few hours. Assistant FBI Director William
Sullivan, Hoover's man in charge of the campaign to destroy King, sent a
memo back to them early that afternoon, asking the Memphis bureau for
answers to a number of questions: "Did MARTIN LUTHER KING [caps in

original] do anything to trigger the violence; what part did he play in the march; how much of the violence is attributable to KING; did he make any statements on joining the march which could have had an effect on the crowd toward violence?" Perhaps he was considering King as a target for a federal anti-riot prosecution. And to make the FBI's line of attack perfectly clear, the memo concluded, "Mr. SULLIVAN has indicated that although MARTIN LUTHER KING preaches non-violence, violence occurs just about everywhere he goes."

The FBI had already formulated its propaganda line on the Memphis march. As part of its COINTELPRO (counterintelligence) actions against "black hate" groups, the FBI's "Racial Intelligence Section" authored two blind memos and sent them out to press contacts on March 28 and 29. The St. Louis *Globe-Democrat*, some of its language identical to the FBI memos, depicted King as a "Judas goat leading lambs to slaughter," who ran away as soon as trouble broke out; it said Memphis would be a "prelude to civil strife," and King's "non-violent masquerade" would lead to a bloodbath in the nation's capital. The U.S. House Select Committee on Assassinations later documented that the *Globe-Democrat* and probably other newspapers, including the *Commercial Appeal*, formulated their anti-King editorials based in part on FBI memos on the "hypocrite" King, which the FBI also forwarded to members of Congress, the White House, the Justice Department, to military intelligence, the attorney general, and various other agencies of government.

In a phone call the morning after the riot, Sullivan again urged Memphis agents to "get everything possible on KING and . . . stay on him until he leaves Memphis." The Memphis FBI field office confirmed, "All racial sources have been alerted to immediately advise of any pertinent info developed by them." Sullivan wanted the identities of the two women who rescued King from Beale Street, but no one discovered who they were.

It seems the best the FBI could come up with was a supplementary memo on another element of King's "hypocrisy": King had urged blacks to boycott white-owned businesses, but he avoided the "fine Hotel [sic] Lorraine . . . owned and patronized exclusively by Negroes," in order to stay at the "plush" and "white-owned, operated and almost exclusively white patronized" Holiday Inn Rivermont. "There will be no boycott of white merchants for King, only for his followers." King had stayed at the dilapidated Lorraine Motel or held meetings there a number of times during visits to Memphis, but the MPD's black Lieutenant Jerry Williams warned him away from it because of its exposed balconies. On March 18, he did not stay there, and on March 28, AFSCME had rented King a room at the Peabody Hotel. Patrolman Nichols had said the riot blocked King's way to either hotel, so he routed him to the Rivermont. The word of King's "hypocrisy" in not going to the Lorraine was soon aired in the media, more or less forcing King to go to the Lorraine the next time he came to Memphis.

At the Rivermont, King had an inkling of this invective being stirred up against him. He canceled his scheduled flight out of Memphis and began to make various calls around the country, not quite sure of what to do next. Reporters discovered his location, and at 5 PM, he felt compelled to hold a press conference, including Lawson and other local leaders. None of King's emotions—despair, fear, anxiety, and an urgent desire to leave— appeared on his face. Instead, he projected the calm, reasonable, soft but determined demeanor that had always made him so acceptable to the white press. In far worse situations, King had been able to steady his nerves. When a raging mob had trapped him and hundreds of others in Brown's Chapel in Selma, threatening to burn it down, King projected a perfect calm and faith that the Movement would prevail, even as tear gas wafted through the church.

THE STORY OF the violence of March 28 was really not about King, no matter what the FBI said. Reverend Starks, Lawson, Jackson, Abernathy, Epps, Baxton Bryant, Ciampa, and Cornelia Crenshaw—all members of the COME strategy committee—attended King's news conference in an attempt to bring the media's focus back to the strike and the root causes of violence. Said Lawson:

The issue is not a question of the violence of today, or of Dr. King's presence. The issue is the same as it was a week ago, namely justice, fairness for the sanitation workers and a new sense of dignity and justice for poor people in this community. We will not let any incident turn us aside from this fundamental issue. . . . Young people who committed violence are excellent students of this very sick society of ours, who have been taught extremely well by this society, and who therefore cannot hear the message of nonviolence, the message of love and reconciliation that many of us have been insisting upon. We do not condone their violence as we do not condone the history of violence of this society of ours.

Lawson ominously voiced the fear "that if violence continues in our city it will become an excuse for the wholesale massacre of innocent people in our midst, including recognizable leadership people of our city and our nation." Nonetheless, the Memphis movement would continue with another march the next day and keep on until the city settled the strike: "We don't intend to let the sanitation workers be sold out under any circumstances." King largely deferred to Lawson, adding, "I thought the march itself was basically a very dignified one," that people on the sidelines, not marchers, had instigated window breaking, and that there would be another nonviolent mass march. Abernathy did his best to correct statements being circulated that King had "fled," saying simply that King left the march because "we won't be a part of violent demonstrations."

City and state authorities held their own "law and order" press conference of white men, featuring Claude Armour representing the governor, Fire and Police Director Holloman, and Shelby County Sheriff William Morris, all of whom stood behind Loeb. The mayor called a curfew, said the march had been "abandoned by its leaders," and vowed that police and National Guard units would "restore law and order"—a theme that quickly dominated media accounts.

King found it all very depressing. With the FBI recording every word, he spoke on the telephone to his longtime adviser Stanley Levison, who urged King to remember that the marchers themselves had not rioted, said that his campaign in Washington would have SCLC staff and marshals to keep things under control, and told him he should get some rest before drawing too many conclusions about the viability of the Poor People's Campaign.

King also spoke to SCLC board member Marion Logan, who feared for King when she saw his dazed expression during the march, on national television news, and urged him to "get your ass out of Memphis." Coretta Scott King also spoke to her husband, trying to calm him by saying, "You mustn't hold yourself responsible, because you know you aren't."

Reassurances did not work. Abernathy recalled that night as a "terrible and horrible experience for him. I had never seen him in all my life so upset and so troubled. I couldn't get him to sleep that night. He was worried, worried. He didn't know what to do, and he didn't know what the press was going to say." Finally, King fell fast asleep. But when he awoke on March 29, reading the morning *Commercial Appeal* must have been a nauseating experience: neither Lawson's comments nor King's reached the public. The commander of the Tennessee National Guard, Brigadier General R. W. Akin, warned that all his men were armed and ready to shoot. Memphis Chamber of Commerce President Thomas Faires called King's role "deplorable," and former Mayor Edmund Orgill demanded that sanitation workers go back to work.

That morning, President Johnson appeared on national television; he denounced "mindless violence," declared "order must be preserved," decried "the tragic events in Memphis," offered federal military assistance to local authorities, and asked them to act firmly and fairly. He also offered to send in a labor mediator, an offer Mayor Loeb declined. The *Washington Post* headline read, "Johnson Warns on Rioting: U.S. Support Is Pledged for Law and Order." The *New York Times*, usually sympathetic to King, called Memphis "a powerful embarrassment to Dr. King" and editorialized that he should call off the Poor People's Campaign because no one could guarantee that another Memphis would not happen in the nation's capital. Only AFL-CIO President George Meany urged Mayor Loeb to recognize the workers' demands, and he offered AFL-CIO assistance to bring about a settlement—an offer Loeb curtly rejected.

For the next several days, the local white media condemned King unequivocally. The *Commercial Appeal* editorial on March 29, "Moment of Truth," said police had contained "the anarchy that was threatened yesterday," and "what could have turned into a full-scale riot was nipped in the bud." It praised the police, who had "exercised restraint," and also the ministers, who had turned the march around. A day later, it accused King of instigating the riot in his March 18 speech, when he urged students to boycott school and said, "We may have to escalate this struggle a bit"—and then, "Having fled the melee, King later issued statements attempting to disassociate himself from the violence that he had instigated." As a result, "Dr. King's pose as a leader of a non-violent movement has been shattered. He now has the entire nation doubting his word when he insists his . . . shanty-town sit-in in the nation's capital . . . can be peaceful." Next to the editorial, a cartoon showed a slightly dopey-looking King, who shrugged his shoulders and said, "Who, me?" In the background, Beale Street was in tatters.

Another editorial backed Loeb's rejection of AFL-CIO offers to help mediate, writing, "Memphis has had enough of Dr. King's help. It can do without George Meany's intrusion." Its editorial cartoon depicted the bandaged white hand of Memphis, slamming the door on the foot of someone trying to get in the door; the foot was marked, "intrusions from outside." On March 31, the *Appeal* ran a short article headlined, "Chicken a La King," painting King as a coward whose "efforts to climb aboard a meat truck were rebuffed" as he tried to leave the riot (a story with no basis in fact). On April 2, it reprinted a *Dallas Morning News* column calling King "the headline-hunting high priest of nonviolent violence," whose staff was willing to "wreck everything for a spot on the evening newscast for the peripatetic preacher." It blamed Black Power militants for turning a strike into a racial confrontation, and King, who, "like a torchbearer sprinting into a powder-house," had brought his "road show" to Memphis. Once the explosion began, he "sprinted down a side street, leaped into an old model car and sped away."

Memphis intelligence officials noted with satisfaction the several days of negative media treatment of King. A nationally published photo in the *Los Angeles Times* was captioned: "Young militants jostled and pushed Dr. King, whose face clouded with apparent fear." The *Providence Sunday Journal* called King "reckless and irresponsible," saying he "scurried to safety" and "took swift refuge in a motel." The Jackson (Mississippi) *Clarion-Ledger* ran a front-page photo of King in the Memphis march titled, "King

Before Disappearing Act." The paper recently had "exposed" King's ties to Jack O'Dell and "Communism," and now it contrasted American troops fighting at the Battle of Khe Sanh in Vietnam with a photo of army tanks in Memphis next to an article titled, "King Vows to Press Attack on Memphis." *Natchez Democrat* cartoons linked King and Carmichael as militant minstrels and also linked King to Fidel Castro, who supposedly was funding America's domestic upheaval. It ran a big story on King's March 23 speech on "noted Communist Negro Educator" W. E. B. Du Bois and exposed a "Kennedy–King Alliance" subverting the country through their appeals to end poverty. Many white southern editors hated Robert Kennedy as much as they hated King.

This nearly unified view of King as a coward, subversive, and hypocrite was not new: the Memphis press and other southern media regularly vilified King as a purveyor of trickery, a meddler in foreign affairs, a man "inflated by ambition," an instigator of mob rule and ghetto violence, an ally of Communists. Lawson and King had explained in their press conference that problems of poverty and racism had given rise to the conflict in Memphis and other cities. But it became standard fare in the mainstream media that King had come in, stirred up trouble, and, coward that he was, fled. As the *Commercial Appeal* put it, King's nonviolent philosophy was merely an excuse "to break laws in the name of a cause." All of these statements echoed FBI Director Hoover's longtime propaganda campaign against King.

Politicians likewise said that Memphis proved King could not lead a peaceful national march on Washington. Tennessee's Republican Senator Howard Baker declared that the Poor People's Campaign march would be "like striking a match to look in your gas tank to see if you're out of gas"; West Virginia's Democratic Senator Robert Byrd called King a "self-seeking rabble-rouser"; Mississippi's Democratic Senator John Stennis called for an injunction to stop the march; Arkansas Democratic Senator John McClellan promised to begin hearings on King's Poor People's Campaign. Even West Tennessee's liberal Democratic Congressman Ray Blanton blamed King for having "contributed to the violence."

Republican Congressman Dan Kuykendall of Memphis denounced King to an all-white audience at East High School the night after the riot and, in a speech before Congress, accused him of "agitating destruction, violence and hatred." He concluded, "I hope this exposure will wake up people to the evil results of his activities before it is too late and freedom is destroyed in America for all, whatever their color." Only Democratic presidential candidate Senator Eugene McCarthy pointed out that the urban crisis and war policies caused racial violence; others simply blamed King. Whites wrote in to the Memphis newspapers, protesting that "white people have civil rights too" and that blacks should pull themselves up by their own bootstraps, and decrying "black hoodlums."

The one local account sympathetic to King came from the *Tri-State Defender*—although it did not appear in print until April 6. The black newsweekly editorially condemned the police for acting like Nazi storm troopers and called Frank Holloman one of "the advocates of genocide of black people." It condemned National Guardsmen and police as "trigger happy cowboys" and described them riding "through peaceful communities, five and six in a car, waving their shotguns out the window and rudely spitting tobacco on streets where Negro women are standing." Its editorial cartoon depicted Holloman firing away with his pistol under the shelter of hooded Klansmen who were labeled "Loeb's Vigilantes." Another editorial, headlined "Memphis on Fire," concluded: "The march was purely incidental to the uprising. A disturbance was bound to occur sooner or later" because of explosive conditions in black Memphis. The authorities—not King or even the Invaders—made the "fatal choice": "Between settling the strike and clubbing the marchers into submission, they chose the latter." The *Defender* said Holloman and other whites, even liberals, ignored the sources of problems in Memphis and instead blamed their effects.

But *Defender* columnist Nat D. Williams also suggested that some in the black middle class saw King as an incendiary figure. Williams described him as "the bomb"—a man "who seemingly came to town reluctantly on invitation" but then "threw the missile" into an explosive situation by calling for a work stoppage and student strike. "His 'call' struck the town like dynamite," setting off "emotionally immature and excitable" high school kids whose teachers "fell back into shaky silence," afraid to moderate them.

The Invaders took great exception to this view of King as a militant leader. On March 29, in front of a deserted downtown lot, NBC-TV reporter Carl Stern interviewed Coby Smith, speaking for the Invaders. Wearing dark sunglasses and a blue work shirt, Smith exuded cool confidence and quiet anger. He blamed the riot on black frustrations over outmoded Movement tactics—namely, "a march, which would have probably been very fruitless," and on police brutality. Smith toyed with the question of whether the Invaders started it, smiling, "We don't organize burnings, we organize people. If people burn, they burn." Nonviolent mass marches were no longer relevant to the temper of the times: "King's attitude has failed. This is a last ditch effort, the Washington march, to get us back to the early sixties and the late fifties I suppose. . . . The people of Memphis have said no to him." If King did not analyze the needs and desires of the people, "He will be faced with this same situation everywhere he goes. . . . Dr. King will have to come over, and if he doesn't, then he is dead . . . in terms of the movement."

King may have been more concerned about his own image than about the plight of blacks, Smith suggested, but an increasingly agitated Stern grew more persistent in questioning him about the damage the riot had done to King. Smith responded, "I don't know why you persist in saying Dr. King. This is Memphis. This city belongs to people here. The black people here have to set the temper of the times. Dr. King is going to have to come in and meet the needs of people here. . . . If he doesn't, the same thing will happen to him everywhere he goes that happened to him here in Memphis." Stern asked, Was this the first outbreak of summer riots? Smith answered, "Of course. . . . People have had it. If that strike lasts any longer, we can look forward to this city going up. . . . We don't have to organize. The police beat heads—they organize for us."

Smith did not see the riot as a setback for the Movement, but rather a promising sign that black people would resist. Stern asked if black youth had a paramilitary-style organization, and Smith frankly responded, "Well, we should." He said 109 Memphians had been killed in Vietnam, probably 75 percent of them blacks, and when those who survived came home with military training, "We can't stop people from using it." NBC's evening *Huntley–Brinkley Report* quoted him saying, "If the community can only respond to force by burning and shooting and looting, we'll do it." Charles Cabbage gave a separate brief interview to a newspaper reporter, saying, "Young black people want black power and they're going to get it." Like Smith, he said people in Memphis should set their own agenda.

A *Los Angeles Times* reporter found that some established black leaders in Memphis now doubted that King could lead a nonviolent march. "Younger Negroes . . . say their allegiance has been promised to no one— least of all to Dr. King." The *Times* headlined its article, "Once Placid Memphis Now a Racial Cauldron." The only cheer in the media came from the Hambone cartoon in the Friday *Commercial Appeal*: "Don' mak no dif-f'unce whut kin' o' face you got, hit look mo' bettuh *smilin'!!*"

AFTER A MISERABLE night of self-doubt, at 10 AM on Friday, March 29, King prepared himself and dressed for a meeting with media representatives. Charles Cabbage, Charles ("Izzy") Harrington, and Calvin Taylor, representing the Invaders, knocked on his door, and Cabbage recalled being shocked that King seemed to have absolutely no security. Abernathy began to cross-examine them, assuming they had touched off the window breaking and looting, and Taylor said, "Cab and me, we got mad because the man hadn't heard what we had to say and already was accusing us as having caused the riot."

When King entered the room, freshly showered and still buttoning his shirt after rising late, the atmosphere changed. Taylor perceived him as not black but brown—or maybe caramel-colored—with soft skin and hands, a gentle man who projected a disarming presence. King said he was surprised to see Cabbage—a "Morehouse man" whom SCLC once had tried to hire for an organizing project in Baltimore—and he sat down with the young men and smoked cigarettes. He told them he had believed there were no Black Power activists in Memphis, and that if he had known this, he would have met with them to agree on a common agenda. Cabbage told King he had tried to send a message to him when he was on the speaker's platform on March 18, but Lawson and the ministers wouldn't give him access, and that he had demanded greater youth participation on the COME strategy committee, to no avail. "We have been trying to talk to

Lawson—he won't hear us." Cabbage also said a man had come to his home warning of a plot to kill King; the SCLC leader blanched, then responded that he heard such threats every day and no one could stop an attempt on his life.

King seemed genuinely depressed by Cabbage's account of failed communications with Lawson, as he relied heavily on Lawson's organizing skill and history of building strong relations with young people in the Movement. An observant young writer working as an intern at the *Commercial Appeal*, of all places, Calvin Taylor described King as genuinely distraught over violence, saying, "Not so much 'Why did you have a riot with me leading it?' But, 'Why would you resort to violence anyway?' As if to say, 'You know that violence hasn't worked for white people. Why would you do that?' The man actually believed that kind of philosophy. . . . I say 'that' philosophy because I don't believe in it, you know." Yet he did believe in King.

Cabbage blamed Lawson for a communications failure, but Taylor felt a bit ashamed during this interchange with King, because he knew there was more to it than that. Cabbage made it appear that the Invaders had done absolutely nothing to set off the street altercations, but "Dr. King wasn't eating that mess up, you know, like we were totally innocent of the thing. And . . . we weren't totally innocent." Members of the Invaders had indeed encouraged young people to take rocks and sticks in their hands before the March 28 riot, then they stayed out of the march and claimed innocence. "The spirit was there. I mean, we had put it there, although we hadn't started it." King now pledged to the Invaders that they would became a part of the COME leadership, but he also wanted to know "what must be done to have a peaceful march, because," he added firmly, "you know I have got to lead one. There is no other way."

Here Cabbage and friends faced a contradiction: To the extent that they could give credibility to any nonviolent leader, they gave it to King, but they actually didn't have much control over their far-flung network in the Memphis youth underground. When King asked for a guarantee of nonviolence, Cabbage laughed and said he had to be kidding. All he could say was that his group would try to keep the next march nonviolent, but his group needed money to be effective. King reassured the trio that they would be involved in planning the next demonstration, and he would help find financial aid, but his demeanor made it clear enough that the Invaders would have to adhere to nonviolent discipline if they wanted to be a part of the Movement.

Calvin Taylor likened this encounter with King to something akin to a "psychotherapy session," a kind of communication with an adult that he hadn't experienced before. "It was unbelievable to me. I mean, the man just looked like peace. He didn't raise his voice . . . you could feel peace all around that man. One of the few times in my life that I wasn't actually fighting something." Even Cabbage, a verbal sharpshooter, "didn't have no comebacks for him. . . . I have never seen Cab sitting in a situation where he couldn't say anything, and he couldn't say a word." King told them he would talk to them again before he left town, and as the Invaders trio left the Rivermont, an elated Cabbage exclaimed that they had just talked to "an extraordinary man," according to Taylor. He had never seen Cabbage give any man the kind of respect he gave King.

Although the Invaders rejected nonviolence as a strategy and a philosophy, King's presence stayed with them. Many years later, Coby Smith viewed King with greater sympathy, saying he was

> a person that was so clear and so committed to the idea that everyone should be involved in his own liberation. That everyone had a right to be involved. And when he talked to you, he talked to you not based on what you had been accused of, but what your reality was. . . . This man talked about nonviolence, not simply as some kind of static philosophy, but he talked about it so as to show you how to strengthen your position. . . . Dr. King's concern was that the community needed all of its resources, especially its young people to be involved.

King went directly from his discussion with the Invaders to an off-the-record media briefing, giving background and analysis that he hoped would lead reporters to more balanced coverage of what had happened. In the same measured, reasonable tones he had used with the Invaders, he explained to reporters that SCLC "had no part in the planning of the march. Our intelligence was totally nil." When reporters asked him why he didn't check out Memphis in advance, King said, "I was completely caught with a miscalculation. . . . I came to speak here two weeks ago where thousands of people assembled inside and outside. Nobody booed, nobody shouted Black Power. . . . I assumed that some of the ideological struggles that we find in most cities over the nation, particularly in the North, were non-existent here." Instead, he found that there had been a breakdown in communication between black ministers and black youth, who were "feeling a sense of voicelessness in the larger society and at the same time a sense of voicelessness in the black community." They "were just angry, and those men were first to say to me that they are willing to engage in a campaign of tactical nonviolence. . . . If we had known that in advance it would have been a matter of meeting with them and giving them a sense of voice, and they would have been the first ones to be marshals."

But the reporters seemed to be less receptive to King than the Invaders. Edgy and skeptical, they sharply questioned King about his role, and he responded that he left the march because "I have always said that I will not lead a violent demonstration." They insisted that he "guarantee" no more violence, but King responded:

I cannot guarantee anybody that Memphis or any other city in this country will not have a riot this summer, if for no other reason than that our government has not done anything . . . about removing the conditions that brought riots into being last summer. We have an extremely recalcitrant Congress, we have an administration that admits it doesn't plan to do anything about the recommendations made by the Kerner Commission. It seems to me that these are the forces that are causing violence in our country, not the people who get so angry and disappointed and disgusted and disenchanted that they engage in the process of breaking a few windows.

This last comment set off a storm of further questions, some of them hostile in tone, about whether King could prevent violence. King pleaded with reporters to remember that this incident had specific causes: "We must not overlook the conditions that led up to yesterday. We must not overlook the fact that people, sanitation workers and ministers, marched nonviolently in this city about three weeks ago and they were maced by the policemen. We must not overlook that students left school by the hundreds yesterday to come to join in the march, and policemen were extremely brutal trying to drive them back into school, and they provoked bottle throwing and other things. So we can't overlook some of what led to what happened yesterday." King cast doubt on police motives, saying they appeared restrained when he was at the head of the march, in front of the television cameras, but out of the range of the cameras, police had attacked.

King also challenged the way the media pictured poor black communities as almost hopelessly violent. Reporters had polled 400 black participants in the Detroit riots, and 92 percent of them said they thought King's nonviolent methods would be more effective, he reminded them. "If you look at the record, you will see that rioters have not been violent toward persons. And nobody can tell me that Negroes can't shoot white people. Some of them are master marksmen, they've been hunting enough to know how to shoot people down." But killings during riots had overwhelmingly been at the hands of police and military units, not ghetto residents. "We haven't had any real violence in this country yet. We haven't had any guerrilla warfare yet. The violence has been vented toward property and not towards persons." King did not see rioters as criminals, and he contradicted Holloman's inference that guerrilla warfare had started, urging reporters to write about police actions and systemic causes of violence.

But reporters pressed again for a personal guarantee that he could stop violence in the future. "I don't know what you mean by guarantee," King said. "I don't want to put myself in the position of being omniscient." King and the reporters seemed to talk past each other, as the press conference came to an inconclusive end.

Although King had tried to reassure the press that nonviolence would triumph in the end, he was not so sure of that himself, and the hostile tone of some reporters unsettled him. He again called Stanley Levison, his phone conversation taped by the FBI, and glumly stated, "I think our

Washington campaign is doomed," because, regardless of the facts or any-thing he or anyone else might say, the media would impose its interpreta-tion on events. Levison told him that people in the Movement shouldn't accept the media's version of events or its assumptions, but King said, "You can't keep them from imposing it. . . . You watch your newspapers. . . . I think it will be the most negative thing about Martin Luther King that you have ever seen." He feared that poor people would not join a campaign that they thought might be taken over by violent people.

He concluded, "Frankly, it was a failure of the leadership here," that The Invaders "were fighting Jim Lawson and the men who ignored them, who neglected them, who would not hear them, wouldn't give them any atten-tion. . . . I know the fellows, and they really do, they love me. They were too sick to see that what they were doing yesterday was hurting me much more than it could hurt the local preachers."

King also predicted that his civil rights critics, such as Roy Wilkins, Adam Clayton Powell, and even Bayard Rustin, would be heavily "influ-enced by what they read in newspapers," and respond accordingly. Indeed, criticism of King came not just from whites but also from blacks in the civil rights movement vying for leadership with King. The controversial New York Congressman Powell had already called him "Martin Loser King," and others suggested King could not control his own movement. A few days after the Memphis riot, Wilkins warned that Memphis showed the danger of a national march; for good measure, he praised the news media for their handling of civil rights issues. NAACP Treasurer Alfred Baker Lewis told an NAACP membership rally in Lynchburg, Virginia: "The Reverend Martin Luther King, Jr., must bear the blame for racial rioting in Memphis, Tennessee, because he exerts no discipline over his followers." A *Press-Scimitar* story titled, "NAACP Official Blames King," quoted Lewis as saying that King was "a leader without a plan, and he has no organization, so that when he gets a group, he has no discipline like we do. He also has a lot of troublemakers, and probably juvenile delinquents. This is evident in what happened in Memphis."

Local organizers might have preferred that King stay for another march planned for Friday afternoon, but a frustrated King asked Ralph Abernathy to "get me out of Memphis" as soon as possible. After his press briefing, King and Abernathy left on the next plane to Atlanta.

The *Commercial Appeal* the next day covered King's press briefing by noting that King said he could not guarantee nonviolence, that he said the march had been "poorly planned," and that there had been a failure of communication with the Invaders. James Lawson held yet another press conference to correct this view, saying, "There had been communication. I don't accept that." The Invaders had been involved since the beginning, he said, and COME had brought in King to strengthen the ministers' campaign of nonviolence, not to start a riot. "We didn't bring in Rap Brown, we brought in King."

AFTER LEAVING MEMPHIS, King was plagued by vast doubts and fears about the direction of events and his responsibility for them. He considered going on a fast against violence, as Gandhi had done in his last days, to unify and purify his movement, but King was far from an ascetic and had never fasted. While eating dinner at the Abernathys' that night in Atlanta, he talked mostly of "the times before the Montgomery bus boycott when we were younger and hadn't taken on the burdens of the black people," Abernathy recalled. Seemingly unconcerned about the company of their wives, whom they hadn't seen for days, both men fell asleep on matching loveseats, and their wives also fell asleep without going to bed. Juanita Abernathy said she had never seen King so depressed. Coretta Scott King said, "He was experiencing a great deal of anxiety."

It must have intensified on Saturday morning, when Jesse Epps showed up at King's office as an emissary from the Memphis movement. Lawson was to have gone to Atlanta, too, but in the middle of the night on Friday, the chief steward of his church had died, so Epps alone had to take on the burden of convincing King to return to Memphis. He met privately with King before the staff meeting and argued that, like the Good Samaritan, King had to make a moral choice to stay on the road he was on, despite the dangers ahead. Epps showed King articles in the Memphis newspapers that claimed he had run away and said, "You as much stuck in Memphis as we are, and you can't leave Memphis no more than we can. And if you do, you're doing in a sense what the press says, you're running." This statement could not have been very welcome to King, disturbed as he already was about this accusation.

King next met with his SCLC executive staff, including Abernathy, Hosea Williams, James Bevel, attorney Chauncey Eskridge, SCLC Executive Director William Rutherford, and SCLC activists Joseph Lowery, Jesse Jackson, James Orange, Dorothy Cotton, and Andrew Young, as well as Epps and SCLC's Washington representative, Walter Fauntroy, and Stanley Levison, who joined them from New York. They met from about 9 AM to 3 PM, and all their doubts about the Poor People's Campaign came raging to the surface. Suffering from a continual migraine, King expressed the urge to quit his leadership role because of divisions in the Movement. Discussion quickly turned acrimonious as a number of King's staff members insisted that he could not afford to get further bogged down in Memphis.

"It was obvious from the beginning that Martin was in an agitated mood," wrote Young. "Never before had I seen him so aggressive in dealing with us. He wanted everyone to drop what they were doing and return with him to Memphis." King talked about going on a fast, sending staff into Memphis to prepare another march, and using it as a launching pad for the Poor People's Campaign—but he did not receive an enthusiastic response. According to Young, King's staff members all had their own concerns. Bevel wanted SCLC to focus on stopping the war, Williams focused mainly on voter registration, Jesse Jackson focused on Operation Breadbasket, a program to demand that businesses employ more African Americans. King's fractious staff, all with strong desires and leadership abilities, sometimes "acted as if Martin was just a symbol under which they operated," wrote Young.

King grew upset with them, "but the staff was upset with him also. There was criticism of his going to Memphis in the first place, and of going ahead with the march when he and Ralph sensed trouble and apparent disorganization." Young believed King had been exhausted: "He had probably been incapable of making a decision, once there, whether to go ahead or not," but he also felt that the whole event had been poorly planned and badly timed in the first place. Had Lawson attended this meeting, a lot of the criticisms now directed at King would have been directed at him.

"Martin didn't usually make those decisions anyway, he depended on us to organize demonstrations and make them work. But we weren't there," wrote Young.

King's staff lectured him about mistakes he had made, but he responded that he went to Memphis, just as he went everywhere, because he was asked. In a phone conversation recorded by FBI wiretaps two days after the meeting, Levison said that King "took the position very sharply that he felt we were in serious trouble as the result of Memphis. And he by no means took for granted that Washington had to go on despite what he had said to the press. That he didn't think we were prepared for it." And yet, King had concluded, according to Levison, "Memphis is the Washington campaign in miniature," and SCLC had to see it through. If it couldn't fight for poor people here, it couldn't do it anywhere.

However, the staff members played upon his doubts, and when Bevel and Jackson preached back at King, he lost his temper. According to Young, King said he had supported various staff in their projects, but, "Now that there is a movement that originated basically from Mississippi-born folk, not from SCLC leadership, you don't want to get involved." In effect, he charged them with putting their interests above that of the Movement. According to Levison, "He did something I've never heard him do before. He criticized the members of the staff with his eloquence and believe me that's murder." Agitated and angry, King asked Abernathy for his car keys and walked out of the meeting. When Jackson (and others) followed him out into the hallway, trying to smooth things over, King rebuked him as if he had been disloyal. Then he left.

"We had never seen Martin explode that way, not with us," said Young. "After he left, people were so stunned they finally began to listen." Young had opposed going to Memphis all along, but now he argued that the Washington campaign was crucial to the war and every other issue, and that the road to Washington led through Memphis. Epps argued that people should see the importance of an alliance with labor, while others, as he recalled, objected that "Labor has always reneged on its promise and haven't kept its word and so on in many instances where the civil rights movement is concerned."

James Orange felt perplexed. He had worked with King at various times since the Birmingham movement, when, as a teenager, he had led students out of the schools and into the jail cells of Bull Connor. At six feet three inches tall and 348 pounds, Orange had played football in college and nearly turned professional. Then he became a conscientious objector to the Vietnam War and SCLC's foremost liaison to gang members in Chicago and Philadelphia. He, too, questioned the wisdom of going to Memphis again, where SCLC had no organized base. He feared "the whole situation was a set up" by the FBI or someone else to discredit King or do something worse. "But Dr. King saw something as far as the coalition with labor and civil rights that a lot of the staff didn't see," said Orange. Aware that King had spoken at numerous union conventions and was well acquainted with union issues and tactics, Orange believed he made a convincing case to go back to Memphis to win this strike, and he ultimately agreed with him.

Finally, the staff unanimously decided that it had the means to control black youth and to pull off a massive nonviolent demonstration. Young wrote, "As somberly and seriously as we had ever done anything, we decided we would support Martin in any way he needed us [and] we would all return to Memphis the next week." Jackson, Orange, Bevel, and Williams would talk to the Invaders and work with ministers to set up the next march.

According to Jesse Epps, "At the conclusion of the staff meeting there was a little prayer meeting in that office. I can never forget that as long as I live. And everybody sort of emerged from the meeting in a very jubilant [mood]—and I came away saying 'Mission accomplished; he's coming back.' And everybody was looking [long sigh], expecting the successful march and we was thinking that this was going to break the camel's back and we'll have this behind us."

EPPS WOULD BE one of those who picked up King when he returned to Memphis on April 3, and he recalled that King told him, "Well, we have come back to Memphis . . . to straighten out the Mayor and go on to Washington. Either the Movement lives or dies in Memphis."

17

STATE OF SIEGE

The crime of racism and segregation and prejudice . . . was already
in our society . . . but it was invisible until there was a catalyst
for making it physical. . . . It wasn't our violence. It was the
violence of the system that came to the surface.
—*James Lawson*

KING ALWAYS SAID VIOLENCE DETERRED A MASS MOVEMENT because it distracted people from the real issues at hand. This is exactly what happened in Memphis. Despite King's efforts to put the Thursday, March 28, events in context, the media focused on the actions of looters and on whether King as a leader could be trusted, blotting out the sanitation workers' strike and the Poor People's Campaign. Meanwhile, the city of Memphis went into a state of siege.

State AFL-CIO leaders continued to block efforts in the Tennessee legislature to suppress the strike, but no one could stop legislation deemed necessary to curb riots. Only hours after the disruption in the streets of Memphis began, the House suspended its rules and voted 70 to 0 to give the state's mayors power to proclaim civil emergencies—for the first time since the 1866 white race riot. Loeb could now impose a curfew for up to fifteen days; ban sales of weapons, gasoline, and liquor; close stores; and prohibit people from being on the street without a permit. That same afternoon, Governor Buford Ellington signed that law, as well as one making it a felony to enter into a conspiracy to incite, organize, promote, encourage, or participate in a riot or to interfere with police or firemen during a riot. Under this elastic language, similar to anti-riot laws already in use against H. Rap Brown, the state could indict almost anyone who played a leadership role in a demonstration or rally that was followed by what might be defined as a riot. A previously passed Tennessee law provided up to fifteen years' imprisonment for looting.

These powers allowed Mayor Loeb to place the city under martial law. He issued an official statement that the march had "degenerated into a riot, abandoned by its leaders," forcing the police "to restore law and order and to protect the lives and property of the citizens of Memphis." "What needs to be done will be done," said Loeb, as police fanned out across the city. Anyone found on the streets without a police pass between 7 PM and 5 AM would be arrested. Loeb's curfew lasted for the next five nights.

By 6 PM on March 28, some 4,000 National Guardsmen, in patrols of twenty men each, had arrived from small towns and rural areas across West Tennessee—all carrying rifles with live ammunition and fixed bayonets. Around 7 PM, a five-mile-long convoy of troops poured into the city. Armored personnel carriers, normally used to transport troops under fire, drove on cleats that tore up the city's pavement. Troops also arrived at the Memphis airport in a U.S. Air Force prop plane. Its front end opened up like a huge mouth, disgorging scores of men in green battle fatigues and helmets and carrying duffel bags and rifles. They dragged ammunition boxes behind them and carried tear-gas canisters around their waists, ready for war.

Nearly all of the guardsmen were young whites from rural areas with no real military experience. One of the very few African Americans, a sergeant, admitted that the National Guard in the South had "traditionally been a white outfit, and Negroes have been reluctant to join it." They were under the direction of the Memphis Police Department's tactical squads, sheriff's deputies, and the Tennessee Highway Patrol, also almost entirely white. During a comparable military occupation of Detroit, scores of African Americans had been shot. With only rudimentary training, and frightened by fires and masses of blacks in the streets, white guardsmen tended to shoot first and ask questions later. Some of them in Memphis had infrared telescopes on their rifles through which they could see the color of a man's shirt 200 yards away in the dark.

One commanding officer told his troops at the National Guard Armory: "How you conduct yourselves downtown will decide whether you're dead or you stay alive." With this alarming send-off, 4,000 National Guardsmen joined 300 policemen, 50 sheriff's deputies, and 250 state troopers careening around Memphis in speeding Jeeps, police cars, and fire trucks. As they drove down narrow roads in neighborhoods filled with "shotgun shacks," showers of bottles and rocks from black residents sometimes greeted them, and the potential for hair-trigger reactions was very high. Anyone walking the street remained subject to arrest, and virtually any black male out in public for the next four nights could expect to be frisked, hands above his head and legs spread on the sidewalk, or to be thrown on the hood of a car.

Authorities sealed off Beale Street and much of black Memphis from the rest of the city. The number of calls for police and fire assistance leapt to 1,115 on Thursday, then declined to 984 on Friday, to 862 on Saturday, and 672 on Sunday. The city answered 517 fire calls over four nights—three times the normal number—and television news showed flames consuming a housing complex. Arkansas also mobilized National Guard troops to patrol the bridge from Memphis into West Memphis, Arkansas, thereby stopping blacks from leaving Memphis and keeping its own black community under tight control.

Scenes of downtown Memphis on the television looked bleak. Signs saying, "I Am A Man" and "Memphis AFL-CIO Labor Council Supports Sanitation Dept. Employees" lay in the streets next to broken windows. A movie theater showing *The Graduate* stood empty. Police held shotguns ready and leaned on billy clubs nearly half the size of their bodies. Helmeted National Guardsmen marched through the streets in formation with bayonets drawn. One or two black traffic cops appeared over the weekend, but otherwise Beale Street seemed to be occupied by an army of white males. Department stores, such as Goldsmith's on Main Street, stood empty—their huge, unsmashed plate-glass windows a testament to the city's resolve. In black neighborhoods, however, a kind of war had begun with the police that would not abate for years to come.

NATIONAL GUARD TROOPS proved to be much more cautious than the police. A few photos showed young black children talking with guardsmen and even curiously touching their weapons, but the children developed no such rapport with white police officers. The *New York Times*, explaining violent police reactions to both African American and student protesters at Columbia University in the spring of 1968, quoted a criminal justice professor: "At some point when police are faced by a mob or crowd, fear erupts and the individual patrolman no longer seems to be able to discriminate and he strikes out at anyone near him." Blacks understood, however, that racism as well as fear motivated the police. Angered by young African Americans insolently dancing, shouting, picketing, and being "boisterous" for the previous three weeks, the police used the March 28 riot as an excuse to strike back.

For five nights, police stopped and searched black people all over the city, often roughing them up and treating them rudely. They ordered people sitting on their porches to go inside, sometimes invaded their homes, and cursed and threatened them. Sanitation worker L. C. Reed and his wife had rushed home before curfew on Thursday night and barely made it; police caught a friend of theirs on his way home and beat him up. A news story told how police jerked a cab-driving minister from his vehicle and cursed and beat him simply for being out on the street; many others experienced similar mistreatment. According to the NAACP, police behavior included frequently using the word *nigger*, crashing down doors, entering without search warrants, confiscating people's personal property, damaging their homes, and cursing, intimidating, and humiliating people of all ages.

Loeb's curfew affected blacks much differently than it did whites. The first night, businesses shut down, but after that, white East Memphis and its environs carried on almost as normal. The central city and the predominantly black areas, however, continued under strict curfew, with restricted bus services, and businesses and government offices closed early. Whites traveled the streets freely while law enforcers stopped and roughly searched any African Americans who dared to venture out.

The difference between the ways blacks and whites experienced the city's state of siege became especially obvious in the schools. On Friday morning, March 29, someone fired several shots at a police car, and isolated incidents of fires and vandalism occurred, but otherwise things remained quiet. Only the Catholic schools closed. Yet Frank Holloman's language of war caused black parents great worry, and many of them kept their children home. Blacks comprised almost all of the 45,000 of the city's 125,000 students who stayed home from school. In white Memphis, few people absented themselves from school, business, or other normal activities.

The militarization of the city affected African Americans in drastic ways, with lives lost or damaged, homes attacked, work and school days lost, and time spent in jail or prison. The Associated Press described Beale Street as a boarded-up "plywood wasteland for ten blocks," where "soldiers and steel-tracked armored vehicles took the place of Saturday shoppers."

For whites, the cost was different: the riot disrupted their sense of innocence, civic pride, and good race relations, and many blamed blacks for it. Thomas Faires, president of the Memphis Chamber of Commerce, told the *New York Times*, "It's going to take maybe forty years before we can make any real progress. You can't take these Negro people and make the kind of citizens out of them you'd like."

Some whites paid a more tangible price in the form of property damage. The Insurance Council of Memphis estimated that rioters smashed 200 storefronts, 155 of them on Beale Street. The council estimated that only about 30 percent of windows and only 5 percent of stores were looted, but business leaders estimated some $400,000 in initial damages, and some people speculated that fire costs would increase that figure to nearly a million dollars. It cost the state legislature $1.5 million to pay for troops and state police.

Yet black Memphians did not respond to police provocations with a general campaign of arson and looting—as had occurred in Watts, Detroit, and Newark—nor did they attack whites. By Saturday, National

Guardsmen had the downtown area almost to themselves, and they looked more bored than anything else. Except for a few policemen injured on Thursday, no white citizens in Memphis experienced personal violence. Police arrested no one for sniping, and blacks committed no homicides. Most fire alarms turned out to be false, just one more method used by black youth for harassing the city. When Assistant Chief Henry Lux assessed the situation, he concluded that none of the fires had been extensive or threatened any lives.

The *Commercial Appeal* called this lack of violence to persons the result of the "overall good performance" of the police. James Lawson, however, credited the existence of a powerful nonviolent movement. "The fact that these thousands of people in a disciplined fashion moved on back to the church in a peaceful way, that's been lost in the whole story." In one sense, the events in Memphis proved King's belief that nonviolent mass action remained viable. He believed it kept the black community in Memphis from really blowing up after the police attack.

On the other hand, the NAACP said that black Memphians "deluged" it with complaints of police brutality; victims included "bank officials, postal employees, unemployed, people with police records, people without police records, housewives." One seventeen-year-old said, "They caught my uncle on the streets and they beat him half to death." Maxine Smith developed a file of fifty-eight sworn affidavits of police brutality and sent many of them to U.S. Attorney General Ramsey Clark and to Shelby County Attorney General Phil Canale.

Heightened police violence continued for months to come. On April 23, police shot the husband of Elizabeth Stevenson in the face and chest, claiming he had run from them, and they subsequently beat a man so severely they paralyzed him. In May, the Tennessee Civil Rights Commission held hearings that documented numerous charges of police brutality; its chairman concluded that if "only a small part of the accusations were true, a serious situation exists in Memphis."

Frank Holloman, a white Mississippian, had always insisted that blacks had equal rights before the Memphis Police Department, but almost no one believed him, and he cast doubt on his own statements after March 28.

"Hollow-man," as the *Tri-State Defender* called him, came out as a hard-line, law-and-order conservative, railing against "long-haired, foul-smelling hippies" and "hostile forces" in black Memphis that threatened to dissolve society from within. A year after the strike, speaking to a white Memphis sorority, he continued to denounce "permissiveness and appeasement" of the city's black movement leaders and warned, "The very future of civilization hangs precariously in the balance" in the police struggle to defeat crime and disorder.

Holloman cited his former boss at the FBI, J. Edgar Hoover, who attributed police-brutality charges to calculated efforts by subversives to undermine law enforcement. (In July, the *Press-Scimitar* headlined Hoover's statements, "Brutality Claims Linked to Communist Plot.") Holloman continued to harp on law-and-order themes. Police were the "thin blue line" protecting society from "the murderers, rapists, robbers, looters, burglars, assassins, arsonists, thieves, bigots and anarchists who threaten our American way of life," he told the Memphis Rotary Club in 1969. "We have stood against anarchy and chaos" and "the revolutionists who would have anarchy in Memphis," Holloman told the City Council in 1970.

Young African American men bore the full brunt of the police crackdown after March 28. Law-enforcement officials arrested 226 people during the day on Thursday, a total of about 300 by Thursday night, another 53 on Friday, and 71 on Saturday. Black teenagers or men in their early twenties made up 80 percent of those arrested; many of them were between the ages of eight and twelve, according to Assistant Chief Lux. Floods of young black men, and at least twenty-seven black women, passed through jails and the courts, some of them held without bail. A reporter described the scene as police booked them at the jail: "Blood streamed down the side of one youth's head. Another was swathed in bandages. A third was pushed to the desk in a wheelchair. About one in eight seemed to be hurt." One woman cried at her inability to get her teenage son out of jail, as young men came into the courts wrapped in bloody bandages. Police shot one black man, age thirty, coming out of a grocery store, and two other men, both twenty-one, in separate incidents—for trying to run. A white store owner wounded a black youth of seventeen with a 12-gauge shotgun.

By April 3, nearly 200 African Americans faced charges of looting, disorderly conduct, or "prowling to intimidate." Some of those arrested after the legislature passed its anti-riot law on March 28 faced even more serious state felony riot charges. Despite the gravity of the situation, some black youths laughed and joked and remained defiant in court.

ACTIVISTS IN MEMPHIS reassessed the situation after March 28, and the possibility of more violence remained heavy on everyone's mind. Reverend Dick Moon said, "We expected Memphis to respond like all of the other cities. We saw Thursday as the first day of rioting, Friday about twice as bad, and by Saturday all hell would break loose." Lawson called for the movement to carry on in a disciplined and peaceful fashion and to take more blows if necessary, while the Invaders saw Thursday's disruption and counterviolence as a kind of victory for black people. Lives hung in the balance over these competing views within the Memphis movement.

Baxton Bryant, who represented the Tennessee Council on Human Relations throughout the strike, told an NBC reporter on Friday, March 29, that the split between youthful militants and the "militant ministers" had been worsening for weeks. Some ministers had walked out of COME meetings when members of the Invaders insulted or criticized them, yet they had been "keeping the militant youth within their own circle, up until yesterday." Bryant doubted whether the ministers could control events any longer: "When you've got two protests with different philosophies going on at the same time it can make it very difficult for all of us."

No one understood the consequences of a breakdown in nonviolent discipline better than the workers themselves. On Friday at noon, when they met at the union hall, AFSCME's staff members hesitated to start marches again, until an older sanitation worker stood up from the back of the room and said, "Ain't we gonna march today?" That settled the issue. Within twenty-four hours of the police attack, 200 to 300 workers would retrace their steps of the previous day. Some of the most famous photos of the strike show these men walking in single file, their signs underscored to read, "I Am A Man," while police and National Guardsmen watched with drawn bayonets.

Whether the Memphis movement would carry on hinged in large measure on the actions of these men: if they folded under pressure, that would end it. Instead, film footage showed them on Friday afternoon moving out again from Clayborn Temple without hesitation, in plain working clothes, walking erect, with a wary but dignified demeanor. As the marchers left in single file, Reverend Starks shook the hand of each man, graciously and with a smile, lending his courage to theirs. Black ministers made sure that strikers marched with signs only: light sticks on picket signs could not break a window, but they might give the police a rationale for attacking marchers. In subsequent days, sanitation workers remained at the core of every march, and they inspired others to keep going.

Lawson and the ministers gathered pictures taken by black photographers of rioters the day before and concluded that few if any of them were marchers or members of the Invaders. Lawson and David Caywood of the American Civil Liberties Union now screened out all teenagers and also used the photos to screen out street people and potential troublemakers, making sure that only workers and adults participated in marches for the next few days. The MPD's Henry Lux, armed with a walkie-talkie, led the marchers in single file, and their ranks stretched out for nearly a mile.

"They marched with these cannons and what not pointed at them . . . so therefore you couldn't say that the men were frightened off," observed T. O. Jones. They detoured past Beale Street, which was blocked off. One of the world's "most famous streets, memorialized in song and verse, was a scene of boarded-up windows, broken glass, scattered merchandise, and armed guards," a reporter wrote. "The rubber-cleated tracks of armored personnel carriers left slashes [that] looked like gigantic zippers." Store owners, angry and silent, stood outside their businesses. When the marchers got to Main Street, they were confronted by four armored personnel carriers with mounted machine guns, two truckloads of guardsmen with fixed bayonets on their rifles, a raft of police in squad cars and motorcycles, and, at one store, four clerks holding shotguns. They continued on, carrying placards reading, "I Am A Man" and "Mace Won't Stop Truth."

Cornelia Crenshaw, white and black college students, black female domestic workers, and a few middle-class white women joined them in another march on Saturday. "Keep Your Money in Your Pockets," read their picket signs. For the duration of the battle in Memphis, black workers and their allies continued to exercise a quiet leadership role on boycott and picket lines, in marches, and in mass meetings, ignoring intimidation and continuing their schedule of daily union meetings and street marches. "Their willingness to go out there day after day in the face of all those white cops is simply amazing. I've never seen a black community so united," said AFSCME's P. J. Ciampa.

Surprisingly, the weekend passed with no major outbreaks of violence or looting. The workers maintained nonviolent discipline, while the Invaders maintained a studied silence. James Lawson believed that the men and their supporters would ride out this crisis and win. AFSCME leaders, however, had reached a real state of panic, because the expenses for the sanitation workers had now reached $50,000 a week. Ciampa reflected, "The mistake we made is that instead of giving a stipend, we started out by saying, 'We will take care of your needs. We'll see that none of your family is hungry. We'll see that you have a roof over your head, that nobody suffers from lack of prescription money or medicine.'" The union ultimately switched to a simple stipend of $40 a week, but the strike still cost AFSCME a total of $300,000 in benefits for the men and their families, not to mention staff costs. Members of Jerry Wurf's staff told him, "We're dead," but Wurf felt, "We had to go on; there was no way back." As Jesse Epps said, Memphis had become "the dam or the gate": a loss here would damage AFSCME's credibility all over the country and perhaps destroy union organizing across the South, while a win could increase the momentum of public-employee unionism.

Wurf, AFSCME's Young Turk of labor, had been in Washington, DC, on March 28 to get more "outsider" support, and he had spent part of his day talking to AFL-CIO President George Meany, the quintessential leader of labor's old guard. Meany boasted that he'd never been on strike in his life, supported the Vietnam War and CIA intervention against labor and peasant movements in Latin America and Africa, and had denounced A. Philip Randolph for demanding the expulsion of unions that excluded blacks. Now Meany opened AFL-CIO coffers to give Wurf $20,000 for the strike and, more important, he sent out a letter to unions across the country asking them also to donate. Based on Meany's letter, Wurf announced a plan to raise $200,000 to support the strikers and their families—enough to keep the strike alive.

Financial support, channeled through the local ministers' group, meant everything; without it, strikers would have been forced back to work. Some of them did better on strike benefits than when they were working, although more than one man had to excuse himself from union meetings to work some other job in order to pay his rent.

The historic march by workers into downtown on Friday, March 29, signaled a quick recovery from the Thursday riot, yet many worried that the law-and-order rhetoric—coming from President Johnson on down—would completely frighten away white supporters. Reverend Dick Wells and a handful of other whites who had participated in Thursday's march had pledged to go down to the Firestone union-hall meeting on the next day, and they kept their promise. As the ministers walked into the hall, the workers, one by one, began to stand. Recalled Wells, "By the time we got to the platform everyone was standing in silence. We had come back in the midst of their defeat, our defeat."

The police attack—far from frightening away sympathetic whites—had galvanized them. On that Friday afternoon, forty white ministers met at Reverend Dick Moon's Westminster House on the Memphis State campus, and a few staff people came into town from the National Council of Churches in New York to help. A handful of religious whites—including Methodist, Catholic, and Episcopal bishops—got together and wrote a manifesto that called for settling the labor issues so that needed racial reconciliation and reform could begin—although the media misinterpreted their statement to say they wanted black ministers to stop their marches. Two Memphis seminary professors also wrote up a support statement signed by a number of theologians. The Memphis Ministers Association over the weekend began talk about a summit meeting of religious, business, and civic leaders.

Dean William Dimmick at St. Mary's Episcopal Cathedral had witnessed the racial polarization in Birmingham in 1963 and was anxious to avoid it in Memphis. On Passion Sunday, March 31, he issued a powerful appeal, calling on Memphians to transcend the black-white divide. A number of other white ministers and rabbis from their pulpits affirmed the Memphis Ministers Association's "Appeal to Conscience," which had been issued on Race Relations Sunday, February 11, the day before the strike began. It simply asked people to "do unto others as you would have them do unto you."

Martin Luther King had always hoped that whites in the South would respond to moral issues raised by the freedom struggle in this way, but it might have been a case of too little, too late. A bruised and battered black community now demanded much more than moral statements from whites. The *Washington Post* reported on Sunday that the strike "has expanded into a broad human rights confrontation in which almost every aspect of Negro life in Memphis is now at issue." Blacks "are beginning to see the basic immutability of their lives, unless they act. They have extrapolated the city's attitude in the garbage strike to everything else—housing, welfare, jobs, education, police." Too few white Memphians understood this change in black consciousness—and least of all those on the City Council.

Councilman Lewis Donelson from the beginning had sharply opposed union recognition and dues checkoff, and in a letter to one of his constituents, he denounced "the Negro racist groups [that] converted the whole matter into a racial question with ugly threats of violence." He blamed "various Negro groups vying for power and in the process trying to outbid each other in violent talk and ridiculous demands." His white constituents in turn called for a hard line: If you "give in to criminals and law violators I hate to think what is going to happen to our good city," wrote one; if you "cower before the union, and intimidation, a wave of strikes can be expected," wrote another. But now the Republican businessman had lost patience with Loeb, and divisions in the white community began to take political shape.

On Friday, Donelson pressed a resolution before the City Council, committing it in vague language to take "affirmative action" to recognize the union and open the way to a settlement. He had earlier proposed to create more training and jobs for blacks, much to the chagrin of many of his white constituents. All day, behind closed doors, council members wrangled over

Donelson's proposal. Unionist Taylor Blair had convinced Council Chairman Downing Pryor that, even if the executive had the power to negotiate contracts, council members had legislative authority to set policy regarding recognition and dues. When a few of them went to Loeb for advice, he simply told them that the workers were wrong and they were wrong. His arrogance incensed Donelson, who pressed on until three black council members—plus Donelson, Pryor, and Jerred Blanchard—voted for a plan to take "affirmative action" to end the strike. Others voted against, creating a 6–6 tie. (It is not clear which council member did not vote.)

The possibility of the City Council settling the strike stalled out once again. As the sixth week of the strike drew to a close, Loeb put eighty-nine garbage trucks on the street, the county court allocated $46,000 to the sheriff to buy more riot-control equipment, and Memphis Police Department officers bolstered their seven-day-a-week, twelve-hour-a-day shifts, all of these measures fixed upon a strategy of breaking the strike.

There were no marches or rallies on Sunday, March 31, but the next day, some 450 people marched again in single file from Clayborn Temple to the downtown and back at 2:30 in the afternoon. Strikers made up the vast majority of the marchers, with COME making no effort yet to bring volatile high school students back into the mix. That day and the next, thousands of strikers and their supporters filed by Larry Payne's body, displayed in an open casket at Clayborn Temple. Payne had been popular among young people in the housing projects where his mother lived, as well as in his father's more middle-class environs of Mitchell Road in southern Shelby County. Fearing the showing of his body would set off an explosion of anti-police sentiments in the streets, police pressured Payne's family to hold the funeral at Payne's home church. At the behest of ministers in COME, his family held the funeral at Clayborn Temple.

During the funeral, the pastor said the sixteen-year-old Payne had been cut down long before his time, and some 500 mourners expressed profound grief and anger at his wanton killing by the police. "They shot you down like a dog," his mother cried out, and teenage girls fainted when they went by the casket. A community source told the FBI, "There will probably not be a Negro in Memphis who is not convinced that he was unarmed when he was shot." Despite seething anger in the black community, sanitation workers marched peacefully to the downtown following the funeral, further demonstrating their ability to maintain nonviolent discipline. The curfew ended, and on Tuesday, April 2, the last of the National Guard pulled out of town.

Meanwhile, King's staff pulled into Memphis. R. B. Cottonreader, James Orange, Jesse Jackson, James Bevel, Hosea Williams, and Poor People's Campaign Mississippi organizer J. T. Johnson all checked into the Lorraine Motel on Sunday and Monday. So did Charles Ballard, John Burl Smith, and Charles Cabbage of the Invaders—on SCLC's bill. Hard feelings persisted between the Invaders and the Memphis ministers, and part of SCLC's job was to smooth over this rift. Ralph Jackson had initially told Cabbage that COME would provide some funds to his Black Organizing Project if he would help keep youths nonviolent, but Jackson thought that instead, the Invaders had instigated trouble at Hamilton High School and downtown, and they virtually had taken over the chapel during the police siege of Clayborn Temple. (Sweet Willie Wine later said some of the Invaders had even stashed weapons in the belfry.) On March 29, the same morning King had interviewed Cabbage, a "fed up" and "disgusted" Jackson had refused to see Cabbage, an FBI source said.

Whatever they might have done to verbally provoke young people on the morning of the march, however, James Lawson saw only one black youth associated with the Invaders—a teenager he knew well—take action, by throwing a brick into a window. Pictures taken by black photographers of Thursday's fracas confirmed their absence from the riot. Reverend Starks cited the main culprits as opportunistic "elements on the sidewalk who were never march participants, and who took advantage of the march to create confusion." Even the FBI agreed that the Invaders were not responsible for the riot. Charles Ballard was the only BOP organizer who showed up on a list of 342 people arrested. But Cabbage and his friends continued purposely to confuse the issue: as leverage to get financial support for their cause, they wanted to maintain the impression that they might have done it and still had the power to stop or start another riot. Yet a black source in the movement told the FBI, "There are only about 12 to

15 hard-core BOP people in Memphis," and the rest "are merely followers or people who tend to imitate them."

These youths nonetheless remained a volatile force. Robert Analavage, a reporter for the New York radical journal the *Guardian*, interviewed Cabbage and his comrades, and an FBI observer said they gave the impression they "all want to destroy the King image." One COME activist called their demands for funds—in return for "keeping the lid on" black youth—a form of "verbal blackmail." Yet the Invaders continued to complain that "the preachers aren't going to do anything" to disrupt the city's garbage collection, and they asked COME to replace James Lawson as its chair. Reportedly, one COME strategy committee member agreed, and some SCLC staff members remained angry at Lawson for the March 28 fiasco, but neither group wanted to lose Lawson's leadership skills, and the answer was no.

At a press conference on Monday, April 1, activists attempted to create at least the image of a black united front. Cabbage and someone named Donnie Delaney represented the Invaders; T. O. Jones, P.J. Ciampa, Joe Paisley, and Bill Lucy represented AFSCME; and Lawson and other local ministers of COME attended, as did SCLC staff members. All called jointly for an end to "plantation rule" in Memphis. Orange said he would hold workshops throughout the week on nonviolence, and Hosea Williams said he would escalate strike actions. Jesse Jackson announced a plan to "redistribute the pain" through a national boycott of goods produced in Memphis as well as against national companies with distribution plants in Memphis, such as Coca-Cola Bottling, Hart's Bread, Wonder Bread, and Sealtest Dairy: "White businesses in the Negro community are going to be told to shape up or ship out," he said. James Bevel announced, "We're here as political psychiatrists. We see the mayor and his group as patients who are mentally sick." He also said, "We unequivocally believe in and advocate Black Power" and "consider ourselves part of the black power movement. We believe in black power and are working toward that aim."

King's SCLC staff highlighted Black Power rhetoric as a way to bring the "militant" and nonviolent wings of the Movement together, but in truth, it was Black Power merged with the Negro-labor alliance. AFSCME and SCLC decided to make the mass march a national event like the march from Selma to Montgomery, the last one that had brought together a powerful national coalition of labor, religious, and civil rights supporters. In New York City, Bayard Rustin and Victor Gotbaum, director of AFSCME's powerful District Council 37, began to mobilize 6,000 people from all over the United States. They chartered a jet for 300 unionists, expecting King to lead a march of as many as 30,000 people. Jesse Epps began to contact as many white unionists as possible, and the COME strategy committee quickly shifted the date of the proposed Memphis march from Friday, April 5, to Monday, April 8, to accommodate this national mobilization.

The situation presented great tactical difficulties. An alliance with King's powerful national allies in the unions surely must have sounded too much like the kind of top-down national march in a local setting that SNCC disdained, and it highlighted the interracial mobilizing that many Black Power advocates rejected. Alternatively, the Black United Front approach presented at the press conference might unify SCLC and COME with the Invaders, but it nearly left out the local unions and whites. Yet King's overriding aim, as always, was to create the largest, most inclusive coalition possible.

The police, meanwhile, increased their pressure on the Invaders. On Tuesday morning, April 2, seven police officers with guns drawn surrounded BOP activist Charles Ballard. The incident could have led to his death, but instead of shooting him, they arrested him for disorderly conduct. This and other threatening incidents by police, who continued to follow the Invaders everywhere they went, made it clear the city planned to crush this group of young black activists.

In his haste to leave Memphis the previous Friday, King had not gotten back to Cabbage as he had said he would. But on Tuesday, James Orange and several other SCLC staff members held long meetings with Cabbage, John Burl Smith, Edwina Harrell (the only woman leader in BOP, and Cabbage's girlfriend), and other Invaders at the Lorraine Motel. The COME strategy committee met on the same day, and Bishop J. O. Patterson of the Pentecostal Church of God in Christ and Bishop Julian Smith of the CME church, who had been in the front row of marchers with King on March 28, insisted that none of the funds raised for strikers should go to The Invaders. (COME, however, ultimately paid out about $3,000 in legal fees to defend them in court for arrests incurred during and after the strike.)

The Invaders now turned to SCLC, asking for hundreds of thousands of dollars to set up a cooperative to sell literature and teach black history. Cabbage later said he had the illusion that King had vast financial resources. Something more sinister developed, the FBI believed, when Black Nationalist minister Reverend Charles Koen (misidentified by the FBI as Reverend Carnes) arrived from Cairo, Illinois, and joined the discussions. The MPD's undercover Invader, Marrell ("Max") McCullough, reported that Koen said his black liberation group in Cairo could provide funds to BOP after April 15 if it could "keep the pressure on the white man"—which meant, "You have to burn his store and virtually have to burn him before you can bring him around." He said the National Council of Churches had raised $2 million to dispense to five cities in danger of racial trouble, and one of the five was Memphis. This rhetoric of burning did not faze Orange, who heard it often from street gangs. Regardless of what anyone said, his job was to turn the Invaders into marshals for the upcoming march. He simply told the BOP that SCLC itself might provide some aid, but no financial decisions could be made without King's approval—and meanwhile, if they wanted funds, they needed to support the nonviolent movement.

Police reports of these discussions went right to the mayor's office, and they must have made city officials extremely uneasy. In addition, economic pressures on the city were becoming unbearable. A couple of small down-town business owners attended the City Council meeting on Tuesday to complain that the economic boycott was hurting them. When Councilman Wyeth Chandler objected that the city had to draw a line somewhere against unions, one of the men responded, "Mr. Chandler, we have just about reached the line. . . . We are not big businessmen like Mr. Pryor or Mr. James. I had salesmen who had to go home the other night without paychecks. If I could find a way to sell my business and leave Memphis, I would do it." It looked like owners of small businesses might now turn against Loeb.

But bigger businesses also worried that riots in Memphis would turn away investors and tourists; auto salesman John T. Fisher thought that the city's business climate might soon fall apart. Adding to businessmen's concerns was the news that AFSCME had begun organizing among kitchen, laundry, and maintenance workers, as well as nurses, at city hospitals. Grain merchant Ned Cook, one of the city's most prominent businessmen, desperate to end the strike, met with Downing Pryor to try to find some solution. Downtown business had fallen by 25 percent even before Thursday's altercations, and sales dropped off much farther after that—and the big sales weekend of Easter was only two weeks away. Blacks also threatened to disrupt the May Memphis Cotton Carnival, the city's biggest tourist attraction.

When Loeb had been the mayor in the early 1960s, business pressures had forced him to pull down the "whites only" and "colored" signs, but this time he showed no sign of bending. On Tuesday, as National Guard troops pulled out of Memphis, Loeb, Holloman, Lux, and city attorneys planned to go to court to place strike leaders under peace and financial responsibility bonds, making them responsible for any further riots and their costs, and to seek a federal injunction to stop King from leading a mass march.

IN ONE SMALL but promising sign of independence from Loeb, the City Council on April 2 asked labor mediator Frank Miles to bring together the city and union negotiators on the council's behalf. Miles immediately tried to restart negotiations, but Jerry Wurf and the city's attorneys could not arrange to meet until April 5. Meanwhile, Tommy Powell invited thirty business and civic leaders to meet with unionists on Thursday, April 4, and John Spence of the Civil Rights Commission planned small discussions with businesspeople on April 5 and 6. They hoped somehow to resolve the strike before King's national march, planned for Monday, April 8.

AFSCME also asked influential Memphis attorney Marx Borod to intervene; he very reluctantly went to the city's attorneys to broach the idea. Ominously, they told him, "We've won the strike. Nothing more needs to be done." A short while later, Loeb called Borod on the phone to reiterate that he had no intention of backing down. The next day, King would return to Memphis.

18

SHATTERED DREAMS AND PROMISED LANDS

> In reply, Jesus said: "A man was going down from Jerusalem to
> Jericho, when he fell into the hands of robbers. They stripped him of
> his clothes, beat him and went away, leaving him half dead. A priest
> happened to be going down the same road, and when he saw the
> man, he passed on the other side. So too, a Levite, when he came to
> the place and saw him, passed by on the other side. But a
> Samaritan, as he traveled, came where the man was;
> and when he saw him, he took pity on him. . . ."
> —*Luke 10:25–37*

ON SUNDAY, MARCH 31, MARTIN LUTHER KING, JR., MADE a powerful moral appeal for justice and peace to an overflowing crowd of more than 4,000 people at the National Cathedral in the nation's capital. Saying, "We must learn to live together as brothers or we will perish together as fools," King beseeched his audience to support his crusade to end poverty, racism, and war. His prayer seemed to be partly answered that very night, as President Lyndon Johnson bowed out of the presidential race, vowing to spend the rest of his time in office avoiding partisan politics and trying to end the Vietnam War. Johnson's top advisers agreed that no path to military victory existed, and increasing numbers of Democrats supported Eugene McCarthy's antiwar campaign within the Democratic Party for withdrawal from Vietnam.

Hoping there might also be a way out of his planned confrontation with the federal government, King told reporters in Washington that he would meet with the president or anyone else in his administration or in Congress who would be willing to implement the Kerner Commission's proposals. "We cannot stand two more summers like last summer without leading inevitably to a rightwing takeover and a fascist state," he warned. In an article slated for publication in *Look* magazine, he used similar language and argued that Americans ignored—at great peril to the nation—the explosive conditions caused by slavery and segregation's legacy of poverty, ill health, and unemployment. In return for positive government action, King seemed willing to call off the Poor People's Campaign. A. Philip Randolph had once won an executive order from President Franklin Roosevelt to stop federal employment discrimination in return for calling off mass demonstrations—an outcome that King might have relished. No one, however, responded to his appeal.

That weekend, Reverend James Jordan, whose historic Beale Street Baptist Church lay right in the middle of the March 28 riot zone, awoke crying in the middle of the night. He went back to sleep but awoke crying again. This time, "Dr. King's picture came before me. . . . And so I saw the Lord had shown me Dr. King's death." He went to the next meeting of the strike strategy committee, pleading with other black clergy not to bring King back to Memphis. One of them retorted, although not reassuringly, "You don't have to worry about any white people doing something to Dr. King. That cat's safe around them. When he gets it, it'll be from some black!" James Lawson said King never let threats stop him; others said the Memphis movement had to march, no matter what. "He was bluntly answered and I felt a little sorry for him," said Maxine Smith. The consensus in Memphis was to push on.

On Monday, April 1, back at home in Atlanta, King wearily asked Ralph Abernathy to delay his return to Memphis by a day. When King finally did board an American Airlines plane for Memphis on Wednesday, April 3, the pilot announced that someone had called in a threat to kill him, and airline employees searched the plane for a bomb for more than an hour. King joked to Abernathy, "Well, it looks like they won't kill me this flight, not after telling me all that." "Nobody is going to kill you, Martin," Abernathy tried to reassure him.

DEATH THREATS AGAINST King, Lawson, and strike leaders came in to the Memphis Police Department in increasing numbers. On April 1, American

Airlines reported to the police that someone who seemed to be white and seemed to be located in Memphis phoned in to say, "Your airlines brought KING to Memphis, and when he comes again a bomb will go off and he will be assassinated." The airline later called again to give the police the exact time of King's arrival. On April 2, a white businessman called from Ohio to pass on a rumor from a business friend who "stated that if KING returned to Memphis Airport for his March, he would be killed by a Negro and that a Memphis Policeman would be blamed for it." Jerry Fanion said Fire and Police Director Holloman told him he received many threats on King's life. Yet neither the Memphis police nor the FBI relayed these death threats to King.

At 10:33 on the morning of Wednesday, April 3, King deplaned at the Memphis airport along with Ralph Abernathy, Bernard Lee, Dorothy Cotton, Andrew Young, and SCLC bookkeeper Jim Harrison, who was secretly passing information to the FBI. Reporters immediately asked King about a statement by NAACP President Roy Wilkins that drew a big headline in the *Press-Scimitar*: "Wilkins Doubts King Can Control March." Wilkins warned, "The great danger of Dr. King's demonstration [in Washington] is that he might not be able to keep control of it. . . . If a maverick in the rear ranks of the march decides to throw a brick through a window, there's nothing Dr. King, up there at the front, can do to stop it." King curtly dismissed the Wilkins comment: "He's said that before. That's not new." King informed them that SCLC had met with the Invaders, and there would be no more violence in Memphis. He added that he would resist any injunction against marching as a violation of First Amendment rights.

As Lawson and about twenty others led King through the lobby of the airport, Tarlese Matthews, one of the Memphis movement's most ardent black community supporters, spotted the MPD's black plainclothes officers and warned Ed Redditt, "If I were a man I would kill you." An MPD squad of four white men also appeared, and when Lieutenant George Kelly Davis asked Matthews about the arrangements to transport King, she retorted, "We have not invited no police if that is what you mean." Don Smith, a leader of the MPD's Red squad, turned to Lawson and told him he and his officers had come to protect King; he then asked where they were headed.

Lawson responded dismissively, "We have not fully made up our minds," and kept walking.

Lawson was not oblivious to the need for security, and he had welcomed it in 1966, when then Police and Fire Commissioner Claude Armour had given King complete protection while he was in the city for the Meredith march. Armour had then assigned a squad of about eight black officers to protect King, including Jerry Williams and Redditt. Lawson had trusted this group, which had been in evidence during King's visit on March 18. But Lawson did not believe the Red squad's white officers had come to protect King; he felt they were there for surveillance purposes and perhaps to do mischief. King himself did not ask for police protection, which he thought was unfitting for a nonviolent leader. In his speeches and writings, King reiterated, "I'm committed to nonviolence absolutely."

As Redditt and Willie Richmond followed King's party by car, an unidentified vehicle seemed to be trying to force them off to the shoulder, but Redditt held to the road. He continued to follow King's car to a strategy meeting at Lawson's church, while the white detectives, led by Smith, set up surveillance around the Lorraine Motel. After the meeting, Redditt and Richmond followed King back to the Lorraine, but when they got there, Smith told Redditt, "I'll take it from here." But later that afternoon, the white detectives left, claiming that SCLC staff had asked them to leave—although Lawson, Samuel Kyles, and Hosea Williams all denied it. The FBI's special agent in charge in Memphis, Robert G. Jensen, with obvious antagonism toward Lawson, reported that he had tried to contact the minister about King's security by phone, but Lawson did not return his call. Perturbed, Jensen did not follow up.

Redditt was disturbed that King seemed to have little or no police protection. He thought it strange: more than anyone in the police department, he knew the characters associated with King and the local movement, but "No one assigned me, no one wanted me around." He drove to Mulberry Street, parked, and took up his duties on his own, as he typically did, watching the streets. Perhaps, he thought, the police department excluded him from a specific assignment to protect King because he was clearly sympathetic to the strikers and to King. He had served as a police escort and eaten with King during one of his previous visits. Redditt had told King of his trials in trying to "integrate" the MPD, including false accusations made against him by white officers. King had advised him, "Just tell the truth. Just tell the truth."

On April 3, both the FBI and the Memphis police had every reason to be concerned about King's safety, yet it appears that neither agency effectively conveyed that concern to King. J. Edgar Hoover had said in 1964 that potential "victims of threatened bodily harm" would be notified by agents about threats, but the U.S. House Select Committee on Assassinations later censured the FBI for doing virtually nothing to prevent an attack on King. Lawson's suspicion that police agencies were there for surveillance rather than protection was correct. Lawson felt that former Police and Fire Commissioner Claude Armour had given King real protection, but under Frank Holloman's control, the MPD seemed interested only in surveillance. Holloman was a protégé of Hoover, and Hoover made a point of not using his powers to protect civil rights workers. Someone told Redditt that Holloman even belonged to the John Birch Society, and Redditt said Holloman refused to answer when he asked him if he did.

Clearly enough, the FBI in Memphis continued the national surveillance policy on King and other civil rights workers such as Lawson. One FBI memo listed twenty-one long-distance calls made by Lawson between January 10 and February 3; the FBI contacted its agents in the various cities, asking them to identify the people he called. FBI agents obviously followed his activities closely, but they never provided any protection or gave him any warnings about threats against his life. Lawson knew from the hateful looks of police and the hate calls in the night that many whites wanted to see him dead. After one late-night bargaining session, he returned to his brightly colored Volkswagen, which he had parked conspicuously under a streetlight. Fearing a bomb could be wired to the ignition switch, he sat in the car sideways, put it in neutral, turned the switch, and leaped out. When it didn't explode, he felt foolish, but after that, he put tape between his hood and his fender: a broken seal meant someone had tampered under the hood. He learned this trick from labor organizer Alzada Clark, who fought KKK anti-union terrorism against her Mississippi organizing campaign, which occurred at the same time as the Memphis sanitation strike. In a separate incident on February 27, a bomb under the hood had killed in Natchez Wharlest Jackson, a rubber worker who had fought to open skilled jobs in his factory to blacks. Lawson knew of other such bombings.

Neither Lawson nor anyone in King's organization felt secure or believed that they could go to the Memphis police or the FBI for help. Indeed, unknown to people at the time, the FBI's counterintelligence program against the New Left and black freedom movements, COINTELPRO, had already hired "ghetto informants" to spy on and disrupt the Movement from within. Such provocateurs frequently served to alienate community supporters, create splits in the Movement, or provoke a pretext for police attacks or arrests. Lawson thought police agents had done all of these things in Memphis already.

Marrell McCullough of the Invaders provided a case in point. One police officer later said that McCullough was so strident in his statements that officers who did not know he was an agent "would have given their eye teeth to have locked him up." Designated for some reason by the MPD as "Agent 500," McCullough had previously spent two years in the U.S. Army as a Military Police officer, perhaps as part of an intelligence unit; then he went through Memphis Police Department basic training. The MPD named him Max and put him on the payroll of an electric company, from which he drew paychecks, as a cover. He grew an Afro and adopted Black Power rhetoric, and Orie McKenzie unwittingly signed him up as an Invader, probably in February 1968. McCullough became the Invaders' "Minister of Transportation," because he had a car, and he soon got "in with" COME strategy committee leaders Jackson, Middlebrook, Bell, and the "potential rough element of Negroes"—specifically, John Henry Ferguson and Willie Kemp, according to a police report.

Infiltration of political organizations had the purpose and the effect of creating suspicion within groups and setting off internal conflict. An FBI report said that Lawson, for instance, "felt that BOP has been infiltrated" by government agencies, possibly the CIA (indeed, McCullough reportedly later worked for the CIA), "and that for this reason the COME group does not fully trust Cabbage and his group." Cabbage, too, suspected some of his associates of working for the police, but he didn't know which ones; he said organizers had little choice but to accept the reality of government snoops or get out of the movement.

As King went about his business on April 3, Richmond watched King's room at the Lorraine from Fire Station Number Two, across the street, recording the names and license plates of those who went in and out of the motel. Redditt, with no specific assignment from his superiors, roamed between the station and the street. Between five and ten agents dressed in civilian clothes reportedly were roaming the streets and monitoring the strike—members of the 111th Military Intelligence Group of the U.S. Army Military Intelligence, which had an office in the downtown Memphis federal building. Military Intelligence Division (MID) units had been tracking King as he spoke across the country, yet another violation of his First Amendment rights.

Like the MPD and the FBI, the MID regarded labor, civil rights, and antiwar protesters, and King, as all potentially subversive, even Communist. MID members later said their Memphis mission did not include surveillance of King, but investigative journalists using the Freedom of Information Act (FOIA) discovered that MID units had in fact tracked King since he was a student at Morehouse, and they began associating him with Communists as soon as he spoke at Highlander Folk School in 1957. The army had long ago monitored King's grandfather, A. D. Williams, founder of Ebenezer Baptist Church, and his father, because of their civil rights activities. Exactly what the army did in Memphis in 1968 may never be known, for it supposedly destroyed its surveillance records, as did the MPD, after revelations of their spying on King.

The U.S. Army's assistant chief of staff for intelligence, William Pelham Yarborough, who led MID work nationally and had commanded Green Berets training and "counterinsurgency" operations in Vietnam during the early 1960s, explained illegal military spying as a reaction to massive antiwar demonstrations, including one he witnessed personally in Washington in October 1967. "What some people don't remember was the terror that all this struck into the hearts of the people that thought the empire was coming apart at the seams," he told a journalist. Army concern focused on King particularly because of his strong antiwar views and an abiding belief within intelligence communities that he was a closet Communist.

The FBI regularly shared its reports with Military Intelligence, the Secret Service and other federal agencies, and the Memphis Police Department, further prejudicing the views of intelligence officials on King. Frank Holloman surely knew of FBI efforts to destroy King, and through its wiretaps on Stanley Levison, the FBI well knew of the great distress that events in Memphis caused him. Assistant FBI Director William Sullivan reveled in it and wanted to play upon King's anxieties as part of the FBI's plan to stop the upcoming Poor People's Campaign, code-named "POCAM."

One thing is certain: None of this illegal surveillance of King's political activities improved his personal security, as evidenced by its failure to apprehend an escaped convict named James Earl Ray, who drove into Memphis in a white Ford Mustang on April 3. Ray grew up in miserable circumstances in Missouri, the poorest of poor whites and one of nine children. Ray's father had a criminal conviction and his mother was an alcoholic; the family grew up during the Depression in complete destitution. Ray was just the sort of poor white to whom King had long tried to reach out—another victim of systemic poverty and injustice. But Ray detested King. He styled himself as a member of George Wallace's American Independent Party and subscribed to Ku Klux Klan leader J. B. Stoner's publication, *The Thunderbolt*, which regularly linked Communism, integration, and King. "Nobody can reason with Jimmy on the two subjects of Niggers and politics," one of Ray's brothers later told journalist William Bradford Huie.

"A habitual criminal, at war with society, hopelessly alone," as Huie described him, Ray escaped from prison in 1967 and survived by his wits and a variety of petty crimes. His brother John ran a tavern in St. Louis, where a "standing offer" of a reward to anyone who would kill King was well known. The offer came from several local businessmen, one of them an associate of the viciously antilabor Southern States Industrial Council (to which Mayor Loeb, like many employers, had belonged), and the American Independent Party. All three of Ray's brothers, who also held racist views, may have helped him after he escaped from prison. In March 1968, Ray had been in Los Angeles, Selma, Birmingham, and Atlanta during King's presence in those areas on behalf of his Poor People's Campaign. According to Huie, Ray had been stalking King.

In Alabama, Ray had bought a Remington Game Master Model 760, "the fastest hand operated big game rifle made"—powerful enough to kill a charging bull, according to its manufacturer. Yet lax federal laws did not even require Ray to register the weapon or be fingerprinted when he purchased it. Ray took it with him to Memphis and stayed at the New Rebel Hotel on the night of April 3. He watched television news as it casually pictured King entering Room 306 at the Lorraine Motel. Ray knew right where to find him.

Intelligence authorities seemed completely unaware of Ray, but Memphis police carefully reviewed a handbill circulating in the black community on April 3 titled, "Yellow Thursday," which warned of another kind of upheaval. It read:

MARTIN LUTHER KING has proven himself to be a yellow uncle Tom. YELLOW instead of BLACK. Now BLACK POWER will have to finish what the YELLOW KING could not. We are going to find out just how good—How Big and Brave the Police Department Is. Sure they are big enough to beat old people and Brave enough to shotgun innocent kids.—But can they stop a march during the Rich White Man's Party? Cotton Carnival. A party the negro [sic] has never been invited to. Just told to go on down to Beale Street <u>Boy</u>. You have your party down there.

It threatened to make Memphis "famous the World over—something that your two bit carnival never could, and <u>you</u> will <u>Burn Baby Burn</u>."

On the day of King's return to Memphis, MPD intelligence officers noted that Black Power activists had been contacting students in the schools, telling them to boycott classes for another King march. Rumors in the community suggested there might be retaliation against the officer who shot Larry Payne. And FBI and police agents tracked a variety of "black militants" coming into town from Alabama, Louisiana, Detroit, and

St. Louis—including, they said, members of the Deacons for Defense and the Revolutionary Action Movement (RAM).

White authorities still hoped, however, that internal disunity would unravel the movement. One local black minister had gone on television to say that black religious leaders should take over from "radical elements" and hold a meeting to "lay this problem at the foot of the cross" as an alternative to King's mass march. White businessman Ned Cook praised him, thinking this "would have been the end of the strike." Another black minister went to the police to accuse Lawson of being a Communist and said Lawson, Jackson, Maxine and Vasco Smith, and Jesse Turner had all failed the black community. White business leaders welcomed such black leaders to speak out against and split the movement, but most blacks remained united behind the strike. That, more than anything, worried the police.

Police and the FBI also worried that Robert Shelton, Imperial Wizard of the United Klans of America and notorious for bombing civil rights activists in Birmingham, might send people to Memphis to attack King or incite other violence. As evidence of the potential for racial agitation, white supremacists tried to publish a quarter-page ad in the *Commercial Appeal* for April 4 that showed the infamous, false photo of King "at a Communist training school." The newspaper, to its credit, refused to run the ad, although it had run the picture as a news item several years earlier. Even without the ad, however, stories about King's disruptive activities, inner-city riots, and "Communist aggression" in Vietnam constantly ran side by side in the mass print media.

MEMPHIS HAD BECOME one of the most dangerous spots on Martin Luther King's journey down Jericho Road. Yet when Harold Middlebrook met him at the airport on April 3, he thought King seemed strangely detached from it all. When a reporter gave him a newspaper announcing an impending injunction against him by Judge Bailey Brown in the U.S. District Court for the Western District of Tennessee, King looked off into space, "just nodding and saying, 'Oh, yes. Is that so?'" A few moments later, he declared, "We are not going to be stopped by Mace or injunctions. . . . We stand on the First Amendment. In the past, on the basis of conscience we have had to break injunctions and if necessary we may do it. We'll cross that bridge when we come to it."

In order to get the power of the federal government on his side against local authorities, King had always avoided defying federal court orders. In Selma, he had even turned around a mass march at the Edmund Pettus Bridge because a federal court order prohibited it, and many in the Movement had excoriated him for doing so. Memphis wanted to put him in a similar bind in order to stop his march entirely or postpone it long enough to kill the strike support momentum. Alternatively, it might be the first city to have King jailed for disobeying a federal court order.

In Judge Brown's courtroom that morning, Memphis Chief of Police J. C. MacDonald said local organizers had refused to make their march plans available to the police, had marched without a permit on March 28, had instigated school walkouts, and had made "inflammatory statements in advance" of the march, until ultimately "the assembled crowd went berserk." For his part, King "took no action whatsoever towards the quietening [sic] or control of the mob, and did in fact, after continuing to march in the presence of said wide spread vandalizm [sic], completely disappear from the scene." Fire and Police Director Holloman accused "negro [sic] leaders" of doing nothing to counter threats by militants "to burn Memphis down." Assistant Chief Henry Lux said he "did not observe any act of disapproval or censure on the part of said Martin Luther King, Jr., towards the widespread acts of vandalism that were being perpetrated within his presence and within his clear vision."

The city's bill of complaint, signed by Henry Loeb, named King, Abernathy, Williams, Bevel, Orange, and Lee and said they should be stopped from crossing state lines to organize another mass march in Memphis. It said that the "defendants knew, or should have known," that actions in support of the march "were likely to cause violence," and that "said conspiracies of said defendants have already caused or resulted in serious breaches of peace, violation of laws, disregard for law and contempt of law," and "defendants threaten through their public announcements to continue to sponsor, foment, encourage and incite riots, mobs, breach of peace and other conduct which is in violation of the laws."

As another reason to stop a second march, City Attorney Frank Gianotti mentioned death threats against King, saying, "We are fearful that in the turmoil of the moment someone may even harm King's life, and with all the force of language we can use we want to emphasize that we don't want that to happen."

At 12:40 PM, Judge Brown issued a temporary (ten-day) restraining order enjoining King and his lieutenants "from organizing or leading a parade or march in the City of Memphis." If King did not comply, he would go to jail for contempt of court, but the city had even more heavy penalties in mind. The city's bill of complaint said "negro" [sic] leaders would be breaking the recently enacted state anti-riot act as well as federal anticonspiracy laws. King could thus be the victim of the kind of "conspiracy" prosecutions used to arrest and jail SNCC's H. Rap Brown for traveling across state lines to "incite" riots. King seemed unperturbed by such prospects. Jesse Epps said King told him, "Even if violence occurred . . . whatever the outcome of Memphis [it] is going to be a success for the men." When some of his staff privately expressed nervousness about the looming confrontation, Abernathy recalled that King said, "There was no more reason to be frightened now than in the past," he was ready to go to jail, and "I would rather be dead than afraid."

Attorneys Louis Lucas and Walter Bailey—backed by the NAACP Legal Defense Fund in New York City—represented King in Judge Brown's court. Bailey noted that King, "of course, had anticipated the injunction . . . was a man of great humility and he was very professional in his approach to problems . . . he'd been through this before." King and Abernathy expected federal marshals to show up at Lawson's church and serve them with Brown's injunction, but when no marshals appeared, they went back to the Lorraine Motel to eat lunch. When marshals finally did serve the warrant outside the Lorraine, King and his lieutenants laughed, apparently because it seemed absurd to think a court injunction at this point could stop the huge march being planned for Memphis.

Meanwhile, the ACLU regional office in Atlanta had called Memphis attorney Lucius Burch. A top establishment lawyer and Democratic liberal who had organized Boss Crump's first political defeat in 1948, Burch had also helped to engineer the new strong-mayor form of city government. He later said, "To be perfectly frank, as I was with Reverend Lawson, I wished at that time he had gone anywhere else in the city of Memphis rather than to call me." He knew that "a very large and reactionary group" in Memphis would start calling him and threatening his family, and he was also wary of Lawson, knowing "that he's been to Vietnam . . . and that the FBI thinks he's a Communist and all that sort of junk."

Burch noted that a CBS News poll the previous week had found that 47 percent of white Americans considered blacks genetically inferior to whites, and he believed that Loeb and most of his business friends also held those sentiments. He called Loeb's handling of the strike "a tragedy of inflexibility." That afternoon, Burch and other members of his firm—David Caywood, Michael Cody, and Charles Newman—met with King, Lawson, and others at the Lorraine. He had never met King, and "I wanted to be sure myself that these people were what they purported to be." King told Burch that "his *whole* future depended on having a non-violent march in Memphis," while Young "completely assured me that it . . . was just exactly what it was represented to be—the right of these people to express by assembly and petition and demonstrations what they felt was a just grievance."

After that reassurance, Burch never hesitated. He went to Brown's courtroom to get a hearing on the injunction set for the next morning; then he worked all night on a brief to defend King's right to march, sleeping only briefly in his office. Burch remarked later, "The white community didn't realize that Martin Luther King was the best friend anybody had. He was the answer to the fire bombing and he was the answer to the looting and he was the answer to Black Power."

LABOR MEDIATOR FRANK Miles, charged by the City Council to find a resolution to the strike, heard from the U.S. District Attorney and the Community Relations Division of the Justice Department that U.S. Attorney General Ramsey Clark was in town. Word also came to Miles through the office of Representative Dan Kuykendall and Clark's deputy, James Laue, that people in touch with King thought he might not march if he could get some kind of concession. An astonished Miles did not think King could back out of Memphis that gracefully, if at all, but several sources said he hoped to do just that.

Reverend Frank McRae on Wednesday met with the mayor at lunch, both of them surrounded by armed guards, saying now was the time to make a deal. "I kept saying, 'Henry, you're sitting on a powder keg. Please realize this.'" Loeb remained unconcerned and opposed to compromise.

A disturbed McRae joined other white ministers that afternoon in a meeting with black ministers that had been postponed almost since the beginning of the strike. It began badly when Rabbi Wax opened the meeting by saying, "We ought to limit this discussion to try to find out what the issues are." Ralph Jackson leapt up, saying everyone knew what the issues were, that the ministers by this time had to take a side, and it was too late to engage in such pointless discussion. "Damn you," he said, walking toward the door—until someone stopped him. The atmosphere went from bad to worse when an older white man talked about the importance of loving "our nigra brethren." Zeke Bell retorted, "The word N-E-G-R-O is not nigra. It's *knee-grow*." Bell couldn't help but point out, "You ministers talk about love, and black people can't even get in the doors of your churches!"

McRae now surprised the ministers by calling for them to march to the mayor's office, finally focusing the attention of the group on doing something together. However, "As soon as a march was suggested, some white ministers began leaving the room like rats off a sinking ship," said Father William Greenspun. Another white minister said it would not be "proper or right" to march without first getting an appointment with the mayor. The meeting dragged on until Wax said he had to leave for an engagement in Arkansas; as he left, at least one black minister muttered that he was a coward. Elsewhere in town, the Chamber of Commerce, Future Memphis, and the Downtown Association jointly issued a call to blacks and whites to unite in support of "law and order" and urged authorities "to prevent and put a stop" to mass demonstrations.

The best the ministers could do was to decide to meet again. The next day, Wax recalled, he frankly told the black ministers, "Many of us who were white found it very difficult to communicate with the Negro leaders

. . . that we were always fearful if we didn't say exactly what the Negroes wanted us to say, that we would be construed or regarded as their enemies." He felt, "In a conversation that's meaningful people should be free to express themselves and not feel compelled to agree." The ministers made painful, incremental headway in their effort to communicate across the racial chasm. That night, Reverend McRae went to the mayor and asked for an appointment for Friday. Loeb agreed but told him, "You're going to waste your time and all you're going to do is get yourselves in trouble with your congregations, and you're going to be misunderstood. And you're not going to change my mind one way or another."

At the Lorraine Motel, King remained on tenuous ground. Early Wednesday afternoon, when he met briefly with Invader leaders, Cabbage complained that King had not yet followed up on his pledge to get funding for BOP's community organizing. An FBI informant among the city's civil rights leaders reported, "The BOP group is still uncontrollable, unpredictable, contentious, avaricious and believed to be 'attempting to con' COME and SCLC out of operating funds." King said he expected Cabbage and BOP to provide at least twenty-five marshals for the upcoming march, but they gave few assurances of nonviolence in return for SCLC financial support. The nonviolent Andrew Young nearly came to blows with John Burl Smith over his aggressive demands for money. According to the FBI's informant, "KING endeavored to convince representatives of BOP that they must assure that they and their followers would create no violence during the scheduled massive march," but they "refused to agree with this and when this meeting was disbanded no agreement had been reached."

Discussions with the Invaders became so fractious that the COME strategy committee canceled a march of sanitation workers and a planned workshop on nonviolence scheduled for that afternoon. One of the FBI's "racial" sources warned, "Unless King spends many hours in direct contact with Memphis Negro youths . . . he will be unable to predictably control youths in any mass march." One of King's lawyers related, "King was very much afraid that if this march went on and there was more violence, that he was going to be irreparably damaged."

King also began to worry that Memphis might disrupt his larger plans for the Poor People's Campaign. He feared that some 6,000 outsiders coming in for the march in Memphis "will spend much money, time and effort in the Memphis project which they should be conserving and holding in abeyance for King's Washington Spring Mobilization Project scheduled to begin April 22," reported an FBI source. Exhausted and ill with a sore throat and a slight fever, King wanted to stay huddled in his hotel room, so he asked Abernathy to take his place at that night's scheduled mass meeting. At this point, Memphis looked not like the starting place for the Poor People's Campaign that King had envisioned, but rather like its graveyard.

WHEN ABERNATHY WALKED into Mason Temple, he realized their mistake: newsmen and television cameras were there, and so were 2,000 to 3,000 Memphians. Sanitation workers probably made up the majority, and they had come at a greater risk to themselves than usual. The air was rent by thunder and lightning, and civil defense sirens wailed across Memphis as a tornado swept through West Tennessee, leveling houses and killing twelve people. The windows at Mason Temple shook from the force of the wind. Workers came out anyway, wanting to hear the power of words that King had and that so many people felt they lacked.

Originally, SCLC had scheduled King to speak the next night, April 4, and Abernathy on April 3, but when Abernathy walked in without King, discernible disappointment rippled through the room, and Abernathy sensed it immediately. Workers had come out in the middle of this storm at great peril to themselves—but not to hear Abernathy. He immediately called King at his hotel and convinced him to come to Mason Temple.

Various people spoke and sang. Lawson made an impassioned indictment of the police for the murder of Larry Payne. Murray Austin Ervin, president of the student body at Northside High School, pledged that students there would take part in King's march and do it nonviolently. King and his assistant Bernard Lee meanwhile drove through high winds and shattering rain to arrive quite late, at about 9 PM. The crowd gave him a standing ovation as he walked in, and King beamed at the warm reception. Striker Clinton Burrows recalled that King wore a black water-repellent jacket with a red inner lining and, "Wherever he would go, people wanted to touch his coat." Lawson thought King seemed composed, as he shook hands with the others seated around the podium, but Middlebrook recalled, "I thought he looked harrowed and tired and worn and rushed."

Abernathy made an unusual move, introducing and lionizing King for twenty-five minutes with anecdotes, jokes, and remembrances. An FBI agent, with some disgust, acidly noted Abernathy's comment, made only half in jest, that, "despite Dr. King's honors, he has not yet decided to be President of the United States. But he is the man who tells the President what to do." After Abernathy sat down, ministers joked with him that it sounded like he had just preached King's eulogy, and King smiled at the joke. But some people thought he was nervous. During the introduction, high winds kept blowing open the outside shutters covering the church's ceiling vents, making a banging noise. Each time, the noise caused King to jump. Lawson finally told someone to switch on the ceiling fans to open the shutters to stop them from banging.

King stepped to the podium at 9:30, while the storms outside reached the height of their power. At age thirty-nine, he looked like an older man—his face lined with the burdens of the world—as he struggled to conjure up that hope he'd felt during his first speech in Memphis. He used no notes and felt very much at home with this audience—typical of the black workers, poor people, and church folk who came to see him as he traveled into the most impoverished communities of the Deep South. King's parents and grandparents came from such folk, and King had known them all his life through the neighborhoods in which he lived as well as his church work. He maintained a visceral kinship with these workers that allowed him to speak to their issues as his own. His audience looked to King for inspiration, and he in turn began emerging from his fear and fatigue.

He thanked them for coming out on such a miserable night, then began quietly by saying, "Something is happening in Memphis, something is happening in our world." As if he were looking out from the beginnings of time, he took them back to Egypt, to Greece, to the Renaissance, to Martin Luther, to the Civil War and Abraham Lincoln, to the Great Depression and Franklin D. Roosevelt. Then he brought them back to the present and said that if the Almighty had asked him when he wanted to live, this would be the time. "Now that's a strange statement to make, because the world is all messed up. The nation is sick. Trouble is in the land. Confusion all around." But from South Africa to Memphis, "The masses of people are rising up." And their cry "is always the same—We want to be free."

Desperation had its advantages: humanity's problems had accumulated to a point of crisis in which survival required that all problems be solved together. "It is no longer a choice between violence and nonviolence in this world: it's nonviolence or nonexistence." The "human rights revolution" demanded a change "to bring the colored people of the world out of poverty, their long years of hurt and neglect, [or] the whole world is doomed."

King painted a picture of despair, yet he said this was the best of all times in which to live. Why? As in Montgomery and at the start of the Poor People's Campaign, he said the most important change wrought by non-violent struggle was in the minds of those who participated in it. Through the freedom struggle, black people already had changed their internal world. They no longer were "scratching where they didn't itch, and laughing when they were not tickled"; they no longer played the fool for the white man. "That day is over. We are determined to be men. We are determined to be people. We are saying that we are God's children. And that we don't have to live like we are forced to live."

Just like any Black Power militant, King saw black unity as the first pre-requisite for further change and division as the way to failure. Centuries earlier, the Pharaoh had kept slaves fighting among themselves, but "when the slaves get together, that's the beginning of getting out of slavery." Second, people had to turn away from the violence that had happened in the streets of Memphis. "Let us keep the issues where they are. The issue is injustice. The issue is the refusal of Memphis to be fair and honest in its dealings with its public servants, who happen to be sanitation workers. Now, we've got to keep attention on that." By focusing on the breaking of windows, the news media had taken the focus off the plight of the workers and a mayor "in dire need of a doctor." King paused as people broke into guffaws and applause at his reference to Loeb.

King then pledged, "We've got to march again, in order to put the issue where it is supposed to be." He called on people to join the Monday march, to remind the world "that there are 1,300 of God's children here, suffering," and only a mass movement could solve their problems. "There is no stopping point short of victory. We aren't gonna let any mace stop us." People cheered heartily as he infused his ideology of hope.

King offered hope by using history, which showed that nonviolence had repeatedly overcome oppression. Through picketing, marching, petitioning, mass meetings, community organizing, singing, and going to jail together, the freedom movement in Birmingham had turned Police Commissioner Bull Connor from a bull "into a steer," King joked. As in Birmingham, the Memphis movement expressed the best in America, because "the greatness of America is the right to protest for right"—embodied in the First Amendment to the Constitution. People cheered him on as he rejected court interference, saying, "We're going to fight this illegal, unconstitutional injunction. All we say to America is, 'Be true to what you said on paper.' " In totalitarian countries like China and Russia, such injunctions against protest could be expected, but freedom to speak and organize remained the bedrock of American justice, and King's whole strategy for change had always depended upon the highest courts in the land ultimately defending that freedom.

King saw the ministers in Memphis doing what he had called for the ministers at the Miami conference to do six weeks earlier. The preacher, he told his audience, "must have a kind of fire shut up in his bones. And whenever injustice is around, he must tell it." He thanked Lawson especially, "who has been in this struggle for many years" and is "still going on, fighting for the rights of his people," as well as Kyles, Jackson, and other preachers who had made the Memphis movement possible. "So often, preachers aren't concerned about anything but themselves," but Memphis ministers had transcended that. "It's alright to talk about 'long white robes over yonder,' in all of its symbolism. But ultimately people want some suits and dresses and shoes to wear down here." His audience laughed and applauded, because they knew just what he meant.

King now moved to his current strategy for attaining economic justice, which included anchoring direct action with "the power of economic withdrawal." If most black people in America were poor as individuals, "collectively we are richer than all the nations in the world, with the exception of nine." The economic boycott in Memphis demonstrated "that's power right there, if we know how to pool it." He endorsed Jesse Jackson's plan to "redistribute the pain" by extending the Memphis boycott to all companies that did not hire blacks or that supported Loeb. Black Memphians should also go further, he said, and trade primarily with black businesses in order to build "a greater economic base."

Building that base required more than setting up accounts in black banks and insurance companies, which would have been of little help to the working poor. Rather King saw a beginning in Memphis through the movement's combination of economic leverage with the other methods of protest and the ballot. With such power, "We don't have to argue with anybody. We don't have to curse and go around acting bad with our words. We don't need any bricks and bottles, we don't need any Molotov cocktails." King may have aimed these words especially at Cabbage and his comrades in the audience, but they hardly registered on Cabbage, who remained focused on his organization's battle for scarce resources and legitimacy.

King had been arguing in the Poor People's Campaign that all classes in the black community should join together to attack larger issues of racial inequality through a movement to support the poorest of the poor—the unemployed in the backwaters of the plantation economy and the inner cities. That campaign had been faltering, but union organizing by the working poor in Memphis, by contrast, had activated nearly the whole black community into a coalition across classes. COME had also expanded the issues, step by step, from justice on the job to justice in the community as a whole. King said the well-off and the not-so-well-off, those with education and those without, should press forward together to a victory:

Now, let me say as I move to my conclusion, that we've got to give ourselves to this struggle until the end. Nothing could be more tragic than to stop at this point, in Memphis. We've got to see it through. And when we have our march, you need to be there. Be concerned about your brother. You may not be on strike. But either we go up together or we go down together.

Perhaps King sensed the hand of destiny that he felt had guided many of his struggles since Montgomery reaching through him again, as he shifted from the specific ways to win in Memphis to a larger spiritual idea at the core of his message: "Let us develop a kind of dangerous unselfishness." King illustrated the concept through one of his favorite lessons from the Bible, in which Jesus recounted the plight of a man who had been robbed and left along the road between Jericho and Jerusalem. Several travelers, including a priest and a member of the Levite tribe, passed by the man beaten and robbed by the side of the road and did nothing for him. Perhaps they had religious duties or worthy and urgent civic goals; perhaps they did not have time to stop, said King.

"But I'm going to tell you what my imagination tells me. It's possible that these men were afraid. You see the Jericho road is a dangerous road." King empathized with these men without courage. He and Coretta had driven the Jericho Road—a steep, winding, downhill path that spiraled to the "bloody pass," a place frighteningly well suited for robbery and crime. Perhaps the man lying on the ground was faking, leading travelers into a trap. "And so the first question that the Levite asked was, 'If I stop to help this man, what will happen to me?' But then the Good Samaritan came by. And he reversed the question: 'If I do not stop to help this man, what will happen to him?'"

King, who traveled a dangerous road for most of his adult life, had reflected on this parable a great deal. Authorities had jailed him at least eighteen times, racist whites had bombed his residence. A storm trooper of the American Nazi Party beat King in the face at a mass meeting in Birmingham, and another one punched him in the face in Selma. White supremacists would have killed him in Mississippi or in the suburbs of Chicago in 1966 if they could have reached him. King had always faced the possibility of premature death by violence, but the story of the Good Samaritan helped him to conquer his fears and, in King's mind, also spoke to the issue of racism. The Samaritan, King emphasized, was of a different race from the Levite and the priest—and perhaps from the unknown victim lying by the road. Yet it was the Good Samaritan who crossed the racial boundary of that era and helped the injured man to an inn, where he was taken care of.

In King's usual telling of the story, the Samaritan's simple decision to stop and help the man made him a great person. By the same token, anyone could be great, because anyone could serve others. As he had said many times, on Judgment Day God would not ask how many degrees a person had or how much wealth they owned. He would ask, "What did you do for others?" The essence of his Poor People's Campaign was to convince the better-off to exercise "dangerous altruism" and "dangerous unselfishness" to aid the poor and oppressed. In Memphis, King had the opportunity to draw the moral of his story directly into the struggle at hand, and he took it: "That's the question for you tonight. . . . The question is not, 'If I stop to help this man in need, what will happen to me?' 'If I do not stop to help the sanitation workers, what will happen to them?' That's the question." Linking Memphis to his larger campaign, King said, "Let us move in these powerful days, these days of challenge to make America what it ought to be. . . . And I want to thank God, once more, for allowing me to be here with you."

Throughout his talk, the audience—Reverend Jackson, especially—had urged King on in the usual way, shouting, "Tell it," "That's right," "Go ahead on," "Amen, brother." Others sat in a kind of hushed awe. Reverend Middlebrook wondered, "Where can the man go next to climax this thing? . . . When he got to a point where he could have climaxed, he didn't." King had hit a number of rhetorical high points, but he kept widening out his theme and embracing larger truths. And he was not finished yet.

"You know, several years ago, I was in New York City autographing the first book that I had written," when a woman asked if he was Martin Luther King, and he said yes. "And the next minute I felt something beating on my chest. Before I knew it, I had been stabbed by this demented woman. . . . The blade was on the edge of my aorta, the main artery. And once that's punctured, you drown in your own blood—that's the end of you." Had he sneezed, he would have died. As the FBI well knew, Ben Davis, formerly the black Communist councilman from Harlem, had donated blood, and District 65 union members and many others had rallied around him. But what King publicly recalled and most remembered was a white girl who wrote to him, "I'm so happy that you didn't sneeze." King said he was happy, too, for if he had sneezed, he would have missed the marvelous black freedom struggle that had taken "the whole nation back to those great wells of democracy which were dug deep by the Founding Fathers in the Declaration of Independence and the Constitution."

Dripping with sweat, King looked back again to the seemingly impossible victories of the past: how student-led sit-ins in 1960 had given new hope to the promise of equal rights; how blacks in Albany in 1962 had straightened their backs against Jim Crow; how hundreds of black children and adults had stood up to fire hoses and dogs in Birmingham, where he had gone to jail exactly five years earlier, on April 3, 1963; how people in Selma in 1965 had stood up to police on horseback who savagely whipped them and cracked their skulls for the crime of wanting to vote.

Had he died in 1958 in New York City, King would have missed the southern struggles that shattered the moral legitimacy of Jim Crow, giving birth to the landmark Civil Rights Act of 1964, which made discrimination in public accommodations and employment a crime; he would have missed the Voting Rights Act of 1965, which once again made voting a national citizenship right, 100 years after the Emancipation Proclamation. He also would have missed this climactic moment that broadened the meaning of the freedom struggle to issues of economic justice: "If I had sneezed, I wouldn't have been in Memphis to see a community rally around these brothers and sisters who are suffering. I'm so happy that I didn't sneeze."

True to form, King electrified and uplifted his audience, overpowering the winds and rain pounding the roof of Mason Temple and the lightning crackling outside. Shouts and applause had continually punctuated his speech as King took himself and his audience beyond the petty tyrannies with which they lived day in and day out. People had been maced by the police, children were hungry, students had walked out of school—but together they formed a vision of a different kind of life and a different relationship among people. People may be poor, they may be tired, King told them, "but whenever men and women straighten their backs up, they're going somewhere. Because a man can't ride your back unless it is bent." That standing up could only be done together.

Lawson had moved off the podium, out into the audience, so that he could better see King do his work. King's eyes focused somewhere else, as if looking at a skyline in the distance; he was beyond the moment, and great emotion seemed to come welling up through his whole body, expressing his commitment to struggle to the end, wherever the Jericho Road might take him. Nearly exhausted, King revealed his personal fears, telling his audience of the bomb threat that had delayed his plane to Memphis. He asked the question on the minds of so many people: "What would happen to me from some of our sick white brothers?" His eyes watered, and his expression seemed to reflect the centuries of struggle King had just reviewed as well as the very hard choices before him. His voice trembling, he cocked his head slightly and seemed to confide his innermost thought: "We've got some difficult days ahead. But it really doesn't matter with me now. Because I've been to the mountaintop."

When he struck this note, ecstatic shouts, cheers, and even laughter rocked Mason Temple. Everyone knew just what he meant, for they too faced fear and anxiety every day, and they had faced more of it than ever during this long strike. Few of the people in that room felt any certainty about the future, but now the preacher and his followers moved together beyond the harsh moment of Memphis to some higher, biblical truth. At Dexter Avenue Baptist Church in Montgomery, in January 1957, King had revealed to his followers that during a sleepless, fearful night after whites had bombed his home, he had "been to the mountaintop." Sensing the power of God supporting the Montgomery movement's struggle for truth and justice, King had then resolved to face death, happy and unafraid. He was doing the same thing now.

A young girl named Barbara Brown watched in awe, later recalling, "He had a strange look on his face" as his voice trembled and water came to his eyes, revealing not fear but a transcendent hope:

And I don't mind. Like anybody, I would like to live a long life. Longevity has its place. But I'm not concerned about that now. I just want to do God's will. And He's allowed me to go up to the mountain. And I've looked over. And I've *s-e-e-n* the promised land. I may not get there with you. But I want you to know tonight, that we as a people will *get* to the promised land. And I'm happy tonight. I'm not worried about anything. I'm not fearing *any* man!

As King's defiant emotions came roaring through him, he abruptly turned away from the audience, shouting a verse from the "Battle Hymn of the Republic": "Mine *e-y-e-s* have seen the glory of the coming of the Lord!" He didn't quite finish his sentence, he didn't wave or gesture to the crowd. He strode a few quick steps, practically falling into the arms of his comrade Ralph Abernathy and collapsing into his chair. The ministers behind rose up around him, shouting and clapping and waving their hands as King sat frozen, momentarily overwhelmed.

Pandemonium swept Mason Temple as people came to their feet— applauding, cheering, yelling, crying. Just as King appeared to have been transported to some other place, so were they. As Reverend Kyles stood with King on the platform, he saw "ministers who ordinarily would keep their composure just break down." Reverend Jordan, who so feared for King's life, said, "You could hear one minister crying all over the building, just at the top of his voice." Middlebrook looked out to see that the chairman of his church's board of trustees stood weeping in the audience.

Middlebrook said that King, who had turned directly toward him to come back to his seat, had tears in his eyes. Reverend Jordan, also on the podium, said, "When he sat down, he was just crying. He sure was." Preachers sometimes cried, he said, but he had never seen King do it. "This time it just seemed like he was just saying, 'Goodbye, I hate to leave.'"

Said Bill Lucy, "It was one of the most dramatic speeches I've ever heard. It was not negative, it was really very, very high. When it ended, the entire church at Mason Temple just went wild with excitement. I mean, he had touched a chord that was so deeply rooted in all of the people—it went far beyond the strikers to community people—and he had shared with them his view of not only himself but of his role in society."

Beyond that, said Reverend James Smith, who later became director of

AFSCME Local 1733, "There was an overcoming mood, an overcoming spirit in that place. When Dr. King spoke that night we knew that we were going to win. There was something about Dr. King. A man who could walk with kings, but he was just as simple when he spoke that all of us understood him. Never met a man like that before."

Sanitation worker James Robinson said that, sitting in the audience that night, he could actually *feel* King's words and *see* the truth of his vision. Moses had gone up to the mountain and looked over into the promised land, and he knew that he would not get there but that the Hebrew people would. "King was like Moses. A lot of that stuff he was talkin' about was true. A lot of that stuff was gonna come to pass. You can't keep treatin' people wrong, you gotta do right some time."

Striker Clinton Burrows, like most people there that night, described King's rhetorical power in religious terms. Burrows had been arrested and his family had suffered privation for two months, but that night, "It was just like Jesus would be coming into my life. . . . I was full of joy and full of determination. Wherever King was, I wanted to be there." He said, "It seemed to me from where I was sitting, his eyes glowed." King's words quieted his own inner turmoil. "He got up and spoke about the plans to kill him if he came to Memphis. He made it very clear that he didn't fear any man. That is a good spirit, to not fear any man. If you believe in right, stick with it."

King's words that night meant something very special to the sanitation workers, Dorothy Crook, later a president of Local 1733, said. "I'm sure a lot of things have been written about why he came. But to these 1,300 guys, it meant a voice speaking for them." King "had his heart on the pulse of people, and that is why they were able to listen to him." As a Baptist preacher, he created a spiritual path they could follow, come what may.

Unlike his famous 1963 "I Have a Dream" speech, broadcast across much of the nation, millions of people did not see King's "Mountaintop" speech in Memphis. This was almost a private moment, as a beleaguered group of several thousand huddled together in a church meant to hold 10,000 or more, with storms raging outside. That moment burned deeply into the consciousness of most of those present, and many of them would carry King's words with them for the rest of their lives.

———————

ATTACKED AS EITHER too radical or too moderate, drained by the massive demands upon his time, depressed by violence and threats of death, ill due to his constant travel and lack of sleep, King had looked both backward and forward, and out of a mountain of despair had hewed one more stone of hope. As Reverend Kyles put it, King had "preached the fear out," of himself and his audience.

Then the moment was over. King briefly stayed at the podium, relaxed, and greeted people. Young Barbara Brown told her babysitter she wanted to shake Dr. King's hand, and she stood in line until her turn came. "His hands were as soft as cotton but very moist," and she would remember that touch a few days later when she marched through the streets of Memphis. Many years later, she recalled, "From that day to this day, my life was changed."

As people walked out of the church, they discovered that the violent storm outside had momentarily passed away.

19

"A CRUCIFIXION EVENT"

The white man has killed his best friend.... There will be
more violence because Martin Luther King's followers will
follow Stokely Carmichael and Rap Brown, not because
they want to but what else is there to do?
—*Middle-aged black man, Memphis*

FTER HIS "MOUNTAINTOP" SPEECH ON APRIL 3, KING'S
spirits rose tremendously, and he stayed in a buoyant mood.
King went to eat at Reverend Ben Hooks's house while the
COME strategy committee met late into the night at the AME Minimum
Salary Building. Reverend Samuel Kyles told Maxine and Vasco Smith
what a great speech King had made, but he also said King's unusual comments about death worried him. Kyles remembered the night when he and
the Smiths had bid Medgar Evers good-bye after a rally in 1963. Maxine
Smith had kissed Evers on the cheek, and within an hour the white
supremacist Byron de la Beckwith had assassinated him.

At 1 AM, King's brother, A. D., arrived by car at the Lorraine Motel, with
Kentucky State Senator Georgia Davis, a SCLC board member, and SCLC
administrative aide Lucy Ward, on their way back to Louisville from a
meeting in Miami. They stayed up until 4:30 AM, when King, Lee, and
Abernathy stepped out of a taxi in the motel courtyard. The King brothers,
Davis, and Ward stayed up visiting—until Martin held a brief SCLC strat-

egy meeting with staff members at 8 AM. SCLC was scheduled to go to federal court, but Young took King's place and King went to bed.

Things were looking up. On Thursday, April 4, in federal district court, Young and Lawson "magnificently" explained to Judge Bailey Brown, according to Lucius Burch, that demonstrations had to continue because poor and minority workers otherwise had "no outlet for expression whatever"—the march was a means of communication, guaranteed by the First Amendment. Police Chief MacDonald counter-argued: "I don't think anybody can have a march next week without violence," but Tennessee Civil Rights Commissioner John Spence testified that pent-up anger in the black community had to be channeled: canceling the march could itself set off violence. Frank Holloman admitted he would much rather see King lead a march than someone else, and Young reassured the judge that further violence in Memphis would repudiate King's whole way of life. Lawson pledged his reputation to keeping Monday's mass march entirely peaceful. Judge Brown said he might allow a march under strict conditions, and he would rule on Friday.

On another front, things were not going so well. At SCLC's expense, a group of well-armed Invaders holed up in Room 315 at the Lorraine, still trying to cut a deal. SCLC staff members Hosea Williams, James Orange, and James Bevel met at 10:30 that morning with Charles Cabbage and his brother Richard, John Burl Smith, John Henry Ferguson, Milton Mack, and a newcomer from Detroit named Theodore Manuel. The young militants still mistakenly thought King could come up with tens of thousands of dollars at the drop of a hat. Cabbage still continued to argue that to prevent youth violence, SCLC would have to fund his organization, yet he still would not make a categorical pledge to support nonviolence. King entered the discussion and said he could not continue to dialogue with the Invaders unless they sincerely supported tactical nonviolence. They insisted that Cabbage's doctrine of "tactical violence" deserved equal respect, but King responded, "I don't negotiate with brothers." He made it clear he wanted them to be marshals, but to do it, they had to adopt nonviolent discipline. At an impasse, the Invaders left.

John Burl Smith felt angry and thought he was being used by King's movement. "I viewed Dr. King much like I saw those around him—not to be trusted." He felt ministers had sold out the strikers several times, and that King, as a speaker and march leader, had "upstaged a valiant fight being waged by black men stooped by decades of de-facto slavery"— namely, the sanitation workers. "We were not interested in joining a national movement" with King to make the Memphis struggle part of the Poor People's Campaign.

King later that afternoon challenged Smith to rethink his position. "Placing a hand on my knee, he looked me in the eyes and said, 'Nobody elected you, so who are you working for? Colored folks need young people willing to lead, and I am offering you that opportunity.' Sometimes, I think I can still feel his grip on my knee." Years later, Smith wrote, "I came to understand his plan."

Meeting with his staff that afternoon, however, King sharply criticized Hosea Williams, who apparently had already proposed to Cabbage and Smith the idea of making them SCLC staff members. Middlebrook said Williams hoped that "exposure to Dr. King and the staff would give them the idea of being nonviolent." According to Abernathy, when King heard about this, he became "grim and businesslike," saying Cabbage would have to be dismissed and no one should be on the payroll unless fully committed to at least tactical nonviolence. He "actually got up . . . and walked around preaching to the staff," said Middlebrook. King feared some of his own staff—Bevel in particular—did not fully support nonviolence, and he said that if they did not, they should leave SCLC immediately. King also reiterated, "I'd rather be dead than afraid. You've got to get over being afraid of death."

Andrew Young later wrote that SCLC staff members also talked about rumors of informers and infiltrators in the Memphis movement. Young believed, as did Bill Lucy, that the FBI had paid provocateurs to disrupt the recent march. In general, wrote Young, "We tended to assume that the most violent, hostile, and angry people were the plants, so much so that I became automatically suspicious of anyone who was supermilitant and wanted to fight and kill people." SCLC tried to channel people's anger into "constructive, nonviolent action," and "to expose the supermilitants for the windbags they were; otherwise, they would get people stirred up to do stupid things."

After this somewhat tense discussion, King returned to a jovial mood. Kyles arrived and started singing old church favorites with Jesse Jackson and members of his Breadbasket Band—songs such as "Yield Not to Temptation," "I've Been 'Buked and I've Been Scorned," and "I'm So Glad Trouble Don't Last Always." King relaxed with his brother and his guests. Then the two brothers spoke to their mother by phone for nearly an hour. When Young returned from his federal court testimony, King teased him and started a lively pillow fight—the King who liked to joke and fool around was back. After the foolishness ended, King and Abernathy prepared for dinner at the Kyles home.

Beyond the cocoon of fellowship at the Lorraine, the area swarmed with police, FBI, and military intelligence (MID) agents. The Memphis Police and Sheriff's Department had nine tactical units—each consisting of three cars and twelve officers—sited at key locations around the city. An additional ten regular police cars, with three to four men per car, cruised the downtown area, and the FBI had numerous agents working out of its Memphis office. Robert Jensen directed FBI surveillance, while black MPD detectives Redditt and Richmond kept watch on King all day through a small hole in newspaper plastered over the window of Fire Station Number Two, across from the Lorraine. Not exactly a high-tech surveillance operation, this more closely resembled the old-fashioned work of Boss Crump's "snitches."

Two black firemen, Norvell E. Wallace and Floyd E. Newsum, worked at the fire station—a segregated, all-black unit in the heart of black Memphis. The city had a history of refusing to advance black firemen beyond the rank of private, so these two men understood clearly the plight of the sanitation workers, and they strongly supported their strike. At the mass meeting at Mason Temple the previous night, they had told people about the surveillance of King by Redditt and Richmond. Reverend Blackburn had warned the two officers, who were in the audience, that people resented their presence, and Reverend Lawson from the pulpit denounced the police officer who had murdered Larry Payne. Others in the audience stared hard at the two plainclothes police agents, and they promptly left. The next day, Holloman promptly removed Wallace and Newsum from the fire station.

This left Redditt and Richmond alone at the fire station to continue watching King and his party on April 4, but members of the 111th Military Intelligence Group, a unit of the MID based in Georgia, were also scouting Memphis on behalf of the Pentagon for signs of an impending riot. At one point, MID investigators allegedly watched SCLC staff members at the Lorraine with binoculars from the fire station's rooftop, but then they abandoned the position as too exposed to public view. Unconvincingly, MID agents later claimed that they relied on police informants for their information, not electronic surveillance, and that they were concerned only about riots, not King.

Meanwhile, the police received multiple warnings of impending violence. Unnamed "intelligence sources" from out of state ominously told the MPD that the Ku Klux Klan had forbidden its members to go to Memphis on April 4, "for fear that they might be blamed for anything which might happen" that day. The police also heard multiple false rumors that Stokely Carmichael was in town to stir up trouble. Federal marshals guarded the homes of the U.S. district attorney, Judges McRae and Bailey Brown, and Mayor Loeb, who had long been under police guard. At 12:50 PM, a woman phoned Redditt at the fire station saying that everyone knew he was there and that spying "was an offense against his people." Philip R. Manuel, from Senator John McClellan's U.S. Senate subcommittee, who was in town investigating King's Poor People's Campaign, also relayed a supposed tip from his Washington office that a black revolutionary from out of state planned to kill Redditt. This threat later proved to be completely erroneous and related not to Redditt but to someone in Knoxville.

Nonetheless, Holloman and Lux removed Redditt from the fire station and told him to take his family into hiding. Redditt protested that if someone was planning to come after him, he would be much safer roaming the streets of Memphis than waiting for them like a sitting duck at home. He did not want to be removed from the area around the Lorraine, feeling that he had some role to play in protecting King. Overruled, he fumed as Lieutenant Ely Arkin drove him home, but Redditt felt so skeptical about the supposed threats that he refused to remove his family from their home. They stayed, but police put them under armed guard for the next several days.

Patrolman Richmond stayed on at the fire station, now apparently the only black officer in the immediate vicinity of the Lorraine Motel. There were no walking police in evidence around the Lorraine, but MPD's TAC Unit 10, made up of three cars and twelve white men, at 5:50 PM joined Richmond at Fire Station Number Two, as its members got refreshments and took a break from their duties. The police were everywhere, yet they were nowhere visible around King.

INSIDE THE LORRAINE, Cabbage resumed a tight game of brinkmanship. When Hosea Williams told him that only supporters of nonviolence would be tolerated within SCLC, he and the other Invaders concluded that SCLC, like the ministers in COME, did not trust them. But Cabbage had no qualms about insisting that his Black Power group get a quid pro quo for its support for a nonviolent mass demonstration, and, according to him, SCLC finally signed over a $10,000 check as a down payment to his group—although congressional investigators later concluded that SCLC had made no such payment.

Around 5 PM, a car pulled into the courtyard with police informant and Invader "Minister of Transportation" "Max" McCullough at the wheel. He had taken SCLC staff members Orange and Bevel shopping for overalls. Orange said that they had spent most of the day explaining to various members of the Invaders how to "get their mind off of doing violence but [instead] sort of protecting people from violence"—for example, by non-violently covering up someone about to throw a brick. He suspected that police infiltrators played a major role in the Invaders, but he also believed that SCLC staff could control any provocateurs.

Around 5:50, the Invaders left the Lorraine Motel, after an emissary from Jesse Jackson—who stood looking at them impatiently from the parking lot—told them that SCLC wanted to put up other people in their room. Cabbage felt particularly conspicuous as he walked out to the parking lot with rifles and guns smuggled in a blanket under his arm. John Burl Smith noticed how quiet it was, with no police in sight, and he thought the whole scene seemed "eerie."

Upstairs, as King and Abernathy prepared to go to dinner, Kyles entered King's room and exchanged pleasantries with him. King buoyantly said of

Memphis, "This is like the old Movement days, isn't it? That first speech here! When I got to the Temple and saw all those people—you couldn't have squeezed two more in if you tried. This really is the old Movement spirit."

From the firehouse, Patrolman Willie Richmond watched King as he stood on the balcony talking to staff members in the courtyard below. King bent over the rail, talking to Solomon Jones, his driver for that night, and then Jesse Jackson, who said from the courtyard, "Hey, you remember Ben Branch?" King knew Branch, the leader of the Breadbasket Band from Chicago, who had been singing in the motel with Kyles and others earlier in the day. He told Branch how much he had enjoyed his version of "Precious Lord," which Branch had played for him in Chicago, and he asked to hear it again at that night's rally: "I want you to play it real pretty."

Abernathy remained inside Room 306, still getting ready to leave for dinner. It was dusk, and time to leave. King had been standing on the balcony for less than five minutes. Orange, Bevel, and Young wrestled around in the parking lot, and King joked to the gentle giant of his staff, "James, don't hurt Andy and Bevel." Orange joked back, " 'Dr. King, it's two of them and one of me, and you should be asking them not to hurt me.' And before he could respond again, the bullet went off," said Orange.

Everyone in the courtyard, including Jackson, Bevel, Young, Williams, Lee, and Orange—most of the top staff of SCLC—instinctively ducked or sprawled onto the pavement. King's attorney, Chauncey Eskridge, black photographers Ernest Withers and Joseph Louw, and Earl Caldwell, a black reporter for the New York Times—all of whom were at the motel—jumped at the sound.

The bullet slammed through King's jaw on a downward trajectory, ripping through his jugular vein and spinal cord. The force of this powerful rifle shot—coming at a speed of 2,670 feet per second from a distance of about 200 feet—twisted him and threw him flat on his back. A woman in the courtyard cried out, "Oh, Lord, they've shot Martin." Abernathy, Kyles, Jackson, and others rushed to his side. Police agent McCullough bounded up the stairs and applied a towel to stanch the wound, as King's blood spurted onto the cement deck outside Room 306. Kyles covered him with a blanket to keep him warm, as cries of anguish rose from the courtyard.

Cabbage heard the shot just as he got into his car, and he did not look up or back; he accelerated out of the parking lot and sped toward his mother's home in South Memphis. Someone had fired a weapon at him in his car earlier in the strike, and he thought the shot was aimed at him. Behind him, Invaders scattered. In the motel, Reverend Kyles could not make a phone call—probably because the co-owner, Lorene Bailey, had gone into shock and wasn't putting calls through the switchboard. Kyles beat the wall, crying, "Oh, Jesus! Oh, Jesus!" but Abernathy told him to get a grip on himself. Solomon Jones drove forward and backward in the parking lot, completely disoriented. A. D. King was in the shower and had not heard the rifle shot. When told what had happened, he went into an emotional breakdown—repeating, between sobs, "They got my brother."

Black patrolman Richmond and a white fireman who had come into the room were horrified at what they had seen through the fire-station peephole. At 6:01, Richmond called the Intelligence Division of the MPD, and within minutes, an order went out to the TAC Unit to close into a ring formation around the Lorraine. TAC Unit 10 members, who had been lounging around the fire station, ran toward the motel. A reporter estimated that some 150 police officers suddenly swarmed around the Lorraine Motel, as King's aides pointed toward a brick rooming house and told them to go in the opposite direction. Jesse Jackson told the *New York Times*, "When I turned around I saw police coming from everywhere. They said, 'Where did it come from?' And I said, 'Behind you.' The police were coming from where the shot came." With anger and bitterness in his voice, he said, "We didn't need to call the police. They were all over the place." He didn't believe they were there to protect King, either.

Some of the police circled around toward the front and back of a two-story brick rooming house that fronted on Main Street and stood directly across from the Lorraine Motel. By 6:06, a police dispatcher sent out a radio communication that the shot had come from the rooming house, and he ordered officers to seal off the whole area. By 6:07, a rifle had been found in a bundle in front of Canipe's Amusement Company, next to the rooming house. A witness said a white man had left it there.

By 6:09, an ambulance sped King toward St. Joseph's Hospital—to the same emergency room where James Meredith had been taken after he was shot in 1966. Reverend Kyles had already seen King's color change, and he remembered having seen this same change in his father's face just before he died. By 6:10, a dispatch over police radio identified a white man fleeing the scene in a white Ford Mustang, driving north on Main Street; Memphis police began looking in that area for the killer. Investigators later concluded that a ham radio operator had contrived this entirely erroneous lead, which drew police attention away from southbound routes. Police dispatcher Lieutenant Frank Kallaher failed to alert police across the nearby state lines of Arkansas and Mississippi to look for an escaping killer. Despite scores of police cars patrolling Memphis, the shooter escaped by driving south and west out of the city.

As Charles Cabbage also drove southward, his car radio announced that Dr. King had been shot, and it soon identified the killer's getaway car as a late-model blue or white Mustang. It sounded too much like Cabbage's powder-blue Mustang, which he had borrowed from Edwina Harrell. He stepped on the gas. By the time he got to his mother's house, police helicopters were flying over the black community, on the lookout for potential rioters. Cabbage quickly drove the car into the backyard and camouflaged it with tree limbs and brush.

He went inside the house and stayed there. Later that night, a twitch in his neck turned into a muscle spasm and then a full-blown seizure; he could not move. In the morning, Cabbage went to the hospital with what looked like a nervous breakdown. Doctors gave him a shot of Demerol to put him out of his pain.

AS WORD OF the shooting spread, Memphis movement activists converged on the Lorraine, hoping that King might still be alive. Joe Warren, Robert Beasley, S. T. Thomas, and other strikers who had been at Clayborn Temple, preparing to go to a mass meeting at Mason Temple, ran toward the hotel. They could not get near it, so Warren went back to his car and drove home. Other workers had already left for Mason Temple, still expecting a mass rally with King.

Maxine Smith, late for her dinner with King at the Kyleses' home, was in her car and trying to drop off two law students who had come into town as civil rights observers for the mass march. When she saw a police car with its siren on and speeding in the direction of the Lorraine, she sped that way too. As she neared the motel, she saw John Henry Ferguson, whom police had attacked or arrested numerous times during the strike, sprinting down the road. He ran so fast that his shoes had come off, and he was carrying them. She stopped and shouted, "'John Henry, what's wrong with you?' And he said, 'They've shot Dr. King.' So I said, 'Get in the car, John Henry.'" She thought that if the police caught him, they would beat or kill him.

Police had sealed off the Lorraine, and she couldn't get past the barricades. Events began to blur: "I remember parking the car and just running. I don't know where I was running or why I was running." When she realized that her young son Smitty was at home alone, she turned around and rushed home, fearful of impending riots. Her two young white law students stayed behind, and the police arrested them as their first possible suspects in the shooting. John Henry slipped away.

Jesse Epps and P. J. Ciampa had also sped to the Lorraine, where they watched the ambulance take King away. Jerry Fanion showed up a few minutes later to find King's bloodstains on the balcony. Bill Lucy and Ralph Jackson rushed to the Lorraine from the Minimum Salary Building, and they stood with others on the perimeter of the parking lot. Lucy and Baxton Bryant quickly obtained passes from Frank Holloman and traveled around the city for the rest of the night, asking people to remain nonviolent. As someone involved in the negotiations, Lucy felt somehow guilty, thinking that perhaps "the adamant position of, maybe both sides of this thing, had caused this to happen."

T. O. Jones at first did not believe the news reports, but when he verified that King had been shot, he decided that a widespread assassination plot was underway, so he locked himself in his room at the Peabody Hotel. He couldn't remember anything about how he felt or what he had done after that. His son Jesse stayed with him, saying that his father just went silent, holding his head in his hands: "He didn't say anything until the rally the next night, and when he did, he began to cry on stage and so did everyone else."

Reverend James Jordan had just returned from the Lorraine Motel when he heard the news. That day, an African American man who had said he was just back from Germany had gone with him to the motel, hoping to see King. Jordan's first thought was that perhaps this black man had shot King: "I'm thinking of what his aide [James Bevel] said, 'When he gets it, it'll be from some Negro.'" The lack of any security for King had been obvious. Jordan jumped in his car and sped back to the Lorraine, fearing that his worst nightmare had come true. He couldn't get anywhere near it.

Gwen Kyles, busy at home preparing dinner for King and his colleagues, did not hear the news until her husband phoned home: "I just went numb. I just felt like somebody had knocked all my senses out. I mean, the light just went out . . . just everything drained out. I couldn't cry. I couldn't do anything. I just went stiff, and when I finally came to myself, I was just walking the floor and I remember saying, 'They've torn it now.'" White society had crossed a line beyond decency, and someone would have to make a loud, militant protest that white America could not ignore.

Reverend James Lawson heard the news while he was home eating dinner with his wife and two sons. He rushed to WDIA, black Memphis's main radio station, and taped a recorded message urging calmness, prayers, and dedication to King's faith in nonviolence. As during the March 28 violence, Lawson's entreaties played a key role in turning people in black Memphis away from mass violence. He was hoping, however, that King had only been wounded.

"The first tape I had made was playing on the radio when we got over the teletype the news that Dr. King was dead. Since I was in the radio station . . . I took it calmly." Lawson made another tape, saying, "It would be a compounding of this death if now Negro people or white people around our country should despair and decide that now is the time to let loose an orgy of violence. It would not be a tribute to Dr. King but a denial of his life and work." Throughout the evening, the station played his tape urging nonviolence.

Alone in his car, Lawson gripped his steering wheel as waves of grief washed over him, and he nearly broke down. But he knew that tears would not get the job done in the middle of an emergency. King's prophetic speech of the previous night had not caused him to have premonitions, but neither was King's death a surprise. He always knew that King could be killed anywhere and at any time, and he also knew that King would want him to do everything he could to help prevent a violent response. Later, he found Judge Benjamin Hooks, and they spent much of the night (with a police pass) moving throughout the city and calling for nonviolence.

Lawson acknowledged, though, that even some of the city's most prominent African Americans felt, "We should have burned the place down." Underneath Lawson's calm exterior, he also had a deep reservoir of anger, and King's death added immeasurably to it. Better than anyone, Lawson understood the disastrous consequences of King's death. He saw it as the triumph of the "moral blindness" created by "interdependent cruelty systems" of racism, war, and institutionalized violence—against which he and King had fought together ever since they first met at Oberlin College in 1957.

Jerry Wurf heard the news in Washington, DC, and reacted with panic: "What's happening to our people in Memphis? Where are they? Are they dead? Are they alive? . . . I had the same feeling as when John Kennedy was killed. Why? How? What kind of a world are we living in? This whole dreadful feeling. What the hell are we doing?"

Wurf spent the night on the phone, tracking down his staff in Memphis and repeatedly calling the White House. He finally spoke to an assistant to Vice President Hubert Humphrey, telling him that the federal government had to intervene in the strike: "I don't know what button to press, but, goddammit, Memphis is going to burn!" Only a maniac, he said, would leave Mayor Loeb in control. Wurf took the first plane he could get and arrived in Memphis the next morning.

Mayor Loeb had been driving south to give a talk to University of Mississippi law students when Sheriff Bill Morris drove up beside him to escort him back to the city. By 6:35 PM, Loeb had called in the state police and the National Guard and had issued a curfew making anyone on the street subject to immediate arrest.

At Mason Temple, where people had gathered for the rally with King, an older black woman cried out, "The Lord has deserted us." Striker Clinton Burrows had first driven to St. Joseph Hospital to find King, but police told him to leave. When he got to Mason Temple and told people King was mortally wounded, "The children began crying and all hell broke loose."

If the Invaders had a secret network ready to attack the town, as the police thought, they didn't use it. To the contrary, one of them told people at the temple, "Just respect the man [King] enough not to go out and do it tonight. Wait till he's buried. Don't you know the policemen are out there waiting for you? . . . That's just what the honkies want us to do. Come right out there like a bunch of wild Indians and they could wipe us out like they did the Indians. Don't do it."

It was a moment of truth for those who thought black Memphians should take guns into the streets against white supremacy. This unidentified Invader later reflected, "We used to have a choice. We could wait for Dr. King to carry out his program and if it didn't work, we could use ours, but now it was as if white people didn't want any other program but ours." He feared that black insurrection, as King had always said, would only lead to massive repression against the black community.

AFSCME organizers arrived and told people to get off the streets. "The people were telling us to go to hell, because it's their night for revenge. And we said, 'It's impossible,' " recalled Ciampa. King's SCLC staff members played the same role, observed ACLU attorney David Caywood: "They were having a terrific argument with a bunch of young Negroes . . . trying to talk them out of burning the town down. . . . And they did a fairly good job of it." Most people went home.

Two white newspaper reporters trying to get to the Lorraine Motel turned back after a group of young blacks broke their car window with bottles and bricks. It was not safe on the streets, and white reporters remained more or less trapped at the city's newspaper offices and television and radio stations. Frantically, they tried to confirm that King had been shot and to find out his condition.

At St. Joseph's Hospital, Abernathy, Bernard Lee, Young, and Chauncey Eskridge stood by as a team of doctors tried to save King. By 7:05, doctors pronounced him dead. For the next twenty-four hours, Abernathy and Lee accompanied King's body through the dreadful process of autopsy and embalming.

Downtown, Frank Miles was meeting with Downing Pryor and other city councilmen, discussing ways to move the mediation forward, when they heard about the shooting. They broke up and went home or to the mayor's office. At city hall, some of the City Council members met with Loeb. "There was an awful shock in the room," said Pryor. Jerred Blanchard later saw it as "Memphis and America damned to hell all over the world. . . . The man who was recognized as the Negro leader of all the leaders, slain, assassinated. Just a modern form of lynching."

Fred Davis began crying uncontrollably, and so did Reverend J. L. Netters. Even Loeb cried—the only time anyone had seen him lose control of his emotions since the strike began. Netters kept repeating in his mind, "If only they had listened." Loeb asked Netters to unite them with a prayer, but Netters could not: he held Loeb responsible for King's death. The mayor moved on and spent the rest of the evening driving around and making statements at television and radio stations to calm people down. Accompanied by a police officer, Loeb carried a pearl-handled revolver in his pocket, supplied by the MPD.

Tommy Powell had been meeting at the Peabody Hotel with businessmen, telling them, "This town is fixin' to blow up if you don't tell Henry Loeb to sign this damn contract." Even Sheriff Morris supported his statement, but these businesspeople weren't ready to buck Loeb. Frustrated at their failure to take the situation as seriously as it deserved, Powell was walking down the stairs when the sheriff's driver ran up to say that King had been shot. "I turned around on the steps and, I will never forget this, I said, 'Laugh now you sons-of-bitches.'" Powell left for the Lorraine Motel.

Rabbi James Wax and friends heard the news at a dinner at the home of Fred and Myra Dreifus. They immediately divided up the food and all went home, believing Memphis was in for another state of siege.

Police reactions to the slaying differed. A black police detective standing outside the Lorraine commented, "Son of a bitch. You remember when they shot Meredith. I'm afraid they're going to just take this town apart. It isn't just black power, it's gonna be everybody—from all over the country." After Tommy Powell got there, though, he saw several white police officers laughing and joking. One recognized Powell and said, "You nigger-loving son-of-a-bitch, we killed Martin Luther King." One white officer later allegedly responded to a question about what King looked like after he was shot, by saying, "Like any other dead nigger."

Someone had shot through Powell's car window as he was driving earlier in the strike, and Powell decided Memphis was not safe. He sent his wife and family to stay with family members in Chattanooga for the next two weeks. White minister Dick Moon had the same feeling, so he sent his wife and family into hiding with friends. No one who supported the strike, white or black, felt safe.

In Mississippi, Charles Evers, the brother of slain NAACP leader Medgar Evers, answered the phone to hear a man telling him, "We just killed that black S.O.B. Martin Luther King and you're next." It was the first of many threats he and other black civil rights advocates throughout the Mississippi Delta would receive that night. The right-wing network of hate callers was activated in Memphis, too. One woman called white attorney Lucius Burch repeatedly, late into the night, asking him why he had agreed to represent "that nigger" King.

Sometime later that evening, Ernest Withers, legendary for his photography of black life and death in Memphis, received police permission to go to the balcony where King was shot. He photographed the pool of blood left behind, which to him looked like a silhouette of King. In King's room, he found a pill container from the pharmacy of Mississippi civil rights leader Aaron Henry and used it to gather some of King's blood, which he took back to his studio for safekeeping. The next morning, Withers photographed King lying in his coffin, just as he had photographed civil rights martyrs Emmett Till, George Lee, Herbert Lee, Medgar Evers, Malcolm X, and Larry Payne before him.

AS NEWS OF King's death flashed across television screens or blared on the radio, sanitation workers and their families suffered through a long, devastating night. Matt Randle, who had been waiting to see King at Mason Temple, recalled, "All of us there went home. It was a death in the family." He decided that the workers could never back off the strike now; they had to have a victory. Jesse Ryan heard the news while dining with his family:

"That stopped everything. When they said he was dead, we all started crying, and for the next few days, we were like that." Taylor Rogers said, "It was like losing a part of your family. . . . We all just had a hurt feeling. The man had done so much good for everybody, black and white." He thought some of the "higher ups" in Memphis had decided, "We don't need this nigger around. I later explained to my family, someone wanted him out of the way."

For Walter Bailey, who co-owned the Lorraine Motel with his wife Lorene, King's death took a heavy personal toll. He and his wife had done everything together to make a living; he had once been a Pullman porter, and they had once tried running a turkey farm. Then they bought a motel and named it after Lorene (though they spelled the name differently), creating an informal, homey atmosphere enjoyed by black entertainers such as B. B. King, the Mighty Clouds of Joy, the Staple Singers, and others. "In your business you gotta be one big family, and a city has gotta be one big family," he believed. "I don't think we'll make it in the world, if we don't get together and make it one big family."

King was their pride and joy. They didn't even charge him for his room, and Bailey said that on April 4, "He just act so different, so happy, than he ever had been before. . . . Look like they had won the world." He remembered King as a sturdy man, "hard as a brick," seemingly indestructible. King's assassination devastated his fifty-two-year-old wife: "She just started shaking like a leaf after we heard the shot." She walked around the motel muttering, "Why? Why? Why?" She had taken to her sickbed for a month when the entertainer Sam Cooke had died some years earlier. After the ambulance took King away, Walter went to work at his side job at the Holiday Inn. While he was gone, a blood vessel to her brain burst and Lorene fell to the floor. She went into a coma and died on Tuesday morning, April 9, the day of King's funeral. Her husband believed the shock of King's death caused hers.

Despair, grief, rage, frustration, and fear gripped black Memphis, as curfew and riot conditions once again descended on the city. Within minutes of the announcement of King's death, young black people began pouring into the streets. In the neighborhood around Tillman and Johnson, blacks with guns pinned down police cars and reportedly wounded two officers—one of only a few incidents in which people directed gunfire at the police.

Someone started a huge fire at O. W. Ferrell Lumber Company on North Second, where dry lumber, turpentine, and other flammable materials shot flames 100 feet into the air. Phone threats against Loeb escalated. Speaking of King, a young black man shouted out at a reporter, "He died for us, and we're going to die for him." Small groups of roving men threw Molotov cocktails and ransacked stores.

During the first three and half hours after King's death, more than 30,000 long-distance calls went out of the city. Phone lines jammed; dial tones sometimes did not appear for fifteen minutes or more. The police, trying to stop a potential riot and find a killer at the same time, feared that some whites, who had been buying increasing numbers of weapons as the strike progressed, might start vigilante action. Fire and Police Director Holloman proclaimed, "Rioting and looting is rampant" in the black community. Some 800 policemen, Tennessee highway patrolmen, and sheriff's deputies tried to take over the streets. By midnight, 3,800 National Guardsmen had joined them.

The news media carried Ralph Abernathy's warning, "If a riot or violence would erupt in Memphis tonight, Dr. King in Heaven would not be pleased." African Americans knew that, but they also wanted to impress their sense of rage upon the authorities. One black youth exclaimed, "I wish that Stokely Carmichael and the other Black Power advocates would come and burn Memphis down!" Another recalled, "Truthfully, I wanted to go out and shoot, mangle, or kill every white person I chanced to meet."

The city pulled Memphis Transit Authority buses off the streets after dark—after rocks and bricks had damaged fifty-six of them. That night, police received 806 emergency phone calls and arrested 245 people, including eighteen women and eleven juveniles. By contrast to the previous weekend, many more of the rioters were adults. Firemen received 229 fire alarms and reported the use of Molotov cocktails in at least seventy-five cases. Several men tried to burn down a Loeb's Laundry but failed. A number of people successfully firebombed a number of other stores.

While flames and smoke engulfed parts of black Memphis, the destruction remained limited compared with what had occurred the previous weekend. Police and the military, already on high alert when King came to town, quickly sealed off black areas. During the 7-PM-to-5-AM curfew, they subjected blacks to preemptory searches and arrests. Once again, the curfew left the white community largely untouched while creating a military occupation in black areas. Memphis looked a bit like the racial police state that King warned against in his last article, published in *Look* magazine after his death.

As on the previous weekend, whites remained safely walled off from riots by geography, the military, and the police. Nevertheless, City Council member Wyeth Chandler said, whites in his neighborhood also went on high alert: "Our neighborhood was like a tomb. We were armed, ready for anything. I think this was generally true throughout the community. . . . If a Negro had stopped to change a tire I don't know whether he'd be left alive or not."

AFRICAN AMERICANS EVERYWHERE recognized King's death as a watershed moment that required a massive response. Riots destroyed black communities most of all, but riots also hurt white owners of capital far more than any economic boycott or nonviolent protest. King's death burst the dam of whatever patience held back the rage of Black America at Depression-level unemployment; job, housing, and school discrimination; pervasive police brutality; useless deaths of black soldiers in Vietnam; and the plethora of ills that stalked the ghettos. Those who thought ghetto residents no longer cared for King were proven wrong.

In Washington, DC, within two hours of King's death, riots began. Stokely Carmichael urged young blacks not to commit suicide by confronting the police, but to get guns and prepare themselves methodically for armed conflict: "When white America killed Dr. King . . . she declared war on us. The rebellions that have been occurring around these cities and this country is just light stuff compared to what is about to happen."

By Friday afternoon, thousands of white civil servants and congressional staffers jammed the roads out of the capital. From the Pentagon,

"You could see the enormous pall of smoke over the District," recalled a government attorney. Flames and billows of smoke ringed a White House and congressional complex surrounded by acres of poverty-stricken black neighborhoods. Military intelligence agents, police, and firemen could hardly get around as enraged people took over the streets.

President Johnson signed an executive order calling out federal troops. On Friday morning, April 5, he proclaimed, "America shall not be ruled by the bullet but only by the ballot of free and just men," and he urged Americans to unify in their support of King's goals. He called on Congress to enact aid to cities, manpower training, laws mandating equal opportunity in housing, and low-income-housing supports. Representative John Conyers from Detroit went further, calling for $80 billion to be spent on a "Marshall Plan" for America's cities. The president said flags would fly at half staff from Friday until King's burial on Tuesday, and he proclaimed Sunday, April 7, as a day of national mourning. Mayor Loeb proclaimed three days of mourning.

It was too late, said SNCC leader Julian Bond in Nashville on Friday: "Brotherhood was murdered in Memphis last night. Nonviolence was murdered in Memphis last night. All that is good in America was murdered in Memphis last night." James Meredith angrily remarked of King's death, "This is America's answer to the peaceful, nonviolent way of obtaining rights in this country." In response, urban riots that King had tried so desperately to prevent now burst forth in Chicago, Detroit, Baltimore, Pittsburgh, and other major cities all across the country. Some lasted for the weekend, others for more than a week.

By Monday, April 8, thirty were dead and 2,000 injured in riots in more than eighty cities; by April 11, forty-three were dead and 20,000 arrested in 125 cities. In one case, a black man killed the first white he saw in retaliation for King's death; otherwise, blacks constituted the vast majority of those killed and hurt. More than $100 million in damages occurred, and the riots forced President Johnson to call off a planned strategic peace conference on Vietnam in Hawaii, as normal life everywhere came to a halt.

Time magazine wrote, "In its sweep and immediacy, the shock wave of looting, arson and outrage that swept the nation's black ghettos after Martin Luther King's murder exceeded anything in the American experience." It tallied 5,117 fires, the wreckage of 1,928 businesses and homes, nearly 24,000 arrests, and a deployment of 72,800 Army and National Guard troops, with 50,000 soldiers standing by at military bases. It was the largest domestic deployment of military forces since the Civil War. The army chief of staff for intelligence told his staff, "We have an insurgency on our hands." Mayor Richard J. Daley ordered his police to shoot to kill when they encountered looters; other authorities reined in police use of deadly force so as not to spread the conflagration.

Governor Buford Ellington put the entire Tennessee National Guard on alert. Police, sheriff's deputies, and National Guardsmen patrolled black Memphis (and Nashville, too) with rifles and machine guns, Jeeps, and heavy vehicles; closed down gasoline stations and liquor stores; and put black men up against walls with their arms and legs spread out. Black children, unlike the previous weekend, kept their distance from the military. Following a night of curfew, schools and colleges were closed on Friday morning, while most businesses remained open, many of them surrounded by troops and police.

The courts arraigned nearly 100 people charged with overnight crimes. In addition, the Shelby County grand jury returned its first indictments under the state's new anti-riot law, passed on March 28. It indicted Willie Henry, striker Willie Kemp, and other movement supporters on a variety of other charges left over from the first riot—as well as Reverend Malcolm Blackburn and five other nonviolent protesters (including Kemp) who had tried to block sanitation trucks with their bodies three weeks earlier.

King's murder on Thursday night had made him the second person (following Larry Payne on March 28) killed during strike-related actions; on Friday night, Memphis police killed a third. Initial police reports said Ellis Tate, twenty-six, fired at officers who interrupted his looting at a liquor store. Several days later, the story changed: police said they interrupted Tate, age forty, who ran and fired one shot at them, but then his rifle jammed. Both reports agreed that the police had shot him nine times.

Behind a veil of police power, Memphians struggled to understand King's death, nervously anticipating the kind of massive riots underway in

Washington, Chicago, and other major cities. The *Commercial Appeal* put Calvin Taylor, a closeted member of The Invaders, into the streets as a reporter to assess the situation. Black people expressed a mixture of rage and apprehension: "I'm scared," "I want them [police] to quit," "Since when did they start hiring black reporters at the *Commercial Appeal*? Get away, boy." One woman said, "I'm 78 years old, and I don't feel like running." A black schoolteacher called it a "horror, when with all the advances of modern civilization it can't solve its problems without killing and rioting." People greatly feared destruction in their community, but most of all they hated military occupation; it only enflamed people and the troops should go home, many said.

Yet African Americans in Memphis that weekend directed their rage mainly at property, not persons, and even property damage proved small by contrast to what happened in the rest of the country. The full damage only became evident later when a police report to the U.S. attorney general totaled the costs of both the March 28 and April 4 weekends. Over a two-square-mile area, 275 Memphis stores had been looted or attacked; all looters were black, 80 percent of them under age twenty-four; whites composed 95 percent of the affected store owners. The report listed only two verified reports of snipers. For Molotov cocktails, arsonists in Memphis often used coal oil in Coke bottles—one indication of their lack of experience at urban warfare. (Gasoline in more breakable beer bottles worked much better.)

It could have been far worse, for something snapped inside many people when King died. For some thirty years, black worker Clarence Coe had fought discrimination in the industrial unions, supported NAACP legal challenges to segregation, performed community and church service, and strictly adhered to nonviolence while supporting the sanitation workers' strike. When King died, however, Coe said good-bye to his Firestone workmates—thinking they might never see each other again—got his rifle and some ammunition, and took command of a small hill at a cemetery near his house. "That's what I thought everybody else was going to do," he recalled. He was surprised when no large-scale rebellion broke out. "And then, when I found out they [blacks] weren't going to do nothing, I'm tellin' you, it took a lot out of me. It took a lot out of me. I just expected to go to war. I mean, that's what I came home for, that's what I was planning on. And I thought that would just happen all over the world."

In a different way, it did happen "all over the world," as Europeans, Africans, and others across the globe expressed outrage and sorrow by demonstrating in the streets. Even *Commercial Appeal* editors had to recognize how the world regarded King: "King's Murder Horrifies World," and "Dark Continent Weeps for King," ran the paper's headlines. In the garment district of New York City, black and white workers on Friday abruptly left their jobs to memorialize King, without employer permission. Union organizers and civil rights advocates continued to hold mass rallies, marches, and memorials to honor King; the movement to declare his birthday a holiday from work had begun.

In Vietnam, many black soldiers, hearing of upheaval back home, lost what little faith they had in the American system. In Memphis, there didn't seem to be an adequate way to express the full extent of grief and rage felt by African Americans. Many predicted that large-scale, armed rebellion would begin after the city honored King with the nonviolent march still planned for April 8.

ON THE NIGHT of King's death, Attorney Walter Bailey went down to the police station to retrieve the two white members of the Law Students Civil Rights Research Council whom the police had picked up near the Lorraine Motel after Maxine Smith left them. He thought it ironic that these civil rights activists were the first two people arrested on suspicion of the King slaying. Ultimately, he got the charges against them dropped.

One of about twelve blacks out of some 800 attorneys in Memphis, Bailey had left Memphis to go to law school and had come back determined to make a difference through the practice of law. But on April 4, as he entered the police station, he was confronted by the same old racism that he had known as a child. Squads of white officers came in and out of the building holding guns and wearing gas masks. One officer at the door held a gun on him; he said, "I don't know whether it was a shotgun or one of these submachine guns or what it was."

Later that night, Fire and Police Director Holloman, who knew that

Bailey was a lawyer for Dr. King, greeted him as "Bailey," and told him he'd be glad to give him a pass so he could get around the city. "I didn't say anything, I didn't respond—I just turned and walked away," said the attorney. He felt that whites still could not give him the simple respect of calling him "Mr. Bailey," or "Attorney Bailey." As a black man, he was, simply, "Bailey." Holloman said he never used titles and perhaps in a casual setting he called everyone by his or her last name, but it didn't matter—Walter Bailey, like thousands of black Memphians, felt a profound white disrespect for his personhood.

For the next few days, Attorney Bailey interviewed dozens of black people assaulted by police officers, many of whom had taken off their badges so they could not be identified: "I noticed that most everybody who had been arrested had some marks about his person"—a head wound, a bandage, blood on their shirt. "I saw no police officers bandaged who had arrested those persons. You see, which indicated that it was all a one-way sort of thing. . . ."

His thoughts flashed back to his meeting with King on April 3, when he had shaken hands with him. King's quiet humility, calmness, and sincerity had been self-evident, and the attorney couldn't believe he was gone.

Reverend Henry Starks felt the same devastating sense of loss. On the evening of King's death, Starks had rushed to the Lorraine like everyone else, but police had forced him to turn back. He felt utterly dejected and miserable as he returned home, and suddenly he wished that the strike had never happened: "Here was a man who could see down the corridor of time and see the road ahead that we were taking would lead to almost a suicidal status . . . destroyed by the very thing that he denounced—violence."

At 1 AM, a handful of King's closest supporters gathered in Room 306 of the Lorraine Motel. Jesse Jackson had gone back to his hometown of Chicago to try to stop one of the country's biggest riots, already in progress. Those who remained met late into the night. James Bevel said that everything SCLC had been doing—especially the Poor People's Campaign and the strike—had to continue, and the group expressed unanimous support for Abernathy, whom King had asked to take his place as SCLC president if he suddenly died. "There was a great sense of unity,"

Lawson recalled, "a great sense of realization that Martin had died on behalf of all of us." As tanks and military vehicles once again rolled down Beale Street, in Room 306 they sang, "We Shall Overcome."

Later that night, one of his aides went through King's coat pockets and found his handwritten note, "The Ten Commandments on Vietnam," refuting the false reasons given for the war. Coretta Scott King would read it at a mass antiwar rally in May 1968. Even without the aid of its most visionary and accomplished leader, the Movement would go on.

James Lawson said they had witnessed "a crucifixion event" in Memphis. That night, he prayed for the resurrection of hope and the will to carry on.

20

RECKONINGS

Here came a man talking love and nonviolence and walking hand
in hand with white people, and they took his head off. . . . It ain't
no such thing as no middle of the road no more. . . . White
America has put itself in one hell of a trick now.
—*Charles Cabbage*

ORETTA SCOTT KING HAD GONE SHOPPING WITH HER
daughter Yolanda on the afternoon of April 4. When she returned
home, Jesse Jackson called to tell her that her husband had just
been shot: "It hit me hard—not surprise, but shock—that the call I seemed
subconsciously to have been waiting for all our lives had come." Trying to
spare her the gruesome details, Jackson told her that Martin had been shot
in the shoulder. Soon, Andrew Young called to tell her his condition was
deathly serious and she should come to Memphis.

Ivan Allen, the mayor of Atlanta, with his wife and city police, escorted
Coretta to the airport, but as she prepared to board the plane, King's secretary, Dora McDonald, approached to say her husband had died. King's
family and friends stood together weeping in the airport. Mrs. King
returned home and spent the night with her four young children—Bernice
(age five), Yolanda (twelve), Martin III (ten), and Dexter (seven)—trying
to explain their devastating loss in terms they might understand. Senator
Robert Kennedy called, as did many others, and he had three phones set up
in her house to take dozens of incoming calls.

Since Montgomery, Coretta had lived with the ever-present possibility that someone would kill her husband. Racists had bombed their home in 1956, nearly killing her and their daughter Yolanda. Many threats, arrests, and physical attacks followed. When they watched television coverage of President John Kennedy's 1963 assassination in Dallas, King had told her, "This is what is going to happen to me." She accepted this reality—not morbidly, but realistically. In 1965, she told a Seattle audience, "You realize that what you are doing is pretty dangerous, but we go on with the faith that what we are doing is right. If something happens to my husband, the cause will continue. It may even be helped."

Coretta knew all about his deep depression and premonitions of death. On recent Sundays, he had preached about his possible death and his legacy. In his prophetic "Drum Major" sermon on February 4, he seemed to preach his own funeral eulogy. "I won't have any money to leave behind. I won't have the fine and luxurious things of life to leave behind. But I just want to leave a committed life behind," he said. On March 12, before he began his whirlwind speaking trip for the Poor People's Campaign, he sent his wife a synthetic red corsage, saying he wanted to give her something to remember him by that would always last. When he died, he left no will, no savings, and few earthly possessions beyond the King family's modest home.

His wife had watched King agonize after the March 28 riot in Memphis and then resolve to return, despite his own great misgivings. King met with his parents and told them to be prepared for his death at any time, that money had been offered and professional killers were being recruited. Said Coretta, "Martin didn't say directly to me that it's going to happen in Memphis, but I think he felt that time was running out. . . . I was aware that any campaign was a dangerous one. But there was something a little different about Memphis." More than anyone, she had supported King during his times of self-doubt and had urged him to go on.

On Friday morning, April 5, she went to Memphis in a plane provided by Senator Kennedy. No viewing of King's body had been announced, but that morning a steady stream of people poured through the R. S. Lewis Funeral Home (only blocks from the riot scene of March 28), most of them in silence. The crowd included "a pitiful handful of whites," wrote strike historian Joan Beifuss, and an array of blacks—"old men, maids and clerk typists and day laborers dressed for work, families with their children, men with button-down collars and teenagers in blue jeans." People came to touch his face, to look upon him, to cry. Tears streamed down Andrew Young's face, and Ralph Abernathy offered a prayer. Then a long procession of cars took King's body to the airport, escorted by police and National Guardsmen.

King's brother A. D. and his sister Christine helped to take King's body on board. Young plaintively recalled that King "would plead with us all the time, don't ever let anybody make you hate, that the world can't live on hate." A band of about 150 forlorn people stood at the runway sobbing, their voices breaking as they tried to sing, "We Shall Overcome." Some of them collapsed as the plane's roar drowned out their refrain, "Yes, we will not fight, Yes, we will not fight, God is on our side, Today." A black man raised a fist in salute as the plane left.

Once home, Coretta opened the casket, surprised that "his face looked so young and smooth and unworried." Embalmers had done a good job of hiding his hideous wound. Coretta's fortitude in the ensuing days helped to stabilize the national temper—much as Jacqueline Kennedy had done after her own husband's shocking, traumatic death five years earlier. Coretta's spirit came from a particularly deep well, much like the one that had nourished Martin. Their partnership came not only from personal love but also from a joint political commitment. Although she had envisioned a career on the concert stage, she largely gave that up to return with him to her native Alabama.

True to the patriarchal society in which they had been raised, Martin felt she should devote herself primarily to making a home and raising the children. She did that, but she did it in the context of two lives absolutely committed to changing the world. She went with him as a peace pilgrim to India and to Scandinavia for the Nobel Peace Prize; marched with him on the dangerous road from Selma to Montgomery; joined the Women's International League for Peace and Freedom (WILPF) and Women Strike for Peace. She spoke for King at a mass peace demonstration in San Francisco in April 1967; on January 15, 1968, King's birthday, she led 5,000 women demonstrators in the nation's capital against the Vietnam War. On March 28, while King was embroiled in the Memphis riot, she presided at a WILPF conference in Washington calling for a cease-fire in Vietnam. "All women have a common bond—they don't want their husbands and sons maimed and killed in war," she said.

Her husband was constantly gone and they had little money, but it seemed she never wavered in her support of King or the freedom movement. Now, as the King family reeled from tragedy, Coretta began to demonstrate her own quiet and steely commitment to nonviolence. "He gave his life for the poor of the world, the garbage workers of Memphis and the peasants of Vietnam," she said on April 6. "The day that Negro people and others in bondage are truly free, on the day want is abolished, on the day wars are no more, on that day I know my husband will rest in a long-deserved peace."

Her resolve would do a great deal to prevent a racial conflagration in Memphis.

JAMES LAWSON SAID that hatred of King symbolized America's "moral blindness," and true change could not occur until whites came to understand his message. Now, white Memphians suddenly caught a glimpse of King through a different lens—as national television and media gave his nonviolent teachings more widespread attention than they did in his life, a *Commercial Appeal* columnist wrote. NBC News anchor Chet Huntley ran excerpts of King's speeches and mourned the loss of King's "restraint, gentleness, charity—virtues we so desperately need." Television networks carried special programs over the weekend and on April 9 would cover the whole three-hour King funeral in Atlanta. Observances of King's life and philosophy began in the streets and in union halls, churches, and synagogues across the country.

Hesitantly, some whites in Memphis joined blacks to publicly mourn the loss of the era's greatest advocate of interracial cooperation. At LeMoyne College on Friday morning, Margaret Valiant, the only white resident of the LeMoyne Gardens low-income housing project, and Midge Wade, a white suburban housewife, joined an overwhelmingly black memorial to King. Wade said, "We had to express something *somewhere*." She felt "numb, hostile, bitter." A white man sitting in front of her tried to offer consoling words to a black woman who ran the LeMoyne business office, but he collapsed into tears. The LeMoyne student choir tried to sing but broke down sobbing. TV crews were there, but Wade thought, "Surely they would not show whites and blacks weeping together in Memphis."

Bishop Joseph Durick led Catholics in numerous memorial masses for King, beginning on Friday. He had been among the white moderates who objected to King's desegregation protests in Birmingham in 1963 as "unwise and untimely," only to be driven out of town by segregationists for his own racial moderation. Now, as senior bishop of the Catholic Church in Tennessee, ministering to 45,000 Catholics in Shelby County (half the state's total), Durick honored King as a man who spoke for the poor and tried "to restore human dignity to every man." Catholic churches across Tennessee read Durick's pastoral letter asking for "a spirit of true love . . . to instill some reality into the dream" of King's "promised land."

The long-delayed gathering of white ministers (led by Rabbi James Wax) and black ministers (led by Reverend Henry Starks) also finally occurred on Friday. Some 300 of them met at St. Mary's Episcopal Cathedral. James Lawson quietly preached from the Book of Isaiah that King had been "wounded for our transgressions; he was bruised for our iniquities." Father Nicholas Vieron of the Annunciation Greek Orthodox Church knelt before Reverend Starks and asked forgiveness for white religious indifference to racism. Presbyterian minister John William Aldridge read a statement, prepared at the home of Southwestern College theologian Carl Walters the night before, mourning the "unspeakable loss" of "our brother" and asking the mayor and the City Council to adopt union recognition and dues checkoff. "We who are white confess our implication in this tragic event by our failure to speak and act . . . with conviction and courage, to the attitudes of prejudice and patterns of injustice which produced the society in which this act could occur."

Wax's vacillation had ended. He asked the ministers to vote on this statement, and they promptly adopted it. Starks and Lawson lined them up, and Episcopal Dean William Dimmick, carrying a gold cross on a black staff, led about 150 of them two by two through the downtown to city hall. Police approached the ministers with their pistols drawn; three police cars, carrying helmeted police with shotguns, followed them. The faint of heart had already dropped out. Starks felt gratified but said, "I was appalled at the number of the clergy who didn't have the courage" to march. It may have been too little, too late, but the annals of the civil rights movement fail to reveal southern white religious leaders joining blacks in taking such a stand anywhere else in the South.

The interracial group soon crowded into the mayor's office and over-flowed into the hall. Loeb, who had hardly slept, greeted them cordially. One minister thought, "He looked as if we were people coming to congratulate him rather than people coming to deliver an ultimatum." Aldridge read their statement, which included an appeal "to create a new community where equality and justice prevail and no man suffers loss of human rights because of racial prejudice and arrogant paternalism." Reverend Jordan asked the mayor to bring the city together with specific commitments to accept union recognition and dues checkoff.

Starks, in such mourning that he could barely speak, said only, "The greatest apostle of peace in our times has died," and it was time for the "white brethren" to speak out. Despite his heartsickness, he believed that communication between whites and blacks had to continue. He said later, "We are getting on ground so dangerous that it will destroy both of us. It will destroy this country. . . . The painful thing about life is that when your trust is betrayed, you must keep on trusting." Otherwise, "Life ends for you right there."

Rabbi Wax took the lead, but not with such a forgiving heart. He addressed the mayor in stern tones of righteous indignation: "We came here with a great deal of sadness in our hearts, but also a great deal of anger, sir. What has happened in our city is the result of injustice, oppression, and lack of human decency and concern." Admonishing Loeb personally, he continued, "I realize we live in a society of law and order. We must have laws. But I would remind you most respectfully, sir, that there are laws that are greater than the laws of Memphis and of Tennessee." With "amens" echoing behind him, Wax accused the mayor of "dodging behind legal technicalities" and ignoring the fact that "the laws of God come before the laws of any man."

Loeb stood listening in silence, but neither his Episcopal nor his Jewish faith moved him to accept this moral appeal. "I understand and share with you sorrow for what happened yesterday," he said. "We don't completely agree but we each have our sincerity in wanting to get this thing behind us." He said that Governor Buford Ellington had asked him to talk to Frank Miles to get mediation started again, and that he would do so that morning. But he made no commitment at all on the issues.

In frustration, Reverend Ralph Jackson, his voice cracking and with tears on his cheeks, asked the mayor: "Will you agree to a dues check off and union recognition? We plead with you. Put it on the backs of the preachers. Put it on us. Please come down." Loeb gave no response. Jackson continued, "If we had been able to get a hearing as ministers of the black community, we would never need to send for Dr. King or anybody else. But you would not hear. You will not hear now." Loeb offered no commitments. Reverend Baxton Bryant of the Tennessee Human Relations Council gave Loeb a graceful way out, saying that he sympathized with the burdens of the mayor's office.

As the meeting began to break up, seemingly in a spirit of reconciliation, a photographer captured the contradictions of Loeb. He stood shaking the hands of black and white ministers on the other side of his desk, the butt end of a loaded shotgun at his feet beneath the desk.

LAWSON STOOD IN the back and said nothing, unsurprised that so little was accomplished. But before everyone could disperse, Memphis State's Presbyterian chaplain, Dick Moon, angry that the ministers seemed to be accepting Loeb's evasions, protested, "He is not going to change his mind. I, for one, am going to stay in his office until he changes his mind. Until the strike is over, I'm going to stay without eating. Anyone who wants to join me, can!" Moon became more angry as the ministers filed past him. Only Sister Marie Hofstetter came to his side, and then a young white tugboat worker named Edward Carter, Jr. MSU instructor Richard Geller and MSU student Jimmy Gates joined them later.

The mayor invited the protesters to stay in the carpeted entryway to his office, and they did so, but at the end of the day, police took the five of them outside to spend the night on wooden benches in the lobby. For the next seven days, they camped out at city hall, fasting and giving moral witness, in the tradition of Gandhi and Cesar Chavez. Moon lost twenty-two pounds and suffered from cold and hunger, but students from MSU and Southwestern soon joined in support.

ON FRIDAY AFTERNOON, U.S. Attorney General Ramsey Clark, ashen-faced, held a press conference in Memphis, accompanied by his distraught and shaken assistant attorney general, Roger Wilkins, nephew of NAACP President Roy Wilkins. They had already met with Mrs. King, talked to the governor and his assistant (former Director of Memphis Public Safety Claude Armour), to Holloman, to Lawson and other black leaders, and to the FBI. Clark presented a profoundly different personal approach than Memphis authorities. Clearly in mourning, he said that he had expressed his "profound sorrow" to Mrs. King and that King's life "teach[es] that nonviolence can bring change within the rule of law." He took the side of the movement in Memphis, saying, "There are many people in this city working with all their hearts . . . for equal justice," and urging the authorities to resolve the current crisis "without repression."

Clark said that "no evidence of a widespread plot" existed, that King's death appeared to be the work of a lone assassin. He cited the "great difficulties inherent" in protecting King. He did not explain how hundreds of police officers in the area and at least thirty officers in the immediate vicinity of the Lorraine Motel could have failed to protect King and then let his shooter get away. African Americans and AFSCME unionists met Clark's lone-gunman theory with massive skepticism, if not complete disbelief. The next day, the *Commercial Appeal* assured its readers: "All evidence indicates it was the work of an individual, a warped, mixed-up, emotional mind." "Mobs Must Not Rule," it editorialized, and there should be "no invasion of Memphis by extremist elements."

Behind the scenes, someone in the FBI sent around an absurd memo suggesting that perhaps black nationalists such as Carmichael or Brown might have ordered King killed—but, to its credit, the FBI also launched the largest manhunt in its history. Within a few days, evidence pointed to a poor white with a variety of aliases, going by the name of Eric Starvo Galt. Few black people doubted that a white man killed King, but they asked, 'Which white man, and how many? *Time* magazine surveyed black Memphians, and most of them thought the Memphis Police Department was involved in King's death. Black Firestone worker Clarence Coe voiced a common feeling at the time and even many years later, saying the circumstances of King's death pointed toward a conspiracy: "If he was shot out of a window on Main Street, why the hell did every police in that area run to the Lorraine? You've fired a gun, you've heard a gun, seen it fired. The noise is where the cap burst, you know. If somebody shoots a gun here, why would you run five or six hundred yards away? . . . Somebody knew what the target was. You know, everybody knew what the target was."

Many black Memphians instinctively believed that white government and police authorities engineered King's death. One white woman conversed with her maid and commented that she hoped the authorities would catch King's killer. "Oh, Mrs. Viar," the woman responded, "we know who did it. Mayor Loeb paid one of those policemen to do it." The FBI "got some sharp-shooters, too," said Coe. People took little comfort from the fact that the authorities had flooded Memphis with about ninety FBI agents and twenty-seven police detectives in the aftermath of King's death. J. Edgar Hoover's second-in-command, Cartha DeLoach, who had engineered years of surveillance and intimidation designed to destroy King, directed the FBI investigation of his death.

Lawson and others wondered why investigators did not even bother to interview all of the people—some fifteen of them—believed to have been in the courtyard at the time of the shooting. James Orange and John Burl Smith claimed to have seen a shooter and a puff of smoke in the bushes. "There is a basic mistrust in the Negro community concerning the Memphis police, FBI and mayor's office," Lawson said. Black City Council members James Netters and Fred Davis both said blacks had no confidence in the mayor or the police, and they began to press for greater citizen control over the police.

The capture of James Earl Ray at a London airport in June did not assuage people's doubts. It seemed logical that Ray—a poor southern white in and out of jail most of his life, a follower of George Wallace and the KKK's J. B. Stoner who seemed to have tracked King around the country, whose fingerprints matched those on the alleged murder weapon—did it. But how did this escaped convict with no visible means of support track King for months, penetrate police and FBI security, and elude them for sixty-five days, let alone obtain a passport and funds to flee the country? London police arrested him at the airport as Ray began his effort to escape to white-supremacist Rhodesia.

A year later, Ray entered a guilty plea in return for a life sentence instead of the death penalty. Shelby County Attorney General Phil Canale said that Ray, like anyone, had the right to a plea bargain, but the government's failure to hold a trial and present its evidence left nagging questions about King's death. Many people agreed with a black minister who told the *Tri-State Defender*: "This fellow was a link in a well planned plot." Investigating conspiracy theories and Ray's guilt or innocence became an industry in itself.

Dr. Benjamin Mays, preaching at King's funeral in Atlanta, said the killer knew that many people wanted King dead and that various whites created the poisoned climate that led to his death. A congressional investigating committee later documented that racist businessmen in the St. Louis area had put out a $50,000 bounty to kill King, and that James Earl Ray surely knew about it. The U.S. House Select Committee on Assassinations in 1977 concluded that Ray pulled the trigger, but he might have been part of a larger conspiracy of racists and extreme anti-Communists.

The mass media also revealed that the FBI had conducted a concerted "counterintelligence" campaign called COINTELPRO to destroy King, and that U.S. Military Intelligence and even the CIA had long conducted surveillance on King and his family. In 1976, the Memphis news media revealed that MPD officials had conducted widespread surveillance on King as well as local movement participants. The MPD burned its surveillance files before the public could see them. None of this ever inspired any confidence in the authorities. In a civil trial in December 1999, twelve

Memphis jurors, six black and six white, heard a wrongful death lawsuit by the King family and reached a verdict that government agencies and private individuals had been involved in a conspiracy to kill Martin Luther King.

In April 1968, many civil rights supporters also asked not just who killed King but what killed him. They blamed racist rabble-rousers such as George Wallace; the Republican "Southern Strategy" of splitting whites from blacks by playing on white racial fears; and they blamed anti-communism, racism, and the violence of the Vietnam War as responsible for engendering a climate of hate that killed King.

Most white Memphians rejected such analyses, or any responsibility for what had happened. "It obviously was not done by a citizen of this city, so there is no reason for us to feel any personal guilt," one white Memphian wrote to the *Commercial Appeal*. Over the years, King had been beaten, stoned, stabbed, bombed, jailed, and condemned by the highest officials in the land. Why should white Memphians accept any blame for his death? Lawson said this "moral blindness" was a "built-in apparatus . . . that tends to insulate us from reality." But black scholar C. Eric Lincoln, raised in Memphis, said the Mississippi Delta provided a climate especially conducive to his murder, going back to the era of slavery. "Memphis was certainly not ready for Martin Luther King or anybody who had King's style or had King's philosophy . . . [and] black life has always been very cheap in Memphis." Lincoln observed that many whites expressed shock when reporters "came down here because 'a nigger's been killed.' Who was Martin Luther King? I mean, 'he's just another nigger.'"

As in life, King in death remained a polarizing figure in Memphis. On Friday, April 5, a rumor spread that someone planned to blow up Memphis State, so authorities called off the weekend's fabled parade and crowning of the Memphis Cotton Carnival's king and queen—an event that romanticized slavery and the virtues of the plantation—thinking it would incite black rebellion. One white woman complained, "All this to-do over King's death—niggers going wild—the curfew and all—are upsetting my schedule." Many white Memphians militarized their households. A group of white businessmen having lunch after King's death decided to arm themselves, one of them vowing to buy a shotgun so that "if they come through my door I'll be prepared to mow them down."

Racists did not guard their comments, assuming that anyone white must have thought the same way they did. Kathy Roop, a young white Southwestern College student who had supported the strike by marching and fasting, was shocked when she heard whites at her local grocery store exulting about King's death. A few white strike supporters began to write down such comments and put them in a file. They found that it was not unusual for white businessmen, professional people, teachers, or workers to refer to King as "Martin Lucifer" or "Martin Luther Coon." Many whites questioned why someone hadn't killed King sooner, and callers sarcastically asked radio stations to play a popular tune, "Bye, Bye, Blackbird." A white insurance agent could not believe the attitude of his coworkers, who said they were glad King had been shot. He worried that bad publicity about Memphis would stop northern investments and hurt the city's business climate.

When Mayor Loeb spoke at the Memphis Sertoma Club the next week, he unconsciously reinforced an idea common in white business circles: "Each of us' heart and prayers are with Mrs. King and the King family. Certainly we wish the incident had happened elsewhere—if it had to happen." Fortunately, he continued on, "Each of us knows that violence begets nothing but trouble for everyone, and each of us sincerely wishes that it hadn't happened and regrets that this thing did happen." A more typical, or perhaps more frank, view came from a white man who said, "King brought violence everywhere. I'm sorry it happened in Memphis, but I'm not sorry it happened."

Some whites made crude and vulgar comments about King even in the presence of blacks. One black teenager first heard about King's death while purchasing equipment at Radio Shack, where a white man "laughed and laughed" when the news came over the radio. Among some white teenagers, the "gross joke" became a fad. "What's black and slower than a speeding bullet?" went one of them. "Do you know why they're looking so hard for the killer of Dr. King? They want to make him president," went another. "Why do the colored people want to send their children to school?

So they can learn to read and 'riot.'" Most uncaring of all, "I hear there's to be a Spider march in Memphis tomorrow. What's a Spider march? It's going to be led by a Black widow!"

An ugly atmosphere pervaded many white schools. When a student teacher distributed *My Weekly Reader*, with a front-page picture of Dr. King, one child scratched out King's face, and most of the other children quickly followed suit. The attitude of a white principal at a black school seemed just as twisted. "How am I going to teach law and order [to children] when they let these damn niggers tear up these cities?" he complained. In a survey of 173 Memphis State University students in three classes, 61 percent disapproved of the killing but 20 percent of the students approved of it, and 19 percent didn't care one way or the other. Sentiments were worse at all-white secondary schools.

Assorted evangelical, anti-union, and segregationist organizations had long depicted the civil rights movement and King as Communist-inspired, and this "political debasement" made it difficult for many whites to separate fantasy from reality concerning King's death, a communications scholar wrote. One man wrote a letter to the *Commercial Appeal* calling King "the biggest Communist in the nation." A well-educated white housewife locked herself and her children inside the house on Thursday night and asked a friend, "Don't you think this is all part of a Communist conspiracy?" Blacks had been happy until "King with his Communist background came in and stirred them all up," said a white suburban housewife, and the Negro was "so stupid he is easy to dupe." A white woman asked in a church discussion, "In the Negro movement, where does Christianity stop and Communism start?" Some claimed Communists had killed King to gain sympathy for the black cause, and a physician blamed his death on a northern–Jewish–Communist conspiracy to destroy the country. Many years later, black attorney and judge Otis Higgs said the pervasive white identification of King with Communism in 1968 dumbfounded him.

With King dead, other civil rights leaders became targets for white animosity. One white Episcopal priest voiced a widespread suspicion about Lawson, who "has been to Russia, studied Communism, but the local newspaper won't print it." Mothers in a school discussion club debated whether Lawson "was organizing a communist revolution." One woman suggested that Ralph Abernathy had King killed so he could take over SCLC; a city fireman said, "Abernathy will never make it to Washington, he'll get his on the way." Another said that Mrs. King would also be killed if she stepped into Movement leadership.

Racist reactions to King's death pervaded the Mississippi Delta. One white store owner in Louisiana recalled various white customers taking him by the arm and saying, "Way to go, fella, way to go," when they heard he was from Memphis. In Hope, Arkansas, a local resident cautioned a motorcyclist on his way to Memphis, "Got a gun?" A white Mississippian, who himself had moved up from sharecropping to prosperity through union membership, said that the "crazy nigger" King had helped blacks take over the unions and should have been killed much earlier.

Many whites verbally attacked black workers and unions, some saying that garbage workers did not deserve higher wages or benefits and that the Poor People's Campaign's demands for expanded social programs discriminated against whites. "I just can't stand feeding lazy people," a white teacher said. "I have been poor all my life, and I have had to work. Why can't they work and take care of their own families and own problems as I have done?" complained a white woman supervisor at a laundry company. One Southwestern College professor said one of his white neighbors told him racial problems could never be solved because, "No matter what else there is, you just can't overlook that black skin."

IN THIS POISONOUS and divided racial climate, union and civil rights organizers struggled to get the Memphis movement back on track. Jerry Wurf flew into town from Washington on Friday, April 5, determined to hold King's march and to get a favorable settlement for the sanitation workers. The costs of losing this strike were now far too great even to contemplate. "You couldn't kill King and then destroy the union," he said. "That would have been too much. That would have been too much for Loeb, which that fool couldn't understand. Do you understand what could have happened to that city had they destroyed the union?"

After King's death on Thursday night, Lawson called Bayard Rustin in

New York, asking for help. Rustin, with whom Lawson had consulted throughout the strike, left for Memphis the next morning, but federal agents diverted his plane to Washington, DC. President Johnson demanded his counsel and that of other civil rights leaders in formulating a federal response to King's death. Rustin and Norman Hill, his assistant from the A. Philip Randolph Institute, got to Memphis that afternoon, as Judge McRae ruled that the April 8 march could go forward, under tight police controls.

On Saturday, Rustin and Lawson convened a twenty-person steering committee to map out details for the march, including members of The Invaders, AFSCME, the NAACP, and church leaders. Rustin, Lawson, and Ralph Jackson led training sessions in nonviolence for marshals, and Rustin told the *New York Times*: "Dr. King understood that political and social justice cannot exist without economic justice," and that the Memphis movement now represented the things King had championed. He called it a "totally new stage" of the civil rights movement, and it all hinged on a successful march. Lawson said of Rustin: "In a very real way, he was my executive director for the march."

King's death galvanized unprecedented national union support for a local strike. Back in New York, King's old union allies, such as Victor Gotbaum of AFSCME District Council 37, Cleveland Robinson and Leon Davis of UAW District 65, Moe Foner and others in Local 1199 of the Hospital Workers Union, Albert Shanker of the American Federation of Teachers, and other union leaders pledged to bring planeloads of demonstrators. Word immediately went out from AFSCME that unionists, civil rights activists, clergy, academics, students, and other "people of good will" should come to Memphis to make King's planned April 8 march a success, and union advocates in Detroit, Chicago, St. Louis, Cairo (Illinois), and elsewhere vowed to go to Memphis.

Infusions of funds from labor and civil rights supporters, particularly unions, gave Local 1733 renewed strength to hold out for a long time to come. George Meany publicly announced his $20,000 donation to support the strike and said that the AFL-CIO's special fund-raising committee had pledged to raise more support as long as necessary. Rustin made an appeal on public television that produced nearly $100,000 in donations, and

AFSCME locals and councils across the country established "Memphis, USA" committees to raise funds. The International Longshoremen and Warehousemen's Union pledged more funds, and the Field Foundation donated $30,000.

The Memphis labor movement also responded to the crisis, with the 35,000-member Memphis Labor Council calling on Loeb to resign. Tommy Powell told the press, "I feel that Henry Loeb is the cause of the national strife we've had in the last 24 hours because of his anti-union and racist attitude." Even the Memphis Building Trades Council finally endorsed the strike. As it had in Selma, tragedy and death stiffened the resolve of civil rights movement and labor supporters everywhere.

The most powerful expression of determination to prevail came from the Memphis sanitation workers themselves, however. When they held their noon meeting on Friday at the United Rubber Workers union hall, L. C. Reed recalled, "Ralph Jackson asked us after the tragedy did happen, were we still willing to stick together, and we all agreed that we was and we wasn't going to stop marching." The police did not want to allow it, but the workers vowed the police would have to arrest them to stop their marches. That afternoon, they marched. Worker self-action remained the key to winning the strike, Reed's wife said. "Mens are mens these days no matter what color they are."

Women were women, too. On Saturday, thirty members of Alpha Kappa Alpha, Coretta Scott King's sorority, marched to city hall from the Lorraine Motel. One lone man—a white auditor named Richard Pullen, who had come down from New York—walked with them. Wearing a suit, a bow tie, and closely cropped hair, he said he hoped to correct the misconception that whites taking part in the civil rights movement were all "beatniks" or "hippies."

Although the court injunction against the Monday march had been lifted, behind the scenes the police still argued that they could not fully protect marchers. Said Lawson, "We made it clear that none of that really mattered, that the central fact was that we were engaged in a struggle for the justice of these men, and that struggle would be paramount." Lawson told Lux and Holloman that on Monday, "We were stepping off and they would simply have to arrest everybody" if they wanted to stop them. Fire and Police Director Claude Armour had prevented violence during the early civil rights movement in Memphis, said Lawson, and police could do it again if they cared to. "Wherever you've had a law enforcement officer who took a fairly strong stand, very rarely did you get violence against the movement. And one of the best illustrations of this would be Memphis."

Nonetheless, many people feared another mass march would produce a disaster of unprecedented proportions. The City Council met all day Friday, trying to find a way to mollify an angry black community. It unanimously sent a resolution of sympathy to Coretta Scott King and underwrote half of a $50,000 fund that businessman Ned Cook had pledged to raise as a reward for any information leading to the arrest of King's killer. The *Commercial Appeal* and the Scripps-Howard Corporation each put up $25,000—for a total of $100,000. An anonymous donor also made an offer of $25,000 to pay the dues of workers to AFSCME as a way to end the strike. Jerry Wurf rejected it out of hand as "more than outrageous, it's laughable." If AFSCME accepted the offer, the city would not have to accept dues checkoff, and it would prove that all the union cared about was money. "We are not going through all this for some union dues but for some recognition and dignity for these men," said Wurf.

The City Council that afternoon also unanimously adopted a resolution by Lewis Donelson requiring city government to provide "full and equal job and promotional opportunities for all of its citizens." The council eliminated civil service tests that blocked less-educated African Americans from getting white-collar jobs and called for a plan to "substantially increase" minority employment and promotion in all administrative divisions of the city. Blacks welcomed this affirmative-action plan, but it did nothing to address the questions at hand: union recognition and dues checkoff. Memphis city government still followed a pattern criticized that very weekend by Illinois Governor Otto Kerner, who blamed riots on white politicians who wouldn't even "take the first step" to resolve their root causes.

But somebody finally took action to break the deadlock in Memphis: President Lyndon Baines Johnson. At 11 AM on Friday, President Johnson asked Undersecretary of Labor James Reynolds why the Labor Department had not already resolved this strike. Reynolds explained that the department did not involve itself in municipal affairs unless invited by local people. "I don't care whether you are asked to do it," Johnson told him. "I am telling you I want you to go down there." Call the governor, tell everyone the president has sent you, Johnson said, and settle the strike. As Reynolds flew out to Memphis, he could see smoke billowing over a burning capital, which would suffer ten deaths and 711 fires. Washington had not looked like this since the British nearly burned it down in 1814.

Front-page newspaper pictures and vivid television documentation showed what looked like the bombings of World War II in places such as Chicago and Washington. By comparison, said a *Commercial Appeal* headline, "National Guardsmen Find Memphis to Be the Place of Good Abode." As Undersecretary Reynolds walked through downtown Memphis on Saturday morning, however, it did not look like a "place of good abode." He observed half-track tanks, National Guardsmen with rifles drawn, and city police (some in civilian clothes) brandishing pistols. Armed guards greeted him outside city hall, on the stairs to the mayor's office, and inside the mayor's office. Reynolds assured the press, "I don't come here as a meddling federal bureaucrat who has all the answers." He expressed the "grave concern" of the president, who wanted to settle "this relatively small labor dispute."

But Reynolds recalled that when he asked Mayor Loeb just what the problem was, Loeb said it was, "We are not ever going to recognize this union. . . . I committed myself in the election that this city would never recognize this union . . . [and] we are not going to do it." Furthermore, the city had spent all its spare money on the new city hall, and it could not afford it.

Aghast at the mayor's unbending attitude, Reynolds sought out Frank Miles, who had been assigned by the City Council to mediate. The two men, who had each worked for business as well as for labor, set to work meeting with various people and trying to restart some semblance of the negotiations that had broken off on March 27. Reynolds realized that negotiations could not start until after the April 8 march and King's funeral on April 9; he thought a conflict in negotiations at that point might touch off a riot. After all, riots still raged out of control in Chicago, Kansas City, Baltimore, and other major cities.

Meanwhile, seventy-five or eighty volunteers, equally divided between blacks and whites, worked out of the Memphis Board of Education building all day Saturday to spread the word by phone and leaflets of a rally for racial reconciliation on Sunday. John T. Fisher, an energetic young white car dealer active in the Chamber of Commerce, lived next door to Loeb and did not support unionization, but he wanted to create a bridge between the white and black communities. To do it, he started a group called "Memphis Cares," and he asked the mayor and Frank Holloman for a permit for the planned gathering. They wouldn't give it, so he went ahead without one.

Many blacks looked askance at this event. Fisher said it should take no position on the strike, nor should it memorialize King, because he didn't want to alienate "moderate" whites. Recalled Maxine Smith, "Memphis came out with a whole lot of hulla-baloo—Memphis cares, you know. . . . It lasted the weekend, maybe. I have no faith in the powers that be in Memphis. We'll only get, in every instance, what we're strong enough to take." Ralph Jackson said the event was simply an attempt by whites to "save face." When rumors spread that Loeb would attend, James Lawson called Fisher and said, "Look, that destroys it for the black community." Fisher assured him that Loeb would not be there, and he made sure he wasn't.

Meanwhile, AFSCME sent out teams of workers to canvass the community, and black ministers pulled together their congregations to channel black-community rage into nonviolent action. Bayard Rustin and James Lawson went ahead with their plan to produce the biggest protest and interracial demonstration held in the South since Selma.

PALM SUNDAY, TYPICALLY a time of joy in Christian churches, marks the entry of Jesus into Jerusalem and Holy Week, a time for remembering the "passion" and then the resurrection of Jesus. On this Palm Sunday, April 7, many people inevitably compared King's death to the crucifixion, but they wondered how there could be a resurrection. Dean William Dimmick of St. Mary's Episcopal Cathedral thought he saw one coming. In his Sunday sermon, distributed in print, he compared King to Jesus as a "messenger of peace" whose message "may speak in death even more powerfully than in life," calling for "love, justice and brotherhood." He asked people to look at their own sins and take responsibility for bringing about change. One female Episcopalian resented any implication of guilt, saying, "Well, I may be a bigot, but I'll be *damned* if I'll pray for Martin Luther King's soul!"

The Sunday *Commercial Appeal* editorial called on people to "Make This [A] Prayerful Day," and those who hated King at least felt largely compelled to keep it to themselves. The liberal side of white Christianity began to be seen in Memphis for almost the first time. Methodists, Lutherans, Baptists, Presbyterians, and the Catholic diocese initiated discussions of urban issues. Memphis Unitarians read excerpts from King's speech in 1966 urging Unitarians to "be maladjusted" to injustice, and they wrote a group letter to Mayor Loeb, asking him to settle the strike. "The quiet, complacent middle class could have averted this tragedy by listening to our consciences and speaking out loud and clear for human brotherhood," it said. During Sunday services, the most segregated hour of the week, most white ministers at least trod lightly over issues relating to King's death rather than stir up more racial animosity.

Complaints about this apparent turn toward moderation in the religious community flooded the Sunday newspaper. Some Catholics indicted "priests and nuns taking part in street demonstrations" and giving donations to strikers. Other people attacked Rabbi Wax for upbraiding the mayor, and one writer indicted Lawson as "a great comfort to our enemies. . . . Treason is treason and should be treated as such." One writer said King's death "supplies the communist cause with exactly what it needs at this time: a martyr." Another expressed the common belief that the hypocrite King preached nonviolence, "but he just goes around causing trouble and then running away." Subsequently, others complained that workers could cure their own poverty if they would only work harder, and that government officials should not give in to the pressure of riots.

Many thought white ministers sympathetic to the strikers had taken leave of their senses, but Dean Dimmick dismissed criticism of his role in leading Friday's ministerial march. Jesus was crucified on a garbage heap between two thieves, he said, so, "If the cross, and the reconciling love of Jesus Christ has no business on the street, then I really don't know where its main business is." A split in white racial thinking emerged, giving some white citizens the courage to write to the newspapers and criticize white racism. A continuing white backlash against activist ministers took its toll, however: Brooks Ramsey, a white Baptist born and raised in Memphis, was threatened for his sympathy for King and called a Communist until he finally left the ministry. Reverend Aldridge left Memphis for a time, and other white, racially liberal religious activists suffered ostracism, threatening phone calls, and nasty letters. Malcolm Blackburn, the strongest and most consistent white minister in support of the strike, after briefly joining the AFSCME staff, ultimately left Memphis.

In the black churches, Palm Sunday produced an extraordinary outpouring of religious feeling fused with anger, sorrow, disgust, and righteous indignation. Most black people saw King, as he saw himself, as a Good Samaritan willing to sacrifice for the betterment of the whole human race. The Memphis movement scarcely needed to organize protests that weekend: black churches of every denomination held their own demonstrations of preaching, singing, and praying for deliverance from racism, war, poverty, and violence. From the pulpit of Lawson's Centenary United Methodist Church, James Bevel spoke of Jeremiah in the Bible, who had also lived in a period when men used murder and other crimes to suppress justice. The spirit of King could not be killed with bullets, said Bevel, because he had already loosed the truths of righteousness and brotherhood upon the land. He said King's name remained synonymous with hope, which could not be killed by any man.

African Americans struggled, however, over whether to adopt the Christian attitude of forgiveness or one of retribution. For many black youth, King's death turned their hopes for a better world into rage. They quickly recalled various racial injustices that they and members of their families had suffered. Charles Warren felt ashamed, as if King's death had been his fault. He decided, "The only thing left to do was to discard non-violence and put violence to work." In a classroom writing exercise at Hamilton High, where students had experienced police violence on March 28, seventeen-year-old Frankie Gross wrote, "You could see and feel the hate in the Negro community after the assassination. . . . People took guns to work the next day just waiting for any white person to do anything wrong. There was burning and looting everywhere." Powerfully affected by the images he saw on television of chaos across the country's urban landscape, he wrote, "I guess I agreed with Stokely Carmichael's philosophy of burning at first, and I wondered why Negroes hadn't burned down more than they had."

King's death shook what little faith black youth had in the possibility of working with whites. Calvin Dickerson questioned whether whites expressing concern about King's death "are sincere or just trying to console the Negro to prevent riots." He concluded, "They are only trying to fool the Negro." Alice Wright wrote, "I was so hurt when I heard about Dr. King's death, that I couldn't stand the sight of a white person. I didn't realize that I could hate anyone that much until the night Dr. King was assassinated." Milton Parson wrote, "I wanted to go out and do as much damage to the white community as I possibly could."

Police violence on April 4 and over the weekend—although not as bad as on March 28—further embittered African Americans. One black woman saw a young black boy beaten by the police in front of her home because he was out after curfew. Her husband tried to explain from the safety of his porch that the boy worked for him as a construction laborer, but the police continued the beating and then nearly attacked her husband. Police threatened grade-school children in housing projects, and the trauma of police and military violence lingered long past the weekend. In a workshop on racism a month later, a black mother asked what she could do "to stop her children from getting hysterical every time they see uniformed men with guns, particularly with fixed bayonets." A workshop participant said, "No one had an answer" to her question.

IN THE MIDST of destabilizing racial violence, a groundswell of support for racial reconciliation emerged when nearly 9,000 people, about 40 percent of them black, turned out at Crump Stadium on Palm Sunday afternoon. Many were still wearing their church clothes. As people filed into the stadium, the "Memphis Cares" organizers asked them to sign a pledge to build a city where people could "trust one another, respect one another and respond to the needs of one another." The fact that only about a dozen police officers attended testified to the nonthreatening character of the event. Black and white businessmen, bishops, educators, politicians, ministers, and labor and civil activists sang "The Star-Spangled Banner" together, many with tears in their eyes. O. Z. Evers, long a supporter of the sanitation workers, chaired the event. The "Memphis Cares" Committee called for a statue to be built in Overton Park in memory of King and for a part of the freeway to be named after him.

The supposedly incendiary Zeke Bell had been asked to give the invocation, but apparently he couldn't bear to do it and did not show up. Mary Collier, a black woman who worked in a white-collar job at Buckman Laboratories, and various others, called for individuals to go beyond race and class to commit themselves to make a better world, but said nothing about King or the strike. Tommy Powell went outside the guidelines for the day's event, demanding an immediate strike settlement, and Ben Hooks went further, by excoriating the city's leadership so sharply that Fisher said he "turned my stomach inside out." Many disgruntled whites began to leave. Advertising man Tom O'Ryan then came to the podium and invoked his Irish immigrant family's assimilation, saying, "America is the greatest country in the world." As he lectured blacks that they should "educate and uplift themselves," as had his forefathers, many of them got up and left.

Fisher's hopes for reconciliation dimmed further when James Lawson, considered by so many whites as a frightful subversive, began to speak. True to his belief in not counting anyone out, Lawson did not boycott the event. Instead, he chose to say what most whites did not want to hear. His voice ringing out over the loudspeakers, Lawson called King's death "God's judgment on you and me and upon our city and our land that it is already too late." The city and the nation could become "nothing more than a roost for vultures and a smoldering heap of debris"—if it did not repent. But, "Repentance is not being concerned whether or not business moves away from Memphis. Repentance is not being concerned whether or not people outside of our city will have a good feeling about us. How can anyone have a good feeling about Memphis when one of the finest sons of this world of ours was shot down in her streets?"

These were just the kinds of statements Fisher had hoped to avoid, but Lawson pressed on: "Memphis will be known for a long time as the place where Martin Luther King was crucified. Yes, crucified. We have witnessed a crucifixion here in Memphis." The only way to atone for such a sin, he said, was by "a determination to work for transformations, real change, a move away from racism to genuine brotherhood." Lawson said that hope for reconciliation and a brighter future could only happen if whites committed to significantly changing themselves and their world.

Whites rarely heard the kind of prophetic, righteous rhetoric that Lawson let loose on April 7. A few days later, Fisher told the Memphis Rotary Club that business leaders in the room had the power to bring about change, whereas "the only power that Jim Lawson has is to disrupt." He had been greatly upset by comments made by Hooks and Lawson at "Memphis Cares," but upon reflection, Fisher came to realize that platitudes about racial harmony would do nothing to change Memphis. He called on businessmen to see King's death as a wake-up call, and a few of them began to do just that. Fisher, Ned Cook, and numerous others in the white establishment later contributed to numerous civic efforts to share more power with African Americans, and Lawson gave them credit for allowing their racial views to be significantly transformed by the events of 1968.

For his part, Fisher came to realize that blacks had no obligation to listen to whites who did nothing more than talk: "If I want a place to walk in the world, then I had better get around to creating that place."

ON MONDAY, APRIL 8, the city braced for a national march in Memphis, even while that city—as well as Nashville, Raleigh, Baltimore, Cincinnati, Pittsburgh, Chicago, and many others—remained under curfew and military occupation. The FBI tracked people coming into Memphis from all around the nation. Twelve charter flights brought at least 1,200 people, and many more came by bus, train, and automobile, including some 350 AFSCME workers and 250 members of the American Federation of Teachers from New York City. Scores of well-known public figures—such as Bill

Cosby, Robert Culp, Sammy Davis, Dr. Benjamin Spock, Harry Belafonte, Percy Sutton (Manhattan borough president)—and religious, political, and union leaders appeared. Many of them went the next day to King's funeral in Atlanta.

By contrast to the situation at the "Memphis Cares" event, police and military authorities massed their forces for the April 8 march. Undercover police and FBI agents, including Marrell ("Max") McCullough, supplemented thousands of uniformed police and members of the military. The Memphis Police Department, after meeting with representatives of the National Guard, Tennessee Highway Patrol, and the sheriff's and mayor's offices, agreed to keep all police officers out of sight in order not to provoke trouble. Instead, 1,500 National Guardsmen out of the 5,000 stationed in Memphis patrolled downtown streets. Lieutenant Arkin of the MPD reported that "talk was rampant" that blacks would loot and riot at the end of the downtown march or else after King's funeral in Atlanta, scheduled for the next day. A police informant claimed that "militant young Negroes" were telling people to store up water for emergency conditions during an urban rebellion.

Some demonstrators braced themselves for possible violence. Before leaving for the march, Episcopal chaplain Ted Hoover gave his will to his secretary in case he didn't come back. Republican lawyer and City Councilman Jerred Blanchard returned to Memphis in the middle of the night after a business trip and stayed up the rest of the night sipping whiskey. Some of his friends had already stopped speaking to him, and many Republicans swore they would never vote for him again because he had tried to resolve the strike. He marveled at his predicament. "I really am a right-wing Republican. I have never liked labor unions," said Blanchard, yet he believed in civil liberties and human rights. Early that morning, Blanchard went to the Clayborn Temple parking lot and lined up in the front row of the march. If someone had told him earlier that he would participate in a civil rights march, "I would have told you that you were crazy."

On a gray, rain-threatening, foreboding day, thousands of marchers gathered, just as they had on March 28, but the feeling in the crowd was much different. Myra Dreifus, the wife of a downtown jeweler, ran a charitable school lunch program that fed impoverished black children for whom school authorities had neglected to get available federal funds. She and her son-in-law from Boston waited an hour and a half for the march to start. Surrounded by a sea of black faces, she felt completely comfortable. March organizers had everything in hand: "We were carefully monitored, so many people to each line." Someone gave her a flyer reading, "HAVE YOU STOPPED TAKING the *Commercial Appeal* and the Memphis *Press-Scimitar*? WHY NOT?" The flyer ticked off the way the newspapers unfairly covered the strike, didn't cover black news or hire blacks, disproportionately covered black crimes, carried "Hambone" cartoons, and ran segregated ads. It read, "They even segregate Negroes in death notices!"

Bayard Rustin's tactical skills prevailed. He, Lawson, and SCLC organizers had apprised the police and the National Guard of all their plans, had set up mobile toilets, and had set aside a place for the media to film the speakers. Workers stayed up all night building a ten-foot-high platform and setting up sound equipment. Rustin walked the march route in advance, step by step, looking for trouble spots, and he ordered semi-trailers parked in certain areas to funnel marchers between them so that no one could leave the march and break store windows. COME passed out flyers with a message from Lawson instructing marchers to walk with heads held high, to follow the marshals' instructions, to keep moving if any disturbance occurred, and to remember their purpose:

> Today we honor Dr. King for the great work he did for all people and particularly for his great love and sacrifice for us. How best can we honor him now? The answer is simply: we honor him by making sure that the Sanitation Workers win their rights non-violently.... Each of you is on trial today. Not only Americans, but people from all over the world will be watching you on TV today. Therefore be considerate, polite and carry yourself with dignity.

Thousands of marchers carried signs that read, "Honor King: End Racism," "Union Justice Now," or, simply, "I <u>Am</u> A Man." John Henry

Ferguson was there with his Invaders jacket but also an orange armband. "Keep it quiet, down to a limited number of people across, and don't let anyone break the line or carry anything as a weapon," he instructed other marshals. Fog delayed a private plane sent to Atlanta for Mrs. King by New York Governor Nelson Rockefeller, so Harry Belafonte chartered a private jet in Atlanta and brought her and three of her children to Memphis. Marchers didn't wait; they went ahead more or less as planned at 11:16 AM. They walked through black neighborhoods, passing shotgun shacks and beauty parlors, past Beale Street's closed-up pawnshops and liquor stores, as National Guardsmen secured the York Arms gun dealership to make sure no one tried to loot it for weapons, as had happened on March 28.

Before the marchers got into the main commercial district, they halted for twenty minutes as motorcycle police escorted Mrs. King into the downtown from the airport. Ferguson and other Invaders held hands to form a protective chain for her as she and her children, escorted by Harry Belafonte and Ralph Abernathy, joined the march. The mass of people began to move forward again down Main Street, past department stores closed for the day, with lootable goods taken out of the windows and a few with signs honoring King. Ferguson said that Mrs. King's entry into the march renewed people's sense of pride, courage, and respect for the peaceful principles for which the Movement stood. "It's beautiful," he summarized to a newsman.

During the last five weeks, police had repeatedly arrested and harassed him, and Ferguson said nonviolence didn't fit his twenty-year-old temperament. "I would much rather be burning than marching . . . like I say, I don't feel we're going to get too far with peaceful marches," he told a reporter. Yet here he was, telling anyone with a cigarette to put it out. Marshals even told people not to chew gum because it was not dignified, and they complied. King had said that black youth attracted to Black Power and armed self-defense could also be brought into the nonviolent movement, and on this day it proved to be true.

Police banned all traffic in the area of the march. Holloman and Lux, peering down side streets and looking at the tops of buildings for possible snipers, walked ahead of Mrs. King, who linked arms with Abernathy on one side and three of her children—Martin III, Yolanda, and Dexter—linked to Belafonte on the other. A phone caller had threatened Lawson in the middle of the night, promising that when he reached Main Street, "You'll be cut down." Ignoring the threat, Lawson led off the march from Clayborn Temple, and he continued to march up front with UAW President Walter Reuther and Mrs. King after she arrived.

Police officers stayed largely out of sight, but National Guardsmen lined the streets, perched on M-48 tanks and on trucks, their bayonets mounted on unloaded rifles. Two helicopters circled overhead. Police ordered people to stay off the roofs and not to open windows. "The most shocking sight was the helmeted, bayonet carrying State Guard standing 'at ease,' guns in hand, with artillery and tanks behind them at most intersections," wrote Myra Dreifus. Marchers moved silently down the streets in lines of eight, "proudly and reverently," arms linked. "The complete silence of the thousands in our armed city of State Guard was eerie, impressive, and quite unbelievable in the 'land of the free, and the home of the brave'—America, Our America. I felt as if the marchers were obedient prisoners in the quiet, closed-up city, so heavily guarded."

Police counted 19,000 marchers, and Rustin estimated 42,000, streaming down Main Street. Many, many more Memphians turned out than had come from out of town. "I never have marched for any cause before," seventy-year-old W. M. Horton told a reporter. He was an older black man who followed the agricultural harvest, making money however and wherever he could. His first political act had been donating $5 to the sanitation workers' strike. "I guess I always favored Dr. King's program and the things he worked for but I was around a long time before anybody worked for the colored people. When all of this business of marches and demonstrations started, I just let the young ones hold up my end." But, no more. "I got friends who's suffering over" the strike, he said. "It ought to be settled. I just, well, I'm here for those reasons and lots more."

This march was perfectly disciplined: no talking, no smoking, and completely silent. Almost the only sound came from the soles of shoes meeting the sidewalk. As they silently merged into the city hall plaza, some people sat on concrete railings or patches of grass; thousands of others stood for hours more, but they remained mostly silent, somber, and vigilant. The marchers "gave Dr. King what he came here for and what was his last wish: a truly nonviolent march," said Rustin.

Memphis on April 8 also represented the coalition King had always sought to build. AFSCME's delegation from New York and the workers from Memphis provided a strong, organized, disciplined group, as did delegations from more than a dozen other international unions. UAW President Walter Reuther and his wife May, Donald Slaiman of the AFL-CIO civil rights committee, international union presidents and local labor leaders, Teamsters truck drivers, Local 1199 Hospital Workers, RWDSU retail, distributive, and department-store workers, AFSCME government workers, UE and IUE farm equipment and electrical workers, UFWA furniture workers, USWA steelworkers, AFT and NEA teachers, American Screen Actors' Guild members, NMU and ILWU maritime workers, United Rubber Workers, and AFL-CIO department heads came from New York, Washington, DC, the Northeast, the Midwest, and other parts of the country. "The town was full of labor people," said Bill Ross.

A full array of religious and political leaders also participated, including rabbis, Catholic and Episcopal bishops, Baptists, Methodists, and a wide array of other religious denominations. Academic and black community activists, national and local, marched arm in arm through the streets and quietly joined forces at the rally. King in life had been the one black leader who could bring together such an interracial alliance of labor, religious, middle-class, and working-class people, and he succeeded at it brilliantly on this day. Marchers in Memphis demonstrated the possibility of a different America.

Rosa Parks sat on the platform with actor Ossie Davis, who opened the ceremonies, and Samuel "Billy" Kyles led people in singing, "Lord, Hold My Hand While I Run This Race." Walter Reuther declared, "Mayor Loeb will somehow be dragged into the twentieth century," and he gave the strikers a $50,000 check from the UAW. He had more than doubled the AFL-CIO's contribution, and there would be more coming if necessary. The problem wasn't money, he said: "We have a nation poor in spirit—

that's where our poverty is." Maybe so, but T. O. Jones adroitly moved in and plucked the check from his hands.

Reuther's check would only cover the costs of the strike for one week, but his gesture meant much more in the eyes of the white establishment, Wurf said. Reuther and King had joined forces in Montgomery, in Detroit, at the 1963 March on Washington, and in Chicago. Reuther remained arguably the most powerful and well-funded social democrat in the country. His presence "create[d] the idea that this was for real," said Wurf, who thought it a crime that local white UAW members in Memphis welcomed Reuther to town but did not join the march.

At the rally, Wurf declared that AFSCME would support the strikers to the end: "Until we have justice and decency and morality, we will not go back to work." Harry Belafonte angrily decried the "bestiality and decay of the white world," going back to genocide against the Indians. James Lawson demanded that the city pull troops out of the black community. "We aren't killing anyone," he said, and "if the curfew doesn't end . . . we're going to break it." Ralph Jackson, Dr. Benjamin Spock, Ben Hooks, Bishop Joseph Durick, James Bevel, and others rededicated the Movement to King's principles. Reverend Ralph Abernathy tried to invoke the power of King's rhetoric, damning the death of black men in Vietnam, denouncing the poverty perpetuated by the capitalist system, demanding "a land free of joblessness where every American citizen that can work can have a job." Many may have felt skeptical about his declaration that God had chosen him to follow King's work, but Jesse Jackson, Andrew Young, Lawson, and other SCLC staff members warmly gathered around and embraced Abernathy as he took up SCLC's mantle of leadership.

The speeches went on at length, as people waited patiently for Coretta Scott King, the person they most wanted to hear. Finally, she stood at the podium—composed, restrained, dressed in black. She spoke quietly, in personal terms, about the love she and her children held for King, of his love for them, and of her family's desire to carry on his work. She challenged the crowd to go on from that day as if King's death were a crucifixion leading toward a time of resurrection that would "make all people truly free and to make every person feel that he is a human being. His campaign for the poor must go on." She spoke, too, of Montgomery and the years in between.

Only in conclusion did her voice break, as she said, "But then I ask the question: how many men must die before we can really have a free and true and peaceful society? How long will it take? If we can catch the spirit, and the true meaning of this experience, I believe that this nation can be transformed into a society of love, of justice, peace, and brotherhood where all men can really be brothers."

Skeptics might have scoffed at such idealistic sentiments, but to Luella Cook, a domestic worker in the audience that day, they meant a great deal. She said Coretta King's courage and composure saved Memphis: "If Mrs. King had cried a single tear, this whole city would have give way."

King's death had engendered feelings of extreme bitterness and even hate in Alice Wright, a Hamilton High School student and granddaughter of a striking sanitation worker. After seeing Mrs. King on television following King's death, however, she decided to spend April 8 marching. "I got very tired but I felt that if a person could give up his life to help you, the least you could do was to show that you appreciated what he had done."

Ernestine Johnson, also from Hamilton High, on April 4 had felt "too stunned to cry. Everything left me. I had no feelings at all." Then she became "very bitter and upset"—as she had when an assassin had killed President Kennedy—and she cried herself to sleep. She thought she had given up hope, but on April 8, she marched. As she listened to King's "courageous wife speak, seeing how she controlled her emotions, I got the courage to go on with life and struggle for the best in life [and] to make something of myself."

Milton Parson, age seventeen, said the mass march also stilled his fury at the loss of King. Instead of burning, "Yes, I marched. All the while that I was marching there was a solemn feeling that all the people in the march wanted to help make this city, and our country, a place where there should be no fear that a person would be shot down in the prime of his life doing something that they believe was right."

As it neared the 5 PM curfew, the program ended and thousands of marchers quietly left the downtown. At least nineteen FBI agents had observed the march, but they found no violence to report. The crime rate dropped drastically that day, and the only violence occurred when a National Guardsman dropped his rifle, which discharged and shot him in the leg. Some young people had talked of instigating riots in the streets after the city paid its nonviolent respects to Dr. King, but Memphis didn't explode that night or any other night after the April 8 mass march. "Memphis was in fact the quietest place in the nation," said Billy Lucy.

THE NEXT DAY in Atlanta, Mrs. King led some 150,000 people, including presidential aspirants and top religious, civic, and labor leaders from across the land; civil rights leaders, ministers, and sanitation workers from Memphis also attended. An old wooden carriage drawn by mules, symbolizing the Poor People's Campaign, pulled King's body through the streets to his resting place. On the day of King's burial, unionized black longshoremen shut down the Mississippi ports of Gulfport and Pascagoula, and African Americans carried out memorial marches throughout Mississippi, while longshoremen from the ILWU shut down many of the ports on the West Coast.

King's mentor, Morehouse College President Benjamin Mays, that day memorialized King in Atlanta as the grandson of a slave called on by God to speak to America "about war and peace; about social justice and racial discrimination; about its obligation to the poor; and about nonviolence as a way of perfecting social change in a world of brutality and war."

King drew no distinctions between rich and poor, said Mays. He "believed especially that he was sent to champion the cause of the man furthest down." He thought King would probably say, "If death had to come, I am sure there was no greater cause to die for than fighting to get a just wage for garbage collectors."

21

"WE HAVE GOT THE VICTORY"

[Union organizers] think they're peddling better wages and working
conditions, but essentially they're offering dignity. And sometimes
the worker who doesn't articulate this very easily has more awareness
than the professional organizer. The civil rights struggle, the
equality struggle or whatever you want to call it, is just one
part of this continuing struggle for dignity.

—*Jerry Wurf*

"A PEBBLE DROPPED INTO A CALM POOL," WHOSE "RESULTING rings have created fantastic national problems," is the way President Lyndon Johnson's emissary, James Reynolds, described the Memphis strike. Memphis had never been a calm pool, but in any case, Reynolds could not swim out of it until he stopped the strike's ripple effects on the nation. He kept negotiators up all night on Palm Sunday. At dawn, Loeb went home to bed, while Jerry Wurf and his men prepared for the April 8 mass march. Sitting on the speakers' podium Monday afternoon, P. J. Ciampa dropped off to sleep, "like a drug addict. . . . I'd wake up and, you know, I'd feel like I wanted to scream."

Loeb lifted martial law following King's funeral on Tuesday, April 9, but on Wednesday, "Mayor Loeb beamed as he showed visitors the stacks of telegrams and mail he has received since Sunday," a *Commercial Appeal* reporter wrote. Loeb claimed to have received 1,000 letters and 3,803 telegrams, all but 100 of which supported his hard line against unions. Businessmen at the Sertoma Club gave him a standing ovation on Friday when he announced that ninety-six sanitation trucks were picking up the garbage.

A front-page *Wall Street Journal* article, titled, "Critics Say the City Where King Died Clings to Old Racial Outlook," declared that the white power structure in Memphis, "as in many cities, is out of touch but doesn't know it." Boss Crump had turned Memphis into an "adolescent city" barren of grown-up leadership, said Myra Dreifus. The City Council majority met on Wednesday, April 10, but still refused to intervene—they feared their "manhood" was on the line against the union, said Councilman J. O. Patterson. Disgusted, he called on all thirteen council members to resign and be replaced in a special election.

"The will to do the type of things that had been so needed in Memphis for so long" now existed for the first time, but no one had the "keys to make things work," insisted Reverend John Aldridge. White Baptists, the predominant religious group, remained silent. The Memphis Committee on Community Relations ran a full-page ad and mailed it to 600 ministers, calling for "100 Days of Love And Prayer." But "the tragedy . . . is that we preach one thing and live another," Reverend Starks responded.

New outbreaks of violence erupted in several cities after King's funeral, and President Johnson prodded Congress until the Senate passed the 1968 Civil Rights Act by a single vote. On April 11, the House passed it too—the last major civil rights bill of the 1960s. Title 8 of the law made it a crime to deny blacks the right to buy or rent in 80 percent of the nation's real estate—a response to King's open-housing campaign in Chicago—and the law also gave federal authorities more power to prosecute killers of civil rights workers and further codified American Indian rights. But the housing section had weak enforcement powers, and law-and-order advocates attached a provision, making it a federal crime to travel or broadcast interstate with the intent to start a riot. A clause protected union organizers from the anti-riot provision, but the law did nothing to enhance the rights of workers, such as those in Memphis, to organize a union.

President Johnson scheduled an address to Congress to propose accelerated antipoverty programs and a tax to pay for them. It would have been a significant response to the Poor People's Campaign, but Johnson had already raised taxes to pay for the Vietnam War, and he quickly canceled the speech and dropped the proposal due to congressional opposition. One hundred House Republicans had split from the conservative wing of their party to join 150 Democrats in passing the Civil Rights Act, but only one Deep South Democrat, Richard Fulton of Tennessee, had voted for it. Georgia Democratic Governor Lester Maddox conjectured that Communists had killed King just to get the law passed (Dan Kuykendall said the same thing). Other potential reforms in the wake of King's death stalled. Only hours before King's death, Mississippi Senator James Eastland had blocked a proposed gun-registration law, one that might have enabled authorities to identify quickly who had purchased the rifle used to kill King. The National Rifle Association, meeting from April 6 to 11, pressured Congress not to pass a registration law; only after another tragic assassination of a public figure, Robert F. Kennedy, would it do so.

In Memphis, on the day after King's funeral, workers resumed daily meetings at the United Rubber Workers union hall and marches from Clayborn Temple through downtown shopping districts. James Lawson announced plans for another massive demonstration and for intensified boycotts of particular businesses, and he demanded increased black employment and civilian review over police, who he said had invaded homes without warrants, brutalized people, and even stolen their money during curfew. "Now all Negroes know, from business executives and doctors on down, how the poorer people have been harassed for decades," he remarked. On April 12, Reverend Gardner Taylor of Brooklyn, president of the Progressive Baptist Convention (which King had long supported), spoke to 600 people at Mason Temple, telling them the "violence of hatred" could not be erased without "a radical change in the hearts of this nation."

Despite these calls for change, "We weren't having any luck at all with the mayor, and the city council had washed its hands of the problem," said Bill Lucy. President Johnson's man, Reynolds, found the mayor and his advisers irrevocably opposed to a settlement. This "group of wellbred, educated Southern gentlemen," from places such as Duke and Harvard and Yale, scorned the "tough little Jewish irascible Northerner" Jerry Wurf and regarded uneducated black garbage workers with disdain, said Reynolds.

"There was a certain condescension on the part of the spokesmen for the city that they would even sit there and talk to these people. . . . They had their finger in the dike and if they gave way . . . the government employees union was going to mushroom and it would be all over the country."

For their part, black workers had a "sullen but deep hurt" after King's death, and Reynolds feared they would walk out and the city would blow up. "The local union leadership was frightfully inept," Reynolds said, and unable to effectively confront Loeb's advisers in negotiations. Reynolds resorted to speaking with the groups separately, and he only brought Wurf and Loeb together periodically. Frustration built up among the workers: "There was nothing that Mr. Wurf could go back to the Rev. Lawson and these people who were meeting in the churches every night and so forth, and say, 'Well, the mayor has agreed to this or that.' There was nothing."

According to Reynolds, Wurf "took a good deal of what I would regard as abuse" from the mayor, and only his exercise of restraint kept the workers from walking out. At one point, however, Wurf himself concluded, "There is no point in going on with this." But Reynolds, whom Wurf called "the best trouble shooter on labor affairs in the United States," would not let him quit. He kept negotiators meeting through Easter weekend and beyond.

"BUSINESS NEVER CLOSES until somebody gets killed," W. C. Handy had written in his "Beale Street Blues." After King's death, half a dozen conventions canceled meetings in Memphis, and on Saturday, April 13, the biggest shopping day before Easter Sunday, some 200 black women intensified the pressure on merchants. Led by Dorothy Evans (a black teacher reputed to be one of the best-dressed women in Memphis), Cornelia Crenshaw, and Tarlese Matthews (strike activist and owner of a beauty shop), they picketed the downtown stores and told shoppers to leave. Black women had increasingly taken charge of AFSCME support work, and they now intensified boycott pressures on white merchants. The *Commercial Appeal* quoted a businessman as saying sales remained "brisk," but it wasn't true. Editor Frank Ahlgren later said merchants had been hiding the boycott's true impact for weeks; on April 14, the newspaper revealed the loss of more than a third of downtown shoppers over the previous month. The story's headline read, "City Must Bear Costly Loss of Goodwill, Money."

Hotel rooms sat empty and tourists avoided the city as though it once again had a yellow fever epidemic. Minuscule audiences came to downtown showings of *The Graduate*, a film packing movie theaters everywhere else. "The riot has knocked hell out" of Memphis, a businessman admitted. Memphis lost taxes on liquor and other goods not sold, while overtime pay for the police had totaled $300,000 since February 12. The city may have sustained up to $1 million in property losses over the course of the strike, according to later police estimates, and many downtown businesses never recovered.

The Invaders said violence would do more than marches to get the establishment's attention, and so did boycotts: Memphis did care, particularly about profits and losses. Jesse Epps threatened to spread the boycott misery by picketing suburban shopping centers. Much more threatening, *Time* magazine on April 12 replaced the city's reputation as the country's cleanest city with the label, "a southern backwater" and described it as a "decaying Mississippi River town." Congressman Dan Kuykendall, seemingly more incensed about *Time*'s comment than about King's death, called this "a vicious character attack upon the people of Memphis and its entire business community." The Memphis Chamber of Commerce and the Rotary Club, both of which had systematically excluded blacks, now feared the city would lose northern investments.

Ned Cook, Allen Morgan, Lewis McKee, and a number of other white businesspeople urged Loeb to settle the strike, while some condemned him for being so shortsighted and inflexible. A group of lawyers and businessmen who had worked on Loeb's election campaign went to the mayor and told him, according to Councilman J. L. Netters, "Man, get this thing settled. If you don't do it, you won't have our support."

The *Commercial Appeal* began to present the strikers in a more favorable light, featuring striker O. D. Wilson, who had six kids but turned over to the police a tourist's lost wallet containing a cashier's check for more than $8,000. My children "aren't that hungry" as to spend other people's money, he said. Both daily papers endorsed the federal Civil Rights Act in

King's honor, perhaps feeling some sense of guilt. James Lawson told *Time* magazine that the newspapers "have attacked and vilified Martin Luther King. They have to share responsibility for his death." On Monday, April 15, the *Press-Scimitar* editorially recognized the importance of the "I <u>Am</u> A Man" slogan and black workers' quest for dignity. The media had shifted toward a pragmatic strike settlement after March 28, and editors at both major newspapers in the city now thought that the longer the mayor stalled, the likelier that more violence could occur.

The Memphis Police Department and the FBI, like the newspapers, feared increased violence in the streets. Loeb received daily death threats, and police reported rumors that Lawson, Ralph Jackson, or Billy Kyles might be assassinated. Anonymous callers made bomb threats to city hall and the county courthouse, while one especially ridiculous rumor claimed that Reverend Jackson had dynamite stored in his church. Someone else sent him an anonymous postcard picturing King at "A Training School for Communists," with a cryptic note, "Ask the men to go back to work. They are wrong." And inside the Memphis movement, Wurf said, "Factionalism of all kinds"—hostilities, resentments, and quarrels—worsened after King's death. Charles Cabbage, John Burl Smith, Edwina Harrell, and Charles Ballard attended COME strategy committee meetings, but Cabbage's talk of "controlled violence" rankled the ministers. And the Invaders and BOP still wanted money for community organizing projects.

John T. Fisher had said that the only power Lawson had was the power to disrupt, and Lawson and others remained willing to use it. SCLC President Ralph Abernathy, at a rally at Metropolitan Baptist Church on April 15, threatened to initiate "some of the most militant nonviolent steps we've ever taken": protesters would block trucks, march through upper-class white areas at night, expand the economic boycott to the suburbs, and close the whole downtown. "I want to call on those Negro scabs who are driving those garbage trucks to leave the keys in the trucks and refuse to work," he said. SCLC leaders hinted at sabotage and mass arrests, and AFSCME leaders warned that a hard struggle lay ahead.

However, negotiators reached a tentative agreement with Loeb that very night. Loeb privately conceded, "After Dr. King was killed, I thought we simply had to get this thing behind us . . . in the country's interest and for many other reasons." One of those reasons might have been concern that northern businesses and the federal government could take their business elsewhere—the same kind of pressures that had forced Boss Crump to leave the CIO alone. James Reynolds, who had been getting phone calls from President Johnson demanding to know when the strike would be settled, did not openly threaten the mayor, but economic pressure was there, and he found ingenious ways to get around Loeb's opposition. Some years later, Bill Lucy facetiously commented of Reynolds, "I think we would still be negotiating had it not been for him."

Reynolds arranged to have a federal credit union available to accept union dues; this provided "an independent, employee-run system over which the mayor had no control," said Lucy. "Our members could have their dues deducted, and there was nothing the mayor could do about it." Reynolds also convinced Loeb to let the City Council sign an agreement with the union and thereby take the blame for union recognition, and the agreement did not make AFSCME the exclusive bargaining agent for the sanitation workers. Pay raises had never been the major issue for the sanitation workers, but the city now balked at giving any money for higher wages. Frank Miles approached industrialist Abe Plough, who owned a huge pharmaceutical company that had viciously fought unionization but failed to stop it in the 1930s. Plough now enjoyed unprecedented profits and anonymously donated close to $60,000 to pay for immediate raises for sanitation workers. This proved to be the key to finalizing a settlement. Reynolds said he had never seen such a thing in all his years of negotiations.

The wage agreement raised pay by 10 cents an hour by May 1 for laborers, crew chiefs, and drivers, and another 5 cents an hour by September 1; Loeb had originally offered an 8-cent raise. To sustain the wage increases, the city would propose a garbage tax that most affected poorer whites and blacks, and it would cause residents to blame the union rather than the mayor for the costs of a settlement. Loeb had already cut garbage collection from twice to once a week, and it would stay that way.

After eleven days of nonstop discussions, Reynolds had found a set of compromises and also a way to let Loeb escape direct responsibility for the settlement. He recalled, "You know the mayor didn't change his attitude. . . . He didn't capitulate one bit."

ON THE MORNING of April 16, a tentative deal was at hand. But Lucy recalled, "As we were going over the final agreement there was one more last stumbling block: T. O. Jones decided not to sign. He wasn't bothered by any particular point: he simply wanted to escalate the demands." T. O. Jones thought the union had watered down its objectives. It was true, Ciampa admitted, that the union "took a beating" on this first agreement—but it could not hope to do any better. Tensions surfaced between Jones and national staff members as they conversed in private. Lucy recalled, only half-jokingly, "While I advised him how nice life would be for him on another planet, Ciampa suggested to him numerous forms of torture he would never forget. Jones decided to sign."

AFSCME promptly took the proposal before members of the COME strategy committee and black church leaders who had gathered at the Peabody Hotel. Wurf told them, "This has been your fight as well as our fight. We think that this should be recommended to the men for approval. If, however, you don't think it should be, you are welcome . . . to say what you will. We want you to." He and his organizers left the room so they could discuss it freely. For a union to give such veto power to people outside the union was unprecedented, but Wurf knew that without broad support from the black community, he could not have a victory. The black leaders quickly approved.

It was the workers who remained the ultimate decision-makers, though. AFSCME staff and strategy committee members together went over to Clayborn Temple, where Lawson was preparing strikers for a march downtown. Said Wurf, "We are here to tell you about some of the agreements we have reached with the city, less than half an hour ago. It is up to you to decide whether you like or don't like the agreements and vote on them today." Especially since city leaders had questioned whether workers really supported this strike or wanted this union, Wurf felt it had to be their decision. For the next half hour, AFSCME staff went through the provisions one by one.

This agreement, which took sixty-five days of struggle to achieve, sounded incredibly simple. But for years to come, it both empowered and limited the sanitation workers and thousands of other public workers in Memphis. As Reverend Jackson had insisted, the words on paper said the city "recognized" the union, which meant that workers had a right to make their own choices and not be dictated to by "the Great White Father," as Jackson put it. No longer would anyone be fired for joining a union; workers could freely pay dues and carry on union activities at work. A year later, the U.S. Court of Appeals ruled, in relation to another organizing campaign, that the First Amendment protected the right of public workers to join a union.

The agreement's second point acknowledged that a dues-checkoff arrangement "is a matter exclusively between the employees and their credit union." Dues checkoff remained crucial, for without it, the union would not survive. Since Tennessee, under the Taft-Hartley Act's section 14(b), had outlawed the "union shop," AFSCME could not require workers to belong to the union as a condition of employment. Nonunion workers could refuse to pay dues and still receive the same benefits as union members— so why should workers join, or pay dues? It was the "Catch-22" of southern right-to-work laws. The checkoff system at least made it possible to collect dues regularly from those who chose to be union members.

The third item simply maintained benefits that the workers already had. The fourth stated: "The City shall make promotions on the basis of senior-ity and competency." White supremacy thus fell, in twelve simple words. When Lucy announced it, a great cheer went up. Industrial workers such as Clarence Coe at Firestone and George Holloway at International Harvester had risked their lives for equal promotion rights, in order to break the back of Jim Crow on the job. Now sanitation workers also had these rights. White supervisors kept their jobs, but blacks now had equal opportunity to compete for those jobs when supervisors retired.

In the meantime, any white boss could be challenged. The longest sec-tion of the agreement set up a detailed, step-by-step grievance procedure. Ed Gillis said, "Now I can go to the union and they'll protect me. See . . . we have a chief steward out there. He speaks for us. . . . This is what the strike did for us." The agreement spelled out steps to be taken, guidelines and timelines. Industrial workers such as Coe and Holloway used grievance procedures as a Bill of Rights, and sanitation workers now had the beginnings of one.

The agreement also contained a nondiscrimination clause, something CIO unions had pioneered in the 1940s. The city would not discharge or otherwise discriminate against workers based on their participation in the strike or in the union, or based on their "age, sex, marital status, race, religion, national origin, or political affiliation." The workers cheered this provision, which declared an end to both racial discrimination and the firing of union activists—as had happened to thirty-three workers after the abortive 1966 strike. This provision's importance became evident when Charles Blackburn announced that all strikers could now return to work.

AFSCME gave up some power in making this agreement, leaving public-employee unions vulnerable for years to come. As Loeb later pointed out to the press, this was a memo of agreement, not a contract; Tennessee law did not require him or any other employer to bargain in good faith; workers did not have to join or pay dues; in case of disagreement during bargaining, arbitration by a third party was advisory only, and the mayor could reject it. Wurf said that the right to belong to a union was a "basic right in a free society," but it should be matched by a requirement that employers bargain in good faith. Loeb hadn't done it, and this agreement still didn't require it.

The agreement also prohibited AFSCME members from going on strike, a right that AFSCME had long struggled to achieve for government workers. With few protections by labor boards or the courts, and without required union membership and the right to strike, AFSCME Local 1733 could only use public pressure to get city leaders to bargain in the future. "All we did was get a premise for staying alive," Wurf later said.

Workers listened tentatively as Wurf and Lucy read off the provisions. It was not all they wanted, but it was an agreement, and it was in writing. Early in the proceedings, they gave Wurf and then Jones standing ovations. Wurf turned over the microphone. Jones was overcome with emotion and could not speak. He sat down with tears streaming from his eyes, as Wurf and Lucy continued to read the agreement.

At 1:05 PM, Wurf again turned over the microphone to Jones, who called the question: "All those who approve the agreement, please stand."

People rose as one to their feet; no one remained seated. "All those who oppose?" There was no one. Jones declared, "The motion has carried!"

Wild jubilation engulfed Clayborn Temple, where tear gas still stained the walls. On the podium, Jones, Ciampa, Lucy, Wurf, Paisley, Epps, and Reverends James Smith, Lawson, Starks, and Bell, as well as Cornelia Crenshaw, O. Z. Evers, Maxine Smith, and others shook hands, hugged, laughed, and cried. Some workers rushed to the front to congratulate their representatives; others danced in the aisles, waved their fingers in a "V for victory" sign or held two thumbs up, and slapped each other on the back. Lawson called it a scene of "great joy and happiness and bedlam."

Jones momentarily silenced the bedlam to say, "We have been aggrieved many times, we have lost many things," tearfully referring to the man who was not there—Martin Luther King. "But we have got the victory." People surged around Jones, patting him and cheering. The audience recognized Jones as a hero. It was a moment of vindication for all he had suffered during nearly eight years of trying to build a union.

Lawson now took the podium, and he too had his mind on the man who was not there. He wanted this victory to count as a first step toward fundamentally changing Memphis and building a lasting alliance between the black community and organized labor. He urged the workers and the union representatives not to forget where they came from or their larger objectives: "We know we have just begun. We want to get to the point where every poor family in this Shelby County can work together in an organization that will allow them to solve their own problems. The fact is that we were able to stand tall and true and together and we have won this glorious victory for you and for America." He reminded AFSCME: "We are not going to let you forget your responsibility to this community."

Reverend Starks rose to say that workers had once "looked askance" at the ministers, but, "Now we are together, let us stay together!" Reverend Bell joked that the workers had done better under Loeb than any other mayor, and he shouted, "Long Live King Henry!" Cornelia Crenshaw said it was time to organize hospital and housing workers. Tommy Powell exulted, "This is one of the biggest days ever for labor in Memphis. I just hope the Negroes and labor can bind themselves together to get some good politicians now." Ralph Jackson said, "COME will not be disbanded. It will be strengthened" to demand "economic equality" (a phrase used by King) and an end to police brutality. It would try also to get relief from the debts workers had incurred to loan sharks (workers subsequently spent years paying these off).

People had high hopes that this would be the beginning of a broader movement for social and economic justice, as they joined hands and sang, "We Shall Overcome." Wurf looked at banker Jesse Turner of the NAACP, "and I felt kind of silly because tears were coming out of my eyes and he was crying, too." People in Memphis still sang, "Black and white together," even when Wurf, Ciampa, Tommy Powell, Joe Paisley, and Malcolm Blackburn were the only whites in the room. "I still am moved by it because we ended every meeting that way," said Wurf.

Workers said the key to the victory was that they had made their own decision. "We're satisfied. They didn't force us to accept anything, we voted on it. That makes the difference," said James Allen. "It's been tough, oh man. They sure have fought for us and I appreciate it," said Sidney Robinson.

The wage increase provided the least cause for celebration. "The raise will help a little, not too much. I would rather have that and go back to work than not be working," said Detroit Luster. Workers remained angry at Loeb. "Anytime a person has to go through this much" to get a few cents extra, said Luby Finney, "I don't like him." Said another worker, "He's a sick man but I'll say one thing for him. He did just what he said he would."

AFSCME shop stewards left Clayborn Temple to plan implementation of the agreement, and the ministers immediately went into a strategy session. Most workers lingered, savoring their victory, relaxing. "Man, it'll feel good to get back to work," said Mack Dean. They could go home to their families that night, satisfied that they had stood up for their rights and prevailed. "There was joy on that day," recalled Clinton Burrows, despite King's death. "I loved him and I am proud I was part of this." He gave thanks to "the Lord, my family, and the International union." The workers also felt a sense of sadness. "We won, but we lost a good man along the way," said one of them.

Mayor Loeb offered this interpretation to the press: "There is no winner, except all of the people of Memphis. The agreement is consistent with
long established policies of the city and laws of this state." He still opposed
the agreement, he said; he had given in on nothing, but, "in the greater
interest of the city I feel we should resolve this issue." He also said that 250
strikebreakers would keep their jobs. Loeb told a top CBS News executive
that he had not changed his views and had "at least 200,000 people backing
us up, and only a handful against." James Reynolds and Frank Miles signed
the document and turned it over to the City Council for ratification; Loeb
never signed anything.

Loeb prided himself on being "stubborn" and "hardheaded," but, Reverend Jackson objected: "When I did that as a child I always got a whip-
ping, and I didn't think that was anything in particular to be proud of." If
Loeb clung to his unilateral decision-making, however, he also needed to
make sanitation workers' raises palatable to other city workers—an important political constituency ever since the Crump era. Laborers, cafeteria
workers, janitors, nurses' aides, and workers in city parks, schools, and the
Memphis Housing Authority, as well as 600 Memphis hospital workers, all
made less than the federal minimum wage of $1.60 an hour. Even firemen
and policemen and many teachers lived at bare survival wages. All of these
city workers needed a raise, and a union. Pay raises had been scheduled for
February 1968, but they had not been implemented because voters had not
approved serving liquor by the drink, thus undermining tax revenues.

Since the start of the strike, employers had feared that an agreement
with AFSCME would set off a tidal wave of wage and unionization
demands. Loeb tried to head this off by pledging, "Those below the minimum wage will be brought up"—but *only* to the minimum wage. In addition, firemen and policemen would also get a long-delayed 10 percent
raise, in two 5 percent increments. As a result of that percentage increase,
white policemen and firemen gained far more in wages than the sanitation
workers did. AFSCME had raised the wage floor for nearly all city workers.
Loeb left it to the City Council to come up with funding.

The city had finally accepted virtually the same agreement that the City
Council subcommittee on public works had agreed to only two weeks after

the strike began; Loeb's own negotiators had accepted a similar agreement on March 5. Now, the City Council approved the "Memorandum of Agreement" on the afternoon of April 16; only Bob James voted against it, saying he did not see how the city could pay for the wage increases. Patterson criticized the council for not having imposed its own version of this agreement weeks earlier.

The mass media acknowledged, finally, that dues checkoff, done routinely for insurance and other purposes, was nothing unusual, and the *Press-Scimitar* editorially praised the settlement as a "Victory for the Community." The *Commercial Appeal* admitted that AFSCME leaders in Washington had not instigated or even known about the strike, and that unions already had similar agreements with various city governments and the Tennessee Highway Department. Its editors praised Jerred Blanchard for putting his "political life on the line" in support of a settlement, and said the agreement paved the way for a "New Era in Memphis."

It would have been nice, Benjamin Hooks said, if the mass media had also acknowledged that "the black community because of their solidarity and togetherness has won a victory." Instead, it seemed to suggest that everything in Memphis would be fine again, as it once used to be. But something had definitely changed. As sanitation worker Luby Finney told a reporter, "We've got a union to fight for us now."

THAT NIGHT, BEFORE some 1,500 celebrants at Golden Leaf Baptist Church, Lawson, Bevel, Bell, Ralph Jackson, and others outlined a fight against police brutality and for educational and economic uplift. A denim-clad Ralph Abernathy called the strike settlement a victory for teachers, janitors, maids, students, and poor people in general. Some people nationally viewed King's death as the end of the civil rights movement, but Martin's brother, A. D. King, told the crowd that the Memphis movement had served notice: "this is just the beginning."

Epilogue

HOW WE REMEMBER KING

They say that freedom is a constant struggle,
Oh Lord, we've struggled so long, we must be free.
—*Freedom movement anthem*

I N MEMPHIS, WORKERS AND MINISTERS, POOR PEOPLE AND THE middle class, unionists and civil rights leaders had reached what Reverend James Lawson called a "threshold moment," connecting struggles for black freedom and economic justice and creating the labor and civil rights alliance that Martin Luther King had long tried to build. In its wake, public employees became the leading force for union expansion in America, and dozens of sanitation strikes by black workers swept the nation. AFSCME, with SCLC support, won recognition in St. Petersburg and Miami, where workers adopted the "I Am A Man" slogan. Black women hospital workers in Charleston, South Carolina—in what *Time* magazine called "echoes of Memphis"—struck for 113 days in 1969, supported by Coretta Scott King and SCLC, against intransigent white politicians who were backed by Nixon administration appointees. Hospital workers obtained recognition but failed to get dues checkoff, and their local floundered.

In Memphis itself, AFSCME's Local 1733 likewise remained on tenuous grounds. Sanitation workers nearly struck again in the summer of 1968 in order to get Loeb's obstinate administration finally to implement its "Memorandum of Agreement," and workers at John Gaston Hospital did strike for forty-nine days in the fall to get recognition and a memo of understanding, supported again by COME and another boycott of the downtown. AFSCME did not get on secure terms with the city until the summer of 1969, when Jesse Epps threatened to "spread the misery" of economic boycotts to the suburbs. He took suburban housewives on a tour of the inner-city homes of impoverished sanitation workers. Appalled at the poverty they witnessed, affluent white women joined with black women to take out ads, write letters, and personally pressure dismissive white men in the city government finally to sign a three-year agreement that gave Memphis one of the highest hourly rates for sanitation workers in the South.

However, the sanitation workers had only opened up the beginnings of a long and difficult battle over union rights and black representation within the city. In the fall of 1969, black workers at St. Joseph's Hospital (where King died) went on strike for recognition and dues checkoff, placing Bishop Durick and others in the difficult position of now opposing AFSCME. The union, the NAACP, and COME joined forces again in a campaign for a contract at St. Joseph's, coupled with demands that the school board and more supervisory positions be opened up to blacks. The movement conducted yet another economic boycott of downtown Memphis and an even more disruptive school boycott by some 65,000 black students, now joined by more than 600 black teachers. They virtually closed some of the schools on successive "Black Mondays," and students smashed windows in some of the schools. Sanitation workers walked off the job and 2,000 demonstrators faced off with the police in a downtown battle on November 10. Students—as well Reverends Lawson, Jackson, Abernathy, Blackburn, Bell, and Bevel, along with Father Milton Guthrie and many others—ended up in jail.

The NAACP ultimately dropped its support for St. Joseph's strikers, who lost, but the movement opened up the school board to black representation, and Maxine Smith soon became its first African American member.

The fault lines between unions and the NAACP remained. In subsequent years, labor and civil rights forces sometimes joined together, other times not.

Across the South, black sanitation workers responded to the Memphis strike of 1968 by organizing and going on strike, but in Memphis itself, AFSCME went through numerous leadership struggles that almost destroyed it. The union's national office asked T. O. Jones to take an organizing job in Florida and then fired him when he did—effectively removing him as president of Local 1733. Jones never obtained a full-time union job again, and he died virtually a pauper on April 12, 1989. He continued to encourage every worker he met to do something to change his or her life; shortly before his death, he asked a reporter to pass on this message to the next generation: "Tell the guys to stay with the union. The union, that's the best salvation." Jesse Epps for a time became AFSCME's regional and local director, but he, Ralph Jackson, and other ministers came under intense legal scrutiny for how they had handled 1968 strike-support funds of some $340,000 (nearly half of which had been contributed by unions and the rest by individuals). Zealous prosecutors pressed allegations of misallocation of funds and accounting errors, forcing Epps to leave Memphis. The momentary black unity that had occurred in the aftermath of King's death wavered.

The Invaders, both perpetrators and victims in a recurring cycle of violence, fell out completely with the movement for worker rights. Charles Cabbage and other Invaders made armed and threatening demands for funds when COME decided to become a permanent organization in the summer of 1968. Although COME had paid $3,000 for Invader legal costs, Cabbage's group threatened to blow up the AFSCME office if it did not provide more funds. The Invaders took over one COME meeting, where Jesse Epps denounced them as "leeches," but AFSCME members outnumbered them at the next meeting. They also tried to get funds from SCLC when it held its convention in Memphis in August 1968. The Invaders played almost no role in subsequent labor and school walkouts, as the police continued to hammer the young activists. They charged John Henry Ferguson with five separate crimes, and the courts handed him a six-year prison sentence for his disruption of Carver High School during the strike. Cabbage was sentenced to prison for draft refusal and for weapons charges left over from the strike, while John Burl Smith, Charles Ballard, and Lance (Sweet Willie Wine) Watson all received jail sentences related to the strike. Petty holdups, the wounding of a police officer, and the accidental shooting death of a black youth by Invaders put thirty-five of them in jail or under indictment by the winter of 1970. It was a time of intense political repression against New Left, Black Power, and antiwar activists during the administration of President Richard M. Nixon. From the perspective of John Burl Smith, who served five years in prison for charges related to the Memphis movement, King's death opened the way to increased state-sponsored terror, as COINTELPRO, in his words, "replaced the KKK."

The aftermath of King's death did not lead to an era of increased understanding across racial lines in the United States or in Memphis, where a war opened up between the police and the black community. Lieutenant Arkin and his superiors in the intelligence division of the Memphis Police Department had apparently learned very little. In reviewing the 1968 strike, Arkin noted that police had arrested 897 people over two months—almost all of them black Memphians—but then he concluded that Memphis had been chosen as a "target city" by outsiders. Arkin proposed as a solution that the city purchase more helicopters, mace, and riot helmets. The angry attitude of white police officers became very public in October 1971, when a mob of them beat sixteen-year-old Elton Hayes to death when he tried to evade them in a speeding car, triggering twenty-three police suspensions and ten days of riots. The NAACP's campaign against unnecessary police use of deadly force took up much of its time and energy.

King's Poor People's Campaign proved to be one of the most disconcerting defeats for social change movements in the wake of the Memphis strike. The march of the poor began from the Lorraine Motel on May 2, with Mrs. King leading the way, as mule teams symbolizing the plight of the rural poor pulled wagons through places King had visited in Mississippi, Alabama, and Georgia, and on to Washington. Thousands of poor people—including Cabbage, T. O. Jones and his son Jesse, and other Memphians—gathered at the "Resurrection City" encampment in the capital, and Mrs. King led the National Welfare Rights Organization's Mother's

Day mobilization on May 12. Delegations visited Congress and departments of government, demanding jobs or income for the poor, and protesters held a large, spirited national demonstration on June 19 ("Juneteenth," a day celebrating emancipation from slavery in the South). But massive rains and organizational chaos engulfed the group's encampment; gang members robbed its residents; Mexican Americans, Native Americans, and poor whites and blacks found it difficult to get along; and government officials hardened their hearts to black economic demands as the Vietnam War sapped the federal tax base.

SCLC hired Bayard Rustin to pull the Movement together, then fired him for emphasizing building coalitions with unions and clergy for moderate demands. No one could provide as credible a leader to the mass media as King; nor could support from unions, churches, Hollywood actors, and college students create a genuine poor people's movement. Capitol police ultimately routed the poor with tear gas and billy clubs and burned down Resurrection City in the middle of the night. The Poor People's Campaign left the capital as "a defeated army," said SCLC Executive Director William Rutherford.

In the midst of this dispiriting campaign, an assassin shot down Robert F. Kennedy in Los Angeles on June 6, the night he virtually secured the Democratic presidential nomination in his California Democratic primary victory. Many African Americans and peace advocates had by now transferred their hopes from King to Kennedy—now a leading opponent of the Vietnam War, and the man who had suggested King bring the poor to the nation's capital in the first place. The premature deaths of Walter and May Reuther in a plane crash on May 9, 1970, and Jerry Wurf's death in 1981 made the enormity of King's loss to the Movement even more apparent. The King family suffered more tragedy too, as Martin's brother, A. D., drowned in a swimming pool and a deranged young black man walked into Ebenezer Baptist Church and shot their mother, Alberta Williams King, dead while she was playing the organ in July 1974. This left Daddy King with no wife and nine fatherless grandchildren.

Despite many setbacks, unionism continued to sweep through the ranks of public employees across the country. In Memphis, discontent and activism among low-wage workers became widespread, and hospital workers, city clerks, car inspectors, jailers, and penal-farm workers created seventeen different AFSCME chapters by the mid-1970s. Black women especially came into the forefront of union, welfare rights, and community organizing. Ortha B. Strong Jones at John Gaston Hospital said she and other black nurses organized because they saw the union as "somebody that we could lean on" and that would speak out for them.

James Robinson, chapter chairperson for the sanitation workers; Taylor Rogers, Local 1733's unpaid president; and James Smith, its paid director, led a relatively stable Local 1733 for the next twenty years. In 1976, AFSCME was the largest union in Memphis and in the state of Tennessee, with some 7,000 members. Its success had the ripple effect that Memphis business leaders had long feared: firemen, police officers, and teachers formed their own organizations, and all of them went on strike in 1977–78, inflicting far more damage on the city's public order than the sanitation workers' strike. Ironically, the police, who had been such vicious opponents of the 1968 Memphis movement, benefited most from desegregation and unionization, gaining increased wages and bargaining power as more and more blacks and women joined the force.

Local 1733 and the Movement veterans of 1968 led the way to increased black voter registration and political action and replaced Republican Representative Dan Kuykendall in 1974 with Harold Ford, the first black congressman elected in the Deep South since Reconstruction. The union helped to elect many others, and, for a time, according to Bill Lucy, "As a political instrument, the union was unmatched." Willie Herenton, who marched with the union in 1968 as a young teacher, in 1978 became the city's first black school superintendent. In 1991, he became the city's first black mayor (albeit without AFSCME's endorsement). Whites voted solidly against black candidates until Herenton's second term, but then they began to vote for him in significant numbers. A new black leadership class, including black women, had emerged from the cauldron of the 1968 mass movement.

But despite public-employee union success, inflation, wage stagnation, and fiscal crises began to undermine both city governments and organized labor. Big industries such as Firestone closed their doors just as black workers like Clarence Coe had finally won equal access to all jobs. The alliance of middle-class black political leaders and unions representing the black working poor increasingly split apart. In April 1977, when 1,300 black sanitation workers went on strike in Atlanta, black Mayor Maynard Jackson fired and replaced them, supported by Martin Luther King, Sr., and even SCLC. Under a reign of fiscal austerity, black mayors felt increasingly compelled to make their alliances with white business leaders and the corporate power structure, instead of unions.

As King had warned, conservative forces now rolled back many of the gains of the labor and civil rights movements. Ronald Reagan, already the "acknowledged master of the imagic art" of television by the time he became California governor in 1966, increasingly made the Right respectable to white workers as well as the middle and business classes as President in the 1980s. The escalating rightward shift devastated efforts to organize the working poor, and plant closings, mechanization, floods of drugs into poor communities, and capitalism's globalization all undercut working-class and minority communities and unions. The loss of unionized workplaces such as Firestone, International Harvester, and RCA destroyed much of the black industrial working class in Memphis and other cities. When black women at Memphis Furniture Company in 1980 went on strike for union recognition and dues checkoff, supported by Mrs. King and SCLC, they won, but soon the company simply closed up shop. It was symptomatic of a new era in which employers shifted their capital and their plants to labor markets even cheaper than the South's, thus gutting unions.

Schisms between the black poor and the better-off intensified: as the percentage of people in the educated black middle class grew, the percentage of people in the black working poor grew even more. Poverty encompassed 58 percent of the Memphis black community in the 1960s; thirty years later, the figure was only about 10 percent less, and de facto school segregation had worsened. Southern cities such as Memphis and New Orleans remained among the poorest in the nation. Black migrants had once left the plantation districts of West Tennessee for jobs in the Memphis sanitation division, but now middle-class blacks and whites moved into the old sharecropping districts and turned them into upscale "exurbs," fleeing the failing schools and declining tax base in the city.

Center-right politics replaced King's Negro–labor–liberal coalition, and religion shifted away from the Social Gospel's vision of uplift for workers and the poor and back to traditional individualistic appeals for personal salvation. Anne Braden of Kentucky, a white woman who spent her life fighting racism, concluded in 1968 that either white southerners would begin to make effective coalitions with blacks, or "the battle in the South will continue to be black against white, instead of what it should be and what we can make it: a battle of people against poverty and injustice." Unfortunately, greed, God, and guns undermined coalition politics, as the tenor of American life swung wildly away from King's vision of a beloved community.

THE POWER OF Dr. Martin Luther King's vision and what happened in Memphis in 1968 is now a matter of historical memory. AFSCME and community advocates saved the Lorraine Motel from destruction and turned it into the National Civil Rights Museum, where tourists and students alike can learn from the history of the freedom movement. For forty years after King's death, sanitation workers came out every year to keep their own memory of King and the Movement alive. They still carried picket signs reading, "Honor King: End Racism," and "I Am A Man," marching on April 4 to the downtown on the well-worn route from Clayborn Temple. Across the nation, union and economic-justice advocates adopted April 4 as a day of action for immigrant and worker rights, and on the eve of the American invasion of Iraq in March 2003, recordings of King's prophetic "Silence Is Betrayal" speech against the Vietnam War rang out across the country.

The shift to remembering King as a labor-rights and peace advocate began, even as corporate and political leaders continued to define him within a narrow framework as "civil rights leader." Hearing, "I Have a Dream," to the exclusion of everything else King had to say, must lead many schoolchildren to think King spent his life sleeping. But Memphis tells us another story.

In Memphis—in a confusing, dispiriting time much like our own—

King found what he needed: an organized, energized movement among those who worked full-time jobs at part-time wages. They had gone beyond the struggle for civil rights to the struggle for human rights, King said, and this gave him hope that a nonviolent movement of the working poor could prevail. James Lawson believed the Memphis strike left a great legacy to the present, as he went on to pastor a large Methodist church in Los Angeles and become one of that community's strongest advocates of unionization for immigrants and the poor. "A dogged coalition builder," according to the *Los Angeles Times*, Lawson held fast to King's goal of creating a mass movement to end poverty: "I don't see going it alone as a viable option for change in America."

For Memphis sanitation workers, the meaning of 1968 and King's sacrifice remained clear. Striker Willie Sain, who later became a minister himself, said King came almost as an emissary from God, a Moses figure who enabled the workers and their allies to win. King broke the media blackout of the strike, energized the community, and came into a new role as a labor leader that he played to perfection.

Taylor Rogers said King had merely followed the model of the Good Samaritan, just as he had urged others to do. "Even if it had been poor white workers, King would have done the same thing. That's just the kind of person he was. . . . All his staff thought it was outrageous of him to stop and come to Memphis. But he went where he was needed, where he could help poor people. . . . He didn't get all accomplished he wanted accomplished, but I don't think he died in vain. Because what he came here to do, that was settled."

FIVE YEARS AFTER King's death, an African American TV news reporter named Ed Harris, whom police had sprayed with mace in 1968, asked an unnamed sanitation worker for his reflections on 1968. "I don't think we can show enough appreciation for what Dr. King give," he said. Implicitly, he believed the strike would have been lost without Dr. King, and for him the benefits of victory were very tangible. Before, he had worked six days a week; now he worked five. Before, he had worked as long as it took to bring in the garbage with no extra pay; now he worked eight-hour shifts. Before, he had had no breaks; now he had at least two fifteen-minute breaks and time for lunch. Before, white supervisors would fire black men on a whim; now they "can't 'buse your round anymore." With a union, his wages and benefits had steadily improved, even as the city mechanized away many sanitation jobs.

With King's help, workers had changed themselves and their relationship to whites: "See, when he was here in the strike, every man wanted to stand up and be a man. And that was the whole story. We wasn't counted as men before then. Every man be counted as a man now. It's no more 'boy'. . . . It's no more of that Uncle Tom now. . . . You be treated like a man."

The struggle itself changes people, King had told his staff when he launched the Poor People's Campaign, and that is why people had to continue to fight, despite the obstacles: "If I didn't have hope, I couldn't go on."

Those involved in the Memphis sanitation workers' strike remembered it as a moment in history that changed everything, because it opened people's eyes to the injustices of poverty and racism, and it gave them hope for a different world. Memphis thus became one of the most important stops on a long road to freedom that people have traveled for generations, and still do.

ACKNOWLEDGMENTS

M Y DEEPEST APPRECIATION GOES OUT TO STRIKE PARTICI-
pants and community supporters interviewed by myself or
others, listed in my oral history source notes, and especially to
James Lawson, Charles Cabbage, Joe Warren, James Robinson, and Taylor
Rogers, who helped to bring this story alive. I am indebted to labor and civil
rights historians, and I list many of their works in my bibliography. I owe a
huge debt of thanks to Kieran Taylor, Martin Halpern, Will Jones, Steve
Estes, and to Patti Krueger, each of whom read and critiqued the entire
manuscript at various stages. Nelson Lichtenstein read parts of it and has
long encouraged me in this project, as have Clayborne and Susan Carson
and the other good people at the King Papers Project at Stanford University.
Beth Kalikoff at the University of Washington, Tacoma, read my very early
drafts and illuminated them with deeper meaning; David Smith, John Lear,
and Nancy Bristow at the University of Puget Sound offered ideas and
scholarly comradeship; Alex Kuo, Joan Burbick, and Ana Solari offered
thoughts and companionship at our scholarly retreat in Bellagio, Italy;

Robin D.G. Kelley, David Montgomery, Timothy Tyson, Pete Daniel, David Roediger, James Barrett, Eileen Boris, Jacquelyn Hall, Robert Korstad, Joe Trotter, Horace Huntley, Dana Frank, Kent Wong, Bill Fletcher Jr., David Garrow, Ira Berlin, Sharon Harley, Zaragosa Vargas, James Gregory, Otto H. Olsen, Charles Payne, David Kennedy, Joe Reidy, Jim Green, Thomas Collins, and other scholars and friends in various ways lit the way forward. Thanks to colleagues in the Labor and Working-Class History Association, the Oral History Association, the Organization of American Historians, and the Southern Historical Association, for promoting our common historical work, and to Julian Bond, Linda Reed, and Juanita Moore, whom I joined in putting on a very special conference at the National Civil Rights Museum in Memphis in 1993 that has informed my work on King (see Bibliography). Thanks to Michele Rubin at Writers House, and to the King Estate for allowing me to quote extensively from King's March 18 and April 3 speeches in Memphis.

Without archivists and librarians serious research would be impossible, and my special thanks go out to them. Ed Frank, archivist at the University of Memphis Mississippi Valley Collection, was tremendously generous in helping me find and use the interviews, films, and great array of documents in the Sanitation Strike Collection. Memphis Public Library archivists Patricia LaPointe and Wayne Dowdy guided me through that library's extensive resources on Memphis history. Mike Smith and his colleagues, including Carrolyn Davis, Thomas Featherstone, and William Gulley at the Walter P. Reuther Archives at Wayne State University in Detroit, helped me find my way through their labor and civil rights treasure trove. The archives of the Martin Luther King, Jr. Center for Non-Violent Social Change and its archives in Atlanta and the online and published Martin Luther King, Jr., Papers at Stanford provided access to crucial collections on King and the freedom movement. Thanks to Gene Dennis Vrana, archivist of the International Longshore and Warehouse Union in San Francisco, to Jess Rigelhaupt for forwarding helpful ILWU documents, and to Eric Gellman for reminding me of important FBI wiretap sources. Thanks to Lisa Phillips for sending me items from District 65 UAW Papers, at the Tamiment Library. Suzanne Klinger at the University of Washington, Tacoma, library provided expert research help. At the University of Memphis Steve Ross gave me early access to transcripts of film interviews for the magnificent film on the strike, *At the River I Stand*, that he and David Appleby and Allison Graham produced. David Cicelski offered insights on current economic conditions in Memphis, and graduate students Robert Masters and Angela Martin provided great research assistance. Gerry Collins and Ken Martin at the Memphis Department of Public Works helped me locate some of the sanitation workers active in 1968. Thanks especially to Richard Copley, Tony Spinoza, and the many fine photographers who are listed at the back of this book for allowing me to reprint their photographs, and to photo archivist Claude Jones at the *Commercial Appeal*. We are indebted to Ernest C. Withers, whose brilliant photographs on the strike, civil rights history, and black life in Memphis illuminate this story so well; they can be viewed in his autobiographical *Pictures Tell the Story*, in the exhibit "I Am A Man: Photographs by Ernest Withers," from Panopticon, and online.

Student research assistants at the University of Washington, Tacoma, proved that this new, interdisciplinary institution (which I have been privileged to help create since 1990) is producing stellar young scholars. These included Eric Stowe, a wizard of newspaper and FBI research who offered much early research support; Benjamin Peters, skilled with secondary documents and fluid thinking; and Margaret Robinson and Gwen Ford, who did newspaper research. Carolyn Braden played a crucial role in bringing this manuscript to completion, and in doing the key phrase notes. I thank her for her commitment to every aspect of the project.

My life partner, Patti Krueger, struggled with me to finish this book for too many years and has been a wonderful comrade in this intellectual endeavor. The warm support of Maureen Honey, my sister; Charles Honey, my brother; and Keith and Betty Honey, my parents, has meant a great deal to me. Special thanks to my other friends/family for many good meals and fellowship: the extended Krueger family in Wisconsin and other parts; Mark Allen, Caledonia and Tim Allen (both of whom helped me with research), Joy Tremewin, Cheryl Cornish, Steve Lockwood, and Mary Durham in Memphis; Martha Leslie Allen, Jonathon Zeitlin, and Zenia in DC; Gordon Jackson and Nancy Bristow and other close friends in Tacoma, and Bobby and Lyle Mercer in Seattle. Special thanks to Barbara Andrews and the National Civil Rights Museum, to Les McLemore and the Fannie Lou Hamer Institute at Jackson State University in Mississippi, and to D'Ann Penner and J. Herbert Nelson at the Benjamin Hooks Institute for Social Change at the University of Memphis, for carrying on the Movement's legacy.

Various academic institutions made extended research and writing possible. My colleagues at the University of Washington, Tacoma, and its director, Bill Richardson, enabled me to take grants and sabbatical time away from teaching, proving the institution's commitment to research and writing. The UW's Helen R. Whiteley Center and its wonderful staff in Friday Harbor, San Juan Island, provided a home for intense periods of writing and reflection. The UW's Harry Bridges Center for Labor Studies funded me with small grants and course release stipends as the Harry Bridges Endowed Chair; it provides a rare nexus of fellowship between scholars of the labor movement. I am deeply indebted to other scholarly institutions that provided places to research, write, and talk with colleagues: the Bellagio Study and Conference Center of the Rockefeller Foundation in Italy; the University of California, Santa Barbara's Interdisciplinary Humanities Center; the Huntington Library, in Pasadena; and the National Humanities Center in North Carolina, where I first began preliminary writing on this project. The National Endowment for the Humanities granted a crucial competitive stipend for a year of writing, without which I could not have completed this book.

Finally, I owe a great debt to Alane Salierno Mason, senior editor at W. W. Norton & Company, who recommended that I write this book. I could not have completed it without her faith in my abilities and her steadfastness in standing behind the project (even when it took many years more than expected). At the crucial moment, she expertly helped to trim a too-long manuscript down into a manageable narrative and made writing an exciting learning experience. Much credit for this book belongs to her. Kathleen Brandes provided expert copyediting, and the ever-reliable Alex Cuadros whipped the photos and the final edits into shape. I feel privileged to work with Alane and the fine people at Norton, an independent, employee-owned publishing house that still puts writing and ideas first.

A NOTE ON SOURCES

S UPPORTED BY GRANTS FROM THE NATIONAL ENDOWMENT FOR the Humanities, Professor David Yellin and Carol Lynn Yellin and others who had lived through the traumatic experiences of 1968 formed the Search for Meaning Committee, a group that compiled the marvelous Sanitation Strike Collection (SSC), now housed in the Mississippi Valley Collection (MVC) of the Ned R. McWherter Library at the University of Memphis. It includes scores of interviews, clippings, video- and audiotapes, correspondence, newsletters, flyers, and more. I relied heavily on this archive for my research, as well as on *At the River I Stand,* an elegant if underappreciated account of the strike, first self-published by English Professor Joan Beifuss in 1983. In this book, I set out to create a more fully historicized account of the strike and its roots in black history, as well as the evolution of Martin Luther King's labor and coalition politics, and the Poor People's Campaign. My narrative is constructed mainly from "primary sources"—eyewitness accounts created at the time events occurred or shortly thereafter—drawing on the strike collection and an array of other sources.

For this purpose, I have drawn heavily on oral histories—some recorded by Beifuss and her colleagues, others by researchers for the Ralph J. Bunche Papers at Howard University, between 1968 and 1972. Interviews recorded in the 1980s and 1990s by me, and by researchers for the *At the River I Stand* film, may be more subject to the memory lapses and embellishments that come with time, yet these, too, remain "primary" sources as eyewitness accounts. Oral history remains crucial to telling what happened and also what people thought about what happened, especially in an era when workers, the poor, and African Americans were largely shut out of the mass media and elective office and could not get their stories told. I use oral history and other sources within a historical context, however, doing my best to compare, contrast, and understand. I list oral histories in the bibliography, but I do not cite them in the source notes, since the reader can infer from the text when I am drawing on an interview and who that interviewee is. Where that may not be clear, I list a citation in the source notes.

The use of intelligence records requires some explanation. I used the FBI's Martin Luther King, Jr., file (100-106670, which I refer to as FBI/MLK), at the FBI Reading Room in Washington, DC. But I relied on scholars who have seen more of those files than I have—namely, David Garrow, Taylor Branch, and Gerald McKnight. I worked most heavily in the Memphis field office files on the Sanitation Strike (157-1092, which I refer to as FBI/MSS), which consist of five files in chronological order. I also used Lieutenant Ely Arkin's "Civil Disorders, Memphis, Tennessee," which is a summary of the Memphis Police Department's surveillance of the strike (referenced as "Arkin Report"). The City's larger collection of "Red squad" files were destroyed by the MPD in 1976 so the public could not see them, making this our only record of their contents. I used all these political surveillance records sources with care and skepticism. Agents were paid for the purpose of finding damning information, and their surveillance reports often distort facts to present a case for prosecution of supposedly "subversive" individuals such as King. Documents were collected in the context of government "counterintelligence" actions to undermine King, the Poor People's Campaign, and other Movement activities through disinformation, provocation, and various forms of intimidation and other illegal actions against citizens exercising First Amendment political rights. Surveillance records often tell us more about the nature of illegal government repression than about the actions of those under surveillance. Yet the taxpayer money used to create surveillance records at least has provided historians with important chronological accounts, a view of how police agencies affected Movement organizing, and information reported to police agencies by people in the community. I list FBI documents by their date and often by the sub-document number, by which any researcher can locate them. All FBI documents used are available under the Freedom of Information Act (FOIA).

I have been cautious in referencing the voluminous and conflicting federal, courtroom, and journalistic investigations of the King assassination, which I do not try to unravel and which has spawned an industry of experts. The FBI moved all its documents dealing with the King assassination into a special file that is code-named "Murkin," which is available on microfilm. I refer to literature on the assassination primarily as it relates to the story of the Memphis movement and how people in Memphis perceived King's death.

In the source notes that follow, I try to provide clear documentation without overwhelming the reader with citations. A voluminous historiography exists on King, civil rights, black workers, and the labor movement, and I humbly invite readers to explore it. Various works on King by David Lewis, David Garrow, Taylor Branch, Peter Ling, Clayborne and Susan Carson and the King Papers Project, Adam Fairclough, Thomas Jackson, Stuart Burns, and others have gone far beyond narrow treatments of King as a "civil rights leader." I also urge readers to consult the many marvelous histories of labor and the black freedom movement, and, for greater depth on issues in Memphis, to see my first two books, listed in the bibliography. I cite secondary accounts only as they directly affect the story, and I avoid repeating sources of common knowledge among scholars or using large numbers of "see also" references. My citations in the source notes are minimized by short titles referring the reader to the bibliography, and key phrases provide documentation in the order in which information appears. My own personal interviews with various people in this book will be placed in an oral history collection and made available to the public.

NOTES

ix "You see, the Jericho road": King, "I See the Promised Land," in Washington, ed., *Testament*, pp. 284–85.

ix "I choose to identify": Jackson, "Recasting the Dream," p. 418.

A PERSONAL PREFACE

xiii "The solidarity of the ages": Bloch, *The Historian's Craft*, p. 43.

xiv "all necessary means": Beifuss, *At the River*, p. 121.

INTRODUCTION: TWO LIVES LOST

1 On this particular day, Cole and Walker: Beifuss, *At the River*, p. 30; T. O. Jones int., SSC, and P. J. Ciampa int., SSC.

2 "He was standing there": CA, February 2, 1968.

2 Two men had already been killed: Earl Green, Jr., "Labor in the South," p. 139.

3 White supervisors, on the other hand: James Robinson int. (M.H.). At the end of the 1968 strike, Public Works Commissioner Charles Blackburn said blacks were thirteen of twenty-one truck and tractor drivers, most of the crew chiefs, seven of twelve foremen, and four of sixteen division superintendents. This is at odds with all other interviews and news articles. Blacks operated trucks and some equipment and several worked as

crew chiefs and foremen in the sanitation division only, but as far as I have found, none were superintendents. PS, April 16, 1968, p. 4.

3   constituted nearly 40 percent: PS, March 16, 1964; Honey, "Martin Luther King, Jr.," in Zieger, ed., *Southern Labor in Transition.*

1. A PLANTATION IN THE CITY

7   "Run tell your mama": McKee and Chisenhall, *Beale*, p. 218.

7   understood their common history: Blight, *Race and Reunion.*

7   Forrest made his fortune: Carney, "Contested Image," pp. 601–30. As recently as August 2005, many whites still defended Forrest as a hero when County Commissioner Walter Bailey tried to change the name of Forrest Park. The *Commercial Appeal* did not even mention the massacre at Fort Pillow.

8   Emancipation unleashed a flood: For an overview, see Honey, *Southern Labor*, ch. 1. Du Bois, *Black Reconstruction*, shows how racism divided southern labor and defeated Reconstruction. Tyson and Cicelski, *Democracy Betrayed*, document how racial division defeated southern populism. See also Honey, "Class, Race and Power," in Tyson and Cicelski.

8   In Tennessee, white Democrats: Wright, *Race, Power.*

9   Black women played a crucial role: Royster, *Southern Horrors.*

9   organized a union in Elaine: Taylor, "We Have Just Begun."

9   "Vendors were on hand": Goings and Smith, " 'Unhidden' Transcripts," p. 375.

10   blacks continued to resist Jim Crow: Brown-Melton, "Blacks in Memphis," pp. 166–69.

10   remained pitifully weak: For examples, see Group I, Series G, Branches, 1913–1939, Box 199, NAACP Papers.

10   Crump as "the big dog": My father, Keith Honey, assigned to the naval air station in nearby Millington during World War II, met Crump on an elevator at the Peabody Hotel one day and was surprised at how ordinary he appeared. See Miller, *Mr. Crump.*

10   "The colored people, they voted": McKee and Chisenhall, *Beale*, p. 52.

11   Only a handful of blacks: Ed Redditt int. (M.H.).

12   Yet most white workers: see Roediger, *Wages of Whiteness*, and Nelson, *Divided We Stand.*

12   white brotherhoods forced black workers out: Arnesen, *Brotherhoods of Color*, pp. 66–71.

12   deadly legacy for public employees: Green, "Labor in the South," pp. 63–64, 70.

12   white firefighters, teachers, and police: Honey, *Southern Labor*, ch. 3.

13   "You had to fight for every inch": Honey, *Black Workers*, p. 78.

15   "I left Memphis to spread the news": Furry Lewis recordings, Kassie Jones Part II. "Masters of Memphis Blues, 1927–1929," liner notes, JSP Records.

16   Union wages spurred bigger donations: Korstad and Lichtenstein, "Opportunities Found and Lost." See also accounts by Coe, Holloway, Davis, and others in Honey, *Black Workers.*

16   "Those supervisors would curse": Honey, *Black Workers*, pp. 96, 98.

16   increasing roles in service work: Green, "Plantation Mentality," and "Race, Gender, and Labor."

17 CIO generated great hopes: Griffith, *Crisis;* Honey, "Operation Dixie," and *Southern Labor,* ch. 9.

17 King protested: Carson, *MLK, Vol. I,* p. 121.

19 hailed Wallace's commitment: O'Dell int. (M.H.), and *MLK, Vol. I,* p. 45.

19 ran black and white candidates: Honey, *Southern Labor,* pp. 248–51.

19 The CIO joined in: On the CIO's "Red scare" in Memphis and the South, see: Honey, *Black Workers,* pp. 114–22 and ch. 5; and Honey, *Southern Labor,* pp. 252–75.

20 frame-up of Willie McGee: see Horne, *Communist Front,* on anti-Communism's effect on the civil rights movement, passim; Honey, *Southern Labor,* pp. 266–67; and "The Case of Willie McGee, A Fact Sheet Prepared by the Civil Rights Congress," UPWA Program Dept., Subject and Correspondence Files, Box 345, Folder 3, UPWA Papers.

20 "If a white person took too much": Honey, *Black Workers,* pp. 202–8. The newspapers even equated the civil rights stand of the Democratic Party to the "fundamental principles of the Communistic Party." CA, February 6, 1964.

20 attacking, among others, Grace Lorch: Fariello, *Red Scare,* pp. 490, 495–96.

21 great reversal of the 1950s: Union membership nearly tripled in Tennessee between 1939 and 1953 but began dropping after Operation Dixie folded in 1953. Green, "Labor in the South," pp. 90, 46.

21 Integrationists tried to use the contradiction: Dudziak, *Cold War Civil Rights.*

21 caused the NAACP increasingly to narrow its framework: Anderson, *Eyes Off the Prize.*

21 Thurgood Marshall collaborated with the FBI: Biondi, *To Stand and Fight,* p. 170. Anderson and Biondi refute the idea that the cold war created a favorable civil rights framework.

21 "Memphis is a hard spot": Van J. Malone to Lucille Black, June 11, 1954, NAACP branch files.

21 "I could really cry": Green, "Plantation Mentality," pp. 307–8.

22 "pronounced apathy and lethargy": Ibid., pp. 307–8.

22 being a Communist front: Ibid., pp. 177–78, 295.

22 The light that CIO unions had once cast: Lichtenstein, *State of the Union.*

22 "a surprising number of the performers": Daniel, *Lost Revolutions,* p. 147.

2. DR. KING, LABOR, AND THE CIVIL RIGHTS MOVEMENT

23 "The two most dynamic": King, "If the Negro Wins, Labor Wins," in Washington, ed., *Testament,* pp. 206–7.

23 "expert organizer" but "no radical": *Time,* February 18, 1957, pp. 17–20.

23 King never confined his politics: Carson et al., *MLK, Vol. I;* Carson, ed., *Autobiography.*

24 "Daddy" King, Martin's father: King, Sr., *Daddy King;* Ling, *Martin,* pp. 17–24.

24 "the inseparable twin": Carson, ed., *Autobiography,* quote p. 10, and *MLK, Vol. I.*

24 King became familiar with Social Gospel indictments: Carson, "Martin Luther King, Jr."

25 When he met Coretta Scott: Scott King, *My Life,* pp. 38–39, 24–34.

25   Their lives changed on December 1: King, *Stride Toward Freedom.*

26   "There comes a time when": Carson et al., *MLK, Vol. III,* pp. 70–79.

26   Nixon embodied: White, " 'Nixon *Was* the One.' "

26   Bayard Rustin and Glenn Smiley: D'Emilio, *Lost Prophet,* pp. 226–48.

27   In 1957, King: Ling, *Martin,* pp. 52, 57–59; Carson, ed., *Autobiography,* chs. 11, 13; reports of Russell Lasley, "Southern Negro Leader's Conference," 1957, in Box 379, UPWA Papers, WHS.

27   "I never intend to adjust myself": King, "The Look to the Future," at Highlander.

27   "The forces that are anti-Negro": King, "Address by Reverend Martin Luther King," October 2, 1957, UPWA Papers.

27   "complete political, economic and social": Carson et al., *MLK, Vol. V,* p. 117. See also Taylor, "Early Ties."

28   picture of King sitting next to: Carson et al., *MLK, Vol. V,* p. 291. The John Birch Society postcard is in the author's possession.

28   Crusade used the allegation: Christian Crusade, "Unmasking Martin Luther King, Jr., The Deceiver." Enclosed in Sylvia Crane to King, February 13, 1963, Box 7, Folder 34, MLK Papers.

28   King's association with the school: Carson et al., *MLK, Vol. V,* pp. 290–93.

28   He petitioned to free integrationists Carl Braden: Braden, *HUAC;* and "A Petition for Clemency to the President of the United States," in the author's files.

28   Drawing on HUAC reports: FBI/MLK, April 13, 1962, April 25, 1962, and numerous other entries tie King to Communists through innuendo and guilt by association.

28   people such as Benjamin Davis: Carson et al., *MLK, Vol. V,* pp. 443–44.

29   King floundered in his efforts: Ling, *Martin,* ch. 2, and Fairclough, *To Redeem the Soul,* ch. 2.

30   formed dozens of civic clubs: Green, "Plantation Mentality," pp. 291–99.

30   Black activists in Nashville: Noting the drive underway in Memphis, Tennessee's black leaders met in Nashville to plan a unified campaign of black voter registration. TSD, February 7, 1959.

30   Three of the five candidates: The ministers running were Reverend Ben Hooks, Reverend Roy Love, and Reverend Henry C. Bunton. TSD, August 1, 1959.

31   "The rally turned out to be": Black doctor B. B. Martin refused to let them use Martin Stadium, giving rise to the comments about Uncle Toms. TSD, August 6, 1959. See also Green, "Plantation Mentality," p. 319.

31   at-large districts and runoff elections: TSD, April 25, 1959, and TSD, August 1, 1959.

31   collaborate with racially moderate: Sivananda, "Public Works," p. 66.

32   "white unity" ticket: PS, January 22, 1958; PS, May 22, 1958; PS June 8, 1959.

32   "Though the white man is divided": TSD, August 29, 1959.

33   Loeb was a personable man: Sivananda, "Memphis Mayor."

33   "Nobody owns a piece of me": PS, May 27, 1952.

33   "two-party system": PS, July 14, 1953.

33   Loeb led "Americanism months": PS, August 14, 1951; PS, May 27, 1952; PS, June 21, 1952; PS, July 1, 1953; PS, July 14, 1953.

34   Loeb built up a following: Sivananda, "Public Works," pp. 67–75.

35   his relationship with blacks: Ibid., pp. 68–71.

35   Loeb went to speak to the men: Lapsley, "Portrait."

36   "I am opposed to integration": Sivananda, "Memphis Mayor," p. 76.

36   "placed the Negro in places": CA, August 24, 1961.

36   Loeb's popularity evaporated: Sivananda, "Memphis Mayor," p. 77.

37   shocking and random police brutality: For examples, see TSD, January 3, 1959; TSD, September 26, 1959; TSD, December 5, 1959; TSD, December 26, 1959; TSD, April 15, 1961; TSD, April 22, 1961; and TSD, February 16, 1963.

38   "no justice for Negroes": TSD, January 3, 1959.

38   "I was the committeeman": Honey, Black Workers, p. 167.

38   "Here in Memphis": Ibid., p. 137.

38   Herbert Hill proved it: Foner, Organized Labor, pp. 325–31.

38   UAW preached equality but practiced white supremacy: Boyle, The UAW, p. 164.

38   "We didn't have CORE": Honey, Black Workers, p. 269.

38   were "prudent realists": Tucker, Memphis Since Crump, p. 118.

39   one of the most active NAACP chapters: TSD, December 19, 1959.

39   "I want to see Mister Joseph": Ibid.

39   Sugarmon went on to earn: Beifuss, At the River, p. 160.

39   a group of black women: Green, "Plantation Mentality," passim.

40   the largest in the South: For details on NAACP, see Turner int., SSC.

41   George Isabell's daughter was among the first to go to jail: Isabell int. (M.H.).

41   "sat in" at several white churches: Green, "Plantation Mentality," pp. 348–50.

43   "This is a quest for equal opportunity": PS, April 30, 1963.

43   the "package deal": Rustin, "From Protest to Politics," in Time on Two Crosses, pp. 116–29, quote on p. 117.

43   black family income averaged one-third: Tucker, Memphis Since Crump, p. 93.

43   pressuring 100 retail firms to change: TSD, May 25, 1963.

43   He and Jesse Turner led some 600: TSD, September 7, 1963.

43   barely escaping Somerville: A mob surrounded Hooks, Willis, Sugarmon, and Lawson on the town square and ten carloads of whites chased them out of town. TSD, July 27, 1963.

44   held workshops on Title VII: TSD, April 17, 1965; TSD, April 24, 1965.

44   "has begun to shine as a beacon": Lentz, "Sixty-five Days," p. 2.

45   He ultimately divested himself: Beifuss, At the River, p. 70.

45   "young, handsome man": TSD, October 12, 1963.

45   The newspaper blamed Loeb: TSD, November 30, 1963.

45   George Grider, a supporter of unions: TSD, March 20, 1965.

45   elect William Ingram as mayor: TSD, November 30, 1963. For background, see Pohlman and Kirby, Racial Politics.

46   The John Birch Society: according to Bill Ross of the Memphis Labor Council, the society had 32 separate clubs in Memphis, including some local newspaper writers.

46   Robert Welch: Arsenault, *Freedom Riders*, p. 346.

46   According to the Memphis *Union News:* The NAM formed the Business–Industry Political Action Committee and donated $100,000 to abolish social welfare programs. *Union News,* October 1963, p. 2. Anti-union groups with business support included Young Americans for Freedom and Harding College in Searcy, Arkansas.

47   "Negroes are almost entirely": King, "If the Negro Wins, Labor Wins," in Washington, ed., *Testament.*

47   The AFL-CIO could expel unions: A. Philip Randolph bitterly criticized first the AFL and then the AFL-CIO for failure to discipline discriminatory unions, and the NAACP's Herbert Hill documented rampant union discrimination. Foner, *Organized Labor,* chs. 21–23. Bruce Nelson devastatingly documents the degree of union racism in *Divided We Stand.*

48   "is a key to unlocking the social and political machinery": MLK to UE convention, 1962, Long Beach, courtesy of Kerry Taylor, MLK Papers Project, Stanford University.

48   "we will find the civil rights movement": King to Reuther, July 19, 1965, Box 253, Folder 2, Reuther Papers.

48   King said the "promissory note": King, "I Have a Dream," in Washington, ed., *Testament,* pp. 217–20.

48   The UAW: The UAW provided strong financial backing and logistical support, March on Washington Files, Box 494, Folders 8–12, Reuther Papers.

48   King stood on picket duty: Hooper, "The Scripto Strike."

49   "had the ability": C. T. Vivian int. (M.H.). See Lichtenstein, *State of the Union,* on the rising moral trajectory of the civil rights movement and the falling moral trajectory of labor in the 1960s.

3. STRUGGLES OF THE WORKING POOR

50   "I was just some sort of slave": For Walker and Stimbert quotes, see U.S. Civil Rights Commission (CRC) Hearings, pp. 126, 158, 162, 175.

51   pervasive racial discrimination: CRC Hearings, pp. 245, 304–6, 313, 325–42, 351–52.

51   "I wish I could answer": Ibid., p. 235.

51   freezing blacks out of craft occupations: The only unions with significant black membership were the bricklayers (12 percent black), plasterers and cement masons (60 percent), and hod carriers (98 percent). Ibid., pp. 344–47.

51   "We have not had a single Negro": Ibid., pp. 342–43.

52   Local, state, and federal agencies: An executive of the Bureau of Apprenticeship and Training in the U.S. Department of Labor office admitted, "I have not made any effort to make the Negro community aware of the President's policy concerning fair employment." Tennessee's Department of Employment Security executive admitted that his

office had to separate locations, one for whites and one for blacks, and that blacks were not admitted to any white training programs. Yet he claimed, "There's no distinction made whatsoever" by race, and even more lamely, "I don't know specifically whether the unions have refused to accept any Negroes or not." Ibid., pp. 195–96, 217–23.

52 mechanization of farming: Wright, *Old South*, pp. 243, 247, 255.

52 unemployment and poverty rates: Marshall, "Industrialization and Race Relations in the Southern States," in Hunter, ed., *Industrialization*, p. 91.

52 suburban employment went to whites: Vivian Henderson, "Region, Race and Jobs," in Hunter, ed., *Industrialization*, p. 80.

52 only 2.2 percent of black workers: Marshall and Van Adams, "The Memphis Public Employee Strike," in Chalmers and Cormick, *Racial Conflict*, p. 77.

53 "Whenever you have a bloc": Ross and Hill, *Employment*, pp. 6–7.

53 "giant housekeeping job": City of Memphis, "Nucleus of the Mid-South, Municipal Report for 1955," p. 42, SSC.

53 "collection and disposal of garbage": Green, "Labor in the South," pp. 110–11.

54 more than a third: Ibid., p. 40.

54 40 percent of their families: Honey, "Martin Luther King, Jr.," in Zieger, ed., *Southern Labor in Transition*, p. 154.

55 "There is no worst job": CA, February 28, 1993, p. 1.

56 "I was born in Earle": Honey, *Black Workers*, p. 302.

56 Brutal struggles over labor rights: Hamburger, *Our Portion of Hell*.

56 day laborers could be fired: PS, April 16, 1968, p. 4.

57 "It was the same thing": CA, February 28, 1993, p. 1.

58 bosses even carried sidearms: Lucy int., SSC.

59 94 cents to $1.14 an hour: TSD, February 6, 1960, p. 1.

59 By 1968, this went up: Sisson int., SSC; CA, April 5, 1997, and February 20, 1993.

60 "We were victims of the system": CA, February 28, 1993, p. 1.

64 difficulty making his ideas understood: Jones sometimes obscured his own statements and contradicted himself in interviews, giving the impression that he was either being coy or simply could not express himself clearly. Jones int., SSC.

66 Evers said some sanitation workers: TSD, May 7, 1960, p. 1.

66 "There will be no union": TSD, March 19, 1960, p. 1.

66 "over 70 workers' wives stomping": TSD, April 9, 1960, p. 1.

67 "I have 1,500 men waiting": TSD, May 7, 1960, p. 1.

67 Teamsters leaders put off a strike: TSD, July 6, 1963.

67 "I think the Union has sold": TSD, June 25, 1960.

67 to create their own structures: Green, *The World*, pp. 103–4; Rachleff, *Hard-Pressed*.

67 a meeting in the Retail Clerks' hall: TSD, July 13, 1963.

67 Loeb and the city commissioners reacted: Memphis *Union News*, July 1963.

68 Farris fired them all: The fired workers included Jesse Stone, 27; Henry Donnerson, 32; Robert Beasley, 38; Jimmy Newson, 40; Tommy Mason, 33; John Lacy, 30; Huria Cotton, 38; John Henry, 34; Sargent Carpenter, 25; Tom Reed, 49; James Beach, 24;

Clarence Milan; Jesse Jackson, 48; Isom Brownlee, 40; Houston Cooperwood; John
Edwardes, 22; Frank Parker, 66; Rochester Milam, 42; John Lee Moore, 46; John Isom,
28; Alonzo McDowell, 62; Forest Stone, 38; John Wesley Jones; and Hardy Savage. TSD,
July 6, 1963. The *Tri-State Defender* later carried a photo of some of the fired men. TSD,
July 13, 1963.

70 He had a quick temper: Wurf's explosive character is evident in his interviews. See also
Goulden, *Jerry Wurf.*

70 And Wurf immediately supported Martin Luther King: Wurf int., Bunche Papers.

70 Before 1964, AFSCME: Billings and Greenya, *Public Worker.* On the change in public-
employee unionism, see Halpern, *Unions, Radicals,* ch. 5; Wurf int., Bunche Papers.

71 no women and only one African American: Spero and Cappozzola, *The Urban Community,* p. 18.

71 about 70 percent white: Green, "Labor in the South," p. 115.

71 "Catholic moral theologians": Memphis *Union News,* November 1964, p. 1.

72 their first slate of officers: Ibid.

72 Jones supported their election: Green, "Labor in the South," pp. 111–12, 116–25.

73 Ingram did nothing for the men: AFL–CIO Memphis Labor Council records, December
8, 1965, minutes, Folder 5, Ms. 346, SSC. For more on the early struggles of Local 1733,
see Jones, Ross, Kyles, Lawson, and Starks ints., SSC.

73 voted four-to-one against: Memphis *Union News,* July 1965 and December 1965.

73 Sisson responded to the union campaign: Beifuss, *At the River,* p. 26.

73 those who did deeply regretted it: James Robinson, for example, dropped the city's earlier insurance policy and was later left destitute as a result of medical bills he had to pay
after a bad car accident. Honey, *Black Workers,* p. 309.

73 talk about taking direct action: Green, "Labor in the South," pp. 118–25.

74 black middle class did not want: Maxine Smith and Sugarmon ints., SSC.

75 at least produced more improvements: Jones int., SSC, and Beifuss, *At the River,* p. 27.

4. STANDING AT THE CROSSROADS

76 "Something is wrong with capitalism": Garrow, *Bearing the Cross,* p. 581.

76 Lawson first learned about: Halberstam, *The Children,* pp. 15–17, 37–43.

77 "And what good did that do": *Los Angeles Times,* January 18, 1993, B3.

79 he met Dorothy Wood: Halberstam, *The Children,* pp. 123–24.

80 "This Movement is not only against": Ling, *Martin,* p. 68.

80 Lawson's teachings: Ibid., pp. 71, 76, 80.

81 threatened to resign in protest: J. Robert Nelson, "The Lawson-Vanderbilt Affair, Letters
to Dean Nelson," Nashville, 1969, SSC.

82 Lawson joined NAACP picketing: Tucker, *Memphis Since Crump,* p. 137.

82 chair of the NAACP's education committee: TSD, February 20, 1965.

82 At least twenty-six: *New York Times,* October 18, 1965.

82   Four days later: documentation in the Kenneth Hahn Papers, the Huntington Library; Horne, *The Fire This Time;* and Branch, *At Canaan's Edge,* chs. 21 and 22.

83   Watts required "a shift in the focus of struggle": untitled address to District 65, UAW, September 17, 1965, MLK Papers.

83   Chicago impressed upon King: Ralph, *Northern Protest,* p. 213.

83   murdered William Moore: Stanton, *Freedom Walk.*

83   Aubrey James Norvell: CA, June 8, 1966, p. 24.

84   "Just a few miles south of here": Ibid.

84   "There is nothing more powerful": TSD, June 11, 1966, p. 4.

84   Later that night at the Lorraine: Carmichael, *Ready for Revolution,* pp. 484–515.

84   a carload of Deacons: Hill, *Deacons for Defense,* pp. 246–51.

84   mass media focused on debates: CA, June 9, 1966; PS, June 27, 1966.

85   Lawson, Reverend Ralph Jackson, the white: PS, June 22, 1966.

85   turning point for twenty-year-old Coby: Smith, "March On."

86   "as if he were out of a straitjacket": Carmichael, *Ready for Revolution,* pp. 511–12.

86   Klansmen in Natchez murdered: Payne, *I've Got the Light,* p. 397.

86   Meredith himself said he would shoot: CA, June 9, 1966, p. 1; PS, June 7, 1966, p. 8; PS, June 27, 1966, p. 13.

87   "Whites can only subvert": *New York Times,* August 5, 1966. Reprinted in Van Deburg, ed., *Black Nationalism,* pp. 119–26. See also Carmichael, *Ready for Revolution,* pp. 566–71.

88   King soberly refuted the idea: King, "Black Power Defined," *New York Times,* June 11, 1967. Reprinted in Washington, ed., *Testament,* pp. 303–12.

88   King returned to Memphis: PS, September 9, 1966, p. 1.

89   "We must persist in the struggle": PS, September 10, 1966, p. 4.

89   "pulling the blankets back": TSD, September 3, 1966.

90   "his professed devotion": CA, September 2, 1966, p. 6.

90   Letters to the editor denounced: CA, June 12, 1966, Sec. 6, p. 5; PS, June 9, 1966, p. 3.

90   He knew King had defended: King maintained a cordial relationship with Benjamin Davis and wrote to the U.S. Board of Parole, urging it to release Communist Party leader Henry Winston from cruel conditions of imprisonment. Carson et al., *MLK, Vol. V,* pp. 442–43.

90   "powerful demagogic speech": Department of Justice, *Security and Assassination Investigations,* p. 165.

90   pinned his accusation that King: Garrow, "The FBI and Martin Luther King, Jr.," *Atlantic Monthly.*

91   COINTELPRO also targeted King: Churchill and Vander Wall, *COINTELPRO Papers,* pp. 95–99.

91   ordered FBI agents not to warn King: Kotz, *Judgment Days,* p. 76.

92   "willing to bear the burden": King, "Revolution and Redemption," August 16, 1964, District 65 UAW Papers, Box 24, SCLC Correspondence, Tamiment Library. Thanks to Lisa Philips for this document.

92   Perhaps this also blinded: King was heckled and jeered at the National Conference for

New Politics in Chicago on August 31, 1967. Branch, *At Canaan's Edge*, pp. 637–40. Agents provocateurs may have also been involved, however.

92   "COUNTERINTELLIGENCE PROGRAM": Churchill and Vander Wall, *COINTELPRO Papers*, pp. 92–93.

93   in a "second phase": King, "Civil Rights at the Crossroads," address to the shop stewards of Local 815, New York, May 2, 1967, MLK Papers.

93   speech at Riverside Church: King, "A Time to Break Silence," April 4, 1967, in Washington, ed., *Testament*, pp. 231–43.

94   "a true revolution of values": *New York Times*, March 4, 1968.

94   "We seek to defeat Lyndon Johnson": United Press International, April 24, 1967, in PS File 5700, SSC.

94   Johnson, for his part, raged: Kotz, *Judgment Days*, pp. 375–77.

95   "an exaggerated appraisal": Garrow, *Bearing the Cross*, p. 576.

95   Lawson and King had worked in tandem: TSD, March 13, 1965, and July 24, 1965.

96   "One voice was missing": King, "The Domestic Impact of the War in America," November 11, 1967, National Labor Assembly for Peace. The group Clergy and Laity Concerned About Vietnam reprinted another version of the speech. See King, "The Domestic Impact of the War in Vietnam," November 11, 1967, Labor Leadership Assembly for Peace, Wisconsin Historical Society, MSS. 470, Madison, Wisconsin.

96   "inadequate protest phase": Garrow, *Bearing the Cross*, p. 581.

96   "a method that will disrupt": Ibid., p. 580.

97   "is forcing America to face all its interrelated flaws": King, "A Testament of Hope," in Washington, ed., *Testament*, p. 315.

97   "This is something like a last plea": Associated Press, August 17, 1967, PS File 5700, MVC.

5. ON STRIKE FOR RESPECT

98   In the fall of 1967: Sugarmon int., SSC; Beifuss, *At the River*, p. 21.

99   only about forty dues-payers: Sabella int., SSC.

99   he called them "fist collections": Beifuss, *At the River*, p. 27.

99   tightened the city's labor policies: Green, "Labor in the South," pp. 133–36; Beifuss, *At the River*, p. 21.

101   They reported the incident: Beifuss, *At the River*, pp. 29–30.

101   Ciampa: Goulden, *Jerry Wurf*, pp. 111–14; Ciampa int., SSC.

101   Two other men had died: Green, "Labor in the South," p. 141; Jones int., SSC.

102   Loeb convened his "kitchen cabinet": Beifuss, *At the River*, p. 31.

102   "We don't have anything no how": Ibid., p. 32.

102   Jones laid out the basic issues: Ibid.

104   "You keep your back bent": Honey, *Black Workers*, p. 298.

105   930 of 1,100 sanitation workers: Beifuss, *At the River*, p. 20.

106   Jones "seems to be the leader": SSC Video 1, February 12, 1968.

110   strikers might last two or three days: Ibid.

110   "just got to the point": Honey, *Black Workers,* p. 296.

111   "I represent these men": CA, February 13, 1968, p. 1.

111   "lack of communication": SSC Video 1, February 12, 1968.

112   "Much planning and study": Arkin Report, p. 2.

112   held their first meeting with Loeb: Beifuss, *At the River,* pp. 37–39.

116   "both morally and financially": CA, February 15, 1968, p. 1.

116   "I can't see anything that necessitates": CA, February 14, 1968, p. 1.

117   the civil rights movement: Wright, *Race, Power.*

117   Loeb tried to command them: CA, February 14, 1968, p. 1.

117   "just as you used to ask me": SSC Video, Reel 2, February 14, 1968.

117   "This is not New York": *New York Times,* February 14, 1968, p. 31.

118   called out a list of demands: The demands discussed on February 11 included a wage increase from $1.80 to $2.35 an hour for laborers and up to $3 an hour for truck drivers. Ciampa's list called for an increase to $2.10 an hour for laborers and $3 an hour for truck drivers, who apparently made a standard wage of $2.40 an hour. Green, "Labor in the South," pp. 145, 155–56.

118   "As a free American citizen": SSC Video 1, February 12, 1968.

119   "I suggested to these men": Beifuss, *At the River,* p. 40.

120   "I don't care what [Governor Nelson] Rockefeller": Ibid., p. 41.

120   could find no common ground: PS, February 14, 1968, p. 1.

121   "suffered uncalled-for insults": CA, February 15, 1968, p. 6.

121   "Looking back, few people remembered": Beifuss, *At the River,* p. 38.

121   "He knew that his support": Ibid., p. 45.

121   Loeb confidently played to a strain: Marshall and Van Adams, "The Memphis Public Employee Strike," p. 83.

122   "As to the legal situation": CA, February 15, 1968, p. 6.

122   Tennessee Supreme Court decision: In the Alcoa case, the Court reasoned that because the National Labor Relations Act "expressly excludes from its coverage employees of a state or any political subdivision of a state . . . neither unions nor employees have a legal right to enforce their demands against such a public body through an organized strike." *City of Alcoa v. Electrical Workers Local 760,* Tennessee Supreme Court, December 6, 1957, Box 5, Folder 13, SSC.

122   "When the governor of the state allows": CA, February 16, 1968, p. 1.

122   twenty states allowed limited union rights: Wurf int., SSC.

123   "says a man has to work": SSC Video 1, February 13, 1968.

124   "Loeb will talk, but will he": Ibid.

124   met without Loeb or Ciampa: According to the *Commercial Appeal,* these discussions reached a compromise agreement on recognition of the union and a grievance procedure. CA, February 15, 1968, p. 1.

125   "broke into angry profanity": Ibid.

126   "If work is not resumed": Ibid.

126   fire and police director, canceled days off: ATR Film Chronology Notes, SSC.

126   endorsed the strike and a boycott: Memphis AFL–CIO Labor Council, Council and Executive Board Minutes, February 14 and February 28, 1968, Box 1, SSC.

126   The council represented 50,000: CA, February 15, 1968, p. 1.

126   the most significant interracial group: Powell int. (M.H.).

126   "We told them there are no hard": CA, February 16, 1968, p. 19.

126   perhaps 300 workers had considered: Ibid., p. 1.

126   Yet fewer than a hundred: The *Commercial Appeal* said thirty regular sanitation workers had refused to go on strike, supplemented by thirty supervisors and twenty new workers. CA, February 16, 1968, p. 1. FBI special agent Jensen thought perhaps 170 workers had gone back. FBI/MSS, February 16, 1968, Doc. 2, p. 1.

6. HAMBONE'S MEDITATIONS: THE FAILURE OF COMMUNITY

128   "We who engage in nonviolent": King, "Letter from Birmingham Jail," in Washington, ed., *Testament,* p. 295.

128   *Hambone's Meditations:* Lentz, "Sixty-five Days," pp. 131–39.

129   *Commercial Appeal* had the largest circulation: Ibid., pp. 141–42.

129   "the principle of quietness": Ibid., p. 136.

130   "moving toward two societies": *Commission on Civil Disorders,* pp. 7–8.

131   "totally unknown to most": Ibid., p. 2.

131   5 percent of newswriters: Ibid., pp. 384–85.

131   "The average black person couldn't": Ibid., p. 374.

131   Loeb spoke "for all of us": Lentz, "Sixty-five Days," p. 149.

131   "a shallow attempt at blackmail": Ibid., p. 145.

131   the "heavy set" T. O. Jones: CA, February 13, 1968.

132   began an editorial barrage: Lentz, "Sixty-five Days," pp. 157–59.

132   "to act as collector of dues": CA, February 15, 1968, p. 6.

132   "Loeb Takes Right Course": Ibid.

132   "Make no mistake about it": Ibid.

132   "union command post": CA, February 23, 1968, p. 1.

133   Newspaper headlines: Ibid.

133   television coverage showed whites applauding: SSC Video 1, Reel 3, February 14, 1968.

133   "would like for us to reach": CA, February 19, 1968.

133   "I don't believe he can be bought": CA, February 21, 1968, p. 6.

134   commercial news media continually played upon: Lentz, "Sixty-five Days," pp. 161–63, 169–70.

135   "beat the living hell": Arkin Report, p. 4.

135   "If a man seeks your job": Ibid., pp. 4–5.

135   Crunk grabbed his .22-caliber rifle: CA, February 16, 1968, p. 1. Washington Butler, the director of the War on Poverty Committee of Memphis/Shelby County, reassured Jones that none of the Youth Corps or other antipoverty workers were involved in strikebreaking. Washington Butler to T. O. Jones, February 22, 1968, AFSCME Washington Correspondence, Box 2, Folder 98, 1968 Strike, SSC.

135   pictured Crunk grim-faced: CA, February 23, 1968, p. 23.

136   "Leave your garbage where it is": *COME Appeal,* Vol. 1, No. 1, p. 4, in FBI/MSS, Sec. 1.

136   he had united white Memphis: Charles Owen to P. J. Ciampa, February 16, 1968, AFSCME Washington Correspondence, Box 42, Folder 98, File 98-8, SSC.

137   "It will be a great day": Jack Boker to P. J. Ciampa, February 22, 1968, AFSCME Washington Correspondence, Box 42, Folder 98, File 98-19, SSC.

137   "Written contracts and due[s] check": J. S. Clark, "Dear Sir," February 20, 1968, Box 42, Folder 98, File 98-15, SSC.

137   letters opposed to his handling: Loeb received letters from both blacks and whites in Memphis and from across the nation urging him to change course. He told one unionist, "Whereas I appreciate your advice, I would like to send you some. At your first opportunity, since you live in California, why don't you go up to Berkeley, instead of writing Tennessee, and get something done to improve the Berkeley foolishness?" Henry Loeb to Melvin Trickey, President, Local 685 AFSCME, Los Angeles, March 18, 1968, AFSCME Washington Correspondence, Box 42, Folder 98, SSC.

137   "Nothing can be gained": Katherine Treanor to Henry Loeb, March 9, 1968, Box 84, Loeb Papers.

138   "the Communist Labor Crew": James W. Hendrick to Henry Loeb, March 28, 1968, Box 84, Loeb Papers.

139   Black packinghouse workers: Halpern and Horowitz, *Meatpackers.*

139   "These are all trade union": Memphis *Union News,* February 1968, p. 1.

140   Powell spoke before the City Council: Beifuss, *At the River,* pp. 145-55.

140   "I'm sorry the council has seen fit": CA, February 17, 1968, p. 19.

141   "but who's going to pay": SSC Video 1, Reel 1, February 15, 1968.

141   "are not qualified to do": Ibid.

141   "the basic dignity of the city": CA, February 17, 1968, p. 19.

141   Elections based on districts: Tucker, *Memphis Since Crump,* p. 151.

142   "ultimate destruction of the country": quoted in Goulden, *Jerry Wurf,* p. 149.

143   Between 900 and 1,000 workers: CA, February 16, 1968. p. 1; Arkin Report, pp. 6-7.

143   not a single African American led: Maxine Smith to Mayor and Board of Commissioners, August 8, 1967, and survey in NAACP, Part IV, Geographic File, Memphis, NAACP Papers, LC.

144   no NAACP statement could be read: Beifuss, *At the River,* p. 49.

145   "This Illegal Strike": PS, February 17, 1968, p. 4.

145   agents began conducting surveillance: Department of Justice, *Security and Assassination Investigations,* p. 24.

145   "injected itself into the strike": Arkin Report, p. 2.

145   the state legislature in Nashville: CA, February 17, 1968, p. 1; Stanfield, "More Than a Garbage Strike."

147   Miles spoke with AFSCME leaders: Beifuss, *At the River,* p. 63.

147   "You take the scabs off the streets": CA, February 19, 1968.

148   pay premiums for workers: J. Gordon Bingham, Jr., to John Massey, Blue Cross–Blue

Shield, June 12, 1968; Bingham to Jerrold More, May 22, 1968; and Henry Loeb to John Massey, Memphis Hospital Service, April 18, 1968, in Series III, Box 84, Sanitation Strike: Food Stamps, Loeb Papers.

148   more than $7,000 for food stamps: The Memphis and Shelby County Welfare Commission Summary Report for February 1968 shows an expenditure of $7,043.50 for food stamps for striking workers. According to Loeb's correspondence, these ended in March, but why or how he had authority to end those payments is not clear. See Series III, Box 84, Sanitation Strike: Food Stamps, Loeb Papers.

148   "wants to play rough": CA, February 17, 1968, p. 1.

149   *Commercial Appeal* reporter Charles Thornton: For Thornton quotes, see CA, February 18, 1968, pp. 1, 10.

149   to speak to every church congregation: Ibid., p. 19.

149   Council members held a secret meeting: Beifuss, *At the River*, p. 64.

150   "The city is going to beat this": Ibid.

7. TESTING THE SOCIAL GOSPEL

151   "I felt that white ministers": Bass, *Blessed Are the Peacemakers*, p. 251.

151   King wrote his "Letter": For King quotes, see Bass, *Blessed*, pp. 247, 252–53.

152   Memphis had more churches: Beifuss, *At the River*, p. 60.

152   "fine to give invocations": Ibid., p. 61.

152   helped to run abolitionists out: Lewis, "Southern Religion," p. 36. David Chappell, however, argues that white religious leaders were not in the forefront of the segregationist movement and many white religious conservatives left open the possibility that God did not sanction racial inequality. See Chappell, *Stone of Hope*.

153   Reverend Roy Love of Mt. Nebo: Honey, *Southern Labor*, p. 203.

153   "Christ, not Crump": Ibid., p. 205.

153   committee of seven black ministers: Other members included J. W. Williams, W. E. Ragsdale, Brady Johnson, A. C. Jackson, and Horace Robinson. Jordan int., SSC.

153   mistakenly invited a black minister: Starks int., SSC.

153   nearly a hundred black ministers: Two or three whites also belonged to the Alliance, including Southwestern University professor Carl Walters, and they provided a small inroad into the white middle class. Starks int., SSC.

153   Association had begun study groups: Dimmick int., SSC.

154   statement condemning racial prejudice: Beifuss, *At the River*, pp. 59–60.

154   selected group of blacks and whites: According to Dimmick, among those present were Reverend Roy Williams, pastor at Lane; Dr. Aldridge of Idlewild Presbyterian; Rabbi James Wax; Frank McRae; Reverend Brooks Ramsey, the only Baptist there; Dr. Paul Tudor Jones; Catholic priests Joseph Leppert and Father Mark Gary; and Dan Cummings of Central Christian Church. Dimmick int., SSC. Reverend Jordan said that J. W. Williams, Brady Johnson, W. A. Ragsdale, A. C. Jackson, H. Horace Robinson, and W. N. Brown were also there. Jordan int., SSC.

154   "Almost all native-born Southerners": Webb, *Fight Against Fear,* p. xvi.

155   quietly taken Jim Crow signs out: Beifuss, *At the River,* p. 53.

155   no Baptist and fundamentalist sects: Lewis, "Southern Religion," p. 78.

155   "vast lower middle class": Lincoln int., SSC.

155   blacks scorned the MCCR: Lewis, "Southern Religion," p. 76.

156   led a committee to see Ciampa: For Wax and Ciampa quotes, see Beifuss, *At the River,* pp. 62–63.

156   nearly two dozen men met: SSC Film and Videotape Record, p. 16.

157   "Father, please!": For Loeb and Ciampa quotes, see Beifuss, *At the River,* pp. 65–66.

157   "Tell those men in no uncertain": SSC Video 1, Reel 6, February 18, 1968.

157   "The right of these men": Ibid.

157   "What *is* that relationship": Ibid.

158   "rumpled gray hair, horn-rimmed": Beifuss, *At the River,* p. 67.

159   disagreements had boiled down: Wax int., SSC.

160   Wurf met nearly 1,300: Arkin Report, p. 8; Green, "Labor in the South," p. 168.

161   "Keep your money in your pockets": Beifuss, *At the River,* p. 70.

161   "There will be no peace": Arkin Report, p. 8.

161   even less able to influence Loeb: CA, February 22, 1968, p. 1. After the all-night session at St. Mary's, negotiators moved on to the First Methodist Church and Father Mark Gary's St. Peter's Roman Catholic Church, but the *Commercial Appeal* on Wednesday declared the talks "fruitless." CA, February 21, 1968, p. 1.

163   "We must stick together": Arkin Report.

164   "Some of the men was goin' back": Honey, *Black Workers,* p. 298.

164   "Twelve or 14 police intelligence men": CA, February 20, 1968, p. 1.

164   E. D. Redditt had attended: Redditt int. (M.H.).

165   tried "to out-do the other": Ibid.

166   "Negro leaders feel that": Ibid.

166   agents cultivated black ministers: Gerald McKnight found that NAACP executive board members maintained regular contact with the FBI. *The Last Crusade,* p. 151. Reverend Kyles spoke regularly to MPD's Henry Lux. Lucy int., SSC, Lawson int. (M.H.), and Redditt int. (M.H.).

166   FBI agents had done very little: Garrow, *The FBI and MLK,* passim.

167   "a darkie on the plantation": Beifuss, *At the River,* pp. 73–74.

8. MINISTER TO THE VALLEY:
THE POOR PEOPLE'S CAMPAIGN

173   "I wish today, that Christians": King, "What Are Your New Year's Resolutions?" Ebenezer Baptist Church, January 7, 1968, Series III, Speeches, MLK Papers.

174   "war on sleep": Young, *An Easy Burden,* p. 433.

174   "like a political campaign": King, *Voices of Freedom,* p. 456.

174 which he defined as a society: For a brilliant summary of King's perspective, see King, "The Future of Integration," Kansas State University, January 19, 1968, Series III, Speeches, MLK Papers.

174 "Two-thirds of the peoples": King, "What Are Your New Year's Resolutions?" Ebenezer Baptist Church, January 7, 1968, Series III, Speeches, MLK Papers.

174 "the plight of the Negro poor": King, "Why We Must Go to Washington," p. 10, MLK Papers.

175 The 1966 SCLC convention: "SCLC 10th Convention Urges Labor-Civil Rights Alliance," *The Mine-Mill Union* 25:9 (September 1966).

175 "We must guard against": King, May 31, 1964, statement on Taft-Hartley, reprinted by MLK Papers Project (mlkpp-liberationcommunity.stanford.edu/launchpads/news/news letter.jsp).

175 proposed to abolish poverty directly: Garrow, *Bearing the Cross*, pp. 593, 600. His guaranteed-income idea was backed by a wide range of humanists and scholars concerned about how to respond to structural unemployment and poverty. Perrucci and Pilisuk, *The Triple Revolution.*

176 "as attention getting and dramatic": King, "Why We Must Go to Washington," p. 11, MLK Papers.

176 "We were prepared to stay": Young, *An Easy Burden,* p. 443.

176 use sit-ins and protests to shut down: Martin Luther King Press Conference Remarks, January 16, 1968, Ebenezer Baptist Church, MLK Papers. See also Garrow, *Bearing the Cross*, pp. 582–83.

176 "Distributive justice" would: King, "Why We Must Go to Washington," p. 16, MLK Papers.

176 Privately, King said American capitalism: Garrow, *Bearing the Cross*, pp. 591–92.

176 "Something is wrong with capitalism": Garrow, *Bearing the Cross*, p. 581.

176 "In this instance, we will": King, "Why We Must Go to Washington," MLK Papers.

176 "In a sense we're going": Martin Luther King Press Conference Remarks, Ebenezer Baptist Church, January 16, 1968, MLK Papers.

177 King said SCLC had 270 affiliates: Martin Luther King Press Conference Remarks, Ebenezer Baptist Church, January 16, 1968, MLK Papers.

177 anyone could understand a simple demand: "Why We Must Go to Washington," King speech, January 15, 1968, MLK Papers.

177 "a radical reordering of our": King, "Why We Must Go to Washington," MLK Papers.

177 felt as if they were adrift: Fairclough, *Redeem the Soul,* p. 362.

177 Speaking to fifty or sixty staff: Garrow, *Bearing the Cross,* pp. 591–93.

178 sense of "dignity and destiny": For King quotes, see King, "See You in Washington," January 17, 1968, MLK Papers.

178 King had specialized: Payne, "The View from the Trenches," in Payne and Lawson, *Debating,* p. 115.

178 Ella Baker: Grant, *Ella Baker,* passim; Ransby, *Ella Baker,* passim.

178   "It is important to keep the Movement democratic": Baker, "Bigger Than a Hamburger,"
       June 1960 in Payne and Lawson, *Debating*.

179   it required a hard sell: Garrow, *Bearing the Cross*, p. 590.

179   Marion Logan, a respected member: Ibid., pp. 600–1.

179   "We've got to find something": King, untitled speech, Chicago, February 6, 1968, MLK
       Papers.

179   campaign as a "capital siege": Associated Press, "King Reveals Strategy for Capital Siege,"
       January 31, 1968. Reproduced in FBI/MLK.

179   SCLC had successfully worked: Martin Luther King Press Conference Remarks, Ebenezer
       Baptist Church, January 16, 1968, p. 9, MLK Papers.

180   "I hope we don't come to": Martin Luther King Press Conference Remarks, Ebenezer
       Baptist Church, January 16, 1968, MLK Papers.

180   he traveled the country speaking: Garrow, *Bearing the Cross,* ch. 12.

180   used the rhetoric of backlash: "Cities in '68," *The New Republic,* December 16, 1967, pp.
       5–7.

181   "This power hungry, evil black devil": FBI/MLK, SAC Cleveland to Director, January 8,
       1968.

181   "guaranteed wages for Negroes": Ibid., December 7, 1967.

181   Congress should stop King: FBI/MLK, Letter to Senator Frank Lausche, November 20,
       1967.

181   "If I am mistaken": FBI/MLK, Attn: J. Edgar Hoover, February 16, 1968.

181   FBI supplied derogatory information: FBI/MLK, January 7, 1968.

181   Ashbrook of HUAC: Ashbrook inserted a *New York Times* article of December 5, 1967,
       and criticized King in the *Congressional Record,* reproduced in FBI/MLK.

182   tapping the phones of his advisers: The FBI regarded King advisersStanley Levison,
       Bayard Rustin, Clarence Jones, Harry Wachtel, Jack O'Dell, Harry Belafonte, Moe Foner,
       Leon Davis, and Cleveland Robinson as subversives. Garrow, *The FBI and MLK*, pp.
       183–86. FBI memos on "Communist Infiltration of the SCLC" noted that King "does not
       make a speech, write a book, or make policy decisions without first consulting with Lev-
       ison," FBI/MLK, December 20, 1967.

182   Campaign might set off: On February 18, 1968, The *Miami Herald* reported that a num-
       ber of black leaders wanted King to direct demonstrators away from Washington and
       into local congressional districts to avoid riots. FBI/MLK, February 21, 1968.

183   "a conscious, alert and informed": King, *Where Do We Go*, p. 184.

183   met with NWRO chairperson: Kotz and Kotz, *Passion for Equality,* p. 76.

183   "You know, Dr. King": ABC News. Partial transcript, MLK Film Project, Subject MLK
       Welfare, Conference Chicago, January 5, 1968, MLK Papers.

183   "You're right, Mrs. Tillmon": Kotz and Kotz, *Passion for Equality,* p. 76.

183   never been criticized so sharply: Garrow, *Bearing the Cross,* p. 595.

184   "In SCLC we were working": Kotz and Kotz, *Passion for Equality,* p. 79.

184   women actually became the backbone: Jackson, "Recasting the Dream," pp. 507–8.

184   Smith of the NWRO organized: on March 30, 1968, King said, "We've had the privilege

of working very closely over the last few weeks with the Welfare Rights Organization," speeches in Mississippi, MLK Papers.

/184   wiretaps by U.S. Army Intelligence: For quotes from the conversation among King, Carmichael, and Brown, see CA, March 21, 1993.

184   meet with Stokely Carmichael: Garrow, *Bearing the Cross*, pp. 595–96.

184   his friends as "black fascists": Ibid.

185   "King, Stokely Join in Capital": *Chicago Defender*, February 6, 1968.

185   "double cross" from Stokely: FBI/MLK, "Washington Spring Project," February 6, 1968.

186   Lack of unity between: Fager, *Uncertain Resurrection*.

186   King met with 600 members: February 16, 1968, FBI/MLK.

186   gave a speech that encapsulated: King, "Mississippi Leaders on the Washington Campaign," St. Thomas AME Church, Birmingham, February 15, 1968, MLK Papers.

188   "You know the Jericho Road": King, "Who Is My Neighbor?" Ebenezer Baptist Church, February 18, 1968, MLK Papers.

188   would not let King or the delegates go: Kyles int., SSC.

188   he addressed the ministers: King, "To Minister to the Valley," February 23, 1968, Miami, MLK Papers.

189   "Our staff has not gotten": Garrow, *Bearing the Cross*, p. 597.

189   "There's no masses in this": Young, *An Easy Burden*, p. 444.

189   "a profoundly weary and wounded": Garrow, *Bearing the Cross*, p. 599.

190   "The bitterness is often greater": Ibid.

9. BAPTISM BY FIRE

192   "What has she got to do with it?": Beifuss, *At the River*, p. 77.

192   "Now we would really like to hear": Ibid.

192   "We insist on hearing": Ibid., p. 76.

192   "There has been an attempt": Ibid., p. 77.

193   Davis tried to keep order: Ibid., pp. 77–78.

193   chambers seemed like a nightmare: Ibid., p. 78.

193   "A whole part of what the black": Ibid., p. 82.

193   Seeing trouble ahead, Councilman: Ibid., p. 78.

194   "A combination union meeting": Ibid., p. 79.

194   142 police officers and thirty: Arkin Report, p. 10.

194   "a hundred loaves of bread": Beifuss, *At the River*, p. 79.

195   "Henry, I don't think you were elected": Ibid., p. 80.

195   "The situation became rather tense": FBI/MSS, February 23, 1968, Doc. 15, p. 2.

195   the most "inflammatory" statement: CA, February 23, 1968, p. 1.

195   "I'm not going to get up there": Beifuss, *At the River*, p. 81.

196   "Those people had been talking": Ibid.

196   "rhetorical conjurer of dark doom": Ibid., p. 284.

196   "The worst thing that happened": Ibid., p. 74.

196 Behind closed doors, Davis and Netters: Arkin Report, p. 10.

197 "When you go home, don't sleep": Beifuss, *At the River,* p. 82.

198 members held a closed session: Ibid., pp. 83–84.

198 Meanwhile, some 600 workers met: Arkin Report, p. 11.

199 "tended to antagonize": FBI/MSS, February 24, 1968, Doc. 18, p. 1.

199 "This is what they think of you": Beifuss, *At the River,* p. 85; Arkin Report, p. 13.

200 "Heretofore, there had been": FBI/MSS, February 24, 1968, Doc. 18, p. 2.

200 "We're going to march": Ibid.

200 "You'd better come down": Beifuss, *At the River,* p. 87.

201 rushed to the office of Mayor Loeb: Ibid.

201 they could march four abreast: Arkin Report, p. 14.

201 "the march could scarcely": FBI/MSS, February 14, 1968, Doc. 18, p. 3.

201 Jones refused to cooperate: Arkin Report, p. 14.

201 Once the march got underway: Beifuss, *At the River,* p. 88.

201 "He was a friendly looking fellow": Ibid.

201 police cars suddenly appeared: SSC Video 1, Reel 8, February 23, 1968.

202 "Get that car back": Beifuss, *At the River,* p. 89.

202 Police claimed that a striker: Arkin Report, pp. 15–16.

202 "a new debilitating type chemical": FBI/MSS, February 24, 1968, Doc. 18, p. 3.

203 "T. O. Jones escaped": FBI/MSS, February 23, 1968, Doc. 14, p. 2.

204 Police had sprayed him: Stanfield, "More Than a Garbage Strike."

204 When Lawson turned: Beifuss, *At the River,* p. 89.

204 "he just wheeled and started": Ibid., p. 90.

208 "you had a bunch of councilmen": Marshall and Van Adams, "The Memphis Public Employee Strike," pp. 178–79.

209 "I feel like we have been assaulted": SSC Video, Reel 11.

209 "I've been pleading": Ibid.

209 "Yesterday, this group was behaved": Ibid.

209 FBI reports made it appear: FBI/MSS, February 24, 1968, Doc. 18, p. 2.

10. MINISTERS AND MANHOOD

211 "treats the workers as though": SSC Video, February 24, 1968, p. 17; Estes, *"I Am A Man!"* p. 162.

212 "From earliest childhood the average Negro": TSD, June 8, 1963.

212 "He's treating you like children": Beifuss, *At the River,* p. 46.

212 Lucy first used the phrase: Lucy told Laurie Green that he and a few other organizers came up with the slogan in March and, after that, its use quickly spread. Green, "Race, Gender, and Labor," p. 483.

212 Waters sing about manhood: Estes, *"I Am A Man!"* pp. 158–59; Gordon, *Can't Be Satisfied,* pp. 3–19, 142–43, 172.

212 exercising one's "manhood" meant: Estes, *"I Am A Man!"*; Tyson, *Radio Free Dixie.*

212   using the first-person pronoun: Benjamin Peters, "I Am A Man: Authoring History in Memphis," spring 2004, unpublished paper in author's possession.

213   "like you was their child": Green, "Race, Gender, and Labor," p. 474.

213   Yarbrough later used: Ibid., p. 483.

213   Jackson concluded that the black: Beifuss, *At the River*, pp. 116–17.

214   "to minister to the valley": Ibid., pp. 99–100.

215   "If these black workers": Ibid., p. 105.

215   barrios in East Los Angeles: See Haney Lopez, *Racism on Trial*.

215   placed the blame on marchers: FBI/MSS, February 24, 1968, Doc. 18, p. 4.

216   "heavy set Negro": CA, February 24, 1968, p. 2.

216   he had "escaped": FBI/MSS, February 23, 1968, Doc. 14, p. 2.

216   the eighth marcher arrested: Jones, O. B. Hicks, O. D. Wilson, James A. Jordan, George E. Jeffries, and John Washington each paid bail of $1,250, while Eugene Brown and John Kearney, Jr., paid bonds of $2,500. Statement of M & M Bail Bond Company, February 26, 1968, SSC.

216   charged him with assault: FBI/MSS, February 24, 1968, Doc. 18, p. 4.

216   *Commercial Appeal* that morning blamed: CA, February 24, 1968, p. 6.

216   internal report later concluded: Arkin Report, p. 17.

216   "No principle of law is more": FBI/MSS, February 26, 1968, Doc. 22, p. 3.

216   Hoffman put his injunction: FBI /MSS, February 26, 1968, Doc. 22.

217. "officers, agents, and members": Richard W. Barnes, Director of Personnel, City of Memphis, February 24, 1968, Series III, Box 84, Loeb Papers.

217   attorneys thought the threat: Beifuss, *At the River*, p. 98.

217   strain on the department's: Ibid., pp. 121–23.

217   to use "all necessary means": For years after the strike, civil libertarians fought to replace that overly broad law, and finally did, but only after many fleeing suspects, most of them young black men, died at the hands of police. Ibid., p. 121.

218   agent Louis McKay: FBI/MSS, February 26, 1968, p. 3; Arkin Report, p. 17.

218   "The ladies at the meeting": CA, February 25, 1968.

219   "Come, let us reason together": Beifuss, *At the River*, p. 106.

219   The meeting included both: Ibid., p. 99.

219   This gathering pulled together: Ibid., pp. 101–2.

220   "racial balance in all kinds of jobs": Ibid., p. 103.

220   "No new clothes for Easter": Ibid., p. 102.

220   Patterson respectfully requested the press: Press conference, SSC Video, February 26, 1968.

220   Matthews came up to officers: Arkin Report, p. 18.

221   Jesse Turner might have been: Maxine Smith int., SSC.

221   every African American congregation: Beifuss, *At the River*, p. 103.

221   Patterson and other ministers broadcast: Patterson, "March On."

222   the Movement's secret weapon: Jack O'Dell int. (M.H.).

222   "Firestone hall should have been": Beifuss, *At the River*, p. 177.

223   "Negro Community, Labor, Ministers": TSD, March 2, 1968.

223   "Negro Pastors Take Reins": CA, March 12, 1968, p. 17.

223   "for one time we're going to": CA, February 26, 1968, p. 1.

223   "Lawbreakers are being led": CA, February 25, 1968, Sec. 5, p. 3.

223   press conference urging employers: SSC Video, February 24–25, 1968.

224   11 AM on Monday: Beifuss, At the River, p. 117.

224   This adherence to strict police rules: FBI/MSS, SAC to Director, `February 26, 1968, p. 6; and Beifuss, At the River, pp. 117–18.

224   Another 122 people marched: CA, February 27, 1968, p. 1.

224   began a strenuous regime: FBI/MSS, February 26, 1968, Docs. 28–30; CA, February 27, 1968, p. 1.

224   let sanitation workers speak: CA, February 27, 1968, p. 1.

225   "Anybody who buys an insult": Stanfield, "More Than a Garbage Strike."

225   "A Negro's Reaction": CA, February 27, 1968, p. 6.

225   "When does a labor problem": CA, February 27, 1968, p. 6. See also Lentz, "Sixty-five Days."

226   "The one thing your scabbing": CA, February 27, 1968, p. 6.

226   immediately put Basinger's letter: Reverend C. O. Basinger, "Untitled," File 9, Box 5, Folder 6, Holloman Papers.

226   FBI reviewed Lawson's leading role: FBI/MSS, February 27, 1968, Doc. 20, p. 9.

226   blandly accepted such falsifications: See O'Reilly, "Racial Matters," and Hoover and the Un-Americans.

228   LeMoyne had a conservative leadership: Halberstam, The Children.

229   "experience themselves as men": Van Deburg, Modern Black Nationalism, p. 127.

230   Black poor people regularly fought: O'Neill, Coming Apart.

230   "This was our approach": Smith, "March On."

232   whites and blacks armed themselves: Frank, An American Death, pp. 1–6.

232   officers surrounded John Burl Smith: TSD, July 8, 1967.

232   "Just look at these people": PS, August 10, 1967; TSD, September 2, 1967.

233   Johnson also expanded domestic spying: McKnight, Last Crusade, pp. 35–48.

233   escalated its COINTELPRO surveillance: McKnight, Last Crusade, pp. 46–47.

233   significant numbers of white votes: Lawson received 8,000 white and 18,000 black votes. Jesse H. Turner, "Analysis of City Election," October 5, 1967, Part IV, Geographic File, NAACP Papers.

234   "Most of us were very religious": Coby Smith, "March On."

234   An FBI informant said Cabbage thought: FBI/MSS, March 21, 1968, Doc. 128.

235   "The name Invaders comes": Beifuss, At the River, p. 133.

235   "When I grew up you couldn't": Coby Smith, "March On."

235   "young, aggressive-minded": Beifuss, At the River, pp. 131–32.

236   Teenagers had no patience: Coby Smith int., SSC.

237   "In 1968, when the sanitation workers": Coby Smith, "March On."

11. CONVERGENCE

240   "Public employees by the hundreds": PS, February 16, 1968, p. 6.

241   In the black community, garbage: CA, February 27, 1968, p. 1.

241   Public employment had increased: PS, February 16, 1968, p. 6.

242   Not "love or affection": CA, February 7, 1968, p. 4.

242   "from protest to politics": D'Emilio, *Lost Prophet*, ch. 17.

242   Rustin, like King, wanted: Rustin, "Civil Rights at the Crossroads," *AFL-CIO American Federationist* 73:11 (November 1966): 16–20.

243   When COME held its first: Lawson int. (M.H.).

243   "can be emotionally stimulated": FBI/MSS, February 29, 1968, Doc. 32, p. 5.

243   5,000 black schoolteachers: Ibid., pp. 2–4.

243   a thousand people filled Clayborn: CA, February 27, 1968, pp. 1, 6.

244   widened the movement's agenda: Stanfield, "More Than a Garbage Strike."

244   "had two or three individuals": FBI/MSS, February 27, 1968, Doc. 30, pp. 4–5.

244   had the name "Invaders" emblazoned: Beifuss, *At the River*, p. 131.

244   "You preachers do the praying": FBI/MSS, February 27, 1968, Doc. 30, pp. 2–3.

244   Starks immediately told the audience: Beifuss, *At the River*, p. 131.

245   "two bearded, natural hair-do": FBI/MSS, February 26, 1968, Doc. 20, p. 5.

245   Police also reported rumors that Loeb's home: CA, February 27, 1968, p. 1.

245   "the incipient SNCC-oriented": FBI/MSS, February 26, 1968, Doc. 20, p. 5.

245   On Tuesday, February 27, some 300 people: Ibid., February 27, 1968, Doc. 30, p. 6.

245   "Whose City Hall is this?": Arkin Report, p. 20.

246   About fifty white businessmen watched: CA, February 28, 1968, p. 1; Beifuss, *At the River*, p. 144.

246   could simply write a letter: CA, February 28, 1968, p. 1.

246   On Sunday night, Wurf and Lawson: Beifuss, *At the River*, pp. 169–70.

246   ended its meeting without taking: CA, March 2, 1968, p. 1.

246   ordered police not to arrest: FBI/MSS, February 27, 1968, Doc. 23, p. 2.

247   Hoffman said he and twenty-two others: Ibid., Doc. 30, p. 7.

247   "These men are not criminals": CA, February 28, 1968, p. 1.

247   fruitless series of appeals: CA, March 1, 1968, p. 1; CA, March 2, 1968, p. 1.

247   "This was a labor issue": Arkin Report, p. 21.

247   black women played a leading role: Kathy Roop (Hunninen), who got much of her grounding as a labor organizer in the Memphis strike, said black women ran many of the activities in the strike and again in the 1978 teachers' strike. Roop Hunninen int. (M.H.).

247   revealed that secret negotiations: Participants in this discussion included John Spence of the city's Civil Rights Commission; Councilmen Pryor, Donelson, and Chandler; white businessmen Carl Carson and Bert Ferguson; LeMoyne College President Hollis Price; NAACP President Jesse Turner; David Caywood, the civil liberties–oriented attorney and friend of Loeb; Jacques Wilmore of the U.S. Civil Rights Commission; and James Lawson. Beifuss, *At the River*, pp. 169–71.

248 "news of a compromise": SSC Video 1, Reel 11, February 27, 1968, p. 23.

248 "We could have ended it that day": Beifuss, *At the River*, pp. 170–72.

248 sent a letter to sanitation workers: FBI/MSS, February 29, 1968, Doc. 32, p. 1; CA, February 29, 1968, p. 16; Arkin Report, p. 21.

248 Lawson met with thirty high school: FBI/MSS, February 29, 1968, Doc. 32, pp. 1–2.

248 mass meeting that night at Mt. Pisgah: FBI/MSS, March 1, 1968, Doc. 34, p. 1; CA, March 2, 1968, p. 1.

249 "The basic issue is not pay": Stanfield, "More Than a Garbage Strike."

249 Blanchard tried to get the City Council: CA, March 1, 1968, p. 1.

249 "helping contain extremist elements": Beifuss, *At the River*, p. 115.

250 "Obscenities! I'll tell you what": Ibid., p. 176.

250 "incipient interlopers": FBI/MSS, February 29, 1968, Doc. 32, pp. 8–9.

251 They identified the leaders: Ibid., February 27, 1968, Doc. 30, p. 7.

251 Police reported trash fires and vandalism: Arkin Report, pp. 21–22.

251 police identified 75 percent: FBI/MSS, March 2, 1968, Doc. 37, p. 3.

251 That night, someone tossed bricks: Ibid.; Arkin Report, pp. 23–24.

251 On Sunday afternoon, twenty-one: CA, March 4, 1968, p. 1.

252 Blacks told Redditt: Arkin Report, pp. 24, 29.

252 "Marchers Draw Little Attention": CA, March 3, 1968, p. 1.

252 "Shoppers either ignored the marchers": CA, March 4, 1968, p. 1.

252 if "any of you are arrested": Ibid.

252 reporters asked Lawson: FBI/MSS, March 3, 1968, Doc. 52, p. 1.

252 "Who's running this thing?": Beifuss, *At the River*, p. 118.

253 triangulated civil rights leadership: FBI/MSS, February 29, 1968, Doc. 32x, p. 5.

253 relinquish day-to-day leadership to Lawson: FBI/MSS, February 28, 1968, Doc. 29x.

253 Few others could keep up: The FBI said Reverend Henry Starks was "sick, virtually physically exhausted." Ibid., March 20, 1968, Doc. 120, p. 1.

253 national and regional leaders: Ibid., February 26, 1968, Doc. 20, p. 2.

254 under tremendous pressure: Rogers int. (M.H.); Warren int. (M.H.).

254 police recording devices: Lucy int.

255 a meeting of black and white: Beifuss, *At the River*, pp. 173–74.

255 A handful of whites played: FBI/MSS, February 26, 1968, Doc. 27.

255 A number of clerics without: Beifuss, *At the River*, pp. 172–76.

255 FBI informants viewed Reverend Blackburn: FBI/MSS, February 29, 1968, Doc. 32x, p. 7.

255 FBI closely tracked white students: White students joined vigils against the Vietnam War under Lawson's leadership during Vietnam Summer in 1967, and the FBI considered them Communists because they were allegedly members of the Southern Student Organizing Committee (SSOC) and the W. E. B. Du Bois Clubs. FBI/MSS, February 29, 1968, Doc. 32x, p. 3.

255 estimated that at least 150: FBI/MSS, March 5, 1968, Doc. 68, p. 1.

255 the movement said 500: Marshall and Van Adams, "The Memphis Public Employee Strike," p. 100.

256 Powell led them in picketing: Beifuss, *At the River,* p. 108.

256 "ultra-conservative community leaders": Memphis *Union News,* March 1968, pp. 1–2.

256 "During the first month": Beifuss, *At the River,* p. 107.

256 bill to create a mediation board: CA, March 16, 1968, p. 10.

257 Seafarers International Union presented: Beifuss, *At the River,* p. 109.

257 "a throw-back to the dark ages": Memphis *Union News,* March 1968, p. 1.

258 "The right-wing people in our plant": G. W. Clark, "A Report to Members Local 186," April 2, 1968, Box 5, Folder 12, SSC.

258 Holloway had battled for years: Honey, *Black Workers,* pp. 59–72.

259 "I want to criticize some folks": CA, February 24, 1968, p. 1.

12. ESCALATION: THE YOUTH MOVEMENT

260 "unfit for the honor of minister": CA, March 5, 1968, p. 1.

260 to widen the Memphis battle: FBI/MSS, March 5, 1968, p. 1; FBI/MSS, March 6, 1968, p. 1.

260 "Memphis is going to be a better": Bell and Starks quoted by a police agent at the Eastern Star meeting. Arkin Report, p. 25.

261 Bell and Moon led workers: FBI/MSS, March 5, 1968, Doc. 53A, pp. 2–3.

261 Another seventy-five protesters: CA, March 6, 1968, p. 1.

261 "the whole basement . . . teeming": Beifuss, *At the River,* p. 156.

261 Lawson said the city could: TSD, March 9, 1968, p. 1.

261 "We will sit in this Council": FBI/MSS, March 6, 1968, Doc. 70, p. 2.

261 "We will burn this city down": Beifuss, *At the River,* p. 156.

261 A white man, his name lost: TSD, March 9, 1968, p. 1.

261 Councilman Patterson hoped to pass: SSC Video, Reel 13, March 5, 1968.

262 "We're not going to leave": FBI/MSS, March 7, 1968, Doc. 54, pp. 2–3, quoting the *Press-Scimitar.*

262 "I say you men don't have": CA, March 6, 1968, p. 1.

262 "Mr. Bell, we have listened": SSC Video, Reel 12, March 5, 1968.

262 "I wanted to find out how the police": Beifuss, *At the River,* p. 157.

263 "before they gas us down": CA, March 6, 1968, p. 1.

263 "You don't want me to have a hernia": Beifuss, *At the River,* p. 158.

263 "It is not dishonorable to go": Ibid.

263 protesters lined up two by two: Ibid., p. 159.

264 kept referring to her as "Maxine": Ibid.

264 "degrading, insulting, and humiliating": Maxine Smith to Frank C. Holloman, March 7, 1968, Box 5, Folder 4, Holloman Papers.

265 "militant young Negroes": CA, March 6, 1968.

265 Charles Cabbage and forty of his followers: FBI/MSS, March 6, 1968, Doc. 70, p. 5.

265 "Afro-American Brotherhood Speaks": Reproduced in FBI/MSS, March 6, 1968, Doc. 70, pp. 6–10.

265   Cabbage and other Invaders: two members of the Invaders formally served on the strategy committee. Stanfield, "In Memphis: Mirror to America?"

266   "Black Power, Black Power": FBI/MSS, March 7, 1968, Doc. 54, p. 5.

266   The escalation in Memphis reverberated: Ibid. March 5, 1968, Doc. 68.

267   Robert Shelton, was complicit: McWhorter, *Carry Me Home*, pp. 514, 529–30.

267   MEMPHIS IS ON THE VERGE: FBI/MSS, March 5, 1968, Doc. 53A, p. 2.

267   "The Negro has been told": CA, March 6, 1968, Sec. 6, p. 3.

267   Lawson's outgoing long-distance phone calls: FBI/MSS, March 28, 1968, Doc. 180, pp.
4–6.

268   "Black and white students have established": Memphis State University, *The Tiger Rag*,
March 8, 1968, Box 26, Folder 55, SSC.

268   "veiled black militancy": William Youngson quoted in FBI/MSS, March 13, 1968, Doc.
84A, p. 1.

268   The FBI now had George Leon: Ibid., March 13, 1968, Doc. 84A.

268   particularly Edwina Harrell: Ibid., March 7, 1968, Doc. 54, p. 8.

269   Downtown, 117 people: *AFL-CIO News,* March 9, 1968, pp. 1, 12; CA, March 7, 1968,
p. 1.

269   T. O. Jones had threatened him: CA, March 7, 1968, p. 1.

269   Hoffman said AFSCME leaders: FBI/MSS, March 6, 1968, Doc. 30, pp. 6–7; Beifuss, *At
the River,* p. 111.

269   leaders claimed they were "helpless": PS, March 7, 1968, p. 17.

270   Sabella appealed: His challenge to the injunction's constitutionality went to the Tennessee Court of Appeals in Jackson, and then to the U.S. Sixth Circuit Court of Appeals,
which turned it down and sent it back to Hoffman. CA, March 8, 1968, p. 1.

270   "Justice Is Dead in Memphis": FBI/MSS, March 7, 1968, Doc. 54, p. 4.

270   "In this casket is justice": CA, March 7, 1968.

270   Marchers hoped to produce: FBI/MSS, March 6, 1968, Doc. 70, p. 5.

270   but the police did nothing: Ibid., March 7, 1968, Doc. 54, p. 5; CA, March 7, 1968, p. 7.

271   On the night of March 6: FBI/MSS, March 7, 1968, Doc. 54, pp. 4–5.

271   "vandalistic youths": Ibid., p. 5.

271   "They [the young people] go to meetings": Ibid., March 8, 1968, Doc. 56, p. 3. Quoting
the *Commercial Appeal.*

271   suspended two students: CA, March 4, 1968, p. 1; CA, March 5, 1968, p. 1.

271   Turner warned adults: CA, March 1, 1968, p. 19.

271   "a loud, boisterous and disorderly": Arkin Report, p. 29.

272   "Memphis is sitting on a powder keg": Ibid., pp. 30–31.

272   began massive riot-control exercises: CA, March 9, 1968, p. 1.

272   "BITTER HATRED ON PART": FBI/MSS, March 8, 1968, Doc. 58.

272   trash fires abounded: Ibid., Doc. 56, pp. 1–3.

272   about fifty black male teenagers: Ibid., March 9, 1968, Doc. 72, p. 1.

273   "some uniformed patrolmen": Ibid., p. 5.

273   "no longer a simple labor dispute": Arkin Report, p. 31.

273   "A few of the kids looked like": Beifuss, *At the River,* p. 178.

273   "ill groomed" white students: FBI/MSS, March 10, 1968, Doc. 150.

273   passed out flyers at school: Ibid., March 12, 1968, Doc. 74, pp. 1–2; Arkin Report, pp. 12–13.

273   After rallying, thirty of them: CA, March 12, 1968, p. 1.

274   They lay down on the floor: A judge fined them for "resisting arrest" and bound them over to the state on charges of disorderly conduct. FBI/MSS, March 12, 1968, Doc. 75A, p. 1.

274   "injecting more youth": FBI/MSS, March 12, 1968, Doc. 74.

274   Jackson led another 175 marchers: CA, March 12, 1968, p. 1.

274   only thirty workers had paid dues: CA, March 7, 1968.

274   Blackburn said 90 percent: SSC Video, Reel 15, March 11, 1968; CA, March 9, 1968, p. 1.

275   "are hopeful that the strike": FBI/MSS, March 13, 1968, Doc. 76, p. 3.

275   Arkin felt confident that strikers: CA, March 9, 1968, p. 1.

275   "no end in sight": FBI/MSS, March 12, 1968, Doc. 74, p. 1.

275   canceled the city's contributions: Lowery to Henry Loeb, March 19, 1968; Henry Loeb to Richard Curran, April 17, 1968. Correspondence in Food Stamps, Box 8, Loeb Papers. See also CA, March 27, 1968.

275   Workers paid 50 cents for $12: CA, March 9, 1968, p. 23.

275   more than 750 of them: CA, March 16, 1968.

276   "No business can be efficiently": CA, March 17, 1968, p. 3.

276   "Negro Pastors Take Reins": *Commercial Appeal* quotes in Arkin Report, p. 33.

276   "I became the fourth 'nigger' ": Beifuss, *At the River,* p. 163.

276   "All right, if you want to leave it": CA, March 12, 1968, p. 1.

277   "only part of a broad spectrum": Ibid.

277   After the council vote: FBI/MSS, March 12, 1968, Doc. 74, p. 3; CA, March 12, 1968; Arkin Report, p. 34.

277   "city for all the people": FBI/MSS, March 13, 1968, Doc. 76, pp. 4–5.

277   At one mass meeting: Stanfield, "More Than a Garbage Strike."

277   The level of threats against: FBI/MSS, March 13, 1968, Doc. 79, pp. 1–2; FBI/MSS, March 13, 1968, Doc. 76, pp. 4–7; FBI/MSS, March 13, 1968, Doc. 80, p. 1.

278   A smaller group split off: FBI/MSS, March 13, 1968, Doc. 75B, pp. 1–3.

278   "shouting, acting boisterous": Ibid., March 14, 1968, Doc. 81A, pp. 1–2.

278   youths went on a rampage: CA, March 14, 1968, p. 1.

278   successful in replacing strikers: CA, March 12, 1968, p. 1; CA, March 14, 1968, p. 1.

279   a more militant response: FBI/MSS, March 14, 1968, Doc. 81, p. 2; FBI/MSS, March 15, 1968, Doc. 82, pp. 1–5.

279   "no matter what they're doing": CA, March 14, 1968, p. 1.

280   150 students confronted him: FBI/MSS, March 15, 1968, Doc. 82, pp. 7–8.

280   purposely stayed in the background: Ibid.

280   bring Stokely Carmichael to town: FBI/MSS, March 14, 1968, Doc. 81C.

281   without a functioning SCLC: Samuel Kyles chaired the SCLC in Memphis, and Hooks and Lawson served on King's board. Middlebrook int., SSC.

282   Rustin's position in the Movement: D'Emilio, *Lost Prophet,* chs. 18, 19.

282   "How can you get rid of poverty": Rustin's Mason Temple speech is in SSC Video, Reels 15, 16.

283   "one of the great struggles": CA, March 15, 1968, p. 23.

283   "This becomes the symbol": Ibid.

285   police arrested five black males: FBI/MSS, March 15, 1968, Doc. 84.

285   "prowling" and "traveling for the": CA, March 15, 1968, p. 1; Arkin Report, p. 36.

285   Weinman's court held in abeyance: Arkin Report, p. 36.

285   reported increasing verbal threats: CA, March 16, 1968, p. 1; Arkin Report, p. 36.

286   black youths picketed downtown: CA, March 17, 1968, p. 1; Arkin Report, p. 37.

286   "Time for Council to Move": CA, March 16, 1968, p. 6.

13. "ALL LABOR HAS DIGNITY"

287   "fundamental patterns of American life": Young, *An Easy Burden,* p. 447.

287   "We had become the enemy": Ibid., p. 446.

288   "Capitalism cannot reform itself": W. E. B. Du Bois, Letter Applying for Membership in the Communist Party of the U.S.A., October 1, 1961, MLK Papers.

288   "our irrational obsessive anti-Communism": King, "Honoring Dr. Du Bois," pp. 108–9.

288   "People become so deluded": *Hattiesburg American,* April 2, 1968.

288   "King, Red Ex-aide Team Up": *Birmingham News,* March 7, 1968.

288   "King Shows Kindly Disposition": *Birmingham News,* March 10, 1968.

288   "Secret FBI records definitely tie": *Clarion Ledger,* March 28, 1968.

288   "prevent the rise of a black messiah": Garrow, *The FBI and MLK,* p. 187.

288   "publicize King as a traitor": Ibid., p. 183.

288   "serve again to remind": FBI/MLK, Security Memorandum, February 29, 1968.

288   FBI also held a "racial conference": McKnight, *Last Crusade,* p. 26.

289   Julia Brown on tour: Ibid., p. 27.

289   Brown had visited Memphis: Bill Ross int., SSC. She visited Memphis again after King's death, SSC clippings file.

289   "As is usually the case": FBI/MLK, February 13, 1968.

289   "playing a last, desperate card": *America,* February 24, 1968.

289   "making a bold play": "Showdown with Insurrection," *National Review,* n.d.

289   "a haphazard series of events": "Principles and Heresies," *National Review,* n.d.

289   "a Washington paralyzed": *Reader's Digest,* April 1968, pp. 65–70.

290   complained to newsman Daniel Schorr: Hampton and Fayer, eds., *Voices of Freedom,* p. 457.

290   Bayard Rustin warned: D'Emilio, *Lost Prophet,* p. 460.

290   "Almost no one on the staff": Hampton and Fayer, eds., *Voices of Freedom,* p. 457.

290   "I'm often disenchanted": King, "The Other America," March 10, 1968, MLK Papers.

290   On March 14 and 15: Branch, *At Canaan's Edge,* pp. 715–17.

291   Harris polls showing: *New York Times,* May 23, 1967.

292 "We had charted out fifteen": Hampton and Fayer, eds., *Voices of Freedom*, p. 459.

292 had to fly from a speaking engagement: FBI/MLK, March 21, 1968.

292 moved SCLC's planning conference: Hampton and Fayer, eds., *Voices of Freedom*, p. 459; CA, March 18, 1968, p. 1.

292 "We had been through this": Young, *An Easy Burden*, p. 449.

292 King flew to Memphis on Monday, March 18: TSD, March 16, 1968, p. 1. The *Defender* covered King's speech on March 18, even though the weekly edition is dated March 16.

293 Powell excoriated Mayor Loeb: CA, March 19, 1968, p. 1; SSC Video, March 18, 1968.

294 "These men tell us that": SSC Video, Reel 18, March 18, 1968.

293 "Loeb said we could pile up": Ibid., Reel 19, March 18, 1968.

293 "We will not stop until": Ibid.

295 O. W. Pickett, AFSCME staff, and COME: PS, March 19, 1968. Crenshaw and Lucy raised one fund; O. W. Pickett and Reverend C. W. Porter of the Church of God in Christ raised another; it seems that they both channeled donations through COME. FBI/MSS, March 12, 1968, Doc. 145, p. 3.

295 "The Negro minister has taken": *COME Appeal*, Vol. 1, No. 1, Box 12, Folder 87, AFSCME Washington Files, SSC.

295 Charleston striker: Seeger, *Where Have All the Flowers Gone*, pp. 32–35.

297 He began quietly: audio recording and annotated transcript, SSC.

304 "We will not go to schools": PS, March 19, 1968.

305 Lucy viewed King's response: Hampton and Fayer, eds., *Voices of Freedom*, pp. 459–60.

306 "saw how many Negroes": CA, March 16, 1968, p. 1.

306 "a series of demagogic appeals": FBI/MSS, March 17, 1968, Doc. 87.

306 "King's Eye on Washington": CA, March 20, 1968, p. 6.

306 "a handy starting point": Arkin Report, p. 40.

306 When he innovated and moved: Halberstam, "The Second Coming."

307 "Nobody knew it except us": Hampton and Fayer, eds., *Voices of Freedom*, p. 459.

307 downtown businesspeople to wonder: Trotter, "The Memphis Business Community."

307 "an undertone of criticism": TSD, March 23, 1968.

307 with Abernathy, Young, Bernard LaFayette: Arkin Report, p. 39.

308 "confer with Negro ministers": FBI/MSS, SAC to Director, March 19, 1968, Doc. 105.

14. "SOMETHING DREADFUL"

309 "It had never snowed that late": Lanetha Jewel Branch int., "Behind the Veil," used by permission.

309 King's strength, said Bayard Rustin: King "did not have the ability to organize vampires to go to a bloodbath," joked Rustin, but rather relied on inspiring speeches and events to make the Movement. D'Emilio, *Lost Prophet*, p. 337. The NAACP's Herbert Hill, for one, considered King more a mystic than a revolutionary. Hill int. (M.H.).

310 eighty-four of the city's 180 trucks: PS, March 19, 1968.

310 "Never before in the history": *COME Appeal*, Vol. 1, No. 1, Box 12, Folder 87, AFSCME Washington Files, SSC.

310 widely distributed a leaflet: COME, "Martin Luther King and the Community on the Move for Equality Invite You to March for Justice and Jobs," 98-19, SSC.

310 "a momentous event for Memphis": COME Memo, 14-12, SSC.

310 "His march will be the most": COME, Flyer to Public School Teachers of Memphis, 97-17, SSC.

310 "be united in harmony": COME, Statement on Purposes of March, 97-20, SSC.

311 "Whites interpreted militant": Marshall and Van Adams, "The Memphis Public Employee Strike," p. 99

311 bringing in Stokely Carmichael: FBI/MSS, SAC to Director, March 19, 1968, Doc. 105.

311 said he would invite Carmichael: FBI/MSS, March 18, 1968, Doc. 112A, p. 4.

311 not stopping the garbage trucks: In a meeting at Dr. Vasco Smith's house, Smith and Harold Middlebrook criticized Lawson for being "too lenient" and advocated lying down in front of garbage trucks. G. P. Tines to J. C. MacDonald, Chief of Police, MPD, March 28, 1968, File 6, Holloman Papers.

311 at the March 18 meeting, Ralph Abernathy: FBI/MSS, March 19, 1968, Doc. 117, p. 2.

311 "We are expecting to have 10,000": PS, March 19, 1968.

311 COME sent a letter: Ezekial Bell et al., "Dear Friends," March 27, 1968, and Lt. E. H. Arkin to G. P. Tines, March 27, 1968. Both in File 9, Box 5, Folder 6, Holloman Papers.

312 used more coercive tactics: Arkin Report, pp. 39–41.

312 had left behind James Bevel: FBI informants observed Bevel at a meeting in the office of the Chicago W. E. B. Du Bois Club. When someone declaimed that he was not a Communist, Bevel responded, "Every thinking American should be," and went on to say, "Negroes have not begun to read yet, but when they do, they will all be socialists." Bevel may have been toying with agents. FBI/MSS, March 21, 1968, Doc. 110; FBI/MSS, March 19, 1968, Doc. 117, pp. 3–4.

312 Bevel spoke at Warren Temple: Ibid., March 30, 1968, Doc. 122, pp. 3–4.

312 "a virulent black power talk": Arkin Report, p. 41.

312 urged students to read Frantz Fanon's: FBI/MSS, March 21, 1968, Doc. 129, pp. 4–5.

313 "Bevel is organizing for": Ibid., pp. 7–8.

313 an excuse to carry matches: Ibid., March 20, 1968, Doc. 122, p. 7.

313 supposedly threatened the Memphis: Arkin Report, p. 42.

313 twelve unemployed "young militants": FBI/MSS, March 21, 1968, Doc. 129, p. 7.

314 "doing his best to talk": Ibid., Doc. 124.

315 sanitation supervisor Leonard Ward: Ibid., March 18, 1968, Doc. 112A, p. 5.

315 Someone even fired a shot: Ibid., March 25, 1968, Doc. 138A.

315 increasingly risky to scab: CA, March 20, 1968.

315 the window of a Loeb's Laundry: Ibid.

315 frequently pulled fire alarms: FBI/MSS, March 20, 1968, Doc. 122, p. 5.

315 striker named Leslie Robinson: Ibid. March 22, 1968, Doc. 134, p. 2; CA, March 22, 1968, p. 19.

315   were both African American: The woman's street address, 1253 Englewood, seems to be in south central Memphis, a black area. CA, March 22, 1968, p. 19.

315   "unlawfully disturbing and disquieting": The law was used only once in its 110-year history. Ibid., March 20, 1968.

315   Police singled out Ferguson: Blackburn int., SCC.

315   sanitation worker Willie Kemp: FBI/MSS, March 22, 1968, Doc. 134, p. 3. Kemp tried to convince black undercover agent Willie Richmond that he had not attacked Ed Redditt. See W. B. Richmond to G. P. Tines, March 26, 1968, File 7, Box 5, Holloman Papers.

315   "Loeb is deeply hated": FBI/MSS, March 19, 1968, Doc. 114, pp. 1–2.

315   Don Stevens reported to the police: Arkin Report, p. 41.

316   "The 'Real' Martin Luther King, Jr.": Enlightened People on Communism, "The 'Real' Martin Luther King, Jr.," 43-9, SSC.

316   "Rev. Dick Moon's wife Glenda": Beifuss, At the River, p. 192.

316   "You black son of a bitch": Ibid.

316   "It was as if a whole host": Ibid., p. 193.

316   "pillage, burn, loot and destroy": Kuykendall, "The Immorality of our Times," March 22, 1968, Box 5, Folder 9, Series II, SSC.

316   "pick pocket party": Kuykendall, "The Republican Party Is the Party for Our Time," February 14, 1968, Box 5, Folder 9, Series II, SSC.

316   effects of "communism everywhere": Kuykendall, "Demonstrations and the War in Vietnam," April 25, 1967, Box 5, Folder 9, Series II, SSC.

317   "shouting and gesturing obscenities": CA, March 20, 1968, p. 6.

317   "To Dr. King and His Marchers": CA, March 21, 1968, p. 1.

318   "Save Our City": flyers, March 4, 1968, in 5-4, SSC.

318   had been holding interracial social meetings: Murray, "White Privilege, Racial Justice," pp. 207–15.

318   "Where were you born, honey?": SSC, anecdotes, 51–33.

318   "I wouldn't do a single thing differently": CA, March 15, 1968.

318   "Upon entering the Union Hall": Mary Doughty, SSC, anecdotes, 51–162.

318   200 strike supporters attended: CA, March 20, 1968, p. 1; CA, March 21, 1968, p. 1.

318   members discussed Patterson's proposal: FBI/MSS, SAC to Director, March 20, 1968, Doc. 106.

319   "deftly fielded questions": CA, March 20, 1968.

319   "I think people found out": Beifuss, At the River, p. 198.

319   "was definitely on the defensive": Louise McComb to Lewis Donelson, March 21, 1968, 8-22, SCC.

320   "and now here comes Dr. King": Beifuss, At the River, p. 109.

320   Any form of mediation: Ibid., p. 187.

320   UAW's Fair Practice Council: Edward Taylor, president; Mark Deason, vice president; James Bridges, recording secretary, to Henry Loeb, March 26, 1968, Donelson File, SSC.

320   gave their workers the day off: FBI/MSS, March 21, 1968, Doc. 129, pp. 2–3.

320   Even the mass media took notice: Beifuss, *At the River,* p. 201.

321   "The printing of that information": Ibid.

321   Council passed Chairman Pryor's resolution: CA, March 22, 1968, p. 1.

321   "If one is to gamble so much": CA, March 20, 1968, p .6.

321   he traveled the Deep South: Garrow, *Bearing the Cross,* p. 608.

322   In Grenada: Branch *Canaan's Edge*, pp. 483–85, 526–29.

322   "We are tired of our men not being able to be men": King, Poor People's Campaign Rally Speech, Grenada, Mississippi, March 19, 1968, Series III, MLK Papers.

322   "The thing wrong with America": King, Poor People's Campaign Rally Speech, Laurel, Mississippi, March 19, 1968, Series III, MLK Papers.

322   "We want some land": King, Poor People's Campaign Rally Speech, Clarksdale, Mississippi, March 19, 1968, Series III, MLK Papers.

322   gave King a hundred-dollar bill: Branch, *At Canaan's Edge,* p. 720.

322   King despaired at Mississippi's poverty: Garrow, *Bearing the Cross,* p. 606; Garrow, *The FBI and MLK,* p. 189.

323   two people raised their hands: FBI/MLK, March 20, 1968, p. 329.

323   he canceled his last speeches: FBI/MSS, March 21, 1968, Doc. 127.

323   stranded at the Birmingham airport: Ibid., Doc. 131.

323   He spent much of the night: FBI/MSS, March 21, 1968, Doc. 131; FBI/MSS, March 22, 1968, Docs. 132, 134.

323   "war on sleep": Young, *An Easy Burden,* p. 433.

323   "Snow Blanket Bundles Dixie": Jackson *Clarion Ledger,* March 24, 1968.

323   Nature had gone on strike: Beifuss, *At the River,* p. 205.

323   "We've got a perfect work stoppage": Ibid.

323   Twenty hardy souls showed up: FBI/MSS, March 22, 1968, Doc. 134; Beifuss, *At the River,* p. 205.

324   "Do Right Mr.? Mayor": Beifuss, *At the River,* p. 205.

324   shot into a strikebreaker's home: Arkin Report, p. 43.

324   "There's no way in the world": Garrow, *Bearing the Cross,* p. 607.

324   flew out again to New York: Ibid., p. 608.

324   "It gets very discouraging sometimes": King, "Unfulfilled Dreams," in Carson and Holloran, eds., *A Knock at Midnight,* pp. 194–99.

325   when union representatives renewed talks: CA, March 23, 1968, p. 1; CA, March 24, 1968, p. 1; CA, March 25, 1968, p. 1.

326   representatives again met behind closed doors: CA, March 26, 1968, p. 1.

326   no longer receive food stamps: CA, March 27, 1968, p. 19.

326   "The strike is illegal": CA, March 28, 1968, p. 1.

326   "'Recognition' meant the rights": Marshall and Van Adams, "The Memphis Public Employee Strike," p. 179.

326   "After three days of meetings": CA, March 28, 1968, p. 1.

327   COME announced that King would lead: CA, March 26, 1968, p. 1.

327   Another giant march: Ibid., March 27, 1968, p. 1.

327 "They were shouting as they walked": Richmond to Tines, March 26, 1968, File 7, Box 5, Holloman Papers.

327 George Wallace indefinitely canceled: Arkin Report, pp. 43–47.

328 to limit mass meetings: FBI/MSS, March 27, 1968, Doc. 151, pp. 1–2.

329 Redditt reported that "Deacons": G. P. Tines to Chief J. C. MacDonald, March 28, 1968, File 9, Box 5, Folder 6, Holloman Papers.

330 "All present agreed": FBI/MSS, March 18, 1968, Doc. 125, p. 3.

15. CHAOS IN THE BLUFF CITY

335 "Be cool, fool": Flyer, March 27, 1968, File 9, Holloman Papers.

335 Eleven incidents of vandalism: Arkin Report, p. 48.

335 strike supporters began confronting: Arkin Report, pp. 47–48; CA, March 29, 1968.

336 "in a rather boisterous manner": FBI/MSS, March 29, 1968.

336 trying to march toward the downtown: SSC Video, Tape 5, Reel 23; Jackson int., SSC.

336 At 9:14, police headquarters sent: CA, March 29, 1968.

336 turned up to defend their children: Middlebrook int., SSC.

336 the FBI reported they had: FBI/MSS, To Director, March 28, 1968, Doc. 160, p. 2.

336 Jo Ann Talbert was hit in the head: Arkin Report, p. 49; Beifuss, *At the River,* p. 212.

336 By 9:30, a torrent of human beings: CA, March 29, 1968.

337 Tommy Powell, Bill Ross, Dan Powell: Beifuss, *At the River,* p. 212.

337 King and the ministers: Ibid., p. 217.

337 Joyce Palmer, a young white mother: Ibid., p. 214.

337 atmosphere changed as word spread: Arkin Report, p. 49.

337 King would be killed: Beifuss, *At the River,* p. 216.

337 Lester High School students joined: Jackson int., SSC.

338 police could hardly keep track: Arkin Report, p. 49.

338 Older people carried placards: Beifuss, *At the River,* p. 217.

338 youngsters created their own signs: Ibid.

338 "We're going to get some white folks": PS, March 29, 1968, p. 15.

338 estimated that only 3,338 to 6,338: Arkin Report, pp. 49–50.

338 Police also identified a number: FBI/MSS, March 29, 1968, Doc. 184, pp .4–5; FBI/MSS, March 28, 1968, Doc. 160, p. 3.

338 BOP organizers stayed behind: FBI/MSS, March 29, 1968, Doc. 184, pp. 1213.

339 "It seemed as though we were": Beifuss, *At the River,* p. 216.

339 disheveled men, young and old: Ibid., p. 219.

339 "a textbook example": Young, *An Easy Burden,* p. 453.

339 did not have enough marshals: Beifuss, *At the River,* p. 219.

339 "drinking anything they could get": Ibid., p. 220.

340 asked such people to leave: Ibid., p. 218.

340 "There was an element in the crowd": Ibid., p. 220.

340 "white presence wasn't exactly": Ibid., p. 214.

340   police had circled the area: Ibid., p. 215.

341   twenty-five men raided a liquor store: CA, March 29, 1968.

341   "LOEB'S HANGING TREE": Beifuss, *At the River,* p. 217.

341   asking them to join a "coalition of conscience": "Conversation with Martin Luther King,"
       pp. 1–19; Garrow, *Bearing the Cross,* p. 608.

342   he was "losing hold": Garrow, *Bearing the Cross,* pp. 608–9.

342   his flight to Memphis: Garrow says King flew to Atlanta and then to Memphis. Young
       says he flew from Newark to Memphis, as do the FBI records. Garrow, *Bearing the Cross,*
       p. 609; Young, *An Easy Burden,* p. 451.

342   "Martin must have been so fatigued": Young, *An Easy Burden,* p. 451.

342   four-foot-long pine sticks: Arkin Report, p. 50.

342   tore the signs off the sticks: Beifuss, *At the River,* p. 219.

342   King an hour to get out: Abernathy, *Walls Came Tumbling,* p. 417. The *Commercial
       Appeal* wrote that it only took ten minutes to get King out of the car. CA, March 29,
       1968, p. 1.

343   Ministers locked their arms: CA, March 29, 1968, p. 1.

343   "The people were trampling": McKnight, *Last Crusade,* p. 66.

343   unruly sea of young people: Beifuss, *At the River,* p. 222.

343   "make the crowds stop pushing": PS, March 29, 1968, p. 15.

343   considered the possibility of aborting: Beifuss, *At the River,* pp. 220–22.

344   Pressed upon by the crowd: *At the River I Stand.*

344   "people were trying to walk": Beifuss, *At the River,* p. 223.

344   Kay Pittman Black remained behind: Ibid., p. 221.

344   observed that a band of youths: Arkin Report, p. 50.

344   a riot had begun behind them: Beifuss, *At the River,* p. 224.

345   "Windows! They're breaking windows!": Ibid.

345   "to interfere with the march": Ibid.

345   "Burn it down, baby!": Ibid., p. 225.

345   Up ahead on Main Street, at Gayoso: FBI/MSS, March 28, 1968, Doc. 159, pp. 1–2; CA,
       March 29, 1968.

345   "Take Dr. King down McCall": Beifuss, *At the River,* p. 225.

345   "Jim, they'll say I ran away": Lawson int., ATR.

345   "Martin balked, so I said": Beifuss, *At the River,* p. 225.

345   "I've got to get out of here": Arkin Report, p. 51; FBI/MSS, To Director, March 28, 1968,
       Doc. 163, p. 3.

346   Bernard Lee flagged down: Young, *An Easy Burden,* p. 454; FBI/MSS, March 28, 1968,
       Doc. 165; FBI/MSS, March 29, 1968, Doc. 171.

346   "only concern was to run": FBI/MSS, March 28, 1968, p. 3.

346   "This is Reverend Lawson speaking": Arkin Report, p. 51.

346   At 11:22, Fire and Police Director Frank Holloman: CA, March 29, 1968.

346   police waded into the crowd: Beifuss, *At the River,* pp. 225–26.

346   shooting tear gas or rolling: CA, March 29, 1968, p. 1.

346   effort to "restore order": Arkin Report, p. 52.

347   "You don't have to show your manhood": CA, March 29, 1968, p. 1.

347   A flying wedge of policemen came: Ibid.

347   resistance infuriated the police: Ibid.

347   John Kearney ran, but the same officer: Wilmore int., SSC; G. P. Tines to J. C. MacDon-
       ald, Chief of Police, MPD, March 28, 1968, p. 4, File 6, Holloman Papers.

347   P. J. Ciampa, with his bum knee: Beifuss, *At the River*, p. 228.

348   "We didn't have trouble": Ibid., p. 227.

348   "I didn't run": Honey, *Black Workers*, p. 310.

348   "It looked like just a big steamroller": Beifuss, *At the River*, p. 229.

348   In the pandemonium, children lost: Ibid., p. 226.

348   "That was an exciting time": AARP et al., "The Voices of Civil Rights: Ordinary People. Ex-
       traordinary Stories," www.voicesofcivilrights.org/Approved_Letters/479-Rogers-TN.html.

349   "came roaring back": PS, March 29, 1968.

349   Only James Lawson with a bullhorn: Beifuss, *At the River*, p. 228.

349   "calmly, but with great dignity": CA, March 29, 1968.

349   Reporters taking pictures: Beifuss, *At the River*, p. 231.

349   "I saw women, young children": Ibid., pp. 215–16.

350   marshals kept control over: Lawson int., SSC; Middlebrook int., SSC.

350   "except the people that had looted": Beifuss, *At the River*, p. 230.

350   "The police seemed slightly reluctant": TSD, April 6, 1968.

350   Barnes Carr, documented: PS, March 29, 1968.

351   Beale Street looked "like a battlefield": PS, March 29, 1968, p. 15.

351   One officer, surrounded by a crowd: CA, March 29, 1968.

351   Numerous officers were hurt: CA, March 29, 1968; PS, March 29, 1968.

351   Looters tried to steal guns: FBI/MSS, March 29, 1968, Doc. 159, pp. 1–2; CA, March 29,
       1968.

352   "I wish this was a real live one": Beifuss, *At the River*, p. 229.

352   people battered and torched a car: Arkin Report, p. 50.

352   "You white folks get on out": Beifuss, *At the River*, p. 229.

352   "Main Street and historic Beale": CA, March 29, 1968.

352   Private ambulances refused to go: Beifuss, *At the River*, p. 237; FBI/MSS, March 28, 1968,
       Doc. 161.

352   Holloman asked Mayor Loeb to call: CA, March 29, 1968; Arkin Report, p. 51.

352   police tactical units that continued: Beifuss, *At the River*, p. 231.

352   "I was terribly frightened": Ibid., p. 224.

352   "Inside the A.M.E. building": PS, March 29, 1968, p. 15.

353   like the aftermath of a war: Beifuss, *At the River*, p. 235.

353   "All of you that are on our side": CA, March 29, 1968; Beifuss, *At the River*, p. 233.

353   Lawson worried about what had happened: Beifuss, *At the River*, p. 231.

353   "looked ashen. His hands were shaking": PS, March 29, 1968, p. 15.

354   police attacked them with mace: TSD, April 6, 1968.

354   "Behind me I could see bottles": PS, March 29, 1968, p. 15.

354   police moved down Hernando: CA, March 29, 1968.

354   thirteen officers with gas masks: TSD, April 6, 1968.

355   "but once the command was given": Beifuss, At the River, p. 234.

355   "Everyone was either hurt or mad": Ibid., p. 236.

355   some 250 people took a stand: CA, March 29, 1968.

355   Holloman called back, asking: Ibid.

355   his officers had not used gas: Beifuss, At the River, p. 237.

356   Charles Cabbage stood on the steps: FBI/MSS, March 28, 1968, Doc. 160, p. 4.

356   "We're trying our damnedest": CA, March 29, 1968.

356   firebomb into a Loeb's Laundry: PS, March 29, 1968.

357   "I told them that there were women": TSD, April 6, 1968.

357   rumor spread that a police officer: FBI/MSS, March 28, 1968, Doc. 160, p. 4.

357   "Get your children from school": Beifuss, At the River, p. 238.

357   "Honey, anything you can name": Ibid.

358   "began swinging at people's legs": Beifuss, At the River, p. 239; Arkin Report, p. 52.

358   Doctors treated many people: Injuries are recorded in John Gaston Hospital Records, SSC.

358   the strike's first fatality: FBI/MSS, To Director, March 28, 1968, Doc. 160.

359   Sixteen-year-old Larry Payne: Beifuss, At the River, pp. 240–42.

359   got a call about youths looting: Arkin Report, p. 52.

360   eyewitnesses claimed that Payne did not: CA, March 30, 1968, p. 25.

360   "He had his hands up": Beifuss, At the River, p. 242.

360   "a muffled sound, like busting a sack": CA, March 30, 1968, p. 25.

360   photo of Leona Jackson: TSD, April 6, 1968, p. 1.

360   More witnesses came forward: CA, March 30, 1968, p. 25.

360   exonerated Jones: McKnight, Last Crusade, p. 56.

360   he was not even suspended: CA, March 31, 1968, p. 14.

360   Payne's parents unsuccessfully sued the police: McKnight, Last Crusade, pp. 56–67; Beifuss, At the River, p. 357.

360   "Yes, we have a war": CA, March 29, 1968, p. 1.

360   "I think you should realize": PS, March 29, 1968.

361   "We were in a civil war": Ibid.

361   "Police charged into the crowd": Ibid.

16. "THE MOVEMENT LIVES OR DIES IN MEMPHIS"

362   people poured into the hospital: John Gaston Hospital Records, March 28, 1968, SSC.

363   "strongly feel some elements": FBI/MSS, Message to Director, March 28, 1968, Doc. 165, p. 2. A second FBI memo later in the afternoon used the language: "Negro group who dislike him and desire to cause KING trouble." FBI/MSS, March 28, 1968, Doc. 168.

363 "the violence was caused by": FBI/MSS, From Atlanta's A. G. Santinella, March 29, 1968, Doc. 168.

363 "really didn't have any idea": Garrow, *Bearing the Cross,* p. 611.

363 Lawson soon arrived, and he and Kyles: Garrow, *The FBI and MLK,* p. 193.

363 investigating committee later concluded: U.S. House of Representatives, House Select Committee on Assassinations, *Final Assassinations Report.*

363 "Did MARTIN LUTHER KING": FBI/MSS, From ASAC C. O. Halter, March 28, 1968, Doc. 167.

364 documented that the *Globe-Democrat:* The U.S. House Select Committee on Assassinations believed that the paper's invective might have encouraged a conspiracy to kill King that was operating out of St. Louis. McKnight, *Last Crusade,* pp. 60–62.

364 "get everything possible on KING": FBI/MSS, March 29, 1968, Doc. 173. The FBI constantly pressured agents to "find something" on King, causing them to twist their reports to that end. An FBI agent in Memphis related Lieutenant Arkin's comments after watching a post-riot television interview in which King "said he did not finish what he set out to do. He didn't elaborate." This suggestion that King wanted violence is clearly wrong: King was saying that he had not done the job of leading a nonviolent march. Such false inferences and political ignorance appear commonly in intelligence files.

364 "All racial sources have been": FBI/MSS, March 29, 1968, Doc. 159, p. 3.

364 avoided the "fine Hotel [sic] Lorraine": Memo from FBI Assistant Director William Sullivan. Reprinted in Friedly and Gallen, *The FBI File,* pp. 575–76. See also Garrow, *The FBI and MLK,* p. 196.

365 King had stayed at the dilapidated: Lawson int. (M.H.); William Bailey int., SSC.

365 When a raging mob had trapped him: *Eyes on the Prize, A Film History,* part 6, "Bridge to Freedom."

365 "The issue is not a question": SSC Video, Reels 25, 26, March 28, 1968, transcript, pp. 693–885.

366 "I thought the march itself": CA, March 29, 1968, p. 1.

366 "we won't be a part of violent": SSC Video, Reels 25, 26, March 28, 1968, transcript, pp. 693–885.

366 "abandoned by its leaders": Ibid.

367 "get your ass out of Memphis": Hampton and Fayer, eds., *Voices of Freedom,* p. 462.

367 "You mustn't hold yourself responsible": Garrow, *Bearing the Cross,* p. 612.

367 "terrible and horrible experience": Garrow, *The FBI and MLK,* p. 194.

367 Faires called King's role "deplorable": CA, March 30, 1968.

367 denounced "mindless violence": *Washington Post,* March 30, 1968, p. 1; Lentz, "Sixty-five Days," p. 274.

367 "Johnson Warns on Rioting": *Washington Post,* March 30, 1968, p. 1.

367 "a powerful embarrassment": Garrow, *Bearing the Cross,* p. 615.

367 Meany urged Mayor Loeb to recognize: CA, March 31, 1968 p. 14; *AFL-CIO News,* April 6, 1968, p. 4.

367   "Moment of Truth": CA, March 29, 1968.

368   "Memphis has had enough": CA, March 31, 1968, p. 6.

368   "Chicken a La King": CA, March 31, 1968. Both Memphis dailies ran consistently anti-King editorials. Lentz, "Sixty-five Days," pp. 203–8.

368   "the headline-hunting high priest": CA, April 2, 1968, p. 6.

368   "Young militants jostled and pushed": Arkin Report, p. 55.

368   "King Before Disappearing Act": *Clarion Ledger,* March 29, 1968, p. 1.

369   "exposed" King's ties to Jack O'Dell: *Clarion Ledger,* March 28, 1968.

369   "King Vows to Press Attack": *Clarion Ledger,* March 30, 1968, p. 1.

369   *Natchez Democrat* cartoons linked King: *Natchez Democrat,* February 1, 1968.

369   "noted Communist Negro Educator": *Natchez Democrat,* March 22, 1968.

369   southern media regularly vilified King: See media scrapbooks collected by Edward Hunvald, retired Memphis department store executive, Container 12, SSC.

369   man "inflated by ambition": CA, March 30, 1965.

369   "to break laws in the name": CA, April 2, 1968, p. 6.

369   Memphis proved King could not lead: CA, April 30, 1968, p. 1; CA, April 2, 1968, p. 21; Garrow, *Bearing the Cross,* p. 616.

369   "like striking a match": CA, March 30, 1968, p. 1.

369   "self-seeking rabble-rouser": CA, April 2, 1968, p. 21.

370   "agitating destruction, violence and hatred": SSC Video, Reel 28; Kuykendall Speech File, SSC.

370   Eugene McCarthy pointed out: CA, March 31, 1968, p. 16.

370   "Memphis on Fire": TSD, April 6, 1968.

370   described him as "the bomb": Ibid.

371   Stern interviewed Coby Smith: SSC Video, Reels 29–32.

371   "If the community can only respond": Branch, *At Canaan's Edge,* p. 740.

372   "Young black people want": CA, April 1, 1968, p. 25.

372   "Younger Negroes . . . say their allegiance": *Los Angeles Times,* March 31, 1968, p. 19.

372   "Don' mak no diff'unce": Branch, *At Canaan's Edge,* p. 737.

372   When King entered the room: Taylor int., SSC. Taylor also recalled King as having said he had met with Stokely Carmichael and Huey P. Newton when he was in California.

372   he was surprised to see Cabbage: Garrow, *Bearing the Cross,* p. 613.

373   warning of a plot to kill King: Cabbage int. (M.H.).

373   "what must be done to have": Garrow, *Bearing the Cross,* pp. 612–13.

373   laughed and said he had to be kidding: Cabbage int. (M.H.); Garrow, *Bearing the Cross,* p. 613; Beifuss, *At the River,* pp. 253–54.

374   "a person that was so clear": Smith, "March On."

374   he explained to reporters: For press conference quotes, see SSC Video, Reels 35–37, March 29, 1968.

376   "I think our Washington campaign": Garrow, *Bearing the Cross,* p. 615.

377   "Frankly, it was a failure": Garrow, *Bearing the Cross,* p. 614.

377   "influenced by what they read": Ibid., p. 614.

377   "Martin Loser King": Lentz, "Sixty-five Days," p. 274.

377   Wilkins warned that Memphis showed: CA, April 3, 1968, p. 1.

377   "NAACP Official Blames King": PS, March 20, 1968. Quoted in Arkin Report, p. 55.

378   "get me out of Memphis": Abernathy, Walls Came Tumbling, p. 422.

378   covered King's press briefing by noting: CA, March 30, 1968.

378   "We didn't bring in Rap Brown": Ibid.

378   "the times before the Montgomery": Abernathy, Walls Came Tumbling, p. 423. Coretta Scott King makes no mention of this dinner, My Life, p. 322. Abernathy's account is riddled with mistakes, but Juanita Abernathy recalls the same dinner, Hampton and Fayer, eds., Voices of Freedom, p. 463.

378   never seen King so depressed: Hampton and Fayer, eds., Voices of Freedom, p. 463.

378   "He was experiencing a great deal": Scott King, My Life, p. 322.

378   "You as much stuck in Memphis": Epps, "March On"; Epps int., SSC.

379   met with his SCLC executive staff: Young, An Easy Burden, p. 457; Branch, At Canaan's Edge, pp. 741–44.

379   Suffering from a continual migraine: Jesse Jackson, in Hampton and Fayer, eds., Voices of Freedom, pp. 463–64.

379   "It was obvious from the beginning": Young, An Easy Burden, p. 458.

379   "but the staff was upset with him": Ibid., p. 457.

380   "took the position very sharply": FBI Levison Wiretap Files, April 1, 1968. 100-111180-9-16227a, on microfilm. Thanks to Erik Gellman for reminding me of this source.

380   King rebuked him as if he: Garrow, Bearing the Cross, p. 616.

381   "As somberly and seriously": Young, An Easy Burden, p. 459.

17. STATE OF SIEGE

382   legislation deemed necessary to curb riots: PS, March 29, 1968.

382   power to proclaim civil emergencies: Public Chapter No. 485, Senate Bill 1360, Series III, Box 84, Sanitation Strike 1968, Loeb Papers. See also Branch, At Canaan's Edge, p. 733.

383   felony to enter into a conspiracy: Public Chapter No. 485, Senate Bill 1169, Series III, Box 84, Sanitation Strike 1968, Loeb Papers.

383   the federal anti-riot law: Most famously, the anti-riot act produced the trial of the Chicago 8, the antiwar protesters charged with inciting the police riot at the Democratic Convention in Chicago in August 1968.

383   fifteen years' imprisonment for looting: Public Chapter No. 485, Senate Bill 1196, Series III, Box 84, Sanitation Strike 1968, Loeb Papers.

383   "degenerated into a riot": PS, March 29, 1968.

383   Loeb's curfew lasted for: Curfews Issued During Sanitation Department Strike, Series III, Box 84, Sanitation Strike 1968, Loeb Papers.

383   some 4,000 National Guardsmen: For details, see Beifuss, At the River, pp. 243–44; SSC Video, Tape 5, Reel 27.

383   "traditionally been a white outfit": CA, March 30, 1968.

383   military occupation of Detroit: Fine, *Violence in the Model City.*

384   infrared telescopes on their rifles: CA, March 30, 1968.

384   "How you conduct yourselves": CA, March 29, 1968, p. 1.

384   300 policemen, 50 sheriff's: CA, April 3, 1968.

384   The number of calls for police: Beifuss, *At the River,* p. 244.

384   news showed flames consuming: SSC Video, Reels 27, 28.

384   Arkansas also mobilized National Guard: PS, March 29, 1968.

385   "At some point when police are faced": *New York Times,* July 7, 1968.

385   police stopped and searched black people: CA, March 31, 1968, p. 14.

385   police jerked a cab-driving minister: CA, April 1, 1968.

385   black areas, however, continued under strict curfew: CA, March 29, 1968.

385   whites traveled the streets: CA, March 31, 1968, p. 14.

386   fired several shots at a police car: PS, March 29, 1968.

386   125,000 students who stayed home: PS, March 30, 1968.

386   "plywood wasteland for ten blocks": *Vicksburg Evening Post,* March 30, 1968, p. 1.

386   "It's going to take maybe forty years": Beifuss, *At the River,* p. 247.

386   rioters smashed 200 storefronts: *Vicksburg Evening Post,* March 30, 1968, p. 1.

386    $400,000 in initial damages: Ibid.

386    $1.5 million to pay for troops: PS, April 1, 1968.

387   Henry Lux assessed the situation: FBI/MSS, March 30, 1968, Doc. 201, p. 3.

387   "overall good performance": Beifuss, *At the River,* p. 247.

387   NAACP said that black Memphians "deluged" it: Maxine Smith to Ramsey Clark, May 10, 1968, Box 5, File 18, SSC; Maxine Smith to Phil Canale, May 10, 1968, Box 5, File 18, SSC.

387   "They caught my uncle": Memphis Branch NAACP News Release, April 15, 1968, Box 5, File 18, and anecdotes files, SSC.

387   shot the husband of Elizabeth Stevenson: Police and Civil Disorders, Box 5, File 18, SSC.

387   "only a small part of the accusations": PS, May 20, 1968.

388   "long-haired, foul-smelling hippies": Holloman, "Where We've Been, Where We Are, Where We Are Going," Memphis Rotary Club, February 18, 1969, Holloman Papers. See also PS, April 20, 1968.

388   "permissiveness and appeasement": Holloman, "Responsibility," Beta Sigma Phi Sorority, November 15, 1969, Holloman Papers.

388   "Brutality Claims Linked": PS, July 13, 1968.

388   "thin blue line" protecting society: Holloman, "Where We've Been, Where We Are, Where We Are Going," Memphis Rotary Club, February 18, 1969, Holloman Papers. See also PS, April 20, 1968.

388   "We have stood against anarchy": Statement of Frank C. Holloman to City Council, January 6, 1970, Holloman Papers.

388   the full brunt of a police crackdown: Beifuss, *At the River,* p. 244.

388   "Blood streamed down the side": CA, March 29, 1968.

388   Police shot one black man: PS, March 29, 1968.

389   200 African Americans faced charges: CA, April 3, 1968.

389   black youth laughed and joked: CA, March 30, 1968, p. 18.

389   "We expected Memphis to respond": Beifuss, *At the River,* p. 249.

389   "keeping the militant youth": SSC Video, Reel 30, Tape 6.

389   "Ain't we gonna march": Billings and Greenya, *Public Worker,* p. 198.

390   film footage showed them: SSC Video, Reel 34, March 29, 1968, pp. 54–55.

390   Starks shook the hand of each man: Ibid.

390   "most famous streets, memorialized": CA, March 30, 1968, p. 1.

390   placards reading, "I Am A Man": SSC Video, Reel 42, April 1, 1968, p. 70.

391   "Their willingness to go out there": *Washington Post,* March 31, 1968.

391   sent out a letter to unions: *AFL-CIO News,* April 6, 1968, p. 4.

392   did better on strike benefits: Beasley int., ATR.

392   "By the time we got to the platform": Beifuss, *At the River,* p. 258.

392   ministers met at Reverend Dick Moon's: Ibid., pp. 249–50.

392   wrote a manifesto: Ibid., p. 250.

392   seminary professors also wrote: *Washington Post,* March 31, 1968.

392   began talk about a summit meeting: Beifuss, *At the River,* p. 251.

393   transcend the black-white divide: Ezekial Bell, depicted as such a firebrand and black nationalist in the press, joined with Darrell Doughty at Parkway Gardens Presbyterian Church in an attempt to form a "truly integrated congregation." On April 4, he would write an open letter to whites asking them to join his interracial church, also suggesting many specific things they could do to increase communication between blacks and whites. See Ezekial Bell, "Open Letter," April 4, 1968, and "Dear Charles," April 4, 1968. Both in Box 5, File 18, SSC.

393   "do unto others": Memphis Ministers Association, "Appeal to Conscience," March 31, 1968, Box 5, File 18, SSC.

393   "has expanded into a broad human rights": *Washington Post,* March 31, 1968, p. 1.

393   "the Negro racist groups [that] converted": Donelson to C. M. Herron, Equitable Life Insurance, March 5, 1968, Folder 8, Item 22, SSC.

393   "give in to criminals and law violators": A "Concerned Citizen" to Councilman Lewis Donelson, March 13, 1968, Donelson File, SSC.

393   "cower before the union": Mrs. B. S. Eastman to Councilman Lewis Donelson, February 23, 1968, Donelson File, SSC.

393   Donelson pressed a resolution: Taylor Blair to Downing Pryor, March 28, 1968, Box 8, Folder 13, SSC.

394   Others voted against: Beifuss, *At the River,* p. 251.

394   As the sixth week of the strike drew: Ibid.

394   450 people marched again in single file: FBI/MSS, April 1, 1968, Doc. 199.

394   Fearing the showing of his body: Ibid., April 2, 1968, Doc. 206, p. 3.

394   "They shot you down like a dog": Ibid., SAC to Director, April 2, 1968, Doc. 210.

394   "There will probably not be a Negro": FBI/MSS, SAC to Director, April 2, 1968, Doc. 206, p. 3; Arkin Report, p. 61.

395 sanitation workers marched peacefully: FBI/MSS, SAC to Director, April 2, 1968, Doc. 210.

395 King's staff pulled into Memphis: FBI/MSS, April 1, 1968, Doc. 199.

395 The Invaders—on SCLC's bill: Cabbage int. (M.H.).

395 Jackson had initially told Cabbage: Cabbage, "Memphis Strike Roundtable."

395 "fed up" and "disgusted" Jackson: FBI/MSS, March 30, 1968, Doc. 201, p. 9.

395 The Invaders were not responsible: An FBI informant verified that though some of the Invaders had been "agitating" young people, "the actual BOP people did not participate in any of the vandalism." FBI/MSS, April 2, 1968, Doc. 206, p. 12. Many students claimed to be Invaders by putting the name on their jackets, but few of them were affiliated with BOP. FBI/MSS, March 29, 1968, Doc. 184, p. 12. An FBI source also said that only one percent of marchers were involved in looting, and many of them were "criminally inclined" rather than movement people. FBI/MSS, March 29, 1968, Doc. 184, p. 13. Another FBI report said that young adults with criminal records started the looting, and it even listed the names and addresses of some of them. FBI/MSS, April 2, 1968, Doc. 228. The Memphis Police had also found black men selling merchandise stolen during the looting. FBI/MSS, April 3, 1968, Doc. 236.

395 Ballard was the only BOP organizer: PS, April 4, 1968, pp. 6, 25.

395 "There are only about 12 to 15": The FBI said Cabbage, John Burl Smith, Charles Ballard, Edwina Jeanetta Harrell, Verdell Brooks, James Phillips, Charles Harrington, and Clifford Taylor had identified themselves to the FBI as Invaders leaders on February 16, 1968. FBI/MSS, March 30, 1968, Doc. 201, p. 11, quote on p. 8.

396 "all want to destroy the King image": FBI/MSS, April 2, 1968, Doc. 206.

396 "keeping the lid on": Ibid., pp. 8–9.

396 "the preachers aren't going": Arkin Report, p. 61.

396 At a press conference on Monday, April 1: SSC Video, Reel 40, April 2, 1968, p. 66.

396 for an end to "plantation rule": Ibid., Reel 42, April 1, 1968, p. 70.

396 a plan to "redistribute the pain": CA, April 3, 1968, p. 8.

396 "White businesses in the Negro community": Arkin Report, p. 61; CA, April 2, 1968, p. 1.

396 "We're here as political psychiatrists": FBI/MSS, April 3, 1968, Doc. 237, p. 3.

396 "We unequivocally believe in": CA, April 2, 1968, p. 1.

396 make the mass march a national event: FBI/MSS, April 2, 1968, Doc. 210. According to Frank, King announced the march as a national event at the airport, but it is not clear who actually made the decision to turn it into a national march, or when. Frank, *An American Death,* p. 43.

397 increased their pressure on the Invaders: FBI/MSS, April 2, 1968, Docs. 230, 249. See also Arkin Report, p. 61.

397 COME Strategy Committee met: FBI/MSS, April 5, 1968, Doc. 273.

398 $3,000 in legal fees: FBI reports tell of the Invaders' continuing struggle for money and legal expenses to be paid by COME. See FBI/MSS, June 1968.

398 The Invaders now turned to SCLC: Jim Bishop wrote that the Invaders had asked for $100,000 from the Memphis ministers, but they told them "they wouldn't get one dol-

lar." Bishop, *The Days of MLK,* p. 35. Branch puts the demand at $200,000, and it may have been more than that. Branch, *At Canaan's Edge,* p. 754; Cabbage int. (M.H.).

398 "keep the pressure on the white man": FBI/MSS, SA Lawrence to SAC, April 13, 1968, Doc. 326. Charles Cabbage corroborated this discussion. Cabbage int. (M.H.).

398 "Mr. Chandler, we have just about": CA, April 3, 1968, p. 8; Beifuss, *At the River,* p. 264.

399 John T. Fisher thought: CA, March 30, 1968; see Fisher File, SSC.

399 Ned Cook, one of the city's most: Beifuss, *At the River,* pp. 286–87.

399 go to court to place strike leaders: Arkin Report, p. 59.

399 "We've won the strike": Beifuss, *At the River,* p. 266.

18. SHATTERED DREAMS AND PROMISED LANDS

400 made a powerful moral appeal: King, "Remaining Awake Through a Great Revolution," in Carson and Holloran, eds., *A Knock at Midnight,* pp. 201–24.

400 Johnson bowed out: Branch, *At Canaan's Edge,* pp. 745–46.

401 "We cannot stand two more summers": CA, April 1, 1968, p. 35. King was not fantasizing about the potential for a fascist state: Congress had funded and actually built federal concentration camps for "subversives," to be used if the president declared a national security emergency under the 1950 McCarran Act.

401 In an article slated for publication: King, "Showdown for Nonviolence," *Look,* April 16, 1968, Vol. 32, pp. 23–25. Reprinted in Washington, ed., *Testament,* pp. 64–72.

401 King seemed willing to call off: "Dr. King Hints He'd Cancel March if Aid Is Offered," *New York Times,* April 1, 1968, p. 20.

401 "Dr. King's picture came before me": Beifuss, *At the River,* pp. 261–62.

401 called in a threat to kill him: The FBI did not tell the MPD about the plane threat until 2 pm, several hours later. Arkin Report, p. 59.

401 "Well, it looks like they won't": Abernathy, *Walls Came Tumbling,* p. 428.

401 Death threats against King: Kotz, *Judgment Days,* p. 119; McKnight, *Last Crusade,* pp. 68–69; FBI/MSS, April 1–3, 1968; Arkin Report, pp. 61–63; and FBI/MLK reports, passim.

402 On April 2, a white businessman: Arkin Report, pp. 61–63.

402 deplaned at the Memphis airport: FBI/MSS, April 3, 1968, Doc. 215.

402 SCLC bookkeeper Jim Harrison: Harrison joined King's staff as a bookkeeper in October 1964, began receiving FBI payments a year later, and remained an FBI informant and staff member at least until July 1971. Garrow, *The FBI and MLK,* pp. 174–75.

402 "Wilkins Doubts King Can Control": PS, April 3, 1968, p. 1.

402 "If I were a man": Redditt int. (M.H.).

402 MPD squad of four white men: Arkin Report, p. 64; Pepper, *Orders to Kill,* pp. 150, 224–25, 281, 291. According to Pepper, the white group included Davis, Lt. William Schultz, Detective Ronald B. Howell, and Inspector J. S. Gagliano. He says D. Hamby and someone named Tucker were also at the Lorraine. See U.S. House of Representatives, *Final Assassinations Report,* p. 547.

402   Davis asked Matthews: Department of Justice, *Security and Assassination Investigations,* p. 27.

402   Don Smith, a leader of the city's: McKnight, *Last Crusade,* p. 67.

403   Lawson was not oblivious: Lawson int. (M.H.).

403   did not ask for police protection: Frank, *An American Death,* p. 46.

403   "I'm committed to nonviolence": King, "Showdown for Nonviolence," *Look,* April 16, 1968, Vol. 32, pp. 23–25, reprinted in Washington, ed., *Testament,* pp. 64–72. See also Branch, *At Canaan's Edge,* p. 746.

403   As Redditt and Willie Richmond followed: Redditt int. (M.H.).

404   Hoover had said in 1964: McKnight, *Last Crusade,* p. 69.

404   later censured the FBI: Ibid., pp. 57–58.

404   listed twenty-one long-distance calls: FBI/MSS, SAC Memphis to SAC Cleveland, March 28, 1968, Doc. 180, pp. 4–6.

404   After one late-night bargaining session: Lawson comments made at the Walter Reuther Library, Wayne State University, tape courtesy of Mike Smith.

404   who fought KKK anti-union terrorism: Alzada Clark int. (M.H.).

405   Wharlest Jackson in Natchez: Payne, *I've Got the Light,* p. 197.

405   McCullough of the Invaders: Pepper, *Orders to Kill,* pp. 431, 444.

405   "would have given their eye teeth": McKnight, *Last Crusade,* p. 154.

405   The MPD named him Max: On April 13, the FBI reviewed its work on the Invaders and said Max had been operating in BOP and The Invaders since at least early March. He worked for the police, not the FBI, which had no black agents, and was apparently the only full-time police officer inside in the Invaders. FBI/MSS, SA Lawrence to SAC, April 13, 1968, Doc. 326. Another report says Max's undercover assignment began in February. Department of Justice, *Security and Assassination Investigations,* p. 25.

405   McKenzie unwittingly signed him up: FBI/MSS, April 3, 1968, Doc. 232; Branch, *At Canaan's Edge,* p. 754.

405   "felt that BOP has been infiltrated": FBI/MSS, April 2, 1968, Doc. 206, p. 7.

405   later worked for the CIA: Posner reports that McCullough was employed by the CIA as late as 1998, but he refused to be interviewed. Posner, *Killing the Dream,* p. 31. Lawson and Cabbage both heard of his later involvement in the CIA.

406   111th Military Intelligence Group: CA, November 30, 1997; CA, March 19, 2003; CA, May 19, 2003.

406   units had been tracking King: Posner concludes MID surveillance activities against King were real, but conspiracy theorists inflated them to include assassinating King. Posner, *Killing the Dream,* ch. 22. For another theory, see Pepper, *Orders to Kill,* pp. 441–43, 446, 448, 449, 454, 457, 459.

406   MID regarded labor, civil rights: CA, November 30, 1997.

406   MID units had in fact tracked King: CA, March 21, 1993.

406   destroyed its surveillance records: CA, November 30, 1997.

406   "What some people don't remember": CA, March 21, 1993.

407   FBI regularly shared its reports: These memos were furnished to William Bray, 111th

Military Intelligence Group, Memphis. FBI/MSS, March 27, 1968, Doc. 152, and others. FBI/MSS, March 26, 1968, Doc. 155.

407   Holloman surely knew of FBI efforts: McKnight, *Last Crusade,* pp. 64–65; Garrow, *The FBI and MLK,* pp. 190, 194–97.

407   Ray grew up in miserable circumstances: For a devastating portrait of the depressed Ray family, see Bishop, *The Days of MLK,* pp. 37–43, and Posner, *Killing the Dream.*

407   "Nobody can reason with Jimmy": Huie, *He Slew the Dreamer,* p. 106.

407   "standing offer" of a reward: U.S. House of Representatives, *Final Assassinations Report,* pp. 471–89.

408   Ray had been in Los Angeles, Selma: Huie, *He Slew the Dreamer,* pp. 122–24, 128–30, 132–33, 135.

408   "the fastest hand operated": Ibid., p. 138.

408   stayed at the New Rebel Hotel: Posner, *Killing the Dream,* p. 22; Beifuss, *At the River,* p. 271.

408   "MARTIN LUTHER KING has proven": Arkin Report, pp. 62–63.

408   On the day of King's return: Arkin Report, pp. 62–63.

409   "would have been the end": Beifuss, *At the River,* p. 286.

409   Another black minister went to the police: Arkin Report, p. 62.

409   tried to publish a quarter-page ad: Beifuss, *At the River,* p. 269.

409   run the picture as a news item: A full picture of this billboard had also been carried by the *Press-Scimitar.* PS, March 23, 1965.

409   stories about King's disruptive activities: Beifuss, *At the River,* p. 263.

409   "We are not going to be stopped": CA, April 4, 1968, p. 1.

410   In Judge Brown's courtroom: The city linked King to a conspiracy whose combined actions "are calculated to lead to great racial agitation and hatred and will disrupt the peace and well being of the entire community, both white and negro." *City of Memphis v. Reverend Martin Luther King, Jr., et al.,* C-68-80, signed by Loeb, Frank Gianotti, E. Brady Bartusch, James Manire, and Frierson Graves, SSC.

411   "We are fearful that in the turmoil": CA, April 4, 1968, p. 1.

411   "from organizing or leading": Temporary Restraining Order, U.S. District Court for the Western District of Tennessee, Western Division, C-68-80. Reproduced in FBI/MSS, April 3, 1968, Doc. 234.

411   "There was no more reason": Abernathy, *Walls Came Tumbling,* p. 437.

411   Memphis attorney Lucius Burch: Beifuss, *At the River,* p. 270; Burch int., SSC.

412   he believed that Loeb and most of his: Burch said Loeb "had no experience at being exposed to what is developing and what has developed among Negroes. Nor does he *know* Negroes very well." Burch int., SSC.

412   Labor mediator Frank Miles: Beifuss, *At the River,* p. 273; Miles int., SSC.

413   a meeting with black ministers: For details, see Beifuss, *At the River,* p. 275.

413   Chamber of Commerce, Future Memphis: SSC Video, Reel 43, April 3, 1968.

414   "The BOP group is still uncontrollable": FBI/MSS, April 4, 1968, Doc. 244.

414   Young nearly came to blows: Garrow says Young and Smith had "a heated exchange"

about demands for money. Garrow, *Bearing the Cross,* p. 622. Cabbage said Smith and SCLC staff had to be restrained early in the evening of April 3, and that Smith physically attacked Young later that night when they went to the Paradise nightclub together. Cabbage int. (M.H.).

414　"KING endeavored to convince": FBI/MSS, April 4, 1968, Doc. 251.

414　"Unless King spends many hours": Ibid., Doc. 244.

414　"King was very much afraid": Garrow, *The FBI and MLK,* p. 199.

415　"will spend much money": FBI/MSS, April 4, 1968, Doc. 244.

415　When Abernathy walked into Mason: Beifuss, *At the River,* p. 277; Branch, *At Canaan's Edge,* pp. 755–56; Abernathy, *Walls Came Tumbling,* pp. 430–31.

415　Various people spoke and sang: SSC Video, Reel 44, April 3, 1968; FBI/MSS, Lowe to SAC, April 4, 1968, Doc. 252.

416　"despite Dr. King's honors": Bishop, *The Days of MLK,* p. 35.

416　some people thought he was nervous: Kyles, Middlebrook, and Lawson, SSC ints.

416　King stepped to the podium at 9:30: Branch, *At Canaan's Edge,* p. 756.

416　"Something is happening in Memphis": For all quotes, see King, "I See the Promised Land," in Washington, ed., *Testament,* pp. 279–86. An earlier transcript with different punctuation and notations on audience response is in the MLK Papers.

419　aimed these words especially at Cabbage: Cabbage int. (M.H.).

420　through one of his favorite lessons: He gave variations on the parable at the New Covenant Baptist Church in Chicago in April 1967; at Dexter Avenue Baptist Church in Montgomery in December 1967; and to his congregation at Ebenezer Baptist Church in Atlanta on March 3, 1968; as well as other places.

421　Ben Davis, formerly the black Communist councilman from Harlem: Friedly and Gallen, *Martin Luther King, Jr.,* pp. 21, 118; District 65 RWDSU stewards and officers to King, September 29, 1958, Western Union, in MLK Papers, 580929-000, Stanford University, courtesy of Kerry Taylor.

423　Lawson had moved off the podium: Frank, *An American Death,* p. 54.

423　King had told his followers: Burns, *To the Mountaintop,* p. 151.

423　"He had a strange look on his face": Barbara Brown, "The Voices of Civil Rights: Ordinary People. Extraordinary Stories," www.voicesofcivilrights.org.

424　"ministers who ordinarily would": Beifuss, *At the River,* p. 280.

425　"There was an overwhelming mood": Hampton and Fayer, eds., *Voices of Freedom,* pp. 465–66.

425　"King was like Moses": Honey, *Black Workers,* p. 309.

426　"His hands were as soft as cotton": Barbara Brown, "The Voices of Civil Rights: Ordinary People. Extraordinary Stories," www.voicesofcivilrights.org.

19. "A CRUCIFIXION EVENT"

427　"The white man has killed": CA, April 8, 1968, p. 8.

427　King went to eat at Reverend Ben Hooks's: Frank, *An American Death,* p. 57.

427   They stayed up until 4:30 AM: According to FBI agents, King arrived in the Lorraine
      Motel courtyard with Abernathy and Bernard Lee at 4:30 am and then stayed up until 8
      am visiting with his brother and Mrs. Davis. FBI, "Report of the Department of Justice
      Task Force," p. 21. Nothing corroborates Abernathy's account, in which he recounts
      King's conflicts with two women earlier that night, in a book loaded with factual mis-
      takes and distortions. *Walls Came Tumbling*, pp. 434–36. King apparently may have had a
      sexual liaison that night and at other times with Kentucky State Senator Georgia Davis.
      Branch, *At Canaan's Edge*, pp. 589–90, 759.

428   "I don't think anybody can have": CA, April 5, 1968, p. 5.

428   met at 10:30 that morning: Frank, *An American Death*, pp. 47, 56.

428   a newcomer from Detroit: Theodore Manuel claimed to have participated in the Detroit
      riot. FBI investigations in Wayne County found no arrest record for him, although they
      did find a record that he had been injured during the Memphis riot on March 28. Arkin
      Report, p. 67.

428   King entered the discussion: Branch, *At Canaan's Edge*, p. 760.

428   John Burl Smith felt angry: Smith, "The Dish," Vol. 2, Issue 1.

429   had already proposed to Cabbage: Cabbage int. (M.H.). SCLC had already listed Cab-
      bage on a staff roster. SCLC Papers, Box 280, Folder 9.

429   "grim and businesslike": Garrow, *Bearing the Cross*, p. 622.

429   "I'd rather be dead than afraid": Garrow, *Bearing the Cross*, p. 622; Abernathy, *Walls
      Came Tumbling*, p. 437.

429   "We tended to assume": Young, *An Easy Burden*, p. 460.

430   started a lively pillow fight: Garrow, *Bearing the Cross*, p. 623; *Eyes on the Prize: The
      Promised Land*, PBS film; and Young, *An Easy Burden*, p. 464.

430   Jensen directed FBI surveillance: Arkin Report, pp. 38–40.

430   refusing to advance black firemen: Black fireman Carl Stotts later sued the city in federal
      court for systemic discrimination against blacks. For NAACP suits and complaints on
      behalf of black firemen, see Box 5, Folder 18, SSC.

430   At the mass meeting: Frank, *An American Death*, pp. 64–65.

430   This left Redditt and Richmond: The Justice Department investigators documented the
      fire-department lookout but said there was no electronic surveillance on King. Depart-
      ment of Justice, *Security and Assassination Investigations*, pp. 24, 29–30. Frank seemed to
      assume that Holloman's police agents were there for King's protection, but Lawson did
      not believe it. Frank, *An American Death*, p. 46, and Lawson int. (M.H.).

431   investigators allegedly watched SCLC: In the fifth official investigation of King's murder,
      the Justice Department interviewed some 200 witnesses relating to the assassination,
      including an ex-Army agent who participated in the MID surveillance. CA, June 9, 2000.
      Freelance investigator William Pepper alleged that MID snipers had King in the sights of
      their rifles at the time of his shooting, but he couldn't prove it: a lawsuit forced his pub-
      lisher to retract his identification of a military officer as false. CA, June 22, 1999. See also
      CA, March 21, 1993, and CA, November 30, 1997.

431   "for fear that they might be blamed": Arkin Report, p. 66.

431 false reports that Stokely Carmichael: Ibid.

431 marshals guarded the homes: Ibid., p. 69.

431 black revolutionary from out of state: One version said the threat came from the Mississippi Freedom Democratic Party, but Holloman and Lux told Redditt it was from the Revolutionary Action Movement. Arkin Report, p. 66 and fn. 345. These were both false reports. Department of Justice, *Security and Assassination Investigations,* pp. 30–31, and Frank, *An American Death,* p. 65.

431 Redditt protested: Redditt int. (M.H.).

432 MPD's TAC Unit 10: Arkin Report, p. 45.

432 signed over a $10,000 check: Cabbage said photographer Ernest Withers even took a picture of the check so that SCLC could not claim it was no good. Cabbage int. (M.H.) The House Select Committee on Assassinations concluded that King rejected any funding for the Invaders, but Cabbage said they did not ask him about this, so he didn't volunteer any information. U.S. House of Representatives, *Final Assassinations Report,* p. 364.

432 SCLC had made no such payment: U.S. House of Representatives, *Final Assassinations Report,* p. 364.

432 a car pulled into the courtyard: Department of Justice, *Security and Assassination Investigations,* p. 25.

432 Around 5:50, the Invaders left: Arkin Report, p. 67. Pepper says some Invaders left with Cabbage and others left on foot. Pepper, *Orders to Kill,* pp. 256, 258.

432 Cabbage felt particularly: Cabbage int. (M.H.).

432 whole scene seemed "eerie": Smith, "The Dish."

433 "This is like the old Movement days": Beifuss, *At the River,* p. 291.

433 he stood on the balcony talking: Beifuss, *At the River,* p. 292; Young, *An Easy Burden,* p. 464; and *New York Times,* April 5, 1968, p. 1.

433 Everyone in the courtyard: Frank, *An American Death,* pp. 77, 81.

433 The force of this powerful rifle shot: The autopsy report came from the Office of the Chief Medical Examiner, Tennessee Department of Health. FBI, "Report of the Department of Justice Task Force," pp. 154–55. See also Bishop, *The Days of MLK,* p. 23.

433 "Oh, Lord, they've shot Martin": Kyles int., SSC.

434 Kyles could not make a phone call: descriptions of the moment in Frank, *An American Death,* p. 76; Beifuss, *At the River,* p. 305; Branch, *At Canaan's Edge,* p. 767; and Kyles int., SSC.

434 150 police officers suddenly swarmed: CA, April 5, 1968, p. 1.

434 "When I turned around": *New York Times,* April 5, 1968, p. 1.

434 By 6:06, a police dispatcher sent: Frank, *An American Death,* p. 84; Arkin Report, pp. 67–68.

434 By 6:09, an ambulance sped King: Arkin Report, p. 68; Kyles int., SSC.

435 identified a white man fleeing: FBI, "Report of the Department of Justice Task Force," p. 47; Arkin Report, pp. 67–68; Beifuss, *At the River,* pp. 292–93; Bishop, *The Days of MLK,* pp. 66, 72. For the most recent investigation of the assassination and theories about King's killer, see Posner, *Killing the Dream.*

435   late-model blue or white Mustang: *New York Times,* April 5, 1968, p. 1.

436   " 'John Henry, what's wrong with you?' ": Smith int., SSC; Beifuss, *At the River,* p. 296.

436   Fanion showed up a few minutes later: Beifuss, *At the River,* p. 294.

436   Lucy and Baxton Bryant quickly obtained passes: Ibid., p. 297.

437   "I just went numb": For reactions to King's death, see Beifuss, *At the River,* pp. 295–306.

439   "Just respect the man [King] enough": Ibid., p. 303.

439   "We used to have a choice": Ibid.

439   "The people were telling us to go to hell": Ibid.

439   "They were having a terrific argument": Ibid.

439   reporters trying to get to the Lorraine: Ibid., pp. 295, 303.

439   At St. Joseph's Hospital: Bishop, *The Days of MLK,* pp. 79–82.

440   "Memphis and America damned to hell": Beifuss, *At the River,* p. 300.

440   "If only they had listened": Ibid.

440   Loeb asked Netters to unite them: Netters interviewed in the film *Eyes on the Prize: The Promised Land.*

440   The mayor moved on and spent: CA, April 5, 1968, p. 8; Beifuss, *At the River,* p. 294.

440   Wax and friends heard the news: Beifuss, *At the River,* p. 297.

440   "Son of a bitch. You remember": CA, April 5, 1968, p. 13.

441   "Like any other dead nigger": SSC, anecdotes, Box 51a, Card 231.

441   Powell decided Memphis was not safe: Michael Loler, "Tommy Powell, the Face of Labor," *Mid-South Magazine;* CA, February 2, 1986.

441   "We just killed that black S.O.B.": CA, April 5, 1968, p. 13.

441   later that evening, Ernest Withers: Frank, *An American Death,* pp. 109–10.

442   "He just act so different": CA, April 6, 1968, p. 8; Beifuss, *At the River,* pp. 305, 366.

442   She went into a coma and died: Beifuss, *At the River,* p. 305.

442   riot conditions once again descended: *New York Times,* April 5, 1968, p. 1.

443   blacks with guns pinned down police: Arkin Report, p. 69.

443   "He died for us": CA, April 5, 1968, p. 1.

443   more than 30,000 long-distance calls: Beifuss, *At the River,* p. 302.

443   "Rioting and looting is rampant": Arkin Report, pp. 69–70.

443   "If a riot or violence would erupt": CA, April 5, 1968, p. 1.

443   "I wish that Stokely Carmichael": Beifuss, *At the River,* p. 308.

443   "Truthfully, I wanted to go out": Ibid.

443   That night, police received 806 emergency: For figures, see CA, April 6, 1968, p. 8.

444   subjected blacks to preemptory searches: TSD, April 6, 1968; Lawson int., SSC; Beifuss, *At the River,* pp. 304–5.

444   "Our neighborhood was like a tomb": Lentz, "Sixty-five Days," p. 110.

444   "When white America killed Dr. King": *Wall Street Journal,* April 8, 1968, p. 1.

445   "You could see the enormous pall": Pyle, *Military Surveillance,* p. 113.

445   smoke ringed a White House: *New York Times,* April 6, 1968, p. 23; Pyle, *Military Surveillance,* pp. 100–3; Gilbert, *Ten Blocks.*

445   "America shall not be ruled": PS, April 5, 1968.

445　He called on Congress to enact aid: CA, April 6, 1968.

445　"Brotherhood was murdered": *National Review,* April 2, 1968, p. 376.

445　"This is America's answer": CA, April 5, 1968, p. 12.

445　In response, urban riots: CA, April 7, 1968, p. 4.

445　$100 million in damages: Lentz, "Sixty-five Days," p. 114. Frank lists $130 million in damages within the first twenty-four hours of the riots. Frank, *An American Death,* p. 78.

445　"In its sweep and immediacy": *Time,* April 19, 1968, pp. 15–16.

446　50,000 soldiers standing by: Pyle, *Military Surveillance,* p. 98.

446　"We have an insurgency": Ibid., p. 104.

446　Guardsmen patrolled black Memphis: SSC Video, Reels 45–51.

446　indicted Willie Henry, striker Willie Kemp: CA, April 6, 1968, p. 8.

446　Initial police reports said Ellis Tate: CA, April 6, 1968, p. 8.

447　Black people expressed a mixture of rage: For quotes, see CA, April 6, 1968, p. 8.

447　police report to the U.S. attorney general: For figures, see International Association of Chiefs Police, "Civil Disorders, After-Action Reports," Box 5, File 16, SSC.

447　Coke bottles: Military veterans in North Carolina favored beer bottles over Coke bottles for Molotov cocktails by a wide margin. Tyson, *Blood Done Sign.*

447　"That's what I thought everybody": Honey, *Black Workers,* p. 313.

448　others across the globe expressed outrage: *New York Times,* April 6, 1968, p. 1.

448　"King's Murder Horrifies World": CA, April 6, 1968, p. 1.

448　"Dark Continent Weeps for King": CA, April 7, 1968, p. 2.

448　In the garment district: *The Dispatcher,* April 12, 1968.

448　the movement to declare his birthday: Will P. Jones, "Working-Class Hero," *The Nation,* January 30, 2006, pp. 23–25.

448　In Vietnam, many black soldiers: *New York Times,* April 8, 1968.

449　"There was a great sense of unity": Beifuss, *At the River,* p. 314.

20. RECKONINGS

451　"Here came a man talking": Cabbage int., Bunche oral history collection.

451　"It hit me hard—not surprise": Scott King, *My Life,* p. 318.

451　Mrs. King returned home and spent: Ibid., pp. 319–21.

452　"This is what is going to happen to me": Garrow, *Bearing the Cross,* p. 307.

452　"You realize that what you are doing": *New York Times,* April 5, 1968, p. 34.

452　Coretta knew all about his deep depression: Scott King, *My Life,* pp. 30915.

452　King met with his parents: King, Sr., *Daddy King,* pp. 186–87.

452　"Martin didn't say directly": CA, April 2, 1978.

452　people poured through the R. S. Lewis Funeral Home: SSC Video, Reel 47, April 4–5, 1968.

452　"a pitiful handful of whites": Beifuss, *At the River,* p. 316.

452　King's brother A. D. and his sister Christine: King, Sr., *Daddy King,* p. 189; Scott King, *My Life,* pp. 324–25.

453   "would plead with us all the time": Beifuss, *At the River,* p. 316.

453   150 forlorn people stood at the runway: CA, April 6, 1968, pp. 22, 36.

453   "his face looked so young": Scott King, *My Life,* p. 324.

453   She spoke for King at a mass: *New York Times,* April 5, 1968, p. 34.

454   she presided at a WILPF conference: Memphis Police and Fire Director Frank Holloman was also in Washington that day to meet with the International Association of Police Chiefs to plan riot control in the cities. Pepper, *Orders to Kill,* p. 452.

454   "All women have a common bond": Press release and photo, United Press International, March 28, 1968, in 5700, PS File, MVC.

454   "He gave his life for the poor": CA, April 7, 1968, p. 9; Scott King, *My Life,* p. 327.

454   white Memphians suddenly caught a glimpse: CA, April 7, 1968; CA, April 8, 1968, p. 26.

454   "restraint, gentleness, charity": SSC Video, Reel 54, transcript, pp. 88–91.

455   "We had to express something": SSC Documents and Artifacts, Folder 40, File 8, Midge Wade.

455   He had been among the white moderates: Bass, *Blessed Are the Peacemakers.*

455   "to restore human dignity": SSC Video, Reel 60, April 7, 1968, transcript, p. 96.

455   "wounded for our transgressions": Lewis, "Southern Religion," p. 128. Joan Beifuss provides a slightly different account of this ministerial gathering. Beifuss, *At the River,* p. 318.

455   "We who are white confess": "Ministers' Statement to Mayor Given after March from St. Mary's Cathedral to City Hall on April 5, 1968," Box 7, Folder 41, SSC.

456   approached the ministers with their pistols: Lewis, "Southern Religion," p. 131.

456   "to create a new community": SSC Video, Reel 49, April 5, 1968, p. 82.

456   "We came here with a great deal of sadness": SSC Video, Reel 47, April 5, 1968, transcript. Accounts differ as to the exact wording of Rabbi Wax's comments. See Beifuss, *At the River,* p. 321, and CA, April 6, 1968, p. 17.

457   "I understand and share with you sorrow": SSC Video, Reel 57, April 5, 1968; Beifuss, *At the River,* p. 320; and CA, April 6, 1968, p. 17.

457   "Will you agree to a dues check off": CA, April 6, 1968, p. 17.

457   "If we had been able to get a hearing": SSC Video, Reel 49, April 5, 1968, p. 83.

457   captured the contradictions of Loeb: *I Am A Man: Photographs,* p. 115.

458   they camped out at city hall: Beifuss, *At the River,* pp. 322–23. "An Open Letter From the Hunger Strikers," April 15, 1968, Box 9, Folder 66, SSC, includes fifteen signatures.

458   Ramsey Clark, ashen-faced: SSC Video, Reel 48, April 5, 1968, transcript, pp. 81–82.

458   "no evidence of a widespread plot": Beifuss, *At the River,* p. 324; CA, April 6, 1968, p. 22.

458   "Mobs Must Not Rule": CA, April 6, 1968, p. 6.

458   FBI sent around an absurd memo: Branch, *At Canaan's Edge,* p. 769.

459   *Time* magazine surveyed black Memphians: An FBI report cited the *Time* survey and said a rumor was going around that a police officer had killed King. FBI/MSS, April 12, 1968, Doc. 307, pp. 1–2.

459   "If he was shot out of a window": Honey, *Black Workers,* p. 312.

459   "Oh, Mrs. Viar," the woman responded: SSC, anecdotes, Box 51a, Card 135.

459 "got some sharp-shooters, too": Honey, *Black Workers*, p. 312.

459 ninety FBI agents and twenty-seven police detectives: CA, April 7, 1968, p. 1.

459 Cartha DeLoach, who had engineered: Ibid.

459 some fifteen of them: *New York Times*, April 5, 1968, p. 1.

459 James Orange and John Burl Smith claimed: Arkin Report, p. 68.

459 "There is a basic mistrust": PS, April 12, 1968, p. 1.

459 Netters and Fred Davis both said blacks: Arkin Report, p. 82.

460 The capture of James Earl Ray: Posner, *Killing the Dream*, pp. 44–47.

460 "This fellow was a link": TSD, April 20, 1968.

460 Dr. Benjamin Mays, preaching at King's funeral: April 20, 1968, p. 1.

460 surveillance on King: U.S. House of Representatives, *Final Assassinations Report*, pp. 471–89.

460 MPD burned its surveillance files: The author was a plaintiff in an ACLU suit (*Kendrick v. Chandler*, 76-449) to stop the Memphis Police Department from burning its files. Despite a court order not to do so, the police burned them on September 10, 1976.

460 In a civil trial: Douglass, "The Martin Luther King Conspiracy Exposed."

461 many civil rights supporters, however, asked: Lawson int., SSC.

461 "It obviously was not done by a citizen": CA, May 5, 1968.

461 "All this to-do over King's death": SSC, anecdotes, Box 51a, Card 56.

462 "if they come through my door": Ibid., Card 214.

462 "Martin Lucifer": SSC, anecdotes, Box 51, Card 49.

462 "Martin Luther Coon": Ibid., Card 106.

462 why someone hadn't killed King sooner: Ibid., Cards 45, 62, 149, 77.

462 A white insurance agent could not believe: SSC, anecdotes, Box 51a, Card 247.

462 "Each of us' heart and prayers": SSC Video, Reel 47, April 10, 1968, transcript, pp. 80–81.

462 "King brought violence everywhere": SSC, anecdotes, Box 51a, Card 201.

462 a white man "laughed and laughed": Ibid., Card 185. Another white man in a restaurant blurted out, "Well, we got one, now we'll get the rest of them."

462 "What's black and slower": SSC, anecdotes, Box 51a.

462 "Do you know why they're looking": Ibid.

462 "Why do the colored people want": Ibid.

463 "I hear there's to be a Spider march": Ibid.

463 teacher distributed *My Weekly Reader:* Ibid., Card 265.

463 "How am I going to teach law and order": Ibid., Card 196.

463 a survey of 173: Beifuss, *At the River*, p. 358.

463 this "political debasement" made it difficult: Wander, "Symbols in the Radical Right," pp. 4–14.

463 "the biggest Communist in the nation": CA, April 7, 1968, pp. 3–4.

463 "Don't you think this is all part": SSC, anecdotes, Box 51a, Card 27.

463 "King with his Communist background": Ibid., Card 60.

463 "so stupid he is easy to dupe": Ibid., Card 76.

463 "In the Negro movement": Ibid., Card 152.

463 "has been to Russia": Ibid., Card 286.

464 "was organizing a communist revolution": Ibid., Card 109.

464 "Abernathy will never make it": Ibid., Card 378.

464 Mrs. King would also be killed: Ibid., Card 327.

464 "Way to go, fella, way to go": SSC, anecdotes, Box 51a.

464 "Got a gun?": Ibid.

464 that the "crazy nigger" King: Ibid., Card 136.

464 "I just can't stand feeding lazy people": SSC, anecdotes, Box 51a.

464 "No matter what else there is": Ibid.

465 Johnson demanded his counsel: D'Emilio, *Lost Prophet,* p. 462.

465 Rustin and Norman Hill: Lawson int., SSC.

465 "Dr. King understood that political": D'Emilio, *Lost Prophet,* p. 462.

465 Infusions of funds from labor: PS, April 16, 1968, p. 1; Wurf int., SSC; Lawson int., SSC; Billings and Greenya, *Public Worker,* p. 187; "AFSCME Wins in Memphis," *The Public Worker,* April 1968, p. 6.

466 Field Foundation donated $30,000: *New York Times,* April 17, 1968, p. 24.

466 "I feel that Henry Loeb is the cause": CA, April 6, 1968, p. 8.

466 "Mens are mens these days": Beifuss, *At the River,* p. 328.

466 white auditor named Richard Pullen: CA, April 9, 1968, p. 17.

467 An anonymous donor also made an offer: CA, April 6, 1968, p. 17.

467 "more than outrageous, it's laughable": Ibid.

467 adopted a resolution by Lewis Donelson: SSC Video, Reel 50, transcript, pp. 83–84.

467 wouldn't even "take the first step": CA, April 18, 1968, p. 16.

468 "I don't care whether you are asked": Reynolds int., SSC.

468 ten deaths and 711 fires: *Time,* April 19, 1968, p. 16. See also Gilbert, *Ten Blocks.*

468 "National Guardsmen Find Memphis": CA, April 7, 1968, p. 12.

468 "I don't come here as a meddling": Ibid., p. 1.

468 "We are not ever going to recognize": Beifuss, *At the River,* pp. 330–31.

469 Meanwhile, seventy-five or eighty volunteers: Ibid., pp. 331–33.

469 Sunday sermon, distributed in print: For quotes, see Dimmick, "Palm Sunday, April 7, 1968," Box 7, Folder 41, SSC.

470 "Well, I may be a bigot": SSC, anecdotes, Box 51a, Card marked, "Bigotry in White Church."

470 "The quiet, complacent middle class": Unitarian Universalist Fellowship of Memphis, To Honorable Henry Loeb, April 7, 1968, Box 41, Folder 17, Church Response, SSC.

470 During Sunday services: The Chamber of Commerce asked 1,146 local ministers to tell their congregations that the chamber was planning a series of meetings to improve black economic and work conditions.

470 Complaints about this apparent turn: For quotes, see CA, April 7, 1968, pp. 8 and 12 and Sec. 6, p. 3.

470 workers could cure their own poverty: CA, April 14, 1968, Sec. 6, p. 3.

470 had taken leave of their senses: Lewis, "Southern Religion," p. 85.

471   write to the newspapers and criticize white racism: For examples, see CA, April 7, 1968, Sec. 6, p. 3; CA, April 10, 1968, p. 7; and CA, April 14, 1968, Sec. 6, p. 3.

471   white backlash against activist ministers: Lewis, "Southern Religion," pp. 137–40, 144, 147–50, 160.

471   James Bevel spoke of Jeremiah: CA, April 8, 1968, p. 17.

471   "The only thing left to do": Charles Rego Warren, Students' Responses, SSC.

472   "You could see and feel the hate": Frankie Gross, age 17, Ibid.

472   "are sincere or just trying to console": Calvin Dickerson, age 17, Ibid.

472   "I was so hurt when I heard": Alice Wright, age 17, Ibid.

472   "I wanted to go out and do as much": Milton Parson, age 17, Ibid.

472   "to stop her children from getting": SSC, anecdotes, Box 51a, Card 298.

472   9,000 people, about 40 percent of them black: Beifuss, At the River, p. 334.

473   "Memphis Cares" organizers asked them: CA, April 8, 1968, p. 1.

473   Mary Collier, a black woman: "Presentation at 'Memphis Cares' Meeting, Sunday, April 7, 1968," Box 7, Folder 39, SSC. New York Times, April 8, 1968, p. 33.

473   "America is the greatest country": Beifuss, At the River, pp. 334–36.

473   "God's judgment on you and me": Ibid., pp. 337–38.

474   "the only power that Jim Lawson has": CA, April 10, 1968, p. 21.

474   "If I want a place to walk": Beifuss, At the River, p. 338; Fisher, "Memphis Strike Roundtable."

474   that city—as well as Nashville, Raleigh: New York Times, April 9, 1968, p. 1.

474   350 AFSCME workers and 250 members: Unionists apparently expected 1,000 workers to participate. CA, April 9, 1968, p. 10.

474   Scores of well-known public figures: FBI/MSS, April 9, 1968, Doc. 292, p. 2.

475   Undercover police and FBI agents: Ibid., April 7, 1968, Doc. 304, pp. 1–2.

475   "militant young Negroes": Ibid., April 11, 1968, Doc. 301, pp. 1–3.

475   Ted Hoover gave his will to his secretary: Beifuss, At the River, p. 342.

475   "I really am a right-wing Republican": CA, April 11, 1968, p. 59. See also Beifuss, At the River, pp. 339–40.

476   "We were carefully monitored": Myra Dreifus, "I'll Tell You Like It Was," Box 40, Folder 6, SSC.

476   "HAVE YOU STOPPED TAKING": Flyer passed out on April 8, 1968, Box 40, Folder 4, SSC.

476   "Today we honor Dr. King": COME Flyer, April 8, 1968, Box 40, Folder 2, SSC.

477   "Keep it quiet, down to a limited number": CA, April 9, 1968, p. 17.

477   "I would much rather be burning": Ibid.

477   Police banned all traffic in the area: Ibid., p. 39.

478   "The most shocking sight": Myra Dreifus, "I'll Tell You Like It Was," Box 40, Folder 6, SSC.

478   "I never have marched for any cause": CA, April 9, 1968, p. 17.

479   "gave Dr. King what he came here for": CA, April 9, 1968.

479   April 8 also represented the coalition: Beifuss, At the River, p. 341; New York Times, April 9, 1968, pp. 1, 33; and Lawson int., SSC.

480   Wurf declared that AFSCME would support: CA, April 9, 1968, p. 10; SSC Video, Reel 64, April 8, 1968, transcript, pp. 100–5.

480   "a land free of joblessness": *New York Times,* April 9, 1968, p. 34.

480   "make all people truly free": *New York Times,* April 9, 1968, p. 34; see also Scott King, *My Life,* pp. 344–47.

481   "If Mrs. King had cried": Luella Cook, SSC, anecdotes, Box 51a.

481   "I got very tired but I felt": Alice Wright, Ibid.

481   "too stunned to cry. Everything left me.": Ernestine Johnson, age 18, Ibid.

481   "Yes, I marched. All the while": Milton Parson, age 17, Ibid.

481   At least nineteen FBI agents had observed: FBI/MSS, April 10, 1968, Doc. 305, p. 5, and Doc. 306.

482   ILWU shut down many of the ports: CA, April 10, 1968, p. 8.

482   "about war and peace": *New York Times,* April 10, 1968.

482   "believed especially that he was sent": Scott King, *My Life,* p. 353.

482   "If death had to come": Ibid., p. 355.

21. "WE HAVE GOT THE VICTORY"

483   "[Union organizers] think they're peddling": Billings and Greenya, *Public Worker,* p. 201.

483   "A pebble dropped into a calm pool": CA, April 19, 1968, p. 19.

483   At dawn, Loeb went home to bed: Beifuss, *At the River,* p. 346; PS, April 8, 1968, p. 20.

483   "Mayor Loeb beamed as he showed": CA, April 10, 1968, p. 1.

483   claimed to have received 1,000 letters: SSC Video, Reel 76, April 10–11, 1968, transcript, pp. 115–16.

484   "Critics Say the City": *Wall Street Journal,* April 8, 1968, p. 1.

484   "The will to do the type of things": Aldridge, "Memphis: The Pain of Transition," *Tempo,* January 15, 1969, pp. 5, 11.

484   "100 Days of Love and Prayer": CA, April 11, 1968, p. 59.

484   violence erupted in several cities: In Kansas City, one man was killed on Tuesday and five more people were killed on Wednesday. CA, April 10, 1968, p. 4; CA, April 12, 1968; and CA, April 13, 1968, p. 5.

484   Senate passed the 1968 Civil Rights Act: *New York Times,* April 12, 1968, p. 1; Public Law 90-284, April 11, 1968.

485   One hundred House Republicans had split: CA, April 11, 1968, p. 1.

485   Maddox conjectured that Communists: *New York Times,* April 12, 1968; Kotz, *Judgment Days,* pp. 356, 361, 367.

485   The National Rifle Association: *The Nation,* April 22, 1968, pp. 522–23; Bijlefeld, ed., *Gun Control Debate,* p. 76.

485   "Now all Negroes know": Arkin Report, p. 77; PS, April 12, 1968, p. 1.

485   "violence of hatred": CA, April 13, 1968.

486   200 black women intensified the pressure: FBI/MSS, April 15, 1968.

487   "City Must Bear Costly Loss": CA, April 14, 1968.

487 $1 million in property losses: Arkin Report, p. 83.

487 "a vicious character attack": PS, May 2, 1968.

487 Memphis Chamber of Commerce and the Rotary: Wurf int., SSC.

487 white businesspeople urged Loeb: Trotter, "The Memphis Business Community," pp. 282–301.

487 turned over to the police a tourist's lost wallet: CA, April 13, 1968. The wallet's owner gave Wilson all the cash he had in the wallet—a $14 reward.

488 "have attacked and vilified Martin": Time, April 26, 1968, p. 44.

488 Press-Scimitar editorially recognized: Lentz, "Sixty-five Days," pp. 210–11.

488 editors at both major newspapers: Ibid.

488 Loeb received daily death threats: Arkin Report, pp. 78, 81.

488 sent him an anonymous postcard: Letters From Donors to COME After Assassination, 57–1, SSC.

488 Cabbage, John Burl Smith, Edwina Harrell: Arkin Report, pp. 78–81.

488 "some of the most militant nonviolent": PS, April 16, 1968, p. 1.

488 "After Dr. King was killed": Beifuss, At the River, p. 345.

489 "I think we would still be negotiating": Billings and Greenya, Public Worker, p. 199.

489 "an independent, employee-run system": Billings and Greenya, Public Worker, p. 199. The city admitted that it "has no control over the relationship between the employees and their Credit Union," and that credit unions "are wholly separate corporations operating under Federal statutes." "Memorandum of Understanding," Folder 38, April 16, 1968, SSC.

489 sign an agreement with the union: "Memorandum of Understanding," Folder 38, April 16, 1968, SSC.

489 city now balked at giving any money: New York Times, April 17, 1968, p. 24.

489 Miles approached industrialist Abe Plough: PS, April 16, 1968, p. 1.

489 a garbage tax that most affected poorer: CA, April 25, 1968. Netters and Patterson called for a sliding-scale tax based on income, but it didn't happen. Cornelia Crenshaw said that even many blacks still objected to the increased fees. Crenshaw int., Bunche Papers.

490 "As we were going over the final": Billings and Greenya, Public Worker, p. 200.

490 T. O. thought the union had watered: Jesse Jones int., ATR.

490 "This has been your fight": Beifuss, At the River, p. 350.

490 "We are here to tell you about": CA, April 16, 1968. See also PS, April 16, 1968, p. 1.

491 the U.S. Court of Appeals ruled: Union News, February 1969, p. 4.

491 "is a matter exclusively between": Beifuss, At the River, p. 346.

492 As Loeb later pointed out to the press: PS, April 17, 1968, p. 1.

492 Workers listened tentatively as Wurf: SSC Video, Reels 77, 78, April 16, 1968, transcript, pp. 118–20; CA, April 17, 1968, p. 1.

493 Lawson now took the podium: PS, April 17, 1968, p. 1.

494 "COME will not be disbanded": CA, April 17, 1968, p. 19.

494 Workers said the key to the victory: Ibid., p. 1.

494 "We won, but we lost a good man": Newsweek, April 29, 1968, p. 22.

495   "There is no winner, except all of the people": PS, April 17, 1968, p. 1.

495   250 strikebreakers would keep their jobs: Ibid.

495   "at least 200,495 people backing us up": Loeb to Charles H. Tower, Executive Vice President, Corinthian Broadcasting Corporation, April 20, 1968, Series III, Box 84, Loeb Papers, SSC.

495   Reynolds and Frank Miles signed: SSC, "Memorandum of Understanding," Folder 38, April 16, 1968.

495   "When I did that as a child": Marshall and Van Adams, "The Memphis Public Employee Strike," p. 179.

495   Even firemen and policemen: Most sanitation workers made about $312 a month; of 1,827 policemen and firemen, 1,045 made between $460 and $570 a month. PS, April 17, 1968, p. 12.

495   long-delayed 10 percent raise: CA, April 17, 1969, p. 1.

495   accepted virtually the same agreement: CA, March 30, 1975.

496   The mass media acknowledged: Lentz, "Sixty-five Days," pp. 216–17.

496   "We've got a union to fight for us now": Ibid., p. 218.

496   That night, before some 1,500 celebrants: FBI/MSS, April 18, 1968, Doc. 331.

EPILOGUE: HOW WE REMEMBER KING

497   Lawson called a threshold moment: Lawson remarks, May 5, 2005, Labor Studies Conference, University of California, Santa Barbara.

497   In its wake, public employees: See McCartin, " 'Fire the Hell Out of Them.' "

497   "echoes of Memphis": Time, April 25, 1969, p. 23. Fink and Greenberg, Upheaval, ch. 7.

498   Appalled at the poverty they witnessed, affluent white women: Murray, "White Privilege, Racial Justice," pp. 204–38.

498   highest hourly rates for sanitation workers: AFSCME's three-year agreement included a $2-per-hour minimum pay; wage hikes of 18 cents an hour two years in a row and 15 cents an hour in the third year; free uniforms; and the banning of involuntary overtime. Union News, July 1969, p. 1.

498   In the fall of 1969, black workers at St. Joseph's: See CA for October 7–8, 1969; October 12, 1969; October 14, 1969; October 16–17, 1969; October 20, 1969; October 24–25, 1969; November 1, 1969; November 4, 1969; November 6, 1969; November 8, 1969; November 10–11, 1969; November 14–19, 1969; and November 22, 1969. Also see Newsweek, November 24, 1969, pp. 38–39; and PS, July 5, 1969. The Memphis Public Library has a file of clippings on unions and strikes.

498   Guthrie and many others—ended up in jail: Jet, January 15, 1969, p. 10. See also Jet, January 22, 1969, p. 9.

499   Jones never obtained a full-time: McKinnon int., (M. H.) Thanks to Mrs. McKinnon for sending me a copy of Jones's funeral program: "A Celebration of Life for a Servant," Union Grove Baptist Church, James Smith, pastor, April 17, 1989.

499   "Tell the guys to stay with the union": Memphis Magazine, April 1988, p. 34.

499   Jackson, and other ministers came under intense: This included a suit against Jackson by AME members. CA, September 11, 1970; PS, June 8, 1970; and CA, July 22, 1970.

499   made armed and threatening demands: FBI agent William Lawrence described the events with words that seemed to come from Cabbage himself. FBI/MSS, SA Lawrence to SAC, August 12, 1968.

499   COME decided to become: Lawson and other ministers tried to make COME a permanent federation of individuals and organizations united around a program of unionization of poor workers, leadership development, direct action, community-wide organizing for better housing, an end to police brutality, and improvement in education. FBI/MSS, July 26 and August 12, 1968.

499   SCLC when it held its convention: "SCLC, Invaders Iron Out Discord," CA, August 17, 1968.

499   Cabbage was arrested: According to Ed Redditt, Cabbage provided information to the FBI in return for federal leniency in sentencing for his draft refusal. Lack of work and health problems also sidelined him from further organizing.

500   Petty holdups: CA, February 2, 1970.

500   the wounding of a police officer: CA, August 28, 1968; CA, February 15, 1969.

500   shooting death of a black youth: CA, November 11, 1969.

500   thirty-five of them in jail or under indictment: PS, February 20, 1969.

500   The aftermath of King's death did not lead: *The Nation,* March 31, 1969, pp. 401–3.

500   In reviewing the 1968 strike: Arkin Report, pp. 83–86.

500   beat sixteen-year-old Elton Hayes to death: PS, May 17, 1973.

500   Poor People's Campaign proved to be: Fager, *Uncertain Resurrection;* Fairclough, *To Redeem the Soul,* pp. 386–91.

501   The King family suffered more: CA, July 1, 1974.

501   Despite many setbacks: Robinson int. (M.H.).

502   Black women especially: Carter, "The Local Labor Union as a Social Movement;" Cornfield, *Becoming A Mighty Voice;* Jones int., by Laurie Green.

502   In 1976, AFSCME was the largest: PS, May 17, 1976.

503   In April 1977: McCartin, " 'Fire the Hell Out of Them,' " pp. 81–83.

503   "acknowledged master of the imagic art": *The New Republic,* April 20, 1968, p. 25.

503   Schisms between the black poor: *Memphis Magazine,* April 1988, p. 89; David Ciscel int. (M.H.).

503   Poverty encompassed 58 percent: PS, March 13, 1964.

503   thirty years later, the figure: *New York Times,* October 5, 1999, p. 14.

505   "A dogged coalition builder": *Los Angeles Times,* January 18, 1993, p. B-3.

505   "Even if it had been poor white workers": Rogers, in Honey, *Black Workers,* p. 301.

505   "I don't think we can show enough": SSC Video, April 1973, transcript, p. 67.

MAIN INDIVIDUALS AND ORGANIZATIONS

Reverend Ralph David Abernathy SCLC treasurer and successor to SCLC president Martin Luther King, Jr.

ACLU American Civil Liberties Union—in our discussion, the West Tennessee chapter.

AFL-CIO American Federation of Labor and Congress of Industrial Organizations.

AFSCME American Federation of State, County and Municipal Employees.

AME African Methodist Episcopal Church.

Frank Ahlgren Editor of *Commercial Appeal.*

Claude Armour Commissioner of the Memphis Police Department.

Robert Beasley First recording secretary and early organizer of AFSCME Local 1733.

Reverend Ezekial Bell Black Presbyterian minister and strike supporter.

Reverend James Bevel SCLC staff member.

Charles Blackburn Commissioner of the Memphis Department of Public Works, including the sanitation division.

Reverend Malcom Blackburn White pastor of the all-black congregation at Clayborn Temple, a scene of mass meetings and mass marches.

Taylor Blair White agent for the International Brotherhood of Electrical Workers who tried to settle the strike.

Jerred Blanchard White Republican City Council member.

BOP Black Organizing Project, started by Charles Cabbage and Coby Smith.

H. Rap Brown Leader of the SNCC.

Reverend Baxton Bryant White director of the Tennessee Council on Human Relations, Nashville.

Clinton Burrows Early organizer of AFSCME Local 1733.

Charles Cabbage SNCC member and organizer of the BOP.

Stokely Carmichael Leader of the SNCC in 1968.

Panfilo Julius (P. J.) Ciampa AFSCME director of field operations, Washington, D.C.

COINTELPRO FBI counterintelligence program to discredit Martin Luther King, Jr., and 1960s social movements.

COME Community on the Move for Equality, a multidenominational minister-led strike support organization.

Commercial Appeal Memphis newspaper with the largest circulation in the mid-South.

Cornelia Crenshaw Community organizer and strike supporter.

E. H. Crump Former mayor (elected 1908) and political boss of Memphis until 1954.

Fred Davis Black Memphis City Council member.

Lewis Donelson White Republican City Council president.

Joseph Durick Bishop of the Catholic Church in Tennessee.

Reverend Jesse Epps AFSCME national organizer assigned to the Memphis strike.

O. Z. Evers Postal worker and early supporter of sanitation workers.

Ed Gillis Older member of AFSCME Local 1733; one of the first to go on strike.

Edwina Harrell Early member of the BOP.

Highlander Folk School Southern organizing center for labor and civil rights movements.

Frank Holloman Memphis fire and police director.

Reverend Benjamin Hooks Baptist minister and lawyer, and the first black judge in Memphis.

J. Edgar Hoover Director of the FBI.

Interdenominational Ministerial Alliance Memphis organization of black ministers.

Invaders Memphis Black Power youth organization started by the BOP.

Reverend Jesse Jackson SCLC staff member.

Reverend Ralph Jackson Director of the minimum salary program of the AME.

Bob James White businessman and Memphis City Council member.

Lyndon Baines Johnson President of the United States, 1963–68.

Thomas Oliver (T. O.) Jones First president and early organizer of AFSCME Local 1733.

Coretta Scott King Antioch College graduate, peace and civil rights activist, and wife of Martin Luther King, Jr.

Reverend Martin Luther King, Jr. Senior minister at Ebenezer Baptist Church in Atlanta, and president of SCLC.

Dan Kuykendall Memphis Republican congressman, 1966–74.

Reverend Samuel (Billy) Kyles Memphis NAACP leader and strike supporter.

Reverend James Lawson Minister of Centenary United Methodist Church in Memphis and chair of COME.

LeMoyne College Historically black college, later merged with Owen Junior College.

Stanley Levison New York attorney, financial and strategic consultant to Martin Luther King, Jr.

Local 1733 Part of AFSCME, chartered in 1963; the Memphis sanitation workers' union.

Henry Loeb Mayor of Memphis, 1960–63 and 1968–72; Commissioner of Public Works, 1956–60.

Lorraine Motel Home to black civil rights activists and musicians on the road, and site of the assassination of Martin Luther King, Jr.

William (Bill) Lucy Memphis native and black field organizer for AFSCME.

Marrell (Max) McCullough Black Memphis Police Department paid informant.

J. C. MacDonald Memphis Police Chief.

Reverend Frank McRae White friend of Henry Loeb and strike sympathizer.

Mason Temple Church of God in Christ mass meeting place in Memphis.

Reverend Harold Middlebrook Youth organizer for Memphis COME.

Frank Miles Labor mediator and personnel director for the E. L. Bruce lumber company.

Reverend Dick Moon Strike supporter and Presbyterian chaplain at the University of Memphis.

NAACP National Association for the Advancement of Colored People.

Jack O'Dell Former leftist union member, fundraiser and strategist for SCLC.

Reverend James Orange SCLC staff member and Poor People's Campaign northern mobilizer.

J. O. Patterson, Jr. Black Memphis City Council member, attorney, and state legislator.

Larry Payne Black youth slain by Memphis police officers on March 28, 1968.

O. W. Pickett Organizer of a black political club and the sanitation strike support fund.

Tommy Powell State legislator and president of the Memphis Labor Council (AFL-CIO).

Downing Pryor White Memphis City Council member and auto dealer.

A. Philip Randolph President of the Brotherhood of Sleeping Car Porters and leader of the March on Washington.

Ed Redditt Black Memphis plainclothes police officer.

L. C. Reed Longtime sanitation worker, one of the first AFSCME members on strike.

Willie B. Richmond Black Memphis plainclothes police officer.

James Robinson Chairperson for the sanitation section of AFSCME Local 1733 after the 1968 strike.

Taylor Rogers President of AFSCME Local 1733 after the departure of T. O. Jones.

James Reynolds Undersecretary of Labor sent by President Johnson to settle the Memphis sanitation strike.

Bill Ross Executive director of the Memphis AFL-CIO Labor Council.

Bayard Rustin Civil rights organizer and advisor to Martin Luther King, Jr.

SCLC Southern Christian Leadership Conference, organized in 1957 to "redeem the soul of America."

Coby Smith Organizer of the BOP and a Southwestern College student.

John Burl Smith Militant leader of the Invaders and former soldier.

Maxine Smith Executive director of the Memphis branch of the NAACP.

Dr. Vasco Smith Board member of the Memphis branch of the NAACP.

SNCC Student Nonviolent Coordinating Committee.

Reverend Henry Starks President of the black Memphis Ministerial Alliance and Memphis sanitation strike leader.

Russell Sugarmon Black attorney, state legislator, and Memphis civil rights activist.

Calvin Taylor Member of the Invaders and intern at *Commercial Appeal.*

Tri-State Defender Major black Memphis newspaper.

Jesse Turner Banker, accountant, and president of the Memphis NAACP.

UAW United Automobile Workers union, led by president Walter P. Reuther.

URW United Rubber Workers union, Local 186, at Memphis Firestone Tire and Rubber Company.

Joe Warren Early organizer and staff member of AFSCME Local 1733.

Rabbi James Wax President of the Memphis Ministers Association, a predominantly white clergy organization.

WDIA Major black radio station.

Roy Wilkins National president of the NAACP, 1955–77.

Hosea Williams Staff member of the SCLC.

WLOK Major black radio station.

Jerry Wurf President of AFSCME, 1964–81.

Andrew Young Leading staff member of SCLC and lieutenant to Martin Luther King, Jr.

BIBLIOGRAPHY

Note: Italicized references in parentheses indicate citation abbreviations used in the Notes section.

ARCHIVES

Tamiment Library, New York University, New York City
   District 65 UAW Papers, SCLC Correspondence

Federal Bureau of Investigation Reading Room, Washington, DC
   Files on the Memphis Sanitation Strike, Memphis Field Office, series 157-1092, five files in
   chronological order *(FBI/MSS)*
   Files on Martin Luther King, Jr., 100-106670, twenty sections, beginning April 25, 1962,
   after King signed a petition to free Morton Sobell *(FBI/MLK)*
   Files on King's murder, code-named MURKIN, starting at 44-1987-D. See: www.fbi.gov/
   foipa/poipa.htm. FBI files are also available on microfilm as David Garrow, ed., "Centers of
   the Southern Struggle: FBI Files on Montgomery, Albany, St. Augustine, Selma, and Memphis (University Microfilms, 1988); and "The Martin Luther King, Jr., FBI File, Part II: The
   King-Levison File" (1991).

Kenneth Hahn Papers
   Huntington Library, San Marino, California

Library of Congress Manuscripts Collection *(LC)*
> National Association for the Advancement of Colored People *(NAACP Papers),* includes: Series G, Branches, 1913–1939; and Part IV, Branch, General Office and Geographical Files, 1966–73

Martin Luther King, Jr., Center for Nonviolent Social Change, Atlanta, Georgia
> Martin Luther King, Jr., Papers *(MLK Papers)*
> Southern Christian Leadership Conference Papers *(SCLC Papers)*

Martin Luther King Papers Project, Stanford University (www.stanford.edu/group/King/mlk-papers/)

Memphis Public Library, Memphis, Tennessee
> Frank Holloman Collection *(Holloman Papers)*
> Papers of Henry Loeb III *(Loeb Papers)*
> Papers of Maxine Smith *(Smith Papers)*
> News clipping files

Ned R. McWherter Library, University of Memphis, Mississippi Valley Collection *(MVC)*
> AFL–CIO Memphis Labor Council records, Ms. 346 AFL–CIO Memphis Labor Council records
> Lt. E. H. Arkin, "Civil Disorders, Memphis, Tennessee," 2/12/68 to 4/16/68, A Report to Frank Holloman, Director of Fire and Police, Beaudoin Collection, box 3, folder 88 *(Arkin Report)*
> Memphis *Commercial Appeal,* clipping and photo files *(CA)*
> Memphis *Press-Scimitar,* File 5700, photos and clippings *(PS)*
> Sanitation Strike Collection *(SSC):* Memphis Multi-Media Archive Project: oral histories, documents, anecdotes, and audio film files, including *A Film and Videotape Record*, a compilation of film news sources from the WHBQ film archive *(SSC Video)*

Walter P. Reuther Archives of Labor and Urban Affairs, Wayne State University, Detroit, Michigan
> American Federation of State, County and Municipal Employees *(AFSCME Papers)*
> United Auto Workers Union President's Office *(Reuther Papers)*

Wisconsin Historical Society, University of Wisconsin, Madison *(WHS)*
> Carl and Anne Braden Papers
> United Packinghouse Workers Union of America *(UPWA Papers)*
> Labor Leadership Assembly for Peace

ORAL HISTORIES AND COMMENTARIES

At the River I Stand (ATR), interviews (undated) by Alison Graham, David Applewhite, and Steve Ross, in MVC: Gwen Awsumb; Robert Beasley; Jerred Blanchard; Lucius Burch; Clinton Burrows; Alzada Clark; Lewis Donelson; Robert James; Jesse Jones; S. B. (Billy) Kyles; Joseph Lowery; J. L. Netters; James Orange; Bill Ross; Coby Smith; Maxine Smith; Taylor Rogers

Michael Honey personal interviews (partial list):
    Fred Ashwell, July 20, 2005
    Charles Cabbage, August 4, 2004, Memphis
    Dorothy Crook, April 1, 1998, Memphis
    W. E. "Red" Davis, January 26–28, 1983, St. Louis, Missouri, and January 14, 1986, Memphis
    Myles Horton, June 1–2, 1981, New Market, Tennessee
    Hosea Hudson, May 28, 1985, Takoma Park, Maryland
    Kathy Roop Hunninen, phone int., October 19, 2004
    Karl Korstad, May 20, 1981, Greensboro, North Carolina
    James Lawson, phone ints., March 24, 2000, and December 14, 2004; personal int., May 5, 2004, Santa Barbara, California; personal int. by Benji Peters, February 26, 2004, Tacoma, Washington
    Jack O'Dell, February 10, 2004, Santa Barbara, California
    Dan Powell, February 1, 1983, Memphis
    Tommy Powell, August 6, 2004, Memphis
    Matt Randle, phone int., August 5, 2004
    Ed Redditt, phone int., January 2, 2006
    Cleveland Robinson, phone int., October 15, 1983
    Taylor Rogers, phone int., August 3, 2004
    William Ross, March 2, 1983, Memphis
    Jesse Ryan, phone int., August 7, 2004
    S. T. Thomas, phone int., August 6, 2004
    C. T. Vivian, November 8, 1997, Atlanta
    Joe Warren, August 7, 2004, Memphis; phone int., August 19, 2004

Additional personal interviews from Honey, *Black Workers Remember:*
    Evelyn Bates, May 25, 1989, Memphis
    Leroy Boyd, February 6, 1983, Memphis
    Irene Branch, May 25, 1989, Memphis
    Alzada Clark, May 24, 1989, Memphis
    Leroy Clark, March 27, 1983, Memphis
    Clarence Coe, May 28, 1989, Memphis
    Matthew Davis, October 30, 1984, Memphis
    George Holloway, March 23, 1990, Baltimore, Maryland

George Isabell, February 7, 1983, Memphis

Ida Leachman, April 9, 1996, and May 10, 1997, Memphis

William Lucy, April 3, 1993, Memphis

Rebecca McKinley, phone int., March 27, 1983

James Robinson, April 10, 1996, Memphis

Taylor Rogers, April 10, 1996

Sanitation Strike Collection *(SSC)*, interviews conducted between 1968 and 1972 by Joan Beifuss, William Thomas, Anne Trotter, David Yellin, and Carol Lynn Yellin: Frank Ahlgren; Walter (Bill) Bailey; Walter Bailey (attorney); Ezekial Bell; Malcolm Blackburn; Taylor Blair; Ben Branch; Lucius Burch; P. J. Ciampa; Edward (Ned) Cook; William Dimmick; Myra Dreifus; Joseph Durick; Jesse Epps; Ed Gillis; Frank Holloman; Benjamin Hooks H. Ralph Jackson; Eddie Jenkins; T. O. Jones; James Jordan; Dan Kuykendall; Gwen Kyles; S. B. (Billy) Kyles; James Lawson; C. Eric Lincoln; Henry Loeb; William Lucy; James Lyke; Frank McRae; Harold Middlebrook; Frank Miles; Richard Moon; James L. Netters; J. O. Patterson, Jr.; Dan Powell; Mr. and Mrs. L. C. Reed; James Reynolds; Bill Ross; Anthony Sabella; Al Sampson; Sengstacke family and Ed Harris; Pete Sisson; Maxine Smith; Henry Starks; Russell and Gina Sugarmon; Joe Sweat; Calvin Taylor; Jesse Turner; James Wax; Roy Wilkins; Jacques Wilmore; Jerry Wurf

Civil Rights Documentation Project, Ralph J. Bunche Oral History Collection, Moorland-Spingarn Research Center, Howard University, Washington, DC *(Bunche);* interviews by James Mosby, Jr., or anonymous:

Charles Cabbage, 1968

Cornelia Crenshaw, July 1968

H. Ralph Jackson, July 10, 1968

Maxine Smith, July 11, 1968

Russell Sugarmon, Jr., May 25, 1968

Jerry Wurf, undated

Behind the Veil Project, Center for Documentary Studies, Duke University

Lanetha Jewel Branch, int. by Doris Dixon, June 16, 1995

Ortha B. Strong Jones, int. by Laurie Green, August 8, 1995

ORAL COMMENTARIES

"March On: Twenty-Five Years Since King," conference held at the National Civil Rights Museum, Memphis, April 2–3, 1994. Speeches of Hattie Jackson, Jesse Epps, Harold Middlebrook, Coby Smith, Thomas Collins, James Orange, Dorothy Cotton, and Bill Lucy; notes and tapes in author's possession.

"Memphis Strike Roundtable," April 2, 2003, at Rhodes College. Comments by Ezekial Bell,

Charles Cabbage, Mattie Bailey Daniels, Hattie Jackson, Otis Higgs, John T. Fisher, Walter Bailey, Jesse Epps, Frank McRae, Lance Watson (Sweet Willie Wine); Honey handwritten notes.

MARTIN LUTHER KING, JR.:
RELEVANT SPEECHES AND ARTICLES (CHRONOLOGICAL)

MIA Mass Meeting at Holt Street Baptist Church, December 5, 1955, *The Papers of Martin Luther King,* vol. III, pp. 71–79.

"The Look to the Future," 25th Anniversary of Highlander Folk School, September 2, 1957, Monteagle, Tennessee.

"Address by Reverend Martin Luther King," The Fourth Biennial Wage and Contract Conference and the Third National Anti-Discrimination Conference and the Third National Conference on Women's Activities of the United Packinghouse Workers of America, AFL-CIO, September 30 to October 4, 1957, Chicago (UPWA Conferences, UPWA Papers, box 526).

"If the Negro Wins, Labor Wins," Fourth Constitutional Convention, AFL–CIO, Bal Harbour, Florida, December 11, 1961, reprinted in Washington, ed., *Testament,* pp. 208–16.

Address before the United Packinghouse Workers of America, May 21, 1962, Chicago, in MLK Papers, Atlanta.

"I Have a Dream," August 28, 1963, in Washington, ed., *Testament,* pp. 217–20.

Closing Address, European Baptist Assembly, Amsterdam, Holland, August 16, 1964, in District 65 Papers, Box 24, SCLC Correspondence, Tamiment Library, New York.

Address (untitled) before District 65, UAW, New York, September 17, 1965, in MLK Papers.

"Dr. King's Speech," Frogmore, South Carolina, staff retreat, November 14, 1966, in MLK Papers.

"A Time to Break Silence," April 4, 1967, reprinted in Washington, ed., *Testament of Hope,* pp. 231–44.

"Civil Rights at the Crossroads," address to the shop stewards of Local 815, Teamsters and Allied Trades Council, New York, May 2, 1967, in MLK Papers.

"Black Power Defined," *New York Times,* June 11, 1967, reprinted in Washington, ed., *Testament,* pp. 303–12.

"The Domestic Impact of the War in America," Address to the National Labor Assembly for Peace, University of Chicago, November 11, 1967. Labor Leadership Assembly for Peace, WHS.

"The State of the Movement," Frogmore, South Carolina, staff retreat, November 28, 1967, in MLK Papers.

Interview with ABC News, Chicago, January 5, 1968, in MLK Papers.

"What Are Your New Year's Resolutions?" Ebenezer Baptist Church, Atlanta, Georgia, January 7, 1968, in MLK Papers.

"Why We Must Go to Washington," Ebenezer Baptist Church, January 15, 1968, in MLK Papers.

Press conference, Ebenezer Baptist Church, January 16, 1968, in MLK Papers.

"See You in Washington," Ebenezer Baptist Church, January 17, 1968, and Poor People's Campaign talks to SCLC staff, January 15–17, 1968, in MLK Papers.

"The Future of Integration," Kansas State University, January 19, 1968, in MLK Papers.

"The Drum Major Instinct," Ebenezer Baptist Church, February 4, 1968, in Carson and Holloran, *A Knock at Midnight*, pp. 169–86.

[Untitled speech], Chicago, February 6, 1968, in MLK Papers.

"In Search of a Sense of Direction," Vermont Avenue Baptist Church, Washington, DC, February 7, 1968, in MLK Papers.

"Mississippi Leaders on the Washington Campaign," speech at St. Thomas AME Church, Birmingham, February 15, 1968, in MLK Papers.

"Pre-Washington Campaign," Selma, Alabama, February 16, 1968

[Untitled speech] at mass meeting, Montgomery, Alabama, February 16, 1968, in MLK Papers.

"Who Is My Neighbor?" Ebenezer Baptist Church, February 18, 1968, in MLK Papers.

"To Minister to the Valley," Miami, Florida, February 23, 1968, in MLK Papers.

"Unfulfilled Dreams," Ebenezer Baptist Church, March 3, 1968, in MLK Papers and in Carson and Holloran, *A Knock at Midnight*, pp. 187–90, 191–200.

"The Other America," Address to Local 1199 Salute to Freedom, Hunter College, New York, March 10, 1968, in MLK Papers.

[Untitled speech], Grosse Pointe High School, Michigan, March 14, 1968, UAW Papers.

"Address of Rev. Martin Luther King, Jr.," Mason Temple Mass Meeting, Memphis, Tennessee, March 18, 1968, in MLK Papers.

Poor People's Campaign Rally Speech, Grenada, Mississippi, March 19, 1968, in MLK Papers.

Poor People's Campaign Rally Speech, Laurel, Mississippi, March 19, 1968, in MLK Papers.

Poor People's Campaign Rally Speech, Clarksdale, Mississippi, March 19, 1968, in MLK Papers.

King, Martin Luther, Jr., "Honoring Dr. Du Bois," *Freedomways* 8:2 (spring 1968), pp.104–11.

"Conversation with Martin Luther King," March 23, 1968, *Conservative Judaism* 22:3, pp. 1–19.

"Remaining Awake Through a Great Revolution," National Cathedral, Washington, DC, March 31, 1968, in Carson and Holloran, *A Knock at Midnight*, pp. 205–24.

"Mountaintop Speech," Mason Temple, Memphis, Tennessee, April 3, 1968, in MLK Papers, SSC; and Washington, ed., *Testament*, pp. 279–86.

"Showdown for Nonviolence," *Look* 32:8 (April 16, 1968), pp. 23–25.

"A Testament of Hope," January 1969, in Washington, ed., *Testament*, pp. 313–28.

NEWSPAPERS

AFL-CIO News (Washington, DC)

American Federationist (AFL–CIO, Washington, DC)

Birmingham News (Alabama)

Clarion Ledger (Jackson, Mississippi)

Commercial Appeal (Memphis) *(CA)*

The Daily Worker (New York City)

The Guardian (New York City)

Hattiesburg American (Mississippi)

I. F. Stone's Weekly

Montgomery Advertiser (Alabama)

Newsweek

New York Times

Press-Scimitar (Memphis) *(PS)*

The Public Employee (AFSCME)

RWDSU Record (New York City)

Selma Times (Alabama)

Southern Patriot (Louisville)

Time

Tri-State Defender (Memphis) *(TSD)*

Union News (Memphis AFL–CIO)

Vicksburg Evening Post (Mississippi)

Washington Post

GOVERNMENT DOCUMENTS

"Civil Disorders, Memphis, Tennessee: February 12 through April 16, 1968" *(Arkin Report),* in SSC/MVC.

Federal Bureau of Investigation. *Report of the Department of Justice Task Force to Review the FBI Martin Luther King, Jr., Security and Assassination Investigations,* January 11, 1977.

Report of the National Advisory Commission on Civil Disorders. New York: E. P. Dutton, 1968.

U.S. Civil Rights Commission. *Hearings Before the United States Commission on Civil Rights.* Hearings held in Memphis, Tennessee, June 25–26, 1962. Washington, DC: U.S. Government Printing Office.

U.S. Congress, Senate Select Committee to Study Governmental Operations with Respect to Intelligence Activities. *Supplementary Detailed Staff Reports on Intelligence Activities and the Rights of Americans.* Book III, *Final Report of the Select Committee.* Washington, DC: U.S. Government Printing Office, 1976 (referred to as the Church Report).

U.S. House of Representatives. *The Final Assassinations Report, House Select Committee on Assassinations.* New York: Bantam, 1979 (referred to as HSCA—House Select Committee on Assassinations).

MAJOR BOOKS AND ARTICLES

Abernathy, Ralph. *And the Walls Came Tumbling Down: An Autobiography.* New York: Harper & Row, 1989.

Anderson, Carol. *Eyes Off the Prize: The United Nations and the African American Struggle for Human Rights, 1944–1955.* New York: Cambridge University Press, 2003.

Arnesen, Eric. *Brotherhoods of Color: Black Railroad Workers and the Struggle for Equality.* Cambridge: Harvard University Press, 2001.

Arsenault, Raymond. *Freedom Riders: 1961 and the Struggle for Racial Justice.* New York: Oxford University Press, 2006.

Bass, S. Jonathan. *Blessed Are the Peacemakers: Martin Luther King, Jr., Eight White Religious Leaders, and the "Letter from Birmingham Jail."* Baton Rouge: Louisiana State University Press, 2001.

Beifuss, Joan. *At the River I Stand.* Memphis: B & W Press, 1985.

Bijlefeld, Marjolijn, ed. *The Gun Control Debate: A Documentary History.* Westport, CT: Greenwood Press, 1997.

Billings, Richard N., and John Greenya. *Power to the Public Worker.* Washington, DC: Robert B. Luce, 1974.

Biondi, Martha. *To Stand and Fight: The Struggle for Civil Rights in Postwar New York City.* Cambridge: Harvard University Press, 2003.

Bishop, Jim. *The Days of Martin Luther King.* New York: G. P. Putnam's Sons, 1971.

Blight, David W. *Race and Reunion.* Cambridge: Harvard University Press, 2001.

Boyer, Richard O., and Herbert M. Morais. *Labor's Untold Story.* New York: Cameron Associates, 1955.

Boyle, Kevin. *The UAW and the Heyday of American Liberalism, 1945–1968.* Ithaca: Cornell University Press, 1995.

Braden, Anne. *HUAC: Bulwark of Segregation.* Los Angeles: National Committee to Abolish HUAC, 1963.

———. "The Southern Freedom Movement in Perspective." *Monthly Review* 17:3 (July–August 1965).

Branch, Taylor. *Parting the Waters: America in the King Years 1954–63.* New York: Touchstone, 1989.

———. *Pillar of Fire: America in the King Years 1963–65.* New York: Simon and Schuster, 1998.

———. *At Canaan's Edge: America in the King Years, 1965–68.* New York: Simon and Schuster, 2006.

Brinkley, Douglas. *Rosa Parks.* New York: Viking, 2000.

Brown-Melton, Gloria. "Blacks in Memphis, Tennessee, 1920–1955." Ph.D. dissertation, Washington State University, 1992.

Burns, Stuart. *To the Mountaintop: Martin Luther King, Jr.'s Sacred Mission to Save America: 1955–1968.* San Francisco: Harper, 2004.

Carbado, Devon W., and Donald Weise. *Time on Two Crosses: The Collected Writings of Bayard Rustin.* San Francisco: Cleis Press, 2003.

Carmichael, Stokely, with Ekwueme Michael Thelwell. *Ready for Revolution: The Life and Struggles of Stokely Carmichael (Kwame Ture).* New York: Scribner, 2003.

Carney, Court. "The Contested Image of Nathan Bedford Forrest." *The Journal of Southern History* 67:3 (August 2001): 601–30.

Carson, Clayborne. *In Struggle: SNCC and the Black Awakening of the 1960s*. Cambridge: Harvard University Press, 1981.

———. "Martin Luther King, Jr., and the African-American Social Gospel," in Paul E. Johnson, ed., *African-American Christianity: Essays in History*. Berkeley: University of California Press, 1994.

———. *The Autobiography of Martin Luther King*. New York: Time Warner Books, 1998.

———, et al., eds., *The Papers of Martin Luther King, Jr.* Vol. I: *Called to Serve, January 1929–June 1951*. Berkeley: University of California Press, 1992. Vol. II: *Rediscovering Precious Values, July 1951–November 1955* (1995); Vol. III: *Birth of a New Age, December 1955–December 1956* (1997); Vol. IV: *Symbol of the Movement, January 1957–December 1958* (2000); Vol. V: *Threshold of a New Decade, January 1959–December 1960* (2005).

Carson, Clayborne, and Peter Holloran, eds. *A Knock at Midnight: Inspiration from the Great Sermons of Martin Luther King, Jr.* New York: Warner Books, 1998.

Carter, Dan T. *The Politics of Rage: George Wallace, the Origins of the New Conservatism, and the Transformation of American Politics*. Baton Rouge: Louisiana State University Press, 1995.

Carter, Deborah Brown. "The Local Labor Union as a Social Movement Organization: Local 282, Furniture Division—IUE, 1943–1988." Ph.D. dissertation, Vanderbilt University, 1988.

Chappell, David L. *A Stone of Hope: Prophetic Religion and the Death of Jim Crow*. Chapel Hill: University of North Carolina Press, 2004.

Churchill, Ward, and Jim Vander Wall. *The COINTELPRO Papers: Documents from the FBI's Secret Wars Against Political Dissent*. Boston: South End Press, 1990.

Collins, Thomas W. "An Analysis of the Memphis Garbage Strike of 1968," in Johnetta B. Cole, ed., *Anthropology for the Eighties: Introductory Readings*. New York: The Free Press, 1982, pp. 353–62.

"Conversation with Martin Luther King." Transcript reprinted in *Conservative Judaism* 22:3 (spring 1968): 1–19.

Cornfield, Daniel B. *Becoming A Mighty Voice: Conflict and Change in the United Furniture Workers of America*. New York: Russell Sage, 1989.

Cowie, Jefferson. *Capital Moves: RCA's Seventy-Year Quest for Cheap Labor*. Ithaca: Cornell University Press, 1999.

Daniel, Pete. *Lost Revolutions: The South in the 1950s*. Chapel Hill: University of North Carolina Press, 2000.

D'Emilio, John. *Lost Prophet: The Life and Times of Bayard Rustin*. New York: The Free Press, 2003.

Dinnerstein, Leonard. "Southern Jewry and the Desegregation Crisis, 1954-1968." *American Jewish Historical Quarterly* 62:3 (1973): 231–41.

———, and Mary Dale Palsson, eds. *Jews in the South*. Baton Rouge: Louisiana State University Press, 1973.

Douglass, Jim. "The Martin Luther King Conspiracy Exposed in Memphis." *Probe Magazine* 7:4 (May–June 2000): 1, 9–15.

Du Bois, W. E. B. *Black Reconstruction in America*. New York: The Free Press, 1998.

Dudziak, Mary L. *Cold War Civil Rights: Race and the Image of American Democracy.* Princeton, NJ: Princeton University Press, 2000.

Dyson, Michael Eric. *I May Not Get There With You: The True Martin Luther King, Jr.* New York: The Free Press, 2000.

Estes, Steve. *"I Am a Man!": Race, Manhood, and the Struggle for Civil Rights.* Chapel Hill: University of North Carolina Press, 2005.

———. "'I Am A Man!' Race, Masculinity, and the 1968 Memphis Sanitation Strike." *Labor History* Spring 2000, 41(2): 153–170.

Fager, Charles. *Uncertain Resurrection: The Poor People's Washington Campaign.* Grand Rapids, MI: Eerdmans, 1969.

Fairclough, Adam. *Martin Luther King, Jr.* Athens: University of Georgia Press, 1995.

———. *To Redeem the Soul of America: The Southern Christian Leadership Conference and Martin Luther King, Jr.* Athens: University of Georgia Press, 1987.

Fariello, Griffin. *Red Scare: Memories of the American Inquisition: An Oral History.* New York: W. W. Norton, 1995.

Fine, Sidney. *Violence in the Model City: The Cavanagh Administration, Race Relations, and the Detroit Riot of 1967.* Ann Arbor: University of Michigan Press, 1989.

Fink, Leon, and Brian Greenberg. *Upheaval in the Quiet Zone.* Urbana: University of Illinois Press, 1999.

Foner, Philip S. *Organized Labor and the Black Worker, 1619–1981.* New York: International Publishers, 1982.

———. *The Black Worker Since the AFL-CIO Merger, 1955-1980.* Philadelphia: Temple University Press, 1984.

Frank, Gerold. *An American Death: The True Story of the Assassination of Martin Luther King, Jr., and the Greatest Manhunt of Our Time.* Garden City: Doubleday, 1972.

Friedly, Michael, and David Gallen. *Martin Luther King, Jr.: The FBI File.* New York: Carroll and Graf, 1993.

Garrow, David. *Bearing the Cross.* New York: William Morrow, 1986.

———. *The FBI and Martin Luther King, Jr.: From "Solo" to Memphis.* New York: W. W. Norton, 1981.

———. "The FBI and Martin Luther King, Jr." *Atlantic Monthly* (July–August 2002): 80–88.

Gilbert, Ben. *Ten Blocks From the White House: Anatomy of the Washington Riots of 1968.* New York: Frederick A. Praeger, 1968.

Goings, Kenneth W., and Gerald L. Smith. " 'Unhidden' Transcripts: Memphis and African American Agency, 1862–1920." *Journal of Urban History* 21 (March 1995): 372–94.

Gordon, Robert. *Can't Be Satisfied: The Life and Times of Muddy Waters.* New York: Little, Brown, 2002.

Goulden, Joseph C. *Jerry Wurf: Labor's Last Angry Man.* New York: Atheneum, 1982.

Grant, Joanne. *Ella Baker: Freedom Bound.* New York: John Wiley, 1998.

Green, Earl, Jr. "Labor in the South: A Case Study of Memphis, the 1968 Sanitation Strike and Its Effects on the Urban Community." Ph.D. dissertation, New York University, 1980.

Green, James R. *The World of the Worker: Labor in Twentieth-Century America.* Champaign: University of Illinois Press, 1980.

Green, Laurie Beth. "Battling the Plantation Mentality: Consciousness, Culture and the Politics of Race, Class and Gender in Memphis, 1940–1968." Ph.D. dissertation, University of Chicago, 1999.

———. "Race, Gender, and Labor in 1960s Memphis: 'I Am A Man' and the Meaning of Freedom." *Journal of Urban History* 30:3 (March 2004): 465–89.

Griffith, Barbara. *The Crisis of American Labor: Operation Dixie and the Defeat of the CIO.* Philadelphia: Temple University Press, 1988.

Halberstam, David. *The Children.* New York: Random House, 1998.

———. "The Second Coming of Martin Luther King," *Harper's* 235:1407 (August 1967): 39–55.

Halpern, Martin. *Unions, Radicals, and Democratic Presidents: Seeking Social Change in the Twentieth Century.* Westport, CT: Praeger, 2003.

Halpern, Rick, and Roger Horowitz. *Meatpackers: An Oral History of Black Packinghouse Workers and Their Struggle for Racial and Economic Equality.* New York: Twayne Publishers, 1996.

Hamburger, Robert. *Our Portion of Hell, Fayette County, Tennessee: An Oral History of the Struggle for Civil Rights.* New York: Links Books, 1973.

Hampton, Henry, and Steve Fayer, eds. *Voices of Freedom: An Oral History of the Civil Rights Movement from the 1950s through the 1980s.* New York: Bantam Books, 1990.

Haney Lopez, Ian F. *Racism on Trial: The Chicano Fight for Justice.* Cambridge: Harvard University Press, 2003.

Hill, Lance. *Deacons for Defense: Armed Resistance and the Civil Rights Movement.* Chapel Hill: University of North Carolina Press, 2004.

Honey, Maureen. *Bitter Fruit: African American Women in World War II.* Columbia: University of Missouri Press, 1999.

Honey, Michael. *Black Workers Remember: An Oral History of Segregation, Unionism, and the Freedom Struggle.* Berkeley: University of California Press, 1999.

———. *Southern Labor and Black Civil Rights: Organizing Memphis Workers.* Urbana: University of Illinois Press, 1993.

———. "Martin Luther King., Jr., the Crisis of the Black Working Class, and the Memphis Sanitation Strike," in Robert H. Zieger, ed., *Southern Labor in Transition, 1940–1995.* Knoxville: University of Tennessee Press, 1997, pp. 146–75.

———. "The Power of Remembering: Black Factory Workers and Union Organizing in the Jim Crow Era," in Charles M. Payne and Adam Green, *Time Longer Than Rope: A Century of African American Activism, 1850–1950.* New York: New York University Press, 2003, pp. 302–35.

———. "Operation Dixie, the Red Scare, and the Defeat of Southern Labor Organizing," in Cherny, Issel, and Taylor, *American Labor and the Cold War: Grassroots Politics and Postwar Political Culture.* New Brunswick, NJ: Rutgers University Press, 2004.

———. "Class, Race, and Power in the New South: Racial Violence and the Delusions of White Supremacy," in Tyson and Cecelski, eds., *Democracy Betrayed: The Wilmington Race Riot of 1898 and Its Legacy.* Chapel Hill: University of North Carolina Press, 1998.

Hooper, Hartwell and Susan. "The Scripto Strike: Martin Luther King's 'Valley of Problems,' Atlanta, 1964–1965." In author's possession.

Horne, Gerald. *Communist Front? The Civil Rights Congress, 1946–1956.* Rutherford, NJ: Fairleigh Dickinson University Press, 1988.

———. *The Fire This Time: The Watts Uprising and the 1960s.* Charlottesville: University Press of Virginia, 1995.

Huie, William Bradford. *He Slew the Dreamer: My Search for the Truth about James Earl Ray and the Murder of Martin Luther King.* Rev. ed. Montgomery, AL: Black Belt Press, 1997.

Hunter, Guy, ed. *Industrialization and Race Relations: A Symposium.* New York: Oxford University Press, 1965.

Huntley, Horace, and David Montgomery. *Black Workers' Struggle for Equality in Birmingham.* Champaign: University of Illinois Press, 2004.

Jackson, Thomas F. "Recasting the Dream: Martin Luther King, Jr., African American Political Thought and the Third Reconstruction." Ph.D. dissertation, Stanford University, 1994.

Kelley, Robin D. G. *Race Rebels: Culture, Politics, and the Black Working Class.* New York: The Free Press, 1994.

King, Coretta Scott. *My Life with Martin Luther King, Jr.* New York: Holt, Rinehart, and Winston, 1969.

King, Martin Luther, Sr. *Daddy King: An Autobiography.* New York: William Morrow, 1980.

King, Martin Luther, Jr. *Stride Toward Freedom.* New York: Harper and Row, 1958.

———. *Where Do We Go From Here? Chaos or Community?* New York: Harper & Row, 1967.

King, Richard H. *Civil Rights and the Idea of Freedom.* New York: Oxford University Press, 1992.

Korstad, Robert. *Civil Rights Unionism: Tobacco Workers and the Struggle for Democracy in the Mid-Twentieth-Century South.* Chapel Hill: University of North Carolina Press, 2003.

———, and Nelson Lichtenstein, "Opportunities Found and Lost: Labor, Radicals, and the Early Civil Rights Movement." *Journal of American History* 75:3 (1988): 786–811.

Kotz, Nick. *Judgment Days: Lyndon Baines Johnson, Martin Luther King, Jr., and the Laws That Changed America.* Boston: Houghton Mifflin, 2005.

———, and Mary Lynn Kotz. *A Passion for Equality: George A. Wiley and the Movement.* New York: W. W. Norton, 1997.

Lapsley, Joe. "Portrait of the Mayor as a Young Man: Henry Loeb as Public Works Commissioner, 1956–1960," University of Memphis, unpublished. In author's possession.

Lentz, Richard. "Sixty-five Days in Memphis: The *Commercial Appeal,* the *Press-Scimitar,* and the 1968 Garbage Strike." M.A. thesis, Southern Illinois University, 1976.

———. *Symbols, the News Magazines and Martin Luther King.* Baton Rouge: Louisiana State University Press, 1990.

Levine, David. *Bayard Rustin and the Civil Rights Movement.* New Brunswick, NJ: Rutgers University Press, 2000.

Lewis, David. *King: A Biography.* Champaign: University of Illinois Press, reprinted 1978.

Lewis, Selma. "Southern Religion and the Memphis Sanitation Strike." Ph.D. dissertation, Memphis State University, 1976.

Lichtenstein, Nelson. *State of the Union: A Century of American Labor.* Princeton, NJ: Princeton University Press, 2003.

———. *The Most Dangerous Man in Detroit: Walter Reuther and the Fate of American Labor.* New York: HarperCollins, 1995.

Ling, Peter. *Martin Luther King, Jr.* London and New York: Routledge, 2002.

MacLean, Nancy. *Freedom Is Not Enough: The Opening of the American Workplace.* Cambridge: Harvard University Press, 2006.

Marshall, F. Ray, and Arvil Van Adams. "The Memphis Public Employee Strike," part three of W. Ellison Chalmers and Gerald W. Cormick, eds., *Racial Conflict and Negotiations: Perspectives and First Case Studies.* Ann Arbor: Institute of Labor and Industrial Relations, University of Michigan/Wayne State University, 1971.

McCartin, Joseph A. " 'Fire the Hell Out of Them': Sanitation Workers' Struggles and the Normalization of the Striker Replacement Strategy in the 1970s." *Labor: Studies in Working-Class History of the Americas* 2:3 (fall 2005): 67–92.

McKee, Margaret, and Fred Chisenhall. *Beale Black and Blue: Life and Music on Black America's Main Street.* Baton Rouge: Louisiana State University Press, 1981.

McKnight, Gerald. *The Last Crusade: Martin Luther King, Jr., the FBI and the Poor People's Campaign.* Boulder, CO: Westview Press, 1998.

McWhorter, Diane. *Carry Me Home: Birmingham, Alabama, the Climactic Battle of the Civil Rights Revolution.* New York: Simon and Schuster, 2001.

Memphis *Commercial Appeal. I Am A Man: Photographs of the 1968 Memphis Sanitation Strike and Dr. Martin Luther King, Jr.* Memphis: Memphis Publishing Co., 1993.

Miller, William D. *Mr. Crump of Memphis.* Memphis: Memphis State University Press, 1957.

Montgomery, David. *The Fall of the House of Labor: The Workplace, the State, and American Labor Activism, 1865–1925.* New York: Cambridge University Press, 1987.

Murray, Gail S. "White Privilege, Racial Justice, Women Activists in Memphis," in Murray, ed., *Throwing Off the Cloak of Privilege: White Southern Women Activists in the Civil Rights Era.* Gainesville: University Press of Florida, 2005.

Needleman, Ruth. *Black Freedom Fighters in Steel: The Struggle for Democratic Unionism.* Ithaca: Cornell University Press, 2003.

Nelson, Bruce. *Divided We Stand: American Workers and the Struggle for Equality.* Princeton, NJ: Princeton University Press, 2001.

O'Neill, William L. *Coming Apart: An Informal History of America in the 1960's.* Chicago: Quadrangle Books, 1971.

O'Reilly, Kenneth. *"Racial Matters": The FBI's Secret File on Black America, 1960–1972.* New York: The Free Press, 1989.

———. *Hoover and the Un-Americans.* Philadelphia: Temple University Press, 1983.

Payne, Charles M. *I've Got the Light of Freedom: The Organizing Tradition and the Mississippi Freedom Struggle.* Berkeley: University of California Press, 1995.

———, and Green, Adam. *Time Longer Than Rope: A Century of African-American Activism, 1850–1950.* New York: New York University Press, 2003.

———, and Steven F. Lawson. *Debating the Civil Rights Movement, 1945–1968.* New York: Rowman and Littlefield, 1998.

Pepper, William F. *An Act of State: The Execution of Martin Luther King*. London: Verso, 2003.

———. *Orders to Kill: The Truth Behind the Murder of Martin Luther King, Jr*. New York: Warner Books, 1995.

Perlstein, Rick. *Before the Storm: Barry Goldwater and the Unmaking of the American Consensus*. New York: Hill and Wang, 2001.

Perrucci, Robert, and Marc Pilisuk. *The Triple Revolution: Social Problems in Depth*. Boston: Little, Brown, 1968.

Pohlman, Marcus D., and Michael P. Kirby. *Racial Politics at the Crossroads: Memphis Elects Dr. W. W. Herenton*. Knoxville: University of Tennessee Press, 1996.

Posner, Gerald. *Killing the Dream: James Earl Ray and the Assassination of Martin Luther King, Jr*. New York: Random House, 1998.

Pyle, Christopher H. *Military Surveillance of Civilian Politics 1967–1970*. New York: Garland Publishing, 1986.

Rachleff, Peter. *Hard-Pressed in the Heartland: The Hormel Strike and the Future of the Labor Movement*. Boston: South End Press, 1993.

Ralph, James R, Jr. *Northern Protest: Martin Luther King, Jr., Chicago, and the Civil Rights Movement*. Cambridge: Harvard University Press, 1993.

Ransby, Barbara. *Ella Baker and the Black Freedom Movement: A Radical Democratic Vision*. Chapel Hill: University of North Carolina Press, 2003.

Roedigger, David R. *The Wages of Whiteness: Race and the Making of the American Working Class*. London: Verso, 1991.

Ross, Arthur M., and Herbert Hill. *Employment, Race and Poverty*. New York: Harcourt, Brace, 1967.

Royster, Jacqueline Jones, ed. *Southern Horrors and Other Writings: The Anti-Lynching Campaign of Ida B. Wells, 1892–1900*. New York: St. Martin's Press, 1996.

Rustin, Bayard. *Down the Line: The Collected Writings of Bayard Rustin*. Chicago: Quadrangle Books, 1971.

Seeger, Pete. *Where Have All the Flowers Gone: A Singer's Stories, Songs, Seeds, Robberies*. Bethlehem, Pa.: A Singout Publication, 1993.

Simonelli, Frederick J. *American Fuhrer: George Lincoln Rockwell and the American Nazi Party*. Urbana: University of Illinois Press, 1999.

Sivananda, Mantri. "Controversial Memphis Mayor Henry Loeb III, 1920–1992: A Biographical Study." Ph.D. dissertation, University of Memphis, 2002.

———. "Henry Loeb III As Public Works Commissioner, 1956-1959." *West Tennessee Historical Society Papers* 66, pp. 67–80.

Smith, John Burl. "The Dish," an online newsletter at www.thedish.org/THEDISHv2no1.htm #Johnv2no1, and other editions.

Sokol, Jason. "Dynamics of Leadership and the Memphis Sanitation Strike of 1968." *Tennessee Historical Quarterly* LX:4 (Winter 2001): 258–83.

Spero, Sterling D., and John M. Cappozzola. *The Urban Community and Its Unionized Bureaucracies: Pressure Politics in Local Government Relations*. New York: Dunellen, 1973.

Stanfield, J. Edwin, "In Memphis: More Than a Garbage Strike"; "In Memphis: Mirror to America?" (March 22, 1968); "In Memphis: Tragedy Unaverted" (April 3, 1968); reprinted by Southern Regional Council, 67-1, SSC, and included on AFSCME "Memphis: We Remember" Website: www.afscme.org/about/jes03tc.htm, unpaginated.

Stanton, Mary. *Freedom Walk: Mississippi or Bust.* Jackson: University Press of Mississippi, 2003.

Sugrue, Thomas J. *The Origins of the Urban Crisis: Race and Inequality in Postwar Detroit.* Princeton, NJ: Princeton University Press, 1996.

Taylor, Kieran. "Martin Luther King's Early Ties to Progressive Movements." *The Dispatcher* (February 2001): 8–9.

———. " 'We Have Just Begun': Black Organizing and White Response in the Arkansas Delta, 1919." *Arkansas Historical Quarterly* 58:3 (autumn 1999): 264–84.

Trotter, Anne. "The Memphis Business Community and Integration," in Elizabeth Jacoway and David R. Colburn, eds., *Southern Businessmen and Desegregation.* Baton Rouge: Louisiana State University Press, 1982, pp. 282–300.

Tucker, David M. *Memphis Since Crump: Bossism, Blacks, and Civic Reformers 1948–1968.* Knoxville: University of Tennessee Press, 1980.

Tyson, Timothy B. *Blood Done Sign My Name: A True Story.* New York: Crown Publishers, 2004.

———. *Radio Free Dixie: Robert F. Williams and the Roots of Black Power.* Chapel Hill: University of North Carolina Press, 1999.

Unger, Irwin, and Debi Unger. *America in the 1960s.* New York: Brandywine Press, 1988.

Van Deburg, William L., ed. *Modern Black Nationalism: From Marcus Garvey to Louis Farrakhan.* New York and London: New York University Press, 1997.

Wailoo, Keith. *Dying in the City of the Blues: Sickle Cell Anemia and the Politics of Race and Health.* Chapel Hill: University of North Carolina Press, 2001.

Ward, Brian. *Radio and the Struggle for Civil Rights in the South.* Gainsville: University Press of Florida, 2004.

Washington, James M., ed. *A Testament of Hope: The Essential Writings and Speeches of Martin Luther King, Jr.* New York: Harper and Row, 1986.

Webb, Clive. *Fight Against Fear: Southern Jews and Black Civil Rights.* Athens: University of Georgia Press, 2001.

White, John. " 'Nixon *Was* the One': Edgar Daniel Nixon, the MIA and the Montgomery Bus Boycott," in Brian Ward and Tony Badger, eds. *The Making of Martin Luther King and the Civil Rights Movement.* London: Macmillan, 1996, pp. 45–66.

Williams, Juan. *Eyes on the Prize: America's Civil Rights Years, 1954–1965.* New York: Viking Press, 1987.

Withers, Ernest C., with contributions by Jack F. Hurley, Brooks Johnson, and Daniel J. Wolff. *Pictures Tell the Story: Ernest C. Withers, Reflections in History.* Norfolk, Va.: Chrysler Museum of Art, 2000.

Woodruff, Nan. *American Congo: The American Freedom Struggle in the Delta.* Cambridge: Harvard University Press, 2003.

Wright, Gavin. *Old South, New South: Revolutions in the Southern Economy Since the Civil War.*
    New York: Basic Books, 1986.

Wright, Sharon. *Race, Power, and Political Emergence in Memphis.* New York: Garland Publish-
    ing, 2000.

Young, Andrew. *An Easy Burden: The Civil Rights Movement and the Transformation of Amer-
    ica.* New York: HarperCollins, 1996.

Zieger, Robert H. *The CIO: 1935–1955.* Chapel Hill: University of North Carolina Press, 1995.

———, ed. *Southern Labor in Transition, 1940–1995.* Knoxville: University of Tennessee Press,
    1997.

INDEX

Page numbers in *italics* refer to illustrations.